Human Relations for Career and Personal Success

Human Relations for Career and Personal Success

Concepts, Applications, and Skills

Tenth Edition

Andrew J. DuBrin
Rochester Institute of Technology

PEARSON

Boston Columbus Indianapolis New York San Francisco Upper Saddle River
Amsterdam Cape Town Dubai London Madrid Milan Munich Paris Montréal Toronto
Delhi Mexico City São Paulo Sydney Hong Kong Seoul Singapore Taipei Tokyo

Editorial Director: Vernon R. Anthony
Acquisitions Editor: Sara Eilert
Editorial Assistant: Doug Greive
Director of Marketing: David Gesell
Senior Marketing Manager: Stacey Martinez
Senior Marketing Coordinator: Alicia Wozniak
Marketing Assistant: Les Roberts
Production Manager: Debbie Ryan
Editor, Digital Projects: Nichole Caldwell
Senior Art Director: Jayne Conte
Cover Designer: Suzanne Benhke
Cover Image: Fotolia
Media Project Manager: Karen Bretz
Full-Service Project Management: PreMediaGlobal
Composition: PreMediaGlobal
Printer/Binder: Courier/Kendallville
Cover Printer: Lehigh/Phoenix Color Hagerstown
Text Font: Utopia Std

Photo Credits: Yuri Arcurs/Shutterstock.com, p. 2; Commercial Eye/Getty Images, p. 30; Dmitriy Shironosov/Shutterstock.com, pp. 60, 216; Image Source/Corbis, pp. 92, 378; Comstock Images/Getty Images.com, pp. 120, 412; Todd Wright/Getty Images, p. 148; Image Source/Getty Images, p. 180; Dorling Kindersley/DK Images, pp. 246, 448; Jim Craigmyle/Corbis, p. 278; Auremar /Shutterstock.com, p. 316; Chris Windsor/Getty Images, p. 348; Denis Opolja/Shutterstock.com, p. 482; Stockbyte/Getty Images, p. 512.

Library of Congress Cataloging-in-Publication Data

DuBrin, Andrew J.
Human relations for career and personal success : concepts, applications, and skills / Andrew J. DuBrin.—10th ed.
p. cm.
Includes index.
ISBN-13: 978-0-13-297440-0
ISBN-10: 0-13-297440-1
1. Success in business. 2. Organizational behavior. 3. Psychology, Industrial. 4. Interpersonal relations. I. Title.
HF5386.D768 2014
650.1—dc23 2012044293

10 9 8 7 6 5 4 3 2 1

PEARSON

ISBN 10: 0-13-297440-1
ISBN 13: 978-0-13-297440-0

To Rosie—and her sparkle
To Clare—and her spirit
To Camila—and her spontaneity
To Sofia—and her self-confidence
To Eliana—and her sweetness
To Julian—and his serenity
To Carson—and his sense of humor
To Owen—and his sociability

Brief Contents

Brief Contents

Contents

Preface

New to This Edition

In addition to thoroughly updating material throughout the text, I have also made other key changes, which include the following:

- Many of the introductory cases, Human Relations in Practice inserts, and case studies have been replaced with contemporary material. Thirteen chapter-introduction cases are new.
- Fourteen Human Relations in Practice inserts have been replaced with new inserts.
- There are twenty new end-of-chapter case studies in this edition. A new appendix has been added that provides an activity for integrating many of the concepts in the text as applied to oneself.
- In many places within the text I have removed some material to reduce complexity, as well as to make room for new material.
- Many new self-assessments, role-plays, and class activities have been added to this edition, including seven new skill-building exercises, eighteen new self-assessment quizzes, sixteen new role-playing exercises (most of them linked to the case studies), and one new class activity. Three Internet skill-building exercises have been replaced with new exercises.
- Detailed chapter-by-chapter revisions and updates—in addition to the changes already mentioned—include the following:

Chapter 1: Human Relations and You

- Self-Assessment Quiz 1-1: My Attitudes Toward Studying Human Relations, including a discussion of the rationale for each answer
- Deletion of discussion presenting an overview of major challenges in the workplace

Chapter 2: Self-Esteem and Self-Confidence

- The consequences of self-esteem are grouped into positive and negative categories
- Information about resilience training and developing self-confidence
- A discussion of how codependence is linked to low self-esteem and low self-confidence

Chapter 3: Self-Motivation and Goal Setting

- Expansion of Maslow's need hierarchy with three extra classes of needs
- Discussion of self-determination as part of employee engagement
- Self-Assessment Quiz 3-3, My Engagement Drivers

Chapter 4: Emotional Intelligence, Attitudes, and Happiness

- Brief discussion of social intelligence in relation to emotional intelligence
- New listing of several of the 100 Best Companies to Work For
- Self-Assessment Quiz 4-1, My Tendencies Toward Organizational Citizenship Behavior
- Self-Assessment Quiz 4-2, The Happiness Checklist

Chapter 5: Values and Ethics

- Socialization as the process for acquiring company values
- New survey about the extent of ethical problems in business
- Engaging in unethical behavior to benefit the company as a cause of ethical problems

Chapter 6: Problem Solving and Creativity

- Human Relations Self-Assessment Quiz 6-1, The Concentration Checklist
- How believing that you are creative can enhance your creativity
- How seeking feedback on your performance can enhance creativity
- How multiple intelligences contributes to problem solving and creativity

Chapter 7: Personal Communication Effectiveness

- Self-Assessment Quiz 7-1, My Communication Effectiveness
- Lie detection through nonverbal communication
- Using social media to enhance communication effectiveness
- Positive communication skills and social networking
- Negative communication skills and social networking
- Soliciting feedback on communication effectiveness
- Gender differences in use of pronouns
- Human Relations Self-Assessment Quiz 7-3, Common Listening Mistakes

Chapter 8: Communication in the Workplace

- The relevance of a positive first impression for relationship building
- Social networking websites as formal communication channels
- Communities of practice as formal communication channels
- Self-assessment Quiz 8-1, The Strength of My Network of Contacts
- Being prepared to think on your feet during a meeting

Chapter 9: Specialized Tactics for Getting Along with Others in the Workplace

- New chapter title to clarify purpose of chapter
- Human Relations Self-Assessment Quiz 9-1, The Civil Behavior Checklist
- Importance of speaking to customer in his or her preferred language even if you can speak his or her native language

Chapter 10: Managing Conflict

- More information about workplace bullying
- Human Relations Self-Assessment Quiz 10-1, Am I Dealing With a Passive-Aggressive Personality?
- Dealing with difficult people shifted from Chapter 9 to Chapter 10

Chapter 11: Becoming an Effective Leader

- Human Relations Self-Assessment Quiz 11-1, The Trustworthiness and Honesty Checklist
- More information about the leader-exchange model

Chapter 12: Motivating Others and Developing Teamwork

- Information about the effectiveness of positive reinforcement as a motivational technique
- The impact of a team leader's positive mood on teamwork.
- Human Relations Self-Assessment Quiz 12-1, My Own Motivators

Chapter 13: Diversity and Cross-Cultural Competence

- Social support seeking as a dimension of cultural values
- Recognizing own personal biases as a way of improving cross-cultural relations
- Human Relations Self-Assessment Quiz 13-2, The Personal Biases and Prejudices Checklist
- Cultural training for domestic employees
- A section on ways in which organizations us diversity to advantage, as follows: diverse teams; matching organizational diversity with community diversity; accommodations for people with physical disabilities; work/personal life accommodations; and employee network (affinity) groups
- State laws protecting the employment rights of gay, lesbian, bisexual, or transgender (LGBT) workers.

Chapter 14: Getting Ahead in Your Career

- Human Relations Self-Assessment Quiz 14-1, Qualifications Sought by Employers
- Expanded discussion of job résumé construction
- Expanded discussion of cover letter
- Expanded discussion of job interview
- Expanded discussion of online reputation and the job search
- Human Relations Self-Assessment Quiz 14-2, Tendencies Toward Being a Proactive Personality

Chapter 15: Learning Strategies, Perception, and Life Span Changes

- Expanded discussion of e-learning
- Shortened section about learning styles
- Human Relations Self-Assessment Quiz 15-1, Should I Be Thinking About a Career Change?

Chapter 16: Developing Good Work Habits

- Boosting your energy to improve work habits and time management
- Human Relations Self-Assessment Quiz 16-2, My Tendencies Toward Wasting or Not Wasting Time

Chapter 17: Managing Stress and Personal Problems

- Reducing stress created by financial problems through using a budget worksheet to help get finances under control
- How role conflict and role ambiguity can have a negative impact on organizational citizenship behavior
- Abusive supervision and uncivil workers as stressors
- Expanded discussion of developing resilience

Welcome to the tenth edition of *Human Relations for Career and Personal Success: Concepts, Applications, and Skills*. This new edition continues the emphasis of the ninth edition on developing effective human relations skills for the workplace, including material on teamwork and motivating and influencing others. The purpose of this book is to show how you can become more effective in your work and personal life through knowledge of and skill in human relations. A major theme of this text is that career and personal success are related. Success on the job often enhances personal success, and success in personal life can enhance job success. Dealing effectively with people is an enormous asset in both work and personal life.

This text is written to help students deal with human relations problems in the workplace and in personal life. It is designed to be appropriate for human relations courses taught in colleges, career schools, vocational-technical schools, and other postsecondary schools. Managerial, professional, and technical workers who are forging ahead in their careers will also find this book immediately useful in improving workplace and personal relationships.

Organization of the Book

The text is divided into four parts, reflecting the major issues in human relations.

Part I covers four aspects of understanding and managing yourself. Chapter 1 focuses on the meaning of human relations, self-understanding, and the interrelationship of career and personal success. Chapter 2 explains how self-esteem and self-confidence are important parts of human functioning. Chapter 3 explains how to use self-motivation and goal setting to improve your chances for success. Chapter 4 deals with the importance of emotional intelligence and attitudes and factors associated with being happy. Chapter 5 explains the contribution of values and ethics to effective human relations. Chapter 6 explains the basics of solving problems and making decisions with an emphasis on creativity.

Part II examines the heart of human relations—dealing effectively with other people. The topics in Chapters 7 through 13 are, respectively, personal communication effectiveness; communication in the workplace; specialized techniques for getting along with others in the workplace; managing conflict; becoming an effective leader; motivating others and developing teamwork; and developing cross-cultural competence.

Part III provides information to help career-minded people capitalize on their education, experiences, talents, and ambitions. The topics of Chapters 14 through 16 are getting ahead in your career; learning strategies, perception, and life span changes; and developing good work habits.

Part IV deals with staying emotionally healthy, while Chapter 17 covers managing stress and personal problems.

About the Author

An accomplished author, Andrew J. DuBrin, PhD, brings to his work years of research experience in human relations and business psychology. He has published numerous articles, textbooks, professional books on such subjects as impression management, and narcissism in the workplace. He also serves occasionally as a peer reviewer of journal articles. Dr. DuBrin received his PhD from Michigan State University and is Professor Emeritus at the E. Philip Saunders College of Business, Rochester Institute of Technology, where he has taught organizational behavior, leadership, and career management.

Experience the DuBrin Total Learning System

Human Relations for Career and Personal Success is not simply a textbook. The tenth edition contains a wealth of experiential exercises, including new cases and self-assessment quizzes that can be completed in class or as homework.

Chapter-Opening Cases Set the Stage

Chapter-opening cases introduce students to the topic and set the stage for the chapter narrative.

Pedagogical Features Relate Concepts to What's Happening Today, Personally and in the Workplace

- **Self-assessment quizzes** give students the opportunity to explore their own opinions, feelings, and behavior patterns as related to chapter topics. All chapters include one or more self-assessment quizzes.
- **Human Relations in Practice** boxes in all chapters illustrate real human relations business practices in today's business world.
- **Motivational "words of wisdom"** from a wide variety of business and world leaders and experts are included in all chapters.

Expanded Assignment Material

End-of-chapter assignment material is organized into two sections:
Concept Review and Reinforcement, featuring exercises that focus on concept retention and developing critical-thinking skills, and **Developing Your Human Relations Skills**, focusing on developing skills that can be used immediately in life and on the job.

Concept Review and Reinforcement	**Key Terms** **Chapter Summary and Review** provides an excellent detailed review of key chapter concepts. **Check Your Understanding** provides questions, reviews key chapter topics, and stimulates thinking about the issues. **Web Corner** provides informational Web sites and asks students to use the power of the Web in researching outside resources. Three of the Internet Skill Builder exercises have been replaced by new exercises.
Developing Your Human Relations Skills	**Skills Exercises** tie together chapter topics and allow students to apply what they have just learned. **New Role-Playing and Class Projects** allow students to practice and model human relations situations in the classroom. **Two Human Relations Case Studies** put students into a realistic scenario so they can practice making decisions in tough situations.

Supplements for Teaching and Learning

Online Course Support

Distance Learning Solutions: Convenience, Simplicity, Success

RESOURCES FOR INSTRUCTORS

To access supplementary materials online, instructors need to request an instructor access code. Go to www.pearsonhighered.com/irc, where you can register for an instructor access code. Within forty-eight hours of registering, you will receive a confirming e-mail including an instructor access code. Once you have received your code, locate your text in the online catalog and click on the Instructor Resources button on the left side of the catalog product page. Select a supplement, and a log-in page will appear. Once you have logged in, you can access instructor material for all Prentice Hall textbooks.

INSTRUCTOR'S MANUAL WITH TEST ITEM FILE

The online instructor's manual for this text contains a large number of multiple-choice and true/false test questions, chapter outlines and lecture notes, answers to discussion questions and case problems, and comments about the exercises.

MYTEST GENERATOR

The computerized test-generation system gives you maximum flexibility in preparing tests. It can be used to create custom tests and print scrambled versions of a test at one time, as well as to build tests randomly by chapter, level of difficulty, or question type. The software also allows online testing and record keeping and the ability to add problems to the database.

POWERPOINT LECTURE PRESENTATION PACKAGE

Lecture presentation screens for each chapter are available online and on the IRC.

JWA HUMAN RELATIONS VIDEOS

JWA videos on human relations and interpersonal communication topics are available to qualified adopters. Contact your local representative for details.

Acknowledgments

A book of this nature cannot be written and published without the cooperation of many people. Many outside reviewers of this and the previous editions provided constructive suggestions for improving the book. The following reviewers provided detailed feedback that drove the refocusing of this edition:

Verl Anderson, Dixie State College

Chet Eric Barney, New Mexico State University

Beverly Bryant, North Carolina Central University

Tommy Gilbreath, The University of Texas

Dorothy Hetmer-Hinds, Trinity Valley Community College

Heidi Hilbert, Eastern Iowa Community College

Norma Johansen, Scottsdale Community College

Daniell Scane, Orange Coast College

Tom Shaughnessy, Illinois Central College

Jim Wilhelm, South Plains College

Previous edition reviewers:

Mary D. Aun, DeVry Technical Institute

Daniel Bialis, Muskegon Community College

Donna Ana Branch and H. Ralph Todd Jr., American River College

Hollis Chaleau Brown, Oakton Community College

Sheri Bryant, DeKalb Technical Institute

Jewel Cherry, Forsyth Technical Community College

Win Chesney, St. Louis Community College

Claudia Cochran, El Paso Community College

Joy Colwell, Purdue University

Dr. Nora Jo Sherman, Houston Community College
Bernice Rose, Computer Learning Center

Ruth Keller, Indiana Vo-Tech College

Jessica Li, University of North Texas

Darlean McClure, College of the Sequoias

Michelle Meyer, Joliet Junior College

Alvin Motley, Metropolitan Community College

Therese Nemec, Fox Valley Technical College

Marcia Polanis, Forsyth Technical Community College

Steve Quinn, Olympic College

Debra Rowe, Oakland Community College

Pamela Simon, Baker College

Rudy Soliz, Houston Community College

Reginald St. Clair, Mountain Empire Community College

Carol Thole, Shasta College

James Van Arsdall, Metropolitan Community College

Susan Verhulst, Des Moines Area Community College

Jim Wilhelm, South Plains College

A special thanks goes to Terese Nemec and Kath Lich from Fox Valley Technical College and Sharon Chacon-Mineau from Northease Wisconsin Technical College for their assistance in revising and expanding the supplementary materials that accompany this textbook.

Thanks also to my family members, whose emotional support and encouragement assist my writing: Melanie, Will, Carson, Owen, Douglas, Gizella, Camila, Sofia, Eliana, Julian, Drew, Rosie, and Clare.

Andrew J. DuBrin

Rochester, New York

Human Relations for Career and Personal Success

1

Human Relations and You

Outline

Sandy Bellows was being honored as the local Woman of the Year by a public relations trade association. Bellows was the executive vice president of a private organization that promoted tourism and convention business in her geographic area. During the awards ceremony, several people who either report directly to Bellows or work closely with her were asked to comment on what makes Sandy Bellows so special.Jack, the director of tourism publicity, spoke first. Among his comments were, "Sandy knows no limits to the kindness and respect she shows to others on her team. When a suggestion of mine might be way off base, Sandy will listen carefully and then compliment me for the good in my idea. But then she will ask me a few sharp questions that point me in the direction of coming up with a better solution to the problem I am facing."

Penny, the convention and banquet manager at a large hotel in the area, opened her comments about Bellows in these terms: "Sandy really knows what it means to partner *with somebody in the community. She works with me and my staff in a fully cooperative way. She keeps emphasizing how the community can prosper only if we truly collaborate in finding ways to bring convention business to our city. Working with Sandy has helped us hotel managers realize that we are not competing against each other but against other areas of the country."*

Megan, who has worked five years as the administrative assistant to Bellows, included this point in her comments: "Sandy makes me feel like the most important person in her workday. She asks my opinion about so many things. She frequently asks me what she *can do to make my job run more smoothly. The impression I get is that Sandy makes a lot of other people feel important too."*

Learning Objectives ▸

After studying the information and doing the exercises in this chapter, you should be able to:

1. Understand how studying human relations will help you.
2. Pinpoint how work and personal life influence each other.
3. Understand how effective human relations begins with self-understanding.
4. Understand the timeline and development of the human relations movement.
5. Understand the major factors influencing job performance and behavior.

The comments made about this public-sector executive focus on the importance of effective human relations. Treating people with kindness helps Sandy Bellows deal effectively with the businesspeople her organization serves, as well as her employees. This book presents a wide variety of suggestions and guidelines for improving your personal relationships both on and off the job. Most of them are based on systematic knowledge about human behavior.

We begin our study of human relations by inviting you to take Human Relations Self-Assessment Quiz 1-1, which will give you an opportunity to think through your attitudes about this field of study and practice.

Human Relations Self-Assessment Quiz 1-1

My Attitudes Toward Studying Human Relations

Indicate whether you think the following statements are mostly true or mostly false.

No.	Statement about Human Relations	Mostly True	Mostly False
1.	High-paying jobs are based on technical skills, so studying human relations will hold you back financially.	______	______
2.	Leadership positions usually require both human relations and intellectual skills.	______	______
3.	Having good people skills is mostly common sense.	______	______
4.	Elite business schools now emphasize human relations skills in addition to analytical skills.	______	______
5.	Because everybody in business has a smart phone these days, you never really have to worry about dealing with people face to face.	______	______
6.	A lot of self-made millionaires are rude and mean, so studying human relations won't get you very far.	______	______
7.	Should I encounter any difficulties in dealing with someone on the job, I will simply find the right app on my smart phone and solve the problem.	______	______
8.	With the right emoticons, such as a smiley face, I will be able to solve almost all my problems involving people.☺	______	______
9.	Taking a course in human relations is mostly a waste of time if it is not in your major.	______	______
10.	Good human relations skills help you hold on to a job, even in highly technical fields.	______	______

Scoring key and interpretation:

The more questions you answered "incorrectly" as suggested by the scoring key, the more you are likely to benefit from studying human relations. The fewer questions you answered "correctly," the more you need to study human relations.

1. **Mostly False.** It is definitely true that technical specialties pay much better to start than nontechnical specialties. Yet in the long run, those people who combine their technical skills with human relation skills generally get more promotions and earn more money than those people who rely exclusively on technical skills. (An exception here is that a great inventor can often get by almost exclusively on technical skill.)
2. **Mostly True.** Few people are promoted to leadership positions who do not combine interpersonal (or human relations) skills with intellectual skills. The highest level leaders in most fields are able to inspire other people and solve difficult business-related problems.
3. **Mostly False.** It would seem that having good human relations skills would be common sense, but sadly this is not true. Relatively few people have good human relations skills. Also common sense is not so common, as indicated by all the problems people experience including drunk driving, spending more than they earn, and not reading directions for the safe use of equipment.
4. **Mostly True.** In recent years the elite business schools such as those at Harvard, MIT, and the University of Pennsylvania have recognized that they went too far in emphasizing analytical, technical, and financial skills. So now these schools place a heavier emphasis on soft skills such as leadership, motivation, and ethics.
5. **Mostly False.** Successful people in all types of organizations still take time to meet face to face with employees and customers and communicate with them. Even technology companies like Dell and IBM still maintain a large sales force that calls on customers.
6. **Mostly False.** It may be true that many self-made millionaires are rude and mean, but they are the exception. Mark Zuckerberg founded Facebook in his early twenties, and is now one of world's best-known CEOs. He continues to refine his human relations skills by meeting regularly with his team to discuss ways in which he can improve his effectiveness with people.
7. **Mostly False.** Dealing with complex human relations problems takes more than a quick access to an app on your smart phone. Even if the app would point you in the right direction, such as an app for dealing with difficult people, you still need to have studied and practiced your skill before an immediate need arises—much like having practiced a maneuver in a sport before it is needed in a big game.

8. **Mostly False.** Emoticons may be cool, and a form of nonverbal communication, but they cannot solve many human relations problems. Much more knowledge than sending an emoticon is needed to deal effectively with people when the issue is complex.
9. **Mostly False.** A course in human relations is rarely part of a student's major, but it is designed to supplement a major. The results from a course in human relations are never guaranteed, but anybody in any field can benefit from knowledge that might help them interact more effectively with others in the workplace.
10. **Mostly True.** During the past twenty-five years large numbers of jobs have been outsourced to other companies, often located in other countries. To the extent that your job involves established relationships with people, the less likely it is to be outsourced. For example, a sales rep with good contacts in the industry is less likely to have his or her job outsourced to a firm that does sales and marketing for other companies.

How Can Studying Human Relations Help You?

Learning Objective 1

In the context used here, **human relations** is the art of using systematic knowledge about human behavior to improve personal, job, and career effectiveness. The field studies individuals and groups in organizations. Human relations is far more than "being nice to people," because it applies systematic knowledge to treating people in such a way that they feel better and are more productive—such as providing a more relaxed work atmosphere to enhance worker creativity.

Human relations
the art of using systematic knowledge about human behavior to improve personal, job, and career effectiveness

From the standpoint of management, human relations is quite important because it contributes to **organizational effectiveness**—the extent to which an organization is productive and satisfies the demands of interested parties, such as employees, customers, and investors. Steve Kent, an equities analyst (not a human relations specialist), made extensive observations about the importance of treating employees well (using principles of human relations). He found that treating employees with respect and paying them fairly contributes to developing an efficient and creative organization. Business firms that go the extra mile to treat employees well often derive tangible benefits, such as a high quality of customer service.[1]

Organizational effectiveness
the extent to which an organization is productive and satisfies the demands of interested parties, such as employees, customers, and investors

Human relations knowledge and skills are also potentially beneficial for the individual as well as the organization.[2] The following case history illustrates how a career-minded person made effective use of human relations principles to resolve a difficult situation that seemed to be blocking her career. You might be able to use the same approach if you face a similar problem.

> Ashley worked as a business analyst at a large hospital. Her responsibilities included searching for ways to improve work processes at the hospital, such as developing better forms for collecting information about patients and reducing the time outpatients spent in the waiting room. Ashley enjoyed her work and believed that she was gaining valuable experience toward her goal of becoming a hospital administrator.
>
> Another contributor to Ashley's job satisfaction was her relationship with Paul, her boss. Ashley perceived her work relationship with him to be ideal. Paul kept feeding Ashley interesting assignments, gave her useful suggestions from time to time, and frequently praised her work. On her most recent performance evaluation, Ashley was described as "an ideal hospital business analyst with great potential."
>
> Ashley's smooth working relationship with her manager quickly changed one January. Paul informed the group that the hospital had offered him a

promotion to a much bigger role at the hospital and that although he enjoyed his present position, he felt obliged to accept the promotion. In Paul's place, the hospital appointed Jody, an experienced supervisor in another department within the hospital.

Within the first three weeks, Jody began criticizing Ashley's work. Jody told Ashley that her approach to improving business processes was not up-to-date, and that it lacked the kind of depth the hospital needed. Ashley then worked diligently on her next project to make the kind of improvements Jody suggested. Jody then found something else to criticize, this time telling Ashley that her PowerPoint presentations supporting her report were too complex, making them difficult for hospital administrators to follow.

Soon Jody found ways to criticize Ashley personally, in addition to the work she was performing. She suggested that Ashley should be careful to never wear heels higher than one and one half inches to the office and that the tattoo on her neck was unprofessional. Jody also suggested to Ashley twice that she should make sure to use the Internet only for job-related purposes during working hours.

After five months of regular criticism from her boss, Ashley decided to talk over the strained relationship with David, a close friend. Ashley explained to David that the negative chemistry between her and her boss was giving her chest pains and interrupted sleep. Ashley also emphasized that she was worried about receiving such a poor evaluation that it would damage her career.

David advised Ashley to "do what she had to do," by confronting her boss about the unjustified criticisms. If that didn't work, Ashley should communicate directly with Jody's manager to get the problem resolved. David explained that "In the modern organization, you are expected to bring problems right out on the table."

Ashley thanked David for his advice and then did some careful reflection. On the surface, David's advice made sense, but with her career potentially at stake, Ashley did not want to operate on common sense alone. She remembered studying about attitude change somewhere in human relations or social psychology. A point that stuck in her mind was that favorable interactions lead to attitude change.

Ashley developed a game plan to look for ways to have positive interactions with Jody whenever possible. One day she thanked Jody for the suggestions she made about preparing less complicated PowerPoint slides. She also incorporated ideas from a recent article about business process reengineering into her next suggestion for improving the workflow in the hospital laundry. Another day Ashley complimented Jody about a business suit she was wearing. At a luncheon meeting with Jody and several other department members, Ashley wore a blouse that covered the tattoo on her neck.

Ashley's game plan of applying a little-known principle of human relations to improving her relationship with her boss soon started to pay off. Jody actually complimented Ashley's report and stated that she was a strong contributor to the hospital. The most concrete evidence of an improved relationship was that Jody rated Ashley as "exceeding expectations" the first time she formally evaluated her performance.

As the case history just presented indicated, another way of understanding the importance of human relations is to examine its personal benefits. A person who carefully studies human relations and incorporates its suggestions into his or her work and personal life should derive the five benefits discussed next. Knowledge itself, however, is no guarantee of success. Because people differ greatly in learning ability, personality, and life circumstances, some will get more out of studying human relations than will others. You may, for example, be getting along well with coworkers or customers, so studying this topic might seem unnecessary from your viewpoint. Or you may be so shy at this stage of your life that you are unable to capitalize on some of the suggestions for being assertive with people. You might have to work doubly hard to benefit from studying that topic. The major benefits from studying human relations are the following:

1. Acquiring valid information about human behavior. To feel comfortable with people and to make a favorable impression both on and off the job, you need to understand how people think and act. Studying human relations will provide you with some basic knowledge about interpersonal relationships, such as the meaning of self-esteem, why goals work, and win–win conflict resolution. You will even learn such things as effective methods of dealing with difficult people.

2. Developing skills in dealing with people. People who aspire to high-level positions or enriched social lives need to be able to communicate with others, work well on a team, manage stress, and behave confidently. Relating well to diverse cultural groups is also an asset. Studying information about such topics, coupled with practicing what you learn, should help you develop such interpersonal skills.

3. Coping with job problems. Almost everyone who holds a job inevitably runs into human relations problems. Reading about these problems and suggestions for coping with them could save you considerable inner turmoil. Among the job survival skills that you will learn about in the study of human relations are how to deal with difficult people and how to overcome what seems to be an overwhelming workload.

4. Coping with personal problems. We all have problems. An important difference between the effective and the ineffective person is that the effective person knows how to manage them. Among the problems studying human relations will help you cope with are self-defeating behavior, dealing with a difficult coworker, overcoming low self-confidence, and working your way out of heavy job stress.

5. Capitalizing on opportunities. Many readers of this book will someday spend part of their working time taking advantage of opportunities rather than solving daily problems. Every career-minded person needs a few breakthrough experiences to make life more rewarding. Toward this end, studying human relations gives you ideas for developing your career, becoming a leader, and becoming more creative.

6. Demonstrating potential for advancement. As implied in the point just made, workers with skill and knowledge about human relations are more likely to be perceived as having advancement potential than workers who lack such skill and knowledge. Supervisors, managers, and other categories of leaders are typically selected from among those individual workers who have good human relations skills in addition to their technical skills and other types of job knowledge. As mentioned in an article about Hollywood studio DreamWorks Animation, "the chief technology officer has to play well with people."[3]

The accompanying Human Relations in Practice box illustrates how human relations skill and understanding can be important even at the highest level of a corporation. You are invited to take the accompanying Human Relations Self-Assessment Quiz 1-2 to think through your current level of human relations effectiveness.

How Do Work and Personal Life Influence Each Other?

Learning Objective 2

Most people reading this book will be doing so to improve their job effectiveness and careers. Therefore, the book centers on relationships with people in a job setting. Keep in mind that human relationships in work and personal life have much in common. Several studies have supported the close relationship between job satisfaction and life satisfaction. One such study conducted by Timothy A. Judge, psychology professor at Notre

Human Relations in Practice

Indra K. Nooyi, Chairman and Chief Executive Officer of PepsiCo: A Combination of Big Thinking and Human Relations Skills

Indra K. Nooyi is Chairman and Chief Executive Officer of PepsiCo, a major multinational corporation whose major product lines are Quaker Oats, Tropicana, Gatorade, Frito-Lay, and Pepsi-Cola. Nooyi worked her way into the top position at PepsiCo based in large part on her ability to think strategically, or defining the overall purpose of what the company is doing (looking at the big picture). She has directed the company's global strategy for fifteen years.

Nooyi is the chief architect of PepsiCo's growth strategy for years to come, called Performance with Purpose. The strategy focuses on delivering sustainable growth by investing in a healthier future for people and the planet. Performance with Purpose involves PepsiCo's major commitments: Build a group of enjoyable and wholesome foods and beverages; find innovative ways to reduce the use of energy, water, and packaging; and provide an outstanding workplace.

In addition to being a strategic leader, Nooyi is recognized as a person who values and practices effective human relations. She strongly believes that employees at all levels should feel free to talk about or handle personal concerns while on the job. She admits that you cannot spend the entire workday talking about your home life, but "a great corporation allows you to bring your whole self to work." Nooyi has stated publically that she has always taken calls from her two daughters during working hours even if the question is "Can I play Nintendo?"

Nooyi has been known to take time from her executive schedule to greet a colleague at the airport who has returned from a long business trip. She emphasizes that communication skills are essential for PepsiCo leaders and that you can never over-invest in them. Nooyi also says that companies that want to prosper must attract talented people to come to work for them. Doing so demands that the company has a work environment that inspires people, motivates them, and cultivates their abilities. The company must be a place where diverse values, beliefs, and practices are respected. Nooyi explains that people must be shown respect by speaking to them with truth and candor, including giving them honest feedback.

According to Nooyi, another key component of good human relations is for managers to be approachable. Workers should feel that they are able to talk to their managers informally to discuss problems and ask questions. Above all, managers and leaders must make employees feel appreciated and show that they are deeply valued.

Nooyi holds a BS degree from Madras Christian College, an MBA from the Indian Institute of Management in Calcutta, and an MA in Public and Private Management from Yale University.

Questions: How might managers having effective human relations skills contribute to the prosperity of a company such as PepsiCo?

Sources: The original story presented above was created based on facts presented in the following: Sue Shellenbarger, "PepsiCo's Indra Nooyi on Tough Calls," *The Wall Street Journal*, April 10, 2011, p. B1; Interview by Tony Bingham and Pat Galagan, "Doing Good While Doing Well," *T & D*, June 2008, pp. 32–36; Indra K.Nooyi, "Our Leadership," www.pepsico.com, p. 1, accessed January 1, 2012; "Biography of Indra Nooyi," *Incredible People*, pp. 1–4, accessed January 2, 2012.

Human Relations Self-Assessment Quiz 1-2

Human Relations Skills

For each of the following statements about human relations skills, indicate how strong you think you are right now. Attempt to be as objective as possible, even though most of us tend to exaggerate our skills in dealing with people. To help obtain a more objective evaluation of your capabilities, ask someone who knows you well (family member, friend, or work associate) to also rate you on these factors. Use the following scale: (1) very weak, (2) weak, (3) average, (4) strong, (5) very strong.

Person	Self-Rating	Rating by Other
1. Listen carefully when in conversation with another person	______	______
2. Smile frequently	______	______
3. Am tactful when criticizing others	______	______
4. Am comfortable in dealing with people from a different generation than myself	______	______
5. Am comfortable in dealing with a person from a different ethnic group than myself	______	______
6. Am comfortable in dealing with a person from a different race than myself	______	______
7. Let my feelings be known when I disagree with another person	______	______
8. Let my feelings be known when I am joyful about something	______	______
9. Have a neat, well-groomed appearance	______	______
10. Congratulate the winner when I lose an athletic or any other type of contest	______	______
11. Concentrate on another person when in conversation instead of accepting a call on my cell phone, making use of call waiting, or responding to e-mail	______	______
12. Compliment others when a compliment is merited	______	______
13. Have a good sense of humor	______	______
14. Am patient with people who do not understand what I am saying	______	______
15. Cooperate with others in a team effort	______	______
16. Have a controllable temper	______	______
17. Am respected for being honest and dependable	______	______
18. Hug people when the situation is appropriate	______	______
19. Am trusted by other people	______	______
20. Motivate others to do something they hadn't thought of doing	______	______
21. Willing to talk to another person to resolve a problem rather than relying exclusively on text messaging	______	______
Total Score	______	______
Combined Score (self plus other)		______

Interpretation

1. **Self-ratings:** If your self-rating is 85 or more, and your scoring is accurate, you have exceptional human relations skills. Scores between 60 and 84 suggest moderate, or average, human relations skills. Scores of 59 and below suggest below-average human relations skills in the areas covered in this quiz.
2. **Rating by other person:** Because people tend to judge us a little more critically than we judge ourselves in human relations skills, use the following scale: 80 or more suggests exceptional human relations skills; 55 to 79 suggests moderate, or average, human relations skills; 54 and below suggests below-average human relations skills.
3. **Combined ratings:** 165 or more suggests exceptional human relations skills; 115 to 163 suggests moderate, or average, human relations skills; 114 or below suggests below-average human relations skills.

Action plan: Whether you scored high, low, or medium on this quiz, there is always room for improvement, just as athletes, actors, and musicians are always looking to improve their art. Scores in the bottom category suggest a more urgent need for improvement in human relations skill.

FIGURE 1-1

HOW WORK AND PERSONAL LIFE INFLUENCE EACH OTHER

1. Job satisfaction enhances life satisfaction.
2. An unsatisfying job can damage physical health.
3. Relationships with people on and off the job influence each other.
4. Certain skills contribute to success in both work and personal life.
5. How we behave at work is closely related to how we behave at home.
6. Workers who achieve a good balance between the demands of work and family life are likely to be more productive and satisfied.

Dame University, and Remus Ilies, psychology professor at Michigan State University, involved seventy-four university employees with administrative support positions, such as secretaries or office managers. The researchers collected reports of mood and job satisfaction at work, mood away from work, and job satisfaction. Data were collected using questionnaires posted on a Web site.

The major findings of the study were that mood influences job satisfaction, with a positive mood increasing satisfaction. The effect decreases rapidly because moods pass quickly. The researchers also found that employee's satisfaction with their jobs, measured at work, influences the mood at home. Workers who are more emotional by nature are more likely to experience these connections, such as joy or anger, on the job spilling over to home life. A related finding was that a mood developed on the job spilled over to the home later in the day.[4] In short, this study confirmed the old cartoons about a worker who is chewed out by the boss coming home and swearing at his or her dog or kicking the furniture!

Work and personal life influence each other in a number of specific ways, as outlined in Figure 1-1. First, the satisfaction you achieve on the job contributes to your general life satisfaction. Conversely, if you suffer from chronic job dissatisfaction, your life satisfaction will begin to decline. Career disappointments have been shown to cause marital relationships to suffer. Frustrated on the job, many people start feuding with their partners and other family members.

Second, an unsatisfying job can affect physical health, primarily by creating stress and burnout. Intense job dissatisfaction may even lead to heart disease, ulcers, intestinal disorders, and skin problems. People who have high job satisfaction even tend to live longer than those who suffer from prolonged job dissatisfaction. These benefits may be attributed to better physical health and passion for life. Finding the right type of job may thus add years to a person's life.

Third, the quality of your relationships with people at work and in personal life influence each other. If you experience intense conflict in your family, you might be so upset that you will be unable to form good relationships with coworkers. Conversely, if you have a healthy, rewarding personal life, it will be easier for you to form good relationships on the job. People you meet on the job will find it pleasant to relate to a seemingly positive and untroubled person.

Another way of explaining the third point is that how we behave at work is closely related to how we behave at home. Psychologist John M. Gottman, executive director of the Relationship Research Institute, has been studying married couples for over thirty-five years. He and his colleagues have used devices such as camcorders, heart monitors, and other biofeedback equipment to measure what takes place when couples experience moments of conflict or closeness. The research results indicate that successful couples look for ways to emphasize the positive and attempt to say yes as often as possible. Successful couples use conflict as a way of working through personality differences rather than to attack each other.

A useful inference from research at the Relationship Research Institute is that the way people manage their relationships in the workplace is closely linked to the way they manage their personal ones. People who frequently use the word *yes* in communications at home are likely to do the same on the job. Also, people who are abusive on the job are likely to be abusive at home.[5]

Personal relationships on the job also influence personal relationships off the job. Interacting harmoniously with coworkers can put one in a better mood for dealing with family and friends after hours. Crossing swords with employees and customers during working hours can make it difficult for you to feel comfortable and relaxed with people off the job.

Fourth, certain skills contribute to success in both work and personal life. For example, people who know how to deal effectively with others and get things accomplished on the job can use the same skills to enhance their personal lives. Similarly, people who are effective in dealing with friends and family members and who can organize things are likely to be effective supervisors.

Fifth, workers who achieve a good balance between the demands of work and family life are likely to be more productive and have more job satisfaction.[6] This idea is often referred to as work/life balance even though "work" and "life" are certainly not opposites. The discussion of balance between work and family will be discussed in Chapter 10 about conflict.

Can you think of other ways in which success in work and success in personal life are related to each other?

How Does Human Relations Begin with Self-Understanding?

Learning Objective 3

Before you can understand other people very well, and therefore practice effective human relations, you must understand yourself. You already know something about yourself. An important starting point in learning more about yourself is self-examination. Suppose that instead of being about human relations, this book were about dancing. The reader would obviously need to know what other dancers do right and wrong. But the basic principles of dancing cannot be fully grasped unless they are seen in relation to your own style of dancing. Watching a video of you dancing, for example, would be helpful. You might also ask other people for comments and suggestions about your dance movements.

Similarly, to achieve **self-understanding**, you must gather valid information about yourself. (Self-understanding refers to knowledge about you, particularly with respect to mental and emotional aspects.) Every time you read a self-help book, take a personality quiz, or receive an evaluation of your work from a manager or instructor, you are gaining some self-knowledge.

Self-understanding
gathering valid information about oneself; self-understanding refers to knowledge about oneself, particularly with respect to mental and emotional aspects

In achieving self-understanding, it is helpful to recognize that the **self** is a complex idea. It generally refers to a person's total being or individuality. To help clarify the meaning of the self, a distinction is sometimes made between the self a person projects to the outside world and the inner self. The **public self** is what the person is communicating about himself or herself and what others actually perceive about the person. The **private self** is the actual person you may be.[7] A similar distinction is made between the real self and the ideal self. Many people think of themselves in terms of an ideal version of what they are really like. To avoid making continuous distinctions between the two selves throughout this text, we will use the term *self* to refer to an accurate representation of the individual.

Self
a complex idea generally referring to a person's total being or individuality

Public self
what a person communicates about himself or herself and what others actually perceive about the person

Private self
the actual person an individual may be

A recent addition to knowledge about the self is that we are also influenced by what could have happened to us or who we could have been. "I could have been a contender" is a famous line from a movie about prize fighting that illustrates the idea of how we think about what our lives might have been. The **alternative self** is an understanding of the self, based on *what could have been* if something in the past had happened differently.[8]

Alternative self
an understanding of the self, based on what could have been if something in the past had happened differently

Imagining what could have been can be a positive force. Tanya might think, "If I had studied math more carefully in the past I could now perform much better in a manufacturing job." Tanya therefore begins to study basic math to serve as a foundation for

FIGURE 1-2

SIX SOURCES OF INFORMATION THAT CONTRIBUTE TO SELF-UNDERSTANDING

1. General information about human behavior
2. Informal feedback from people
3. Feedback from superiors
4. Feedback from coworkers
5. Feedback from self-assessment quizzes
6. The Johari Window

new learning in manufacturing technologies. The alternative self might also be a negative force if it leads to discouragement. Brad might think, "If I hadn't married and had a family so early in life, I could have taken more risks in my career. Now instead of having started my own business, I'm stuck in a dead-end job."

Some scientific evidence suggests that the self is based on structures within the brain. According to the research of Joseph LeDoux at New York University, the self is the sum of the brain's individual components, or subsystems. Each subsystem has its own form of memory, along with its interactions with other subsystems.[9] Two examples of subsystems in the brain are the centers for speech and hearing. The implication to recognize here is that the self could be an entity that is both psychological and biological.

While we discuss the self in depth in the first chapter, the chapters that follow also deal with the self. Most of this text is geared toward using human relations knowledge for self-development and self-improvement. Throughout the text you will find questionnaires designed to improve insight. The self-knowledge emphasized here deals with psychological (such as personality traits and thinking style) rather than physical characteristics (such as height and blood pressure). As outlined in Figure 1-2, we discuss six types of information that contribute to self-understanding, along with potential problems in self-evaluation.

GENERAL INFORMATION ABOUT HUMAN BEHAVIOR

As you learn about people in general, you should also be gaining knowledge about yourself. Therefore, most of the information in this text is presented in a form that should be useful to you personally. Whenever general information is presented, it is your responsibility to relate such information to your particular situation, such as in studying sources of conflict. One such general cause is limited resources—that is, not everyone can have what he or she wants. See how this general principle applies to you. Here is an example involving others: "That's why I've been so angry with Melissa lately. She was the one given the promotion, whereas I'm stuck in the same old job."

In relating facts and observations about people in general to yourself, be careful not to misapply the information. Feedback from other people will help you avoid the pitfalls of introspection (looking into yourself).

INFORMAL FEEDBACK FROM PEOPLE

Feedback
information that tells one how well he or she has performed

As just implied, **feedback** is information that tells you how well you have performed. You can sometimes obtain feedback from the spontaneous comments of others or by asking them for feedback. An auto-insurance claims investigator grew one notch in self-confidence when coworkers began to call him "Super Sleuth." He was given this name because of his ability to quickly detect accident fraud. His experience illustrates that a valuable source of information for self-understanding is what the significant people in your life think of you. Although feedback of this type might make you feel uncomfortable, when it is consistent, it accurately reflects how others perceive you.

With some ingenuity you can create informal feedback. (In this sense, the term *informal* refers to not being part of a company-sponsored program.) For example, you might send an e-mail or social media post to ten people in your social network asking them for a candid evaluation of your strengths and weaknesses. Make the promise that you will not retaliate if you don't like what you hear.

A few skeptics will argue that friends never give you a true picture of yourself but, rather, say flattering things about you because they value your friendship. Experience has shown, however, that if you emphasize the importance of their opinions, most people will give you a few constructive suggestions. You also have to appear sincere. Because not everyone's comments will be helpful, you may have to sample many people.

FEEDBACK FROM SUPERIORS

Virtually all employers provide employees with formal or informal feedback on their performances. A formal method of feedback is called a *performance evaluation*. During a performance evaluation (or appraisal) your superior will convey to you what he or she thinks you are doing well and not so well. These observations become a permanent part of your human resources record. Informal feedback occurs when a superior discusses your job performance with you but does not record these observations.

Many companies have moved toward supplementing annual performance evaluations with frequent, informal feedback. Part of the reason for the shift to more frequent feedback is the growing number of millenials (the latest generation) entering the workforce, many of whom prefer immediate and frequent feedback. Sussane Bond, director of professional services for Halogen Software Inc., says, "It's no longer a sit-down once a year. Performance reviews mean timely feedback face to face with employees."[10]

The feedback obtained from superiors in this way can help you learn about yourself. For instance, if two different bosses say that you are a creative problem solver, you might conclude that you are creative. If several bosses tell you that you are too impatient with other people, you might conclude that you are impatient.

FEEDBACK FROM COWORKERS

A sometimes-used practice in organizations is **peer evaluations**, a system in which teammates contribute to an evaluation of a person's job performance. Although coworkers under this system do not have total responsibility for evaluating each other, their input is taken seriously. The amount of a worker's salary increase could thus be affected by peer judgments about his or her performance. The results of peer evaluations can also be used as feedback for learning about yourself. Assume that coworkers agree on several of your strengths and needs for improvement. You can conclude that others who work closely with you generally perceive you that way.

Peer evaluations
system in which teammates contribute to an evaluation of a person's job performance

Teammates might rate each other on performance dimensions such as cooperation with other members of the team, customer service attitude, productivity, and contributions to meetings. If several teammates rated you low in one of these dimensions, it could indicate a **developmental opportunity**, an area for growth, or weakness.

Developmental opportunity
area for growth or weakness

FEEDBACK FROM SELF-ASSESSMENT QUIZZES

Many self-help books, including this one, contain questionnaires that you fill out by yourself, for yourself. The information that you pick up from these questionnaires often provides valuable clues to your preferences, values, and personal traits. Such self-examination questionnaires should not be confused with the scientifically researched test you might take in a counseling center or guidance department or when applying for a job. Another source of useful self-assessment quizzes is www.queendom.com, which offers a variety of tests that contribute to self-understanding, including the classical intelligence quotient (IQ), mental toughness, risk-taking, and self-esteem tests, among many others.

The amount of useful information gained from self-examination questionnaires depends on your candor. Because no outside judge is involved in these self-help quizzes, candor usually is not a problem. An exception is that we all have certain blind spots. Most people, for example, believe that they have considerably above-average skills in dealing with people.

As a starting point in conducting self-examination exercises, you already completed Human Relations Self-Assessment Quiz 1-1. Quiz 1-3 gives you an opportunity to write some things down about yourself.

Human Relations Self-Assessment Quiz 1-3

The Written Self-Portrait

A good starting point in acquiring serious self-knowledge is to prepare a written self-portrait in the major life spheres (or aspects). In each of the following spheres, describe yourself in about twenty-five to fifty words. For example, interpersonal sphere, a person might write, "I'm a little timid on the surface. But those people who get to know me well understand that I'm filled with enthusiasm and joy. My relationships with people last a long time. I'm on excellent terms with all members of my family. And my significant other and I have been together for five years. We are very close emotionally and should be together for a lifetime."

A. Occupational and school: ______________________________

____

____

____

B. Interpersonal (interactions with people): ______________________________

____

____

____

C. Beliefs, values, and attitudes: ______________________________

____

____

____

D. Physical description (body type, appearance, grooming): ______________________________

____

____

____

A general point about all forms of feedback is that it takes mental toughness to benefit from the negative type. Yet according to writer Karen Wright, without negative feedback we would be stuck in the Stone Age, unable to learn or improve our chances for attaining success. Negative feedback is useful for negotiating life and interpersonal relations. Much of our growth and development depends on interactions and other experiences that feel bad.[11] For example, suppose that early in his career, an information technology (IT) specialist keeps telling his coworkers how badly he is overloaded with work. Soon a few coworkers tell him essentially to shut up and stop complaining. The IT specialist might profit from the negative feedback and come to understand that he should spend much less time complaining to his coworkers about his heavy workload.

LOOKING AT THE SELF THROUGH THE JOHARI WINDOW

A systematic approach to looking at yourself is through a model of communication called the Johari Window, which focuses on self-disclosure. The **Johari Window** is a grid showing how much information you know about yourself as well as how much other people know about you. (The term *Johari* came about because the method was created by Joseph Loft and Harry Ingram.)

Johari Window
a grid showing how much information you know about yourself as well as how much other people know about you

The basics of the model are outlined in Figure 1-3. One axis of the grid is the degree to which information about you is known to or understood by you. The other axis is the degree to which information about you is known to others. The horizontal dimension involves soliciting, or obtaining, feedback from others about you; the vertical dimension involves feedback about you to others, or self-disclosure.[12]

The basic premise of the model, as well as the lesson it teaches, is that we can improve our personal and professional relationships through understanding ourselves in depth. But you also have to take the next step of selecting those aspects of the self that are appropriate to share with others. A packaging specialist might want to reveal to coworkers that he does his best creative thinking when jogging alone. However, he might not want to reveal that he finds coworkers to be an annoying distraction while he is attempting to think creatively.

Another premise of the model is that the more we share of ourselves with others, the higher the probability of developing high-quality relationships. To develop these positive relationships, we need to be aware of the four areas (or four panes of the window) indicating what is known about us and what is hidden. Observe that the four areas, or panes, of the window are the basics of the communication model.

FIGURE 1-3 THE JOHARI WINDOW

Solicit Feedback →

Give Feedback ↓

	Known to Self	Unknown to Self
Known to Others	**Open Area:** known to self and others	**Blind Area:** blind to self, seen by others
Unknown to Others	**Hidden Area:** open to self, hidden from others	**Unknown Area:** unknown to self and others

Open area
pane of Johari Window consisting of information that is known to us and others

- The **open area** consists of information that is known to us and others. Among these readily observable aspects would be hair color, skin color, physical appearance, and spoken communication skills. As a relationship builds we enlarge the open area by revealing more about ourselves. As the open area expands, relationships with others improve—unless you annoy others with too many details about your work and personal life.

Hidden area
pane of Johari Window that contains information known to us about ourselves but is hidden from others

- The **hidden area** contains information known to us about ourselves but is hidden from others. Frequent hidden areas are ambitions and dislikes of specific individuals. Over the long term, fewer hidden areas lead to more openness and closeness in relationships with others. Yet it is prudent to keep some areas hidden, such as describing a strong physical attraction toward your coworker's or manager's spouse.

Blind area
pane of Johari Window that contains information that others are aware of but we cannot see in ourselves in reference to both positive and negative qualities

- The **blind area** contains information that others are aware of but we cannot see in ourselves in reference to both positive and negative qualities. Many people suffer from thinking that they are not physically attractive, yet others in general have an opposite perception. In the opposite direction, many people perceive themselves to be highly skilled in getting along with other people, yet most people might have an opposite point of view. Feedback from others, if not blocked by defensiveness, will help reduce the blind area. As your blind area decreases, you are likely to enlarge your open area because you will have more accurate data to work with.

Unknown area
pane of Johari Window that contains information that you and others do not know about you

- The **unknown area** contains information that you and others do not know about you. It sometimes takes an unusual situation to bring out this unknown information, such as emerging as a leader when a crisis, such as a hurricane, hits your unit of the company.

The Johari Window is useful in reminding you of the importance of self-disclosure, such as in enlarging your open area. As you disclose more about yourself, others will reciprocate and disclose more about themselves. The mutual disclosures lead to enhanced positive feelings among people in both work and personal life.

TWO SELF-EVALUATION TRAPS

The theme of this section of the chapter is that self-awareness is a positive force in our lives. Yet, self-awareness also has two negative extremes or traps. One of these extremes is that focusing on the self can highlight shortcomings the way staring into a mirror can dramatize every blemish and wrinkle on a face. Certain situations predictably force us to engage in self-reflection and become the object of our own attention. When we talk about ourselves, answer self-quizzes, stand before an audience or camera, or watch ourselves on a video, we become more self-aware and make comparisons to some arbitrary standard of behavior. The comparison often results in negative self-evaluation in comparison to the standard and a decrease in self-esteem as we discover that we fall short of standards.[13] Keeping the self-awareness trap in mind will help you minimize needless underevaluation, thereby benefiting from gathering feedback about yourself.

In contrast to underevaluation, it is also true that many people tend to overestimate their competence, such as thinking they deserve a bigger raise or an A in every course. A particular area in which people overestimate their competence is in the moral domain. Many people suffer from a "holier than thou" syndrome. A study with college students, for example, found that they consistently overrated the likelihood that they would act in generous or selfless ways. Eighty-four percent of the students initially predicted that they would cooperate with their partner, but in reality only 61 percent did.[14]

Cultural differences help explain at least some of the differences in underevaluation versus overevaluation. Several studies have shown, for example, that East Asians tend to underestimate their abilities, with an aim toward improving the self and getting along with others. North Americans are more likely to overestimate their abilities and not be so prone to look for areas of self-improvement.[15] Cultural differences reflect stereotypes that apply to the average individual from a culture.

The antidote to the twin self-evaluation traps is to search for honest and objective feedback from others to help you supplement your self-evaluation. Competing against peers, such as in school, sports, and contests on the job (for example, a sales contest or creative suggestion contest), can help you evaluate yourself more realistically. Next, we look more at human relations from the standpoint of the workplace rather than the individual.

How Did the Human Relations Movement Develop?

Learning Objective 4

The **human relations movement** began as a concentrated effort by some managers and their advisers to become more sensitive to the needs of employees or to treat them in a more humanistic manner. In other words, employees were to be treated as human beings rather than as parts of the productive process. As diagrammed in Figure 1-4, the human relations movement was supported directly by three different historic influences: the Hawthorne studies, the threat of unionization, and industrial humanism.[16] Scientific management, which predated the growth of human relations in industry, contributed indirectly to the movement.

Human relations movement movement that began as a concentrated effort by some managers and their advisers to become more sensitive to the needs of employees or to treat them in a more humanistic manner

SCIENTIFIC MANAGEMENT

The study of management became more systematized and formal as a byproduct of the Industrial Revolution, which took place from the 1700s through the 1900s. Approaches to managing work and people needed to be developed to manage all the new factories that were a central part of the Industrial Revolution. The focus of **scientific management** was on the application of scientific methods to increase individual workers' productivity. Frederick W. Taylor, considered the father of scientific management, was an engineer by background. He used scientific analysis and experiments to increase worker output. Taylor's goal was to remove human variability so each worker could become essentially an interchangeable part. His model for human behavior was a machine, with inexpensive parts, each of which has a specific function. Using the principles of scientific management, a worker might assemble a washing machine with the least number of wasted motions and steps. United Parcel Service (UPS) relies heavily on the principles of scientific management to get the most productivity from carriers and shipping personnel, including tightly timing their deliveries.

Scientific management theory that focuses on the application of scientific methods to increase individual workers' productivity

With scientific management sounding so dehumanizing, how could the movement have contributed to good human relations? Taylor also studied problems such as fatigue

FIGURE 1-4 INFLUENCES SUPPORTING THE HUMAN RELATIONS MOVEMENT

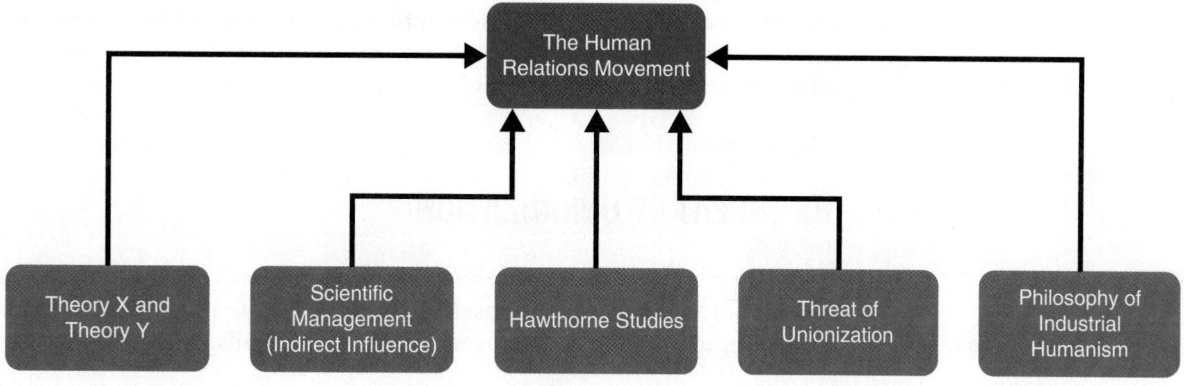

and safety. He urged management to study the relationship between work breaks and the length of the workday and productivity. He convinced some managers that work breaks and shorter workdays could increase productivity. Furthermore, scientific management proposed that workers who produced more be paid more.

Scientific management also contributed to the human relations movement by creating a backlash against what many people thought was mistreatment of workers. The industrial engineer with his or her stopwatch and clipboard, hovering over a worker measuring each tiny part of the job and the worker's movements, became a hated figure.[17] The objection to this approach called for a better way to treat people, which came to be known as the human relations movement.

THE HAWTHORNE STUDIES

The human relations school of management is generally said to have begun in 1927 with a group of studies conducted at the Chicago-area Hawthorne plant of an AT&T subsidiary. These studies were prompted by an experiment carried out by the company's engineers between 1924 and 1927. Following the tradition of scientific management, these engineers were applying research methods to investigate problems of employee productivity.

Two groups were studied to determine the effects of different levels of light on worker performance. As prescribed by the scientific method, one group received increased illumination, whereas the other did not. A preliminary finding was that when illumination was increased, the level of performance also increased. Surprisingly to the engineers, productivity also increased when the level of light was decreased almost to moonlight levels. One interpretation of these findings was that the workers involved in the experiment enjoyed being the center of attention. In other words, they reacted positively because management cared about them. Such a phenomenon taking place in any work or research setting is now called the **Hawthorne effect**.[18]

Hawthorne effect
applying research methods to investigate problems of employee productivity using the scientific method; in the study, employees reacted positively because management cared about them

As a result of these preliminary investigations, a team of researchers headed by Harvard professors Elton Mayo and Fritz J. Roethlisberger conducted a series of experiments extending over a six-year period. The conclusions they reached served as the foundations for later developments in the human relations approach to management. It was found that economic incentives are less important than generally believed in influencing workers to achieve high levels of output. Also, leadership practices and work group pressures profoundly influence employee satisfaction and performance. An example of an effective leadership practice would be coaching and encouraging workers to higher performance. The researchers noted that any factor influencing employee behavior is embedded in a social system. For instance, to understand the impact of pay on performance, you have to understand the atmosphere that exists in the work group and how the leader approaches his or her job.

A major implication of the Hawthorne studies was that the old concept of an economic person motivated primarily by money had to be replaced by a more valid idea. The replacement concept was a social person, motivated by social needs, desiring rewarding on-the-job relationships and more responsive to pressures from coworkers than to control by the boss.[19] Do you believe that workers are more concerned with social relationships than with money?

THE THREAT OF UNIONIZATION

Labor union officials and their advocates contend that the benefits of unionization extend to many workers who themselves do not belong to unions. Management in nonunion firms will often pay employees union wages to offset the potential advantages of unionization. A similar set of circumstances contributed to the growth of the human relations movement. Labor unions began to grow rapidly in the United States during the late 1930s. Many employers feared that the presence of a labor union would have negative consequences for their companies. Consequently, management looked aggressively for ways to stem the tide of unionization, such as using human relations techniques to satisfy workers.[20] Their reasoning is still valid today: Dissatisfied workers are much more likely to join a labor union, in hope of improving their working conditions.[21]

Today the threat of unionization is primarily in the public sector. Although unionization has declined considerably in manufacturing, about 36 percent of government workers, including those in education, are union members, compared with about 7 percent of workers in private-sector industries. In 1945, about 36 percent of the U.S. workforce was unionized, versus about 12 percent today.[22] The decline of manufacturing jobs has contributed to the decline of union membership. Much of the decline can be attributed to the outsourcing of manufacturing jobs to other countries and the use of information technology to replace workers.

THE PHILOSOPHY OF INDUSTRIAL HUMANISM

Partly as a byproduct of the Hawthorne studies, a new philosophy of human relations arose in the workplace. Elton Mayo was one of the two key figures in developing this philosophy of industrial humanism. He cautioned managers that emotional factors (such as a desire for recognition) were a more important contributor to productivity than physical and logical factors. Mayo argued vigorously that work should lead to personal satisfaction for employees.

Mary Parker Follett was another key figure in advancing the cause of industrial humanism. Her experience as a management consultant led her to believe that the key to increased productivity was to motivate employees, rather than simply ordering better job performance. The keys to both productivity and democracy, according to Follett, were cooperation, a spirit of unity, and a coordination of effort.[23]

THEORY X AND THEORY Y OF DOUGLAS MCGREGOR

The importance of managing people through more effective methods of human relations was advanced by the writings of social psychologist Douglas McGregor. His famous position was that managers should challenge their assumptions about the nature of people. McGregor believed that too many managers assumed that people were lazy and indifferent toward work. He urged managers to be open to the possibility that under the right circumstances people are eager to perform well. If a supervisor accepts one of these extreme sets of beliefs about people, the supervisor will act differently toward them than if he or she believes the opposite. These famous assumptions that propelled the human relations movement are summarized as follows:

Theory X Assumptions

1. The average person dislikes work and therefore will avoid it if he or she can.
2. Because of this dislike of work, most people must be coerced, controlled, directed, or threatened with punishment to get them to put forth enough effort to achieve organizational goals.
3. The average employee prefers to be directed, wishes to shirk responsibility, has relatively little ambition, and highly values job security.

Theory Y Assumptions

1. The expenditure of physical and mental effort in work is as natural as play or rest.
2. External control and the threat of punishment are not the only means for bringing about effort toward reaching company objectives. Employees will exercise self-direction and self-control in the service of objectives to which they attach high valence.
3. Commitment to objectives is related to the rewards associated with their achievement.
4. The average person learns, under proper conditions, not only to accept but also to seek responsibility.
5. Many employees have the capacity to exercise a high degree of imagination, ingenuity, and creativity in the solution of organizational problems.
6. Under the present conditions of industrial life, the intellectual potentialities of the average person are only partially utilized.[24]

The distinction between Theory X and Theory Y has often been misinterpreted. McGregor was humanistic, but he did not mean to imply that being directive and demanding with workers is always the wrong tactic. Some people are undermotivated and dislike work. In these situations, the manager has to behave sternly toward group members to motivate them. If you are a Theory Y manager, you size up your group members to understand their attitudes toward work.

RELEVANCE OF THE HISTORY OF HUMAN RELATIONS TO TODAY'S WORKPLACE

Many of the pioneering ideas described in the history of human relations are still relevant, partly because human nature has not undergone major changes. Most of the core ideas in the history of the human relations movement are still part of the human relations and organizational behavior curriculum today, even though they have more research substantiation and new labels. A good example is the push toward creativity and innovation based on the involvement of many different workers, not only specialists from one department. The link to history is that Theory Y encourages empowering employees to use their ingenuity and creativity to solve organizational problems. Next is a bulleted summary of ideas from the human relations movement that still influence the practice of human relations today.

- Many principles of scientific management are useful in making workers more productive so business firms can compete better in a global economy.
- Ideas from the Hawthorne studies have helped managers focus on the importance of providing both congenial work surroundings and adequate compensation to motivate and retain workers.
- Industrial humanism is widely practiced today in the form of looking for ways to keep workers satisfied through such methods as flexible work arrangements, family leave, and dependent care benefits.
- Theory Y has prompted managers to think through which style of leadership works best with which employees. Specifically, a modern manager is likely to grant more freedom to employees who are well motivated and talented. Spurred partially by Theory X, few managers today believe that being the "bull of the woods" is the best way to supervise all workers.

What Major Factors Influence Job Performance and Behavior?

Learning Objective 5

Part of understanding human relations is recognizing the factors or forces that influence job performance and behavior. In overview, the performance and behavior of workers is influenced by factors related to the employee, manager, job, and organization as discussed next and outlined in Figure 1-5. Here we present a sampling of these many factors, because a comprehensive understanding of them would encompass the study of human relations, organizational behavior, and management.

1. **Factors related to the employee.** The major influence on how a worker performs and behaves, or acts, on the job stems from his or her personal attributes. The worker's mental ability influences how quickly and accurately he or she can solve problems. Physical ability would influence some types of performance, such as the ability to stand up for long periods of time as a store manager or lift boxes as a warehouse attendant. Job knowledge is obviously important, such as a financial consultant being knowledgeable about a variety of investments. Employees who are well motivated and interested in the work are likely to perform better and behave in a more professional manner. Workers who receive encouragement from friends and family are likely to perform better. Being distracted, such as frequently accessing Facebook

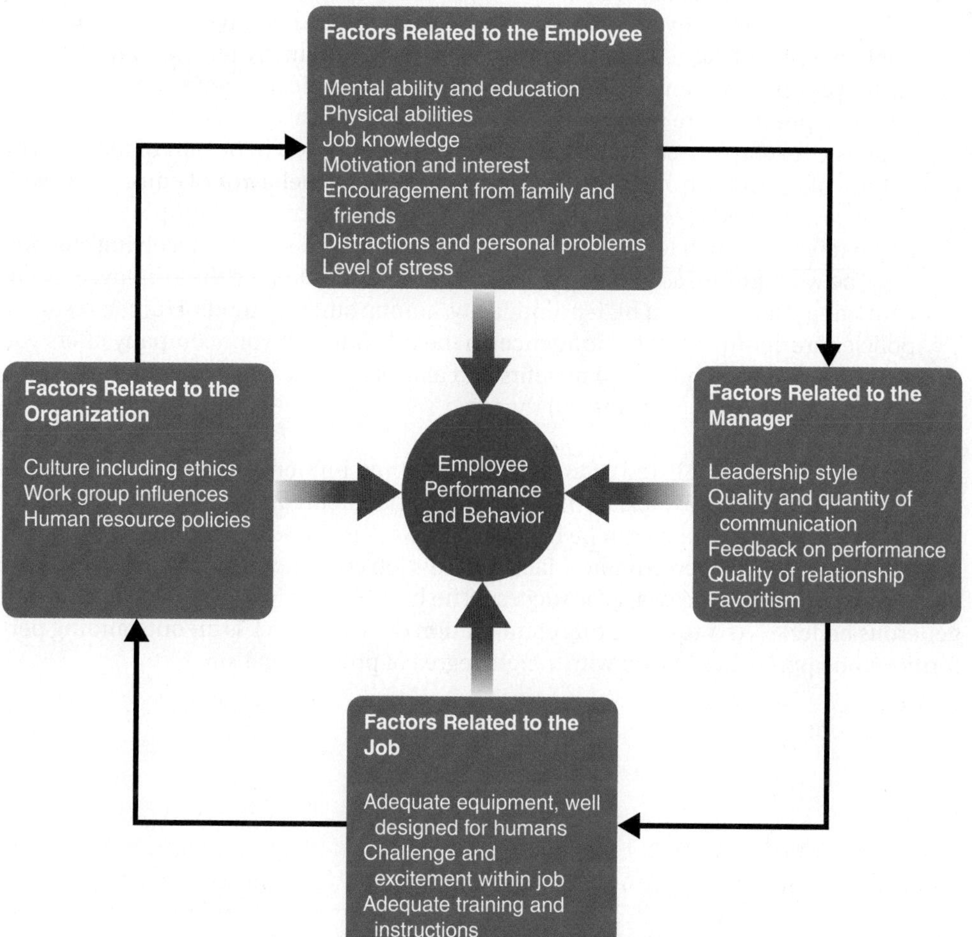

FIGURE 1-5
FACTORS CONTRIBUTING TO PERFORMANCE AND BEHAVIOR IN THE WORKPLACE

and Twitter during the workday or experiencing heavy personal problems, can influence performance negatively. Having the right amount of stress can boost performance, whereas being overstressed can lower performance and lead to distracting behavior, such as being confused.

2. **Factors related to the manager.** The manager, or supervisor, is another major influence on work behavior. A manager whose style, or approach, is warm and supportive is likely to bring out the best in many employees. But some workers require a more directive and demanding supervisor to perform at their best. Ample communication among the manager and group members is likely to enhance performance and guide employees toward doing what is expected of them. Most workers need considerable feedback from their supervisor to stay on track and be highly motivated. A high-quality relationship between the manager and group members leads to high performance, more loyalty, and lower absenteeism. Favoritism is another key factor related to the manager. A manager who plays favorites is less likely to gain the cooperation of the entire group.
3. **Factors related to the job.** The job itself influences how well the worker might perform and behave. Given the right equipment, designed well for human use, a worker is likely to perform better, such as being less likely to have aches, pains, and wrist injuries as a result of many hours of keyboarding. A proven strategy for improving worker motivation is to give the employee an exciting, challenging job, such as the opportunity to make presentations to management about a project. Adequate training and instructions can also be a big boost to job performance.
4. **Factors related to the organization.** The organization as a whole can have a profound influence on the individual worker's performance and behavior. The *culture,* or atmosphere and values of a company, establishes an unwritten standard for how employees perform and behave. At Google, for example, employees are placed in an atmosphere where being creative and making suggestions is expected. And all Zappos.com employees know that having fun is supposed to be part of the job. The culture of the organization also influences the ethical behavior of employees, with some companies expecting honest treatment of workers and employees. Other companies are much less ethical and encourage tactics such as deceiving customers. The work group, as part of the organization, can influence the employee by encouraging teamwork and high productivity, among other methods. Human resource policies are another notable influence on the individual. If your company offers you generous medical and dental benefits and allows time off for family emergencies, it becomes easier to concentrate on the job.

The four factors just listed often have a combined influence on the worker. Let us take an extreme example: Jack, a well-motivated and talented assistant hotel manager, reports to a manager with whom he has a great relationship, which includes giving Jack ample feedback on his performance. Jack finds his job challenging, and his hotel has the advanced equipment necessary for success. The hotel has a friendly climate, along with generous benefits. As a result of this combination of factors, Jack is an outstanding performer who approaches his job with a high degree of professionalism.

Key Terms

Human relations, 5
Organizational effectiveness, 5
Self-understanding, 11
Self, 11
Public self, 11
Private self, 11
Alternative self, 11
Feedback, 12
Peer evaluations, 13
Developmental opportunity, 13
Johari Window, 15
Open area, 16
Hidden area, 16
Blind area, 16
Unknown area, 16
Human relations movement, 17
Scientific management, 17
Hawthorne effect, 18

Summary and Review

Human relations is the art and practice of using systematic knowledge about human behavior to improve personal, job, and career effectiveness.

From the standpoint of management, human relations is important because it contributes to organizational effectiveness. Treating employees with respect and paying them fairly contributes to developing an efficient and creative organization. Major benefits of studying human relations include the following:

- Acquiring information about human behavior
- Developing skills in dealing with people
- Coping with job problems
- Coping with personal problems
- Capitalizing on opportunities
- Demonstrating potential for advancement

Work and personal life often influence each other in several ways, as follows:

- Mood influences job satisfaction, but the effect passes quickly.
- Job satisfaction influences the mood at home, with more emotional employees more likely to experience this relationship.
- A high level of job satisfaction tends to spill over to your personal life. Conversely, an unsatisfactory personal life could lead to negative job attitudes.
- Your job can affect physical and mental health. Severely negative job conditions may lead to a serious stress disorder, such as heart disease.
- The quality of relationships with people at work and in one's personal life influence each other.
- Certain skills (such as the ability to listen) contribute to success at work and in one's personal life.
- How we behave at work is closely related to how we behave at home.
- Workers who achieve a good balance between the demands of work and family life are likely to be more productive and satisfied.

To be effective in human relationships, you must first understand yourself. Six sources of information that contribute to self-understanding are as follows:

1. General information about human behavior
2. Informal feedback from people
3. Feedback from superiors
4. Feedback from coworkers
5. Feedback from self-examination exercises
6. Looking at the self through the Johari Window

Be aware of the self-evaluation traps of highlighting your shortcomings and unrealistically overevaluating your competence. Cultural differences help explain some of the differences in underevaluation versus overevaluation.

The human relations movement was a concentrated effort to become more sensitive to the needs of employees and to treat them in a more humanistic manner. Along with the indirect influence of scientific management, the movement was supported directly by four historic influences:

1. Scientific management applied scientific methods to increase worker productivity.

2. The Hawthorne studies showed that concern for workers can increase their performance as much as or more than improving physical working conditions.
3. Employers used the threat of unionization, in which management employed human relations techniques to deter workers from joining a labor union.
4. The philosophy of industrial humanism, in which motivation and emotional factors are important.

Many of the pioneering ideas described in the history of human relations are still relevant, partly because human nature has not undergone major changes. An example of a pioneering idea in use is that Theory Y has prompted managers to think through which leadership style works best with which employees.

Check Your Understanding

1. Why do you think good human relations skills are so important for supervisors who direct the work activities of entry-level workers?
2. How might participation in team sports enhance an individual's human relations skills? How might such participation encourage a person to develop poor human relation skills?
3. Give an example from your own experience of how work life influences personal life and vice versa.
4. How might a person improve personal life to the extent that the improvement would also enhance job performance?
5. How might a person improve his or her job or career to the extent that the improvement would actually enhance personal life?
6. Of the six sources of information about the self described in this chapter, which one do you think is likely to be the most accurate? Why?
7. Imagine yourself as a manager or small-business owner. How might you apply the Hawthorne effect to increase the productivity of workers reporting to you?
8. How do you think having good human relations skills and knowledge might add to your job security in a competitive workplace?
9. In your current job, or any previous one, which set of factors had the biggest impact on your performance and behavior—those related to the employee, manager, job, or organization? How do you know?
10. Based on what you have studied so far, in what way does human relations involve more than "being nice to people"?

Web Corner

The Dale Carnegie organization has long been associated with teaching human relations effectiveness. The company stemmed from the work of Dale Carnegie, who many years ago popularized the idea of "winning friends and influencing people." Visit www.dalecarnegie.com to understand what type of skills Dale Carnegie Training teaches. Compare the course listing to subjects listed in the table of contents in this text. What similarities do you see?

INTERNET SKILL BUILDER

The Importance of Human Relations Skills in Business

One of the themes of this chapter and the entire book is that human relations skills are important for success in business. But what do employers really think? To find out, visit the Web sites of five of your favorite companies, such as www.ge.com. Go to the employment section and search for a job that you might qualify for now or in the future. Investigate which human relations or interpersonal skills the employer mentions as a requirement, such as "Must have superior spoken communication skills." Make up a list of the human relations, or interpersonal, skills you find mentioned. What conclusions do you reach from this exercise?

Developing Your Human Relations Skills

Human Relations Application Exercises

Applying Human Relations Exercise 1-1

Learning about Each Other's Human Relations Skills

A constructive way of broadening your insights about human relations skills is to find out what other people perceive as their strengths in dealing with others. Toward this end, each class member comes to the front of the class, one by one, to make a two-minute presentation on his or her best ability in dealing with people. To help standardize the presentations, each student answers the following question: "What I do best with people is __________."

In this exercise, and all other class presentation exercises contained in the text, students are asked to share only those ideas they would be comfortable in sharing with the class. Here, for example, you might be very good at doing something with people about which you would be embarrassed to let others know.

As the other students are presenting, attempt to concentrate on them and not be so preoccupied with your presentation that you cannot listen. Make note when somebody says something out of the ordinary. When the presentation is over, the class will discuss answers to the following questions:

1. What was the most frequent human relations capability mentioned?
2. To what extent do classmates appear to be exaggerating their human relations skills?
3. What omissions did you find? For example, were there any important human relations skills you thought a few students should have mentioned but did not?

Applying Human Relations Exercise 1-2

My Human Relations Journal

A potentially important aid in your development as a person with effective human relations skills is to maintain a journal or diary of your experiences. Make a journal entry within 24 hours of carrying out a significant human relations action or failing to do so when the opportunity arose. You therefore will have entries dealing with human relations opportunities both capitalized on and missed. Here is an example: "A few of my neighbors were complaining about all the vandalism in the neighborhood. Cars were getting dented and scratched, and lamplights were being smashed. A few bricks were thrown into home windows. I volunteered to organize a neighborhood patrol. The patrol actually helped cut back on the vandalism." Or, in contrast, given the same scenario: "I thought that someone else should take care of the problem. My time is too valuable." (In the first example, the key human relations skill the person exercised was leadership.)

Also include in your journal such entries as feedback you receive on your human relations ability, good interpersonal traits you appear to be developing, and key human relations ideas about which you read.

Review your journal monthly, and make note of any progress you think you have made in developing your human relations skills. Also consider preparing a graph of your human relations skill development. The vertical axis can represent skill level on a 1 to 100 scale, and the horizontal axis might be divided into time internals, such as calendar quarters.

Human Relations Case Study 1–1

Amanda, the Rejected Job Candidate

Amanda had several years of experience in Web site development at one company. She also had studied Web site development at college, and had five years of experience in developing Web sites for friends and family as a hobby. The company she worked for was acquired by a larger firm that had Web site development staff of its own, so Amanda's position was eliminated.

Although she received two months of severance pay, and would soon be eligible for unemployment insurance, Amanda began a job search immediately. She concentrated her online job search for Web site developer positions within fifty miles of her apartment that she shared with her sister. After sending twenty-one inquiries and job résumés, Amanda landed a job interview with Noble Properties, a large regional real estate sales company.

The interview began with a discussion of Amanda's technical qualifications for the job. Amanda described her experience in Web site development, and also accessed on the interviewer's desktop computer and her smart phone, two different Web sites she had developed. During her presentation, Amanda noticed that she had a text message waiting from a friend. She motioned to the interviewer with her index finger and a nod that she would take a brief pause from the interview to read the message and respond. Amanda said to the interviewer, "My friends won't stop texting me."

Later in the interview, Amanda was asked how well she got along with other workers in her past employment. Amanda replied, "I'm kind of a lone wolf, but who cares? I'm not applying for a job in sales. I work best alone. When coworkers ask me questions, it breaks my concentration."

At approximately twenty-five minutes into the interview, the manager explained to Amanda that after a ten-minute break, she would have a group interview with several other Noble Properties staff members.

Amanda was called into a small conference room where four Noble staffers and the interviewing manager were waiting. At first, Amanda said nothing while she sat staring at her hands. She then said, "What do you want from me?"

The CEO said to Amanda, "One thing I would like from you is to remove your sports cap. It interferes with seeing your facial expressions." Amanda replied, "I would hate to take off my cap because my hair is awful today, but I'll do it anyway. But I don't see how facial expressions are important for a Web site developer."

The interviewing manager concluded the interview by asking Amanda if she had any questions or comments. Amanda responded, "Please text me with your decision. I really prefer text messages to talking on the phone."

After Amanda left the conference room, the interviewing manager said, "So what if this woman is an effective Web site developer. Her people skills are unsuited for Noble Properties. I recommend that we do not make her a job offer."

Questions

1. What evidence do you see from the information presented that Amanda has poor people (human relations) skills?
2. Why should the interviewing manager at Noble Properties care if a Web site developer has good human relations skills?
3. What advice might you offer Amanda to increase her chances of being more successful during an interview for the position of a Web site developer?

Human Relations Case Study 1–2

Feedback Shortage at the Call Center

Derek is proud of his job as a supervisor in a large call center that deals with technical and customer service problems for twenty different companies. The call center is located in Utah for three key reasons. First, Utah is perceived to be one of the most business-friendly states because of low energy costs and low taxes. Second, Utah residents speak a type of English that is relatively easy for a large part of the U.S. population to understand, including those for whom English is a second language. Third, Utah residents have a strong work ethic, and employees tend to be loyal in terms of staying with their employer.

A key part of Derek's job as a supervisor is to encourage the call center specialists to stay motivated and perform well. The specialists have to work rapidly, yet be polite to customers (the callers). At the same time, the specialists can become discouraged because many of the callers become hostile because of problems with their equipment or the customer service problems they are facing. Derek's usual approach to supervising call center specialists, both those dealing with technical problems and customer-service problems, is to smile and tell the workers how well the call center is functioning.

During a meeting with Angela, his manager, Derek was told that he wasn't providing enough specific feedback to the call center workers in his group. (Angela had received a few complaints from workers reporting to Derek.) He explained that the workers in his unit absorbed enough negativism from clients, so he didn't want to add to make their lives any worse by adding his own criticism. Derek also explained that he provided general positive feedback by pointing out how well the department is performing. Also, he added, "If a call center specialist is doing something right, he or she receives immediate positive feedback from the customer."

Angela explained to Derek, "I read the results of Gallup survey conducted with 1,000 employees. Thirty-seven percent of the employees said their managers focused mostly on their strengths, and 11 percent said their managers focused mostly on their weaknesses. And 25 percent of employees said that managers just about ignored them in the sense of not saying much about strengths or weaknesses. The surprising result was that workers who were placed in the "ignored category" were the least committed to their jobs. The take-away from this study is that not giving feedback to employees can result in them not caring much about the job or the company."

"Angela, thanks for the feedback about the feedback I'm giving our employees," said Derek "Yet our situation could be different. The workers in my department get plenty of feedback from customers. And besides, it is difficult to find the time to provide feedback to our workers when they are so busy stuck to their telephones."

Angela said, "The issue is not yet resolved. We will have to talk about it some more."

Questions

1. Why do you think the call center workers mentioned in this case want more feedback on their performance?
2. What do you think of Angela's tactic of providing Gallup survey evidence to support her contention that workers benefit from feedback?
3. What do you recommend that Derek do to find a way to give more feedback to the call center technicians in his group?

Human Relations Role-Playing Exercise

Kindness and Recognition

Here, as in all chapters, a role-playing (or role-assuming) exercise will be presented to provide practice in implementing a specific human relations skill or technique. The role-plays will typically be presented in front of others for about five to ten minutes. A natural and easy way of carrying out most of these role-plays is for you to get a general idea of the role and then spontaneously say and do what you think a person in that role might do and say. For many of the role-plays, it will be helpful for you to read the relevant text material to assist you in refining your skill. For these two introductory role-plays, just rely on whatever knowledge and skills you already have.

Scenario 1: Kindness at the Not-for-Profit Agency Getting back to the chapter-opening story, one person plays the role of Sandy Bellows who is presented with what appears to be a way-off-base suggestion from a staff member. The staff member suggests that their organization should raise more funds by requiring each person who works at the agency to be assigned a monthly collection quota. The money would be collected from anybody in their network, including family members, friends, neighbors, and work associates. The staff members who failed to meet quota for three consecutive months faced the possibility of being fired. One person plays the role of the staff member who makes the suggestion. Another person plays the role of Bellows, who will reject the suggestion with kindness. Run the conversation for about six minutes.

Scenario 2: Giving Feedback to a Call Center Technician Getting back to Case Study 1-2, one person plays the role of Derek, the supervisor. While walking down the halls he overhears Jessica, a customer-service representative engaged in a heated discussion with a customer. In a loud, annoyed tone, Jessica says to the customer on the other end of the line, "What don't you understand? I have told you four times that you were not over-charged. We simply added sales tax to your purchase. What planet are you from?" Derek decides to wait until Jessica is on break to provide her feedback about her aggressive approach to dealing with the customer in question.

Another student plays the role of Jessica who thinks that some customers are too difficult to service well. She is a little peeved that Derek does not understand her point of view, and will attempt to defend her approach to dealing with the customer who thought he was overcharged.

For both scenarios, observers rate the role-players on two dimensions, using a 1 to 5 scale from "very poor" to "very good." One dimension is "effective use of human relations techniques." The second dimension is "acting ability." A few observers might voluntarily provide feedback to the role-players in terms of sharing their ratings and observations. The course instructor might also provide feedback.

Human Relations Class Activity

The Unique People

Most of the self-assessment quizzes and human relations exercises presented throughout this book are performed by students working individually or in small groups. At the end of each chapter we present an additional activity geared toward enhanced human relations knowledge or skill that is to be performed by the entire class, often interacting with each other. The unit of contribution might be you working alone, but at some point the contributions become collective.

Our first class activity is geared toward reinforcing the idea that part of effective human relations is to recognize that people are different in many ways, stemming from their group characteristics, culture, personality, problem-solving ability, experiences, and interests, among many other factors. Each student in the class, or only those who volunteer, come up to the front of the class one at a time to make a one-minute presentation about any way in which he or she is unique. Here are three statements of uniqueness among an infinite number of possibilities: "I graduated number one in my high school class of fifty-seven students." "I was born and raised in China, but I don't like to eat in Chinese restaurants. I prefer Applebee's and Outback Steakhouse." "I rigged up my house to be smart. I can use my BlackBerry to start the air-conditioning or the oven in my house from miles away."

After the unique aspects of each class member are presented, volunteers might offer feedback to participants by completing the following statements:

1. "What really surprised me was _________."
2. "What made me really think positively about _________ was the fact that he (or she) _________."
3. "I really learned something about human relations today. Now I know that _________."

REFERENCES

1. Steven Kent, "Happy Workers Are the Best Workers," *The Wall Street Journal,* September 6, 2005, p. A20.
2. Jeffery Pfeffer, *The Human Equation* (Boston: Harvard Business School Press, 1998), p. 59; Pfeffer, "Producing Sustainable Competitive Advantage through the Effective Management of People," *Academy of Management Executive,* November 2005, pp. 95–108.
3. Timothy A. Judge and Remus Ilies, "Affect and Job Satisfaction: A Study of Their Relationship at Work and Home," *Journal of Applied Psychology,* August 2004, pp. 661–673.
4. "Making Relationships Work: A Conversation with Psychologist John M. Gottman," *Harvard Business Review,* December 2007, pp. 45–50.
5. "The Multitasking Tech Exec," *Fortune,* August 31, 2009, p. 42.
6. Kathy Gurchiek, "Not a 'Mommy' Issue," *HR Magazine,* April 2011, pp. 40–41.
7. C. R. Snyder, "So Many Selves," *Contemporary Psychology,* January 1988, p. 77.
8. Otila Obodaru, "The Self Not Taken: How Alternative Selves Develop and How they Influence Our Professional Lives," *Academy of Management Review,* January 2012, p. 36.
9. Cited in Etienne Benson, "The Synaptic Self," *Monitor on Psychology,* November 2002, p. 40.
10. Rita Pyrillis, "The Reviews Are In," *Workforce Management,* May 2011, pp. 21.
11. Karen Wright, "A Chic Critique," *Psychology Today,* March/April 2011, p. 55.
12. Joseph Luft, *Group Process: An Introduction to Group Dynamics* (New York: Mayfield Publishing Company/McGraw-Hill, 1984); Luft, *Of Human Interaction* (Palo Alto, CA: National Press, 1969); Suzanne C. De Janasz, Karen O. Dowd, and Beth Z. Schneider, *Interpersonal Skills in Organizations* (New York: McGraw-Hill, 2002), pp. 31–32.
13. Saul Kassin, *Psychology,* 3rd ed. (Upper Saddle River, NJ: Prentice Hall, 2001), p. 74.
14. Research summarized in Tori DeAngelis, "Why We Overestimate Our Competence," *Monitor on Psychology,* February 2003, p. 61.
15. Ibid.
16. Robert Kreitner, *Management,* 5th ed. (Boston: Houghton Mifflin, 1992), pp. 51–52.
17. Edward G. Wertheim, "Historical Background of Organizational Behavior." Retrieved March 15, 2006, from: http://web.cba.neu.edu/~Wertheim/introd/history.htm.
18. Elton Mayo, *The Human Problems of Industrial Civilization* (New York: Viking Press, 1960).
19. James A. F. Stoner and R. Edward Freeman, *Management,* 4th ed. (Upper Saddle River, NJ: Prentice Hall, 1989), p. 49.
20. Kreitner, *Management,* p. 50.
21. Alan B. Krueger, "Job Satisfaction Is Not Just a Matter of Dollars," *New York Times.* Retrieved December 8, 2005, from: www.nytimes.com§.
22. "Union Members Summary," *Economic News Release: Union Member Summary,* January 21, 2011, from: www.bls.gov/news.
23. Kreitner, *Management,* p. 62.
24. Douglas McGregor, *The Human Side of Enterprise* (New York: McGraw-Hill, 1960), pp. 33–48.

2

Self-Esteem and Self-Confidence

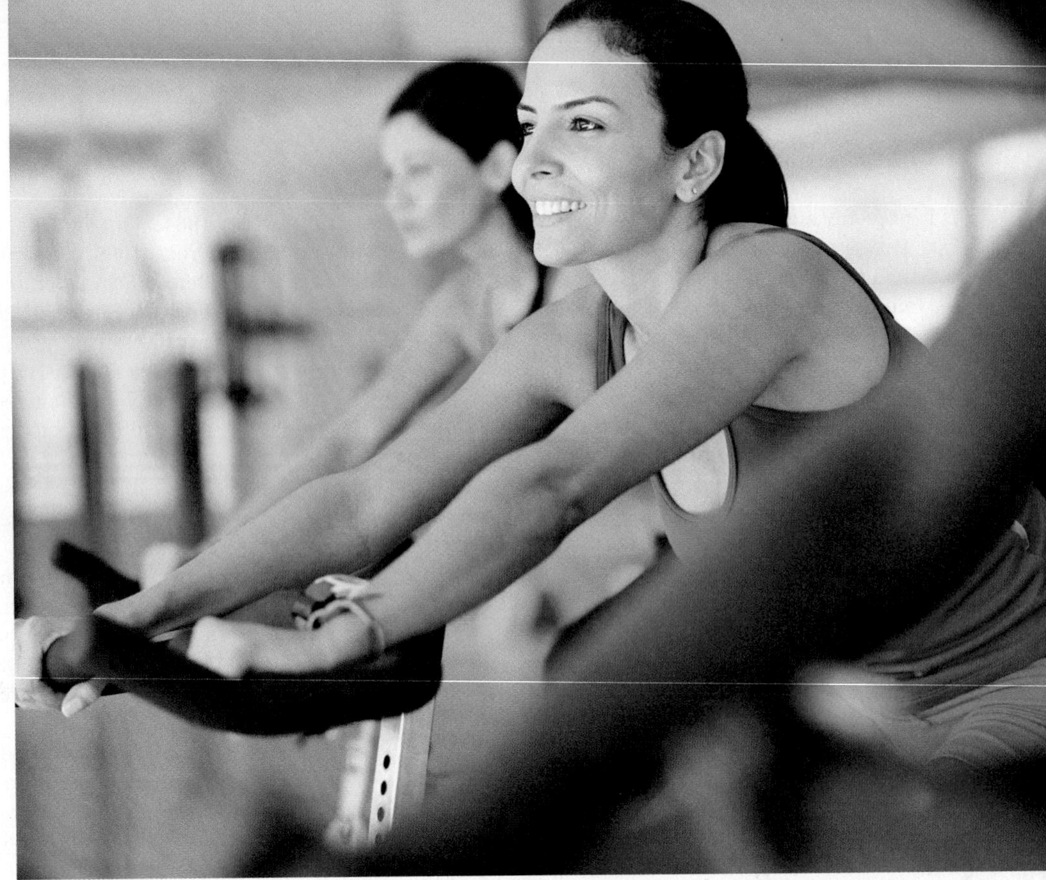

Outline

Emilio Romano, an experienced media and aviation executive, was appointed as the new president of Telemundo, the second largest Spanish-language television network in the United States. A proud and confident man, Romano said in a press release in October 2011 that he was honored to be joining this team of professionals. He also expressed excitement about being part of the transformation taking place within the Hispanic/Latino media market in the United States.

Praise for Romano's appointment was plentiful. Lauren Zalaznic, Chairman of NBC Universal Entertainment & Digital Networks and Integrated Media said that Emilio Romano was the ideal executive to lead Telemundo during a time when the company was achieving outstanding business results. He also noted that the company would benefit greatly from his expertise in various types of media. Romano's experience in the Mexican market is an asset as Telemundo continues to broaden its appeal to the Latino community.

Throughout his career Romano has been confident enough to occupy a variety of roles. For three years he was CEO of Mexicana de Aviacion airline. He has also served as the president and chief executive officer of Grupo Puerta Alamedi (GPA), a real estate and investment company with operations in the United States and Mexico. An attorney by profession, he served as a professor in the doctoral program in tax laws at the Escuela Libre de Derecho. He was well liked as a professor because of his passion for his work and the high standards he set for students.

By age 46 Romano's career had spanned the media, aviation, and Internet industries where he held a number of leadership positions over a twenty-year period, from start-up entrepreneurial roles to the head of large business firms. During his tenure with the Mexican airline company, he organized the launch of Click Mexican, the first low-cost carrier in Mexico.

Roman typically assumes a positive attitude toward any new challenge he faces, and his pride in taking on the challenge impresses his colleagues and subordinates. His typical business attire includes a fashionable suite and tie. He is an accomplished executive who keeps his ego in check.[1]

The story just presented illustrates how self-confidence, such as being willing to take risks and try something new, helps a person succeed in a competitive field. Romano also has to have high self-esteem to think that his analytical skills are so good that he can compete in the worlds of aviation, real estate, and language broadcasting. Many other people you will meet in this book score high in self-esteem and self-confidence—otherwise they would never have been so successful. In this chapter the focus is on two of the biggest building blocks for more effective human relations: the nature and development of self-esteem and self-confidence.

Learning Objectives ▸

After studying the information and doing the exercises in this chapter, you should be able to:

1. Describe the nature, development, and consequences of self-esteem.
2. Explain how to enhance self-esteem.
3. Describe the importance of self-confidence and self-efficacy.
4. Pinpoint methods of strengthening and developing your self-confidence.
5. Describe the problem of codependence and how it is linked to low self-esteem and self-confidence.

Learning Objective 1

What Is the Nature of Self-Esteem, Its Development, and Consequences?

Self-esteem
the experience of feeling competent to cope with the basic challenges in life and of being worthy of happiness

Understanding the self from various perspectives is important because who you are and what you think of yourself influences many facets of your life, both on and off the job. A particularly important role is played by **self-esteem,** the experience of feeling competent to cope with the basic challenges in life and of being worthy of happiness.[2] In more general terms, self-esteem refers to a positive overall evaluation of oneself.

A useful distinction is that our self-concept refers to what we *think* about ourselves, whereas self-esteem is what we *feel* about ourselves.[3] People with positive self-esteem have a deep-down, inside-the-self feeling of their own worth. Consequently, they develop positive self-concepts. Before reading further, you are invited to measure your current level of self-esteem by taking the Human Relations Self-Assessment Quiz 2-1. Next the nature of self-esteem and many of its consequences are examined.

THE DEVELOPMENT OF SELF-ESTEEM

Part of understanding the nature of self-esteem is to know how it develops. Self-esteem comes about from a variety of early life experiences. People who were encouraged to feel good about themselves and their accomplishments by family members, friends, and teachers are more likely to enjoy high self-esteem. The basis for a healthy level of self-esteem grows out of a secure attachment to a parent. Self-esteem later in life can be weak if a parent is inconsistently supportive or lacks empathy and concern for the child. Self-esteem is enhanced if the parent is emotionally supportive toward the child even when the latter does something wrong, such as spilling a glass of diet soda on a beige carpet.[4]

As just implied, early life experiences play a key role in the development of both healthy self-esteem and low self-esteem, according to research synthesized at the Counseling and Mental Health Center of the University of Texas.[5] Childhood experiences that lead to healthy self-esteem include the following:

- Being praised
- Being listened to
- Being spoken to respectfully
- Getting attention and hugs
- Experiencing success in sports or school

In contrast, childhood experiences that lead to low self-esteem include the following:

- Being harshly criticized
- Being yelled at or beaten
- Being ignored, ridiculed, or teased
- Being expected to be "perfect" all the time
- Experiencing failures in sports or school
- Often being given messages that failed experiences (losing a game, getting a poor grade, and so forth) were failures of one's whole self

A widespread explanation of self-esteem development is that compliments, praise, and hugs alone build self-esteem. Yet, many developmental psychologists seriously

Human Relations Self-Assessment Quiz 2-1

The Self-Esteem Checklist

Indicate whether each of the following statements is mostly true or mostly false as it applies to you.

	Mostly True	Mostly False
1. I love me.	______	______
2. Most of any progress I have made in my work or school can be attributed to luck.	______	______
3. I often ask myself, "Why can't I be more successful?"	______	______
4. When my manager or team leader gives me a challenging assignment, I usually dive in with confidence.	______	______
5. I believe that I am truly a person of high value.	______	______
6. I am able to set limits to what I will do for others without feeling anxious.	______	______
7. I regularly make excuses for my mistakes.	______	______
8. Negative feedback crushes me.	______	______
9. I care very much how much money other people make, especially when they are working in my field.	______	______
10. I feel like a failure when I do not achieve my goals.	______	______
11. Hard work gives me an emotional lift.	______	______
12. When others compliment me, I doubt their sincerity.	______	______
13. Complimenting others makes me feel uncomfortable.	______	______
14. I find it comfortable to say, "I'm sorry."	______	______
15. It is difficult for me to face up to my mistakes.	______	______
16. My coworkers think I am not worthy of promotion.	______	______
17. People who want to become my friends usually do not have much to offer.	______	______
18. If my manager praised me, I would have a difficult time believing it was deserved.	______	______
19. I'm just an ordinary person.	______	______
20. Having to face change really disturbs me.	______	______

Scoring and Interpretation:

The answers in the high self-esteem direction are as follows:

1. Mostly True
2. Mostly False
3. Mostly False
4. Mostly True
5. Mostly True
6. Mostly True
7. Mostly False
8. Mostly False
9. Mostly False
10. Mostly False
11. Mostly True
12. Mostly False
13. Mostly False
14. Mostly True
15. Mostly False
16. Mostly False
17. Mostly False
18. Mostly False
19. Mostly False
20. Mostly False

17–20 You have very high self-esteem. Yet if your score is 20, it could be that you are denying any self-doubts.

11–16 Your self-esteem is in the average range. It would probably be worthwhile for you to implement strategies to boost your self-esteem (described in this chapter) so that you can develop a greater feeling of well-being.

0–10 Your self-esteem needs bolstering. Discuss your feelings about yourself with a trusted friend or with a mental health professional. At the same time, attempt to implement several of the tactics for boosting self-esteem described in this chapter.

Questions:
1. How does your score on this quiz match your evaluation of your self-esteem?
2. What would it be like being married to somebody who scored 0 on this quiz?

"Even the most accomplished, beautiful, and celebrated human beings don't get a steady stream of compliments and positive feedback."
—Harriet Brown
Assistant professor of magazine journalism at the S. I. Newhouse School of Public Administration, Syracuse University. *Psychology Today*, January/February 2012, p. 69.

question this perspective. Instead, they believe that self-esteem results from accomplishing worthwhile activities and then feeling proud of these accomplishments.[6] Receiving encouragement, however, can help the person accomplish activities that build self-esteem.

Leading psychologist Martin Seligman argues that self-esteem is caused by a variety of successes and failures. To develop self-esteem, people need to improve their skills for dealing with the world.[7] Self-esteem, therefore, comes about by genuine accomplishments, followed by praise and recognition. Heaping undeserved praise and recognition on people may lead to a temporary high, but it does not produce genuine self-esteem. The child develops self-esteem not from being told he or she can score a goal in soccer but from scoring that goal.

Although early life experiences have the major impact on the development of self-esteem, experiences in adult life also affect self-esteem. David De Cremer, of the Tilburg University (Netherlands), and his associates conducted two studies with Dutch college students about how the behavior of leaders and fair procedures influence self-esteem. The study found that self-esteem was related to procedural fairness and leadership that encourages self-rewards. The interpretation given of the findings is that a leader/supervisor can facilitate self-esteem when he or she encourages self-rewards and uses fair procedures.[8] A takeaway from this study would be that rewarding yourself for a job well done, even in adult life, can boost your self-esteem a little.

THE CONSEQUENCES OF SELF-ESTEEM

No single factor is as important to career success as self-esteem, as observed by psychologist Eugene Raudsepp. People with positive self-esteem understand their own competence and worth and have positive perceptions of their abilities to cope with problems and adversity.[9] Here we look at the major positive and negative consequences of self-esteem, as outlined in Figure 2-1.

POSITIVE CONSEQUENCES

The right amount of self-esteem can have many positive consequences, as described next.

Good Mental Health

One of the major consequences of high self-esteem is good mental health. People with high self-esteem feel good about themselves and have positive outlooks on life. One of the links between good mental health and self-esteem is that high self-esteem helps prevent many situations from being stressful. Few negative comments from others are likely to bother you when your self-esteem is high. A person with low self-esteem might crumble if somebody insulted his or her appearance. If you have high self-esteem you might shrug off the insult as simply being the other person's point of view. If faced with an everyday setback, such as losing keys, if you have high self-esteem you might think, "I have so much going for me, why fall apart over this incident?"

FIGURE 2-1
CONSEQUENCES OF SELF-ESTEEM

1. Good mental health
2. Profiting from negative feedback
3. Career success
4. Organizational prosperity
5. Serves as a guide for regulating social relationships
6. Negative consequences (narcissism, envying too many people, romance problems)

Profiting from Negative Feedback

Although people with high self-esteem can readily shrug off undeserved insults, they still profit well from negative feedback. Because they are secure, they can profit from the developmental opportunities suggested by negative feedback. Workers with high self-esteem develop and maintain favorable work attitudes and perform at high levels. These positive consequences take place because such attitudes and behaviors are consistent with the personal belief that they are competent individuals. The late Mary Kay Ash, the legendary founder of a beauty products company, put it this way: "It never occurred to me I couldn't do it. I always knew that if I worked hard enough, I could." Furthermore, research has shown that high-self-esteem individuals value reaching work goals more than do low-self-esteem individuals.[10]

Career Success

A major consequence of having high self-esteem is that you have a better chance of attaining career success, as mentioned at the beginning of this section, and supported by long-term research. The study in question was known as the National Longitudinal Survey of Youth, involving over 12,000 young men and women. The group was studied over a twenty-five-year period beginning in 1979. Human Relations Self-Assessment Quiz 2-2 gives you the opportunity to take the same survey used in the study to measure core self-evaluations.

The components of core self-evaluations include high self-esteem, self-efficacy (an aspect of self-confidence described later in this chapter), beliefs in personal control over events, and emotional stability. Individuals with high core self-evaluations are better motivated, perform better on the job, tend to hold more challenging jobs, and have higher job satisfaction.

Among the many results of the study were that people with higher core evaluations performed better in their first jobs. Furthermore, over time those people with high core evaluations increase their career success at a faster pace than those with below-average core evaluations. Over a twenty-five-year span, the career success they have over others doubles. Success was measured in terms of job satisfaction, pay, and holding a higher-status position.[11] A practical conclusion to take away from this study is that if you have a high core self-evaluation, it will pay impressive career dividends.

Later research suggests that people with core high core self-evaluations are more likely to have high job performance when they combine positive attitudes toward the self with a concern for the welfare of others. (Consistently good job performance enhances career success.) For example, call-center employees with positive core self-evaluations tended to perform better when they worried about letting other people down. The call center work involved telemarketing to generate funds to support new jobs at a university.[12]

Organizational Prosperity

The combined effect of workers having high self-esteem helps a company prosper. Self-esteem is a critical source of competitive advantage in an information society. Companies gain the edge when, in addition to having an educated workforce, employees have high self-esteem, as shown by such behaviors as the following:

- Being creative and innovative
- Taking personal responsibility for problems
- Feeling of independence (yet still wanting to work cooperatively with others)
- Trusting one's own capabilities
- Taking the initiative to solve problems[13]

Human Relations Self-Assessment Quiz 2-2

National Longitudinal Survey of Youth Measure of Core Self-Evaluations

	True	False
1. I have little control over the things that happen to me.	_____	_____
2. There is little I can do to change many of the important things in my life.	_____	_____
3. I feel that I am a person of worth, on an equal basis with others.	_____	_____
4. I feel that I have a number of good qualities.	_____	_____
5. All in all, I am inclined to feel that I am a failure.	_____	_____
6. I feel I do not have much to be proud of.	_____	_____
7. I wish I could have more respect for myself.	_____	_____
8. I've been depressed.	_____	_____
9. I've felt hopeful about the future.	_____	_____
10. What happens to me in the future depends on me.	_____	_____
11. What happens to me is of my own doing.	_____	_____
12. When I make plans, I am almost certain to make them work.	_____	_____

Scoring and Interpretation:

The answers in the high core self-evaluations direction are as follows:

1. False	**5.** False	**9.** True
2. False	**6.** False	**10.** True
3. True	**7.** False	**11.** True
4. True	**8.** False	**12.** True

Although there are no specific categories for scores, the more statements you answered in the direction of high core self-evaluations, the more likely it is that you have the type of core self-evaluations that will facilitate career success.

Questions:

1. How does your score on this quiz match your evaluation of your core self-evaluations?
2. How does your score on this quiz compare to your score on Self-Assessment Quiz 2-1 ?
3. How can you explain the fact that responses to the above statements were found to be related to long-term career success?

Source: The statements are from the National Longitudinal Survey of Youth (NLSY79), a study commissioned and operated by the Bureau of Labor Statistics, U.S. Department of Labor. The statements are also reported in Timothy A. Judge and Charlice Hurst, "How the Rich (and Happy) Get Richer (and Happier): Relationship of Core Self-Evaluations to Trajectories in Attaining Work Success," *Journal of Applied Psychology*, July 2008, p. 863.

Behaviors such as these help you cope with the challenge of a rapidly changing workplace where products and ideas become obsolete quickly. Workers with high self-esteem are more likely to be able to cope with new challenges regularly because they are confident that they can master their environments.

A research study conducted with college students and working adults suggests that high self-esteem is more likely to lead to enhanced job performance when the employee's self-esteem does not depend on performing well.[14] If your self-esteem is dependent to some extent on your own feelings of self-worth related to factors external to the job, you are more likely to perform better on the job. For example, a person might base his or her feelings of self-esteem mostly on factors such as relationships with people, success in school, and technology skills but not so much on job performance. A possible explanation for these findings is that if your self-esteem is heavily dependent on job performance you might become a little anxious and not perform at your best.

Serves as a Guide for Regulating Social Relationships

Another consequence of self-esteem is that you can use it as a guide in regulating social relationships. According to Mark Leary, director of social psychology at Duke University, self-esteem provides a gauge of performance during social interactions: "Self-esteem rises and falls, acting as an internal barometer of how well you're faring, telling you to fix this problem here, and helping you understand that you don't have to worry about it there."[15]

Following this reasoning, fluctuations in self-esteem provide information that is useful in working your way through social relationships. For example, if you are talking and the person you are talking to yawns, your self-esteem drops, signaling you to change the topic. When you tell a joke, and people laugh, your self-esteem climbs rapidly. If we did not feel bad when we bored or offended others, or satisfied when we delighted them, we would not be inclined to change course.[16]

POTENTIAL NEGATIVE CONSEQUENCES

High and low extremes in self-esteem can create problems for individuals, as described next.

1. **Exaggerated levels of self-esteem can lead to narcissism.** Self-esteem can elevate to the level whereby the individual becomes self-absorbed to the point of having little concern for others, leading to narcissistic attitudes and behaviors. **Narcissism** is an extremely positive view of the self, combined with limited empathy for others. Quite often extreme narcissism can hamper success because the narcissist irritates and alienates others in the workplace. A frequent human relations problem with office narcissists is that they are poor listeners because they attempt to dominate conversations by talking about themselves. Yet, the right amount and type of narcissism can at times facilitate success because the narcissist appears to be self-confident and charismatic.[17]

Narcissism
extremely positive view of the self, combined with little empathy for others

2. **Envying too many people.** A potential negative consequence of low self-esteem is envying too many people. If you perceive that many individuals have much more of what you want and are more worthwhile than you, you will suffer from enormous envy. To decrease pangs of envy, it is best to develop realistic standards of comparison between you and other people in the world.

   If high school basketball player Joshua measures his self-esteem in terms of how well he stacks up with basketball superstar and super-millionaire LeBron James, young Joshua will take a lot of blows to his self-esteem. However, if Joshua compares himself to other players on his team and in his league, his self-esteem will be higher because he has chosen a more realistic reference group. For example, Joshua might think that Kent, the starting point guard on his team, has a good chance of winning a basketball scholarship to college, speaks intelligently, and is well groomed. Joshua works hard to develop the same potential and behaviors. When he believes he has succeeded, Joshua will experience a boost in self-esteem.

   Kristin Neff, a professor of educational psychology at the University of Texas at Austin, supports the idea that making social comparisons can lead to problems with self-esteem. She explains that in American culture, people tend to acquire a sense of self-worth from feeling special. A musician who compares herself to a musician of less talent will feel superior, and even have a boost in self-esteem. But if she compares herself to a more talented musician, she will feel a decrease in self-esteem even if her talent and skills have not diminished.[18]

3. **Poor romantic relationships when self-esteem is low.** Low self-esteem can have negative consequences for romantic relationships because people with self-doubts consistently underestimate their partners' feelings for them. People with low **self-respect** distance themselves from the relationship—often devaluing their partner—to prepare themselves for what they think will be an inevitable breakup. John G. Holmes, a psychologist at the University of Waterloo in Ontario, Canada, says, "If people think negatively about themselves, they think their partner must think negatively about them—and they're wrong."[19]

Self-respect
how you think and feel about yourself

Learning Objective 2

How Do You Enhance Self-Esteem?

Improving self-esteem is a lifelong process because self-esteem is related to the success of your activities and interactions with people. Following are approaches to enhancing self-esteem that are related to how self-esteem develops.

ATTAIN LEGITIMATE ACCOMPLISHMENTS

To emphasize again, accomplishing worthwhile activities is a major contributor to self-esteem in both children and adults. Self-esteem therefore stems from accomplishment. Giving people large trophies for mundane accomplishments is unlikely to raise self-esteem. More likely, the person will see through the transparent attempt to build his or her self-esteem and develop negative feelings about the self. The general-information point of view is the opposite: accomplishment stems from a boost in self-esteem. The two different viewpoints are diagrammed in Figure 2-2.

What about you? Would your self-esteem receive a bigger boost by (a) receiving an A in a course in which 10 percent of the class received an A or by (b) receiving an A in a class in which everybody received the same grade?

Another way of framing the attainment of legitimate accomplishments is that to boost your self-esteem, you must engage in behaviors and make choices that are worthy of esteem. To implement this strategy, you must first size up what your reference group regards as esteemed. For most reference groups, or the people whose opinion matters to you, esteem-worthy behavior would include the following:

- Successfully completing a program of studies
- Occupying a high-status job and staying long enough to accomplish something worthwhile

FIGURE 2-2
GOAL ACCOMPLISHMENT AND SELF-ESTEEM

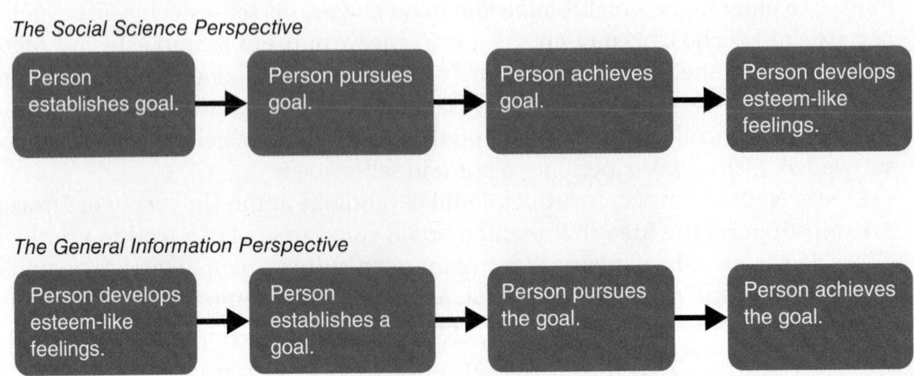
The Social Science Perspective
Person establishes goal.
Person pursues goal.
Person achieves goal.
Person develops esteem-like feelings.
The General Information Perspective
Person develops esteem-like feelings.
Person establishes a goal.
Person pursues the goal.
Person achieves the goal.

- Investing time and money in charitable activities
- Taking pride in your physical appearance and condition
- Having a social networking page that is filled with honorable and sensible content

As you have probably observed, all these esteem-worthy accomplishments reflect values about what is important. For example, a person might have criminals and swindlers in his or her reference group. Self-esteem for this person based on the acclamation of others would therefore stem from such activities as defrauding others of money and not paying taxes.

Closely related to attaining legitimate accomplishments is to have constructive goals that can make a difference for others. When a person's self-esteem is low, helping others can take the attention away from oneself thereby taking away some of the discomfort associated with low self-esteem. In this sense, a person's self-esteem would feel elevated. Jennifer Crocker, a psychology professor at the University of Michigan explains that by taking your ego out of the situation—and focusing on helping others, your self-esteem will gain a legitimate boost.[20] An example of a constructive goal that would be to develop a plan to directly help others is to distribute donated food to families in dire need.

BE AWARE OF PERSONAL STRENGTHS

Another method of improving your self-esteem is to develop an appreciation of your strengths and accomplishments. Appreciating your strengths and accomplishments requires that you engage in **introspection,** the act of looking within oneself. Although introspection may sound easy, it requires considerable discipline and concentration to actually observe what you are doing. A simple example is that we are often not even aware of some of our basic habits, such as biting the lip when nervous or blinking when attempting to answer a difficult question. A good starting point is to list your strengths and accomplishments on paper. This list is likely to be more impressive than you expected.

Introspection
the act of looking within oneself

You can sometimes develop an appreciation of your strengths by participating in a group exercise designed for such purposes. A group of about seven people meet to form a support group. All group members first spend about ten minutes answering the question, "What are my three strongest points, attributes, or skills?" After each group member records his or her three strengths, he or she discusses them with the other group members.

Each group member then comments on the list. Other group members sometimes add to your list of strengths or reinforce what you have to say. Sometimes you may find disagreement. One member told the group, "I'm handsome, intelligent, reliable, athletic, self-confident, and very moral. I also have a good sense of humor." Another group member retorted, "And I might add that you're unbearably conceited."

The late Leo Buscaglia (aka Dr. Hug) was a major contributor to emphasizing the importance of people appreciating their strengths to boost their self-esteem. Part of his program for enhancing human relationships was for people to love others as well as themselves. He wanted people to understand that they were unique.[21]

MINIMIZE SETTINGS AND INTERACTIONS THAT DETRACT FROM YOUR FEELINGS OF COMPETENCE

Most of us have situations in work and personal life that make us feel less than our best. If you can minimize exposure to those situations, you will have fewer feelings of incompetence. The problem with feeling incompetent is that it lowers your self-esteem. An office supervisor said she detests company picnics, most of all because she is forced to play softball. At her own admission, she had less aptitude for athletics than any able-bodied person she knew. In addition, she felt uncomfortable with the small-talk characteristic of picnics. To minimize discomfort, the woman attended only those picnics she thought were absolutely necessary. Instead of playing on the softball team, she volunteered to be the equipment manager.

A problem with avoiding all situations in which you feel incompetent is that it might prevent you from acquiring needed skills. Also, it boosts your self-confidence and self-esteem to become comfortable in a previously uncomfortable situation.

TALK AND SOCIALIZE FREQUENTLY WITH PEOPLE WHO BOOST YOUR SELF-ESTEEM

Psychologist Barbara Ilardie says that the people who can raise your self-esteem are usually those with high self-esteem themselves. They are the people who give honest feedback because they respect others and themselves. Such high-self-esteem individuals should not be confused with yes-people who agree with others simply to be liked. The point is that you typically receive more from strong people than weak ones. Weak people will flatter you but will not give you the honest feedback you need to build self-esteem.[22]

A related approach to boosting self-esteem is to create a web page blog in which you enter positive comments, still photos, and videos about you. You invite others to respond with positive comments about you, thereby boosting your good feelings about yourself. A downside here, however, is that some people respond to warm invitations with negative and hurtful commentary. An underlying problem here is that many people are quite uninhibited when responding to a social media site. Have you ever noticed how nasty and uninhibited people can be on the Internet?

MODEL THE BEHAVIOR OF PEOPLE WITH HIGH SELF-ESTEEM

Observe the way people who are believed to have high self-esteem stand, walk, speak, and act. Even if you are not feeling so secure inside, you will project a high-self-esteem image if you act assured. Eugene Raudsepp recommends, "Stand tall, speak clearly and with confidence, shake hands firmly, look people in the eye and smile frequently. Your self-esteem will increase as you notice encouraging reactions from others."[23] (Notice here that self-esteem is considered to be about the same idea as self-confidence.)

Choose your models of high self-esteem from people you know personally as well as celebrities you might watch on television news and interview shows. Observing actors on the large or small screen is a little less useful because they are guaranteed to be playing a role. Identifying a teacher or professor as a self-esteem model is widely practiced, as is observing successful family members and friends.

Learning Objective 3

What Is the Importance of Self-Confidence, and Its Sources?

Self-efficacy
confidence in your ability to carry out a specific task in contrast to generalized self-confidence

Although self-confidence can be considered part of self-esteem, it is important enough to study separately. **Self-efficacy** is confidence in your ability to carry out a specific task in contrast to generalized self-confidence. When self-efficacy is high, you believe you have the ability to do what is necessary to complete a task successfully. If you have self-efficacy in relation to many tasks, you are likely to be self-confident.

THE IMPORTANCE OF SELF-CONFIDENCE AND SELF-EFFICACY

Self-confidence has also long been recognized as a trait of effective leaders. A straightforward implication of self-efficacy is that people who think they can perform well on a task do better than those who think they will do poorly. Various studies have shown that people with a high sense of self-efficacy tend to have good job performance, so being self-confident is important for your career. They also set relatively high goals for themselves.[24]

Self-efficacy also contributes to goal setting because the higher your level of self-efficacy, the more likely you are to think that a goal is realistic. A person with high self-efficacy for learning German might say, "I think learning two German words per day is realistic."

The importance of self-confidence for your career can be illustrated by the tactics of Jack Welch, the former CEO of General Electric (GE), who is regarded by many business writers as one of the most influential leaders of all time. Welch has become a well-known business author and columnist, in addition to remaining active in directing several companies. Welch once said that his most important responsibility at GE was building the self-confidence of managers throughout the company. Although an intimidating and demanding boss, Welch would help managers develop their self-confidence by giving them lots of opportunities to succeed on major assignments.

THE SOURCES OF SELF-CONFIDENCE

Research by college professors and psychological consultants George P. Hollenbeck and Douglas T. Hall suggests that our feelings of self-confidence stem from five sources of information.[25] The first source is the *actual experience,* or *things we have done.* Having done something before and having succeeded is the most powerful way for you to build self-confidence. If you successfully inserted a replacement battery in your watch without destroying the watch, you will be confident in making another replacement.

The second source of self-confidence is the *experiences of others,* or *modeling.* You can gain some self-confidence if you have carefully observed others perform a task, such as resolving conflict with a customer. You might say to yourself, "I've seen Tracy calm down the customer by listening and showing sympathy, and I'm confident I can do the same thing."

The third source of self-confidence is *social comparison,* or *comparing yourself to others.* If you see other people with capabilities similar to your own perform a task well, your will gain in confidence. A person might say, "If that person can learn how to work with enterprise software, I can do it also. I'm just as smart."

The fourth source of self-confidence is *social persuasion,* or *the process of convincing another person.* If a credible person convinces you that you can accomplish a particular task, you will often receive a boost in self-confidence large enough to give the task a try. If the encouragement is coupled with guidance on how to perform the task, your self-confidence gain will be higher. So the boss or teacher who says, "I know you can do it, and I'm here to help you," knows how to build self-confidence.

The fifth source of self-confidence is *emotional arousal,* or *how you feel about events around you and manage your emotions.* People rely somewhat on inner feelings to know if they are self-confident enough to perform the task. Imagine a person standing on top of a high mountain ready to ski down. However, he or she is trembling and nauseous with fear. Contrast this beginner to another person who simply feels mildly excited and challenged. Skier number one has a self-confidence problem, whereas skier number two has enough confidence to start the descent. (Have your emotional sensations ever influenced your self-confidence?)

The more of these five sources of self-confidence are positive for you, the more likely your self-confidence will be positive. Human Relations Self-Assessment Quiz 2-3 provides some insight into your level of self-confidence.

Human Relations Self-Assessment Quiz 2-3

How Self-Confident Are You?

Indicate the extent to which you agree with each of the following statements. Use a 1 to 5 scale: (1) disagree strongly, (2) disagree, (3) neutral, (4) agree, and (5) agree strongly.

	DS	D	N	A	AS
1. I frequently say to people, "I'm not sure."	5	4	3	2	1
2. I perform well in most situations in life.	1	2	3	4	5
3. I willingly offer advice to others.	1	2	3	4	5
4. Before making even a minor decision, I usually consult with several people.	5	4	3	2	1
5. I am generally willing to attempt new activities for which I have very little related skill or experience.	1	2	3	4	5
6. Speaking in front of the class or other group is a frightening experience for me.	5	4	3	2	1
7. I experience stress when people challenge me or put me on the spot.	5	4	3	2	1
8. I feel comfortable attending a social event by myself.	1	2	3	4	5
9. I'm much more of a winner than a loser.	1	2	3	4	5
10. I am cautious about making any substantial change in my life.	5	4	3	2	1
Total score: ______					

Scoring and Interpretation:

Calculate your total score by adding the numbers circled. A tentative interpretation of the scoring is as follows:

45–50 Very high self-confidence with perhaps a tendency toward arrogance

38–44 A high, desirable level of self-confidence

30–37 Moderate, or average, self-confidence

10–29 Self-confidence needs strengthening

Questions: **1.** How does your score on this test fit with your evaluation of your self-confidence?
2. What would it be like working for a manager who scored 10 on this quiz?

▶ Learning Objective 4 ▶

How Do You Develop and Strengthen Your Self-Confidence?

Strengthening your confidence often facilitates success. As explained by motivational speaker and author Valorie Burton, a lack of authentic confidence holds most people from attaining their goals. People who are more successful are not necessarily better equipped than others, but they are bolder in their belief in themselves.[26] Career specialist Anthony Balderrama explains that workers at all levels should speak to work associates in a confident, self-assured manner.[27]

Self-confidence is generally achieved by succeeding in a variety of situations. A confident civil engineering technician may not be generally self-confident unless he or she also achieves success in activities such as forming good personal relationships,

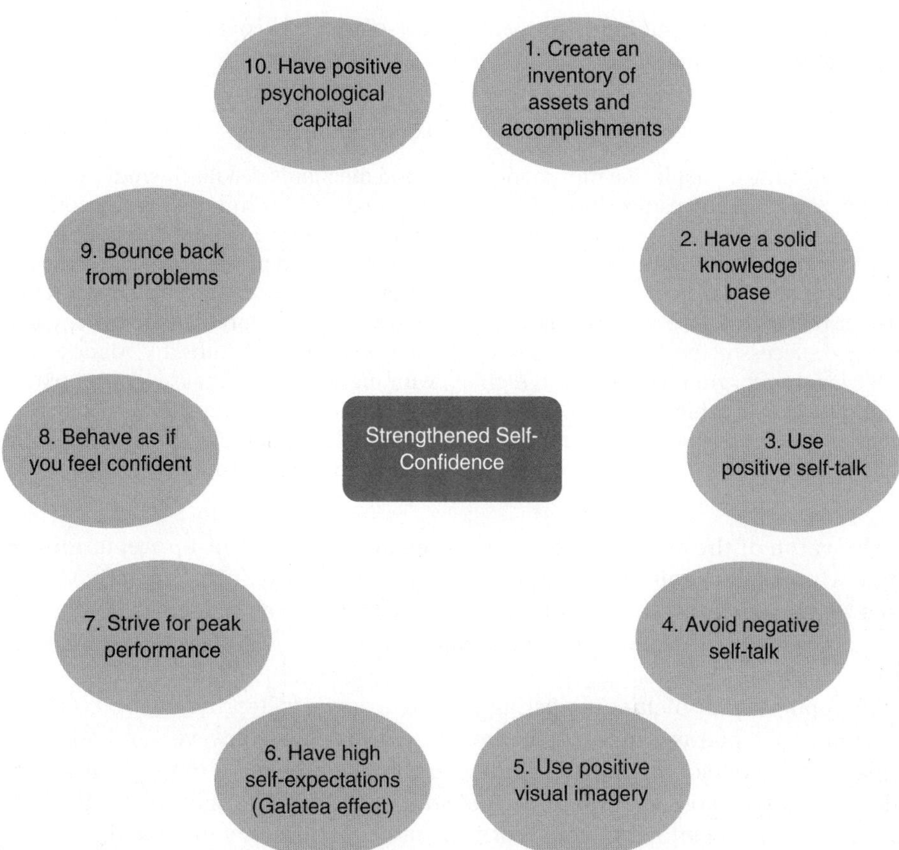

FIGURE 2-3
TECHNIQUES FOR STRENGTHENING YOUR SELF-CONFIDENCE

navigating complex software, writing a letter, learning a second language, and displaying athletic skills.

Although this general approach to building self-confidence makes sense, it does not work for everyone. Some people who seem to succeed at everything still have lingering self-doubt. Low self-confidence is so deeply ingrained in this type of personality that success in later life is not sufficient to change things. Following are ten specific strategies and tactics for building and elevating self-confidence. They will generally work unless the person has deep-rooted feelings of inferiority. The tactics and strategies described here and outlined in Figure 2-3 are arranged approximately in the order in which they should be tried to achieve best results.

TAKE AN INVENTORY OF PERSONAL ASSETS AND ACCOMPLISHMENTS

Many people suffer from low self-confidence because they do not appreciate their own good points. Therefore, a starting point in increasing your self-confidence is to take an inventory of personal assets and accomplishments. A slight variation of this activity was offered previously as a method of developing self-esteem. Personal assets should be related to characteristics and behaviors rather than tangible assets, such as an inheritance or an antique car.

Accomplishments can be anything significant in which you played a key role in achieving the results. Try not to be modest in preparing your list of assets and accomplishments. You are looking for any confidence booster you can find. Two lists prepared by different people will suffice to give you an idea of the kinds of assets and accomplishments that might be included.

Amy

Good listener; most people like me; good messaging skills; good posture; inquisitive mind; good at solving problems; above-average Internet search skills; good sense of humor; patient with people who make mistakes; better-than-average appearance. Organized successful fund drive that raised $40,000 for church; graduated tenth in high school class of 500; achieved first place in industrial bowling league; daughter has an excellent career.

Todd

Good mechanical skills, including automotive repair and computer repair; work well under pressure; good dancer; friendly with strangers; great physical health (drug and disease free); good cook; can laugh at my own mistakes; favorable personal appearance; respectful of authority. Made award-winning suggestion that saved company $45,000; scored winning goal in college basketball tournament; dragged child out of burning building; dynamite blogger.

The value of these asset lists is that they add to your self-appreciation. Most people who lay out their good points on paper come away from the activity with at least a temporary boost in self-confidence, and perhaps self-esteem. The temporary boost, combined with a few successful experiences, may lead to a long-term gain in self-confidence.

An important supplement to listing your own assets is hearing the opinion of others on your good points. This tactic has to be used sparingly, however, and mainly with people who are personal-growth minded. A good icebreaker is to tell your source of feedback that you have to prepare a list of your assets for a human relations exercise. Because that person knows of your work on your capabilities, you hope that he or she can spare a few minutes for this important exercise. For many people, positive feedback from others does more for building self-confidence than does feedback from you. The reason is that self-esteem depends to a large extent on what people think others think about them. Consequently, if other people—whose judgment you trust—think highly of you, your self-image will be positive.

DEVELOP A SOLID KNOWLEDGE BASE

A bedrock strategy for projecting self-confidence is to develop a base of knowledge that enables you to provide sensible alternative solutions to problems. Intuition is very important, but working from a base of facts helps you project a confident image. Formal education is an obvious and important source of information for your knowledge base. Day-by-day absorption of information directly and indirectly related to your career is equally important. A major purpose of formal education is to get you in the right frame of mind to continue your quest for knowledge.

In your quest for developing a solid knowledge base to project self-confidence, be sensitive to abusing this technique. If you bombard people with quotes, facts, and figures, you are likely to be perceived as an annoying know-it-all.

USE POSITIVE SELF-TALK

Positive self-talk
saying positive things about yourself to yourself

A basic method of building self-confidence is to engage in **positive self-talk,** saying positive things about you to yourself. The first step in using positive self-talk is to objectively state the incident that is casting doubt about self-worth.[28] The key word here is *objectively*. Terry, who is fearful of poorly executing a report-writing assignment, might say, "I've been asked to write a report for the company, and I'm not a good writer."

The next step is to objectively interpret what the incident *does not* mean. Terry might say, "Not being a skilled writer doesn't mean that I can't figure out a way to write a good report or that I'm an ineffective employee."

Next, the person should objectively state what the incident *does* mean. In doing this, the person should avoid put-down labels such as *incompetent, stupid, dumb, jerk,* or *airhead.* These terms are forms of negative self-talk. Terry should state what the incident does mean: "I have a problem with one small aspect of this job."

The fourth step is to objectively account for the cause of the incident. Terry would say, "I'm really worried about writing a good report because I have very little experience in writing along these lines."

The fifth step is to identify some positive ways to prevent the incident from happening again. Terry might say, "I'll get out my textbook on business communications and review the chapter on report writing" or "I'll enroll in a course or seminar on business report writing."

The final step is to use positive self-talk. Terry imagines his boss saying, "This report is really good. I'm proud of my decision to select you to prepare this important report."

Positive self-talk builds self-confidence and self-esteem because it programs the mind with positive messages. Making frequent positive statements or affirmations about the self creates a more confident person. An example would be, "I know I can learn this new equipment rapidly enough to increase my productivity within five days."

Business coach Gary Lockwood emphasizes that positive self-talk is also useful for giving you the confidence to get people past difficult times. He explains that you are in charge of your feelings, as well as your attitude. He says, "Instead of berating yourself after making a mistake, learn from the experience and move on. Say to yourself something of the nature, "Everyone makes mistakes," or "What can I learn from this?"[29]

AVOID NEGATIVE SELF-TALK

In addition to making positive statements, you should minimize negative statements about yourself to bolster self-confidence. A lack of self-confidence is reflected in statements such as, "I may be stupid, but . . .," "Nobody asked my opinion," "I know I'm usually wrong, but . . .," "I know I don't have as much education as some people, but. . . ." Self-effacing statements such as these serve to reinforce low self-confidence.

It is also important not to attribute to yourself negative, irreversible traits, such as "idiotic," "ugly," "dull," "loser-type," "hopeless," "nerdy," and "dorky." Instead, look on your weak points as areas for possible self-improvement. Negative self-labeling can do long-term damage to your confidence. If a person stops that practice today, his or her self-confidence may begin to increase.

USE POSITIVE VISUAL IMAGERY

Assume you have a situation in mind in which you would like to appear confident and in control. An example would be a meeting with a major customer who has told you by e-mail that he is considering switching suppliers. Your intuitive reaction is that if you cannot handle his concerns without fumbling or appearing desperate, you will lose the account. An important technique in this situation is **positive visual imagery,** or picturing a positive outcome in your mind. To apply this technique in this situation, imagine yourself engaging in a convincing argument about why your customer should retain your company as the primary supplier. Imagine yourself talking in positive terms about the good service your company offers and how you can rectify any problems.

Positive visual imagery picturing a positive outcome in your mind

Visualize yourself listening patiently to your customer's concerns and then talking confidently about how your company can handle these concerns. As you rehearse this moment of truth, create a mental picture of you and the customer shaking hands over the fact that the account is still yours.

Positive visual imagery helps you appear confident because your mental rehearsal of the situation has helped you prepare for battle. If imagery works for you once, you will be even more effective in subsequent uses of the technique.

SET HIGH EXPECTATIONS FOR YOURSELF (THE GALATEA EFFECT)

Galatea effect
a type of self-fulfilling prophecy in which high expectations lead to high performance

If you set high expectations for yourself, and you succeed, you are likely to experience a temporary or permanent boost in self-confidence. The **Galatea effect** is a type of self-fulfilling prophecy in which high self-expectations lead to high performance. The term *Galatea effect* stems from Greek mythology. Galatea was a maiden who was originally a statue carved by Pygmalion. She was later brought to life by Aphrodite in response to the sculptor's pleas. Similar to positive self-talk, if you believe in yourself, you are more likely to succeed. You expect to win, so you do. The Galatea effect does not work all the time, but it does work some of the time for many people.

Workplace behavior researchers D. Brian McNatt and Timothy A. Judge studied the Galatea effect with seventy-two auditors within three offices of a major accounting firm for a three-month period. The auditors were given letters of encouragement to strengthen their feelings of self-efficacy. Information in the letters was based on facts about the auditors, such as information derived from their résumés and company records. The results of the experiment showed that creating a Galatea effect bolstered self-efficacy, motivation, and performance. However, the performance improvement was temporary, suggesting that self-expectations need to be boosted regularly.[30]

STRIVE FOR PEAK PERFORMANCE

Peak performance
exceptional accomplishment in a given task

A key strategy for projecting confidence is to display **peak performance,** or exceptional accomplishment in a given task. The experience is transient but exceptionally meaningful. Peak performance refers to much more than attempting to do your best. Experiencing peak performance in various tasks over a long time period would move a person toward self-actualization (full use of potential).[31] To achieve peak performance, you must be totally focused on what you are doing. When you are in the state of peak performance, you are mentally calm and physically at ease. Intense concentration is required to achieve this state. You are so focused on the task at hand that you are not distracted by extraneous events or thoughts. To use an athletic analogy, you are *in the zone* while you are performing the task. In fact, many sports psychologists and other sports trainers work with athletes to help them attain peak performance.

The mental state achieved during peak performance is akin to a person's sense of deep concentration when immersed in a sport or hobby. On days when tennis players perform way above their usual game, they typically comment, "The ball looked so large today. I could read the label as I hit it." On the job, focus and concentration allow the person to sense and respond to relevant information coming both from within the mind and from outside stimuli. When you are at your peak, you impress others by responding intelligently to their input. While turning in peak performance, you are experiencing a mental state referred to as *flow.*

Although you are concentrating on an object or sometimes on another person during peak performance, you still have an awareness of the self. You develop a strong sense of the self, similar to self-confidence and self-efficacy, while you are concentrating on the task. Peak performance is related to self-confidence in another important way. Achieving peak performance in many situations helps you develop confidence. Here are two representative examples of peak performance:

- A real estate agent sells $17 million of homes in her region in one year, 40 percent higher than any other agent in her area.
- A customer-service specialist becomes certified as a Black Belt in the quality-improvement process called Six Sigma and then leads a team that moves a call center from a customer satisfaction rating of 75 to 98 percent.

BEHAVE AS IF YOU FEEL CONFIDENT

A principle of psychology developed about 100 years ago states that your behavior leads to attitudes. As you change your behavior, your attitudes will begin to change. This same idea can be used to project confidence. A useful example is the often-feared situation of making a presentation. Executive coach Gail Golden says that you should enter the room purposefully, holding your back straight. Look up and out at the audience instead of looking down at your notes or at the screen of your computer graphic presentation. Speak in a loud, clear voice, and look the audience in the eye or on their foreheads.[32] Behaving in this manner will often make you feel more confident within several minutes.

BOUNCE BACK FROM SETBACKS AND EMBARRASSMENTS

Resilience is a major contributor to personal effectiveness. Overcoming setbacks also builds self-confidence. An effective self-confidence builder is convincing yourself that you can conquer adversity, such as setbacks and embarrassments, thus being resilient. The vast majority of successful leaders have dealt successfully with at least one significant setback in their careers, such as being fired or demoted. In contrast, crumbling after a setback or series of setbacks will usually lower self-confidence.

Overcoming some adversity not only builds self-confidence but it also contributes to a person's long-term well-being. A study involving 2,398 participants surveyed over a three-year period found that people who had experienced a few adverse events reported better mental health and well-being than people with a frequent history of adversity and people with no reports of misfortune. Mark Seery a researcher at the Department of Psychology at the University of Buffalo, concluded "that a history of some lifetime adversity—relative to no adversity or high adversity—predicted lower global distress, lower functional impairment, lower PTS (post-traumatic stress) symptoms and higher life satisfaction.[33]

The accompanying Human Relations in Practice box describes how one of the world's largest organizations attempts to build resilience within its workforce, and their family members.

Three key suggestions for bouncing back from setbacks and embarrassments are presented next.

Get Past the Emotional Turmoil

Adversity has enormous emotional consequences. The emotional impact of severe job adversity can rival the loss of a personal relationship. The stress from adversity leads to a cycle of adversity followed by stress, followed by more adversity. A starting point in dealing with the emotional aspects of adversity is to *accept the reality of your problem.* Admit that your problems are real and that you are hurting inside. The next step is *not to take*

Human Relations in Practice

The U.S. Army Trains Its Soldiers to Be Resilient

The army's senior noncommissioned officer, Sgt. Major of the Army Kenneth O. Preston, talked to a crowd of 200 soldiers about how the army is ensuring its Soldiers' well-being through Comprehensive Soldier Fitness (CSF), whether at home or deployed at another country.

"That is what Comprehensive Soldier Fitness is about," Preston said. "When soldiers are faced with adversity, army leadership wants Soldiers to come out of those stressful situations stronger than they were before. Preston talked about the four tools to enhance CSF and how Soldiers can become more resilient toward the different changes and challenges in life. The CSF is a holistic fitness program for Soldiers, families, and army civilians to enhance performance and build resilience. The goal is to have an army of balanced, healthy, self-confident people whose resilience and total fitness enables them to excel in an era of high operational tempo and persistent conflict.

The first tool is an online assessment that gives Soldiers an awareness of their strengths and weaknesses based on the five dimensions of CSF. The Global Assessment Test (GAT) is designed to show Soldiers their strengths and weaknesses in the physical, social, emotional, social, spiritual, and family pillars of strength, Preston said. He elaborated how the GAT is for self-improvement, and how results are private.

"The GAT doesn't replace good leadership," Preston said. "The GAT is designed as an individual tool to show individuals where they stand. Nobody sees how you answer these questions. It is confidential because we want you to be honest with yourself so that you can see yourself exactly how you feel inside."

Preston said that more than 800,000 of the 1.1 million active duty, reserve, and National Guard Soldiers in the army have taken the GAT. Preston also recommended that Soldiers complete the 20 online resilience modules available through CSF, the second tool of the program. Preston said the modules were interactive and had good vignettes.

The third tool of the CSF is the Master Resilience Trainer course, which is offered at Victory University in Fort Jackson, South Carolina. The ten-day course teaches soldiers resiliency techniques on how to solve challenges within the five dimensions of CSF. It teaches Soldiers how to ask the right questions so they can understand problems from a bigger perspective, Preston said. From there, they come up with their own solutions to fixing problems. "Nobody can fix your own problems or challenges except you," Preston emphasized.

The last tool is the incorporation of resiliency training into other Training and Doctrine Command schools, Preston said. Soldiers will receive CSF training from the time they start their careers to the time they leave. It is a tool to help you to make a better Soldier and to make you a better person."

Questions: How does Comprehensive Soldier Fitness tie in with the development of self-confidence?

Source: Adapted slightly from "Comprehensive Soldier Fitness," *Army Reserve* (www.usar.army.mil/arweb/soldiers), accessed January 30, 2012.

the setback personally. Remember that setbacks are inevitable as long as you are taking some risks in your career. Not personalizing setbacks helps reduce some of the emotional sting. If possible, *do not panic.* Recognize that you are in difficult circumstances under which many others panic. Convince yourself to remain calm enough to deal with the severe problem or crisis. Also, *get help from your support network.* Getting emotional support from family members and friends helps overcome the emotional turmoil associated with adversity.

A type of emotional turmoil that faces many people at some point in their careers is to be fired for what the company thinks is poor performance. Being fired hurts most people deeply, but by following the steps previously described, the impact can be softened and can ultimately lead to heightened self-confidence. A surprisingly large number of successful entrepreneurs were at one time fired from a corporate job, often because they were seen as mavericks who would not follow rules well.

Find a Creative Solution to Your Problem

An inescapable part of planning a comeback is to solve your problem. You often need to search for creative solutions. Jason, a business student in Chicago, ran a sub shop to earn a living and support himself through college. Layoffs at nearby companies had driven his sales way down below the point at which it paid to keep the sub shop open. In the process of exploring all the possibilities of what he could do in a hurry to earn a living, Jason observed that loads of old buildings in downtown Chicago were being rebuilt and turned into apartments and retail space. Jason then thought of starting an "interior demolition" company, combining efforts with two relatives in the home repair business. Jason's creative solution accomplished what needed to be done to regain his financial equilibrium. His self-confidence continues to surge as his interior demolition business has prospered. If the preceding steps work for you and you bring your level of self-confidence to where you want it to be, you will have achieved a major milestone in applying human relations to yourself.

Regain Confidence by Relaxing a Little

Even the most successful business people face a slump from time to time. The performance of sales representatives is highly measurable, so they are likely to be more aware of and pained by a slump. When the slump occurs, workers tend to lose self-confidence, obsess about past mistakes, and become anxious about performing tasks they once enjoyed. The loss of self-confidence tends to deteriorate performance further.

As recommended by some sports psychologists, an effective way to regain self-confidence when in a slump is to stop overworking and allow yourself to relax. A case in point is Dan Di Cio, a Pittsburg account executive who was hoping for an excellent season selling high-tech equipment but the big sales were not forthcoming. He became discouraged and self-doubting as he watched other sales professionals win awards. Di Cio contacted sports psychologist Gregg Sternberg after hearing him speak. The psychologist told the account executive that he was working so hard that he risked driving his sales results even lower. Di Cio's outlook improved so much that he doubled his sales over the previous year.[34]

STRIVE TO DEVELOP POSITIVE PSYCHOLOGICAL CAPITAL

A comprehensive way of becoming more self-confident is to develop **positive psychological capital,** a positive psychological state of development in which you have hope, self-efficacy, optimism, and resilience. Note that self-efficacy and resilience have

Positive psychological capital
a positive psychological state of development in which you have a storehouse of hope, self-efficacy, optimism, and resilience

already been included in our study of self-confidence. In more detail, the components of positive psychological capital are as follows:

- *Hope* refers to persevering toward goals and, when necessary, redirecting paths to a goal in order to succeed. In everyday language, don't give up when pursuing your goals.
- *Self-efficacy* refers to having the confidence to take on and invest the necessary effort to succeed at challenging tasks. Experience is a big help here, because if you have successfully completed the same task, or a similar one, previously you will be more confident that you can succeed.
- *Optimism* refers to making a positive attribution about succeeding now and in the future. If you are a natural pessimist you will have to work harder at looking for the positive aspects of a given situation.
- *Resiliency* refers to dealing with problems and adversity by sustaining effort and bouncing back to attain success. Conquering a major setback would be an enormous contributor to your self-confidence.

An encouraging note about positive psychological capital is that people can develop it. An experiment conducted with 187 working adults found that a Web-based, highly-focused two-hour training program raised the average level of psychological capital. The increase in psychological capital was measured by more positive responses after training to such statements as, "If I should find myself in a jam at work, I could think of many ways to get out of it" (hope).[35] Should the participants in the study really do a better job of getting out of jams in the future, you could be even more confident about how well training improves psychological capital.

AVOID OVERCONFIDENCE

As with most human qualities, self-confidence can be a negative factor if carried to the extreme. The overly self-confident individual might become intimidating and unwilling to listen to the advice of others. During a group meeting, the highly self-confident person might typically make a comment before giving others their fair turn to speak. Overconfident individuals are so self-centered that they do not even notice eyes rolling when they hog the meeting.

The potential disadvantages of extremely high self-confidence also apply to too much concern about the self in general, including self-esteem. Too much attention to the self can lead a person to be self-centered, self-conscious, and uninterested in other people and the outside world. As mentioned above, a narcissist can be annoying. You have probably met people who include in almost every conversation a statement about their health or an activity of theirs, indicating their self-centeredness.

The right balance is to be concerned about yourself, your self-esteem and self-confidence, and your personal growth yet still focus on the outside world. Focusing on the outside world can ultimately strengthen you because you develop skills and interests that will enhance your self-esteem and self-confidence.

Learning Objective 5

What Is Codependence, and How Is It Linked to Low Self-Esteem and Low Self-Confidence?

A substantial negative consequence of having low self-esteem and low self-confidence is that it can lead people to look for something outside of the inner self to make them feel better. Some try to feel better through alcohol, drugs, or nicotine, and become addicted.

Another way people with low self-esteem attempt to take care of the problem is to play a martyr role and become the benefactor of someone else.

In personal life, as well as on the job, codependence can create unhealthy, dysfunctional relationships. Here we take a quick overview of the meaning, symptoms, and control and overcoming of codependence. Recognize, however, that codependency is a vast, complicated problem with millions of articles, books, and Web sites about the topic.[36] The topic of codependence could also fit into the section in Chapter 17 about personal problems. Yet codependence can also affect other topics in human relations such as coworker relationships and leadership.

MEANING OF CODEPENDENCE

Codependency is a state of being psychologically influenced or controlled by, reliant on, or needing another person who is addicted to substances such as alcohol and drugs, or behavior such as gambling or Internet use. The codependent is mutually dependent because he or she relies on the other person's dependence. The codependent has a tendency to place the needs and wants of others first, to the exclusion of acknowledging one's own needs. Such behavior is closely tied to low self-esteem. Codependency is also regarded as an emotional and behavioral condition that affects an individual's ability to have a healthy, mutually satisfying relationship.

Codependency
a state of being psychologically influenced or controlled by, reliant on, or needing another person who is addicted to substances such as alcohol and drugs, or behavior such as gambling or Internet use.

Codependency is also referred to as *relationship addiction* because codependent people often form or maintain relationships that are one-sided, emotionally destructive, and abusive. Codependent behavior is usually learned by watching and imitating other family members who display this type of behavior. Yet it is possible for a person to drift into codependent behavior later in life in attempting to meet the needs of a partner or boss with intense personal problems.

Figure 2-4 illustrates the major transaction that takes place in a codependent relationship, whether or not the two people explicitly understand what is happening.

The two people in a codependent relationship rely on each other.

FIGURE 2-4
A KEY ASPECT OF A CODEPENDENT RELATIONSHIP

SYMPTOMS AND DESCRIPTION OF THE PROBLEM

1. The codependent feels responsible for the dependent by covering up the other person's addiction, such as excessive alcohol use for fear of discovery. (For example, Jim is drunk today, so when his boss calls, Jim's wife, Jane, says, "I am sorry but Jim is terribly ill today. He seems to have caught a wicked virus.") The problem with the cover up is that the addicted person's behavior becomes sustained.
2. The codependent will often only feel good when the dependent person feels good, so the codependent tries hard to please the dependent person. As a result the codependent person is extremely dependent, eager to please, and easily yields to the wishes of others.
3. A higher percentage of women than men are codependent, perhaps because some cultures emphasize the nurturing and supportive role of women, with men being more indifferent to the problems of others. (This is a broad gender stereotype that might apply to a small majority of men and women.)
4. The codependent will have difficulty leading a satisfying and productive life because he or she invests so much energy in taking care of a person with a dependency. Quite often the codependent invests considerable time in keeping the other person addicted so as to feel useful.
5. The codependent has a strong need to be needed, so she or he gains some satisfaction from the partner having problems and needing to be rescued. As a result, the codependent's helping behavior goes beyond a healthy limit, such as arranging a loan for the gambling addict who spent his entire paycheck with online sports betting.
6. The codependent often believes that she or he is a victim of being trapped by a person who requires help. An example would be an administrative assistant who feels victimized because her boss spends a couple of hours per day accessing pornography on a company computer. She feels it is unfair that she is subject continually to this form of environmental sexual harassment.
7. The codependent has a strong need to rescue or fix another person—even though an unconscious motive might be present to keep the other person addicted and helpless.
8. The codependent may feel resentful for reasons such as the other person not appreciating the help, or because that person will not change.
9. Codependents have an unhealthy dependence on relationships, and will do anything to hang on to a relationship to avoid feeling abandoned.

HOW TO CONTROL AND OVERCOME CODEPENDENCE

1. Codependency often stems from growing up in a dysfunctional family, so psychotherapy and counseling may be required to overcome the behavior pattern and attitudes of a codependent.
2. With or without therapy the codependent must become aware of the problem, and carefully process information about codependency. The codependent must examine thoroughly his or her caretaking. Good questions to ask the self are: "Is my behavior preventing this person from functioning independently?" "Do I really want him (or her) to get better?" "Am I making it easier for him (or her) to stay addicted?"
3. The codependent person must learn to say "No," perhaps in small steps. For example, "No, I am not going to bring you a meal into the den so you can sit up for a few more hours and work the Internet." "No, I am not going to bring you back a 12-pack of beer from the convenience store." "No, you call in sick to the office yourself or write your own e-mail explaining why you can't work today."
4. The codependent person must recognize that it is often not in his or her power to change the behavior of another person. That other person must first want to become independent and healthy.

Key Terms

Self-esteem, 32
Narcissism, 37
Self-respect, 38
Introspection, 39
Self-efficacy, 40
Positive self-talk, 44
Positive visual imagery, 45
Galatea effect, 46
Peak performance, 46
Positive psychological capital, 49
Codependence, 51

Summary and Review

- *Self-esteem* refers to feeling competent and being worthy of happiness. People with high self-esteem develop positive self-concepts.
- Self-esteem develops from a variety of early-life experiences. People who were encouraged to feel good about themselves and their accomplishments by key people in their lives are more likely to enjoy high self-esteem.
- Of major significance, self-esteem also results from accomplishing worthwhile activities and then feeling proud of these accomplishments. Praise and recognition for accomplishments also help develop self-esteem.
- Self-esteem is important for career success. Good mental health is another major consequence of high self-esteem. One of the links between good mental health and self-esteem is that high self-esteem helps prevent many situations from being stressful. High self-esteem helps us profit from negative feedback.
- Workers with high self-esteem develop and maintain favorable work attitudes and perform at a high level. A company with high self-esteem workers has a competitive advantage.
- High self-esteem is associated with long-term career success, including job satisfaction, higher pay, and occupying high-status positions. Companies also prosper when workers have high self-esteem.
- Self-esteem can be useful in guiding social relationships because you can adjust your behavior as your esteem feelings fluctuate.
- Potential negative consequences of excessively high or low self-esteem include becoming narcissistic, envying too many people, and relationship problems. Our own reference group has the biggest impact on self-esteem.

Self-esteem can be enhanced in many ways:

- Attain legitimate accomplishments, including engaging in behaviors and making choices that are esteem worthy. Setting constructive goals is also helpful.
- Be aware of your personal strengths.
- Minimize settings and interactions that detract from your feelings of competence.
- Talk and socialize frequently with people who boost your self-esteem.
- Model the behavior of people with high self-esteem.

Various studies have shown that people with a high sense of self-efficacy tend to have good job performance, so self-confidence is important for your career. Our feelings of self-confidence stem from five sources of information:

- Actual experiences, or things that we have done
- Experiences of others, or modeling
- Social comparison, or comparing yourself to others
- Social persuasion, the process of convincing another person
- Emotional arousal, or how people feel about events around them and managing emotions

A general principle of boosting your self-confidence is to experience success (goal accomplishment) in a variety of situations. The specific strategies for building self-confidence described here are as follows:

- Take an inventory of personal assets and accomplishments.
- Develop a solid knowledge base.
- Use positive self-talk.

- Avoid negative self-talk.
- Use positive visual imagery.
- Set high expectations for yourself (the Galatea effect).
- Strive for peak performance.
- Behave as if you feel self-confident.
- Bounce back from setbacks and embarrassments. (Get past the emotional turmoil; find a creative solution to your problem; regain confidence by relaxing a little.)
- Strive to develop psychological capital (hope, self-efficacy, optimism, and resiliency).

Avoiding overconfidence will help you make more effective use of your self-confidence. To achieve the right level of self-confidence and self-esteem, maintain focus on others also.

A substantial negative consequence of low self-esteem and self-confidence is that it can prompt the person to develop a codependent relationship. The codependent is psychologically controlled by or reliant upon another person who is addicted to a negative substance or behavior. The codependent person must learn to say "No" to the other person, perhaps in small steps.

Check Your Understanding

1. Imagine an accountant being told by a client, "I think that you are really stupid, and I am going to report you to your boss." Give one example of how a high-self-esteem accountant might respond, and one of how a low-self-esteem accountant might respond.
2. Identify a public figure, such as a business executive, professional athlete, or politician whose self-esteem is so extreme that he or she is a narcissist. Give a couple examples of his or her narcissistic behavior.
3. In what way has a teacher, instructor, or professor ever raised your self-esteem? How long-lasting was the effect?
4. How might you improve your self-efficacy for a specific job that you are performing?
5. When you meet another person, on what basis do you conclude that he or she is self-confident?
6. What steps could you take in the next thirty days to increase your positive psychological capital?
7. In what way does your program of studies contribute to building your self-esteem and self-confidence?
8. Many pharmaceutical firms actively recruit former cheerleaders as sales representatives to call on doctors to recommend their brand of prescription drugs. The firms in question say that cheerleaders make good sales reps because they are so self-confident. What is your opinion on this controversial issue?
9. Visualize yourself applying for your dream job, and because you want the job so badly you do not feel highly self-confident. What steps can you take to appear self-confident?
10. Interview a person whom you perceive to have a successful career. Ask that person to describe how he or she developed high self-esteem. Be prepared to discuss your findings in class.

Web Corner

INTEGRATING SELF-ESTEEM INTO THE FABRIC OF SOCIETY

www.self-esteem-nase.org

BUILDING YOUR SELF-CONFIDENCE

www.mindtools.com/selfconf.html (includes video)

INTERNET SKILL BUILDER 2-1

Learning More about Your Self-Esteem

The National Mental Health Information Center has a Web site (listed below) that provides a self-help guide to building self-esteem. Many of the suggestions in the booklet the Web site provides reinforce what you have studied in this chapter. The help offered is mostly from the perspective of people who have low esteem and are working to improve their situation. As you read the booklet and do the self-esteem-building exercises, you are asked to keep the following statement in mind: "I am a very special, unique, and valuable person. I deserve to feel good about myself." (http://mentalhealth.samhsa.gov)

INTERNET SKILL BUILDER 2-2

Developing Your Self-Confidence Online

As described in this chapter, self-confidence is a major contributor to leadership effectiveness in a variety of situations.www.self-confidence.co.uk offers a free self-confidence course online. After you sign up for the course, you will receive your first installment immediately. After that you will receive one tutorial a week for six weeks. The lessons include self-confidence-boosting stories, information and quotes, and skill-development exercises. Sponsors of the site will invite you to take related courses for a fee.

Developing Your Human Relations Skills

Human Relations Application Exercises

Applying Human Relations Exercise 2-1

The Self-Esteem-Building Club

You and your classmates are invited to participate in one of the most humane and productive possible human relations skill-building exercises: membership in the "self-esteem-building club." Your assignment is for three consecutive weeks to help build the self-esteem of one person. Before embarking on the exercise, review the information about self-esteem development in the chapter. One of the most effective tactics would be to find somebody who has a legitimate accomplishment and give that person a reward or thank-you. Record carefully what the person did, what you did, and any behavioral reactions of the person whose self-esteem you attempted to build. The incident could become part of your human relations journal. An example follows, written by a 46-year-old student of human relations:

> *Thursday night two weeks ago I went to the athletic club to play racquetball. Different from usual, I had a date after the club. I wanted to look good, so I decided to wear my high school class ring. The ring doesn't have much resale value, but I was emotionally attached to it, having worn it for special occasions for twenty-eight years. I stuffed the ring along with my watch and wallet in my athletic bag.*
>
> *When I was through with racquetball, I showered and got dressed. My ring was missing from my bag even though my wallet and watch were there. I kind of freaked out because I hate to lose a prized possession. I shook the bag out three times, but no luck. Very discouraged, I left my name, telephone number, and e-mail address at the front desk just in case somebody turned in the ring. I kept thinking that I must have lost the ring when I stopped at the desk to check in.*
>
> *The next morning before going to class, I got a phone call from a front-desk receptionist at the club. The receptionist told me that Karl, from the housekeeping staff, heard a strange noise while he was vacuuming near the front desk. He shut off the vacuum cleaner immediately and pulled out my ring. To me, Karl was a hero. I made a special trip to the club that night to meet with Karl. I shook his hand, and gave him a $10 bill as a reward. I also explained to Karl what a difference he had made in my mood. I told him that honest, hardworking people like him who take pride in their work make this world a better place. It made my day when Karl smiled and told me it was a pleasure to be helpful.*

Your instructor might organize a sharing of self-esteem-building episodes in the class. If the sharing does take place, look for patterns in terms of what seemed to work in terms of self-esteem building. Also, listen for any patterns in failed attempts at self-esteem building.

Applying Human Relations Exercise 2-2

Building Your Self-Confidence and Self-Efficacy

Most people can use a boost to their self-confidence. Even if you are a highly confident individual, perhaps there is room for building your feelings of self-efficacy in a particular area—for example, as a proud and successful business owner learning a new skill such as editing digital photos or speaking a foreign language. For this skill-building exercise, enhance your self-confidence or self-efficacy in the next two weeks by trying out one of the many suggestions for self-confidence building described in the text.

As part of planning the implementation of this exercise, think about any area in which your self-confidence could use a boost. A candid human relations student, who was also a confident cheerleader, said, "Face it, I suck at PowerPoint presentations. I put up so many details on my slides that the audience is trying to read my slides instead of looking at me. I have to admit that my PowerPoint presentation consists mostly of my reading my slides to the audience. I'm much better at cheerleading." So this student studied information in her human relations text about making better graphic presentations. She revamped her approach to using her slides as headlines and talking points. She tried out one presentation in class and one at her church. She received so many compliments on her presentations that she now has much higher self-efficacy with respect to PowerPoint presentations.

Human Relations Class Activity

The Self-Esteem and Self-Confidence Survey

Here is an opportunity to engage in data collection about a vital human relations topic. Each class member is required to obtain survey data from five people, asking each person four questions, as follows: (Survey anybody convenient, including yourself.)

1. What is your sex (gender)?
2. What is your age?
3. How would you rate your self-esteem from 1 (low) to 10 (high)?
4. How would you rate your self-confidence from 1 (low) to 10 (high)?

Use any method of data collection you would like, including face-to-face interviews, e-mail, chat, instant messaging, social networking site, or phone. The results of the survey are entered into a class database run by one or two volunteers. After all data have been collected, one of the volunteers analyzes the data in terms of the following results:

1. Percent of respondents who are male and percent female
2. Average age
3. Average self-esteem rating
4. Average self-confidence rating
5. Average self-esteem and self-confidence ratings of men and women
6. Average self-esteem and self-confidence ratings of respondents of (a) those twenty-five and younger and (b) those twenty-six and older

Class discussion might include any conclusions drawn from the results and how the results fit expectations. For example, a few students might comment about what they predicted would be the average score on self-esteem and self-confidence or any sex or age differences they might have predicted. What about you? How do your self-esteem and self-confidence ratings compare to the survey average?

Human Relations Case Study 2-1

Cindy Struggles in Customer Service

Cindy, age twenty-four, had never looked forward to frequent conflict at home or on the job. She is good natured and gets along with most people as long as they are not abrasive and rude. Despite knowing that she does not feel at her best in dealing with angry people, Cindy accepted a position as a customer service representative in big-box discount department store. The position requires her to work thirty-seven and one half hours per week, split among days and evenings, including weekends. Customer service at this store involves mostly exchanges of merchandises, granting refunds for returned merchandise, and occasionally listening to complaints about service at the store or about advertised merchandise not being available.

Cindy's supervisor, Derek, explained that the most demanding part of the job would be refusing refunds to customers who had obviously abused merchandise or had bought the merchandise with the intent of using it for a while and then expecting a full refund. Cindy cringed at the thought of standing up to angry customers, but she told Derek that she was up to the challenge.

After a three-day training and orientation program at the store, Derek said that Cindy was ready to work at the customer service desk on her own. Cindy accepted Derek's decision that she was ready to deal with customer demands, but she was trembling underneath. She thought, "How will I handle it if one of those abusive customers tries to rip us off?"

For the first few days, the customer requests were relatively easy for Cindy to manage. Many of the customers brought back merchandise neatly packed in the original boxes, with no visible damage to the merchandise. Several other customers wanted to exchange merchandise for a different size or color. One Friday evening, the relative tranquility of Cindy's job changed suddenly.

A woman around thirty-five years old brought back a long overcoat, saying, "I want my money back. I don't like this coat." Cindy noticed that the coat had a mud stain, so she politely asked, "Ma'am, is it possible that you have worn this coat, and maybe gotten it a little bit dirty?"

"I just wore the coat once. What's wrong with that? I want my money back right now, or I am going to complain to your supervisor." Cindy began to tremble and thought that she just didn't want to get in a fight with a cheat and a thief. She thought that the customer really never intended to keep the coat but just wanted to pretend to buy the coat, all the time expecting a refund after wearing the coat once or twice. So Cindy replied to the customer, "I might be stretching store policy a little, but I think I can give you a full refund."

Later that night Cindy wondered if she had the courage to go back to the job tomorrow. She kept thinking about whether she had enough nerve to deal with demanding customers, even when she knew they were being unreasonable.

Questions

1. In what way does this case deal with self-confidence?
2. What steps do you recommend that Cindy take to enhance her self-confidence?
3. What steps do you recommend that Derek take to boost Cindy's self-confidence?
4. What should Cindy have told the customer who wanted to return the mud-stained coat?

Human Relations Role-Playing Exercise 2-1

Dealing with an Unreasonable Customer

Human Relations Case 2-1 provides the background information and story line for this role-play. One person plays the role of the customer attempting to obtain a full refund on the mud-stained overcoat. The other student plays the role of Cindy, who intends to quite confidently reject the customer's demand as being unreasonable.

Observers rate the role-players on two dimensions, using a 1 to 5 scale, from very poor to very good. One dimension is "effective use of human relations techniques." The second dimension is "acting ability." A few observers might voluntarily provide feedback to the role-players in terms of sharing their ratings and observations. The course instructor might also provide feedback.

Human Relations Case Study 2-2

High-Self-Esteem Brandy

As Brandy Barclay navigated the challenging highways toward her job interview in Los Angeles, she rehearsed in her mind the importance of communicating that she is a unique brand. "I have to get across the idea that I am special, even if my brand is not as well established as Godiva Chocolates or Dr Pepper. (A brand is a basket of strengths that sets you apart from others.) This administrative assistant position at the hotel and resort company will be a good way to launch my career and brand. After all, I am a very special person."

An excerpt of her job interview with the hiring manager Gloria Gomez follows:

Gomez: Welcome Brandy, I am pleased that you made it through the online job application and the telephone screening interview. Tell me again why you would like to join our hotel company as an administrative assistant.

Barclay: Oh, I really don't want to join you as an administrative assistant. I would prefer a vice president job, but I have to start somewhere. (Smiling) Seriously, I like the hotel field. It fits my brand called Brandy. I am a great support person, and a great people person. I'm so unique because I'm great with details and great with people. Many people have told me that I am a very special person."

Gomez: Tell me specifically what key strengths would you bring to this job?

Barclay: As found in my brand called Brandy, I am high info tech and high touch. I'm a whiz at Microsoft Office Suite, and I'm sweet with people. Kind of catchy, don't you think? Come to think of it, have you seen my business card? It contains loads of details about my skills and strengths on the back. The card is laminated so it will last, and it contains my photo, and even is like a hologram with a 3-D look.

Gomez: Yes, Brandy, I do have your card. You gave one to the receptionist, and she gave it to me. And why do you keep referring to yourself as a brand? Is this just a gimmick to get you noticed?

Barclay: Being a brand is the modern way to tell you that Brandy Barclay is one of a kind. I've got a skill set that is hard to beat. Besides, I want to build a reputation fast that will propel me to the top as an executive in the hotel field. I am quite proud of who I am.

Gomez: On your trip to the top, what do you plan to do for us as an administrative assistant?

Barclay: I will live up to the brand called Brandy by getting the job done big time. Just ask me to do something, and it will be done. Don't forget I will be building my brand image while in this beginning assignment.

Gomez: Now let's talk about details like the job assignment, salary, and benefits.

Barclay: Fine with me. We have to deal with the mundane at some point.

Case Questions

1. How effectively is Brandy Barclay presenting herself as a brand (or a unique individual)?
2. What suggestions can you offer Barclay for presenting herself as a strong individual more effectively?
3. To what extent do you think that Brandy's high self-esteem has reached the point of narcissism?

Human Relations Role-Playing Exercise 2-2

Brandy Becomes More Humble

Assume that Brandy receives an e-mail that Gloria Gomez is not going to extend her a job offer because she appeared to be more interested in boosting her career than helping the company. Brandy decides that she will appear a little more humble in her next job interview, yet still present a positive self-picture. She lands an interview with another company for an administrative position. Her interviewing manager is Gus, who likes positive people but dislikes arrogance.

One student plays the role of Brandy who wants to impress, yet plans to tone down her self-admiration. Another student plays the role of Gus, who is unaware of Brandy's recent rejection as a job candidate. Observers rate the role-players on two dimensions, using a 1 to 5 scale, from very poor to very good. One dimension is "effective use of human relations techniques." The second dimension is "acting ability." A few observers might voluntarily provide feedback to the role-players in terms of sharing their ratings and observations. The course instructor might also provide feedback.

REFERENCES

1. Original story was created from facts presented in the following sources: Tanzina Vega, "Emilio Romano Named President of Telemundo," *Media Decoder* (http::/ /mediadecoder .blogs.nytimes.com), September 21, 2011, pp. 2–3: "Emilio Romano: President, Telemundo," www.nbcun.com/ corporate/management/executives, p. 1 (accessed January 3, 2012); "Emilio Romano," (http://people.forbes.com?profile/ print), accessed January 2, 2012; "Telemundo Gets New Boss," *Latin American Herald Tribune,* December 29, 2011, pp. 1–3
2. Nathaniel Branden, *Self-Esteem at Work: How Confident People Make Powerful Companies,* (San Francisco: Jossey-Bass, 1998).
3. April O'Connell, Vincent O'Connell, and Lois-Ann Kuntz, *Choice and Change: The Psychology of Personal Growth and Interpersonal Relationships,* 7th ed. (Upper Saddle River, NJ: Pearson/Prentice Hall, 2005), p. 3.
4. Harriet Brown, "The Boom and Bust Ego," *Psychology Today,* February 2012, p. 70.
5. "Better Self-Esteem." Retrieved February 1, 2006, from: www .utexas.edu/student/cmhc/booklets/selfesteem/selfest.html.
6. A review of the scholarly research on this topic is contained in Mark R. Leary and Ray F. Baumeister, "The Nature and Function of Self-Esteem: Sociometer Theory," in *Advances in Experimental Social Psychology,* Vol. 32 (New York: Academic Press, 2000), pp. 1–49.
7. Cited in Randall Edwards, "Is Self-Esteem Really All That Important?" *APA Monitor,* May 1995, p. 43.
8. David De Cremer et al., "Rewarding Leadership and Fair Procedures as Determinants of Self-Esteem," *Journal of Applied Psychology,* January 2005, pp. 3–12.
9. Eugene Raudsepp, "Strong Self-Esteem Can Help You Advance," *The Wall Street Journal.* Retrieved August 10, 2004, from: www.careerjournal.com.
10. Jon L. Pierce, Donald G. Gardner, Larry L. Cummings, and Randall B. Dunman, "Organization-Based Self-Esteem: Construct Definition, Measurement, and Validation," *Academy of Management Journal,* September 1989, p. 623.
11. Timothy A. Judge and Charlice Hurst, "How the Rich (and Happy) Get Richer (and Happier): Relationship of Core Self-Evaluations to Trajectories in Attaining Work Success," *Journal of Applied Psychology,* July 2008, pp. 849–863.
12. Adam M. Grant and Amy Wrzenesniewki, "I Won't Let You Down . . . or Will I? Core Self-Evaluations, Other-orientation, Anticipated Guilt and Gratitude, and Job Performance," *Journal of Applied Psychology,* January 2010, pp. 108–121.
13. Nathaniel Branden, *Self-Esteem at Work: How Confident People Make Powerful Companies,* (San Francisco: Jossey-Bass, 1998); Timothy A. Judge and Joyce E. Bono, "Relationship of Core Self-Evaluations Traits—Self-Esteem, Generalized Self-Efficacy, Locus of Control, and Emotional Stability—With Job Satisfaction and Job Performance: A Meta-Analysis,"*Journal of Applied Psychology,* February 2001, pp. 80–92.
14. D. Lance Ferris, "Self-Esteem and Job Performance: The Moderating Role of Self-Esteem Contingencies," *Personnel Psychology,* Autumn 2010, pp. 561–593.
15. As quoted in Erika Casriel, "Stepping Out," *Psychology Today,* March/April 2007, p. 73.
16. Ibid.
17. Andrew J. DuBrin, *Narcissism in the Workplace: Research, Opinion, and Practice,* (Cheltenham UK: Edward Elgar, 2012), p. 1.
18. Cited in Brown, "The Boom and Bust Ego," p. 73.
19. Cited in Julia M. Klein, "The Illusion of Rejection," *Psychology Today,* January/February 2005, p. 30.
20. Cited in Brown, "The Boom and Bust Ego," p. 73.
21. A good sampling of his thinking is Leo Buscaglia, *Living, Loving, and Learning,* (New York: Ballantine Books, 1985).
22. Cited in "Self-Esteem: You'll Need It to Succeed," *Executive Strategies,* September 1993, p. 12.
23. Raudsepp, "Strong Self-Esteem."
24. Marilyn E. Gist and Terence R. Mitchell, "Self-Efficacy: A Theoretical Analysis of Its Determinants and Malleability," *Academy of Management Review,* April 1992, pp. 183–211.
25. George P. Hollenbeck and Douglas T. Hall, "Self-Confidence and Leader Performance," *Organizational Dynamics,* Issue 3, 2004, pp. 261–264.
26. Ayana Dixon, "The Center of Success: Author Explains How Confidence Can Get You Further," *Black Enterprise,* March 2008, p. 123.
27. Anthony Balderrama, "Soft Skills Job Seekers Needed," *Democrat and Chronicle,* August 7, 2011, p. 2F.
28. Jay T. Knippen and Thad B. Green, "Building Self-Confidence," *Supervisory Management,* August 1989, pp. 22–27.
29. "Entrepreneurs Need Attitude: Power of Being Positive Can Help You to Succeed in Spite of Setbacks," Knight Ridder, September 16, 2002.
30. D. Brian McNatt and Timothy A. Judge, "Boundary Conditions of the Galatea Effect: A Field Experiment and Constructive Replication,"*Academy of Management Journal,* August 2004, pp. 550–565.
31. Frances Thornton, Gayle Privette, and Charles M. Bundrick, "Peak Performance of Business Leaders: An Experience Parallel to Self-Actualization Theory," *Journal of Business and Psychology,* Winter 1999, pp. 253–264.
32. Cited in "Present with Panache," June 2007, p. 8. *Manager's Edge,*
33. Mark Seery, Alison E. Holman, and Roxanne Cohen Silver, "Whatever Does Not Kill Us: Cumulative Lifetime Adversity, Vulnerability, and Resilience," *Journal of Personality and Social Psychology,* December 2010, pp. 1025–1041.
34. Sue Shellenbarger, "Slumping at Work? What Would Jack Do?" *The Wall Street Journal,* October 13, 2010, p. D1.
35. Fred Luthans, James R. Avey, and Jaime L. Patera, "Experimental Analysis of a Web-Based Training Intervention to Develop Positive Psychological Capital," *Academy of Management Learning and Education,* June 2008, pp. 209–221.
36. Much of the discussion here about codependence is based on "Co-dependency," pp. 1–3; *Mental Health America* (www .nmha.org/go/dependency), © 2012 Mental Health America; "Codependency," *AllAboutCounseling.com.,* pp. 1–2. Accessed February 14, 2012.

3

Self-Motivation and Goal Setting

Outline

Peyton is on the administrative staff of a health-maintenance organization (HMO). Among her varied responsibilities are preparing reports about patterns of patient visits and reviewing reimbursements from insurance companies to search for any discrepancies between requests by the HMO and payments from the insurers. Peyton majored in business administration and took several courses in office procedures, giving her a solid educational background for her position. Despite her good educational credentials and prior office experience, Peyton is experiencing performance problems. She explains her problems in these words:

I can't help it. I want to get all my work done, especially those reports. But it takes me so long to get something done. It's so difficult to stay focused. I look at my smart phone and I see that there are a bunch of Facebook notifications waiting for me. And my friends keep sending me text messages during the day. I don't want to be rude and not text back right away.

Also, I need a little break from concentrating so hard on my work. So I go get a coffee from the break room, or I take a quick peek at ESPN on my phone, or maybe see what specials Amazon or Overstock is running.

I also run into problems in my life off the job. Last year I didn't renew my driver's license on time, and also I got pulled over because the inspection sticker on my SUV had expired. This morning my mother told me that she was ticked off at me because I forgot her birthday.

Exasperated with Peyton's lack of focus on the job, her boss Max said to Peyton, "If you want to succeed as a hospital administrator, and even hold your job, you have to make some big changes. Right now I see you as a wheelbarrow personality—useless unless loaded, pointed, and pushed by somebody else."

Learning Objectives ▸

After studying the information and doing the exercises in this chapter, you should be able to:

1. Explain how needs and motives influence motivation.
2. Identify several needs and motives that could propel you into action.
3. Pinpoint how the hierarchy of needs could explain your behavior.
4. Explain why and how goals contribute to self-motivation.
5. Describe how to set effective goals and the problems sometimes created by goals.
6. Describe several specific techniques of self-motivation.
7. Apply the self-discipline model to achieving your goals.

Whether or not you are interested in hospital administration as a career, the story about Peyton illustrates that without being self-disciplined enough to focus on the job, good performance is unattainable. Unless you direct your energies toward specific goals, such as improving your productivity or meeting a new friend, and stay focused you will accomplish very little. Knowledge of motivation, goal setting, and self-discipline as applied to yourself, therefore, can pay substantial dividends in improving the quality of your life. Knowledge about motivation and goal setting is also important when attempting to influence others to get things accomplished. Motivating others, for example, is a major requirement of the manager's job.

Being well motivated is also important simply to meet the demands of employers. Most organizations insist on high productivity from workers at all levels. Assuming that you have the necessary skills, training, and equipment, being well motivated will enable you to achieve high productivity.

The general purpose of this chapter is to present information that can help you sustain a high level of motivation, centering on the importance of needs and goals. Chapter 12 contains information that you will find useful for motivating other people. Here is an example that might apply to you personally.

> Assume that similar to many readers of this book, you are ambitious. You have many interesting career goals. You want to finish your formal education, you want to obtain professional certification in your field, you want to attain a high level of responsibility in your career, and you want to be among the top 10 percent of income earners. Your plate is also filled with personal goals: You want to improve substantially in your favorite sport, become fluent in your second language, network all your electronic devices together, and double your network of friends.

Despite all your exciting goals, you are not making much progress in attaining them. Could the problem be that your level of self-discipline is not quite high enough to propel you toward accomplishing these goals one by one? Not having sufficient self-discipline is the major reason most people fall short of reaching their goals. Later in the chapter, we describe a well-developed system for developing enough self-discipline for getting things done that are important to you.

Learning Objective 1

How Needs and Motives Influence Motivation

Need
an internal striving or urge to do something, such as a need to drink when thirsty

According to a widely accepted explanation of human behavior, people have needs and motives that propel them toward achieving certain goals. Needs and motives are closely related. A **need** is an internal striving or urge to do something, such as a need to drink when thirsty. It can be regarded as a biological or psychological requirement. Because the person is deprived in some way (such as not having enough fluid in the body), the person is motivated to take action toward a goal. In this case the goal might be simply getting something to drink.

A discussion of needs often triggers a discussion of the difference between *needs* and *wants.* A need is essentially a craving or urge that must be satisfied to maintain your equilibrium. In contrast, a want refers to more of a luxury—something you would like to have but is not necessary to keep your system balanced. A need is a more technical concept than is a want. Here is an example of the difference between a need and a want:

> Visualize yourself jogging in 90-degree weather. Suddenly your need for water surfaces, so any old fountain water will satisfy your physiological craving. But at the same time, you want a prestige brand of flavored bottled water to drink. You don't need the bottled water, you want it.

Motive
an inner drive that moves a person to do something

A **motive** is an inner drive that moves you to do something. The motive is usually based on a need or desire and results in the intention to attain an appropriate goal. Because needs and motives are so closely related, the two terms are often used interchangeably. For example, "recognition need" and "recognition motive" refer to the same thing.

THE NEED THEORY OF MOTIVATION

The central idea behind need theory is that unsatisfied needs motivate us until they become satisfied. When people are dissatisfied or anxious about their present status or performance, they will try to reduce this anxiety. This need cycle is shown in Figure 3-1.

FIGURE 3-1
THE NEED CYCLE

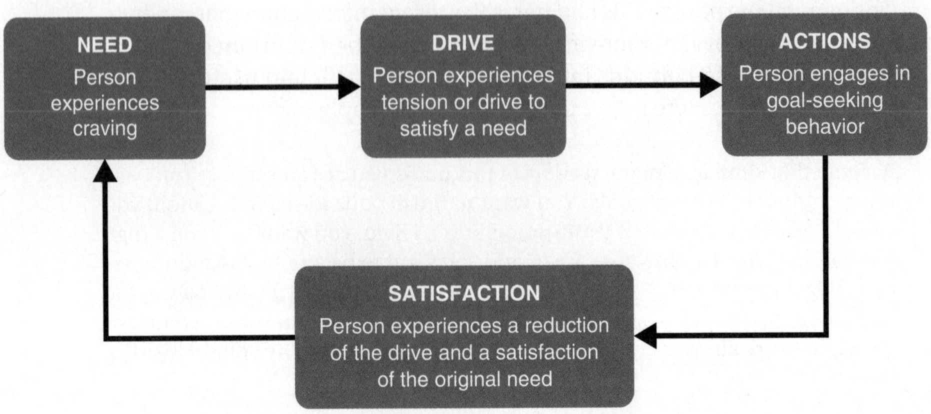

Assume that you have a strong need or motive to achieve recognition. As a result, you experience tension that drives you to find some way of being recognized on the job. The action you take is to apply for a position as the team leader of your group: Being appointed as team leader would provide ample recognition, particularly if the team performs well. You are appointed to the position, and for now your need for recognition is at least partially satisfied as you receive compliments from your coworkers and friends. Once you receive this partial satisfaction, two things typically happen. Either you will soon require a stronger dose of recognition, or you will begin to concentrate on another need or motive, such as achievement. In either case, the need cycle will repeat itself. You might seek another form of recognition or satisfaction of your need for power. For example, you might apply for a position as department manager or open your own business. Ideally, in this former situation, your boss would give you more responsibility. This could lead to more satisfaction of your recognition need and to some satisfaction of your need for achievement. (The needs mentioned so far, and others, are defined next.)

The need theory suggests that self-interest plays a key role in motivation.[1] People ask, "What's in it for me?" (or "WIIFM," pronounced *wiff'em*), before engaging in any form of behavior. In one way or another, people act to serve their self-interest. Even when people act in a way that helps others, they are doing so because helping others helps them. For example, you may give money to poor people because this act of kindness makes you feel wanted and powerful.

IMPORTANT NEEDS AND MOTIVES PEOPLE ATTEMPT TO SATISFY

Work and personal life offer the opportunity to satisfy dozens of needs and motives. In this and the following section, important needs that propel people into action are described. As you read about these needs and motives, relate them to yourself. For example, ask yourself, "Am I a power-seeking person?"

Achievement

The **need for achievement** is the desire to accomplish something difficult for its own sake. People with a strong need for achievement frequently think of how to do a job better. Responsibility seeking is another characteristic of people with a high need for achievement. They are also concerned with how to progress in their careers. Workers with a high need for achievement are interested in monetary rewards primarily as feedback about how well they are achieving. They also set realistic yet moderately difficult goals, take calculated risks, and desire feedback on performance. (A moderately difficult goal challenges a person but is not so difficult as to most likely lead to failure and frustration.) In general, those who enjoy building businesses, activities, and programs from scratch have a strong need for achievement. Figure 3-2 outlines the preferences of workers with strong achievement needs.

Need for achievement
the desire to accomplish something difficult for its own sake

Power

People with a high power need feel compelled to control resources, such as other people and money. Successful executives typically have a high power motive and exhibit

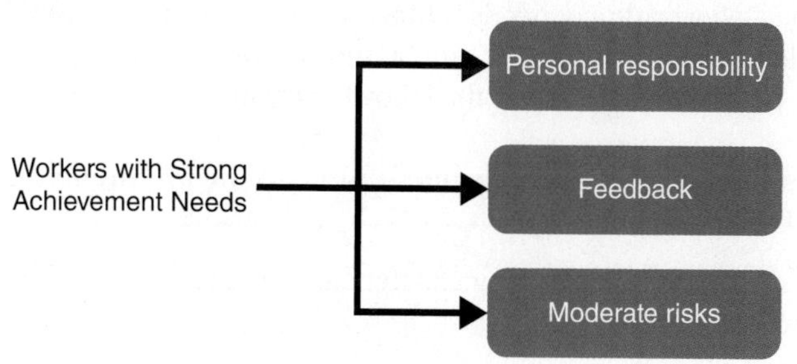

FIGURE 3-2
PREFERENCES OF WORKERS WITH STRONG ACHIEVEMENT NEEDS

three dominant characteristics: (1) They act with vigor and determination to exert their power, (2) they invest much time in thinking about ways to alter the behavior and thinking of others, and (3) they care about their personal standing with those around them.[2] The power need can be satisfied through occupying a high-level position or by becoming a highly influential person. Or you can name skyscrapers, hotels, and golf courses after yourself, following the lead of Donald Trump.

Affiliation

People with a strong affiliation need seek out close relationships with others and tend to be loyal as friends or employees. The affiliation motive is met directly through belonging to the "office gang," a term of endearment implying that your coworkers are an important part of your life. Many people prefer working in groups to individual effort because of the opportunity the former provides for socializing with others.

Recognition

People with a strong need for recognition want to be acknowledged for their contribution and efforts. The need for recognition is so pervasive that many companies have formal recognition programs in which outstanding or long-time employees receive gifts, plaques, and jewelry inscribed with the company logo. The recognition motive can be satisfied through means such as winning contests, receiving awards, and seeing your name online or in print. A major reason the need for recognition is such a useful motivator is that most people think they are underappreciated (and overworked).

Order

People with a strong need for order want to achieve arrangement, balance, neatness, and precision. The order motive can be quickly satisfied by cleaning and organizing your work or living space. Occupations offering the opportunity to satisfy the order motive almost every day include accountant, computer programmer, and paralegal.

Risk Taking and Thrill Seeking

Some people crave constant excitement on the job and are willing to risk their lives to achieve thrills. The need to take risks and pursue thrills has grown in importance in the high-technology era. Many people work for employers, start businesses, and purchase stocks with uncertain futures. Both the search of giant payoffs and daily thrills motivate these individuals.[3] A strong craving for thrills may have some positive consequences for the organization, including willingness to perform such dangerous feats as setting explosives, capping an oil well, controlling a radiation leak, and introducing a product in a highly competitive environment. However, extreme risk takers and thrill seekers can create such problems as being involved in a disproportionate number of vehicular accidents and making imprudent investments. Take Human Relations Self-Assessment Quiz 3-1 to measure your tendency toward risk taking.

MASLOW'S HIERARCHY OF NEEDS

Maslow's hierarchy of needs the best-known categorization of needs; according to psychologist Abraham H. Maslow, people strive to satisfy the following groups of needs in step-by-step order: physiological needs, safety needs, social needs, esteem needs, and self-actualizing needs

The best-known categorization of needs is **Maslow's hierarchy of needs**. At the same time, it is the most widely used explanation of human motivation. According to psychologist Abraham H. Maslow, people strive to satisfy the following groups of needs in step-by-step order:

1. *Physiological needs* refer to bodily needs, such as the requirements for food, water, shelter, and sleep.
2. *Safety needs* refer to actual physical safety and to a feeling of being safe from both physical and emotional injury.

Human Relations Self-Assessment Quiz 3-1

The Risk-Taking Scale

Answer true or false to the following questions to obtain an approximate idea of your tendency to take risks or your desire to do so.

		True	False
1.	I open e-mail attachments from completely unknown sources.	❑	❑
2.	I would rather be a stockbroker than an accountant.	❑	❑
3.	I think that amusement park roller coasters should be abolished.	❑	❑
4.	I enjoy doing creative work.	❑	❑
5.	I enjoy (or did enjoy) the excitement of looking for new dates.	❑	❑
6.	I don't like trying foods from other cultures.	❑	❑
7.	I would choose bonds over growth stocks.	❑	❑
8.	Friends would say that I do not like to take risks.	❑	❑
9.	I like to challenge people in positions of power.	❑	❑
10.	I don't always wear seat belts while driving.	❑	❑
11.	I sometimes talk on my cell phone or send text messages while driving at highway speeds.	❑	❑
12.	I would love to be an entrepreneur (or I love being one).	❑	❑
13.	I purposely avoid traveling overseas to any country that is known to have civil unrest, including riots.	❑	❑
14.	Most days are boring for me.	❑	❑
15.	I would like helping out in a crisis such as a product recall.	❑	❑
16.	On the highway, I usually drive at least 10 miles per hour beyond the speed limit.	❑	❑
17.	I would like to go cave exploring (or already have done so).	❑	❑
18.	I like to have a daily dose of stimulation.	❑	❑
19.	I would be willing to have at least one-third of my compensation based on a bonus for good performance.	❑	❑
20.	I would be willing to visit a maximum-security prison on a job assignment.	❑	❑

Scoring and Interpretation:

1. True	**5.** True	**9.** True	**13.** False	**17.** True
2. True	**6.** False	**10.** True	**14.** False	**18.** True
3. False	**7.** False	**11.** True	**15.** True	**19.** True
4. True	**8.** False	**12.** True	**16.** True	**20.** True

Give yourself one point each time your answer agrees with the key.

16–20 You are probably a high risk taker.
10–15 You are a moderate risk taker.
5–9 You are cautious.
0–4 You are a very low risk taker.

Questions: **1.** How does your self-evaluation of your risk-taking tendencies compare with your score on this quiz?
2. Do you see any needs for improvement in terms of becoming more (or less) of a risk taker?

Source: The idea of a test about risk-taking comfort, as well as several of the statements on the quiz, come from psychologist Frank Farley.

3. *Social needs* are essentially love, affection, or belonging needs. Unlike the two previous levels of needs, they center on a person's interaction with other people.
4. *Esteem needs* represent an individual's demand to be seen as a person of worth by others—and to him- or herself.
5. *Self-actualizing needs* are the highest level of needs, including the needs for self-fulfillment and personal development.

Maslow recognized that the five classes of needs in the hierarchy are only a partial description of human needs. Three other classes of needs are also important, *cognitive need, aesthetic needs,* and *transcendence needs* (or *B-values*).

- *Aesthetic needs* relate to the needs for symmetry, order, and beauty. This class of needs fits below the self-actualization needs on the hierarchy.
- *Cognitive needs* relate to the needs to know, understand, and explore. This class of needs fits above the esteem needs—and just below the aesthetic needs—on the hierarchy.
- *Transcendence needs* or *B-values* refer to needs to contribute to human welfare and to find higher meanings in life. This class of needs is an extension of self-actualization needs and fits above those needs on the hierarchy.[4]

A diagram of the needs hierarchy is presented in Figure 3-3. Notice the distinction between higher-level and lower-level needs. With few exceptions, higher-level needs are more difficult to satisfy. A person's needs for affiliation might be satisfied by being a member of a friendly work group. Yet, to satisfy self-actualization need, such as self-fulfillment, a person might have to develop an outstanding reputation in his or her company.

The needs hierarchy implies that most people think of finding a job as a way of obtaining the necessities of life. Once these are obtained, a person may think of achieving friendship, self-esteem, and self-fulfillment on the job. When a person is generally satisfied at one level, he or she looks for satisfaction at a higher level. As Maslow described it, a person is a "perpetually wanting animal." Very few people are totally satisfied with their lot in life, even the rich and famous.

FIGURE 3-3
MASLOW'S HIERARCHY OF NEEDS

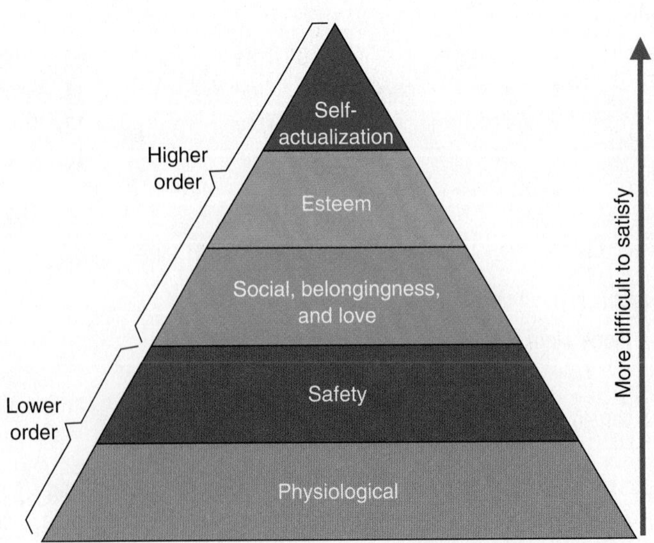

Note: Modern additions to the need hierarchy are (1) cognitive needs, (2) aesthetic needs, and (3) transcendent needs. The cognitive and aesthetic needs fit above the esteem needs, and the transcendent needs would fit above the self-actualization needs.

The extent of need satisfaction is influenced by a person's job. Some construction jobs, for example, involve dangerous work in severe climates, thus frustrating both physiological and safety needs. Ordinarily there is much more opportunity for approaching self-actualization when a person occupies a prominent position, such as a top executive or famous performer. However, a person with low potential could approach self-actualization by occupying a lesser position. In the current era, workers at all levels are threatened with the frustration of security needs because so many companies reduce the number of employees to save money.

How do Maslow's needs and the other needs described in this chapter relate to self-motivation? First you have to ask yourself, "Which needs do I really want to satisfy?" After answering the question honestly, concentrate your efforts on an activity that will most likely satisfy that need. For instance, if you are hungry for power, strive to become a high-level manager or a business owner. If you crave self-esteem, focus your efforts on work and social activities that are well regarded by others. The point is that you will put forth substantial effort if you think the goal you attain will satisfy an important need.

To learn more about how the needs hierarchy fits your need makeup, take Human Relations Self-Assessment Quiz 3-2. The class activity presented toward the end of the chapter will also enlarge your understanding of the need hierarchy.

ENGAGEMENT AS PART OF SELF-MOTIVATION

Another way of looking at self-motivation is that if you are strongly motivated you are engaged in your work, or committed to the job and company. Employees engaged in their work are more willing to help supervisors and coworkers and to voluntarily promote the company outside of work. An engaged employee also feels connected to the organization. An analysis of many studies indicates that **work engagement** refers to high levels of personal investment in the work tasks performed in a job.[5] As a result the self is injected into the job. The engaged worker would therefore feel personally responsible for good and poor job performance, and would take pride in accomplishment. An inventor would be likely to experience engagement, but so might a bookkeeper.

Work engagement
high levels of personal investment in the work tasks performed in a job

Several studies have found that most American workers are not fully engaged in their work. They do what is expected of them but do not contribute the extra mental and physical effort to be outstanding. A survey of over 100,000 workers and managers by LeadershipIQ, found that 69 percent of North American workers said they were either disengaged or unengaged.[6]A Gallup study showed that employee engagement levels have a big impact on the organization. Business units in the top quartile on engagement had 18 percent higher productivity, 16 percent higher profitability, and 49 percent fewer safety accidents versus those in the bottom quartile on engagement.[7]

Employee engagement can have life and death consequences. LifeGift, a Houston nonprofit, receives human organs and tissue from recently deceased donors and matches them to patients on transplant waiting lists across the United States. Samuel Holtzman III, President and CEO says, "So in our organization, engagement means having employees who never give upon on finding a donor. Not ever." When a survey indicated that employee engagement at LifeGift was declining, managers spent more time ensuring that employees received the training, emotional support, and other resources they needed to cope with the heavy demands of their job.[8]

Among the many initiatives companies take to enhance engagement are (a) opportunities for career advancement, (b) celebration of job successes, (c) encouraging workers to bring forth problems to managers, and (d) giving employees breathing room in how they should complete their tasks.

The link between employee engagement and self-motivation is that self-motivated workers are more likely to be engaged, or committed to their companies. "Breathing room"

Human Relations Self-Assessment Quiz 3-2

My Standing on the Need Hierarchy

Respond to each of the following statements in terms of its importance to you, as follows: (1) not important, (2) a little bit important, (3) average importance, (4) important, and (5) very important.

Statement Number	Statement	Importance (1 to 5)
1.	Having a good reputation	______
2.	Loving another person	______
3.	Having a high evaluation of myself	______
4.	Being somebody special and important	______
5.	Having coworkers who are not physically abusive	______
6.	Being respected by others	______
7.	Feeling emotionally close to another person	______
8.	Becoming much more than I am now	______
9.	Avoiding big surprises in my work routine	______
10.	Feeling useful and necessary in the world	______
11.	Being a member of a group I care about	______
12.	Feeling well rested	______
13.	Feeling that I have the right balance of nutrients and chemicals in my body	______
14.	Having a workplace that is relatively free of harmful germs	______
15.	Being confident that I will achieve my full potential	______
16.	Having an affectionate relationship with another person	______
17.	Feeling completely self-fulfilled	______
18.	Feeling comfortable rather than too hot or too cold	______
19.	Not having to commute during hazardous road conditions	______
20.	Eating food that has a pleasant taste	______
21.	Being loved by another person	______
22.	Becoming who I am capable of becoming	______
23.	Having self-respect	______
24.	Having enough food to eat	______
25.	Avoiding loud, irritating noises	______

Source: The ideas for the statements in the quiz stem from Abraham H. Maslow, "A Theory of Human Motivation," *Psychological Review*, July 1943, pp. 370–396.

Scoring and Interpretation:

The scoring key follows the five categories in the Maslow needs hierarchy. Enter your rating (1–5) for each statement, and compute your total for each of the five categories of needs.

Ranking

Physiological

12______ 13______ 18______ 20______ 24______ Physiological total______ ______

Safety

5______ 9______ 14______ 19______ 25______ Safety total______ ______

Love

2_______ 7_______ 11_______ 16_______ 21_______ Love total_______ _______

Esteem

1_______ 3_______ 6_______ 10_______ 23_______ Esteem total_______ _______

Self-actualization

4_______ 8_______ 15_______ 17_______ 22_______ Self-actualization total_______ _______

The total for each of the five needs will be somewhere between 1 and 25. The highest score receives a rank of 1, and the lowest score receives a rank of 5. A tentative interpretation here is that your most important need category is the one with the highest rank, whereas the least important need category receives the lowest rank. A high-importance ranking might suggest that you are actively attempting to satisfy the need category in question. A low-importance ranking would suggest that you are not currently attempting to satisfy that need category because that category is already satisfied. It is also possible that you just don't care about the need category, such as not worrying about becoming self-actualized.

Questions:

1. What importance ranking to these needs categories might a person give who is unemployed and currently living in his or her SUV or minivan? Why?
2. Visualize one of your favorite celebrities. What importance rankings might one of your favorite celebrities give to these needs categories? Why?

is particularly helpful because people who have control over the method of solving a problem tend to feel that they are acting independently. An example would be a manager telling a worker, "See if you can find a way to decrease shipping costs by 5 percent. I won't give you any hints." A theory relating to self-motivation and engagement is presented next.

SELF-DETERMINATION AND ENGAGEMENT

Why and how employees become engaged in their work can be explained to some extent by **self-determination theory**. The theory contends that we are most deeply engaged, and that we do our most creative work, when we feel that we are acting according to our own will and pursing goals we find meaningful. Self-determination theory closely relates to self-motivation because it explains that motivation develops internally, grounded in three basic human needs. The *competency* needs refers to wanting to develop our skills; the *autonomy* need refers to acing on our own accord; and *relatedness* refers to connecting with others in our environment.

Self-determination theory the motivation theory contending that we are most deeply engaged, and do our most creative work, when we feel that we are acting according to our own will and pursuing goals we find meaningful

An important focus of self-determination theory is that doing exciting work that meets our needs is more important than external rewards in staying motivated. Although external rewards, such as money and prizes, can influence motivation, the truly engaged worker focuses mostly on working somewhat independently on exciting tasks and connecting with coworkers.[9] (No wonder social media are so popular!)

Human Relations Self-Assessment Quiz 3-3 will help you think through job factors that are likely to engage you in your work.

As you review the five factors most likely to bring about your commitment, what pattern do you notice? For example, would the work itself be the most important for you? Or, are you more likely to feel engaged with respect to factors not directly related to the job, such as free lunches?

The accompanying Human Relations in Practice illustrates what a company might do to foster engagement.

Human Relations Self-Assessment Quiz 3-3

My Engagement Drivers

A checklist follows of ten factors that have been observed to get many professional-level workers engaged in (or committed to) their employer. Check off the five factors that would be most likely to bring about your engagement.

1. An opportunity to learn new skills almost every month. ❑
2. Receiving frequent coaching from my manager. ❑
3. Free lunches served in the company cafeteria. ❑
4. Well above-average pay and benefits. ❑
5. The opportunity to make use of the latest high-tech gadgets related to my work. ❑
6. Company leaders who are inspiring and warm. ❑
7. A manager who really listened to my concerns and problems. ❑
8. A beautiful physical facility including and onsite gym and showers. ❑
9. An opportunity to be promoted if I were an outstanding performer. ❑
10. Interesting, friendly, well-motivated, and intelligent coworkers. ❑
11. Work that challenged me almost every day. ❑
12. Good professional and social networking opportunities at the company. ❑

Human Relations in Practice

High-Tech Cobham Sensor Systems Strives for Employee Engagement

Cobham Sensor Systems designs and manufactures a variety of active and passive microwave components, assemblies and subsystems for the aerospace and defense industries, including homeland security. In recent years, the company has achieved outstanding financial success. Company leadership attributes much of the success to developing an engaged workforce.

President Dave Schmitz says that the company put in motion a series of initiatives designed to engage all members of the workforce. A positive workplace creates opportunities for all employees to participate in a meaningful way. "By helping employees reach their potential both personally and professionally, they execute strategies that support our customer and our ultimate success."

In order to get employees engaged, company management placed a focus on professional growth and special projects as a means to get all employees involved in producing exceptional results. Employees are offered ample opportunity to advance and collaborate with some of the brightest people in leading-edge defense technology. Another Cobham approach to engaging employees is to offer demanding, exciting work and at the same time guiding and mentoring the workforce. The company believes that enriching the work experience captures employee commitment.

Before the company focused on employee engagement, most of the decisions were made by the managers. Getting employees to participate more in making decisions about technology and productivity helped them identify more with their jobs. At one point, each employee developed a *flight plan*—a description of a skill, job, or achievement that he or she would master or improve upon in the upcoming year. The flight plan represented a new height of achievement, such as taking a leadership role on a committee or analyzing some complex data.

After a goal in the flight plan had been achieved, employees were recognized in a ceremony attended by their supervisor and the area vice president. Furthermore, they received wings of achievement and their photos and flight plans were placed on a Wall of Fame in the cafeteria.

Question: Why would performing exciting work and being coached bring about commitment?

Source: The original story above is created from facts presented in the following: John F. Schierer, "When Workers Support the 'Flight Plan'," *HR Magazine*, July 2011, pp. 32–34; "Working at Cobham,"www.cobhamcareers.com, accessed January 6, 2012; "Cobham Takes Top Award in Large Company Category at Workplace Excellence Awards for the Second Time," www.redorbit.com/news/business, accessed January 13, 2012, pp. 1–2; "Workplace Excellence Awards 2011: What Workplace Excellence Awards Means to Winners,"www.sdshrm,org/, January 5, 2011, pp. 1–2.

How Goals Contribute to Motivation

◀ Learning Objective 2 ◀

At some point in their lives, almost all successful people have established goals, attesting to the importance of goals. A **goal** is an event, circumstance, object, or condition a person strives to attain. A goal thus reflects your desire or intention to regulate your actions. Here we look at six topics to help you understand the nature of goals: (1) the advantages of goals, (2) different goal orientations, (3) goal setting on the job, (4) personal goal setting, (5) guidelines for goal setting, and (6) potential disadvantages of goals.

Goal
an event, circumstance, object, or condition a person strives to attain

ADVANTAGES OF GOALS

Goals and goal setting have become embedded into our society both on and off the job. Sales quotas and New Year's resolutions are examples of goal setting. Five of the potential advantages of goals are outlined in Figure 3-4.

Setting specific, reasonably difficult goals improves performance. One of many possible examples involves the American Pulpwood Association, which wanted to increase the productivity (employee cords per hour) of independent loggers in the southern United States. Based on goal-setting theory, Pulpwood crew supervisors assigned a specific high goal for the loggers. They also handed out tally meters to enable the workers to keep count of the number of trees they cut down. Productivity soared in comparison

1. Reasonably difficult goals improve performance.
2. Goals can instill purpose, challenge, and meaning into ordinary tasks.
3. Goals focus our efforts in a specific direction.
4. Goals increase our chances for success because they serve as a standard for measuring success.
5. Goals serve as self-motivators and energizers.

FIGURE 3-4
ADVANTAGES OF GOALS

to those crews who were simply urged to do their best. According to Gary Latham, professor of organizational behavior at the Rotman School of Management, goal setting instilled purpose, challenge, and meaning into what was previously seen as a boring, tiresome task.[10]

Another advantage of goals is that when we guide our lives with goals, we tend to focus our efforts in a consistent direction. Your conscious goals affect what you achieve. Without goals, our efforts may become scattered in many directions. We may keep trying, but we will go nowhere unless we happen to receive more than our share of luck.

Goal setting increases our chances for success, particularly because success can be defined as the achievement of a goal. The goals you set for accomplishing a task can serve as a standard to indicate when you have done a satisfactory job. A sales representative might set a goal of selling $400,000 worth of merchandise for the year. By November, she might close a deal that places her total sales at $410,000. With a sigh of relief she can then say, "I've done well this year."

Goals serve as self-motivators and energizers. People who set goals tend to be motivated because they are confident that their energy is being invested in something worthwhile. Aside from helping you become more motivated and productive, setting goals can help you achieve personal satisfaction. Most people derive a sense of satisfaction from attaining a goal that is meaningful to them. Breakthrough goals are particularly good at generating excitement and inspiration because they stretch the imagination of people. Workers at Apple Inc. and Google Inc. have for years been pursuing the goal of "changing the world."

THE LEARNING AND PERFORMING ORIENTATIONS TOWARD GOALS

Another useful perspective on understanding how goals influence motivation is that goals can be aimed at either learning or hoping to perform well.[11] A learning-goal orientation means that an individual is focused on acquiring new skills and mastering new situations. For example, you might establish the goal of learning how to develop skill in using social media to market a product. You say to yourself, "My goal is to learn how to use social media so I know even more about how to apply communication technology."

A performing-goal orientation is different. It is aimed at wanting to demonstrate and validate the adequacy of your competence by seeking favorable judgments about your competence. At the same time, the person wants to avoid seeking negative judgments. For example, your goal might be to make Facebook posts that would highly impress whoever watched them. Your focus is on looking good and avoiding negative evaluations of your postings.

Desire for Feedback

A person's goal orientation usually affects his or her desire for feedback. People with a learning-goal orientation are more likely to seek feedback on how well they are performing. In contrast, people with a performing-goal orientation are less likely to seek feedback. If you focus too much on setting performance goals, you might have a tendency to overlook the value of feedback. Yet, the feedback could help you improve your performance in the long run.

Impact on Work Performance

Goal orientation is also important because it can affect work performance. Attempting to master skills often leads to better results than does attempting to impress others. A study of the effects of the two different goal orientations was conducted with 167 salespeople working for a medical supplies distributor. The salespeople were paid mostly on the commission of the gross profits they generated. The researchers found that a learning-goal orientation was associated with higher sales performance. In contrast, a performing-goal orientation was unrelated to sales performance. An important implication of the study is that even if you are an experienced worker, a focus on skill development is likely to lead to higher performance.[12]

Better Relationships with Supervisors

Another positive consequence of a mastery (or learning-goal) orientation is that it often prompts workers to develop better relationships with their supervisors. Workers with a mastery orientation are likely to have stronger job performance and job satisfaction than those workers with a performance orientation. The positive outcomes of stronger job performance and satisfaction appear to take place because the workers develop better relationships with their supervisors.[13]

A good reason exists as to why a learning-goal (or mastery) orientation is so important in today's business world. The purpose of a learning goal is to stimulate a person's imagination, to engage in discovery, and to think imaginatively. A performance goal focuses more on exerting effort to attain an objective using the knowledge one already possesses. When an effective strategy requires innovation that has yet to emerge—as is often the case—specific, high-learning goals should be set.[14] An example of a learning goal of high importance would be figuring out how to dispose of debris after a hurricane.

GOAL SETTING ON THE JOB

Virtually all organizations have come to accept the value of goal setting in producing the results they want to achieve. Goal-setting programs designed to boost performance or personal development are in frequent use. The personal aspects of goal setting are described in the following section. In most goal-setting programs, executives at the top of the organization are supposed to plan for the future by setting goals such as "Improve profits 10 percent this year." Employees at the bottom of the organization are supposed to go along with such broad goals by setting more specific goals. An example is "I will decrease damaged merchandise by 10 percent this year. I will accomplish this by making sure that our shelving is adequate for our needs."

You participate in the goal-setting process by designing goals to fit into the overall mission of the firm. A bank teller might set a personal goal of this nature: "During rush periods, and when I feel fatigued, I will double count all the money that I handle." In some goal-setting programs, employees are requested to set goals that will lead to their personal improvement. An auditor for the state government set this goal for herself: "Within the next 12 months, I will enroll in and complete a supervisory training course in a local college." This woman aspired toward becoming a supervisor.

The points made in the two previous paragraphs merit repetition because of their importance. In a well-designed organization, the goals the individual sets contribute to the company organizational goals. The construction supervisor who establishes a goal to regularly consult a checklist to make sure that safety procedures are being followed is contributing to the company goal of reducing accidents on the construction site.

A sample set of work goals is shown in Figure 3-5. The service and repair department supervisor who set these objectives took into account the requirements of his boss and the automobile dealership. Even if you set goals by yourself, they must still take into account the needs of your employer.

PERSONAL GOAL SETTING

If you want to lead a rewarding personal life, your chances of doing so increase if you make plans. Personal goals heavily influence the formulation of career goals as well. For this reason, it is worthwhile to set personal goals in conjunction with career goals. Ideally,

FIGURE 3-5

FORM USED IN AUTOMOBILE DEALERSHIP FOR STATEMENT OF GOALS

JOB TITLE AND BRIEF JOB DESCRIPTION

Manager, Service Department:
Responsible for supervision of service department of automobile dealership. Responsible for staffing service department with appropriate personnel and for quality of service to customers. Work closely with owner of dealership to discuss unusual customer problems. Handle customer complaints about mechanical problems of cars purchased at dealership.

Objectives for Scott Gilley

1. By December 31 of this year, decrease by 10 percent customer demands for rework.
2. Hire two general mechanics within 45 days.
3. Hire two body specialists within 45 days.
4. Decrease by 30 percent the number of repairs returned by customers for rework.
5. Reduce by 10 percent the discrepancy between estimates and actual bills to customers.
6. Schedule at least 20 percent of our service appointments through our Web site by January 15 of next year.

they should be integrated to help achieve a balance between the demands of work and personal life. For example, if your preferred lifestyle would be to live in a rural area, a career in manufacturing or food processing would be more sensible than a career in advertising. This is true because manufacturing and food processing within North America has moved mostly to rural areas, whereas advertising remains mostly in large cities.

Types of Personal Goals

Personal goals can be subdivided into those relating to social and family life, hobbies and interests, physical and mental health, career, and finances. An example of each type follows:

Social and family life. "By age 30 I would like to have a spouse and two children."

Hobbies and interests. "Become a black belt in karate by age 28."

Physical and mental health. "Be able to run four miles without stopping or panting for breath by April 15 of next year."

Career. "Become office manager by age 28."

Finances. "Within the next four years be earning $70,000 per year, adjusted for inflation."

Other categories of personal goals are possible, yet the list presented represents convenient categories for most people.

ACTION PLANS TO SUPPORT GOALS

Action plan
describes how you are going to reach your goal

Ideally, reading this chapter and doing the exercises in it will start you on a lifelong process of using goals to help you plan your life. But before you can capitalize on the benefits of goal setting, you need a method for translating goals into action. An **action plan** describes how you are going to reach your goal. The major reason you need an action plan for most goals is that without a method for achieving what you want, the goal is likely to slip by. If your goal were to build your own log cabin, part of your action plan would be to learn how to operate a buzz saw, to read a handbook on log cabin building,

1. State each goal as a positive statement.
2. Formulate specific goals.
3. Formulate concise goals.
4. Set realistic as well as stretch goals.
5. Set goals for different time periods.
6. Strive for synergy among your goals.

FIGURE 3-6
GUIDELINES FOR GOAL SETTING

to learn how to operate a tractor, and so forth. Some goals are so difficult to reach that your action plan might encompass hundreds of separate activities. You would then have to develop separate action plans for each step of the way.

Some immediate goals do not really require an action plan. A mere statement of the goal may point to an obvious action plan. If your goal were to start painting your room, it would not be necessary to draw up a formal action plan such as, "Go to hardware store; purchase paint, brush, and rollers; borrow ladder and drop cloth from Ken; put furniture in center of room" and so on.

GUIDELINES FOR GOAL SETTING

Goal setting is an art in the sense that some people do a better job of goal setting than others. Following are suggestions on setting effective goals—those that lead to achieving what you hoped to achieve, as outlined in Figure 3-6.

Express Each Goal as a Positive Statement

Expressing your goals in positive statements is likely to be more energizing than focusing on the negative.[15] An example of a positive statement would be, "During the next year when I am attending networking events, I will create a positive, professional impression on everybody I meet." The negative counterpart would be, "During the next year, I will avoid making a fool of myself when I am attending networking events." Despite this suggestion, there are times when a negative goal is useful, such as in reducing errors.

Formulate Specific Goals

A goal such as "attain success" is too vague to serve as a guide to daily action. A more useful goal would be to state specifically what you mean by "success" and when you expect to achieve it. For example, "I want to be the manager of customer service at a telecommunications company by January 1, 2018, and receive above-average performance reviews."

Formulate Concise Goals

A useful goal can usually be expressed in a short, punchy statement—for example, "Decrease input errors in bank statements so that customer complaints are decreased by 25 percent by September 30 of this year." People new to goal setting typically commit the error of formulating lengthy, rambling goal statements. These lengthy goals involve so many different activities that they fail to serve as specific guides to action.

Set Realistic as Well as Stretch Goals

A realistic goal is one that represents the right amount of challenge for the person pursuing the goal. On the one hand, easy goals are not very motivational—they may not spring you into action. On the other hand, goals that are too far beyond your capabilities may lead to frustration and despair because there is a good chance you will fail to reach them. The extent to which a goal is realistic depends on a person's capabilities. An easy goal for an experienced person might be a realistic goal for a beginner. Self-efficacy is also a factor in deciding whether a goal is realistic. The higher your self-efficacy, the more likely you are to think that a particular goal is realistic. A person with high self-efficacy for learning Chinese might say, "I think that learning two new Chinese words a day is realistic."

Several goals that stretch your capability might be included in your list of goals. An extreme stretch goal might be for a store manager trainee to become the vice president of merchandising for Target Corp., within four years. Another type of stretch goal is striving for a noble cause. A logging supervisor may not get excited about having the crew load a certain number of felled trees on a flatbed truck, but she might get excited about the trees being used to build homes, schools, and hospitals.

Set Goals for Different Time Periods

Goals are best set for different time periods, such as daily, short range, medium range, and long range. Daily goals are essentially a to-do list. Short-range goals cover the period from approximately one week to one year into the future. Finding a new job, for example, is typically a short-range goal. Medium-range goals relate to events that will take place within approximately two to five years. They concern such things as the type of education or training you plan to undertake and the next step in your career.

Long-range goals refer to events taking place five years into the future and beyond. As such, they relate to the overall lifestyle you wish to achieve, including the type of work and family situation you hope to have. Although every person should have a general idea of a desirable lifestyle, long-range goals should be flexible. You might, for example, plan to stay single until age 40. But while on vacation next summer, you might just happen to meet the right partner for you.

Short-range goals make an important contribution to attaining goals of longer duration. If a one-year work goal is to reduce mailing and shipping costs by 12 percent for the year, a good way to motivate workers is to look for a 1 percent saving per month. Progress toward a larger goal is self-rewarding.

Strive for Synergy among Your Goals

A powerful approach to goal setting is to make your goals synergistic, or fit together in a way that makes them work together. Executive coach Joelle K. Jay explains that synergy takes place when one idea advances another.[16] Goals that are not synergistic run the risk of becoming a group of unrelated chores. Smaller, short-term goals fitting a long-range purpose (vision) brings about synergy. Assume that business student Tony has established the major goal of "Help hundreds of people have financially secure retirements." Two synergistic goals for Tony would be, "Get an A in my personal finance course," and "Start preparing for Chartered Financial Analyst certification two years after graduation." (Do you think we are putting too much pressure on Tony?)

PROBLEMS SOMETIMES CREATED BY GOALS

Despite the many advantages of goals, they can create problems.

1. **Inflexibility.** A major problem is that *goals can create inflexibility*. People can become so focused on reaching particular goals that they fail to react to emergencies, such as neglecting a much-needed machine repair to achieve quota. Goals can also make a person inflexible with respect to missing out on opportunities. You develop tunnel vision and ignore important events not directly related to your goal. Sales representatives sometimes neglect to invest time in cultivating a prospective customer

because of the pressure to make quota. Instead, the sales rep goes for the quick sale with an established customer. A person on a diet might establish the goal of avoiding networking events in restaurants because fattening foods and beverages are served. The person might lose weight but at the same time miss out on the development of useful professional contacts.

A problem related to inflexibility is that goals can sometimes become obsessions, leading you to neglect other phases of work or life. A worker might become so obsessed with accomplishing work by the end of a quarter that he or she refuses to take the time to help a coworker in need. Executive coach Marshall Goldsmith cautions that he sees too many older people damaging their physical health in pursuit of their next accomplishment. He also sees too many younger people "missing their youth, then postponing their love life, then not having children—all in the service of their career."[17]

A recommended approach to combating the potential inflexibility and obsessive nature of goals is to recognize and admit when you might be pursuing the wrong goal. Imagine that you decide to start a vineyard so you can create and market wine that retails for less than $15 per bottle. Among the hurdles you encounter are that (a) nobody wants to finance such a venture and (b) the world already has far too many brands of wine. You finally surrender your wine-venture idea and look for a business activity with a greater chance of success. Life coach Pamela Mitchell explains the problem of pursuing wrong goals. She observes that when we make the strategic decision to stop investing in actions that offer little return or negative outcomes, we capture the power of positive quitting. "It is important to discontinue activities that steal our time, drain our energy, waste our money, or diminish self-esteem and respect."[18]

2. **Loss on interest in the task.** Another problem is that *performance goals can sometimes detract from an interest in the task.* People with a performance-goal orientation (focusing on being judged as competent) will sometimes lose interest in the task. The loss of interest is most likely to occur when the task is difficult. Assume that your primary reason for working as an information technology specialist is to perform well enough so that you can earn a high income. If carrying out your responsibilities encounters some hurdles, you may readily become discouraged with information technology as a field. But if your orientation is primarily to advance your knowledge about a dynamic field, you will not be readily frustrated when you encounter problems. You might even look on it as a learning opportunity.
3. **Engaging in unethical behavior.** A tight focus on goals can also encourage unethical behavior and a disregard for *how* the goals are attained. A sales representative might give kickbacks simply to gain a sale, and a CEO might lay off needed workers and neglect investing in new-product research simply to make certain profit figures. Too much emphasis on goals can also contribute to cheating in the form of people falsely reporting that they met a performance level.[19] An example would be a meat inspector claiming to have visited more meat packers than she actually did.

Despite the problems that can arise in goal setting, goals are valuable tools for managing your work and personal life. Used with common sense and according to the ideas presented in this chapter, they could have a major, positive impact on your life.

Self-Motivation Techniques

Learning Objective 3

Many people never achieve satisfying careers and never realize their potential because of low motivation. They believe they could perform better but admit that "I'm simply not a high-initiative type" or "I'm simply not that motivated." Earlier we described how identifying your most important needs could enhance motivation. Here we describe six additional techniques for self-motivation.

1. Set goals for yourself. As shown throughout this chapter, goal setting is one of the most important techniques for self-motivation. If you set long-range goals and support them with a series of smaller goals set for shorter time spans, your motivation will increase.

Intrinsic motivation
the natural tendency to seek out novelty and challenges, to extend and use one's capacities, to explore, and to learn

2. Find intrinsically motivating work. A major factor in self-motivation is to find work that is fun or its own reward. **Intrinsic motivation** refers to the natural tendency to seek out novelty and challenges, to extend and use one's capacities, to explore, and to learn.[20] The intrinsically motivated person is involved in the task at hand, such as a technology enthusiast surfing the Internet for hours at a time. Finding a job that offers you motivators in ample supply will help enhance your intrinsic motivation. For example, you might have good evidence from your past experience that the opportunity for close contact with people is a personal motivator. Find a job that involves working in a small, friendly department or team.

Intrinsically motivating work often takes the form of *meaningful work,* or work that has personal meaning to you based on your values and interests. One person might think that working as a store manager for the Salvation Army is meaningful. Another person might think that working as an electronics technician at a missile defense systems company is meaningful.

Based on circumstances, you may have to take whatever job you can find, or you may not be in a position to change jobs. In such a situation, try to arrange your work so you have more opportunity to experience the reward(s) that you are seeking. Assume that solving difficult problems excites you but that your job is 85 percent routine. Develop better work habits so that you can take care of the routine aspects of your job more quickly. This will give you more time to enjoy the creative aspects of your job.

3. Get feedback on your performance. Few people can sustain a high level of motivation without receiving information about how well they are doing. Even if you find your work challenging and exciting, you will need feedback. One reason positive feedback is valuable is that it acts as a reward. If you learn that your efforts achieved a worthwhile purpose, you will feel encouraged. For example, if a graphics display you designed was well received by company officials, you would probably want to prepare another graphics display.

A study conducted with management students demonstrated that participants adjusted their goals upward after receiving positive feedback and downward after negative feedback. It was also found that when the students were more emotional about the feedback, the positive and negative results were more pronounced.[21] The link here to self-motivation is that when goals are higher, motivation will be higher.

Behavior modification
system of motivation that emphasizes rewarding people for doing the right things and punishing them for doing the wrong things

4. Apply behavior modification to yourself. Behavior modification is a system of motivation that emphasizes rewarding people for doing the right things and punishing them for doing the wrong things. Many people have used behavior modification to change their own behavior. Specific purposes include overcoming eating disorders, tobacco addiction, Internet abuse, nail biting, and procrastination. To boost your own motivation through behavior modification, you would have to first decide what specific motivated actions you want to increase (such as working thirty minutes longer each day). Second, you would have to decide on a suitable set of rewards and punishments. You may choose to use rewards only because rewards are generally better motivators than punishments.

Expectancy theory of motivation
people will be motivated if they believe that their efforts will lead to desired outcomes

5. Improve your skills relevant to your goals. The **expectancy theory of motivation** states that people will be motivated if they believe that their efforts will lead to desired outcomes. According to this theory, people hold back effort when they are not confident that their efforts will lead to accomplishments. You should, therefore, seek adequate training to ensure that you have the right abilities and skills to perform your work. The training might be provided by the employer or on your own through a course or self-study. Appropriate training gives you more confidence that you can perform the work. The training also increases your feelings of self-efficacy.[22] By recognizing your ability to mobilize your own resources to succeed, your self-confidence for the task will be elevated. Another motivational advantage of self-efficacy is that you are likely to commit more resources, such as time and money, to attaining a goal when you feel confident that you can perform the task.[23] For example, if you had confidence in your skills to develop an eBay business, you might be willing to spend a lot of time in designing the business and money in buying products to sell on the site.

6. Raise your level of self-expectation. Another strategy for increasing your level of motivation is to simply expect more of yourself. If you raise your level of self-expectation, you are likely to achieve more. Because you expect to succeed, you do succeed. The net effect is the same as if you had increased your level of motivation. The technical term for improving your performance through raising your own expectations is the Galatea effect. In one experiment, for example, the self-expectations of subjects were raised in brief interviews with an organizational psychologist. The psychologist told the subjects they had high potential to succeed in the undertaking they were about to begin (a problem-solving task). The subjects who received the positive information about their potential did better than those subjects who did not receive such encouragement.[24]

High self-expectations and a positive mental attitude take a long time to develop, but they are critically important for becoming a well-motivated person in a variety of situations.

7. Develop a strong work ethic. A highly effective strategy for self-motivation is to develop a strong work ethic. If you are committed to the idea that most work is valuable and that it is joyful to work hard, you will automatically become strongly motivated. A person with a weak work ethic cannot readily develop a strong one because the change requires a profound value shift. Yet, if a person gives a lot of serious thought to the importance of work and follows the right role models, a work ethic can be strengthened. The shift to a strong work ethic is much like a person who has a casual attitude toward doing fine work becoming more prideful.

8. Develop psychological hardiness. A comprehensive approach to becoming better self-motivated would be to develop a higher degree of **psychological hardiness**—a mental state in which the individual experiences a high degree of commitment, control, and challenge. (The importance of commitment to company goals was described earlier in the chapter.) *Commitment* is a tendency to involve oneself in whatever one is doing or encounters, such as being committed to developing a successful computer game. Commitment also refers to a strong desire to follow through on the action plan in support of a goal. Many people set goals without following through. Commitment has also been defined as being willing to do whatever it takes.[25]

Psychological hardiness
mental state in which the individual experiences a high degree of commitment, control, and challenge

Control is a tendency to feel and act as if one is influential, rather than helpless, in facing twists and turns in life. *Challenge* is a belief that change rather than stability is normal in life and that changes lead to growth and are not threats to security. (Moving in these three directions would involve substantial personal development.) A study with more than 600 college students demonstrated that those who scored higher on psychological hardiness tended to have stronger motivation to study and learn.[26] Psychological hardiness would also be helpful in work motivation.

Remind yourself that you have personal power, and that you can make things happen. Erase those negative mental tapes that say "No, I can't."

—E. Carol Webster
Clinical Psychologist, quoted in *Black Enterprise*, September 2005, p. 157.

How to Develop the Self-Discipline to Achieve Goals and Stay Motivated

◀ Learning Objective 4 ◀

Another perspective on achieving goals and staying motivated is that they require **self-discipline**—the ability to work systematically and progressively toward a goal until it is achieved. If you are self-disciplined, you work toward achieving your goals without being derailed by the many distractions faced each day. Self-discipline incorporates

Self-discipline
the ability to work systematically and progressively toward a goal until it is achieved

self-motivation because it enables you to motivate yourself to achieve your goals without being nagged or prodded with deadlines.

Our discussion of how to develop self-discipline follows the model shown in Figure 3-7. You will observe that the model incorporates several of the ideas about goals already discussed in this chapter. Without realizing it, you have already invested mental energy into learning the self-discipline model. To think through your own tendencies toward being self-disciplined, you are invited to take Human Relations Self-Assessment Quiz 3-4. The components of self-discipline are described next.

Component 1: *Formulate a mission statement.* Who are you? What are you trying to accomplish in life? If you understand what you are trying to accomplish in life, you have the fuel to be self-disciplined. With a mission, activities that may appear mundane to others become vital stepping stones for you. An example would be learning Spanish grammar to help you become an international businessperson. To help formulate your mission statement, answer two questions: What are my five biggest wishes? What do I want to accomplish in my career during the next five years?

Component 2: *Develop role models.* An excellent method of learning how to be self-disciplined is to model your behavior after successful achievers who are obviously well disciplined. To model another person does not mean you will slavishly imitate every detail of that person's life. Instead, you will follow the general pattern of how the person operates in spheres related to your mission and goals. An ideal role model is the type of person whom you would like to become, not someone you feel you could never become.

Component 3: *Develop goals for each task.* Your mission must be supported by a series of specific goals that collectively will enable you to achieve your mission. Successfully completing goals eventually leads to fulfilling a mission. Each small goal achieved is a building block toward larger achievements.

Component 4: *Develop action plans to achieve goals combined with if-then planning.* Self-disciplined people carefully follow their action plans because they make goal attainment possible. It is helpful to chart your progress against the dates established for the sub-activities. *If-then planning* supports your action plan because it suggests what to do in case something happens while implementing the action plan. (An if-then plan is a variation of a contingency plan.) The if-then plan points to what you

FIGURE 3-7

THE SELF-DISCIPLINE MODEL

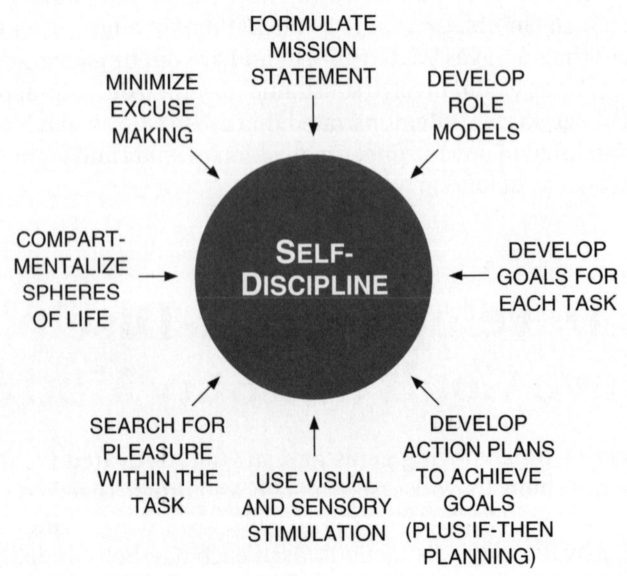

Human Relations Self-Assessment Quiz 3-4

The Self-Discipline Quiz

On the following scale, indicate the extent to which each of the following statements describes your behavior or attitude by circling one number for each: disagree strongly (DS), disagree (D), neutral (N), agree (A), agree strongly (AS). Consider asking someone who knows your behavior and attitudes well to help you respond accurately.

	DS	D	N	A	AS
1. I have a strong sense of purpose.	1	2	3	4	5
2. Life is a pain when you are always chasing goals.	5	4	3	2	1
3. My long-range plans in life are well established.	1	2	3	4	5
4. I feel energized when I have a new goal to pursue.	1	2	3	4	5
5. It is difficult for me to picture an event in my mind before it occurs.	5	4	3	2	1
6. When success is near, I can almost taste, feel, and see it.	1	2	3	4	5
7. I consult my daily planner or a to-do list almost every day.	1	2	3	4	5
8. My days rarely turn out the way I had planned.	5	4	3	2	1
9. What I do for a living is not (or would not be) nearly as important as the money it pays.	5	4	3	2	1
10. Some parts of my job are as exciting to me as any hobby or pastime.	1	2	3	4	5
11. Working sixty hours per week for even a short period of time would be out of the question for me.	5	4	3	2	1
12. I have personally known several people who would be good role models for me.	1	2	3	4	5
13. So far I have never read about or known anybody whose lifestyle I would like to emulate.	5	4	3	2	1
14. My work is so demanding that it's difficult for me to concentrate fully on my personal life when I'm not working.	5	4	3	2	1
15. When I'm involved in an important work project, I can enjoy myself fully at a sport or cultural event after hours.	1	2	3	4	5
16. If it weren't for a few bad breaks, I would be much more successful today.	5	4	3	2	1
17. I am easily distracted.	5	4	3	2	1
18. I get bored easily.	5	4	3	2	1
19. Planning is difficult because life is so unpredictable.	5	4	3	2	1
20. I feel that I'm moving forward a little bit each day toward achieving my goals.	1	2	3	4	5

Scoring and Interpretation:

Calculate your score by adding the numbers circled.

90–100 points: You are a highly self-disciplined person who should be able to capitalize on your skills and talents. Studying about self-discipline might help you capitalize even further on your strong self-discipline.

60–89 points: You have an average degree of self-discipline, so studying the self-discipline model could point to areas for personal improvement.

40–59 points: You may be experiencing problems with self-discipline. Start putting into practice the ideas contained in the self-discipline model.

20–39 points: If your answers are accurate, you have enough problems with self-discipline to limit achieving many of the things in life important to you. In addition to studying the self-discipline model, study about work habits and time management.

Questions:
1. How does this score agree with your evaluation of your self-discipline?
2. Who might you use as a role model of a person with high self-discipline?

will do in the critical situation. "If X happens, I will do Y." Y is the specific action you will take whenever X occurs. Studies have shown that people who use if-then planning are more likely to attain self-improvement goals.[27]

Here is an example of if-then planning. You are determined to enter a company contest for developing a new product idea. Yet, as you go about your regular job responsibilities, your attempts to develop your product idea keep getting interrupted. Without if-then planning you might just give up on entering the contest. Instead, you find the time to develop your new-product idea through if-then planning: "If I get interrupted more than once in developing my new-product idea, I will spend four hours the next Sunday morning digging away on the project."

Component 5: *Use visual and sensory stimulation.* A self-disciplined person relentlessly focuses on a goal and persistently pursues that goal. To accomplish this consistent focus, self-disciplined people form images of reaching their goals—they actually develop a mental image of the act of accomplishing what they want. As mysterious as it sounds, visualization helps the brain convert images into reality. The more senses you can incorporate into your visual image, the stronger its power. Imagine yourself seeing, tasting, hearing, smelling, and touching your goal. Can you imagine yourself sitting in your condo overlooking the ocean, eating a great meal to celebrate the fact that the business you founded now has ten thousand employees?

Component 6: *Search for pleasure within the task.* A self-disciplined person finds joy, excitement, and intense involvement in the task at hand and therefore finds intrinsic motivation. Instead of focusing on the extrinsic (or external) reward, the love of the task helps the person in pursuit of the goal. An axiom of becoming wealthy is not to focus on getting rich. Instead, focus on work. If the task at hand does not thrill you, at least focus on the pleasure from the most enjoyable element within the task. A bill collector might not find the total task intrinsically motivating, but perhaps he or she enjoys developing skill in resolving conflict.

Component 7: *Compartmentalize spheres of life.* Self-disciplined people have a remarkable capacity to divide up (or compartmentalize) the various spheres of their lives to stay focused on what they are doing at the moment. While working, develop the knack of concentrating on work and putting aside thoughts about personal life. In the midst of social and family activities, concentrate on them rather than half thinking about work. This approach will contribute to both self-discipline and a better integration of work and family life.

Component 8: *Minimize excuse making.* Self-disciplined people concentrate their energies on goal accomplishment rather than making excuses for why work is not accomplished. Instead of trying to justify why they have been diverted from a goal, high-achieving, self-disciplined people circumvent potential barriers. Undisciplined people, in contrast, seem to look for excuses. If you are an excuse maker, conduct a self-audit, writing down all the reasons blocking you from achieving any current goal. Be brutally honest in challenging each one of your excuses. Ask yourself, "Is this a valid excuse, or is it simply a rationalization for my getting sidetracked?"

"Nothing in the world can take the place of persistence. Persistence and determination alone are omnipotent. The slogan 'press on' has solved, and always will solve, the problems of the human race."

—Calvin Coolidge
Thirtieth President of the United States

The belief that self-discipline contributes to goal attainment and success is about as strong as the belief that a healthy diet and exercise contribute to physical health. Nonetheless, a study conducted with 325 working adults provides reassurance about the benefits of self-discipline. The study participants completed the self-discipline questionnaire previously presented, and they also answered questions about their age, education, salary, and how they felt about their career success and goal accomplishment. As shown in Figure 3-8, positive relationships were found between being self-disciplined and education, salary, career success, and goal attainment. Self-ratings of career success and goal accomplishment were the most strongly related. In conclusion, self-discipline

FIGURE 3-8 RELATIONSHIP BETWEEN SELF-DISCIPLINE SCORE AND KEY FACTORS

Key Factor	Average Score on Factor for 325 Adults	Relationship to Self-Discipline Score
1. Age	34.7 years	Almost zero
2. Years of formal education	15.9	Slightly positive
3. Salary in U.S. dollars	$45,899	Slightly positive
4. Self-rating of career on scale of 1 to 7	4.9	Quite positive
5. Self-rating of goal accomplishment on scale of 1 to 7	5.6	Quite positive
6. Self-discipline score on scale of 20 to 100	76.9	------

Source: Table derived from data presented in Andrew J. DuBrin, "Career-Related Correlates of Self-Discipline," *Psychological Reports*, 2001, Vol. 89, p. 109.

pays.[28] Why do you think it was found that self-discipline was positively associated with years of formal education?

Another useful perspective on self-discipline is that a self-disciplined person is able to delay gratification. An important aspect of self-discipline is to focus on the present at the moment in order to attain longer-range goals. For example, if you want to improve your credit rating for the future, it is essential not to make an impulse purchase that you cannot afford. In the words of Meghan Clyne, managing editor of *National Affairs,* "self-control means valuing the future more than the present."[29] For many people this aspect of self-discipline could mean forgoing income now to complete a degree, and eventually earn more money. The ability to delay gratification begins early in life. An amusing study gave eighth-graders the opportunity to receive one dollar at the moment, or two dollars if they were willing to wait a week. The students who had the self-discipline to delay gratification consistently outperformed their more impulsive counterparts on grades and achievement test scores.[30]

Key Terms

Need, 62
Motive, 62
Need for achievement, 63
Maslow's hierarchy of needs, 64
Work engagement, 67
Self-determination theory, 69
Goal, 71
Action plan, 74
Intrinsic motivation, 78
Behavior modification, 78
Expectancy theory of motivation, 78
Psychological hardiness, 79
Self-discipline, 80

Summary and Review

Self-motivation is important for achieving success in work and personal life. A well-accepted explanation of human behavior is that people have needs and motives propelling them toward achieving certain goals.

- The central idea behind need theory is that unsatisfied needs motivate us until they become satisfied.
- After satisfaction of one need, the person usually pursues satisfaction of another, higher need.

Work and personal life offer the opportunity to satisfy many different needs and motives. Among the more important needs and motives are achievement, power, affiliation, recognition, and order. The need for risk taking and thrill seeking is also important for some people.

According to Maslow's hierarchy of needs, people have an internal need pushing them toward self-actualization.

- Needs are arranged into a five-step ladder. Before higher-level needs are activated, certain lower-level needs must be satisfied.
- In ascending order, the groups of needs are physiological, safety, social, esteem, and self-actualization (such as self-fulfillment).
- Additional classes of needs for the hierarchy are cognitive needs, aesthetic needs, and transcendent (or B-value) needs.

Another way of looking at self-motivation is that if you are strongly motivated you are engaged in your work, or committed to the job and company. Work engagement refers to high levels of personal investment in the work tasks performed in a job. Several studies have found that American workers are not fully engaged in their work.

Substantial research indicates that setting specific, reasonably difficult goals improves performance. Goals are valuable because they

- Will improve performance if reasonably difficult
- Can instill purpose, challenge, and meaning into ordinary work
- Focus our efforts in a specific direction
- Increase our chances for success
- Serve as self-motivators and energizers

Goals can be aimed at either learning or performing. A learning-goal orientation means that an individual is focused on acquiring new skills and mastering new situations. A performing-goal orientation is aimed at wanting to demonstrate and validate the adequacy of your competence by seeking favorable judgments of competence. People with learning-goal orientations are more likely to

- Seek feedback on how well they are performing
- Focus on skill development that will lead to higher job performance
- Develop better relationships with their supervisors
- Be innovative in solutions to problems

Goal setting is widely used on the job. Goals set by employees at lower levels in an organization are supposed to contribute to goals set at the top.

Goal setting in personal life can contribute to life satisfaction. For maximum advantage, personal goals should be integrated with career goals. Areas of life in which personal goals may be set include

- Social and family
- Hobbies and interests

- Physical and mental health
- Career
- Financial

To increase their effectiveness, goals should be supported with action plans. Effective goals are

- Specific and concise
- Expressed as a positive statement
- Realistically challenging, yet also include stretch goals
- Set for different time periods
- Synergistic with other goals you set

Goals have some problems associated with them. They can create inflexibility or become an obsession. Performing goals can detract from an interest in the task, and goals can encourage unethical behavior. To combat the potential inflexibility and obsessive nature of goals, recognize and admit when you are pursuing the wrong goal.

Key techniques of self-motivation include the following:

- Setting goals for yourself
- Finding intrinsically motivating work
- Getting feedback on your performance
- Applying behavior modification to yourself
- Improving your skills relevant to your job
- Raising your level of self-expectation
- Developing a strong work ethic
- Developing psychological hardiness (a high degree of commitment, control, and challenge)

Achieving goals and staying motivated require self-discipline. A model presented here for developing self-discipline consists of eight components:

- Formulate a mission statement.
- Develop role models.
- Develop goals for each task.
- Develop action plans supported by what-if planning.
- Use visual and sensory stimulation.
- Search for pleasure within the task.
- Compartmentalize spheres of life.
- Minimize excuse making.

A study found positive relationships between self-discipline scores and education, salary, satisfaction with career success, and satisfaction with goal attainment. Also, self-disciplined people are able to delay self-gratification.

Check Your Understanding

1. One of the biggest concerns of workers is that they want employers to pay more of their health-care insurance. What does this issue tell us about the importance of satisfying the lower-level needs of workers?
2. Identify two business-related jobs for which a high need for risk taking and thrill seeking would be an advantage. Also, identify two business-related jobs for which a high need for risk taking and thrill seeking would be a *disadvantage.*
3. Identify any self-actualized person you know or have heard of and explain why you think that person is self-actualized.
4. How realistic is it for managers to expect workers earning close to a minimum wage to be engaged? Explain your reasoning.
5. Why does a learning-goal orientation often contribute to more peace of mind than a performing-goal orientation?
6. Many students have observed that it is easier to be self-motivated after you have decided on a major. What might this be true?
7. Give examples of two jobs in your chosen field you think are likely to be intrinsically motivating. Explain your reasoning.
8. Explain how you might be able to use the Galatea effect to improve the success you achieve in your career and personal life.
9. What sacrifices might a highly self-disciplined person have to make in contrast to a lowly self-disciplined person?
10. Ask a person who has achieved career success how much self-discipline contributed to his or her success.

Web Corner

Self-motivation

www.secretsofmotivation.com/self-motivation-tips.html

Self-discipline

www.personal-development.com

INTERNET SKILL BUILDER

Personal Goal Setting

At www.mindtools.com/page6.html you will find a program for personal goal setting useful for both career and personal success. The program includes a thoughtful, brief video. An important feature of the personal goal-setting plan is that it urges you to set goals in nine areas of life: artistic, attitude, career, education, family, financial, physical, pleasure (really recreation), and public service. After reviewing the program, give your opinion of the usefulness of SMART goals. Also, how does the use of SMART goals compare to the suggestions for goal setting presented in this chapter?

Developing Your Human Relations Skills

Human Relations Application Exercises

Applying Human Relations Exercise 3-1

Goal-Setting and Action Plan Worksheet

Goal setting, along with developing action plans to support the goals, is a basic success strategy. Here you are being asked to refine a process you may have already begun. Consider entering more than one goal and accompanying action plan in each category. To clarify the meaning of the following entries, we provide examples in italics of a recent graduate entering the retail field. Before writing down your goals, consult the section "Guidelines for Goal Setting." If you are not currently employed, set up hypothetical goals and action plans for a future job.

Long-Range Goals (Beyond Five Years)

Work: *Ultimately become CEO of a major division of a retail company, perhaps the CEO of Bloomingdales.*

(Place your entry here.)

Action plan: *Work my way up, position by position, starting as assistant merchandising manager.*

(Place your entry here.)

Personal: *Married, with children, home ownership.*

(Place your entry here.)

Action plan: *Continue to develop relationship with my boyfriend as life partner. We will both save and invest at least 10 percent of our incomes each year.*

(Place your entry here.)

Medium-Range Goals (Two to Five Years)

Work: *Become merchandising manager for one store in a large retail chain.*

(Place your entry here.)

Action plan: *Will work hard as assistant merchandising manager, listen to and act on feedback from my supervisors, take courses in human relations and merchandising management.*

(Place your entry here.)

Personal: *Continue to develop relationship with my boyfriend and marry him within three years.*

(Place your entry here.)

Action plan: *Communicate in depth with each other regularly to build relationship. We will work on not criticizing each other so often. After he proposes marriage, we will use our business skills to plan the wedding.*

(Place your entry here.)

Short-Range Goals (within Two Years)

Work: *Do an outstanding job as assistant merchandising manager this month.*

(Place your entry here.)

Action plan: *Will take care of more e-mail and other routine work when not in the store. In this way I can put more time and energy into merchandising. I will ask my supervisor for feedback from time to time so I can make adjustments to my performance.*

(Place your entry here.)

Personal: *Get further into digital photography, particularly learning how to take action shots. Will go beyond the "point and click" approach to photography.*

(Place your entry here.)

Action plan: *I will study the camera manual more carefully and attend one of the digital photography workshops given at my former community college.*

(Place your entry here.)

Applying Human Relations Exercise 3-2

Setback in Goal Setting and Developing Action Plans

Goal setting does not always go as well as planned because barriers to goal attainment might arise such as running out of money or motivational energy. In these cases you may need to develop contingency plans, or back up goals, to avoid not accomplishing something important or feeling totally frustrated. In this exercise reflect on what you would do (or have done) in response to a goal you did not attain. Sometimes that backup plan is referred to as "Plan B."

Important goal that I might not attain (or did not attain):

____

Backup goal (or contingency goal): ______________________________

____

Action plan to attain back up goal (or Plan B): ______________

____

Human Relations Class Activity

How Important Is Need Satisfaction to People?

Here is an opportunity to engage in data collection about a major human relations topic. Each class member agrees to obtain survey data about need satisfaction by having five people complete Human Relations Self-Quiz 3-2. Perhaps a student will volunteer to make an electronic copy of the test. Obtain the sex and age of each participant. (Survey anybody convenient, including yourself.)

For each completed self-quiz, record the importance ratings for each of the five need categories: physiological, safety, love, esteem, and self-actualization. To quantify the fact that people may differ in the strength of certain needs, choose participants who appear to be in quite different life situations. For example, you might look for a full-time student, an unemployed person, a professional worker, an entry-level worker, and a retired person. (The research lesson here is that you obtain more interesting results when your sample is diverse.)

A couple of class volunteers will then compile the data for all the completed self-quizzes. Average importance ratings will be calculated for each of the five needs. An example result might be, "For the total group, the average importance rating for safety needs is 3.24." Also calculate average importance ratings by sex and age group, such as above and below age twenty-five.

Among the questions for class discussion are these:

1. Does our sample appear to show much variation in the importance ratings attached to needs?
2. Which need appears to be the most frustrated among the participants in our sample?
3. Which need appears to be the most satisfied among the participants in our sample?

You might also compare your pattern of importance ratings to the averages obtained for the sample. If your need-importance profile seems to be quite different, you might explain to yourself why this fact is most likely true.

Human Relations Case Study 3-1

Unengaged Monique at Shea, Cohen, Antonelli and Armstrong

Monique was happy to receive her associate's degree with a major in paralegal studies. At a minimum, she could now satisfy her parents' demands that she work in the legal field. Monique's father frequently told her something to this effect: "Even if we have an occasional recession, people are going to keep suing each other. They might even sue more during hard times just to get some money." Monique's mother kept emphasizing that being a paralegal would give her status and make other people think that she is somebody important.

After a brief job hunt, Monique found a position at the legal firm of Shea, Cohen, Antonelli and Armstrong (often referred to as SCAA by insiders). Wanting to appear as professional as possible, Monique joined the South Carolina Paralegal Association, although she rarely attended meetings.

After an orientation period of several days, Monique was assigned to the residential and small business real estate department. Her work activities focused on the paperwork and electronic searches needed to support lawyers in closing on houses and small buildings. Monique thought to herself that it was curious that she and other paralegals did most of the work in preparing for closings, yet the lawyers were paid considerably more.

One evening while at the athletic club where she was a member, Monique met Kurt, one of her former classmates. When asked, "How's the job going at the law firm?" Monique replied, "To tell you the truth, Kurt, house closings are a lot like airplane rides. After a half dozen or so, they are all the same. I get no thrill out of all the prep work for the closing. Yet, I do like to see the happy faces of the people when the deal is done."

One afternoon Monique was standing in line at Quizno's to order a toasted sub for lunch. Right in front of her was Louise, the database manager at SCAA. Louise invited Monique to sit together after they paid the cashier. During lunch, Louise said to Monique that she had some curious feedback she had been thinking of sharing with her.

"Please tell me, Louise. I hope I didn't make an error in providing background data for one of those dumb properties."

"No error in facts, but maybe an error in attitude. One of the attorneys was telling me that he and a couple of his colleagues refer to you as 'Monique Zombie.' Of course, I asked why. He said that it seems like you are just going through the motions with no passion about what you are doing."

"Honestly, Louise," responded Monique. "I would show a little more passion at SCAA if I were closing on skyscrapers or being paid what some of the partners in the firm are earning. Give me a break."

Questions

1. What can Monique do to become more engaged in her work?
2. What can Monique do to overcome the reputation of being a zombie on the job?
3. In what way might Monique's parents have contributed to her lack of commitment to paralegal work?
4. What might be the career consequences for Monique if she does not become more enthusiastic about her present work assignments?

Human Relations Role-Playing Exercise

Getting Monique More Engaged

The scenario presented in Case Study 3-1 hints at a major challenge facing many managers: How to get a group member more excited about (or engaged in) the work. One student plays the role of partner Shea who is concerned that Monique is not as excited about the work and the firm as a paralegal should be. He decides to hold a discussion with her about her laid-back attitude. Shea does not want to fire Monique, but Shea wants to get her fired up. Another student plays the role of Monique who did not think that being a passionate, committed employee was part of her job description as a paralegal.

Observers rate the role-players on two dimensions, using a 1 to 5 scale from very poor to very good. One dimension is "effective use of human relations techniques." The second dimension is "acting ability." A few observers might voluntarily provide feedback to the role-players in terms of sharing their ratings and observations. The course instructor might also provide feedback.

Human Relations Case Study 3-2

Trevor Aims for the Top

Trevor is employed as a sales representative for a company that sells storage space to individuals and small companies. The storage space consists of garage-like compartments placed at four locations in and around Phoenix, Arizona. The storage space is concept has been growing rapidly for several groups of customers. One group is small enterprises who lack the space to keep all their supplies but do not want to invest in a larger office or manufacturing facility. The major group of retail customers is home owners who have excess furniture and other belongings they do not need urgently but still want to keep. Another group of retail customers is people who have sold their houses yet are not sure whether they want to get rid of all their belongings that do not fit in their new reduced-size living quarters.

Trevor's boss Mike, the owner of the storage company, has recently established a goal-setting program for every company employee as a way of expanding the business and improving operating efficiencies. Mike gave Trevor some general guidelines about goal setting and told him to also consult articles online that might help him with establishing goals for the new fiscal year. Four days later, Trevor sent Mike an e-mail, as follows:

Hi Mike,

As you requested, I've put together a bunch of goals for the upcoming year that I think will help me boost sales for the year, and win that big prize of a company-paid trip to Las Vegas. ☺

- Be the best storage-space sales rep in the greater Phoenix area.
- Strive to do my best every day.
- Improve my sales by 30 percent by trying extra hard.
- Network like crazy to increase my potential customer base.
- Talk up the company whenever I have the chance.

Yours truly,
Trevor

Mike thought to himself, "I like the sincerity that Trevor has shown, but I think he needs some more guidance about goal setting in business."

Questions:

1. What is your evaluation of the effectiveness of the goals set by Trevor?
2. What specific suggestions can you offer Trevor to make his goals more likely to be attained?
3. How relevant is a program of goal setting for Mike's company?

REFERENCES

1. For a theoretical explanation of the principle of self-interest, see Dale T. Miller, "The Norm of Self-Interest," *American Psychologist,* December 1999, pp. 1053–1060.
2. David C. McClelland and Richard Boyatzis, "Leadership Motive Pattern and Long-Term Success in Management," *Journal of Applied Psychology,* December 1982, p. 737.
3. Marvin Zuckerman, "Are You a Risk Taker?" *Psychology Today,* November/December 2000, p. 53.
4. The original statement is Abraham H. Maslow, "A Theory of Human Motivation," *Psychological Review,* July 1943, pp. 370–396. See also Maslow, *Motivation and Personality* (New York: Harper & Row, 1954); *Motivation and Personality,* 2nd edition, 1970.
5. Michael S. Christian, Adela S. Garza, and Jerel E. Slaughter, "Work Engagement: A Quantitative Review and Test of Its Relations with Task and Contextual Performance," *Personnel Psychology,* Number 1, 2011, p. 89.
6. Data reported in Garry Kranz, "Losing Lifeblood," *Workforce Management,* July 2011, p. 24.
7. Ed Frauenheim, "Commitment Issues," *Workforce Management,* November 16, 2009, p. 20.
8. Kranz, "Losing Lifeblood," pp, 24–25. The quote is from p. 24.
9. Edward L. Deci, James P. Connell, and Richard My. Ryan, "Self-Determination in a Work Organization," *Journal of Applied Psychology,* August 1989, p. 580; Karen McCally, "Self-Determined," *Rochester Review,* July–August 2010, p. 18.
10. Gary P. Latham, "The Motivational Benefits of Goal Setting," *Academy of Management Executive,* November 2004, pp. 126–129.
11. Don VandeWalle and Larry L. Cummings, "A Test of the Influence of Goal Orientation on the Feedback-Seeking Process," *Journal of Applied Psychology,* June 1997, pp. 390–400; VandeWalle, William L. Cron, and John W. Slocum, Jr., "The Role of Goal Orientation Following Performance Feedback," *Journal of Applied Psychology,* August 2001, pp. 629–640.
12. Don VandeWalle, Steven P. Brown, William L. Cron, and John W. Slocum, Jr., "The Influence of Goal Orientation and Self-Regulation Tactics on Sales Performance: A Longitudinal Field Test," *Journal of Applied Psychology,* April 1999, pp. 249–259.
13. Onne Janssen and Nico W. Van Yperen, "Employee Goal Orientations, the Quality of Leader-Member Exchange, and the Outcomes of Job Performance and Job Satisfaction," *Academy of Management Journal,* June 2004, pp. 368–384.
14. Gerard H. Seijts and Gary P. Latham, "Learning versus Performance Goals: When Should Each Be Used?" *Academy of Management Executive,* February 2005, p. 130.
15. Susan B. Wilson and Michael S. Dobson, *Goal Setting: How to Create an Action Plan and Achieve Your Goals,* 2nd ed. (New York: American Management Association, 2008).
16. Joelle Jay, "Make Your SMART Goals WISE Goals," *Communication Briefings,* December 2011, Number 2, pp. 2–3.
17. "Personal Goal Setting: Find Direction. Live Life Your Way," www.mindtools.com/page6.html © Mind Tools Ltd, 1995–2008.
18. Quoted in "Too Obsessed with Personal Goals?" *Executive Leadership,* June 2008, p. 5. Adapted from "Are You Too Obsessed with Your Goals?" www.HarvardBusiness.org
19. Lisa D. Ordóñez, Maurice E. Schweitzer, Adam D. Galinsky, and Max H. Bazerman, "Goals Gone Wild: The Systematic Side Effects of Overprescribing Goal Setting," *Academy of Management Perspectives,* February 2009, p. 10.
20. Richard M. Ryan and Edward L. Deci, "Self-Determination Theory and the Facilitation of Intrinsic Motivation, Social Development, and Well-Being," *American Psychologist,* January 2000, p. 70.
21. Remus Ilies and Timothy A. Judge, "Goal Regulation across Time: The Effects of Feedback and Affect," *Journal of Applied Psychology,* May 2005, pp. 453–467.
22. P. Christopher Earley and Terri R. Lituchy, "Delineating Goals and Efficacy: A Test of Three Models," *Journal of Applied Psychology,* February 1992, p. 96.
23. Jeffrey B. Vancouver, Kristen M. More, and Ryan J. Yoder, "Self-Efficacy and Resource Allocation: Support for a Nonmonotonic, Discontinuous Model," *Journal of Applied Psychology,* January 2008, pp. 35–47.
24. Taly Dvir, Dov Eden, and Michal Lang Banjo, "Self-Fulfilling Prophecy and Gender: Can Women Be Pygmalion and Galatea?" *Journal of Applied Psychology,* April 1995, p. 268.
25. Tamara E. Holmes, "The Power of Commitment: Mere Motivation Is Often Not Enough to Achieve Your Goals," *Black Enterprise,* November 2007, p. 113.
26. Michael S. Cole, Hubert S. Field, and Stanley G. Harris, "Student Learning Motivation and Psychological Hardiness: Interactive Effects on Students' Reactions to a Management Class," *Academy of Management Learning and Education,* March 2004, pp. 64–85. The definition of *psychological hardiness* is from citations on page 66 of the same source.
27. Heidi Grant Halvorson, "The If-Then Solution," *Psychology Today,* February 2011, p. 48.
28. Andrew J. DuBrin, "Career-Related Correlates of Self-Discipline," *Psychological Reports,* 2001, Vol. 89, pp. 107–110.
29. "Saying Yes to Saying No," (book review), *The Wall Street Journal,* January 5, 2011, p. A13.
30. Ann Pleshette Murphy, "Teach Your Kids Patience, Now," *USA Weekend,* August 4-6, 2006, p. 6.

4

Emotional Intelligence, Attitudes, and Happiness

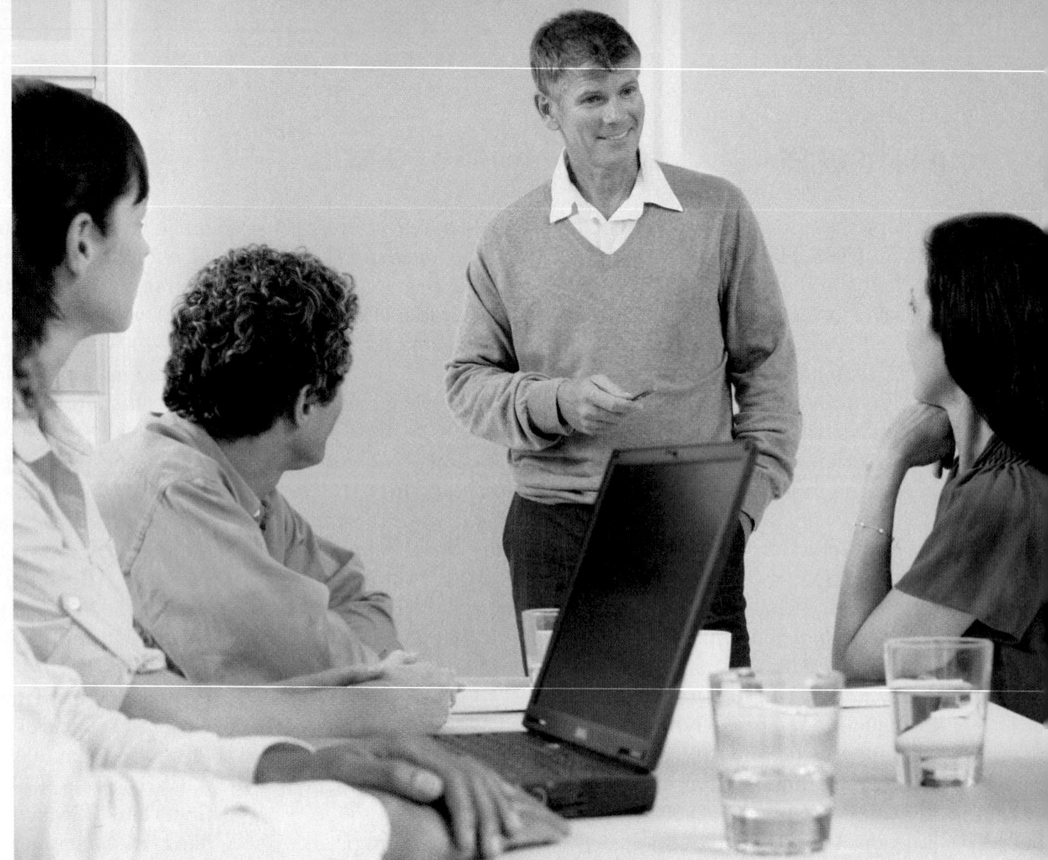

Outline

At Star Automatic Merchandising, sales were down 45 percent for December in comparison to the previous December, and 26 percent for the year. Ben, the general manager, knew that business had to improve to keep his staff of twenty-five workers intact. He had recently received a visit from the corporate director of marketing and sales, who advised Ben to improve his region's sales or cut his division down enough to match its current sales volume.

Ben replied to the director that his sales staff was trying hard to get more business but that the business recession was a formidable force facing the group. The director said, "Just tell your sales force that they have to improve sales by 20 percent, or half of them will lose their jobs. And while you are at it, tell the service people to keep the vending machines we have in force closer to full capacity. Tell them their jobs are in jeopardy also."

Ben explained to the director that the entire staff was trying hard, and that motivation wasn't the problem. To which the director responded, "No excuses, Ben. We are facing an emergency need for revenue growth."

Ben called a meeting for Thursday at 4 p.m. with every member of Star who could possibly attend. With business down so much, rumors flew among the employee group that Ben would be making a layoff announcement.

At the meeting, Ben served pastries, bagels, fruit, and coffee. His gesture drew applause and good-natured kidding from the group. Karen, the administrative assistant, said to the group, "Please don't report Ben to the corporate group for having served non-vended food at our meeting."

As the meeting began, Ben could detect the fearful mood in the group. He said to the staff, "We're here today for a problem-solving meeting, not for a hatchet job. Let's begin by talking about how you feel about business prospects and your jobs."

With a collective sigh of relief, each Star worker expressed his or her attitude about business prospects. Phil, one of the junior sales representatives, volunteered to speak first, and said: "Of course, I'm frightened about poor sales right now. Yet, if we can just have a little more time, I know business will improve. I have been showing a few small companies how a Star Automatic Merchandising system can actually add a few hundred dollars to their bottom line each month. We offer the business owner a nice, fat little commission."

In turn, the other Star employees talked about how they felt about their jobs as well as the overall business.

Ben's approach to working with his employees illustrates how important emotions are to workers and that they should be dealt with to achieve good business results. By dealing with employee feelings, Ben displayed good emotional intelligence, one of the major topics in this chapter. Other major sections of the chapter deal with related aspects of using emotion constructively: attitudes and happiness.

Learning Objectives ▸

After studying the information and doing the exercises in this chapter, you should be able to:

1. Explain how emotional intelligence contributes to effective human relations.
2. Understand the components of attitudes and how they are acquired and changed.
3. Appreciate the importance of positive attitudes.
4. Pinpoint why organizational citizenship behavior is so highly valued in the workplace.
5. Understand the nature of happiness and how it can be acquired and enhanced.

▶ Learning Objective 1 ▶

What Is Emotional Intelligence?

How effectively people use their emotions has a major impact on their success. The term *emotional intelligence* has gathered different meanings, all relating to how effectively a person makes constructive use of his or her emotions. John D. Mayer, a professor of psychology at the University of New Hampshire, along with Yale psychology professor Peter Saloey, originated the concept of emotional intelligence. Mayer explained that from a scientific (rather than a popular) viewpoint, **emotional intelligence** is the "ability to accurately perceive your own and others' emotions; to understand the signals that emotions send about relationships; and to manage our own and others' emotions."[1]

Emotional intelligence
the ability to accurately perceive emotions, to understand the signals that emotions send about relationships, and to manage emotions

Expressed more simply, emotional intelligence is the ability to perform emotional tasks. An example of an emotional task would be informing a homeowner whose house was destroyed in a flood that she did not have flood insurance. A more general, and widely used, definition of emotional intelligence is that it refers to a grab-bag of everything that is not cognitive (intellectual) intelligence.[2] A person with high emotional intelligence would be able to engage in such behaviors as sizing up people, pleasing others, and influencing them.

KEY COMPONENTS OF EMOTIONAL INTELLIGENCE

Four key factors included in emotional intelligence are as follows:[3]

Self-awareness
the ability to understand moods, emotions, and needs as well as their impact on others; self-awareness also includes using intuition to make decisions you can live with happily

Self-management
the ability to control one's emotions and act with honesty and integrity in a consistent and acceptable manner

Social awareness
having empathy for others and having intuition about work problems

Relationship management
the interpersonal skills of being able to communicate clearly and convincingly, disarm conflicts, and build strong personal bonds

1. **Self-awareness.** The ability to understand your moods, emotions, and needs as well as their impact on others. Self-awareness also includes using intuition to make decisions you can live with happily. (A person with good self-awareness knows whether he or she is pushing other people too far.)
2. **Self-management.** The ability to control one's emotions and act with honesty and integrity in a consistent and acceptable manner. The right degree of self-management helps prevent a person from throwing temper tantrums when activities do not go as planned. Effective workers do not let their occasional bad moods ruin their day. If they cannot overcome the bad mood, they let coworkers know of their problem and how long it might last. (A person with low self-management would suddenly decide to drop a project because the work was frustrating.)
3. **Social awareness.** Includes having empathy for others and having intuition about work problems. A team leader with social awareness, or empathy, would be able to assess whether a team member has enough enthusiasm for a project to assign him or her to that project. Another facet of social skill is the ability to interpret nonverbal communication, such as frowns and types of smiles.[4] (A supervisor with social awareness, or empathy, would take into account the most likely reaction of group members before making a decision affecting them.)
4. **Relationship management.** Includes the interpersonal skills of being able to communicate clearly and convincingly, disarm conflicts, and build strong personal bonds. Effective workers use relationship management skills to spread their enthusiasm and solve disagreements, often with kindness and humor. (A worker with relationship management skill would use a method of persuasion that is likely to work well with a particular group or individual.)

Emotional intelligence thus incorporates many of the skills and attitudes necessary to achieve effective interpersonal relations in organizations. Many topics in human relations, such as resolving conflict and helping others develop, and positive political skills would be included in emotional intelligence. Figure 4-1 outlines and illustrates how emotional intelligence relates many other topics in human relations.

FIGURE 4-1 THE LINK BETWEEN EMOTIONAL INTELLIGENCE AND OTHER TOPICS IN HUMAN RELATIONS

Chapter Number	Illustrative Links to Emotional Intelligence (EI)
1. Human Relations and You	To understand yourself well, the self-awareness aspect of EI is essential.
2. Self-Esteem and Self-Confidence	Self-esteem focuses heavily on understanding your feelings, which makes EI quite important.
3. Self-Motivation and Goal Setting	Some aspects of self-motivation involve being able to read your own emotions. The self-management aspect of EI contributes to self-discipline.
4. Emotional Intelligence, Attitudes, and Happiness	EI is linked to attitudes because they have an emotional content. You need to understand your own emotions and feelings to be happy.
5. Values and Ethics	Values are colored with emotions, so understanding emotions helps develop your values. An important test of being ethical is to understand how you would feel if your behavior were made public. EI helps you understand these feelings.
6. Problem Solving and Creativity	Emotions and intuition contribute heavily to problem solving and creativity, so having good EI can be an asset.
7. Personal Communication Effectiveness	Personal communication includes relationship building, such as being supportive of others. A key part of EI is relationship building. Dealing with emotions and attitudes is also a contributor to overcoming barriers to communication.
8. Communication in the Workplace	Behaving effectively in meetings includes being able to understand the impact you are making on others and also reading the emotions of others. Both skills are part of EI.
9. Specialized Tactics for Getting Along with Others in the Workplace	Managing relationships is one of the major components of EI. The social awareness aspect of EI includes having empathy for others, which is helpful in developing workplace relationships.
10. Managing Conflict	The relationship-management aspect of EI includes disarming conflict, so your emotional intelligence will help you deal with conflict. Also, being able to read the emotions of others will help you resolve conflict.
11. Becoming an Effective Leader	Several researchers believe that EI is the most important trait and characteristic of an effective leader. Your EI will also help you develop good relationships with subordinates.
12. Motivating Others and Developing Teamwork	When attempting to motivate others, it is helpful to understand their emotions and feelings and identify their major needs. Also, if your EI is good, you will be able to more readily praise others.
13. Diversity and Cross-Cultural Competence	A major contributor to effective cross-cultural relations is to have the cultural sensitivity to size up your environment and then act appropriately. Having cultural sensitivity and empathy is part of EI.
14. Getting Ahead in Your Career	Having good EI will help you build the relationships you need to succeed, such as during a job interview and with network members. Also, appropriate etiquette can contribute to career advancement, and EI helps you size up which standards of behavior are expected.
15. Learning Strategies, Perception, and Life Span Changes	EI can help in such ways as having the self-awareness to understand your learning style and being able to recognize the subtle changes you need to make at various stages of life. Strong EI can also help you sharpen your perception because you will be able to recognize potential emotional biases.
16. Developing Good Work Habits	An important part of having good work habits is to understand your potential tendencies toward procrastination. The self-awareness aspect of EI is a major contributor to this type of self-reflection.
17. Managing Stress and Personal Problems	To understand how stress from work and personal life might be affecting you, you have to be able to read your emotions. Dealing well with personal problems also requires enough EI to read your emotions.

Tests of emotional intelligence typically ask you to respond to questions on a 1 to 5 scale (never, rarely, sometimes, often, consistently). For example, indicate how frequently you demonstrate the following behaviors:

I can laugh at myself.	1 2 3 4 5
I help others grow and develop.	1 2 3 4 5
I watch carefully the nonverbal communication of others.	1 2 3 4 5

Social intelligence
an understanding of how relationships with bosses and colleagues, family, and friends, shape our brains and affect our bodies

Another type of intelligence contributing to effective human relations is **social intelligence,** an understanding of how relationships with bosses and colleagues, family, and friends, shape our brains and affect our bodies. Social intelligence is therefore somewhat similar to emotional intelligence. Social intelligence is a book-length subject; yet, we can take away a couple of basic lessons that are linked to positive human relations.[5] Social intelligence tells us that good relationships act like vitamins, energizing us to perform well. In contrast, bad relationships are like poison that undermines our cognitive efficiency and creativity. The person with good social intelligence would work at having positive relationships with others on the job, so as to being able to concentrate on the task and perform well.

Another aspect of having social intelligence would be to recognize that being arrogant or derisive toward others can cause emotional distress that impairs the brain's ability to learn and think clearly. So a good team player or a manager would relate more positively toward others in order to help attain a productive workplace.

CONSEQUENCES OF HIGH AND LOW EMOTIONAL INTELLIGENCE

Demonstrating good emotional intelligence is impressive because it contributes to performing well in the difficult arena of dealing with feelings. A worker with good emotional intelligence would engage in such behaviors as (a) recognizing when a coworker needs help but is too embarrassed to ask for help, (b) dealing with the anger of a dissatisfied customer, (c) recognizing that the boss is facing considerable pressure also, and (d) being able to tell whether a customer's "maybe" means "yes" or "no."

A synthesis of a large number of studies indicated that for high emotional labor jobs (those that require positive emotional displays) emotional intelligence contributes to good performance. Also of note, emotional intelligence makes a contribution beyond cognitive intelligence and personality traits when the job calls for emotional display. A sales manager who had the responsibility of firing up the sales force would therefore benefit from having good emotional intelligence. For jobs with low emotional content, such as an accounts payable specialist, emotional intelligence would typically make a very small contribution to job performance. In some situations, having high emotional intelligence in a low-emotion job could even lower job performance because the worker might feel emotionally suppressed.[6]

Emotional contagion
the automatic and unconscious transfer of emotions between individuals based on cues the one person observes in another

Another positive consequence of emotional intelligence is that if you know how to project positive emotion you will spread that positive feeling to others in your immediate workplace. **Emotional contagion** is the automatic and unconscious transfer of emotions between individuals based on cues the other person observes. The contagion takes place because people have a tendency to mimic and synchronize the facial expressions, sounds, postures, and movements of another person. As a result of the mimicking, the second person experiences the emotion of the first person.[7] Here is how you might use emotional contagion to solve a human relations problem: You are the team leader of a group of discouraged, disgruntled, and downtrodden people working in a distribution center of a large online retailer. You hear regular complaints such as, "We get treated like prison labor in a third-world country," "The computer system keeps going down so we can't get our work done on time," "Even the Rollerblades management gives us to scoot around the center are in drastic need of repair." From time to time you tell the group to cheer up, but your words are not taken seriously.

Being skilled at emotional intelligence, you give emotional contagion a try. You enlist the help of the most cheerful member of the group, Willy, to duplicate your act so the effects of emotional contagion will be doubled. You and your confederate Willy come to work smiling, expressing positive thoughts, standing up straight, and making fist-to-fist contact with anybody who says something positive. Soon the positive mood and actions of you and Willy begin to rub off a little on other teammates. The mood becomes positive enough to start working on problems instead of simply moaning and complaining.

A review of many studies concluded that employees with low emotional intelligence are more likely than their high-emotional-intelligence counterparts to experience negative emotional reactions to job insecurity, such as high tension. Furthermore, workers with low emotional intelligence are more likely to engage in negative coping behaviors, such as expressing anger and verbally abusing an immediate supervisor for the organization failing to provide job security.[8]

ACQUIRING AND DEVELOPING EMOTIONAL INTELLIGENCE

Many people believe that emotional intelligence can be acquired and developed, much like a person can learn to become more extraverted or learn to control his or her temper. Many consultants offer training programs for helping employees develop emotional intelligence, and school systems throughout North America provide students some training in emotional intelligence. Elkhonon Goldberg, a clinical professor of neurology at New York University School of Medicine, explains that emotional intelligence can be learned to a degree, much like musical talent or numerical ability can be developed. Having the right natural talent, however, is an important starting point. The combination of biological endowment (such as being aware of your emotions) and training will enable most people to enhance their emotional intelligence.[9]

Given that emotional intelligence is composed of different components, to acquire and develop such ability would usually require working on one component at a time. For example, if a person had difficulty in self-management, he or she would study and be coached in an aspect of self-management such as anger control. Training in anger management is widespread today because so many people have difficulty in managing their anger. Skill-Building Exercise 4-1 presented later in the chapter provides a step-by-step approach to the development of emotional intelligence.

CONCERNS AND CROSS-CULTURAL CONSIDERATIONS

A criticism of the idea of emotional intelligence is that it might simply be part of analytical (or traditional) intelligence. For example, if you can read the feelings of other people, aren't you just being smart? Another concern is that the popularized concept of emotional intelligence has become so broad it encompasses almost the entire study of personality. Emotional intelligence has become an all-inclusive term for many ideas about human behavior that were studied before and since the popularization of the term. Yet, when emotional intelligence is regarded as a series of skills that can be developed, it has more scientific backing.[10]

As with all dimensions of human relations, in some situations it will be helpful to be aware of possible cross-cultural differences in what constitutes effective emotional intelligence. For example, an overt display of emotion might be more effective in a meeting conducted in Mexico City than London, because the typical Mexican businessperson is more open in expressing emotion than his or her typical British counterpart.

Learning Objective 2

What Are the Components of Attitudes, and How Are They Acquired and Changed?

Attitude
a predisposition to respond that exerts an influence on a person's response to a person, a thing, an idea, or a situation

"You've got an attitude," said the supervisor to the store associate, thus emphasizing the importance of attitude to job performance. For mysterious reasons, the term *attitude* in colloquial language often connotes a *negative* attitude. More accurately, an **attitude** is a predisposition to respond that exerts an influence on a person's response to a person, a thing, an idea, or a situation. Attitudes are an important part of human relations because they are linked with perception and motivation. For example, your attitude toward a coworker influences your perception of how favorably you evaluate his or her work, and you will be better motivated if you have a positive attitude toward your work. Having and displaying positive attitudes will also help you build better relationships with coworkers, managers, and customers.

Our study of attitudes includes the components of attitudes, how attitudes are acquired, how they are changed, the importance of positive attitudes, how companies attempt to enhance positive attitudes and job satisfaction, and organizational citizenship behavior.

COMPONENTS OF ATTITUDES

Attitudes are complex, having three components, as shown in Figure 4-2. The **cognitive component** refers to the knowledge or intellectual beliefs an individual might have about an object (an idea, a person, a thing, or a situation). A market researcher might

FIGURE 4-2
THE THREE COMPONENTS OF ATTITUDES
Observe that the three components of attitudes influence each other and that the attitude toward a subject, person, object, or thing is the combined effect of the cognitive, affective, and behavioral components.

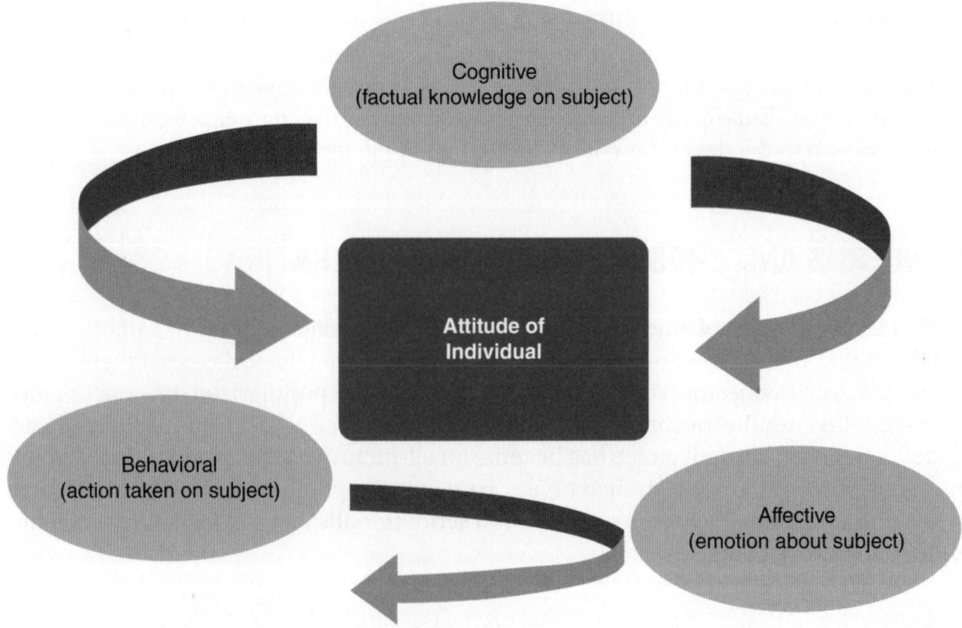

have accumulated considerable factual information about statistics (such as sampling procedures) and software for running data. The researcher might, therefore, have a positive attitude toward statistics.

The feeling or **affective component** refers to the emotion connected with an object or a task. The market researcher mentioned might basically like statistical analysis because of some pleasant experiences in college associated with statistics. The **behavioral component** refers to how a person acts. The market researcher might make positive statements about statistical methods or emphasize them in his or her reports.

Affective component
(of attitude) the emotion connected with an object or a task

Behavioral component
(of attitude) how a person acts

The cognitive, affective, and behavioral aspects of attitudes are interrelated. A change in one of the components will set in motion a change in one or more of the others. If you have more facts about an object or process (cognitive), you form the basis for a more positive emotional response to the object (affective). In turn, your behavior toward that object would probably become more favorable. For example, if you have considerable information about the contribution of feedback to personal development, you might have a positive feeling toward feedback. When receiving feedback, therefore, you would act favorably.

Moods are similar to the affective component of an attitude, yet are not the same thing. A mood is a short-term response associated with one stimulus, such as being in a bad mood because your vehicle was dented while in the company parking lot.[11] An attitude is a longer-term disposition or inner tendency such as having a favorable attitude about the work ethic of Mexicans.

At times, people do not experience the type of consistency previously described and feel compelled to search for consistency. **Cognitive dissonance** is the situation in which the pieces of knowledge, information, attitudes, or beliefs held by an individual are contradictory. When a person experiences cognitive dissonance, the relationship between attitudes and behaviors is altered. People search for ways to reduce internal conflicts when they experience a clash between the information they receive and their actions or attitudes. The same process is used when a person has to resolve two inconsistent sets of information.

Cognitive dissonance
situation in which the pieces of knowledge, information, attitudes, or beliefs held by an individual are contradictory

A typical example of cognitive dissonance on the job might occur when a worker believes that the report she submits to team members is of high quality; her teammates, however, tell her the report is flawed and requires substantial revisions. To reduce the dissonance, the worker might conveniently ignore the criticism. Or the worker might reason that she is the resident expert on the topic of the report, and her teammates, therefore, are not qualified to judge the merits of her report.

HOW ATTITUDES ARE FORMED

Attitudes usually are based on experience. Assume that you visited a convenience store, and you left your wallet on the counter without realizing it. Your wallet contained your credit cards, debit cards, driver's license, $150 in cash, and personal items. On your way home you receive a phone call from the clerk, informing you that he is holding your wallet for you. You most likely develop an immediate positive attitude toward the convenience store, the clerk, and perhaps toward other people of his ethnic group. Next we look more closely at the processes underlying attitude formation.[12]

A starting point in developing attitudes is to receive direct instruction from another individual. A friend whose opinion you respect tells you that e-filing of income tax is fast, efficient, and modern. You might quickly have a positive attitude toward e-filing. Similarly, you might develop a positive attitude through modeling the behavior of another person. You have seen that your trusted friend e-files her income tax, so you develop a positive attitude toward e-filing.

Conditioning, or making associations, also contributes to attitude formation, as in the example of the convenience store. The attitudes that we develop based on conditioning or associations usually develop after at least several exposures. You might develop a favorable attitude toward the human resources (HR) department if you asked for help several times, and each time you received useful advice. In contrast, you might have developed negative attitudes toward HR if a department representative was unhelpful at each visit.

The way we think about things, or our *cognitions,* can influence attitude formation. You might be quite content with your salary and benefits provided by your employer. You then visit www.salary.com and discover that you make much less than other workers in your city performing the same work. As a result, your attitude toward your salary and benefits plunges.

The deepest contributor to attitude formation could be a person's standing on the personality trait of optimism. People with a high degree of optimism are predisposed toward viewing events, persons, places, and things as positive, which in turn leads to a positive attitude. In contrast, people who have a high standing on pessimism will harbor many negative attitudes. Many workers who have chronically low job satisfaction are pessimistic at the core.[13]

THE IMPORTANCE OF POSITIVE ATTITUDES

Positive attitudes have always been the foundation of effective human relations, as reflected in the writings of Dale Carnegie, the pioneer of the popular (rather than scientific) approach to human relations. He emphasized such truisms as "Don't criticize, condemn, or complain," and "Talk in terms of the other person's interests."

In recent years positive attitudes have also become of interest to human relations specialists, as reflected in the fields called positive psychology and positive organizational studies. A major thrust of these fields is to enhance our experiences of enjoyment of work, as well as love and play. The assumption is that when employees are in a positive mood, they are typically more creative, better motivated to perform well, and more helpful toward coworkers.[14]

A worker who consistently maintains a *genuine* positive attitude will accrue many benefits. Being genuine is important because people with good emotional intelligence can readily detect a phony smile used as a cover-up for anger. Assuming the worker with a positive attitude backs it up with good performance, he or she is more likely to (a) be liked by customers, (b) close more sales, (c) receive good performance reviews, (d) receive favorable work assignments, and (e) be promoted.

Another potential benefit of having a positive attitude is that it makes you a more desirable coworker. Denise Keller, the chief operating officer of Benchmark Email, contends that because nobody wants to work with a complainer, an optimistic attitude is essential. These are the "glass is always half full" workers who readily perceive the good in a situation.[15]

Positive moods also make a positive impact on job performance and company productivity. A study with customer service representatives found that at a large company found that reps who were happy at the start of the day usually stayed that way as the day progressed. The reps in a good mood generally felt more positively after talking with customers. As a result, they provided better service on subsequent calls. One of the conclusions drawn in the study was that reinforcing good moods, such as offering cookies in the break room, may lead to in improvement in work quality.[16]

A mild note of caution is that there is a negative side to workers being too positive. As analyzed by Judge and Ilies, putting on a happy face can lead to stress, burnout, and job dissatisfaction. Workers who have an unrealistically positive self-concept might become self-centered and manipulative and think they deserve more attention and rewards than other workers.[17] Also a little negativity and cynicism is helpful in jobs such as auditor, budget analyst, tax accountant, and store detective. Sometimes being suspicious and negative contributes to a job role. Pessimism about a potential outcome can help mobilize us to act quickly to avoid future problems, such as the person who purchases an offsite backup service for valuable computer files.[18]

HOW ATTITUDES ARE CHANGED

In general, attitudes can be changed by reversing the processes by which they were formed. Yet, we can look at the process of attitude change more specifically. First, we might receive information from a source we trust. A manager might have negative attitudes toward the value of employee training but then reads in a reliable business magazine that IBM spends more than $5,000 per employee annually on training. As a consequence, the manager develops a more favorable attitude toward training. A person might also be reconditioned to bring about attitude change. A small-business owner might have a negative attitude toward e-filing income taxes because of the need to learn new skills combined with a fear of lack of security. After trying e-filing for two consecutive years because of being almost forced to by the law, the business owner receives refunds promptly and find the process not really so complicated. So her attitude toward e-filing becomes reconditioned in a positive direction.

Another way to change attitudes is to learn to look at the positive or negative aspect of situations, if you are a pessimist or optimist, respectively. A pessimistic person should concentrate on searching for the positive elements of a situation, such as a supervisor saying to himself or herself, "Okay, this employee is a pill, but maybe there is something good about him."

In contrast, a naturally optimistic person might learn to say, "I tend to fall in love with the credentials of most job candidates. So maybe I should scrutinize this candidate more carefully."

Looking at the positive aspects of a situation to change your attitude is often a question of where you choose to focus your attention. What we see tends to shape how we feel. Suppose you dislike your job. The way to change your attitude is to write down every single thing you like about your job, even something small, like the free espresso. It is also helpful to maintain a list of anything positive that happens to you during the workday. An example might be, "Today Laura showed me how to position my mouse over a false e-mail address to uncover the true address. I found that interesting." Keep in mind also that you are being paid, and without paid work a person cannot live independently.[19]

HOW COMPANIES ENCOURAGE POSITIVE ATTITUDES AND JOB SATISFACTION

From the standpoint of management it is beneficial for employees to have positive attitudes and job satisfaction. These two emotional states contribute to better customer service, less absenteeism and tardiness, less turnover, and often higher productivity. The logic is that satisfied employees will lead to satisfied customers, resulting in a more profitable business. Much of the effort of human resource professionals is aimed at making employees more content. Among the hundreds of possible company initiatives to foster positive attitudes and high job satisfaction among employees are flexible working hours, recognition awards, company picnics, financial bonuses, time off for birthdays, on-site haircuts, and on-premises child-care centers. Following are three specific examples of companies voted among the 100 Best Companies to Work For (as evaluated by *Fortune* magazine) to enhance employee attitudes and satisfaction.[20]

SAS Institute, Cary, North Carolina (Enterprise software for organizations, 6,046 employees). Voted in the top 100 for fifteen years, this software giant is known for its employee perks including onsite health care, summer camp for children, car cleaning, intramural sports leagues, and a full-size gym.

Carmax, Richmond, Virginia (retail used-car chain, 15,565 employees). The company survived a two-year recession in the used-car business, and then rebounded in 2010–2011 by hiring 1,200 new employees, and awarding the largest bonuses it its history. Each used-car location is sparkling clean and is staffed by well-mannered, pleasant workers.

Scott Trade, St. Louis, Missouri (discount brokerage, 3,138). Employees are entitled to earn 5 percent on their checking accounts if they use the company-owned bank. A feeling of job security pervades the company because so far they have never had a layoff.

Although companies invest considerable money in satisfying employees, a good deal of job satisfaction stems from positive interpersonal relationships in the work environment. A comprehensive study about job satisfaction was conducted with 540 people in a variety of positions, including teachers, physicians, and construction workers. The nature of the work, such as having a variety of interesting tasks to perform, contributed to job satisfaction. A bigger impact on job satisfaction, however, stemmed from frequent interaction with others, office friendship, and receiving emotional support from supervisors and coworkers.[21]

ORGANIZATIONAL CITIZENSHIP BEHAVIOR

Organizational citizenship behavior (OCB)
the willingness to go beyond one's job description to help the company, even if such an act does not lead to an immediate reward

An employee attitude highly valued by employers is **organizational citizenship behavior (OCB)**—the willingness to go beyond one's job description to help the company, even if such an act does not lead to an immediate reward. Being a good organizational citizen is also tied in with values, because the person who goes beyond the job description to help others most likely has a strong work ethic and values helping others. Human Relations Self-Assessment Quiz 4-1 offers you an opportunity to think through your actual or potential tendencies toward organizational citizenship behavior. Several examples of good organizational citizenship follow:

- Melissa helps an employee in another department with a currency exchange problem because she has skill in this area, but Melissa's job does not involve working with currency exchange.
- Joshua, a business intern, observes that the office in which he works seems glum. So he goes out of his way to be cheerful to others and offers compliments for work well done.

Penelope, a gifted information technology person, is walking down the aisle toward her cubicle. She notices a worker from another department with a panicked look on his face as he stares into his computer monitor. Penelope asks if there is anything she can do to help and proceeds to transfer valuable data from a corrupted file to a new file for the employee in panic.

Organizational citizenship behavior is so important to organizations that this set of attitudes has been the subject of many studies. A general finding has been that as a

Human Relations Self-Assessment Quiz 4-1

My Tendencies Toward Organizational Citizenship Behavior

Describe whether each of the statements in the quiz below is mostly true or mostly false about you. If you have not experienced the situation, estimate whether it would be most likely true or most likely false about you.

Number	Statement about Organizational Citizenship Behavior	Mostly True	Mostly False
1.	I have helped a coworker with a work problem without being asked.	❑	❑
2.	I pick up litter in the company parking lot or outside of the building, and then dispose of the litter properly.	❑	❑
3.	Helping others is an important part of my job even if I am not a manager.	❑	❑
4.	I make a special effort to say thank you and smile when somebody helps me in any way on the job.	❑	❑
5.	I volunteer to do a nonglamorous task when nobody in particular has responsibility for the task.	❑	❑
6.	If I found an apparently intoxicated person sleeping on the ground outside my workplace, I would call for help rather than leaving him or her lying there.	❑	❑
7.	I am pretty good at putting myself in another worker's place and understanding his or her perspective.	❑	❑
8.	I do my best to give effective comforting messages to other workers in distress.	❑	❑
9.	I am able to initiate, maintain, and terminate casual conversations with coworkers.	❑	❑
10.	During group meetings, I listen carefully to whomever is speaking to the group without performing another task such as looking at a smart phone placed on my lap.	❑	❑
11.	If my company faced an emergency such as a flood or hurricane, I would tell my supervisor that I will be on call twenty-four hours per day to help out.	❑	❑
12.	I have covered for workers who were absent or out on a break.	❑	❑
13.	I check with others before doing something that would affect their work.	❑	❑
14.	Even if I disliked a coworker, I would help him or her with a difficult problem.	❑	❑
15.	I help people outside my workgroup when I have the right knowledge or skill.	❑	❑
16.	I am willing to do work not in my job description even if the effort means that I will have to work a couple of extra hours.	❑	❑
17.	I am willing to point to things the workgroup might be doing wrong, even if others disagree with me.	❑	❑
18.	I am willing to risk disapproval in order to do what is best for the company.	❑	❑
19.	I challenge work procedures and rules that seem to be nonproductive.	❑	❑
20.	I have tried to resolve person-to-person conflicts between workers in my department or unit.	❑	❑
21.	I do what I can to raise the spirits of coworkers having problems on the job.	❑	❑
22.	If I pick up some new job-related knowledge, I will share it with team members for whom the knowledge is useful.	❑	❑
23.	When I think of something that will help the entire company, I will share that knowledge with my manager and/or company leadership.	❑	❑
24.	I have politely voiced my concerns about something I think the company is doing wrong.	❑	❑
25.	If I see a social media comment about our company that seems significant, I will forward that comment to the right person in my company.	❑	❑

(continued)

Scoring and Interpretation:

Count the number of statements that you indicated are mostly true.

18–25 points You have strong tendencies toward displaying positive organizational citizenship behavior. Your initiative and other proactive behavior will probably be an asset in your career.

7–17 points You have about average tendencies with respect to engaging in positive organizational citizenship behavior. It would be helpful for you in your career to seek out ways to help coworkers and the company besides performing well in your own job.

0–7 points You take very little initiative to work outside the limits of your job description. You run the risk of being perceived as not caring about the welfare of coworkers to the company. Such a negative perception could be a negative in terms of you being regarded as eligible for promotion.

Source: Several of the statements in this quiz are based on Scott B. MacKenzie, Philip M. Podaskoff, and Nathan P. Podaskoff, "Challenge-Oriented Organizational Citizenship Behaviors and Organizational Effectiveness: Do Challenge-Oriented Behaviors Really Have an Impact on the Organization's Bottom Line?" *Personnel Psychology*, Number 3, 2011, p. 574; Theresa M. Glomb, Devasheesh P. Bhave, Andrew G. Miner, and Melanie Wall, "Doing Good, Feeling Good: Examining the Role of Organizational Citizenship Behaviors in Changing Mood," *Personnel Psychology*, 2011, Number 1, p. 204; Nicole M. Dudley and Jose M. Cortina, "Knowledge and Skills that Facilitate the Personal Support Dimension of Citizenship," *Journal of Applied Psychology*, November 2008, p. 1253.

result of many workers being good organizational citizens, the organization functions more effectively in such ways as improved productivity, reduced costs, customer satisfaction, and reduced turnover. Employees who are good organizational citizens also benefit because they are more likely to perform better, and as a result obtain better performance reviews and salary increases.[22]

Personal support assisting others in the workplace through the use of interpersonal skills

The personal support dimension of OCB will help you understand how citizenship behavior contributes directly to effective human relations in the workplace. **Personal support** refers to assisting others in the workplace through the use of interpersonal skills. As outlined in Figure 4-3, and presented next, the personal support dimension has four components, or subdimensions.[23] The three examples presented above involve a mixture of personal support and task-related assistance. Here is the difference: Penelope, just mentioned, is providing personal support when she helps the frustrated computer user calm down. She provides task-related assistance when she transfers the data to a new file.

FIGURE 4-3
THE FOUR COMPONENTS OF THE PERSONAL SUPPORT DIMENSION OF ORGANIZATIONAL CITIZENSHIP BEHAVIOR

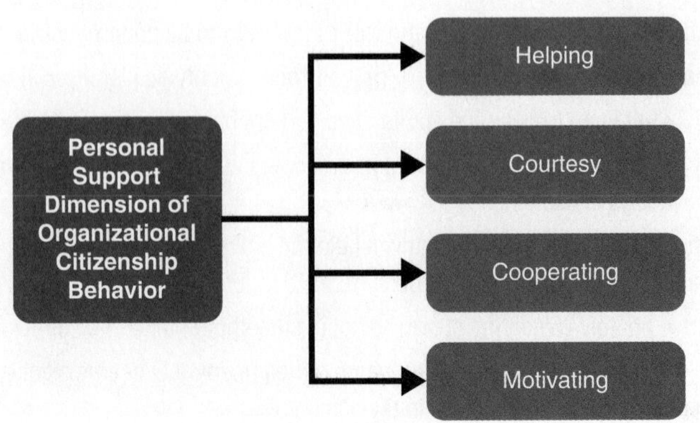

1. ***Helping.*** Person-focused helping includes self-esteem maintenance and other more personal problem-solving behaviors. Penelope would be engaged in self-esteem maintenance if she said to the man she was helping, "Don't feel bad; even IT support staff have trouble with corrupted files." Helping behavior contributes to organizational effectiveness when the help is of high technical quality. If Penelope calms down the man she is trying to help but does not help him with the corrupted file, not much has been accomplished for the organization.
2. ***Courtesy.*** In general, courtesy involves showing consideration and tact in interpersonal relationships. Although courtesy might be regarded as expected behavior on the job, many workers are rude and discourteous toward each other. Being courteous therefore stands out as part of organizational citizenship behavior. An example of courteous behavior during a department meeting would be to listen intently to the presenter without engaging in other activities, even if the person bored you.
3. ***Cooperating.*** A person who cooperates on the job willfully contributes time, effort, and resources to accomplish joint tasks. As a member of a team, you are expected to cooperate. In terms of citizenship behavior, cooperating includes accepting the suggestions of work associates, following their lead, and placing team objectives over personal interests. Included also in cooperation is informing others of events or requirements that may affect them. Cooperation is mostly clearly part of OCB when you go out of your way to cooperate with people outside of your immediate work unit. An example would be sending a job-relevant Web link to someone in another department.
4. ***Motivating.*** As related to organizational citizenship behavior, motivating behaviors include applauding the achievements and successes of coworkers, encouraging them when they face adversity, and helping them overcome setbacks. Expressing confidence in coworkers, and perhaps supervisors, is also part of the motivating component of personal support. In the example of Melissa presented above, she might have to encourage the person she is helping to study more about currency exchange. In sum, you are a good organizational citizen if you are helpful, courteous, cooperative, and motivational, even if these behaviors are not part of your job description.

What Is Happiness, and How Can It Be Acquired and Enhanced?

◀ Learning Objective 3 ◀

When asked "What is the most important thing in life?" many people respond, "Happiness." (Happiness is a positive emotion.) Psychology professor at Harvard Daniel Gilbert, argues that happiness is the ultimate goal of virtually all decisions we make. The measure of a good decision is whether it leads to well-being, pleasure, happiness, joy, or contentment. Research and opinion on the topic indicate that people can take concrete steps to achieve happiness.[24] Happier people have better physical health, live longer, achieve more career success, work harder, and are more caring and socially engaged. Misery can lead to self-obsession and inactivity.[25] Based partially on the importance of happiness for well-being, there has been a surge of writing and study about happiness in recent years. Companies have developed an interest in developing specific ways of elevating employee happiness, as illustrated in the accompanying Human Relations in Practice.

Human Relations in Practice

Companies Hire Happiness Coach Shawn Achor

If you see Shawn Achor in person or a photo of him, he always has a positive expression on his face—never a scowl. Little wonder because he is one of the world's best known happiness coaches. Achor holds a Master's degree from the Harvard Divinity School, and for several years taught one of the most popular classes at Harvard, "Positive Psychology." He is hired regularly by business firms to help get the workforce to think positively and be happy in order to be more productive, and experience less sick time.

Among Achor's clients have been UBS, Credit Suisse, and American Express. He says that the first day he visited UBS in 2008, employees were ashen faced. They were so stressed that they hardly even looked at their smart phones. "All these banks were in such dire straits, that employees had just stopped working," says Achor. To jumpstart the finance specialists, Achor held happiness seminars that explained the contagious nature of positive emotion, and emphasized the value of psychological wealth in contrast to financial wealth.

At client firms, Achor urges employees to meditate, send regular e-mail messages thanking coworkers for their help, and help others without expecting something in return. Employees are also encouraged to keep a journal of happenings they are grateful for.

Achor provides research evidence to companies suggesting that workers with more positive attitudes have higher job performance, get stronger performance reviews, are more creative, and better team players. He also makes the case that the single greatest advantage in the modern economy is a happy and engaged workforce. According to Achor, a decade of research demonstrates that the happiness increases nearly every business and educational outcome. Sales increase by 37 percent, productivity by 31 percent, and task accuracy by 19 percent, as well as numerous health and quality-of-life improvements.

Question: Some critics of Achor and other happiness coaches say "hogwash," that pushing positive thinking is simply a way for management to improve morale while managers burden employees with threats of job loss and heavy workloads. What is your opinion of this criticism?

Source: The original story above is created based on facts from the following: Shawn Achor, "Positive Intelligence," *Harvard Business Review*, January–February 201, pp. 100–102; Achor,"The Happiness Dividend," *SpeakersOffice, Inc.* (http://blog.speakersoffice.com), October 19, 2011, pp. 1–4; Sue Shellenbarger, "Thinking Happy Thoughts at Work," *The Wall Street Journal*, January 27, 2010, p. D2; Achor, "Make Stress Work for You," http://blogs.hbr.org, February 15, 2011, pp. 1–2; "Workplace Blues? Call a 'Happiness Coach'," http://blogs.wsj.com/juggle, January 27, 2010, pp. 1–2; Michelle Conlin, "Wall Street: Paging Dr. Happy," *Businessweek*, December 7, 2009, p. 057.

Our approach to the unlimited topic of understanding how to achieve happiness involves a model of happiness and a summary description of keys to happiness. To start thinking of happiness as it applies to you, take Human Relations Self-Assessment Quiz 4-2.

THE SPHERES OF LIFE AND HAPPINESS

A practical way of understanding happiness is that it is a byproduct of having the various components of life working in harmony and synchrony. To understand this approach, visualize about six gears with teeth, spinning in unison. As long as all gears are

Human Relations Self-Assessment Quiz 4-2

The Happiness Checklist

Indicate whether you agree (A) or disagree (D) with the following statements.

Number	Statement about Happiness	A	D
1.	I look forward to almost every day.	_____	_____
2.	I love at least two other persons including family members.	_____	_____
3.	I have no interests outside of work or school	_____	_____
4.	It doesn't bother me when I learn that somebody else earns more money than I do now or will earn in the future.	_____	_____
5.	It disturbs me when I recognize that so many people are better looking than I am.	_____	_____
6.	I like my body.	_____	_____
7.	I am passionate about at least one interest outside of work or school.	_____	_____
8.	Thinking about how happy or unhappy I am makes me anxious.	_____	_____
9.	It makes me happy to see other people happy.	_____	_____
10.	Some things that are free or cost very little make me happy.	_____	_____

Scoring and Interpretation:

Happiness is difficult to measure on a scale, but the more the number of items you scored in the direction of happiness, the happier you probably are. "Agree" in response to the following items suggests happiness: 1. 2, 4, 6. 7, 9, and 10. "Disagree" in response to the following items suggests happiness: 3, 4, and 8.

moving properly (and no teeth are broken), a state of equilibrium and fluid motion is achieved. Similarly, imagine that life has six major components. The exact components will differ among people. For most people, the components would be approximately as follows:

1. Work and career
2. Interpersonal life, including loved ones and romantic life
3. Physical and mental health
4. Financial health
5. Interests and pastimes, including reading, surfing the Internet, and sports
6. A spiritual life or belief system, including religion, science, or astrology

When you have ample satisfactions in all six spheres, you achieve happiness. However, when a deficiency occurs in any of these six factors, your spheres are no longer in harmony, and dissatisfaction or unhappiness occurs. Yet, sometimes if you are having problems in one sphere, satisfaction in the other spheres can compensate temporarily for a deficiency in one. For the long range, a state of happiness depends on all six spheres working in harmony. In short, the theme of this book surfaces again: Work and personal life are mutually supportive. Figure 4-4 presents the spheres-of-life model of happiness.

FIGURE 4-4

THE SPHERES-OF-LIFE MODEL OF HAPPINESS

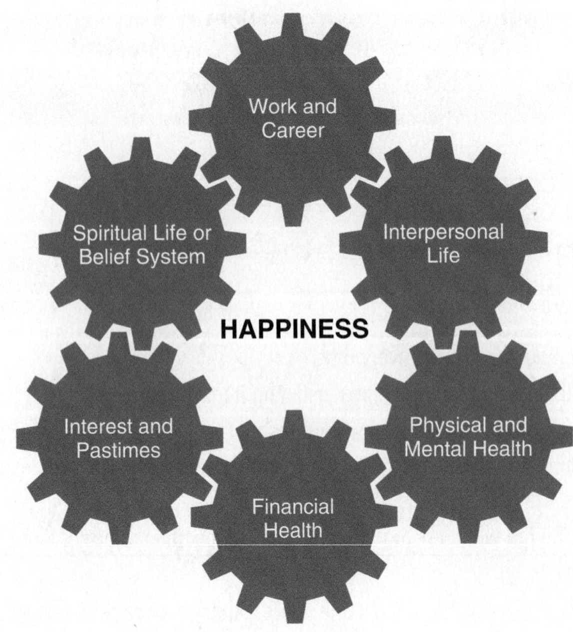

People vary as to how much importance they attach to each sphere of life. A person with intense career ambitions, for example, might place less weight on the interests sphere than would a more leisure-oriented person. However, if any of these spheres are grossly deficient, total happiness will not be forthcoming. Another source of variation is that the importance people attach to each sphere may vary according to the stage of life. If you are a full-time student, for example, you might need just enough money to avoid worrying about finances. However, after about ten years of full-time career experience, your expenses might peak. You would then attach more importance to the financial sphere.

THE KEYS TO HAPPINESS

If you are aware of known contributors to happiness, you might be able to enhance your happiness. Fortunately there is some consistency in information about what makes people happy. Here we summarize and synthesize a wide range of research and opinion on the keys to happiness.[26]

Give High Priority to the Pursuit of Happiness

Having the intention or goal of being happy will enhance your chances of being happy. A key principle is to discover what makes you happy and make the time to pursue those activities, as spending time doing what you enjoy contributes directly to happiness. University of California–Riverside psychology professor Sonja Lyubormirsky has researched routines to help people become happy by focusing on happiness, thereby systematically pursuing happiness. Her research shows that you need to put intentional effort into becoming happier. If people think about happy life events every day for three days, within four weeks they are happier than they were before they started this routine.[27] If you are going through a particularly unhappy period, you may have to stretch to think of a few happy life events. For example, did anybody pay you a compliment about anything you did or said recently? Did you help anybody recently who thanked you for your kindness?

Develop and Maintain Friendships with Happy People

An overwhelming finding about happiness is that positive interactions with people facilitate being happy. To quote Daniel Gilbert, "If I had to summarize all the scientific literature on the causes of human happiness in one word, that would be 'social' ".[28] (*Social* in this context means interaction with people, not exclusively social media on the Internet.) Evidence indicates that getting connected to happy people is especially important for improving a person's own happiness. Nicholas Christakis, a professor of medical sociology at Harvard Medical School, and James Fowler, a political scientist at the University of California–San Diego, surveyed the emotional state of about 5,000 people and the 50,000 social ties they shared. Happiness level, or emotional state, was measured at various points. Happiness was measured by asking people how often during the past week they could say, (a) I enjoyed life, (b) I was happy, (c) I felt hopeful about the future, and (d) I felt that I was just as good as other people.

The study found that happiness is contagious. If a participant's friend was happy, that participant was 15 percent more likely to be happy. If the friend of a participant's friend was happy, the original participant was 10 percent more likely to be happy. The happiness chain even extended further out, with a happy friend of a friend, of a friend giving a 5.6 percent boost to the original participant's happiness.

Another key finding was that people with the most social connections, including friends, spouses, neighbors, and relatives, were also the happiest. Each additional person in your network makes you happier. Spouses and other live-in partners who are happy increase the likelihood of their partners being happy by 8 percent. Happy siblings living nearby boosted life satisfaction 14 percent, and happy neighbors increased happiness levels by 34 percent.

The "friends" in this study were mostly traditional friends, not the type of "friends" you contact on social networks like Facebook and Twitter. Yet, the study also found that people who are smiling on their Facebook photos tend to cluster together, forming an online social circle.[29]

Develop a Sense of Self-Esteem

Self-love must precede love for others. High self-esteem enables one to love and be loved. Developing a good self-image leads to the self-esteem required for loving relationships. An early contributor to the importance of thinking positively about oneself was Emile Coué, a French psychologist. He made a name for himself in the twentieth century by teaching that mental health could be achieved by repeating the sentence, "Every day and in every way I'm becoming better and better."[30]

A feeling of self-worth is important because it helps prevent being overwhelmed by criticism. An important part of developing self-esteem is to not want financial success more than other things. Insecure people seek society's approval in the form of purchasing consumer goods and accumulating investments. (In this way the person might be admired by others.) The accompanying Core Self-Evaluations Scale (Human Relations Self-Assessment Quiz 4-3) is a scientifically developed instrument that gives you an opportunity to assess how positively you think about yourself.

Work Hard at What You Enjoy and Achieve the Flow Experience

To achieve happiness, it is necessary to find a career that fits your most intense interests. In addition, it helps to achieve regularly the flow experience of total involvement in what you are doing at the moment. Happiness stemming from flow is powerful because it is not dependent on favorable external circumstances, such as recognition or love. The individual creates the happiness that follows from flow. Hard work contributes to happiness in another important way. A fundamental secret of happiness is accomplishing things and savoring what you have accomplished. Happiness researcher

Human Relations Self-Assessment Quiz 4-3

The Core Self-Evaluations Scale

Below are several statements about you with which you may agree or disagree. Using the response scale below, indicate your agreement or disagreement with each item by placing the appropriate number on the line preceding that item.

1	2	3	4	5
Strongly Disagree	Disagree	Neutral	Agree	Strongly Agree

1. ________ I am confident I get the success I deserve.
2. ________ Sometimes I feel depressed.
3. ________ When I try, I generally succeed.
4. ________ Sometimes when I fail, I feel worthless.
5. ________ I complete tasks successfully.
6. ________ Sometimes, I do not feel in control of my work.
7. ________ Overall, I am satisfied with myself.
8. ________ I am filled with doubts about my competence.
9. ________ I determine what will happen in my life.
10. ________ I do not feel in control of my success in my career.
11. ________ I am capable of coping with most of my problems.
12. ________ There are times when things look pretty bleak and hopeless to me.
________ Total Score

Scoring and Interpretation:

The scoring for items 1, 3, 5, 7, 9, and 11 proceeds as follows: 5, 4, 3, 2, 1 to indicate a positive attitude toward yourself. The scoring for questions 2, 4, 6, 8, 10, and 12 proceeds as follows: 1, 2, 3, 4, 5 to indicate a positive attitude toward yourself. Add all your scores to attain your total score. The higher the score, the more positive your attitude toward yourself. Scores of 48 and higher suggest a very positive attitude, scores between 37 and 47 suggest a neutral attitude, and scores between 12 and 35 indicate a negative attitude toward yourself. The mean score for several different groups of people, including working adults and students, is 45.

Source: Timothy A. Judge, Amir Erez, Joyce E. Bono, and Carl J. Thoresen, "The Core Self-Evaluation Scale: Development of a Measure," *Personnel Psychology*, Summer 2003, p. 315. This measure is nonproprietary (free) and may be used without permission.

David T. Lykken argues that happiness is available to anyone who develops skills, interests, and goals that he or she finds meaningful and enjoyable.[31] The successful pursuit of goals therefore contributes enormously to happiness. A log cabin dweller who lived off the land and whose goal was to be close to nature would therefore be happier than a wealthy person in a luxurious house who was not leading the lifestyle he or she wanted.

Appreciate the Joys of Day-to-Day Living

Hedonic adaptation
the tendency to adapt to regard exciting new aspects of life as routine after a while

A major obstacle to happiness is **hedonic adaptation**—the tendency to adapt to regard exciting new aspects of life as routine after a while.[32] Imagine a person who wants a luxurious lifestyle finally purchases a fiftieth-story condominium penthouse overlooking a harbor.

At first the view is breathtaking, yet after a while looking at the harbor becomes routine. To overcome the hedonic adaptation you therefore have to learn to appreciate the joys of day-to-day living. The essence of being a happy person is to savor what you have right now. As Benjamin Franklin said, "Happiness is produced not so much by great pieces of good fortune that seldom happen as by the little advantages that occur every day."

Part of the same key to happiness is the ability to live in the present without undue worry about the future or dwelling on past mistakes. Be on guard against becoming so preoccupied with planning your life that you neglect to enjoy the happiness of the moment.

Be Fair, Kind, and Helpful, and Trust Others

The Golden Rule is a true contributor to happiness. It is also important to practice charity and forgiveness. Helping others brings personal happiness. Knowing that you are able to make a contribution to the welfare of others gives you a continuing sense of satisfaction and happiness. Related to fairness and kindness is trust of others. Happy people have open, warm, and friendly attitudes.

Have Recreational Fun in Your Life

A happy life is characterized by fun, zest, joy, and delight. When you create time for fun (in addition to the fun in many kinds of work), you add an important element to your personal happiness. But if you devote too much time to play, you will lose out on the fun of work accomplishments. In choosing fun activities, avoid overplanning. Because novelty contributes to happiness, be ready to pursue an unexpected opportunity or to try something different.

Learn to Cope with Grief, Disappointment, Setbacks, and Stress

To be happy, you must learn how to face problems that occur in life without being overwhelmed or running away. It is also important to persevere in attempting to overcome problems rather than to whine or engage in self-pity. Once you have had to cope with problems, you will be more able to appreciate the day-to-day joys of life. An example of an everyday problem that ranks high on the misery list is lengthy commutes to work, by private or public transportation.[33] If you cannot change the length of the commute for now, find ways to make commuting more enjoyable, such as finding a radio station that provides information useful for your professional growth or is simply enjoyable.

Live with What You Cannot Change

Happiness guru Martin Seligman says that attempting to change conditions unlikely to change sets us up for feeling depressed about failing. Weight loss is a prime example. Nineteen out of twenty people regain weight they lost. It is, therefore, better to worry less about weight loss and concentrate on staying in good physical condition by engaging in moderate exercise. Good condition contributes much more to health than does achieving a weight standard set primarily to achieve an aesthetic standard. You can then concentrate on being happy about your good physical condition instead of being unhappy about your weight.[34]

Energize Yourself through Physical Fitness

Engage in regular physical activity, such as dancing or sports that make you aerobically fit. Whether it is the endorphins released by exercise, dopamine released by the excitement, or simply the relaxed muscles, physical fitness fosters happiness. Physical fitness also contributes to happiness because it helps us minimize the unhappiness linked to physical and mental illness. Another important part of energizing yourself is to attain adequate rest. Happy people invest time in revitalizing sleep and solitude.

Satisfy Your Most Important Values

Based on a survey of more than 6,000 individuals, social psychologist Steven Reiss concluded that people cannot find lasting happiness by aiming to have more fun or seeking pleasure. Instead, you have to satisfy your basic values or desires and take happiness in passing. To increase your value-based happiness, you have to first identify your most important desires and then gear your life toward satisfying these values. Among these key values are curiosity, physical activity, honor, power, family, status, and romance.[35] For example, if power and romance are two of your basic values, you can achieve happiness only if your life is amply provided with power and romance. Religion also fits into the realm of values, and religious people tend to be happier than nonreligious people, particularly in societies under stress such as facing adequate food, job, and healthcare.[36]

To attain happiness by living your values, you first have to know what your values are. Physician and happiness counselor Russ Harris suggests that you answer the following question to identify your key values: "Imagine you could wave a magic wand to ensure that you would have the approval and admiration of everyone on the planet, forever. What, in this case, would you choose to do with your life?"[37] (The topic of values will be explored in Chapter 5.)

Earn Enough Money to Do Meaningful Things and Avoid Misery

The role of money as a contributor to happiness is the subject of endless debate. Money cannot buy happiness, but having enough money to purchase the things that make you happy is important. Whether an iPad or owing a high-performance sports car would make you happy, they both require money—even though the amounts differ. It is widely acknowledged that helping less fortunate people contributes to a person's happiness. A person who decides to purchase a holiday meal for 100 residents of a mission for the homeless would need discretionary money to execute this act of generosity. Feeding the homeless would in turn contribute to his or her happiness. However, the pursuit of money for its own sake is less likely to contribute to happiness.

Recent data suggest that earning more than $75,000 per year does not yield additional happiness. Even more important than a specific income level is which group we use for comparison. If your comparison group has elevated income, such as big-company CEOs or successful investment bankers, your cutoff point for contentment will be higher.

More revealing than statistics about money and happiness is what we do with our money. Harvard Business School professor, Michael Norton observes that people often spend money to give them a short-term emotional lift, such as purchasing a rhinestone-studded smart phone case. Norton explains that spending money on experiences such as leisure and travel or friends or loved ones offers a better return on investment. Such purchases enhance the feelings of meaning and social connection than are the foundation of happiness.[38]

Another consideration is that not being able to pay for what you consider a necessity may lead to low self-esteem and unhappiness. Even if a person does not equate money with happiness, having a car repossessed or a house foreclosed contributes to at least a temporary state of unhappiness. As long as you have enough money to pay for what you consider to be necessities, money is not a factor in your happiness.

Lead a Meaningful Life

Most of the principles previously stated, as well as the spheres-of-life happiness model, all point toward the conclusion that having a meaningful life is a major contributor to happiness. For example, if you are a greeting card designer and you perceive that you are contributing to improved personal relationships, you are likely to be happy.

A major conclusion about attaining happiness is that it is the byproduct of working toward meaningful goals. For most people the maximum positive feelings are generated, and negative feelings avoided, when they attain a goal that stretches their capabilities, but is still within reach.[39] A meaning or an important purpose helps a person get through periodic annoyances that temporarily lower happiness.

Key Terms

Emotional intelligence, 94
Self-awareness, 94
Self-management, 94
Social awareness, 94
Relationship management, 94
Social intelligence, 96
Emotional contagion, 96
Attitude, 98
Affective component (of attitude), 99
Behavioral component (of attitude), 99
Cognitive dissonance, 99
Organizational citizenship behavior (OCB), 102
Personal support, 104
Hedonic adaptation, 110

Summary and Review

Emotional intelligence generally refers to how effectively a person makes constructive use of his or her emotions. The four key components of emotional intelligence are

1. Self-awareness (understanding the self)
2. Self-management (emotional control)
3. Social awareness (includes empathy and intuition)
4. Relationship management (includes interpersonal skills)

Demonstrating good emotional intelligence is impressive because it contributes to performing well in the difficult area of dealing with feelings. Another positive consequence of emotional intelligence is that if you know how to project positive emotion you will spread those positive feelings to others in the workplace. In some situations it will be helpful to be aware of possible cross-cultural differences in what constitutes effective emotional intelligence.

The combination of biological endowment and training will enable most people to enhance their emotional intelligence.

Attitudes are complex, having three components

1. Cognitive (knowledge or beliefs)
2. Affective (emotional)
3. Behavioral (how a person acts)

Cognitive dissonance occurs when the three components are not consistent with each other. Attitudes are formed based on experience, including receiving instruction from another person, conditioning, and cognitions (the way we think about something). The trait of optimism versus pessimism influences attitudes strongly. A worker who maintains a genuine positive attitude will accrue many benefits, yet being too positive can have disadvantages.

Attitudes can be changed by reversing the process by which they were formed. Looking at the positive or negative aspect of a situation can also lead to attitude change. From the standpoint of management it is beneficial for employees to have positive attitudes and job satisfaction. Much of job satisfaction stems from good interpersonal relationships in the workplace. Organizational citizenship behavior is highly valued by employers because such attitudes can lead to improved product quality and quantity. Personal support is one aspect of organizational citizenship behavior and includes helping, courtesy, cooperating, and motivating.

A practical way of understanding happiness is that it is a byproduct of having the spheres of life working in harmony and synchrony. For most people these spheres would be the following:

- Work and career
- Interpersonal life, including romance
- Physical and mental health
- Financial health
- Interests and pastimes
- Spiritual life or belief system

Contributors or keys to happiness include the following:

- Giving priority to happiness
- Developing and maintaining friendships with happy people
- Self-esteem

- Working hard at things enjoyed, and achieving the flow experience
- Appreciation of the joys of day-to-day living
- Fairness, kindness, helpfulness, and trust
- Recreational fun
- Coping with grief, disappointment, setbacks, and stress
- Living with what you cannot change
- Energizing yourself through physical fitness
- Satisfying your most important values
- Earning enough money to accomplish meaningful things and avoid feeling miserable

Check Your Understanding

1. What has one of your professors or instructors done recently to demonstrate good emotional intelligence in dealing with students?
2. Describe what a business executive, entertainer, or well-known athlete has done recently to demonstrate low emotional intelligence. Explain your reasoning.
3. Suppose the vast majority of company managers had high emotional intelligence. How might this fact give the company a competitive advantage?
4. Imagine yourself as a manager or team leader. What could you do to make positive use of emotional contagion with the people in your group?
5. How is a person supposed to maintain a positive attitude when major things in life are going wrong, such as a job loss, a personal bankruptcy, a broken relationship, or the premature death of a loved one?
6. Why do people often feel better when working with co-workers and a supervisor who have positive attitudes?
7. How do your "spheres of life" compare with those in Figure 4-4?
8. When you are happiest, are you more productive professionally/academically?
9. Assume that you are a business owner who is granted $15,000 to improve company productivity, and you are given two alternatives: software to improve operating efficiency or happiness training for employees. Make a choice and explain your reasoning.
10. Happiness researchers agree that having a high income is not necessarily associated with happiness. Yet at the same time activities that bring happiness, such as dining in restaurants, or taking vacations with friends and family, require considerable money. How does a person resolve this conflict?

Web Corner

Emotional intelligence:
www.eiconsortium.org; http://bx.businessweek.com/emotional-intelligence/news/

The Happiness Test:
www.pathwaytohappiness.com/happiness_test.htm

Positive attitudes:
www.attitudeiseverything.com.

Positive Psychology Center:
www.ppc.sas.upenn.edu

INTERNET SKILL BUILDER

Daily Doses of Happiness on the Web

Visit www.thehappyguy.com to receive your "daily dose of happiness." This site offers you happiness quotes and suggestions for self-actualization. The "Happy Guy" promises to help you achieve such ends as becoming inspired about life, discovering the meaning of happiness, and achieving personal growth. After trying out this program of happiness and personal growth, you be the judge. Have you made strides toward becoming happier? Do you feel any better emotionally? What impact do the Daily Happiness mugs have on your personal well-being? Be happy!

Developing Your Human Relations Skills

Human Relations Application Exercises

Applying Human Relations Exercise 4-1

Enhancing Your Emotional Intelligence

A realistic starting point in improving your emotional intelligence is to work with one of its four components at a time, such as the empathy aspect of social awareness. A complex behavior pattern or trait such as emotional intelligence takes considerable time to improve, but the time will most likely be a good investment. Follow these steps:

1. Begin by obtaining as much feedback as you can from people who know you. Ask them if they think you understand their emotional reactions and how well they think you understand them. It is helpful to ask someone from another culture or someone who has a severe disability how well you communicate with him or her. (A higher level of empathy is required to communicate well with somebody much different from you.) If you work with customers, ask them how well you appear to understand their position.
2. If you find any area of deficiency, work on that deficiency steadily. For example, perhaps you are not perceived as taking the time to understand a point of view quite different from your own. Attempt to understand other points of view. Suppose you believe strongly that only people with lots of money can be happy. Speak to a person with a different opinion and listen carefully until you understand that person's perspective.
3. At a minimum of a few weeks later, obtain more feedback about your ability to empathize. If you are making progress, continue to practice.
4. Prepare a document about your skill development. Describe the steps you took to enhance your empathy, the progress you made, and how people react differently to you now. For example, you might find that people talk more openly and freely with you now that you are more empathetic.
5. Then repeat these steps for another facet of emotional intelligence. As a result you will have developed another valuable interpersonal skill.

Applying Human Relations Exercise 4-2

Achieving Happiness

The following exercises will help you develop attitudes that contribute mightily to happiness.

1. **Start the day off right.** Begin each day with five minutes of positive thought and visualization. Commit to this for one week. When and how do you plan to fit this into your schedule?

   ____

   ____

   ____

2. **Make a list of five virtues in which you believe.** Examples would include patience, compassion, and helping the less fortunate.

   ____

   ____

   ____

3. **Each week, for the next five weeks, incorporate a different virtue into your life.** On a simple index card, write this week's virtue in bold letters, such as "helping the less fortunate." Post the card in a prominent place. After you have completed one incident of helping the less fortunate, describe in about ten to twenty-five words what you did. Also record the date and time.

   ____

   ____

   ____

4. **Look for good things about new acquaintances.** List three students, customers, or coworkers you have just met. List three *positive* qualities about each.

   ____

   ____

   ____

5. **List the positive qualities of fellow students or coworkers you dislike or have trouble working with.** Remember, keep looking for the good.

___

___

___

6. **Think of school assignments or job tasks you dislike, and write down the merits of these tasks.** Identify the benefits they bring you.

___

___

___

7. **Look at problems as opportunities.** What challenges are you now facing? In what way might you view them that would inspire and motivate you?

___

___

___

Source: The idea for this exercise stems from Stu Kamen, "Turn Negatives into Positives," *Pryor Report Success Workshop*, May 1995, pp. 1–2.

Human Relations Class Activity

The World's Happiest Person

Hundreds of thousands of articles and Web sites have been devoted to the subject of the world's happiest, man, woman, or person. Class time and resources most likely prohibit you from searching the globe for that person, but you and your classmates can search for that person in your classroom. If you are taking this course online, the work can be accomplished by e-mail or course Web site.

After about five minutes of reflection, each class member should decide whether he or she is totally happy, or almost totally happy. Several class members who feel that they might qualify for the title of World's Happiest Person (at least who comes closest within this classroom) volunteer to explain why to the rest of the class. Candidates for the Happiest Person category will make about a three-minute presentation of precisely why they feel so happy. As you listen to these presentations, attempt to identify any of the principles of happiness covered in this chapter.

After the presentations are completed, spend a few minutes looking for trends to arrive at a few conclusions. For discussion points, you might complete these sentences:

1. All the happy people seem to think that ___________.
2. I notice that each candidate for the World's Happiest Person seemed to ___________.
3. A difference I noticed between me and the volunteers (or between me and the rest of the volunteers) is that ___________.
4. In terms of the candidates smiling, I noticed that ___________.

The conclusions you reach can become information for class discussion. Look to see if many class members arrived at similar conclusions—perhaps in response to the four questions.

Human Relations Case Study 4-1

Alex Explodes in Anger

Alex worked as an accountant in the fraud investigation unit of the welfare department of a state government. He said that one of the things he liked about his job was that he was indirectly helping people in need. Although he was not dealing directly with welfare clients, he helped the state uncover fraud in providing financial assistance to hordes of people. Alex reasoned that when fraudulent applications for public assistance are uncovered, more money is available for families that really need the money. One such case Alex helped uncover involved a woman making $30,000 per year selling stolen electronics goods on her Web site, yet she claimed to be unemployed.

Although Alex did not have major problems with his coworkers and management, he incurred some difficulties. He would become quite irritated when his work was interrupted by an e-mail message or a phone call from a work associate. He would often respond in writing: "I can't answer you now. I'm busy with something important." By phone he would respond in an abrupt tone: "Call me later. I'm busy now."

One day Alex came to work in a particularly bad mood. He smashed the bumper on his car by backing into a two-foot-high guardrail in a parking lot, he had a fight with his girlfriend, and his favorite NFL team was eliminated from the playoffs. The same day, Alex was due for a performance and salary review. Marilyn, his supervisor, told him that he would not be receiving merit pay because he was a poor team player. (Merit pay is a bonus for good performance beyond a cost-of-living adjustment.) Alex became red in the face and explained that he was one of the most valuable people in the agency because his detection of fraud saved the agency over $500,000 during the past year. Alex left the evaluation interview without even saying thank you or goodbye to Marilyn.

Before leaving the office, Alex sent an e-mail to Marilyn with distribution to every e-mail account in the agency, with the subject line, "Getting Ripped Off." The rest of the e-mail explained in a couple of hundred words how much he had contributed to the agency and how because of office politics he was not receiving merit pay.

Still feeling mistreated when he returned home, Alex made the following entry in his blog:

> *Our investigation unit should be investigated itself. I have personally found five instances in which state funds are being diverted to personal use. Did you know that our director uses a state limousine for trips to racetracks and gambling casinos? Did you know that three of the officials in our department ran up a $650 tab at a fancy restaurant and charged it to the state as a business expense?*

Two hours after Alex arrived at the office the next morning, Marilyn and the agency head came to his cubicle to tell Alex he was immediately suspended from his job because of insubordination. Also, a strong recommendation was being made to the state review board that he be fired and never allowed to work for the state again. As he left the office, Alex said angrily, "Don't you guys believe in free speech?"

Questions

1. Which aspects of low emotional intelligence did Alex display?
2. How justified is Alex's suspension along with the recommendation for termination?
3. You be the career coach: What can Alex do to patch the problems he has created with his career?

Human Relations Role-Playing Exercise

Dealing with an Angry Worker

The case about Alex provides the setting for this role play. One person plays the role of Marilyn who decides not to suspend Alex, but instead to see if she can encourage him to get help with his anger, such as attending an anger-management workshop. However, Marilyn does not intend to permit Alex to continue his angry behavior for too much longer. Another student plays the role of Alex who thinks that his impatience is a virtue on the job, and that he is misunderstood by management.

For both scenarios, observers rate the role-players on two dimensions, using a 1 to 5 scale from "very poor" to "very good." One dimension is "effective use of human relations techniques." The second dimension is "acting ability." A few observers might voluntarily provide feedback to the role-players in terms of sharing their ratings and observations. The course instructor might also provide feedback.

Human Relations Case Study 4-2

Margot Pursues Happiness

Margot is a vehicle claims adjuster for a regional branch of the property and casualty division of a large insurance company. She is responsible for preparing field reports on cars and small trucks that have been involved in an accident. In addition to making written observations, Margot photographs the vehicles that have been damaged.

Although Margot enjoys her work, she is not totally satisfied or happy. She said, "My personal life, including my relationship with my husband, daughter, parents, and relatives is fine. I also love playing in a woman's softball league. But something is missing. My job is okay, but something is missing. I'm not joyful every day."

After reading a couple of articles and two books about happiness, Margot develops a plan for being happier on the job. Her plan centers on a bulleted list of activities to make her work life happier and more joyful, as follows:

- Look at each vehicle wreck as a chance to give some much needed funds to a person in trouble.
- Walk out my door each morning with a smile on my face, even if I have to force it a little.
- Place a few smiley face decals in my cubicle and on the windshield of my car.
- Read the comic strips in my local newspaper at least five times per week.
- Watch at least one good comedy on television each night.
- Each month, think through all the good a property and casualty insurance company does for society.
- Find a different unfortunate person each week to hug.

Questions

1. What is your evaluation of Margot's plan for attaining happiness on the job?
2. Give Margot two more suggestions for attaining happiness through her work.

REFERENCES

1. Quoted in "Leading by Feel: Be Realistic," *Harvard Business Review,* January 2004, p. 28.
2. Dana L. Joseph and Daniel A. Newman, "Emotional Intelligence: An Integrative Meta-Analysis and Cascading Model," *Journal of Applied Psychology,* January 2010, p. 55.
3. Daniel Goleman, Richard Boyatzis, and Annie McKee, "Primal Leadership: The Hidden Driver of Great Performance," *Harvard Business Review,* December 2001, pp. 42–51.
4. David A. Morand, "The Emotional Intelligence of Managers: Assessing the Construct Validity of a Nonverbal Measure of 'People Skills,'" *Journal of Business and Psychology,* Fall 2001, pp. 21–23.
5. Daniel Goleman, *Social Intelligence: The New Science of Human Relationships* (New York: Bantam, 2006).
6. Joseph and Newman, "Emotional Intelligence," p. 72.
7. Stefanie K. Johnson, "I Second That Emotion: Effects of Emotional Contagion and Affect at Work on Leader and Follower Outcomes," *Leadership Quarterly,* February 2008, p. 2.
8. Peter J. Jordan, Neal M. Ashkanasy, and Charmine E. J. Hartel, "Emotional Intelligence as a Moderator of Emotional and Behavioral Reactions to Job Insecurity," *Academy of Management Review,* July 2002, pp. 361–372.
9. Cited in "Leading by Feel: Train the Gifted," *Harvard Business Review,* January 2004, p. 31.
10. This is one of the major themes from Kevin R. Murphy, ed., *A Critique of Emotional Intelligence: What Are the Problems and How Can They Be Fixed?* (Mahwah, NJ: Lawrence Erlbaum, 2006).
11. Nancy P. Rothbard and Steffanie L. Wilk, "Waking Up On the Right or Wrong Side of the Bed: State-of-Workday Mood, Work Events, Employee Affect, and Performance," *Academy of Management Journal,* October 2011, p. 959.
12. Based to some extent on information synthesized in Dodge Fernald, *Psychology,* (Upper Saddle River, NJ: Prentice Hall, 1997), pp. 562–563.
13. L. A. Burke and L. A. Witt, "Personality and High-Maintenance Employee Behavior," *Journal of Business and Psychology,* Spring 2004, pp. 349–363.
14. Timothy A. Judge and Remus Ilies, "Is Positiveness in Organizations Always Desirable?" *Academy of Management Executive,* November 2004, 152.
15. Cited in Anthony Balderrama, "10 Traits of Successful Workers: Employers Seek Good Attitude," *Democrat and Chronicle,* June 12, 2001, p. 2F.
16. Nancy Rothbard, "Put on a Happy Face. Seriously," *The Wall Street Journal,* October 24, 2011, p. R2. Report based on Rothbard and Wilk," Waking Up on the Right Side," pp. 959–980.
17. Judge and Ilies, "Is Positiveness in Organizations Always Desirable," pp. 153–155.
18. Anne Murphy Paul, "The Uses and Abuses of Optimism (and Pessimism)," *Psychology Today,* November/December, 2011, p. 61.
19. Judith Sills, "Take This Job and Love It," *Psychology Today,* November/December 2008, pp. 58–59.
20. "The 100 Best Companies to Work for 2008," pp. 61–94; Milton Moskowitz, Robert Levering, & Christopher Tkaczyk, "The 100 Best Companies to Work for 2009,"; Moskowitz and Lervering, "The 100 Best Companies to Work For," *Fortune,* February 2, 2012, pp. 117–127.
21. Frederick P. Morgeson and Stephen E. Humphrey, "The Work Design Questionnaire (WDQ): Developing and Validating a Comprehensive Measure for Assessing Job Design and the Nature of Work," *Journal of Applied Psychology,* November 2006, pp. 1321–1339.
22. Nathan P. Podaskoff, Steven W. Whiting, Philip M. Podaskoff, and Brian D. Blume, "Individual- and Organizational-Level Consequences of Organizational Citizenship Behavior: A Meta-Analysis," *Journal of Applied Psychology,* January 2009, pp. 122–141; Scott B. MacKenzie, Philip M. Podaskoff, and Nathan P. Podaskoff, "Challenge-Oriented Organizational Citizenship Behaviors and Organizational Effectiveness: Do Challenge-Oriented Behaviors Really Have an Impact on the Organization's Bottom Line?" *Personnel Psychology,* Number 3, pp. 559–592.
23. Nicole M. Dudley and Jose M. Cortina, "Knowledge and Skills That Facilitate the Personal Support Dimension of Citizenship,"*Journal of Applied Psychology,* November 2008, pp. 1249–1270.
24. Cited in Rebecca A. Clay, "Stumbling on Happiness," *Monitor on Psychology,* May 2010, p. 29.
25. Research reported in Hara Estroff Marano, "Clues to Character," *Psychology Today,* May/June 2011, pp. 59-60; Nick Powdthavee, *The Happiness Equation* (New York: icon, 2011); Amy Novotney, "The Happiness Diet: Sonjya Lyubomirsky Argues that Limiting Overthinking Can Improve Our Emotional Well-Being," *Monitor on Psychology,* April 2008, pp. 24–25.
26. The major sources of information for this list are Mihaly Csikzentmihalyi, "Finding Flow," *Psychology Today,* July/August 1997, pp. 46–48, 70–71; Carlin Flora, "The Pursuit of Happiness," *Psychology Today,* January/February 2009, pp. 60–69; Interview with Daniel Gilbert, "The Science Behind the Smile," *Harvard Business Review,* January/February 2012, pp. 85–90.
27. Cited in Novotney, "The Happiness Diet," p. 24.
28. Gilbert, "The Science Behind the Smile," p. 88.
29. Study cited in Alice Park, "The Happiness Effect. How Emotions and Even Behaviors Can Spread Like an Epidemic," *Time,* December 22, 2008; Maggie Fox, "Happiness Is Contagious, Study Finds," *Scientific American,* www.sciam.com. Accessed December 5, 2008.
30. Quoted in George Melloan, "The Rich Are Getting Richer, but So Are Others," *The Wall Street Journal,* December 23, 2003, p. A15.
31. David T. Lykken, *Happiness: What Studies on Twins Show Us about Nature, Nurture, and Happiness Set Point* (New York: Golden Books, 1999), p. 67.
32. Jonathan Clements, "The Pursuit of Happiness: Six Experts Tell What They've Done to Achieve It," *The Wall Street Journal,* December 6, 2006, p. D1.
33. Clements, "The Pursuit of Happiness," p. D1.
34. Martin Seligman, "Don't Diet, Be Happy," *USA Weekend,* February 4-6, 1994, p. 12.
35. Steven Reiss, "Secrets of Happiness," *Psychology Today,* January/February 2001, pp. 50–52, 55–56.
36. Corliss, "Is there a Formula for Joy?" p. 74.
37. Quoted in Flora, "The Pursuit of Happiness," p. 69.
38. Cited in Colleen Walsh, "Money Spent on Others Can Buy Happiness," *Harvard Gazette,* April 2008, p. 1.
39. Corliss, "Is there a Formula for Joy?" p. 74.

5

Values and Ethics

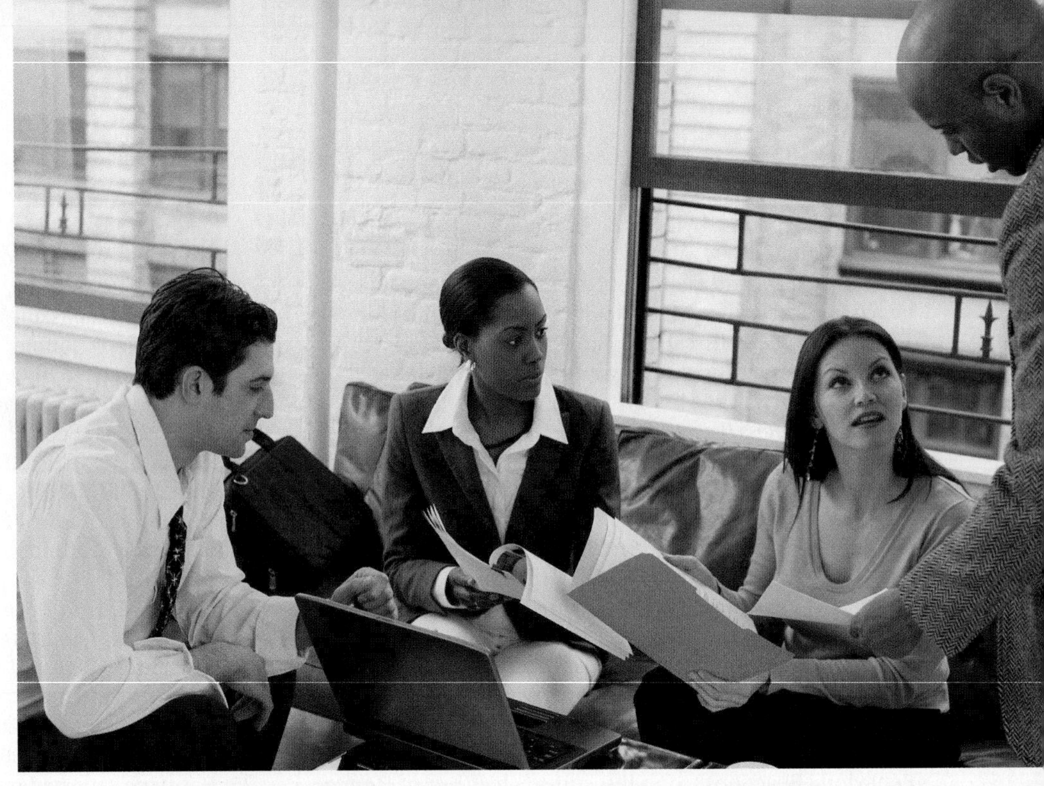

Outline

Tanya is an automobile underwriting specialist at the mid-western division of a small insurance company. She believes that in helping set premium prices for automobiles she helps protect customers against risk, as well as bringing a fair return on investment for her employer. Tanya believes strongly that by establishing fair premiums, everybody benefits—including the company, the policy holder for whom the rate is set, and other policy holders also. "If a given policy holder pays too little, that means that somebody else pays too much. So I attempt to set the fairest rates possible based on the data given my department by the actuaries."

Tanya has been bothered lately by some information presented to the company by car owners who live in areas with few farms. She has noticed that among the vehicles being classified as farm vehicles include Porcshe Carrera, a BMW Z4, a Cadillac DTS, and a Lexus. The insurance applications indicate that these luxury cars are being used for such purposes as spraying pesticides among corn rows, pulling tillers, and hauling fertilizer.

Tanya doesn't like what she sees particularly in light of a report by Quality Planning, a company that verifies the accuracy of policyholder data for the auto insurance company. The assessment indicates that some of the drivers of luxury vehicles claim them as farm equipment to reap hefty discounts on insurance premiums. One conclusion reached by the report was that about 8 percent of 80,000 vehicles for which a farm-use insurance discount was claimed were in zip codes where less than 1 percent of the population was agricultural workers. The report also estimated that insurance companies are losing about $150 million annually through unpaid premiums based on the application of farm-use discounts on luxury vehicles.

Tanya's biggest concern was that honest insurance customers wind up subsidizing the insurance premiums of dishonest people. She brought her concerns to management, and the company has since started a practice used by several of the larger insurance companies. Underwriters now use Google Maps to verify whether the address given for a vehicle receives the agricultural discount that corresponds to ranch or farm land. Tanya now feels that justice is being served.[1]

The story about the insurance company underwriter illustrates how valuing fair play and having higher ethical standards can reduce cheating by some at the expense of others. In this chapter we study values, an important force contributing to a person's level of ethical behavior, as well as ethics. Values and ethics are foundation topics in human relations because our values and ethics influence how we treat others and how we are treated in return.

Learning Objectives ▸

After studying the information and doing the exercises in this chapter, you should be able to:

1 Understand the nature of values and how they are learned.

2 Be able to classify values and explain generational differences in values.

3 Pinpoint the nature of value clarification and how the meshing of individual and organizational values is important.

4 Understand the importance of business ethics, the difficulty of being ethical, and the extent of ethical problems in business.

5 Identify workplace situations that often present ethical dilemmas.

6 Follow the guidelines for making ethical decisions and behaving ethically.

Learning Objective 1

In What Ways Are Values a Part of Understanding Human Relations?

Value
the importance a person attaches to something; values are also tied to the enduring belief that one's mode of conduct is better than another mode of conduct

Ethics
the moral choices a person makes

Morals
an individual's or a society's determination of what is right and wrong

One group of factors influencing how a person behaves on the job is that person's values and beliefs. A **value** refers to the importance a person attaches to something. Values are also tied to the enduring belief that one's mode of conduct is better than another mode of conduct. If you believe that good interpersonal relations are the most important part of your life, your humanistic values are strong. Similarly, you may think that people who are not highly concerned about interpersonal relations have poor values.

Values are closely tied in with **ethics**—the moral choices a person makes. A person's values influence which kinds of behaviors he or she believes are ethical. Ethics converts values into action. A business owner who highly values money and profits might not find it unethical to raise prices higher than needed to cover additional costs. A corporate executive who strongly values family life might suggest that the company invest company funds in an on-premises dependent-care center. Another concept that ties in closely with values and ethics is **morals**, which are an individual's or a society's determination of what is right or wrong. Your morals are influenced by your values. If you value truth telling, for example, you would consider it immoral to lie to a coworker.

According to the late Stephen Covey, values play an important role in our work life. You should understand what is important in your life, and what gives you meaning and fulfillment. Knowing the answer to these issues will help cope with the inevitable ups and downs in most work roles.[2] A supervisor at a customer care center might be having a bad day because of equipment failure and two people quitting. Yet, focusing on her values, she thinks, "Our purpose is to make life more satisfying for our customers, and we are doing that. Today might be tough, but in the long run our group is helping customers."

HOW VALUES ARE LEARNED

People are not born with a particular set of values. Instead, people acquire values in the process of growing up, and many values are learned by the age of four. One important way we acquire values is through observing others, or modeling. Models can be teachers, friends, brothers, sisters, and even public figures. If we identify with a particular person, the probability is high that we will develop some of his or her major values, such as those of a parent, instructor, or coach.

Given that values are acquired in the process of growing up, your culture influences your values, as will be explained more in detail in Chapter 13. For now, consider this illustration. People growing up in a Malaysian culture, as well as other Far East cultures, learn to value age, hierarchy, and wisdom. When meeting the 70-year-old CEO of his company, the young Malaysian customer service rep might say, "Sir, I am honored to have the opportunity to speak with you and benefit from your wisdom." In contrast, a young American worker might say, "Hi, Joe. How's it going?" (Of course, we are exaggerating a stereotype.)

Another major way values are learned is through the communication of attitudes. The attitudes that we hear expressed directly or indirectly help shape our values. Assume that using credit to purchase goods and services was considered an evil practice among your family and friends. You might, therefore, hold negative values about installment purchases.

Unstated but implied attitudes may also shape your values. If key people in your life showed a lack of enthusiasm when you talked about work accomplishments, you might not place such a high value on achieving outstanding results. If, however, your family and friends centered their lives on their careers, you might develop similar values. (Or, you might rebel against such a value because it interfered with a more relaxed lifestyle.) Many key values are also learned through religion and thus become the basis for society's morals. For example, most religions emphasize treating other people fairly and kindly. To "knife somebody in the back" is considered immoral both on and off the job.

Later Life Influences on Values

Although many core values are learned early in life, our values continue to be shaped by events late in life. The media, including dissemination of information about popular culture, influence the values of many people throughout their lives. The aftermath of Hurricane Katrina intensified a belief in the value of helping less fortunate people. Volunteers from throughout the United States invested time, money, and energy into helping rebuild New Orleans and several other Gulf Coast cities. Influential people, such as NBA players, were seen on television building houses for Katrina victims. Such publicity sent a message that helping people in need is a value worth considering.

The publicity given to building a sustainable environment, or "being green," has shaped the values of countless thousands of people throughout the world. Many people regard being green as an important value and are attracted to business firms, such as Ford Motor Company and Wal-Mart that have a green agenda.

The media, particularly advertisements, can also encourage the development of values that are harmful to a person intent on developing a professional career. People featured in advertisements for consumer products, including snack food, beer, and vehicles, often flaunt rudeness and sloppy grammar. The message comes across to many people that such behavior is associated with success.

Changes in technology can also change our values. As the world has become increasingly digitized, more and more people come to value a *digital lifestyle* as the normal way of life. The changes in values lead to curious changes in the behavior of people. Eastman Kodak Co. Chair and Chief Executive Antonio Perez commented on how people have shifted away from storing prints of photos in shoeboxes, thereby being in danger of losing many important memories. Perez said, "As much as we complain about the old shoebox, it was brilliant. Because it was just a matter of going through the attic. This is going to be a lot more difficult in digital, as you all know. Formats are going to change. Hard drives will crash."[3] Of course, people who truly value stored memories can make prints.

The Influence of Company Values

Values can sometimes be learned later in life when we are introduced to values that did not capture our attention earlier. It is possible that the teaching and demands of an employer will help us acquire new values. A relevant example is the effort and time IBM invests in teaching company values to employees. For example, company leadership emphasizes that IBM employees should be dedicated to the success of all the company's customers.[4]A sales representative when meeting a customer might say to himself or herself, "What IBM product or service might help this company be more successful," rather than, "What IBM product or service can I sell this company so I can meet my sales quota?" Three other examples of important company values are presented next.

Kindness and Compassion. Most people would probably think of kindness and compassion as individual rather than corporate values, yet some companies do promote kindness and compassion as a corporate value. For example, several companies including the clothier Genesco Inc. and Whole Foods Market Inc. provide funds to families facing emergencies. At Genesco, circumstances that may qualify for a grant include a natural disaster, life-threatening or serious illness or injury, death of employee or dependent, and catastrophic or extreme circumstances.

A head physician who perceives kindness as a basic staff development strategy made this statement: "It's my job to make the people who work for me happy; if they're happy, they'll work harder . . ."[5]

Being kind to employees may benefit the company because kindness contributes to job satisfaction, which in turn can lead to less turnover and higher productivity.

Sustainability. As mentioned above, sustainability, or protecting the environment, has surged in importance as a corporate value. Sustainability has also been perceived as a business megatrend, like electrification, mass production, and information technology and will profoundly affect the competiveness and survival or business firms.[6]

A survey about business social responsibility found that approximately 75 percent of companies engage in sustainable practices. Among these practices are recycling, eco-efficient waste management practices, and the use of alternative energy sources such as wind turbines. Among the benefits to employers from emphasizing sustainability are improved employee morale, stronger public image, and increased employee loyalty. Green initiatives can also save a company directly, such as lowered energy costs.[7]

Corporate Spiritualism. Another value that individuals may acquire as a result of being part of an organization is *corporate spiritualism.* This type of spiritualism takes place when management is just as concerned about nurturing employee well-being as they are about profits. A practice such as a work/life program contributes to this style of corporate spiritualism.[8] The purpose of a work/life program is to make it easier for workers to effectively manage both work and personal life responsibilities. Flexible working hours and dependent-care assistance are prime examples, but even the presence of a dry cleaner on company premises can help workers balance the demands of work and personal life.

Socialization
the process of coming to understand the values, norms, and customs essential for adapting to the organization

Company values are passed along to organization members as part of the process of **socialization**, the process of coming to understand the values, norms, and customs essential for adapting to the organization. As the individual observes others, he or she picks up hints as to what is acceptable behavior by watching company employees in action. For example, a newcomer to the organization might observe the manager authorizing emergence funds for a worker whose house burned down. This would be an example of the value of kindness and compassion in action.

THE CLASSIFICATION AND CLARIFICATION OF VALUES

Because values can be related to anything we believe in, a large number of values exist. Several attempts have been made to classify values, and each one is closely tied to psychological needs. If you value something strongly, such as accomplishing worthwhile activities, it leads to a need such as achievement. If you value independence, it will most likely lead to a need for autonomy. The following classification of values involves needs and is linked to both career and personal life. The basis of the value classification is to categorize people into four types emphasizing different values and needs.[9]

Humanists are driven primarily by a need for self-awareness, personal growth, and a sense of being individual and unique. Humanism is their most important value. A humanist is likely to devote considerable time to self-help activities including personal reflection and attending a workshop designed for personal growth, such as one given by Anthony Robbins.

Strategists highly value a sense of mastery and personal achievement. They are likely to say, "I am what I do." Strategists might believe that insight and understanding are important, but they place the highest value on tangible accomplishments. A typical strategist activity would be to undertake and complete a project such as fund raising for a community center.

Pragmatists strive for a corner in the world anchored by power, influence, stability, and control. They search for roles and settings that provide them with formal power, respect, and prestige. A pragmatist, therefore, highly values career success in the traditional meaning of the term—high compensation and rank. A pragmatist would enjoy being a high-ranking manager in a business, government, or non-profit organization.

Adventurers place low value on status and conformity. Instead, they have a powerful drive for excitement and adventure. The adventurer might say, "I don't want to play it safe. I want to play often and big. Play is good. Just do it." The adventurer has high standing on the traits of risk taking and thrill seeking. An adventurer might enjoy working in the Arctic Circle as part of a team searching for underground petroleum reserves.

Another key value that influences both work and personal life is *conscientiousness*. As a personality trait, conscientiousness is regarded as one of the basic components of personality. But the same trait also functions as a value, with the conscientious person striving to be industrious, well organized, self-controlling, responsible, traditional, and virtuous.[10] Dozens of studies have demonstrated that workers with a high standing on conscientiousness tend to perform well in a wide variety of positions. As a result, employers look for conscientious workers when choosing among job candidates for both initial hiring and later promotion.[10]

Loyalty to the organization as manifested in wanting to stay with or make supportive statements about an employer, is another key individual value with an impact on the job. Some people think that loyalty as a value is diminishing partly because employers are quick to lay off employees when sales decrease or expenses mount. During the Great Recession that began in 2008—and whose effect was still being felt in 2012—employee loyalty increased. Reasons for the increase include an appreciation for a job when so many other people are being fired. Another factor is that after organizations have shrunk due to downsizing, some employees feel that they are now part of a stable organization.[12]

Generational Differences in Values

Differences in values among people often stem from age, or generational differences. Workers older than fifty, in general, may have different values than people who are much younger. A subtle point, however, is that quite often generational values and attitudes we pick up at a certain age may persist for many years.[13] Assume that as a teenager and young adult, Jen develops a passion for using communication technology devices, as well as for living a balanced lifestyle (a fair balance between work and personal life). Although Jen has acquired these values early in life, the same values are likely to persist for many years. However, as Jen gets older she may become more risk averse, such as not changing jobs unless forced to and obeying speed limits—with the increased conservatism being linked to age rather than her generation.

Generational differences in values have often been seen as a clash between baby boomers and members of Generation X and Generation Y. According to the stereotype, boomers see Generation X and Generation Y as disrespectful of rules, not willing to pay their dues, and being disloyal to employers. Generation X and Generation Y see boomers as worshipping hierarchy (layers of authority), being overcautious, and wanting to preserve the status quo.

An emerging tendency is a new generation to follow the Milennials (1981-2002) referred to as the iGeneration. These are the individuals so preoccupied with smart phones that they prefer to text than talk with other individuals, and want to stay connected electronically to friends.[14] A few athletic coaches have complained that players miss out on some key plays because they will not talk to each other on the field. Also, some customers complain that the youngest store associates hesitate to speak to a customer because talking to people is less preferred than sending them text messages.

Figure 5-1 summarizes these stereotypes with the understanding that massive group stereotypes like this are only partially accurate because there are literally millions

FIGURE 5-1 VALUE STEREOTYPES FOR SEVERAL GENERATIONS OF WORKERS

Baby Boomers (1946–1964) Including Generation Jones (1954–1965)	Generation X (1961–1980)	Generation Y (1981–2002) Millenials
Uses technology as a necessary tool, but not obsessed with technology for its own sake	Tech-savvy	Tech-savvy, and even questions the value of standard IT techniques such as e-mail, with a preference for communications on a Web site
Appreciates hierarchy	Teamwork very important	Teamwork very important, highly team focused
Tolerates teams but values independent work	Dislikes hierarchy	Dislikes hierarchy, prefers participation
Strong career orientation	Strives for work-life balance but will work long hours for now; prefers flexible work schedule	Strives for work-life balance, and may object to work interfering with personal life; expects flexible work schedule
More loyalty to organization	Loyalty to own career and profession	Loyalty to own career and profession and feels entitled to career goals
Favors diplomacy and tact	Candid in conversation	Quite direct in conversation
Seeks long-term employment	Will accept long-term employment if situation is right	Looks toward each company as a stepping stone to better job in another company
Believes that issues should be formally discussed	Believes that feedback can be administered informally, and welcomes feedback	Believes that feedback can be given informally, even on the fly, and craves feedback
Somewhat willing to accept orders and suggestions	Often questions why things should be done in certain way	Frequently asks why things should be done in a certain way, and asks loads of questions
Willing to take initiative to establish starting and completion dates for projects	Slight preference for a manager to provide structure about project dates	Prefer structure on dates and other activities based on childhood of structured activities
Regards rewards as a positive consequence of good performance and seniority	Expects frequent rewards	Feels strong sense of entitlement to rewards, including promotions
Will multitask in front of work associates when it seems necessary	Feels comfortable in multitasking while interacting with work associates	Assumes that multitasking, including listening to music on earphones while dealing with work associates, is acceptable behavior
Prefer working at desk in company office	Eager to have the option of working from anywhere at any time	Prefer working from anywhere at any time; feel constrained when having to work in company office full-time

Note: Disagreement exists about which age brackets fit baby boomers, Generation X, and Generation Y, with both professional publications and dictionaries showing slight differences.

Source: The majority of ideas in this table are from Sommer Kehrli and Trudy Sopp, "Managing Generation Y: Stop Resisting and Start Embracing the Challenges Generation Y Brings to the Workplace," *HR Magazine,* May 2006, pp. 113–119; Ron Alsop, *The Trophy Kids Grow Up: How the Millenial Generation Is Shaking Up the Workforce* (San Francisco: Jossey-Bass/Wiley, 2008); Alsop, "Schools, Recruiters Try to Define Traits for Future Students," *The Wall Street Journal,* February 14, 2006, p. B6; Kathryn Tyler, "Generation Gaps: Millennials May Be Out of Touch with the Basics of Workplace Behavior," *HR Magazine,* January 2008, pp. 69–72; Lindsay Holloway, "Stick Together," *Entrepreneur,* March 2008, p. 30; Martha Irvine, "Recession Intensifies Gen X Discontent at Work," *The Detroit News* (*www.detnews.com*), November 16, 2009; Chris Penttila, "Talking about My Generation," *Entrepreneur,* March 2009, pp. 53–55; Cindy Krischer Goodman, "Meeting in the Middle: Generations X and Y," *The Miami Herald* (www.miamiherald.com), August 18, 2010, pp. 1–3.

of exceptions. For example, many baby boomers are fascinated with communication technology, and many members of Generation Y like hierarchy. Also, you may have observed that many people in their fifties and sixties are so wedded to communication technology that they incessantly use their smart phone on and off the job. Now the vast majority of workers are tethered to communication technology, not just members of Generation X and Generation Y.

Heather Huhman, a person who has mentored people seeking entry-level positions, offers a useful perspective for understanding value-based generational difference. She contends that earlier generations have developed negative stereotypes about Gen Y people and offers the following advice for members of Gen Y to overcome such stereotypes—including dealing with these four stereotypes.[15]

Above all, Gen Y is tech savvy. Their lifestyle is all about technology. They are consumed by entertainment and accomplished at multitasking.
—Elizabeth Gillespie
President of marketing for Jones Lang LaSalle Americas Inc., a real estate firm.

1. *They are entitled.* Remember to say frequently, "What can I do to help?" Offering help to others helps overcome the stereotype of being self-centered. Another approach is to suggest something of benefit to the organization, and volunteer to develop it.
2. *They have a weak work ethic.* Ask your supervisor to be specific about what he or she expects. The supervisor is likely to perceive the questioning as a sign of interest and commitment. At the same time you are likely to get the information you need to perform your job well.
3. *They are self-centered.* Show that you are a team player by being a good organizational citizen. (A team player is the opposite of being self-centered.) At the same time, displaying initiative and leadership will show that you want to help the company as well as coworkers.
4. *They are too casual in their speech (such as vocalized pauses and overuse of "like" and "you know").* Using a camcorder and/or a speech coach, most people can learn to speak in a more refined and polished manner

Although stereotypes do give us some general ideas, they can be insulting and patronizing. For example, many Gen Y people have highly polished speaking skills. At the same time, being a baby boomer does not automatically grant a person refined speaking skills.

Value Clarification

The values that you develop early in life are directly related to the kind of person you are and to the quality of the relationships you form.[16] Recognition of this fact has led to exercises designed to help people clarify and understand some of their own values. At times the values you clarify will match with the value categories previously listed, including company values and generational differences in values. At other times, your personal value list will be different. The Human Relations Skill-Building Exercise at the end of the chapter gives you an opportunity to clarify your values.

THE MESH BETWEEN INDIVIDUAL AND JOB VALUES

Under the best of circumstances, the values of employees mesh with those required by the job. When this state of congruence exists, job performance is likely to be high. Suppose that Jacquelyn strongly values giving people with limited formal education an opportunity to work and avoid being placed on welfare. So she takes a job as a manager of a dollar store that employs many people who would ordinarily have limited opportunity for employment. Jacquelyn is satisfied because she and her employer share a similar value.

When the demands made by the organization or a superior clash with the basic values of the individual, he or she suffers from **person–role conflict.** The individual wants

Person–role conflict
the demands made by the organization or a superior clash with the basic values of the individual

FIGURE 5-2
AN EXAMPLE OF PERSON–ROLE CONFLICT

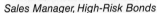

Sales Manager, High-Risk Bonds

Sales Rep with Strong Ethical Code

to obey orders but does not want to perform an act that seems inconsistent with his or her values. A situation such as this might occur when an employee is asked to produce a product that he or she feels is unsafe or is of no value to society. Another example of person–role conflict is illustrated in Figure 5-2.

> A manager of a commercial weight-reduction center resigned after two years of service. The owners pleaded with her to stay based on her excellent performance. The manager replied, "Sorry, I think my job is immoral. We sign up all these people with great expectations of losing weight permanently. Most of them do achieve short-term weight reduction. My conflict is that more than 90 percent of our clientele regain the weight they lost once they go back to eating standard food. I think we are deceiving them by not telling them up front that they will most likely gain back the weight they lose."

What constitutes a good fit between personal values and organizational values may change at different stages of a person's career because of a change in values. At one point in a person's career, he or she may think that founding a business is important because the new firm might create employment. At another stage of the same person's career, he or she might believe that working for the nonprofit sector is more meritorious.

A starting point in finding a good fit between individual and organizational values is to identify what type of work would be the most meaningful to you. Po Bronson, a writer specializing in social documentaries, observes that people "thrive by focusing on the question of who they really are—and connecting to work that they truly love (and, in so doing, unleashing a productive and creative power that they never imagined)."[17] After identifying your passion in terms of work, you would then seek an employment opportunity that provides such work. For example, a manager might discover that helping young people learn useful job skills brings her the most professional excitement. She might then seek an opportunity to manage a manufacturing apprenticeship program in her company.

A study with managers enrolled in an MBA program illustrates the importance of value congruence between the individual and the organization. When leaders were able to help group members perceive how the organization matched its values, work group effectiveness tended to increase.[18]

The accompanying Human Relations in Practice presents an example of a businessperson whose values dominate her work.

Human Relations in Practice

Human Relations in Action: Green Technology and Youth Advocate Alicia Abella

AT&T scientist Alicia Abella occupies a major leadership role on the job and in the broader society. In her role as Executive Director of the Human Computer Interface Services Research Department, Abella heads a group of researchers who are intent on decreasing the need for aircraft travel and other commuting methods that potentially harm the environment or heavily consume nonrenewable energy sources. Her technical staff also specializes in data mining, user interfaces, mobile services, teleconferencing, and other emerging technologies.

Chuck Kalmanek, Vice President of Networking & Services Research at AT&T, regards Abella as a change agent. He says that she has a vision of innovative services based on her extensive experience in the interaction between humans and computers. She also has a natural understanding of how social networks change the way that users interact with each other, and with the services we offer.

In relation to her technical work, Abella explains that she and her colleagues are trying to enhance the way people are communicating with each other. The innovations she and her group accomplished have best interests of people in mind.

In terms of community involvement, Abella is committed to developing the careers of women and minority researchers. She has been the Vice President of the Young Science Achievers Program and Chair of the AT&T Labs Fellowship Committee. In these capacities, Abella has worked hard to bring an interest and excitement in science and engineering to high school girls and minority students. The programs involve mentoring and the encouragement of scientific achievement, such as laboratory experiments.

In 2011, Abella expanded her role substantially as a leader of young women and minorities. (The two categories overlap because at least one-half of people classified as minorities are women.) She was appointed to the Presidential Advisory Commission on Educational Excellence for Hispanics. The initiative provides advice on matters relevant to the educational achievement of the Hispanic (or Latino) community.

Upon accepting the appointment, Abella said, "I am honored to serve on this important commission whose mission is aligned with my long-standing effort to help minority and female students achieve their educational objectives. I owe my professional success to my education."

Abella's formal education includes a PhD and an MS in computer science from Columbia University. She also holds a BS from NYU, with a major in computer science. A first-generation child of Cuban immigrants, Abella says that her parents are still her key mentors and sources of inspiration. Her mother was a commercial artist, and her father a marketing manager.

Questions:
1. What evidence does this story give that Abella has strong scientific as well as humanistic values?
2. What concerns might an airline industry and hotel executives have about the work of Alicia Abella and her group?

Source: This story was created from facts and observations found in the following sources: Joshua Molina, "Alicia Abella: Youth Mentor, and 'Change Agent' for Green, Innovative Research at AT&T," *Hispanic Business,* April 2010, p. 28; Sylvia Aguilera, "Dr. Alicia Abella Honored for Developing Innovative Green Technologies," *Hispanic Technology & Telecommunications Partnership* (http://httponline.org, September 21, 2009, p. 1; "ATT&T Scientist Dr. Alicia Abella Appointed to Presidential Advisory Commission on Educational Excellence for Hispanics," *PR Newswire* (www.printthisclickability.com), May 23, 201, pp. 1–2; "Alicia Abella," *AT&T Labs Research—Leading, Invention, Driving Innovation,* 2010, AT&T, pp. 1–2.

Learning Objective 2

Why Be Concerned About Business Ethics?

When asked why ethics (the moral choices a person makes) is important, most people would respond something to the effect that, "Ethics is important because it's the right thing to do. You behave decently in the workplace because your family and religious values have taught you what is right and wrong." All this is true, but the justification for behaving ethically is more complex, as described next.[19]

A major justification for behaving ethically on the job is to recognize that people are motivated by both self-interest and moral commitments. Most people want to maximize gain for themselves. At the same time, most people are motivated to do something morally right. As one of many examples, vast numbers of people donate money to charity, although keeping that amount of money for themselves would provide more personal gain.

Corporate ethics are a major component of ethical behavior for workers. Many business executives want employees to behave ethically because a good reputation can enhance business. A favorable corporate reputation may enable firms to charge premium prices and attract better job applicants. A favorable reputation also helps attract investors, including mutual fund managers whose primary responsibility is to purchase stock in companies. Certain mutual funds, for example, invest only in companies that are environmentally friendly. Managers want employees to behave ethically because unethical behavior—for example, employee theft, lost production time, and lawsuits—is costly.

Behaving ethically is also important because many unethical acts are also illegal, which can lead to financial loss and imprisonment. A company that knowingly allows workers to engage in unsafe practices might be fined and the executives may be held personally liable. Furthermore, unsafe practices can kill people. Low ethics have also resulted in financial hardship for employees as company executives raid pension funds of other companies they purchase, sharply reducing or eliminating the retirement funds of many workers.

Extreme acts of unethical behavior can lead a company into bankruptcy, such as the famous scandals at Enron Corporation. Among the worst ethical violations were hiding financial losses by passing the losses on to phony subsidiaries, encouraging employees to invest their life savings in company stock that was doomed to failure, and creating power shortages in California to artificially inflate energy prices. Furthermore, company executives sometimes held business meetings at strip clubs—at company expense.[20]

A subtle reason for behaving ethically is that high ethics increases the quality of work life. Ethics provides a set of guidelines that specify what makes for acceptable behavior. Being ethical will point you toward actions that make life more satisfying for work associates. A company code of ethics specifies what constitutes ethical versus unethical behavior. When employees follow this code, the quality of work life improves. Several sample clauses from corporate (or company) ethical codes are as follows:

- Demonstrate courtesy, respect, honesty, and fairness.
- Do not use abusive language.
- Do not bring firearms or knives to work.
- Do not offer bribes.
- Maintain confidentiality of records.
- Do not harass (sexually, racially, ethnically, or physically) subordinates, superiors, coworkers, customers, or suppliers.

TRANSWORLD ENTERTAINMENT CORPORATION CODE OF ETHICS

General Statement of Policy

- Honesty and candor in our activities, including observance of the spirit, as well as the letter of the law;
- Avoidance of conflicts between personal interests and the interests of the Company, or even the appearance of such conflicts;
- Avoidance of Company payments to candidates running for government posts or other government officials;
- Compliance with generally accepted accounting principles and controls;
- Maintenance of our reputation and avoidance of activities which might reflect adversely on the Company; and
- Integrity in dealing with the company's assets.

Violations of Codes of Ethics

Violations of the Code of Ethics or any of the Company's rules of conduct in effect with constitute grounds for disciplinary action, up to and including termination. Associates are expected to act fairly and honestly in all transactions with the Company and with others to maintain the high ethical standards of the Company in accordance with this Code of Ethics.

Source: Abridged from www.twec.com/corpsite/corporate/code.cfm

FIGURE 5-3
A CORPORATE CODE OF ETHICS

A specific example of a corporate code of ethics for an entertainment company is presented in Figure 5-3. To the extent that all members of the organization abide by an ethical code, the quality of work life will improve. At the same time, interpersonal relations in organizations will be strengthened. To help raise your awareness of your own ethical thoughts and behaviors, take Human Relations Self-Assessment Quiz 5-1.

WHY BEING ETHICAL ISN'T EASY

As analyzed by Linda Klebe Treviño, an organizational behavior professor at Pennsylvania State University, and Michael E. Brown, a management professor at Penn State–Erie, behaving ethically in business is more complex than it seems on the surface, for a variety of reasons.[21] To begin with, ethical decisions are complex. For example, someone might argue that hiring children for factory jobs in overseas countries is unethical. Yet, if these children lose their jobs, many would starve or turn to crime to survive. Second, people do not always recognize the moral issues involved in a decision. A handyman on a work assignment who finds a butcher knife under the bed might not think that he has a role to play in perhaps preventing murder. Sometimes language hides the moral issue involved, such as when the term *file sharing* replaces *stealing* in terms of online music.

Another complexity in making ethical decisions is that people have different levels of moral development. At one end of the scale, some people behave morally simply to escape punishment. At the other end of the scale, some people are morally developed to the point that they are guided daily by principles of justice and right, such as wanting to help as many people as possible. The environment in which we work also influences our behaving ethically. Suppose a restaurant owner encourages such practices as serving customers food that was accidentally dropped on the kitchen floor. An individual server is more likely to engage in such behavior to obey the demand of the owner.

Human Relations Self-Assessment Quiz 5-1

The Ethical Reasoning Inventory

Describe how well you agree with each of the following statements. Use the following scale: disagree strongly (DS), disagree (D), neutral (N), agree (A), agree strongly (AS). Circle the number in the appropriate column.

	Statement	DS	D	N	A	AS
1.	When applying for a job, I would cover up the fact that I had been fired from my most recent job.	5	4	3	2	1
2.	Cheating only a few dollars in one's favor on an expense account is okay if a person needs the money.	5	4	3	2	1
3.	Employees should report on each other for wrongdoing.	1	2	3	4	5
4.	It is acceptable to give approximate figures for expense account items when one does not have all the receipts.	5	4	3	2	1
5.	I see no problem with conducting a little personal business on company time.	5	4	3	2	1
6.	Simply to make a sale, I would stretch the truth about a delivery date.	5	4	3	2	1
7.	I think it is okay for most workers to spend about one hour per day during work using Facebook or Twitter.	5	4	3	2	1
8.	I would flirt with my boss simply to get a bigger salary increase.	5	4	3	2	1
9.	If I received $500 for doing some odd jobs, I would report it on my income tax return.	1	2	3	4	5
10.	I see no harm in taking home a few office supplies.	5	4	3	2	1
11.	It is acceptable to read the e-mail messages and faxes of coworkers, even when not invited to do so.	5	4	3	2	1
12.	It is unacceptable to call in sick to take a day off, even if only done once or twice a year.	1	2	3	4	5
13.	I would accept a permanent, full-time job even if I knew I wanted the job for only six months.	5	4	3	2	1
14.	I would first check company policy before accepting an expensive gift from a supplier.	1	2	3	4	5
15.	To be successful in business, a person usually has to ignore ethics.	5	4	3	2	1
16.	If I felt physically attracted toward a job candidate, I would hire that person over a more qualified candidate.	5	4	3	2	1
17.	On the job, I tell the truth all the time.	1	2	3	4	5
18.	If a student were very pressed for time writing a paper, it would be acceptable to either have a friend write the paper or to purchase one.	5	4	3	2	1
19.	I would authorize accepting an office machine on a thirty-day trial period, even if I knew we had no intention of buying it.	5	4	3	2	1
20.	I would never accept credit for a coworker's ideas.	1	2	3	4	5

Scoring and Interpretation:

Add the numbers you have circled to obtain your total score.

90–100 You are a strongly ethical person who may take a little ribbing from coworkers for being too straitlaced.

60–89 You show an average degree of ethical awareness and therefore should become more sensitive to ethical issues.

41–59 Your ethics are underdeveloped, but you at least have some awareness of ethical issues. You need to raise your level of awareness of ethical issues.

20–40 Your ethical values are far below contemporary standards in business. Begin a serious study of business ethics.

Closely related to moral development is that some people have a tendency to *morally disengage,* or think in such a way that avoid being moral without feeling distress. A product development specialist might morally disengage from selling a trade secret to a competitor by rationalizing that he or she is underpaid and therefore deserves supplementary income from working so hard. Workers with a strong tendency to morally disengage have been shown to engage in such behaviors as committing fraud, and self-reported lying, cheating, and stealing.[22]

Another major reason for unethical behavior in business is that goals sometimes reward unethical behavior, such as sales representatives being rewarded for sales with less attention to how the sale is accomplished. To enhance sales, the representative might then offer a bribe (or kickback) to the customer in order to attain the sale.

Ethics professors Max H. Bazerman of Harvard and Ann E. Tenbrunsel at the University of Notre Dame explain that another reason for poor corporate ethics is *motivated blindness.* People tend to see what they want to see and easily block out contradictory information when it is in their interest to remain uninformed.[23] A mortgage broker intent on placing a lot of mortgages may be almost unconsciously motivated to overlook certain credit red flags on a mortgage application, such as the applicant having no savings account. To find red flags in the application represents a conflict of interest between selling the mortgage to a bank and making an honest appraisal of the mortgage application.

THE EXTENT OF ETHICAL PROBLEMS

The ethical misdeeds of executives have received substantial publicity in recent years. But ethical violations by rank-and-file employees also take place. Here are the major findings of a survey conducted by the Ethics Resource Center:[24]

- The percentage of employees who felt under pressure to compromise standards to accomplish their jobs rose to 13 percent in 2011 from 9 percent in 2009.
- The share of companies with weak ethic cultures climbed to near record levels.

As the economy improves, with companies and employees becoming optimistic about their financial futures, it appears that ethical misconduct will increase and reporting will drop.

Going beyond surveys of what individuals believe, some company practices of today might be considered unethical in terms of people getting harmed. Today, there is much less disgrace in a company declaring bankruptcy, thereby leaving many debts unpaid and abandoning employees' pensions. (The federal government is then forced to take over the pension plan and pays the workers a small percentage of the pension for which they were hoping.)

Figure 5-4 presents seven examples of unethical and/or criminal behavior in business and government. As you scrutinize the examples, you will notice the variety of organizations and types of unethical behavior.

FREQUENT ETHICAL DILEMMAS

Certain ethical mistakes, including illegal actions, recur in the workplace. We refer to these as *ethical dilemmas,* because a person is not certain as to which is the best course of action. The uncertainty creates the dilemma. Familiarizing yourself with these mistakes can be helpful in monitoring your own behavior. Here we describe a number of common ethical problems faced by business executives as well as workers at lower job levels.[25]

FIGURE 5-4 EXAMPLES OF UNETHICAL BEHAVIOR IN THE WORKPLACE BY EXECUTIVES AND CORPORATE PROFESSIONALS

Person and Organization	Ethical and/or Criminal Offense
Bernard L. Madoff, former NASDAQ chairman and then chairman of own investment company	Charged with having perpetrated a mammoth Ponzi scheme in which investors may have lost as much as $50 billion. The victims included prominent families, charities, and high-risk investment funds (hedge funds). (A Ponzi scheme involves taking people's money without really investing it and paying them returns with money collected from new investors.) The Madoff firm was liquidated. Madoff was later sentenced to 150 years in prison.
Facebook executives	The company hired a public relations firm to post negative stories about Google's privacy policies (Google and Facebook are competitive in social media.) Facebook then tried to hide its involvement in the rumor campaign. Because nastiness is not illegal, no charges were filed against Facebook.
Department head and workers in the Royalty in Kind division of Mineral Management Services of the U.S. Interior Department, Denver, Colorado	Thirteen workers were charged by government investigators with having engaged in secret sex and drug abuse with oil company employees and accepted thousands of dollars in gifts while managing billions of dollars of energy contracts. Employees were also accused of rigging contracts, helping workers fix problems in their contracts, and working part-time as private oil consultants.
Executives at Goldman Sachs & Co.	Company executives and brokers encouraged some of their major clients to place investment bets against California bonds, even though Goldman Sachs had collected millions of dollars in fees to help the state sell some of the same bonds. The company did not inform the California treasurer that it was proposing a way for investment clients to profit from California's deepening financial problems. (The bets involved selling clients credit default swaps that are essentially an insurance policy against a bond default.)
Seven town board members in Franklin County, New York	Undue influence was placed on board members to approve multimillion-dollar wind farms, with turbines two hundred feet or taller. Some of the public officials who approved the contract were leasing their own land to the developers.
Executives at Apple Inc.	Apple management has been accused (not legally charged) of relying on brutal factory conditions at Chinese suppliers to manufacture their most popular products. Audits by Apple have revealed that hundreds of its suppliers in China require employees to work more than 60 hours per week often in highly hazardous conditions. Workers assembling iPhones, iPads, and other devices often work in harsh conditions, with some workers standing so long that their legs swell until walking is exceedingly difficult. To reduce these problems, Apple has developed a supplier code of conduct that incorporates work standards and safety protections.

Sources: In order of use, as follows: Roger Parloff, "As if a Credit Tsunami Weren't Enough: The Case of Accused Ponzi Schemer Bernard L. Madoff," *Fortune*, January 19, 2009, p. 6; L. Gordon Crovitz, "Facebook's Anti-Google Fiasco," *The Wall Street Journal*, May 16, 2011, p. A15; November 6, 2007; "Interior Dept. Scandal: Sex, Drugs, Energy Deals Probed at Denver Office," *Denver Post* (denverpost.com), September 20, 2008; Sharona Coutts, Marc Lifsher, and Michael A. Hiltzik, "Goldman Sachs Urged Bets against California Bonds It Helped Sell," *Los Angeles Times*, November 11, 2008; Christine Harper, "Lending or Trading? That's the Question for Goldman," *Bloomberg Business Week*, April 4–April 10, 2011, pp. 49–50; Joseph Spector, "Whistle Blown on Wind Power," *Democrat and Chronicle* (Rochester, NY), July 28, 2008, pp. 1A, 10A; Charles Duhigg and David Barboza, "In China, Human Costs Are Built Into an iPad," *The New York Times* (www.nytimes.com), January 25, 2012, pp. 1–14.

The Temptation to Illegally Copy Software

A rampant ethical problem is whether to illegally copy computer software. According to the Business Software Alliance, approximately $59 billion was lost to software piracy during a recent year. In the United States, about 20 percent of software is stolen.[26] The illegal copying of software deprives software developers of profits they deserve for having produced the software. Such pirating also leads to the loss of potential jobs for many software developers because the companies that produce the software have less revenue.

Treating People Unfairly

Being fair to people means equity, reciprocity, and impartiality. Fairness involves the issue of giving people equal rewards for accomplishing equal amounts of work. The goal of human resource legislation is to make decisions about people based on their qualifications and performance—not on the basis of demographic factors such as sex, race, or age. A fair working environment is where performance is the only factor that counts (equity). Employer-employee expectations must be understood and met (reciprocity). Prejudice and bias must be eliminated (impartiality).

Treating people fairly—and therefore ethically—requires an under-emphasis on political factors. Yet, this ethical doctrine is not always easy to implement. It is human nature to want to give bigger rewards (such as fatter raises or bigger orders) to people we like.

Follow the Platinum Rule: Treat people the way *they* wish to be treated.

—*Eric Harvey and Scott Airitam* Authors of *Ethics 4 Everyone.*

Sexual Harassment

Sexual harassment is a source of conflict and an illegal act. Sexual harassment is also an ethical issue because it is morally wrong and unfair. All acts of sexual harassment flunk an ethics test. Before sexually harassing another person, the potential harasser should ask, "Would I want a loved one to be treated this way?"

Conflict of Interest

Part of being ethical is making business judgments only on the basis of the merits or facts in a situation. Imagine that you are a supervisor who is romantically involved with a worker within the group. When it comes time to assign raises, it will be difficult for you to be objective. A **conflict of interest** occurs when your judgment or objectivity is compromised. Conflicts of interest often take place in the sales end of business. If a company representative accepts a large gift from a sales representative, it may be difficult to make objective judgments about buying from the representative. Yet, being taken to dinner by a vendor would not ordinarily cloud one's judgment. Another common example of a conflict of interest is making a hiring decision about a friend who badly needs a job but is not well qualified for the position.

Conflict of interest judgment or objectivity is compromised because of two competing ends that must be satisfied

Dealing with Confidential Information

An ethical person can be trusted by others not to divulge confidential information unless the welfare of others is at stake. Suppose a coworker tells you in confidence that she is upset with the company and therefore is looking for another job. Behaving ethically, you do not pass this information along to your supervisor, even though it would help your supervisor plan for a replacement. Now suppose the scenario changes slightly. Your coworker tells you she is looking for another job because she is upset. She tells you she is so upset that she plans to destroy company computer files on her last day. If your friend does find another job, you might warn the company about her contemplated activities.

The challenge of dealing with confidential information arises in many areas of business that affect interpersonal relations. If you learned that a coworker was indicted for a crime, charged with sexual harassment, or facing bankruptcy, there would be a temptation to gossip about the person. A highly ethical person would not pass along information about the personal difficulties of another person.

Misrepresentation of Employment History

Many people are tempted to distort in a positive direction information about their employment history on their job résumé, job application form, and during the interview. Distortion, or lying, of this type is considered unethical and can lead to immediate dismissal if discovered.

Possible Ethical Violations with Computers and Information Technology

As computers dominate the workplace, many ethical issues have arisen in addition to pirating software. One ethical dilemma that surfaces frequently is the fairness of tracking the Web sites a person visits and those from which he or she buys. Should this information be sold, like a mailing list? (Sometimes this tracking is harmless and humorous. A human relations professor was searching the Internet for articles about the *proactive personality*. Soon he would regularly see advertisements for the acne medication *Proactiv*® when he visited Web sites.) Another issue is the fairness of having an employee work at a keyboard for sixty hours in one week when such behavior frequently leads to repetitive-motion disorder. And is it ethical for workers to spend so much time doing online shopping and placing bets online during the working day?

Causing Problems in Order to Take Credit for Fixing Them

A longstanding workplace problem involves employees who quietly cause problems so they can later take the credit for their resolution.[27] The advantage derived from fixing problems is that such behavior is considered quite valuable by most employers. The problem repaired might be fictitious, or simply exaggerated. For example, a service manager at an automobile dealership pretended that many customers were complaining about the dimly lit waiting room. So he proceeded to improve the lighting, and then told the owners of the dealership about how he enhanced customer satisfaction.

You may have observed that these common ethical problems are not always clear-cut. Aside from obvious matters, such as prohibitions against stealing, lying, cheating, and intimidating, subjectivity enters into ethical decision making.

Engaging in Unethical Behavior to Benefit the Company

A final ethical dilemma here is whether to engage in unethical behavior in order to help the company. This type of dilemma is also a reason contributing to unethical behavior in the workplace. Employees will be tempted to engage in unethical acts in order to benefit the company, in such ways as the following: (1) "Cooking" numbers to boost the prediction of financial analysts' projections and stock values. (2) Withholding information about the hazards of a pharmaceutical product. (3) Neglecting to give customers correct change when the amount is small, such as 25 cents.

Two studies found that workers were more likely to engage in unethical behavior when they identify with their employer, and at the same time expect they will be rewarded for such behavior.[28] An example would be receiving a favorable performance evaluation for benefiting the company with unethical behavior.

▶ Learning Objective 3 ▶

What Are Some Guidelines for Making Ethical Decisions and Behaving Ethically?

Following guidelines for ethical behavior is the heart of being ethical. Although many people behave ethically without studying ethical guidelines, they are usually following guidelines programmed into their minds early in life. The Golden Rule exemplifies a guideline taught by parents, grandparents, and kindergarten teachers. In this section we approach ethical guidelines from six perspectives: (1) developing the right character traits, (2) following a guide for ethical decision making, (3) developing close relationships with work associates, (4) using corporate programs for ethics, (5) following an ethical role model, and (6) following an applicable professional code of conduct.

DEVELOPING THE RIGHT CHARACTER TRAITS

Character traits develop early in life, yet with determination and self-discipline many people can modify old traits or develop new ones. A **character trait** is an enduring characteristic of a person that is related to moral and ethical behavior that shows up consistently. For example, if a person has the character trait of untruthfulness, he or she will lie in many situations. Conversely, the character trait of honesty leads to behaving honestly in most situations.

Character trait
an enduring characteristic of a person that is related to moral and ethical behavior that shows up consistently

The Character Counts Coalition is an organization formed to encourage young people to develop fairness, respect, trustworthiness, responsibility, caring, and good citizenship. The coalition has developed a list of ten key guidelines as a foundation for character development.[29] If you develop, or already have, these traits, it will be easy for you to behave ethically in business. As you read the following list, evaluate your own standing on each character trait. Remember, however, that extra effort is required to evaluate one's character traits, because most people have an inflated view of their own honesty and integrity.

1. **Be honest.** Tell the truth; be sincere; do not mislead or withhold information in relationships of trust; do not steal.
2. **Demonstrate integrity.** Stand up for your beliefs about right and wrong; be your best self; resist social pressure to do wrong.
3. **Keep promises.** Keep your word and honor your commitments; pay your debts and return what you borrow.
4. **Be loyal.** Stand by family, friends, employers, community, and country; do not talk about people behind their backs.
5. **Be responsible.** Think before you act; consider consequences; be accountable and "take your medicine."
6. **Pursue excellence.** Do your best with what you have; do not give up easily.
7. **Be kind and caring.** Show you care through generosity and compassion; do not be selfish or mean.
8. **Treat all people with respect.** Be courteous and polite; judge all people on their merits; be tolerant, appreciative, and accepting of individual differences.
9. **Be fair.** Treat all people fairly; be open-minded; listen to others, and try to understand what they are saying and feeling.
10. **Be a good citizen.** Obey the law and respect authority; vote; volunteer your efforts; protect the environment.

If you score high on all of the preceding character traits and behaviors, you are an outstanding member of your company, community, and school. Your ethical behavior is superior.

USING A GUIDE TO ETHICAL DECISION MAKING

Ethical screening
running a contemplated decision or action through an ethics test, particularly when a contemplated action or decision is not clearly ethical or unethical

A powerful strategy for behaving ethically is to follow a guide for ethical decision making. Such a guide for making contemplated decisions includes testing their ethics. **Ethical screening** refers to running a contemplated decision or action through an ethics test. Such screening makes the most sense when the contemplated action or decision is not clearly ethical or unethical. If a sales representative were to take a favorite customer to Pizza Hut for lunch, an ethical screen would not be necessary. Nobody would interpret a large pizza to be a serious bribe. Assume, instead, that the sales rep offered to give the customer an under-the-table gift of $1,000 for placing a large offer with the rep's firm. The sales representative's behavior would be so blatantly unethical that conducting an ethical screen would be unnecessary.

Several guidelines, or ethical screens, have been developed to help the leader or other influence agent decide whether a given act is ethical or unethical, with all of them asking similar questions.[30] We present a typical guide here.

How morally correct was my decision? This question is based on the idea that there are certain universally accepted guiding principles of rightness and wrongness, such as "thou shall not steal." A person dining at a restaurant who is trying to cut back in expenses might contemplate giving tips of 5 percent. Before doing so, he or she wonders, "Is this right?"

Was justice served by my decision? According to the concept of justice, certain actions are inherently just or unjust. For example, it is unjust to fire a high-performing employee to make room for a less competent person who is a relative by marriage. Justice includes the idea that it is not just for people to get hurt by a decision, such as selling food supplements with dangerous side effects.

How comfortable would I be if the details of my decision or actions were made public in the media? For example, would you be willing to post on Facebook or Twitter the outcome of a decision you made with respect to an ethical temptation, such as potential job discrimination?

What would you tell a young family member to do? Would you say to a younger family member, "The way to write a good term paper is to pluck one from the Internet"?

Ethical issues that require a run through the guide are usually subtle rather than blatant, a decision that falls into the gray zone. You can use an ethical decision-making guide to help solve important human relations problems. Visualize yourself in the same or similar predicament faced by Danielle.

> Danielle and an acquaintance of hers, Ashley, were rivals for a promotion to supervisor of the pension department at a financial services firm. Ashley was often rude toward Danielle, making the rivalry more intense. Both were attending the same barbeque. It soon became apparent that Ashley was drinking way too much beer. Finally, Ashley jumped into the pool dressed in a tank top and cutoff jeans, while holding a bottle of beer in her left hand. Danielle was taking videos anyway, so she filmed Ashley's leap into the pool and obvious drunken behavior.
>
> That night Danielle thought she could place her rival Ashley in an unfavorable light by posting the video on YouTube and then having a friend alert an executive at the financial services firm to the availability of the video. Danielle hesitated long enough to think through the ethics of what she was doing, including how she would feel if her decision were made public. As a result, Danielle did not transmit the video to YouTube, and she also deleted the pool scene from her camcorder.

DEVELOPING STRONG RELATIONSHIPS WITH WORK ASSOCIATES

A provocative explanation of the causes of unethical behavior emphasizes the strength of relationships among people.[31] Assume that two people have close professional ties to each other, such as having worked together for a long time or knowing each other both on and off the job. As a consequence, they are likely to behave ethically toward one another on the job. In contrast, if a weak professional relationship exists between two individuals, either party is more likely to engage in an unethical relationship. The owner of an auto service center is more likely to behave unethically toward a stranger passing through town than toward a long-time customer. The opportunity for unethical behavior between strangers is often minimized because individuals typically do not trust strangers with sensitive information or valuables.

The ethical-skill-building consequence of information about personal relationships is that building stronger relationships with people is likely to enhance ethical behavior. If you build strong relationships with work associates, you are likely to behave more ethically toward them. Similarly, your work associates are likely to behave more ethically toward you. The work associates we refer to are all your contacts.

USING CORPORATE ETHICS PROGRAMS

Many organizations have various programs and procedures for promoting ethical behavior. Among them are committees that monitor ethical behavior, training programs in ethics, and vehicles for reporting ethical violations. The presence of these programs is designed to create an atmosphere in which unethical behavior is discouraged and reporting on unethical behavior is encouraged.

Ethics Hotlines

Ethics hotlines are one of the best-established programs to help individuals avoid unethical behavior. Should a person be faced with an ethical dilemma, the person calls a toll-free line to speak to a counselor about the dilemma. Sometimes employees ask questions to help interpret a policy, such as, "Is it okay to ask my boss for a date?" or "Are we supposed to give senior citizen discounts to customers who qualify but do not ask for one?" At other times, a more pressing ethical issue might be addressed, such as, "Is it ethical to lay off a worker only five months short of his qualifying for a full pension?"

At times an ethical problem of such high moral intensity is presented that employee confidentiality cannot be maintained. But the ethics office handles the inquiries in as confidential a manner as practical and assigns them case identification numbers for follow-up.[32]

Ethics Training Program

Wells Fargo & Co., a mammoth bank, emphasizes both a code of conduct and ethics training. The company Code of Ethics and Business Conduct specifies policies and standards for employees, covering a variety of topics from maintaining accurate records to participating in civic activities. Each year, employees also participate in ethics training. Any Wells Fargo employee may ask questions or report ethical breaches anonymously using an ethics hotline or dedicated e-mail address. The company fires violators, dismissing about one hundred people a year for misconduct ranging from conflicts of interest to cheating on incentive plans. Patricia Callahan, Executive Vice President and Chief Administrative Officer at the bank, says that you cannot have a worker who lies or cheats representing the company.[33]

A group of human resource professionals said that no amount of training will ensure that employees will choose the ethical path in every situation. Also, which behavior is the most ethical is not always clear-cut. Nevertheless, the human resource specialists noted that training can start a useful dialogue about right and wrong behavior that employees could recall when faced with an ethical temptation.[34]

The Right Corporate Culture

A corporate ethics program works best when placed in a corporate culture that promotes ethical behavior. When top management holds meetings at strip clubs, such as Enron executives did on occasion, it is difficult to seriously preach the importance of ethics. Executives have to communicate regularly about the importance of high ethics and corporate values. For example, when sales representatives are asked about their total sales, they should also be asked how ethically they behaved in attaining the sales.

FOLLOW AN ETHICAL ROLE MODEL IN THE COMPANY

An important influence on your ethical behavior can be the behavior of other people whom you regard as ethical role models. The role model is not necessarily a top-level manager. He or she could be the purchasing agent who refuses to accept tickets to sporting events from vendors, the coworker who goes on a business trip and returns the part of the travel advance not spent, or the supervisor who tells workers the truth about company problems that might affect them. According to a series of interviews, general categories of attitudes and behaviors that characterize ethical role models in organizations are as follows:

- Everyday interpersonal behaviors, such as taking responsibility for others
- High ethical expectations for oneself, such as working extra hours simply to make sure performance evaluations of group members were completed on time
- High ethical expectations for others, such as expecting others to avoid favoritism, including not recommending unqualified friends and relatives for jobs at the company
- Fairness in dealing with others, such as getting their input on a problem situation involving them

Quite often these role models were managers the participants in the study knew well rather than distant executives. As one of the interviewees in the study responded, "I had an opportunity to interact with him on a daily basis in close confines. I had the chance to see that the actions matched the verbal message."[35]

FOLLOW AN APPLICABLE CODE OF PROFESSIONAL CONDUCT

Professional codes of conduct are prescribed for many occupational groups, including physicians, nurses, lawyers, paralegals, purchasing managers and agents, and real estate salespeople.

A useful ethical guide for members of these groups is to follow the code of conduct for their profession. If the profession or trade is licensed by the state or province, a worker can be punished for deviating from the code of conduct specified by the state. The code of conduct developed by the profession or trade is separate from the legal code but usually supports the same principles and practices. Some of these codes of conduct developed by the professional associations are fifty and sixty pages long, yet all are guided by the kind of ethical principles implied in the ethical decision-making guide described earlier. A representative principle would be to avoid conflicts of interest, such as a purchasing agent making a major purchase from a company he or she operated on the side.

Key Terms

Value, 122
Ethics, 122
Morals, 122
Socialization, 124
Person–role conflict, 127
Conflict of interest, 135
Character trait, 137
Ethical screening, 138

Summary and Review

Values, morals, and beliefs influence how a person behaves on the job, and values are closely tied in with ethics, the moral choices a person makes. Values are learned in several ways, as follows:

- Observing others or modeling
- Communication of attitudes by others
- Unstated but implied attitudes of others
- Later life influences, such as stories reported by the media
- Demands of employers that may help us acquire new values, including corporate spiritualism

Values are closely tied to psychological needs. One way of categorizing values is as follows:

- Humanists (includes personal growth)
- Strategists (mastery and personal achievement)
- Pragmatists (power and control)
- Adventurers (excitement and adventure)

Conscientiousness, and kindness and compassion, are other values that influences both work and personal life.

Differences in values often stem from generational differences, such as members of Generation X and Generation Y being less concerned about hierarchy than are baby boomers. Earlier generations have developed negative stereotypes about Gen Y people, yet Gen Y people can often overcome these stereotypes.

Value clarification can lead to a better understanding of your values. When individual and job values mesh, performance may be higher. A person may suffer from person–role conflict when personal and job values clash. To find a good value fit, it helps to identify the type of work that would be most meaningful to you.

Business ethics are important to study for many reasons, including the following:

- People are motivated by both self-interest and moral commitments.
- A good ethical reputation can enhance business.
- Many unethical acts are illegal.
- High ethics increases the quality of work life because they provide guidelines for acceptable behavior.

Being ethical isn't easy, because ethical decisions are complex, people have different levels of moral development, our work environment influences our ethical behavior, workers are sometimes rewarded for being unethical, and people may engage in motivated blindness. Surveys reveal that unethical behavior is widespread. Also, much questionable unethical behavior exists, including companies declaring bankruptcy while at the same time granting top-level executives extraordinary compensation.

Common ethical problems faced by business executives as well as workers at lower job levels include the following:

- The temptation to illegally copy software
- Sexual harassment
- Conflict of interest
- Dealing with confidential information
- Accurate presentation of employment history
- Possible ethical violations with computers and information technology
- Causing problems in order to take credit for fixing them

Guidelines for making ethical decisions and behaving ethically include the following:

- Develop the right character traits (such as honesty, integrity, and loyalty).
- Use a guide to ethical decision making (the process of ethical screening).
- Develop strong relationships with work associates.
- Use corporate ethics programs.
- Follow an ethical role model in the company.
- Follow an applicable code of professional conduct.

Check Your Understanding

1. Identify several of your values that you think will help you succeed. Why do you think these values will help you?
2. What evidence would you need to conclude that there was a good fit between your values and those of your employer?
3. Get together in a brainstorming group to identify what you think might be a few values important to (a) Wal-Mart and (b) Nike. Support your reasoning.
4. To what extent have you found it true that some of the youngest members of the workforce are hesitant to talk to people because they prefer to send text messages?
5. Give an example of an action in business that might be unethical but not illegal.
6. A work associate or an acquaintance says to you "Don't worry about me. I am totally honest." How does such a statement influence you evaluation of the person's ethical behavior?
7. A 25-year-old is applying for a position as an assistant loan officer at a bank, and the bank is ready to make an offer. The hiring manager then decides against the offer when she discovers by Internet that the candidate spent one night in jail seven years ago after being arrested as an antiwar demonstrator. How ethical is the hiring manager's decision?
8. If so many successful business executives and people in public office have been charged with ethical violations, why should you worry about being ethical?
9. The number of deaths and serious injuries caused by automobile and small-truck drivers sending and receiving text messages while driving continues to increase. What ethical responsibility should cell phone manufacturers and phone service providers have for preventing or reducing these accidents?
10. Some hospitals prohibit doctors from accepting any gift but a free lunch from pharmaceutical companies. Are these hospitals going overboard on ethics? Explain your reasoning.

Web Corner

Choosing a Career Based on Values

www.careersonline.com.au/disc/vwp.html

Learning More About Business Ethics

www.ethicsandbusiness.org/links/

Making Ethical Business Decisions

http://www.decision-making-solutions.com/ethics_in_decision_making.html

INTERNET SKILL BUILDER

Demonstrating Company Values

Assume that you have accepted a position in your field with Levi Strauss & Co., the manufacturer of work and casual clothing. You want to fit in well with the company. One of your strategies is to demonstrate regularly that you conform to the company values of empathy, originality, integrity, courage, and vision. Details about these values are found by visiting http://www.levistrauss.com/company/valuesandvision.aspx, or simply visit the company Web site and look for the values statement.

The skill aspect of this exercise is for you to explain in about twenty-five words how you will demonstrate that you have incorporated each one of these values into your thinking and actions. For example, to demonstrate *integrity,* you might say something to the effect of, "Whenever I tell a supervisor or coworker that I will do something, I will follow through promptly. If the activity will take a long time, I will furnish a couple of progress reports."

Developing Your Human Relations Skills

Human Relations Application Exercises

Applying Human Relations Exercise 5-1

Value Clarification

Learning how to clarify your values can be uplifting and, at the same time, can help you make career choices based on these values. Ideally, you might pursue career opportunities that give you an opportunity to satisfy your most important career values, such as a person who highly values "making an above-average income" pursuing a career in industrial sales. And a person who values "helping people less fortunate than me" might pursue a career in youth work.

Rank from 1 to 20 the importance of the following values to you as a person. The most important value on the list receives a rank of 1; the least important a rank of 20. Use the space next to "Other" if the list has left out an important value in your life.

__________ Having my own place to live
__________ Having one or more children
__________ Having an interesting job and career
__________ Owning a car
__________ Having a good relationship with coworkers
__________ Having good health
__________ Sending and receiving e-mail messages and instant messages and using the Web
__________ Being able to stay in frequent contact with friends by smart phone and text messaging
__________ Watching my favorite television shows
__________ Participating in sports or other pastimes
__________ Following a sports team, athlete, music group, or other entertainer
__________ Being a religious person
__________ Helping people less fortunate than me
__________ Loving and being loved by another person
__________ Having physical intimacy with another person
__________ Making an above-average income
__________ Being in good physical condition
__________ Being a knowledgeable, informed person
__________ Completing my formal education
__________ Other

1. Discuss and compare your ranking of these values with the person next to you.
2. Perhaps your class, assisted by your instructor, can arrive at a class average on each of these values. How does your ranking compare to the class ranking?
3. Look back at your own ranking. Does it surprise you?
4. Are there any surprises in the class ranking? Which values did you think would be highest and lowest?

Applying Human Relations Exercise 5-2

Ethical Decision Making

The NY Pizza Burger, introduced at the Burger King Whopper Bar restaurant in New York City a few years ago, is four times the size of the chain's Whopper. The pizza burger is served on a nine-and-one-half inch sesame bun, and contains 2,520 calories. (The recommended daily calorie allowance for the average adult male is 2,500 calories.) The Pizza Burger consists of four Whopper patties on a 9.5 inch sesame bun, sliced into six pieces. The giant burger is topped with pepperoni, mozzarella, Tuscan pesto, and marinara sauce. The burger contains more than the recommended daily allowance of calories for the average man, with 144 grams of fat, 59 grams being saturated fat. The Pizza Burger also contains more than double the recommended amount of salt for adults. A Burger King executive explains that the burger is not intended to feed only one person. He also said, that the Pizza Burger "demonstrates the type of menu offering our guests can expect."

Working in a group, evaluate the ethics of the decision to offer the NY Pizza Burger to the public. You are specifically requested to take the decision through the guide for ethical decision making presented in the text. Before using the guide or screen, the group might first briefly discuss why anyone would think there are any ethical issues involved with the Pizza Burger.

Source: The facts supporting this exercise are found in the following articles: Larry McShane, "NY Pizza Burger, Set to Debut at Burger King, Includes Four Whoppers and a Whopping 2,520 Calories," *Daily News* (NTDailyNews.com), August 19, 2010, p. 1; "Burger King Introduces the 2,500 Pizza Burger," *The Telegraph* (www.telegraph.co.uk/news), August 23, 2010, p. 1.

Human Relations Class Activity

My Biggest Ethical Challenge and Its Resolution

The first step in this class activity is for each student to think of an ethical challenge, or temptation, he or she has faced in recent years and how he or she resolved the challenge. You may need about five minutes to think through your ethical challenge and its resolution. Students should keep in mind that they will be asked to share the scenario with classmates, so a scenario should be chosen that they would be comfortable sharing with others. Each student in the class, or perhaps volunteers, then makes about a two-minute presentation of his or her challenge and resolution. Here is an example contributed by a student named Danielle:

> About five years ago, I was facing financial pressures because of bills and things like that. I was due a $357 tax refund form the IRS, and I really needed the money. Then something bizarre happened. I received a refund for $357 one Monday, which pleased me no end. Then it blew my mind when I received refund checks for $357 on Tuesday and Wednesday also. The money would have been so helpful. But then I thought of the ethical problems. The federal government is in worse shape than me and needs every penny. Also, what if I got audited?
>
> My resolution of the ethical dilemma was to contact the IRS on its Web site and explain my dilemma. Five weeks later I received a letter from the IRS instructing me to return the money. I hated sending those two extra refunds back, but I can sleep better knowing that I did the right thing.

The class will vote by secret ballot as to which three students presented ethical challenges and resolutions that were the most instructive for the rest of the class. The votes can be made on small slips of paper, or by computer if the classroom is so equipped. After the votes are tallied, the class might discuss why the scenarios receiving the most votes were so instructive.

PS: What would you have done if you had been in Danielle's position?

Human Relations Case Study 5-1

Am I Paid to Be My Manager's TV Repair Technician?

Karen worked for a division of a pharmaceutical company as a member of the technical support team. Among her many responsibilities were keeping the division's desktop computers, laptop computers, printers, and smart phones in working order. Gus, her manager, who had been with the company for about ten years, had a general understanding of what the tech support staff was doing, but he was more of an administrator than a specialist in communication technology.

Several times in recent weeks Gus complained to Karen and a few other team members about a problem he was having with a digital television set connected to an internal (rabbit ears) antenna. During a lunch break, he explained to Karen, "I'm going a little crazy. I have four television sets at home. The two big ones are satellite connected and they work just fine. I have a small set in the family room in the basement connected to rabbit ears, and the reception is reasonably good. I am picking up the digital signals with a few halts here and there, but I am getting the reception I need."

"The problem I have is with a relatively new set connected in our upstairs bedroom. I did the channel scan about one year ago, and I was getting the network channels I needed. A few weeks ago I stopped receiving the channels I needed. All that was left was HSN (Home Shopping Network). I must have done a channel scan twenty times to try to fix the problem. Plus, I rotated the antenna a few times. I called tech support at the manufacturer of my set, and the rep couldn't help. He told me to telephone the FCC (Federal Communication Commission). I did that, followed the rep's instructions, and still no signal."

Karen agreed that Gus was facing a frustrating problem, but that many people using antennas on their TV sets have lost reception since the conversion from analog to digital in 2009.

A week later, Gus spoke to Karen again about his TV reception woes. He then asked Karen, "How about you coming over after work some night to help straighten out my TV problem? My wife and I would really appreciate your help. You're a great tech fixer."

Karen pondered for a moment, thinking that Gus was making an unreasonable demand. She replied, "Gus, let me think about your request. I really don't know a lot about TV reception. Also, I am pretty much tied up after work for a couple of weeks."

With a frown on his face, Gus said, "Karen, I know you can help. Please don't let me down."

Questions

1. What do you see as any potential ethical issues in Gus's request that Karen attempt to fix his TV set reception problem?
2. What advice might you offer Karen for dealing with this problem?
3. How do Gus's demands fit into the category of expecting Karen to exhibit strong organizational citizenship behavior?

Human Relations Role-Playing Exercise 5-1

Dealing with an Unusual Request from the Boss

The case about the manager's request for tech support for this television set provides the background information for this role play. The scenario is another meeting between Gus and Karen. One student plays the role of Gus who is now increasingly frustrated that he cannot get the reception he wants. Just last week he telephoned a television repair service, and was told politely that he should simply hook up the set to cable or satellite TV. But Gus and his wife do not want any more wires running through their house. So this time, Gus is more insistent that Karen come over to his house to fix the problem.

Another person plays the role of Karen who has thought through Gus's request some more, and she feels that his demand is both inappropriate and unethical. However, Karen still wants to maintain a good professional relationship with Gus.

Run the role play for about five minutes. For both scenarios, observers rate the role players on two dimensions, using a 1-to-5 scale from very poor to very good. One dimension is "effective use of human relations techniques." The second dimension is "acting ability." A few observers might voluntarily provide feedback to the role players in terms of sharing their ratings and observations. The course instructor might also provide feedback.

Human Relations Case Study 5-2

Should We Introduce Ultimate Energy?

Jason is the marketing and new product director at Cambridge Beverages, a small niche player in the beverage industry. Among Cambridge's products are ice tea in a can, vitamin water, fruit drinks made from natural ingredients, and bottled water stemming from underground springs.

Despite some success, sales and profits at Cambridge are barely enough for the 65-employee company to survive. Today Jason is meeting with the owner Tim, and the sales director, Brenda.

"The bad news," said Jason, "is that we are scarcely surviving. Even the big players like Coca-Cola, Pepsi, and Cadbury are invading our niches. But the good news is that I have a product in mind that should vastly improve our business outlook.

"My new product idea will be called Ultimate Energy. It's a caffeinated alcoholic drink. As you know this category is a small but fast-growing beverage popular among people under age 30. Because of the caffeine, and a high dose of sugar, we can call it an energy drink. The alcohol will give the consumer the same good feeling as beer or wine, thereby taking away a little of their spending on beer, wine, and liquor.

"My tentative design for the can will pull no punches. We'll have a drawing of a dynamite stick, along with young people having a great celebration."

Scratching his head, Tim commented, "I recently read some scientific research reported in a trade journal that people who consume caffeine and alcohol at the same time increase their risk of alcohol-related injuries or other problems. Suppose a few of our customers downed a six-pack of Ultimate Energy and then had a multiple-vehicular accident? Would we be liable?

"I have also read that the Food and Drug Administration, as well as the Federal Trade Commission might be cracking down on beverages that combine alcohol and caffeine."

Brenda said, "I kind of like the idea of Ultimate Energy. It will be years before the government agencies get around to placing any real restrictions on this product. Also, we can post a warming on the label about the potential dangers, like they do with medicine. Consumers have to act responsibly with whatever product they use. Look, peanut butter is composed of about 50 percent fat. And that can do more harm to the body than an occasional drink of caffeine and alcohol."

Jason said, "I'm glad you two are at least listening."

Tim said, "Before we move forward, we've got to study the pros and cons more carefully. But by the way Jason, how long do you think it would take to launch Ultimate Energy?"

Questions

1. What is your evaluation of the ethics of introducing Ultimate Energy to the market?
2. How far should Tim push his objections about Ultimate Energy?
3. How might generational differences in values influence concerns about the ethics of introducing Ultimate Energy to the market?

Human Relations Role-Playing Exercise 5-2

Ethics of a Product Launch

One student plays the role of Tim, who after thinking for a few days about the potential launch of Ultimate Energy is deeply concerned. He knows that he is the owner, but wants to collaborate with the members of his team. Two other students play the roles of Jason and Brenda who feel that the company must move forward even if ethics are stretched just a little. The three role players engage in an emotional discussion about the potential launch of Ultimate Energy.

Run the role play for about five minutes. Observers rate the role players on two dimensions, using a 1-to-5 scale from very poor to very good. One dimension is "effective use of human relations techniques." The second dimension is "acting ability." A few observers might voluntarily provide feedback to the role players in terms of sharing their ratings and observations. The course instructor might also provide feedback.

REFERENCES

1. Story created from facts in the following sources: Jerry Hirsch, "Insurance Cheaters Call Their Luxury Cars Farm Vehicles,"*Los Angeles Times* (www.latimes.com/business, July 9, 2001, pp. 1–2; "Wealthy Insurance Cheaters Call Their Porsches and Cadillac Sevilles 'Farm Vehicles'," http://thepoliticalcarvinal.net, July 9, 2001, p. 1; "Car Insurance Fraud on the Farm," *Car-Insurance.com,* July 11, 2001, p. 1.
2. Stephen Covey, *The 7 Habits of Highly Successful People* (New York: The Free Press, 1989).
3. Ben Rand, "'On Track' at Kodak," *Democrat and Chronicle* (Rochester, NY), May 21, 2006, p. 4E.
4. Paul Hemp and Thomas A. Stewart (interview with Samuel J. Palmisano), "Leading Change When Business Is Good," *Harvard Business Review,* December 2004, p. 63.
5. Quoted in Judith Sills, "Kindness and Corporation," *Psychology Today,* March/April 2009, pp. 62–63.
6. David A. Lubin and Daniel C. Esty, "The Sustainability Imperative," *Harvard Business Review,* May 2010, pp. 42–50.
7. Jennifer Schramm, "Promoting Sustainability," *HR Magazine,* March 2001, p. 88.
8. Joanne Cole, "Building Heart and Soul," *HRfocus,* October 1998, pp. 9–10.
9. Douglas B. Richardson, "Know Thyself: An Easy Approach," www.Vault.com, Inc., 2012.
10. Brent W. Roberts, Oleksandr S. Chernyshenko, Stephen Stark, and Lewis R. Goldberg, "The Structure of Conscientiousness: An Empirical Investigation Based on Seven Major Personality Questionnaires," *Personnel Psychology,* Spring 2005, pp. 103–139.
11. A review of the evidence is Nicole N. Dudley et al., "A Meta-Analytic Investigation of Conscientiousness in the Prediction of Job Performance: Examining the Intercorrelations and the Incremental Validity of Narrow Traits," *Journal of Applied Psychology,* January 2006, pp. 40–57.
12. Nick Staffieri, "Employee Loyalty Making a Comeback in Recession Economy," *Philadelphia Workplace Examiner* (www.examiner.com), March 30, 2010.
13. Opinion of Peter Cappelli cited in Erin White, "Age Is as Age Does: Making the Generation Gap Work for You," *The Wall Street Journal,* June 30, 2008, p. B6.
14. Cindy Krischer Goodman, "Meeting in the Middle: Generations X and Y," *The Miami Herald* (www.miamiherald.com), August 18, 2010, p. 2; Sharon Jayson, "Tech Savvy 'iGeneration' Kids Multi-Task, Connect," *USA Today* ((www.usatoday.com), February 10, 2010, p. 1.
15. Heather Huhman, "Avoiding Gen Y Stereotypes on the Job," *San Francisco Examiner* (www.examiner.com), December 3, 2008.
16. David C. McClelland, "How Motives, Skills, and Values Determine What People Do," *American Psychologist,* July 1985, p. 815.
17. Po Bronson, "What Should I Do with My Life?" *Fast Company,* December 2002, p. 68.
18. Brian J. Hoffman, Bethany H. Bynum, Ronald F. Piccolo, and Ashley W. Sutton, "Person-Organization Value Congruence: How Transformational Leaders Influence Work Group Effectiveness," *Academy of Management Journal,* August 2011, pp. 779–796.
19. Linda K. Treviño and Katherine A. Nelson, *Managing Business Ethics: Straight Talk about How to Do It Right* (New York: Wiley, 1995), pp. 24–35; O. C. Ferrell, John Fraedrich, and Linda Ferrell, *Business Ethics: Ethical Decision Making and Cases,* 4th ed. (Boston: Houghton Mifflin, 2000), pp. 13–16; Anita Bruzzese, "Tools Take Ethics to the Real World," Gannett News Service, May 16, 2005.
20. Erin Kelly, "Unethical Behavior Is on Rise, Experts Fear," Gannett News Service, March 5, 2006.
21. Linda Klebe Treviño, "Managing to Be Ethical: Debunking Five Business Ethics Myths," *Academy of Management Executive,* May 2004, pp. 69–72.
22. Celia Moore et al, "Why Employees Do Bad Things: Moral Disengagement and Unethical Organizational Behavior," *Personnel Psychology,* Number 1, 2012, pp. 1–48.
23. Max H. Bazerman and Ann E. Tenbrunsel, "Ethical Breakdowns," *Harvard Business Review,* April 2011, p. 58.
24. *2011 National Business Ethics Survey* (www.ethics.org/nbes/findings.html), pp. 1–2.
25. Treviño and Nelson, *Managing Business Ethics,* pp. 47–64.
26. Reported in Dina Bass, "Software Piracy Jumps to $59 Billion in 2010, Report Says," *www. Businessweek.com/new,* May 12, 2011, p. 1.
27. Phred Dvorak, "'Munchausen at Work': Employees Advance by Fixing Problems They Had Created," *The Wall Street Journal,* August 25, 2008, p. B4.
28. Elizabeth E. Umphress, John B. Bingham, and Marie S. Mitchell, "Unethical Behavior in the Name of the Company: The Moderating Effect of Organizational Identification and Positive Reciprocity Beliefs on Unethical Pro-Organizational Behavior," *Journal of Applied Psychology,* July 2010, pp. 769–780.
29. Michael S. Josephson, "Does Character Still Count?" *USA Weekend,* September 23–25, 1994, p. 20; www.charactercounts.org. Accessed January 18, 2012.
30. Two such guides are James L. Bowditch and Anthony E. Buono, *A Primer of Organizational Behavior* (New York: Wiley, 2001), p. 4, and Curtis C. Verschoor, "What's Ethical? Here's a Simple Test," *Strategic Finance,* March 2000, p. 24.
31. Daniel J. Brass, Kenneth D. Butterfield, and Bruce C. Skaggs, "Relationships and Unethical Behavior: A Social Network Perspective,"*Academy of Management Review,* January 1998, pp. 14–31.
32. Daryl Koehn, "An Interview with William Griffin." Accessed March 8, 2006, from www.stthom.edu/cbes/griffin.html.
33. Quoted in "The Optima Awards: They've Got Game," *Workforce Management,* March 2005, p. 44; www.wellsfargo.com, March 2011.
34. Jean Thilmany, "Supporting Ethical Employees," *HR Magazine,* September 2007, p. 106.
35. Gary R. Weaver, Linda Klebe Treviño, and Bradley Agle, "'Somebody I Look Up To': Ethical Role Models in Organizations," *Organizational Dynamics,* Issue 4, 2005, pp. 313–330.

6

Problem Solving and Creativity

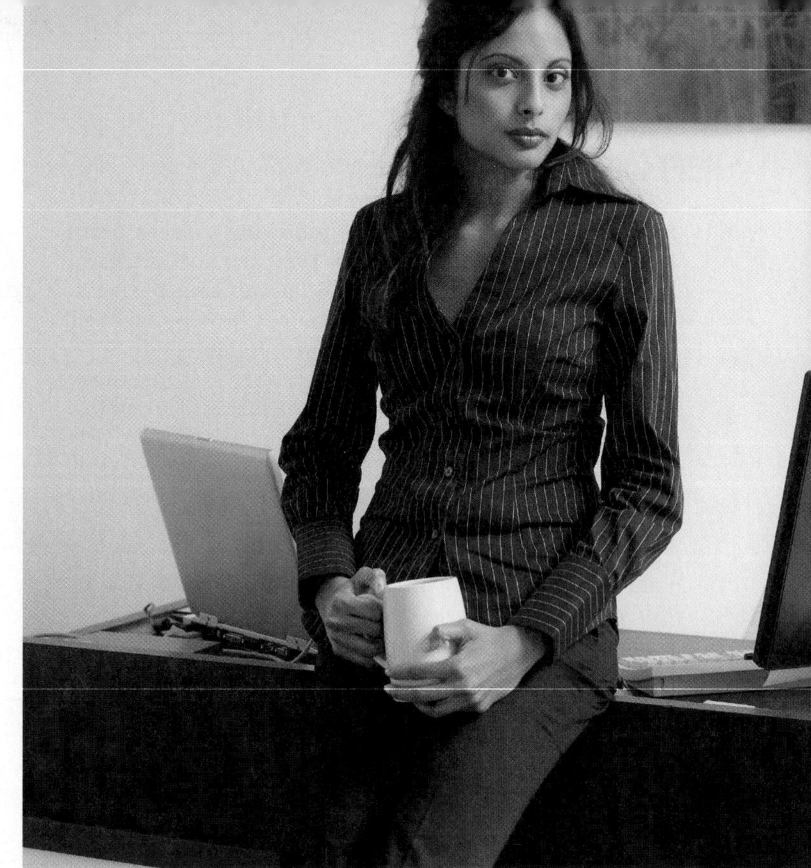

Outline

Parking lots in suburban areas take up a lot of space and quite often are physically unattractive. The Long Island Index, a nonprofit research group, decided to search for solutions to this problem, by running the Build a Better Burb contest. The contest offered a $10,000 grand prize for generating creative ideas to transform some or all of the 4,341 acres of parking lots on Long Island into a feature that makes life better on the island. (Long Island is a section of New York State that contains four counties, two of which are part of New York City.) The contest called for bold ideas from architects, urban designers, and visionaries. The idea was not to eliminate parking but to include alternatives to flat, over-ground parking lots such as multilevel parking ramps and underground garages.

The competition solicited ideas to help Long Island master several challenges: to build affordable housing and wider housing choice, particularly rentals; to reduce vehicle dependency and congestion; to unify Long Island's diverse community in a shared public realm; to improve access to opportunity for all; to meet the needs of baby boomers who do not want to relocate; and to fight the brain drain of younger residents who depart for locations with a better future.

June Williamson, associate professor of architecture, City College of New York, was the consultant for the project. The winners were selected by a diverse jury of distinguished academics and professionals in the field of urban and suburban design. Build a Better Burb attracted 212 submissions from more than 30 countries. Most of the entries showcased designs for retrofitting Long Island's 156 downtowns and areas adjacent to trains. Three of the seven winners (composed of teams) were as follows:

- *AgISLAND hoped to put the "farm" back in Farmingdale by proposing the replacement of office parks with organic farms.*
- *BuildingC-Burbia is a landscape proposal for addressing climate changes with an exciting new kind of infrastructure designed to efficiently trap carbon in plantings.*
- *Upcycling 2.0 (student winner) is a comprehensive approach that employs a creative, optimistic reading of the suburb and its building blocks, which it proposes to combine in interesting ways.*[1]

The story about the Build a Better Burb contest illustrates that putting aside time for exploring ideas can result in creative solutions to societal and business problems. At the same time, the story illustrates a major theme of this book—work life and personal life often support each other. The contest generated ideas that would improve both the work and personal life physical atmospheres. An important side message for this chapter is that students are smart enough to think of award-winning ideas for improving our physical environment. The general purpose of this chapter is to help you become a more effective and creative problem solver when working individually or within groups.

Two key definitions will help you understand the nature of the material in this chapter. A **problem** is a gap between what exists and what you want to exist. If you are a Web site developer, and far fewer people are visiting your site than your company is hoping for, you have a problem. **Decision making** refers to choosing one alternative from the various alternative solutions that can be pursued. After exploring a number of possibilities for your Web site, you must choose one.

Learning Objectives ▸

After studying the information and doing the exercises in this chapter, you should be able to:

1. Understand how personal characteristics influence the ability to solve problems and make decisions.
2. Apply the problem-solving and decision-making steps to complex problems.
3. Summarize the characteristics of creative people.
4. Describe various ways of improving your creativity.
5. Know the basic steps in critical thinking.
6. Explain how multiple intelligences might help in problem solving and creativity.

Problem
gap between what exists and what you want to exist

Decision making
choosing one alternative from the various alternative solutions that can be pursued

▶ Learning Objective 1 ▶

What Are Some Personal Characteristics That Influence Your Problem-Solving Ability?

Many personal characteristics influence the type of problem solver and decision maker you are or are capable of becoming. Fortunately, some personal characteristics that influence your decision-making ability can be improved through conscious effort. For instance, if you make bad decisions because you do not concentrate on the details of the problem, you can gradually learn to concentrate better. Most of the personal characteristics described next can be strengthened through the appropriate education, training, and self-discipline. Figure 6.1 outlines these characteristics.

COGNITIVE INTELLIGENCE, EDUCATION, AND EXPERIENCE

In general, if you are intelligent, well educated, and well experienced, you will make better decisions than people without these attributes. (The term *cognitive intelligence* refers to the intellectual, or traditional, type of intelligence that is necessary for such tasks as solving math problems and conjugating verbs.) Cognitive intelligence helps because, by definition, intelligence denotes the ability to solve problems. Education improves the problem-solving and decision-making process because it gives you a background of principles and facts on which to rely.

Experience facilitates decision making because good decisions tend to be made by people who have already faced similar situations in the past. All things being equal, would you prefer to take your computer problem to an experienced or an inexperienced specialist? Or what about flying with an experienced airline pilot?

> On January 16, 2009, airline pilot Chesley "Sully" Sullenberger, age fifty-seven, became an international hero after landing an engine-damaged jet airplane safely into the Hudson River in New York City. Captain Sullenberger had forty years of flying experience, including twenty-eight years with U.S. Airways. He was also well educated, including degrees from the U.S. Air Force Academy and two other universities, and a specialist in airline safety. In short, Sullenberger's intelligence, education, and experience contributed to his heroic feat.

FIGURE 6-1

INFLUENCES ON PROBLEM-SOLVING SKILL

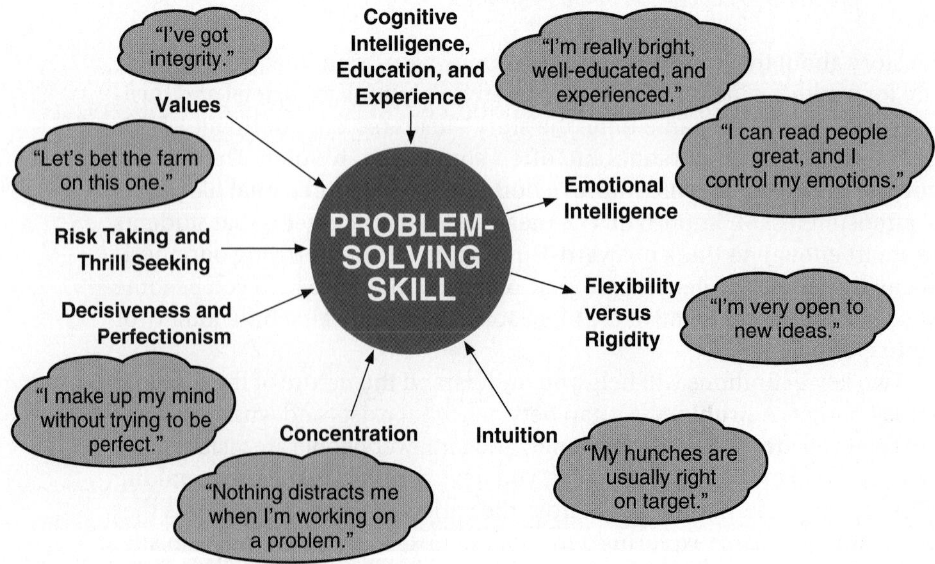

EMOTIONAL INTELLIGENCE

Being able to deal effectively with your feelings and emotions and those of others can help you make better decisions. A worker with high emotional intelligence would be able to engage in such behaviors as sizing up people, pleasing others, and influencing them.

Emotional intelligence is important for decision making because how effective you are in managing your feelings and reading those of other people can affect the quality of your decisions. For example, if you cannot control your anger, you are likely to make decisions that are motivated by retaliation, hostility, and revenge. An example would be shouting and swearing at your team leader because of a work assignment you received. Your emotional intelligence could also influence your career decision making. If you understand your own feelings, you are more likely to enter an occupation or accept a position that matches your true attitude.

Another part of emotional intelligence related to problem solving is that contrary to common knowledge, experiencing intense emotions can facilitate decision making. Instead of attempting to block your emotions, you allow them to surface to facilitate making sharper decisions. A study with 101 members of stock investment clubs found that the investors who experienced more intense feelings achieved higher decision-making performance. Among the dozens of emotions and feelings recorded were "happy," "enthusiastic," "nervous," and "depressed." An equally important finding was that investors who were better able to identify and distinguish among their current feelings made better investment decisions. Understanding their feelings apparently enhanced their ability to control possible biases induced by these feelings.[2] For example, you might have exceptionally positive feelings about any company that directly assists animals, such as a pet-food manufacturer. If you are aware of these feelings, it could prevent you from making the mistake of investing in a poorly managed dog and cat food company based on your love of animals.

FLEXIBILITY VERSUS RIGIDITY

Some people are successful problem solvers and decision makers because they approach every problem with a fresh outlook. They are able to avoid developing rigid viewpoints. Flexible thinking enables the problem solver to think of original—and therefore creative—alternative solutions to solving a problem. Another perspective on the same issue is that being open-minded helps a person solve problems well. In recent years several major retailers have become more flexible in their thinking about inner cities as profitable locations for their stores. For example, Wal-Mart has been successful with many of its new inner-city stores. The link between flexibility and creativity will be described in more detail in the discussion of the characteristics of creative people.

INTUITION

Effective decision makers do not rely on careful analysis alone. Instead, they also use their **intuition,** an experience-based way of knowing or reasoning in which weighing and balancing of evidence are done automatically. Judgments and decisions reached through intuition are rapid, and they are largely unconscious—we are not completely aware of how we reached the decision.[3] Intuition appears to be composed of the interplay between knowing (intuition-as-expertise) and sensing (intuition-as-feeling).

Intuition
an experience-based way of knowing or reasoning in which weighing and balancing of evidence are done automatically

The best use of intuition, therefore, involves both bringing past facts in mind to deal with the situation and a sudden emotional hunch at the same time.[4] An experienced real estate developer might look at an old building and within ten minutes decide it would be a good investment to rehabilitate the structure. Based on hundreds of property evaluations, the developer knows that rehabilitating an old building can be profitable. At the same time, the developer visualizes what the old building would look like when rehabilitated.

Relying on intuition is like relying on your instincts when faced with a decision. Intuition takes place when the brain gathers information stored in memory and packages it as a new insight or solution. Intuitions, therefore, can be regarded as stored information that is reorganized or repackaged. Developing good intuition may take a long time because so much information has to be stored.

Despite its merits, intuition has its drawbacks. Our hunches based on the combination of experience and emotion can sometimes lead us astray when a more analytical approach would have led to a better decision. For example, a charming and articulate job candidate might be chosen mostly on the basis of intuition. A background check based on rational analysis might have revealed that the candidate is a procrastinator and a criminal. One way to improve intuition is to get feedback on the decisions we make, so we can sharpen future decisions.[5] For example, a credit analyst in a bank profits from feedback about the future payment records of the loans he or she approved.

CONCENTRATION

Flow experience
total absorption in work; when flow occurs, things seem to go just right

Mental concentration is an important contributor to making good decisions. Many people who solve problems poorly do so because they are too distracted to immerse themselves in the problem at hand. In contrast, effective problem solvers often achieve the **flow experience**—total absorption in their work. When flow occurs, things seem to go just right. The person feels alive and fully attentive to what he or she is doing. As a by-product of the flow experience, a good solution to a problem may surface. If you fail to concentrate hard enough, you may overlook an important detail that could affect the outcome of the decision. For example, a person about to purchase an automobile might be excited about the high gas mileage but forget to check the vehicle's ability to withstand a crash.

A major factor affecting your ability to concentrate is how well rested you are. Being well rested helps you concentrate more, and being sleep deprived lowers concentration.[6] Negative stress can also adversely affect concentration, resulting in poorer decisions. Many serious automobile accidents are caused by fatigued drivers who could not concentrate well at the moment.

DECISIVENESS AND PERFECTIONISM

Some people are ill suited to solving problems and making decisions because they are fearful of committing themselves to any given course of action. "Gee, I'm not sure, what do you think?" is their typical response to a decision forced on them. If you are indecisive, this characteristic will have to be modified if you are to become successful in your field. A manager has to decide which person to hire. And a photographer has to decide which setting is best for the subject. As the old saying goes, at some point "you have to fish or cut bait." The combination of being indecisive and a perfectionist can lead to procrastination. Also, being a procrastinator can make one indecisive. Perfectionism

Human Relations Self-Assessment Quiz 6-1

The Concentration Checklist

Check whether each of the following statements tends to apply to you.

	Yes	No
1. I can concentrate on one thing for more than a few minutes at a time.	❑	❑
2. I have to stop doing this quiz right now to check my phone for messages or e-mails.	❑	❑
3. I cannot read more than one page of written information at a time without taking a break.	❑	❑
4. I can work on my favorite sport or hobby for an hour without interruption.	❑	❑
5. I can sit through an entire film without having to get up and take a break.	❑	❑
6. I am able to sit through an entire lecture, or speech, and focus intently on what is being said.	❑	❑
7. It takes me at least two sittings to balance my checkbook.	❑	❑
8. I can usually remember a person's name after he or she tells me it once.	❑	❑
9. I can tell you the name of the instructor for this course, and the course title, without looking at the syllabus.	❑	❑
10. When I'm involved in a task I enjoy, I'm not aware of anything else that is happening around me.	❑	❑

Scoring and Interpretation:

Good powers of concentration are suggested by "Yes" responses to statements 1, 4, 5, 6, 8, 9, and 10. Poor powers of concentration are suggested by "No" responses to statements 2, 3, and 7. A person with a score of 7 or higher, would usually have good concentration. A score of 6 or less suggests poor concentration, and a score of 3 or less suggests problems in concentrating on work and personal life.

contributes to delayed decision making because the person keeps working on a project before deciding to submit it to somebody else.

RISK TAKING AND THRILL SEEKING

The need for taking risks and seeking thrills is yet another personality characteristic that influences problem-solving skill. For some types of problems, the high risk taker and thrill seeker is at an advantage. Firefighters have to take risks to save people from burning buildings and remove people trapped in collapsed buildings. An information technology specialist might have to engage in a risky maneuver to salvage data from a crashed hard drive. Risk taking and thrill seeking can also lead to poor problem solving and decision making, such as a merchandiser buying a huge inventory of a highly original fashion. The experienced decision maker needs to know when to take high risks and seek thrills and when to be more conservative.

Another influence on decision making related to risk is the common tendency to focus on avoiding loss—or being averse to taking a risk. According to the Nobel Prize-winning research of Daniel Kahneman and Amos Tverseky, an individual's response to loss is much more intense than his or her response to gains. This is one reason why so many people are tempted to hold on to a losing stock or refuse to leave a casino despite a long losing streak.[7] The same phenomenon of loss aversion helps explain why flat-rate telephone plans are so popular, even when they cost more than variable-rate plans.[8]

VALUES OF THE DECISION MAKER

Values influence decision making at every step. The right values for the situation will improve problem solving and decision making, whereas the wrong values will lead to poor decisions. Ultimately, all decisions are based on values. A manager who places a high value on the well-being of employees tries to avoid alternatives that create hardships for workers. Another value that significantly influences problem solving and decision making is the pursuit of excellence. A worker who embraces the pursuit of excellence (and is, therefore, conscientious) will search for the high-quality alternative solution.

▶ Learning Objective 2 ▶

What Are the Problem-Solving and Decision-Making Steps?

Whatever complex problem you face, it is best to use the standard problem-solving and decision-making steps as a guide. These steps are similar to the systematic approach used in the scientific method and also contribute to critical thinking as explained later in the chapter. Figure 6.2 summarizes the steps involved in problem solving and decision making. It assumes that problem solving should take place in an orderly flow of steps. Paying attention to this model is important because deviating too far will often result in decision failure. Paul C. Nutt studied 356 decisions in medium to large organizations in

FIGURE 6-2
PROBLEM-SOLVING AND DECISION-MAKING STEPS

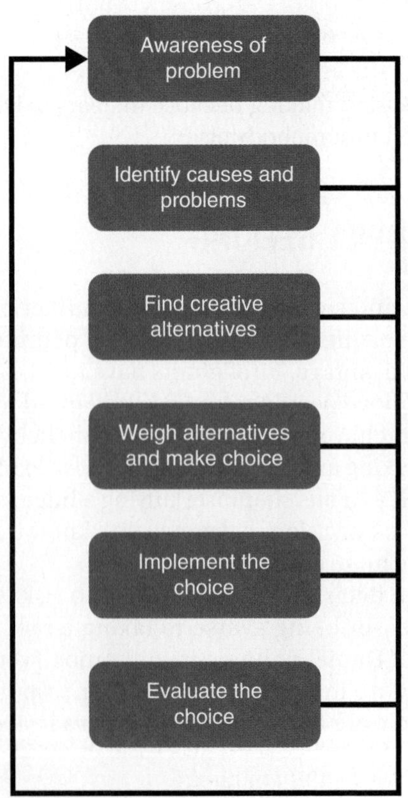

the United States and Canada. He found that one-half of these decisions failed, meaning that the decision was not fully used after two years. The typical reason for failure is that the decision makers did not take a systematic approach, such as searching for many alternative solutions. The managers involved also committed the human relations error of not involving enough people in the decisions.[9]

Although the problem-solving and decision-making steps appear logical, we emphasize again that people are frequently not entirely rational when making decisions. Emotions and personality traits can cloud decision making.

BE AWARE OF THE PROBLEM

Problem solving and decision making begins when somebody is aware that a problem exists. In most decision-making situations, problems are given to another person. At other times, people create their own problems to solve, or they find problems. Scotch tape had its origins in 1930, when somebody noticed a problem. The story goes like this:

> Richard Drew, a banjo-playing engineer, was working for the Minnesota Mining and Manufacturing Co. (3M today), whose only product at the time was sandpaper. Drew was product testing one brand of sandpaper at a local body shop when he noticed that car painters were having trouble making clean dividing lines on two-color paint jobs. In 1925, as a solution to the problem, Drew invented a masking tape using crepe paper with lines of pressure-sensitive glue running along the edges. A problem encountered was that the tape kept falling off.
>
> An automotive painter told a 3M representative to "Take this tape back to those Scotch [negative stereotype that Scotch people are cheap] bosses of yours and tell them to put more adhesive on it." The bosses did, the tape worked, and the name was soon applied to the entire line of 3M tapes. Five years later, Drew overcame numerous production hurdles and developed the Scotch Brand Cellulose Tape that has become a worldwide staple. The first trial shipment of the new tape was sent to a Chicago firm specializing in package printing for bakery products. The response to the new cellulose tape was so positive that it was introduced to the market.[10]

After you are aware that a problem exists or have identified it, recognize that it may represent an important opportunity. For example, if you are bothered enough by a problem facing your company, you might volunteer to be the person in charge of overcoming the problem.

IDENTIFY CAUSES OF THE PROBLEM

The causes of problems should be diagnosed and clarified before any action is taken because they are not always what they seem to be on the surface. Some may be more complicated than suspected or may even be the wrong problem you need to solve in a particular situation. Five key elements to ask questions about (along with some sample questions) are as follows:

1. **People.** What do the people involved contribute to the problem? Are they competent? Do they have an attitude problem?
2. **Materials.** Do we have the right materials available? Is the quality of the materials adequate?
3. **Machines and facilities.** Do we have the right machines and facilities to do the job? Have the machines and facilities changed?

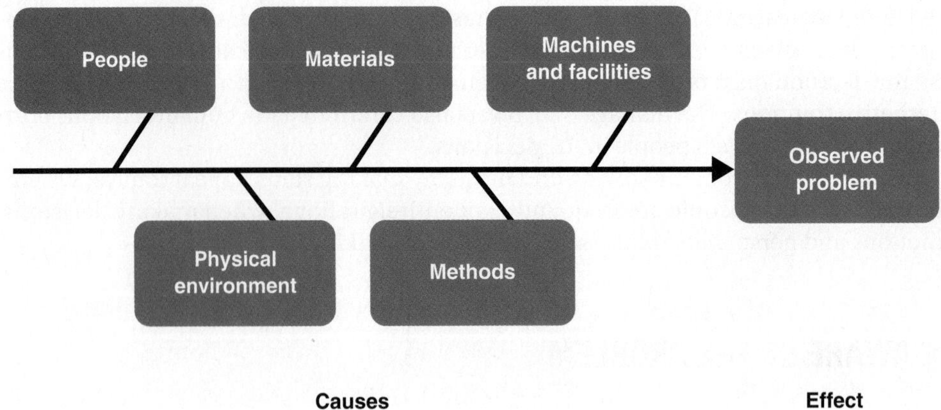

FIGURE 6-3
BASIC CAUSE-AND-EFFECT DIAGRAM

4. **Physical environment.** Is anything wrong with the environment (such as toxic fumes making people sick)? Has the environment changed?
5. **Methods.** Are the processes and procedures adequate? Have new methods been introduced that workers do not understand?

The approach to analyzing causes is often placed in a cause-and-effect diagram, as shown in Figure 6.3. The approach is sometimes referred to as a *fishbone diagram* because of the angles of the lines leading to the various causes. Notice that all the causes contribute to the problem at the right. Even when you have identified the general source of a problem, you may still need to dig further as to what, when, and where a problem *did not* occur. Suppose a friend talks about a fear of public speaking. By asking a few "but not" questions, you might be able to identify a major cause of the problem. Let's try out the method:

Your friend: I'm horribly afraid of public speaking. I hate going up in front of class.

You: But have you ever not been afraid of speaking to a group of people?

Your friend: Yes, I can remember once feeling okay speaking at a victory dinner for my high school soccer team. We came in first place in the region.

You: What did you talk about?

Your friend: I told a cute story about how my mother and father put a soccer ball in my crib. I hugged it every day like it was a teddy bear.

You: So why weren't you afraid of giving that talk?

Your friend: I knew what I was talking about. I didn't have to rehearse.

You: What else was different about the talk?

Your friend: It wasn't like talking to strangers. I was just there with my buddies and our coaches.

You: What you are really telling me is that public speaking is okay when you are well prepared and you are in a comfortable surrounding?

Your friend: Thanks for helping me understand my problem.

FIND CREATIVE ALTERNATIVES

Creativity and imagination enter into problem solving and decision making. Successful decision makers have the ability to think of different alternatives. The person who pushes to find one more alternative to a problem is often the person who finds a breakthrough solution. The more alternatives you generate, the more likely you will find a useful solution to your problem. In the words of business strategy expert and consultant Gary Hamel, "Innovation is a numbers game. It takes 1,000 wacky ideas to find 100 things worth putting any money at all on, to find 10 ideas worth really investing in, to wind up with one really great idea."[11]

WEIGH ALTERNATIVES AND MAKE THE CHOICE

This stage refers simply to examining the pros and cons of the various alternatives in the previous stages and then making a choice. In a major decision, each alternative would have to be given serious consideration. In practice, weighing alternatives often means jotting down the key good and bad points of each possible choice. The essence of decision making is selecting the right course of action to follow. You have to choose an alternative, even if it is not to go ahead with a new plan of action. For instance, after conducting a job campaign, you could decide *not* to change jobs. Instead of coming to a decision, some people overanalyze a problem. Do you suffer from "analysis paralysis," or do you make up your mind after a reasonable amount of thought?

In choosing an alternative, it is helpful to remember that most problems really have multiple solutions. You therefore do not have to be overly concerned with finding the only correct answer to your problem. For instance, there might be several effective ways of reducing the costs of running a department.

Another useful consideration about choices is that it is best to reduce the number of possible choices you have to make. With too many choices, you might freeze in terms of decision making, such as trying to choose one among fifteen different television sets. Psychology professor Barry Schwartz of Swarthmore College notes that as we face more and more options we become overloaded. "Choice no longer liberates, but debilitates. It might even be said to tyrannize."[12]

IMPLEMENT THE CHOICE

After you decide which course of action to take, you have to put the choice into effect. Some decisions are more difficult to implement than others. Decisions made by top management, for example, are sometimes so difficult to implement that they have to be reversed. An executive at a major online retailer announced a new policy that all customer problems would have to be resolved by e-mail and that the toll-free number for customer assistance would be disbanded. Hundreds of customers complained about the new policy by e-mail, and many customer accounts became inactive. The executive reconsidered the decision in terms of its effect on customer service and goodwill and reinstated the toll-free line. The general point is that to implement many decisions, the human element must be taken into consideration.

EVALUATE THE CHOICE

The decision-making sequence is not complete until the decision has been evaluated. Evaluation may take a considerable period of time because the results of your decision are not always immediately apparent. Suppose you receive two job offers. It might take several months to a year to determine whether you are satisfied with the job you accepted. It would be necessary to look at the factors you think are most important in a job. Among them might be "Is there opportunity for advancement?" "Are the people here friendly?" "Is the work interesting?"

Evaluating your choice would be further complicated by the difficulty of determining how you might have fared in the job you didn't accept. Now and then, you might obtain some information to suggest what that alternative held in store for you, as did a woman who turned down a job offer with a new and promising company. She questioned that decision until she read one morning a year later that the company had gone into bankruptcy.

Worst-case scenario helpful decision-making aid that involves visualizing what you would do if the alternative chosen proved to be dreadful

Exit strategy determining in advance how to get out of a bad decision, such as having joined a failing family business

What happens when your evaluation of a decision is negative? You go back to the drawing board, as the line and arrow on the left-hand side of Figure 6.2 indicates. Because your first decision was not a good one, you are faced with another problem situation. A helpful decision-making aid is to visualize what you would do if the alternative you chose proved to be dreadful—the **worst-case scenario.** Suppose, for example, you choose a job that proves to be unsuited to your talents. Would you resign as soon as your mistake became apparent, or would you sweat it out for a year to show some employment stability? Or would you retain the job while starting to look for a more suitable job? Developing a worst-case-scenario plan helps prevent you from becoming overwhelmed by a bad decision. Closely related to the worst-case scenario is establishing an **exit strategy** that determines in advance how you will get out of a bad decision, such as having joined a failing family business.

A classic example of changing directions after discovering that a wrong decision was made took place in relation to the marketing of beer. Problem-solving expert, the late Russell Ackoff, studied the marketing strategy of Anheuser Busch, the producer of Budweiser brand beer. Ackoff reached the startling conclusion that increasing the advertising budget had little effect on sales. The former director of strategy for the beer company said that the negative finding was extremely valuable. "It gave Anheuser-Busch the confidence to maintain its marketing budget flat from 1961 to 1976. We quadrupled sales." [13] Today, the cool advertising campaign for Bud Lite may have a positive impact on sales, but the situation was different many years ago.

The accompanying Human Relations in Practice box illustrates a successful application of elements of the problem-solving and decision-making steps.

BRAIN TEASERS FOR IMPROVING YOUR PROBLEM-SOLVING ABILITY

A widely accepted belief is that solving difficult problems and puzzles enhances your problem-solving ability. Among these brain teasers could be crossword puzzles, some types of video games, and various types of word puzzles. Just to give you a brief mental workout, here we present an example of the well-known Sudoku (Figure 6.4). A brain

FIGURE 6-4

SUDOKU

Fill in the Sudoku grid so that every row, every column, and every 3 × 3 box contains the digits 1 through 9.

	6		1		4		5	
		8	3		5	6		
2								1
8			4		7			6
		6				3		
7			9		1			4
5								2
		7	2		6	9		
	4		5		8		7	

Human Relations in Practice

Boland Inc. Solves Its Problem with Rick's Quick Fit

Boland Inc., provides clients with sustainable and energy efficient solutions for many types of buildings in the Washington DC/Baltimore metropolitan area. The company works closely with clients to provide energy efficient HVAC (heating, ventilation, and air conditioning) systems with state-of-the-art controls supported by a factory trained staff.

As a provider of air conditioning systems, Boland management is well aware that sweating on the job can be a problem. Yet at the same time, management recognizes that physical movement during the workday is essential for health. A few years ago, management observed that not enough of the employees appeared to be in good physical condition.

Management reasoned that an obvious reason for not being in good physical condition was not obtaining enough exercise. Digging into the possible causes of the problem were facts such as workers not being staying committed to an exercise program, and the discomfort of doing physical exercise during the day. Even though the Boland facility has superior air conditioning, the outside temperature in the DC area is quite warm eight months a year. An employee might think, "It is 98 degrees outside. I'm not going to work out when I get into the building."

If employees are asked to engage in heavy physical exercise on company premises, Boland management would have to provide shower facilities. Furthermore, exercising and showering can take a big chunk of time out of the workday. Another contributing factor to the problem of insufficient physical exercise is that many people look for excuses to avoid the effort involved in engaging in full workouts.

"What we need is relatively effortless workouts that don't result in much sweating," thought Boland managers. The alternative chosen by Boland management was Rick's Quick Fit, a program that requires only simple exercises than can be done in work clothes, suits included. Quick Fit is a thorough, no-sweat workout designed to be accomplished in as little as fifteen minutes daily. (Note than people differ considerably in how readily they perspire.) Because clothing does not have to be changed before starting the workout, and post-exercise showers are not needed, Quick Fit can be done in the workplace. Quick Fit includes a 10 minute treadmill walk; four minutes of strengthening exercises; and one minute of stomach crunches.

The solution chosen to the physical exercise problem appears to be a good one. It has helped some of the 200 participants lose weight and lower their blood pressure. Boland employees can run through the daily program in the office gym during breaks or at home.

Questions: What might have made selecting a known exercise program such as Rick's Quick Fit have been more effective than simply encouraging Boland employees to exercise for 15 minutes every day?

Source: The facts supporting this story are derived from the following sources: "15-Minute Workout (in Work-Clothes) Cuts Excuses to Skip Exercise," *HR Specialist: Compensation & Benefits,* August 2010, p. 7; www.boland.com; "About QF," www.ricksquickfit.com, pp. 1–2, accessed January 24, 2012; "Quick Fit," www.ltwell.com/quick_fit_article.htm. Copyright © 2012, L&T Health and Fitness.

teaser based on verbal skills is the frame game, so in this example: The words in the box below symbolize a popular saying ("dog days"):

Sunday Collie
Monday Cocker Spaniel
Tuesday German Boxer
Wednesday Golden Retriever

Performing activities such as these regularly might sharpen your mental acuity for problem solving on the job and in school. The answers to the Sudoku and the frame games are presented following the references in this chapter.

Learning Objective 3

What Do I Need to Know About Creativity in Decision Making?

Creativity is helpful at any stage of problem solving but is essential for being aware of problems, analyzing their causes, and searching for alternative solutions. Simply put, **creativity** is the ability to develop good ideas that can be put into action. Finding a creative idea usually involves a flash of insight as to how to solve a problem, such as that experienced by the person who thought of Scotch tape. The flash of insight might take place at the workplace or while engaged in other activity, such as jogging, walking, showering, or watching a movie. If you are aware that you have a problem to solve, the sudden insight is more likely to flash into your mind. For example, you might want to solve the problem of adding a couple of more influential people into your network. So while you are taking out the garbage, the names of a couple of potential contacts might surface into your brain. Your mind has been working on your problem below your level of awareness.

Creativity
the ability to develop good ideas that can be put into action

Imagination is a very special thing, and we always try to find students with that ability.
—*David Greenberg*
Senior Vice President, human resources, for L'Oréal USA. Quoted in the *Wall Street Journal*, September 12, 2006, p. B8.

When many people see or hear the word *creativity,* they think of a rarefied talent. A more helpful perspective is to recognize that not all creativity requires wild imagination. The emphasis here is on creativity applied to business and personal life rather than on creativity in science, technology, and the arts.

A major theme of this chapter is that for the vast majority of people, it is possible to improve their creativity. Creativity can be taught, learned, enhanced, and mastered. Current thinking is that creativity is a skill rather than a trait we inherit. Anyone can therefore learn to be somewhat creative.[14] Creativity is highly valued in the workplace because it precedes **innovation**, the commercialization or implementation of creative ideas. A global positioning system (GPS) for consumer vehicles was a creative idea, but it was not truly innovative until it became a product on the market. Recognize, however that creativity and innovation are sometimes used almost as synonyms. This is particularly true when an idea must be useful to be classified as creative.

Innovation
the commercialization or implementation of creative ideas

MEASURING YOUR CREATIVE POTENTIAL

One way to understand creativity is to try out exercises used to measure creative potential. Begin with Human Relations Self-Assessment Quiz 6-2, which measures creativity based on verbal ability.

Human Relations Self-Assessment Quiz 6-2

Creative Personality Test

Answer each of the following statements as mostly true or mostly false. We are looking for general trends, so do not be concerned that under certain circumstances your answer might be different in response to a particular statement.

	Mostly True	Mostly False
1. I think movies based on fictional stories are a waste of time, so I am more likely to watch a documentary.	______	______
2. You have to admit, some crooks are ingenious.	______	______
3. I pretty much wear the same style and colors of clothing regularly.	______	______
4. To me most issues have a clear-cut right side or wrong side.	______	______
5. I enjoy it when my boss hands me vague instructions.	______	______
6. When I'm surfing the Internet, I sometimes investigate topics about which I know very little.	______	______
7. Leisure activities without a known purpose have very little appeal to me.	______	______
8. Taking a different route to work is fun, even if it takes longer.	______	______
9. From time to time I have made friends with people of a different sex, race, religion, or ethnic background from myself.	______	______
10. Rules and regulations should be respected, but deviating from them once in a while is acceptable.	______	______
11. People who know me say that I have an excellent sense of humor.	______	______
12. I have been known to play practical jokes or pranks on people.	______	______
13. Writers should avoid using unusual words and word combinations.	______	______
14. Detective work would have some appeal to me.	______	______
15. I am much more likely to tell a rehearsed joke than make a witty comment.	______	______
16. Almost all advertising on television bores me.	______	______
17. Why write letters or send e-mail greetings to friends when there are so many clever greeting cards already available in the stores or online?	______	______
18. For most important problems in life, there is one best solution available.	______	______
19. Pleasing me means more to me than pleasing others.	______	______
20. I'm enjoying taking this test.	______	______

Scoring and Interpretation:

Give yourself a plus 1 for each answer scored in the creative direction as follows:

1. Mostly False
2. Mostly True
3. Mostly False
4. Mostly False
5. Mostly True
6. Mostly True
7. Mostly False
8. Mostly True
9. Mostly True
10. Mostly True
11. Mostly True
12. Mostly True
13. Mostly False
14. Mostly True
15. Mostly False
16. Mostly False
17. Mostly False
18. Mostly False
19. Mostly True
20. Mostly True

A score of 15 or more suggests that your personality and attitudes are similar to those of a creative person. A score of between 9 and 14 suggests an average similarity with the personality and attitudes of a creative person. A score of 8 or less suggests that your personality is dissimilar to that of a creative person. You are probably more of a conformist and not highly open-minded in your thinking at this point in your life. To become more creative, you may need to develop more flexibility in your thinking and a higher degree of open-mindedness.

CHARACTERISTICS OF CREATIVE WORKERS

Creative workers tend to have different intellectual and personality characteristics from their less creative counterparts. In general, creative people are more mentally flexible than others, which allows them to overcome the traditional ways of looking at problems. This flexibility often shows up in practical jokes and other forms of playfulness, such as making up a rap song about the company's product line. The characteristics of creative workers can be grouped into three broad areas: knowledge, intellectual abilities, and personality.[15]

Knowledge

Creative thinking requires a broad background of information, including facts and observations. Knowledge supplies the building blocks for generating and combining ideas. This is particularly true because, according to some experts, creativity always comes down to combining things in a new and different way. A team of innovation researchers found that the most important discovery skill of a cognitive nature is the associating, defined as making connections across seemingly unrelated fields. You can therefore become more creative by searching for associations.[16]

Auto Trader's iPhone app for the United Kingdom illustrates how combining ideas can result in a creative idea. Users take a photo of a vehicle license plate number to search a vehicle's history, thereby combining a camera with a database about the history of a vehicle. The app was so popular that it overloaded the servers and had to be temporarily shut down until Auto Trader upgraded its server capacity.[17]

Intellectual Abilities

Insight
an ability to know what information is relevant, to find connections between the old and the new, to combine facts that are unrelated, and to see the "big picture"

In general, creative workers tend to be bright rather than brilliant. Extraordinarily high intelligence is not required to be creative, but creative people are good at generating alternative solutions to problems in a short period of time. According to Tufts University dean of the School of Arts and Sciences and professor of psychology Robert Sternberg, the key to creative intelligence is **insight**, an ability to know what information is relevant, to find connections between the old and the new, to combine facts that are unrelated, and to see the "big picture."[18](Again, the importance of combining ideas is emphasized.) Creative people also maintain a youthful curiosity throughout their lives, and the curiosity is not centered on only their own field of expertise. Instead, their range of interests encompasses many areas of knowledge, and they generate enthusiasm toward almost any puzzling problem.

Creative people are able to think divergently. They can expand the number of alternatives to a problem, thus moving away from a single solution. Yet the creative thinker also knows when it is time to think convergently, narrowing the number of useful solutions. For example, the divergent thinker might think of twenty-seven different names for a Web site to sell high-fashion buttons. Yet at some point, he or she will have to converge toward choosing the best name, such as www.chicbutton.com.

Personality

Creative self-efficacy
the belief that one has the knowledge and skills to produce creative outcomes.

The emotional and other nonintellectual aspects of a person heavily influence creative problem solving. Creative people tend to have a positive self-image without being blindly self-confident. Because they are self-confident, creative people are able to cope with criticism of their ideas. The self-confidence associated with worker creativity has been labeled **creative self-efficacy**—the belief that one has the knowledge and skills to produce creative outcomes. Creative self-efficacy is therefore a key psychological mechanism that supports solving problems creativity.[19] The marketing manager at MasterCard might say to her staff, "We have the same old problem. Only about 15 percent of the world's purchases are made with a credit card. How can we capture more of the 85 percent?" A staff member with high creative self-efficacy might respond, "Please let me form a small task force to work on this problem for a week. We will find you the answer you need."

Creative people have the ability to tolerate the isolation necessary for developing ideas. Talking to others is a good source of ideas. Yet at some point, the creative problem solver has to work alone and concentrate.

Creative people are frequently nonconformists and do not need strong approval from the group. Many creative problem solvers are thrill seekers who find developing imaginative solutions to problems to be a source of thrills. Creative people enjoy dealing with uncertainty and chaos. A creative person, for example, would enjoy the challenge of taking over a customer service department that was way behind schedule and ineffective. Less creative people become frustrated quickly when their jobs are unclear and disorder exists.

THE CONDITIONS NECESSARY FOR CREATIVITY

Creativity is not simply a random occurrence. Well-known creativity researcher and professor of business administration at Harvard Business School, Teresa M. Amabile, summarized twenty-two years of her research about creativity in the workplace. Her findings are also supported by others.[20] Creativity takes place when three components come together: expertise, creative thinking skills, and the right type of motivation. *Expertise* refers to the necessary knowledge to put facts together. The more ideas floating around in your head, the more likely you are to combine them in some useful way, as already described.

Creative thinking refers to how flexibly and imaginatively individuals approach problems. If you know how to keep digging for alternatives and to avoid getting stuck in the status quo, your chances of being creative multiply. Along these same lines, you are much more likely to be creative if you are intentionally seeking ideas, such as always being on the lookout for ways to save money. Persevering, or sticking with a problem to a conclusion, is essential for finding creative solutions. A few rest breaks to gain a fresh perspective may be helpful, but the creative person keeps coming back until a solution emerges. Or the creative idea might surface outside of the work setting, as described earlier.

Because creative ideas can surface at odd times, daydreaming is regarded as a contributor to creative output. Daydreaming is seen by some researchers as a source of creativity, especially for those who pay attention to their daydreams. Allegedly, the visionary daydreams of Albert Einstein facilitated his developing theory of relativity while he worked at an ordinary position in the Swiss patent office.[21] A modern example might be a father daydreaming about new product ideas while his waits for his daughter to complete her ride on a carousel.

The right type of *motivation* is the third essential ingredient for creative thought. A fascination with or passion for the task is much more important than searching for external rewards. Passion for the task and high intrinsic motivation contribute to a total absorption in the work and intense concentration, resulting in the flow experience. A creative businessperson, such as an entrepreneur developing a plan for worldwide distribution of a product, will often achieve the experience of flow. One analysis of creativity suggests that hard work and the love of the task can be at least as important as raw talent in ensuring creative success.[22] In addition to the internal conditions that foster creativity, five factors outside the person are key:

1. **An environmental need must stimulate the setting of a goal.** This is another way of saying, "Necessity is the mother of invention." For example, several years ago independent hardware stores were faced with the challenge of large chains, such as Home Depot and Lowe's, driving them out of business. Many of these independent stores survived by forming buying alliances with each other so that they could purchase inventory in larger quantities—and therefore at lower prices. The independents also emphasize doing home repairs, such as fixing ripped screens and broken windows.

2. **Another condition that fosters creativity is enough conflict and tension to put people on edge.** Robert Sutton, professor of engineering at Stanford University, advises managers to prod happy people into fighting among themselves to stimulate creativity. The fights should be about ideas, not personality conflicts and name-calling. For example, a group member should be given time to defend his or her work, and then the ideas should be sharply criticized by the other group members.[23]

3. **Another external factor for creativity is encouragement, including a permissive atmosphere that welcomes new ideas.** A manager or team leader who encourages imagination and original thinking and does not punish people for making honest mistakes is likely to receive creative ideas from people. W. L Gore is often cited among the world's most innovative companies. You may be familiar with their waterproof fabrics and guitar strings. The cornerstone of Gore's innovative culture has been a permissive atmosphere. In the words of human resources associate Jackie Brinton, "We believe in the power of the individual who is given the freedom to do great things and in the beauty of small teams, even though we're now operating on a global, coordinated scale."[24]

4. **Humor is a key environmental condition for enhancing creativity.** Humor has always been linked to creativity. Humor gets the creative juices flowing, and effective humor requires creativity. Thomas Edison started every workday with a joke-telling session. Mike Vance, chair of the Creative Thinking Association of America, says, "Humor is unmasking the hypocritical. What makes us laugh often is seeing how things are screwed up—then sometimes seeing how we can fix them. Whenever I go into a company and don't hear much laughter, I know it's not a creative place.[25]

5. **A final key environmental condition to be considered here is how much time pressure the problem solver should face to trigger creativity.** Conventional wisdom says that people produce the best when pressure is highest—for example, thinking of ways to keep a business running after a disaster, such as a fire, flood, or terrorist attack. Yet studies show that the more workers feel pressed for time, the less likely they are to produce creative output, such as solving a tricky problem or envisioning a new product, or to have other such "ah ha!" experiences that result in innovation. Time pressures may diminish creativity because they limit a worker's freedom to think through different options and directions. A subtle finding, however, is that time pressures may help creativity if the worker is focused on a single task that he or she considers important.[26] So if you are under heavy time pressure to arrive at a creative solution, focus on one task.

Despite the theme of permissiveness in several of the conditions for enhancing creativity, constraints also have their place. Individuals or teams with budget constraints and time constraints sometimes find that these constraints help them rise to the occasion. Marissa Ann Mayer, CEO of Yahoo!, contends that constraints can actually speed product development. Google often gets a sense of just how good a new concept is if they simply prototype it (try it out) for a single day or week. Another constraint would be limiting team size to two or three people.[27]

▶ Learning Objective 4 ▶

How Do I Improve My Creativity?

Because of the importance of creative problem solving, many techniques have been developed to improve creativity. Here we look at both specific techniques and general strategies for becoming more creative. The goal of these experiences is to think like a creative problem solver. Such a person lets his or her imagination wander. He or she ventures beyond the constraints that limit most people. The result of thinking more creatively is to bring something new into existence. *Something new* can be a totally new creation or a combination of existing things and ideas. To focus again on the subject, when we refer to creativity in business we are not necessarily thinking of revolutionary ideas that create a new industry. The new design of containers for prescription medicine is a representative example. Old prescription bottles were difficult to open and read, whereas the new prescription bottles are color coded to specific medicines and easy to read and open. Nevertheless, many of the older-style prescription bottles are still in use.

BELIEVE THAT YOU CAN BE CREATIVE

As implied by creative self-efficacy, a starting point in increasing your creativity is to believe that you can. Acknowledge that you can solve problems with more imagination if you approach them with a different mindset.[28] David Kelley, the founder of the design firm, IDEO, writes that innovators are not necessarily exceptional, as much as they are confident.[29] The message here is to recognize that you have the capacity to be a creative problem solver, and to push forward and keep trying when faced with a problem that lacks a standard solution.

CONCENTRATE INTENSELY ON THE TASK AT HAND

The ability to concentrate was mentioned earlier as a characteristic that contributes to effective problem solving in general. The ability to eliminate distractions also contributes mightily to generating new ideas. At times we think we are thinking intently about our problem, yet in reality we may be thinking about something that interferes with creativity. Among the office distractions that interfere with concentration are phone calls, a computer beep informing you of an incoming message, a person in the next cubicle talking loudly on the phone, and a friendly hello from a work associate walking past your cubicle. All the methods that follow for creativity enhancement require concentration.

OVERCOME TRADITIONAL MENTAL SETS

An important consequence of becoming more intellectually flexible is that you can overcome a **traditional mental set,** a fixed way of thinking about objects and activities. Overcoming traditional mental sets is important because the major block to creativity is to perceive things in a traditional way. All creative examples presented so far in this chapter have involved this process, and here is another one. You may be familiar with the Nalgene sports bottle for carrying water and other fluids. Aside from its decorative colors, a key feature is its durability. The bottle had its origins in chemical laboratories—the traditional use for a durable plastic bottle. However, by the 1970s, managers at Nalgene noticed that scientists were using the durable bottles to hold water for camping and hiking. The company soon started a division to market its "laboratory" bottles to Boy Scouts and other hikers. Today a strong demand still exists for the Nalgene sports bottle, despite a claim in 2008 that a toxic substance in the bottle could leach into the bottles' contents and make consumers ill. In response to the potential problem, Nalge Nunc International Corp removed the offending agent (Bisphenol A, or BPA) in the manufacture of the sports bottle.[30]

Traditional mental set
fixed way of thinking about objects and activities

An effective way of overcoming a traditional mental set (or thinking outside the box) is to challenge the status quo. If you want to develop an idea that will impress your boss or turn around an industry, you must use your imagination. Question the old standby that things have always been done in a particular way.

DISCIPLINE YOURSELF TO THINK LATERALLY

Vertical thinking
analytical, logical process that results in few answers; the vertical thinker looks for the one best solution to a problem, much like solving an equation in algebra

Lateral thinking
process of spreading out to find many different alternative solutions to a problem

A major challenge in developing creative thinking skills is to learn how to think laterally in addition to vertically. **Vertical thinking** is an analytical, logical process that results in few answers. The vertical thinker is looking for the one best solution to a problem, much like solving an equation in algebra. In contrast, **lateral thinking** spreads out to find many different alternative solutions to a problem. In short, critical thinking is vertical, and creative thinking is lateral. A vertical thinker might say, "I must find a part-time job to supplement my income. My income is not matching my expenses." The lateral thinker might say, "I need more money. Let me think of the various ways of earning or having more money. I can find a second job, get promoted where I am working, cut my expenses, run a small business out of my home. . . ."

CONDUCT BRAINSTORMING AND BRAINWRITING SESSIONS

Brainstorming
technique by which group members think of multiple solutions to a problem

The best-known method of improving creativity is **brainstorming**, a technique by which group members think of multiple solutions to a problem. Using brainstorming, a group of six people might sit around a table generating new ideas for a product. During the idea-generating part of brainstorming, potential solutions are not criticized or evaluated in any way. In this way, spontaneity is encouraged. Brainstorming continues as a standard procedure for producing creative ideas in all types of organizations. If you engage in brainstorming on the job or in personal life, you will be both solving a real problem and enhancing your creative thinking skills at the same time. Rules for brainstorming are presented in Figure 6.5. Brainstorming has many variations, including individuals submitting ideas via e-mail or a shared Web page, and brainwriting.

An important strategy for enhancing the outcome of brainstorming is to have intellectually and culturally diverse group members. Some group leaders purposely choose people of different problem-solving styles to encourage more diverse thinking. The logical type might have more "brainstorms" based on facts, whereas the intuitive type might have more brainstorms based on hunches. Cultural diversity is likely to improve brainstorming because people with different cultural experiences often bring different viewpoints to bear on the problem. A basic example is that when developing new food products, members with different ethnic backgrounds are chosen for a brainstorming group.

Brainwriting

Brainwriting
arriving at creative ideas by jotting them down

In many situations, brainstorming alone produces as many or more useful ideas than does brainstorming in groups. **Brainwriting** is arriving at creative ideas by jotting them down yourself. The creativity-improvement techniques discussed so far will help you develop the mental flexibility necessary for brainstorming. After you have loosened up your mental processes, you will be ready to tackle your most vexing problems. Self-discipline is very important for brainwriting because some people have a tendency to postpone something as challenging as thinking alone. A variation of brainwriting is for group members to pass along their ideas from working alone to another member who reads them and adds his or her own ideas.

FIGURE 6-5
RULES AND GUIDELINES FOR BRAINSTORMING

1. Use groups of about five to seven people.
2. Encourage the spontaneous expression of ideas. All suggestions are welcome, even if they are outlandish or outrageous. The least workable ideas can be edited out when the idea-generation phase is completed.
3. Quantity and variety are very important. The greater the number of ideas, the greater the likelihood of a breakthrough idea.
4. Encourage combination and improvement of ideas. This process is referred to as *piggybacking* or *hitchhiking*.
5. One person serves as the secretary and records the ideas, perhaps posting them on a whiteboard or a computer with a projection device.
6. Do not over-structure by following any of the preceding rules too rigidly. Brainstorming is a spontaneous process.

Brainwriting supports group brainstorming in two important ways. One approach is for team leaders to alert participants of the upcoming brainstorming session and encourage them to bring creative ideas into the meeting. David Perkins, a professor at the Harvard Graduate School of Education, says, "The best way to get good ideas is to get people to write them down privately and then bring them in."[31] A second approach is to permit participants to submit additional ideas up to twelve hours after the meeting. In this way participants who were shy about submitting a particular idea in a group will have a voice.[32] Also, we often think of the right thing to say after an event—the phenomenon of "I wish I would have thought of that then instead of now."

In the various types of brainstorming just discussed, collecting wild ideas is only the start of the process. After ideas are collected, the group or each member carefully evaluates and analyzes the various alternatives. (You also need to refine your ideas from brainwriting.) It is usually important to also specify the implementation details. For example, how do you actually convert an industrial robot into an amusement park ride?

The term *brainstorming* is so much part of everyday language that the structured process of brainstorming is often confused with any group discussion. A major problem with unstructured group meetings, however, is that they often result in tangential discussions that tend to dampen the creativity of meeting participants. Business author David Sherwin writes that groups "risk filling time with consensus, rather than exploring divergent, multidisciplinary viewpoints. It is in the friction between these views that we explore new patterns of thought."[33]

ESTABLISH IDEA QUOTAS FOR YOURSELF

To enhance creativity, many companies assign idea quotas to workers. For example, workers might be instructed to bring one good idea for earning or saving money to every meeting. Establishing idea quotas is similar to brainwriting with a goal in mind. An easy way of getting started is to establish a monthly minimum quota of one creative idea to improve your personal life and one to improve your job or school performance. Although this exercise might take only about five minutes of thinking each month, it could have a tremendous impact on your life. After you have gained the skill of developing one good idea per month, you might up your quota to two or three ideas. As with any creative idea, you will need an action plan to make the idea a reality. For example, one creative idea might be "I will sell buried treasure on eBay." Next, you have to find the buried treasure or find a supplier, photograph the treasure, and so forth.

ENGAGE IN MULTICULTURAL EXPERIENCES

A current analysis of many studies supports the assumption that multicultural experience fosters creativity.[34] *Multicultural experience* in this context refers to all direct and indirect experiences of encountering or interacting with people from foreign cultures. This definition is helpful because it suggests that travel to other countries is not the only way to obtain multicultural experience. For example, eating in a foreign-themed restaurant or interacting with people from another culture via the Internet would give you at least some multicultural experience.

Multicultural experience fosters creativity in several ways. First, you might obtain direct access to novel ideas and concepts from other cultures. For example, an American visitor to Japan might observe that many Japanese people read novels on their cell phones and then convince his or her company to start a similar service in the United States.

Second, multicultural living experience may allow people to recognize that the same surface behavior has different functions and implications. For example, in some cultures leaving food on your plate is a compliment to the host, implying that you had enough food. In another culture, leaving food on the plate would suggest the food wasn't good. A stretch application of this concept is that the act of using a fountain pen might be perceived as (a) a means of signing an important document or as (b) a gesture of status. The latter is why expensive fountain pens still sell even if their practical use is limited.

Third, exposure to foreign cultures might shake up a person's thinking enough to access unconventional knowledge when back in their own cultures. For example, you might observe that people in parts of Canada and Iceland actually pay to stay in a hotel made of ice and sleep in sleeping bags in their ice beds. As a hotel manager, you might say to yourself, "Maybe we can charge people to stay overnight in a swamp here in Florida."

Fourth, exposure to other cultures may lead to a psychological readiness to recruit ideas from unfamiliar sources and places. The well-traveled manager might now be more willing to ask entry-level workers for their suggestions on improving products, services, and work procedures. Or during "Bring Your Child to Work Day," the manager might ask the visiting children for useful suggestions.

Fifth, cultural exploration might foster a willingness to synthesize seemingly incompatible ideas from diverse cultures. For example, the rickshaws used in Asia sparked the idea for a similar service to provide transportation to businesspeople and tourists in crowded cities such as New York City and London. The modern rickshaw is usually bicycle driven and referred to as a pedicab.

OBTAIN ADEQUATE PHYSICAL EXERCISE

Physical exercise plays an important role in preparing you for creative thinking. Physical movement stimulates the brain by bringing it more blood and oxygen. At the same time, the exercise may reduce stress that makes it difficult to concentrate enough to think creatively. Exercise also enhances activity in the frontal lobe, the region of the brain involved in abstract reasoning and attention. Participating in physical activity may also foster creativity because many flashes of insight occur while engaged in leisure pursuits.

Phillip A. Newbold, the CEO of Memorial Hospital in South Bend, Indiana, runs the Innovation Café, a laboratory for collecting creative ideas. He holds regular brainstorming sessions in which participants are often required to stand up for the entire twenty-one-minute exercise so they practice thinking on their feet. Newbold, 61 years old, runs, bikes, swims, and competes in ironman triathlons. He says, "I couldn't do my innovation marathon if I weren't in marvelous physical shape."[35] The fact that physical activity can boost creative thinking should not be interpreted in isolation. Without other factors going for you, such as a storehouse of knowledge and passion for the task, physical exercise will not lead to mental breakthroughs.

SOLICIT FEEDBACK ON YOUR PERFORMANCE

An effective way of enhancing creativity on the job is to seek feedback on your performance from both your manager and coworkers. Even if you are not asking for feedback on creative suggestions exclusively, the feedback process is likely to sharpen your imagination. An example of a feedback-seeking question would be, "What did you think of my suggestion for reducing energy costs by encouraging employees to bring sweaters to the office?" The feedback refines your thinking, helping you develop ideas that others perceive to be imaginative.

A study demonstrating the link between feedback seeking and job creativity was conducted with 456 supervisor-employee pairs in four management consulting firms. Employees who asked for feedback directly, as well as looking around for indirect feedback, tended to be rated more highly on displaying creativity.[36] Examples of indirect feedback would be seeing positive mention of your performance in an e-mail or hearing a spontaneous comment about your work during a meeting.

PLAY THE ROLES OF EXPLORER, ARTIST, JUDGE, AND LAWYER

A method for improving creativity has been proposed that incorporates many of the suggestions already made. The method calls for you to adopt four roles in your thinking.[37]

1. **Be an explorer.** Speak to people in different fields and get ideas that you can use. For example, if you are a telecommunications specialist, speak to salespeople and manufacturing specialists.
2. **Be an artist by stretching your imagination.** Strive to spend about 5 percent of your day asking "what if" questions. For example, a sales manager at a fresh-fish distributor might ask, "What if some new research suggests that eating fish causes intestinal cancer in humans?" Also remember to challenge the commonly perceived rules in your field. Years ago, a bank manager challenged why customers needed their canceled checks returned each month. This questioning led to some banks not returning canceled checks unless the customer paid an additional fee for the service. (As a compromise, most banks send customers photocopies of about ten checks on one page.)
3. **Know when to be a judge.** After developing some wild ideas, at some point you have to evaluate them. Do not be so critical that you discourage your own imaginative thinking, but be critical enough to prevent attempting to implement weak ideas.
4. **Achieve results by playing the role of a lawyer.** Negotiate and find ways to implement your ideas within your field or place of work. The explorer, artist, and judge stages of creative thought might last only a short time toward developing a creative idea. Yet, you may spend months or even years getting your brainstorm implemented. For example, it took a long time for the developer of the electronic pager to finally get the product manufactured and distributed on a large scale.

How Does Critical Thinking Relate to Problem Solving and Creativity?

Learning Objective 5

Another way of understanding and improving problem solving and creativity is to regard both processes as being part of critical thinking. Probably any course you have ever taken, including mathematics, chemistry, history, political science, and English literature, was aimed partially at improving your critical thinking. This is true because critical thinking is a broad concept that includes many different cognitive, or intellectual, behaviors that focus on problem solving. **Critical thinking** refers to solving problems and making decisions through a systematic evaluation of evidence.[38] A person who thinks clearly and rationally is engaged in critical thinking, and the problem-solving steps described in this chapter help you think critically. Also, the suggestions for improving creativity will help you attain high-quality solutions to problems. Critical thinking proceeds in steps, as shown in Figure 6.6.

Critical thinking solving problems and making decisions through a systematic evaluation of evidence

Step 1 is to have a healthy degree of skepticism about the argument or proposition being presented. Probe for logical flaws in the argument the other person might have made. The other person's emotional state might have made him or her a little irrational. Visualize yourself as a store manager in a chain of furniture stores. The CEO introduces a plan for saving money by firing two-thirds of the experienced full-time store associates and replacing them with part-time workers at modest wages. You are quite skeptical that this plan will help the company in the long run.

Step 2 is to evaluate the stated or unstated assumptions underlying the argument. You say to yourself, "The CEO is assuming that part-time, inexperienced associates will sell as much furniture and accessories as our experienced associates

FIGURE 6-6
STEPS IN CRITICAL THINKING

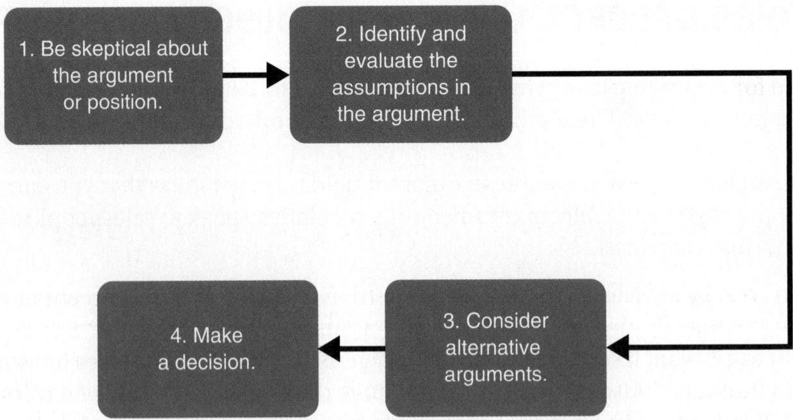

did. He is also assuming that knowledge of the business does not account for much. Another assumption is that the part-timers who replace the full-timers will be as loyal, even if not given benefits. I doubt these assumptions are correct." Evaluating assumptions is important because a persuasive speaker will often influence us not to carefully evaluate the logic of his or her position.

Step 3 is to imagine and attempt to evaluate alternative arguments. Here are a couple of other assumptions you might make: "Experienced and knowledgeable store associates are the lifeblood of our business. They are worth the compensation they receive because they generate more business and create a greater base of satisfied customers. Many part-time workers might sell furniture as a supplement to their regular job. Instead of feeling committed to our company, they might have high turnover."

Step 4 is to make a decision. You have given careful thought to top-management's plan, including having conducted some research. Your decision is to write an e-mail to the CEO that includes these thoughts: "I know we want to trim costs and increase profits. Our best profit generators are experienced, dedicated store associates. They give great decorating ideas to customers. Home Depot once tried to save money by dumping full-time associates. Customer service became so bad that the plan was reversed. Circuit City tried the same stunt of saving money by firing experienced store associates, and they went bankrupt."

Critical thinking is often difficult to accomplish for a variety of personal and situational factors that might prevent or limit us from critically evaluating a problem. The factors that influence problem-solving skill listed in Figure 6.1 might be considered potential constraints on critical problem solving. Here we highlight a few possible constraints.

One personal factor is a person's emotional state. When we are too emotional in a negative or positive direction, our ability to critically evaluate a situation is diminished. Another personal factor is cognitive skills, including knowledge and wisdom. A person who is mentally sharp and has more knowledge is better able to think critically than a person with less cognitive skills and less knowledge. (In the above example, being familiar with the Home Depot and Circuit City experiences in reducing the number of full-time associates was quite useful.)

Situational factors, including the atmosphere of the company, also influence critical thinking. For example, in some companies critical thinking by employees about major issues is welcomed. In some other company atmospheres, critical thinking of issues outside your immediate area is discouraged. Another situational factor would be a crisis situation, such as a worker not taking time to reflect carefully on alternatives when he or she is charged with using company resources to establish a child pornography Web site. (The worker also did not engage in critical thinking when establishing the Web site.)

How Do Multiple Intelligences Contribute to Problem Solving and Creativity?

◀ Learning Objective 6 ◀

Another approach to understanding the diverse nature of mental ability is the theory of **multiple intelligences**. According to Howard Gardner, people know and understand the world in distinctly different ways and learn in different ways. The concept of multiple intelligences also provides insights into problem solving and creativity because is suggests that people have different types of intelligences, or mental abilities, that can be called upon as needed to solve a particular problem. Individuals possess the following eight intelligences, or faculties, in varying degrees:

Multiple intelligences the idea that people know and understand the world in distinctly different ways and learn in different ways and that the possess eight intelligences, or faculties, in varying degrees.

1. **Linguistic.** Enables people to communicate through language, including reading, writing, and speaking.
2. **Logical-mathematical.** Enables individuals to see relationships between objects and solve problems, as in calculus and statistics.
3. **Musical.** Gives people the capacity to create and understand meanings made out of sounds and to enjoy different types of music.
4. **Spatial.** Enables people to perceive and manipulate images in the brain and to recreate them from memory, as is required in making graphic designs.
5. **Bodily kinesthetic.** Enables people to use their body and perceptual and motor systems in skilled ways such as dancing, playing sports, and expressing emotion through facial expressions.
6. **Intrapersonal.** Enables people to distinguish among their own feelings and acquire accurate self-knowledge.
7. **Interpersonal.** Makes it possible for individuals to recognize and make distinctions among the feelings, motives, and intentions of others as in managing or parenting.
8. **Naturalist.** Enables individuals to differentiate among, classify, and utilize various features of the physical external environment.

The list of multiple intelligences is dynamic with new possibilities emerging such as *existential intelligence* that focuses on a concern about ultimate issues, such as the nature of human existence. Existential intelligence would be similar to spirituality, and would therefore be quite helpful for a religious leader.

Your profile of intelligences influences how you best learn and to which types of jobs you are best suited. Gardner believes that it is possible to develop these separate intelligences through concentrated effort. However, any of these intelligences might fade if not put to use.[39] The components of multiple intelligences might also be perceived as different talents or abilities. Having high cognitive intelligence would contribute to high standing on each of the eight intelligences.

The application of multiple intelligences applied to an everyday problem implies that the problem solver reaches into his or her bag of intelligences to use the right mix to solve the problem at hand. For example, if the problem facing you was how to raise some quick cash for a small business, you might decide to sell surplus equipment and furniture on an auction Web site such as eBay. To make the sale successful you might use your logical-mathematical intelligence to figure out reasonable pricing; your linguistic intelligence to accurately describe your offerings; and your spatial intelligence to post esthetically pleasing photos of the furniture and equipment.

Key Terms

Summary and Review

Problem solving occurs when you try to remove an obstacle that is blocking a path you want to take or when you try to close the gap between what exists and what you want to exist. Decision making takes place after you encounter a problem and you select one alternative from the various courses of action that can be pursued. Many traits and characteristics influence the type of problem solver you are now or are capable of becoming. Among them are the following:

- Cognitive intelligence, education, and experience
- Emotional intelligence
- Flexibility versus rigidity
- Intuition
- Concentration
- Decisiveness and perfectionism
- Risk taking and thrill seeking
- Values of the decision maker

The decision-making process outlined in this chapter uses both the scientific method and intuition for making decisions in response to problems. Decision making follows an orderly flow of events:

1. You are aware of a problem or create one of your own.
2. You identify causes of the problem.
3. You find creative alternatives.
4. You weigh the alternatives and make a choice.
5. You implement the choice.
6. You evaluate whether you have made a sound choice. If your choice was unsound, you are faced with a new problem, and the cycle repeats itself.

Creativity is the ability to look for good ideas that can be put into action. Innovation occurs when a creative idea is commercialized. Creative workers tend to have different intellectual and personality characteristics than their less creative counterparts. In general, creative people are more mentally flexible than others, which allows them to overcome the traditional way of looking at problems. These characteristics are as follows:

- **Knowledge.** Creative thinking requires a broad background of information, including facts and observations. The most important discovery skill of a cognitive nature is making connections across seemingly unrelated fields.
- **Intellectual abilities.** Creative workers tend to be bright rather than brilliant. The key to creative intelligence is insight, including the combination of ideas (associating). Creativity can stem from both fluid (raw) intelligence and crystallized (accumulated) intelligence.
- **Personality.** The emotional and other nonintellectual aspects of a person heavily influence creative problem solving. For example, creative people are frequently nonconformists and thrill seekers.

Creativity takes place when three components come together:

1. Expertise
2. Creative thinking skills (being flexible and imaginative)
3. The right type of motivation (passion for the task and intrinsic motivation)

Four factors outside the person play a key role in fostering creativity: an environmental need, enough conflict and tension to put people on edge, encouragement from management, and the presence of humor. Unless a person is working on a highly focused task, time pressures are likely to diminish creativity. Constraints, such as time and budgets, can often enhance creativity.

Methods of improving your creativity include the following:

- Concentrate intensely on the task at hand.
- Overcome traditional mental sets.
- Discipline yourself to think laterally.
- Conduct brainstorming and brainwriting sessions.
- Borrow creative ideas.
- Establish idea quotas for yourself.
- Engage in multicultural experiences.
- Obtain adequate physical exercise.
- Solicit feedback on your performance.
- Play the roles of explorer, artist, judge, and lawyer.

Another way of understanding and improving problem solving and creativity is to regard both processes as part of critical thinking. The process has four steps:

1. Be skeptical of the argument or proposition offered.
2. Evaluate the stated or unstated assumptions underlying the argument.
3. Imagine and attempt to evaluate alternative arguments.
4. Make a decision.

The idea of multiple intelligences can contribute to both problem solving and creativity because it recognizes that at least eight different types of intelligence, or faculties, can be applied to the problem at hand.

Check Your Understanding

1. What would be some of the symptoms or signs of a "flexible thinker"?
2. How might being a low risk taker limit a person's chances for attaining a high level of career success?
3. Provide an example of how you have used intuition to your advantage in work or personal life.
4. Furnish an example from your own life in which you became aware of a problem. What led to this awareness?
5. Why does knowledge lead to creativity?
6. Provide an example of how a supervisor or teacher of yours encouraged you to be creative. How effective was this encouragement?
7. Why is being passionate about the task at hand almost essential for being creative?
8. The Lincoln automobile design chief, Max Wolf, has a short beard and has a tuft in his hair (somewhat of a point). A magazine writer said that this appearance suggests that Wolf is creative. What is your opinion of this physical stereotype of a creative male worker?
9. How might having just a couple of creative ideas during your work life have a major impact on the success of your career?
10. Ask an experienced manager or professional how important creative thinking has been in his or her career. Be prepared to report back to class with your findings.

Web Corner

Problem-Solving and Decision-Making Tools:
www.mindtools.com

Development of Creative Thinking:
www.cre8ng.com

INTERNET SKILL BUILDER

Creativity Training

Many Web sites offer creativity training and an opportunity for self-assessment with respect to creativity. One such site is www.creax.com, which offers creativity services as well as a comprehensive forty-question test of creativity tendencies. The CREAX creativity test measures your creativity in eight different areas and visually depicts how your score compared to others who took the test. After you take the test, compare your results to the creativity test you took in this chapter. Also decide if the CREAX test is measuring personal characteristics that contribute to creative thinking, or if actual creative thinking is being tested. If CREAX is no longer in operation, insert "creativity training" in your search engine to find a comparable site.

Developing Your Human Relations Skills

Human Relations Application Exercises

Applying Human Relations Exercise 6-1

Using the Problem-Solving Process

Imagine that you have received $2 million in cash with the income taxes already paid. The only stipulation is that you will have to use the money to establish some sort of enterprise, either a business or a charitable foundation. Solve this problem using the following worksheet. Describe what thoughts you have or what actions you will take for each step of problem solving and decision making.

I. *Be Aware of the Problem.* You have already been assigned the problem.
II. *Identify causes of the problem.* How did this problem come about?
III. *Find creative alternatives.* Think of the many alternatives facing you. Let your imagination flow and be creative.
IV. *Weigh alternatives and make the choice.* Weigh the pros and cons of each of your sensible alternatives, and choose one course of action.

	Alternatives	Advantages	Disadvantages
1.			
2.			
3.			
4.			
5.			

V. Implement the choice. Outline your action plan for converting your chosen alternative into action.
VI. Evaluate the choice. Do the best you can here by speculating how you will know if the decision you reached was a good one.

Applying Human Relations Exercise 6-2

Stretch Your Imagination

A global contest was organized by Stanford University through its Technology Ventures program. Anyone in the world was permitted to enter. The assignment was to take ordinary rubber bands and "add value" to them. Entries were submitted by video, posting them on YouTube. Entrants included people from many different occupations, including computer scientists. The winner received the Genius Award.

Here is where you fit in. By brainwriting or brainstorming, come up with at least six ways of adding value (making more useful) to a rubber band, or a bunch of rubber bands. You must stretch your imagination to be successful. After the brainstorming sessions have been completed, perhaps taking ten minutes of class time, a representative of each group might share results with the class. Students might then assign a Genius Award to the entry that seems the most useful. Or the instructor might be the judge.

Source: The facts about the contest stem from Lee Gomes, "Our Columnist Judges a Brainstorming Bee, and Meets a Genius," *The Wall Street Journal,* March 5, 2008, p. B1.

Human Relations Class Activity

Creative Problem Solving and Traffic Congestion

Traffic congestion has become a major problem in many large cities. Any solution to the problem must be simple, effective, and not too expensive to administer. The basic approach to this exercise is for problem-solving (or brainstorming) groups to suggest about several solutions to resolving traffic congestions in a city of their choice. Because this problem is so complex, with easy solutions not available, the groups may want to consult outside sources such as Web sites while engaging in problem solving.

After the various groups have completed their problem solving, it will be useful to compare solutions. Class discussion can then be held to answer the following questions:

1. Which solution to the problem of downtown traffic suggestion seems the most feasible, and why?
2. What objections might the owners of vehicles have to the best suggestions?

The idea for this exercise stems from Edward de Bono, "Creative Problem-Solving: An Exercise in Creative Problem-Solving Using the Example of Traffic Congestion," www.thinkingmanagers.com, July 7, 2008, pp. 1–4.

Human Relations Case Study 6-1

Budget Vision Care Needs Ideas

Seth is the CEO of Budget Vision Care, a chain of twenty-five stores whose business is to provide low-price eyeglasses to consumers who cannot afford, or who do not choose to pay, standard prices for eyeware. The stores are located in neighborhoods with below-average income level. Each store has a state-certified optician on premises. Most of the staff except for the store manager is part-time workers which helps reduce payroll costs. The bottom line of eyeglasses begins with a price of about $20. The frames and lenses are purchased from the lowest-price possible supplier from third-world countries.

Customer satisfaction has not been a major problem for Budget Vision Care because most of their customers understand that the eyeglasses they purchase at Budget are a good buy. The most consistent complaint, however, is that the eyeglasses are of low quality and break and bend easily. The frames often become misshapen after a few month of wear, and the lenses usually become detached if the eyeglasses fall on a hard surface.

With most of his customers having access to the Internet, Seth worries that dissatisfied customers might make negative social media posts, including Yelp, about Budget Vision Care. Several media posts, for example, have stated that the company exploits the poor by selling them very low-quality frames. Seth is also concerned that the optician stores in major discount retailers such as Walmart and Target will erode Vision's market share.

Seth is so worried about the forces against his business that he decides to work on the problem with his top-management team. Seth said that he has been casually talking about the problem with his team, but he hasn't really put the problem on his agenda. Seth sends his team an e-mail about the necessity of finding new sources of revenue for the firm, and he alerts them to a meeting to work on the problem.

At the meeting, Seth says to the group, "Budget Vision Care is in trouble. Our revenues declined only 12 percent last year, but the handwriting is on the wall. The criticism of our business model is getting more vocal, with even the Better Business Bureau inquiring about the quality of our product. The big box stores are breathing down our neck.

"I want you as the executive team to come up with a way of finding new sources of revenue for Budget Vision."

"No disrespect," said Kathy the director of marketing. "But you are our leader. You are supposed to provide the breakthrough idea that will create a solid future for Budget Vision Care. We've often talked about broadening our services, but we usually hit the same brick wall. The most notable idea was the one about installing tattoo parlors in our stores because so many of our customers wear tattoos.

"I think the best idea we had was the one about selling lottery tickets in all the stores. But I think we ran into some potential legal problems."

Seth then said, "I don't disagree that as CEO maybe I should have the next great idea for Budget Vision. But I don't right now, so that's why I'm asking you for your creative suggestions."

José, the CFO said, "I think that we need to ask an even deeper question than where we can find new sources of revenue. We need to ask where to look and whom to ask about new lines of business."

Questions

1. To what extent do you think it is Sam's individual responsibility to furnish creative ideas for generating new business for Budget Vision Care?
2. In response to José's comment, where should the management team look for creative ideas for enlarging the revenue of Budget Vision Care?
3. From the standpoint of ethics, do you think Budget Vision Care should stay in business? Explain your reasoning.

Human Relations Role-Playing Exercise 6-1

Group Decision Making and Creativity

One student plays the role of Seth, who, during his meeting with the executive team, presses them to suggest at least one useful idea for expanding Budget Vision Care's top line (revenue) by either selling more of existing services or creating a new service. Several other students play the roles of members of the executive team. They enjoy this opportunity of group decision making as well as the chance to engage in creative thinking. Yet, they also believe that it is Seth's role to exercise strong leadership by pointing Budget Vision Care in the right direction. Observers will look to see if this problem-solving session is likely to result in any innovations for Budget Vision Care.

Human Relations Case Study 6-2

Stefanie Ponders a Career Decision

Four years ago when Stefanie was 21 years old, she secured a position as a data-entry specialist in the customer support center for business software at a telecommunications company. For Stefanie, this position was an important starting point for moving up the career ladder. Within one year, Stefanie's advancement began. She was promoted to the position of customer support representative, in which she helped customers resolve software problems related to large-size commercial printers. Stefanie worked on problems both online and by telephone.

Two years ago, Stefanie received some disappointing news from her manager. As company revenues declined, Stefanie's position was eliminated. Her boss reassured Stefanie that she was an above-average performer and that she could possibly be called back should business conditions improve.

Stefanie was quite discouraged, yet she took action to move to what she thought be a more stable career. Stefanie enrolled in a three-month course at a beauty school, which would certify her as a cosmetologist. One week after graduating, Stefanie found a position as a hair stylist and nail specialist with a cosmetology studio in a home for seniors. She worked an average of thirty hours per week as a contract employee. Most of her work consisted of styling and shampooing the hair of women in their seventies and eighties.

Four months into her new position, Stefanie's manager at the telecommunications company telephoned her with positive news. Stefanie would be invited back to the company just four months from the date of the call. Stefanie expressed her appreciation for the exciting news and said she would get back to her manager with a decision soon.

Stefanie explained to her best friend, "I don't know what to do. I loved my job at the company. My work as a cosmetologist is going okay, and I'm kind of still learning. If I go back to the company, maybe I would be laid off again. Also, I don't know if it's such a good idea to quit a job so soon after beginning."

Questions

1. How should Stefanie systematically go about deciding whether to return to the company that laid her off?
2. What might be an imaginative solution to Stefanie's dilemma?
3. To what extent might Stefanie be facing an ethical issue if she leaves her position as a cosmetologist in a few months?

Source: Case researched by Stefanie Donaldson.

Human Relations Role-Playing Exercise 6-2

Helping Stefanie Make a Career Decision

The case about Stefanie's dilemma serves as background material and the story line for this role-play. One person plays the role of Stefanie, who meets with her best friend to discuss what kind of decision she should reach about being called back to the company. Another student plays the role of the best friend, who will do more than simply listen. The best friend will attempt to facilitate Stefanie using the problem-solving and decision-making steps to help her arrive at a sound decision.

For both scenarios, observers rate the role-players on two dimensions, using a 1 to 5 scale from very poor to very good. One dimension is "effective use of human relations techniques." The second dimension is "acting ability." A few observers might voluntarily provide feedback to the role-players in terms of sharing their ratings and observations. The course instructor might also provide feedback.

Answer to the brain teaser is as follows:

9	6	3	1	7	4	2	5	8
1	7	8	3	2	5	6	4	9
2	5	4	6	8	9	7	3	1
8	2	1	4	3	7	5	9	6
4	9	6	8	5	2	3	1	7
7	3	5	9	6	1	8	2	4
5	8	9	7	1	3	4	6	2
3	1	7	2	4	6	9	8	5
6	4	2	5	9	8	1	7	3

REFERENCES

1. Original story based on facts in the following sources: "Build a Better Burb Competition Winners," *Bustler* (www.bustler.net/index), October 4, 2010, pp. 1–6; "An Idea Competition to Retrofit Long Island Downtowns," *Planetizen* (www.planetizen.com). © 2000–2010 Urban Insight Inc., p. 1; Lisa Selin Davis, "Extreme Makeover: Parking Edition," *Time,* May 31, 2010, pp. 46–47; Matt Ball, "Time Magazine Features the Build a Better Burb Contest," (www.vectormedia.com), May 21, 2010, pp. 1–5.
2. Myeong-Gu Seo and Lisa Feldman Barrett, "Being Emotional During Decision Making—Good or Bad? An Empirical Investigation,"*Academy of Management Journal,* August 2007, pp. 923–940.
3. Erik Dane and Michael G. Pratt, "Exploring Intuition and Its Role in Managerial Decision Making," *Academy of Management Review,* January 2007, pp. 33–54.
4. Eugene Sadler-Smith and Erella Shefy, "The Intuitive Executive: Understanding and Applying 'Gut Feel' in Decision-Making,"*Academy of Management Executive,* November 2004, p. 76.
5. Lea Winerman, "What We Know without Knowing," *Monitor on Psychology,* March 2005, p. 52.
6. Christopher M. Barnes and John R. Hollenbeck, "Sleep Deprivation and Decision-Making Teams: Burning the Midnight Oil or Playing with Fire?" *Academy of Management Review,* January 2009, p. 64.
7. Research reported in Amy Cynkar, "A Towering Figure," *Monitor on Psychology,* April 2007, pp. 38–39.
8. David A. Shaywitz, "Free to Choose but Often Wrong," *The Wall Street Journal,* June 24, 2008, p. A17.
9. Paul C. Nutt, "Surprising but True: Half the Decisions in Organizations Fail," *Academy of Management Executive,* November 1999, pp. 75–90; Nutt, *Why Decisions Fail* (San Francisco: Berrett-Koehler, 2002).
10. Carol Polsky, "This Invention Is So Useful, It Has Stuck around for 75 Years," *Newsday* syndicated story, May 13, 2000; Mary Bellis, "The History of Scotch Tape: Richard Drew (1886-1982)," *About.com Inventors,* p. 1. Accessed January 25, 2012.
11. Quoted in Ann Pomeroy, "Cooking Up Innovation," *HR Magazine,* November 2004, pp. 49–50.
12. Cited in Dan Heath and Chip Heath, "Analysis of Paralysis," *Fast Company,* November 2007, p. 68.
13. Stephen Miller, "A Management Philosopher with Heady Ideas About Beer," *The Wall Street Journal,* November 11, 2009, p. A18.
14. Jonah Lehrer, *Imagine: How Creativity Works* (Boston: Houghton Mifflin Harcourt, 2012).
15. Richard W. Woodman, John E. Sayer, and Ricky W. Griffin, "Toward a Theory of Organizational Creativity," *Academy of Management Review,* April 1993, pp. 293–321; Greg R. Oldham and Anne Cummings, "Employee Creativity: Personal and Contextual Factors at Work,"*Academy of Management Journal,* June 1996, pp. 607–634; Robert J. Sternberg, "Creativity as a Decision," *American Psychologist,* May 2002, p. 376; Zak Stambor, "Self-Reflection May Lead Independently to Creativity, Depression," *Monitor on Psychology,* June 2005, p. 13.
16. Research reported in Carolyn T. Geer, "Innovation 101," *The Wall Street Journal,* October 17, 2011, p. R5.
17. Bridget Carey, "A Culture of Creativity," www.miamiherald.com, February 1, 2011, p. 2.
18. Robert J. Sternberg, ed., *Handbook of Creativity* (New York: Cambridge University Press, 1999).
19. Yaping Gong, Jia-Chi Huang, and Jiing-Lih Farth, "Employee Learning Orientation, Transformational Leadership, and Employees Creativity: The Mediating Role of Employee Creative Self-Efficacy," *Academy of Management Journal,* August 2009, p. 766.
20. Teresa M. Amabile, "How to Kill Creativity," *Harvard Business Review,* September–October 1998, pp. 78–79.
21. Josie Glausiusz, "Devoted to Distraction," *Psychology Today,* April 2009, pp. 84–91.
22. Teresa M. Amabile, "Beyond Talent: John Irving and the Passionate Craft of Creativity," *American Psychologist,* April 2001, p. 335.
23. Robert I. Sutton, "The Weird Rules of Creativity," *Harvard Business Review,* September 2001, p. 101.
24. Patrick J. Kiger, "Small Groups: Big Ideas," *Workforce Management,* February 27, 2006, p. 2.
25. Cited in Robert McGarvey, "Turn It On," *Entrepreneur,* November 1996, pp. 156–157.
26. Research cited in Bridget Murray, "A Ticking Clock Means a Creativity Drop," *Monitor on Psychology,* November 2002, p. 24; Interview with Teresa M. Amabile in Bill Breen, "The 6 Myths of Creativity," *Fast Company,* December 2004, pp. 77–78.
27. Marissa Ann Mayer, "Creativity Loves Constraints," *Business Week,* February 13, 2006, p. 102; Alexia Tsotsis, "Marissa Mayer, Google's 'De Niro,' Reveals What She Asks Job Candidates," www.techcrunch.com, December 8, 2011, p. 1.
28. Carlin Flora, "Everyday Creativity," *Psychology Today,* November/December 2009, p. 65.
29. Cited in Carolyn T. Geer, "Innovation 101," *The Wall Street Journal,* October 17, 201, p. R5.
30. "Sports Bottles Oh So Cool," *Democrat and Chronicle* (Rochester, NY), August 23, 2003, p. 14D; "Nalgene Sports Bottle Maker Sued Over Toxic Claims," *Business & Financial News* (http: www,reuters.com), April 23, 2008, p. 1.
31. Quoted in Jared Sandberg, "Brainstorming Works Best if People Scramble for Ideas on Their Own," *The Wall Street Journal,* June 13, 2006, p. B1.
32. "Expand Brainstorming," *Manager's Edge,* November 2008, p. 6.
33. Quoted in Douglas French, "Do Group Discussions Squelch Creativity?" *The Christian Science Monitor* (www.csmonitor.com), April 24, 2011, pp. 1–2.
34. Angela Ka-yee Leung, William W. Maddux, Adam D. Galinksy, and Chi-yue Chiu, "Multicultural Experience Enhances Creativity: The When and How," *American Psychologist,* April 2008, pp. 169–181.
35. Joann S. Lublin, "A CEO's Recipe for Fresh Ideas," *The Wall Street Journal,* September 2, 2008, p. D4.
36. Katleen E, De Stobbeleir, Susan J. Ashford, and Dirk Buyens, "Self-Regulation of Creativity at Work: The Role of

Feedback-Seeking Behavior in Creative Performance," *Academy of Management Journal,* August 2011, pp. 811-831. 37.

37. "Be a Creative Problem Solver," *Executive Strategies,* June 6, 1989, pp. 1–2.
38. Saul Kassin, *Psychology,* 2nd ed. (Upper Saddle River, NJ: Prentice Hall, 2001), p. 278. The critical-thinking steps described in this section are from the same source.
39. Howard Gardner, *Intelligence Reframed: Multiple Intelligence in the 21st Century* (New York: Basic Books, 1999); Mark K. Smith, "Howard Gardner and Multiple Intelligences," *The Encyclopedia of Informal Education* (www.infed.or/thinkers/gardner.htm), pp. 1–12; 2002, 2008.

7

Personal Communication Effectiveness

Outline

Psychologist Elizabeth Prial doesn't like liars, and she has developed techniques for detecting lies by studying nonspoken, or nonverbal, indicators of lying. She spent a good part of her career with the Federal Bureau of Investigation looking for false statements by mobsters and terrorists. Prial then went into the private sector to focus on untruths expressed occasionally by Wall Street fund managers (those who manage large mutual funds). Her clients are the prospective purchasers of those funds, such as pension managers and institutional fund managers. She also still works as a consultant to the government in the departments of defense and homeland security.

Prial's employer is Insite Security, a firm that helps other companies detect and combat fraud. She says, "It's usually very clear. I'm 90 percent confident in most of the things that I see." Insite's management says that Prial's expertise in human factor analysis can help avert disaster by providing on-site observation and real-time feedback regarding the truthfulness of a subject's statements. She also observes the congruence between a subject's verbal (spoken) and nonverbal behavior.

The president of Insite says that Dr. Prial brings skills to the due diligence process that are vital to ferreting out the truth. She has exceptional ability to detect deception. She brings investors a peace of mind that other approaches to due diligence cannot provide.

When Prial is observing whether a prospective fund manager is telling the truth she looks for certain micro-expressions which hint that the speaker is hiding something. Among these indicators are pupils changing size (a fear indicator); motionlessness (often occurs when person is focused on telling a lie); and an extremely quick verbal response (indicates a prepared answer).

Prial as well as other lie detection professionals admit that their work is not 100 percent accurate, and background investigations are therefore still important in sorting out fraud. Also, some people are polished liars. Prial believes that many Wall Street finance specialists may be better liars than most people because they are somewhat narcissistic (self-adoration to the extreme), a trait that is linked to deception.[1]

Learning Objectives ▸

After studying the information and doing the exercises in this chapter, you should be able to:

1. Explain the basic communication process.
2. Explain the relationship-building aspect of interpersonal communication.
3. Describe the nature and importance of nonverbal communication in the workplace.
4. Identify roadblocks to communication.
5. Know how to build bridges to communication.
6. Overcome many gender communication barriers.
7. Enhance your listening skills.

Understanding the behavior of others by means of their nonverbal communication is but one aspect of communication studied in this chapter. However, the story just presented illustrates the relevance of studying communication skills. Communication is so vital that it has been described as the glue that holds organizations and families together. Most job foul-ups and personal relationship disputes are considered to be a result of communication problems. Furthermore, to be successful in work or personal life, you usually have to be an effective communicator. You can't make friends or stand up against enemies unless you can communicate with them. And you can't accomplish work through others unless you can send and receive messages effectively.

In this chapter we explain several important aspects of interpersonal communication, such as the communication process, communicating with others via the social media, and overcoming various communication barriers. Many factors contribute to enhanced communication, leading in turn to more effective human relations. Explanation should also lead to skill improvement. For example, if you understand the steps involved in getting a message across to another person, you may be able to prevent many communication problems.

To personalize the subject of interpersonal communication effectiveness, you are invited to take Human Relations Self-Assessment Quiz 7-1.

Human Relations Self-Assessment Quiz 7-1

My Communication Effectiveness

Indicate the extent of your agreement with the following statements, using the following scale: Agree strongly (AS); Agree (A); about equal between agree and disagree (N); Disagree (D); Disagree strongly (DS). Because it is so easy to overrate our own communication effectiveness, it would be useful to also have somebody who has frequently observed you communicate to respond to the questions. Circle the best response to each of the ten statements.

Statement about Communication Effectiveness	AS	A	N	D	DS
	5	4	3	2	1
1. When I talk, people listen.	5	4	3	2	1
2. I almost never telephone or speak in person to another individual if it is possible to send him or her a text message.	1	2	3	4	5
3. I have received several compliments about the quality of presentations I have made in front of a group.	5	4	3	2	1
4. I have been told by at least a few people that I am a good listener.	5	4	3	2	1
5. I look away rather than maintain eye contact during a conversation with others.	1	2	3	4	5
6. My vocabulary continues to grow because I look up the meaning of words unfamiliar to me.	5	4	3	2	1
7. I often keep my hand over my mouth when I have an important message to deliver to another person.	1	2	3	4	5
8. During a conversation, I vary the loudness of my voice.	5	4	3	2	1
9. I often use text style spelling when sending messages about work or school. (For example, r u ok? LOL)	1	2	3	4	5
10. My social media postings are polite as well as being and professional in appearance.	5	4	3	2	1

Scoring and Interpretation:

Add your scores, as indicated by the numbers you have circled. Assuming that your evaluations are reasonably accurate, use the following guide:

40 or higher high communication effectiveness and a positive communication style.

21–39 average communication effectiveness and an average communication style.

20 or less you need to improve your communication effectiveness and develop a comment.

▶ Learning Objective 1 ▶

How Does Communication Take Place?

Communication
the sending and receiving of messages

A convenient starting point in understanding how people communicate is to look at the steps involved in communicating a message. **Communication** is the sending and receiving of messages. A diagram of how the process takes place is shown in Figure 7-1. The theme of the model is that two-way communication involves three major steps and that each step is subject to interference or noise. Assume that Crystal, a customer, wishes to inform Tony, a used-car sales representative, that she is willing to make an offer of $8,000 on a used car. The price tag on the car is $8,750.

Encoding
the process of organizing ideas into a series of symbols, such as words and gestures, designed to communicate with a receiver

Step 1 **Sender encodes the message.** **Encoding** is the process of organizing ideas into a series of symbols, such as words and gestures, designed to communicate with the receiver. Word choice has a strong influence on communication effectiveness. The better a person's grasp of language, the easier it is for him or her to

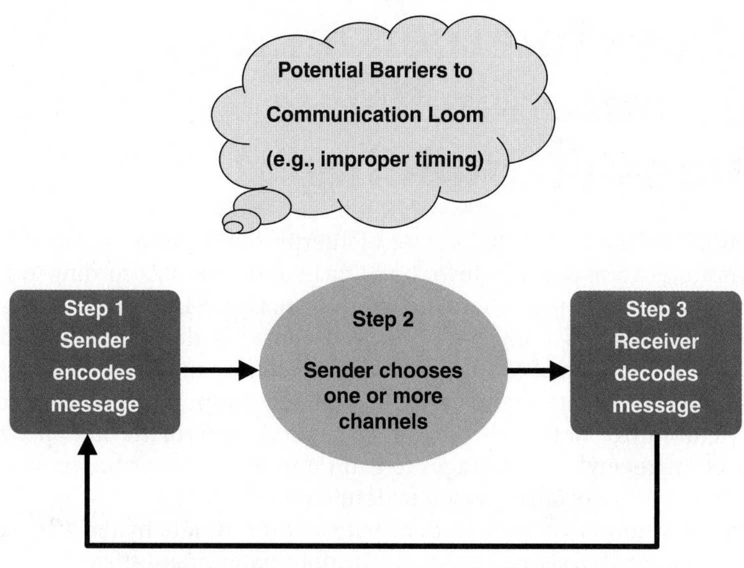

FIGURE 7-1

THE COMMUNICATION PROCESS

When sending a message to another person, one has to take into account potential barriers to communication. Feedback from the receiver helps clarify if the message has been sent as intended.

encode. Crystal says, "Tony, this car obviously is not in excellent condition, but I am willing to give you $8,000 for it."

Step 2 **Sender chooses one or more channels.** The message is sent via a communication channel or medium, such as voice, telephone, paper, e-mail, or messaging. It is important to select a medium that fits the message. It would be appropriate to use the spoken word to inform a coworker that he swore under his breath at a customer. It would be less appropriate to send the same message through e-mail. Many messages on and off the job are sent nonverbally through the use of gestures and facial expressions. For example, a smile from a superior during a meeting is an effective way of communicating the message "I agree with you." Crystal has chosen the oral medium to send her message.

Step 3 **Receiver decodes the message.** In **decoding**, the receiver interprets the message and translates it into meaningful information. Decoding is the process of understanding a message. Barriers to communication are most likely to surface at the decoding step. People often interpret messages according to their psychological needs and motives. Tony wants to interpret Crystal's message that she is very eager to purchase this car. Therefore, he may listen attentively for more information demonstrating that she is interested in purchasing the car. Effective decoding is also dependent on the receiver understanding the words chosen by the sender. Breadth of vocabulary as well as cultural factors can influence the interpretation of a word or phrase. For example, if Crystal says the car is "bad," she could mean that the car is in poor condition *or* that it is wonderful, depending on her vernacular.

Decoding
the process of understanding a message; the receiver interprets the message and translates it into meaningful information

Decoding the message leads naturally to action—the receiver does something about the message. If the receiver acts in the manner the sender wants, the communication has been successful. If Tony says, "It's a deal," Crystal had a successful communication event. Many missteps can occur between encoding and decoding a message. **Barriers to communication** or unwanted interference or **noise** can distort or block a message. If Crystal has an indecisive tone and raises her voice at the end of her statement, it could indicate that she is not really serious about offering a maximum of $8,000 for the car.

Barriers to communication (or noise)
missteps that can occur between encoding and decoding a message; unwanted interference that can distort or block a message

▶ Learning Objective 2 ▶

How Does Interpersonal Communication Relate to Relationship Building?

Another way of understanding the process of interpersonal communication is to examine how communication is a vehicle for building relationships. According to Texas Tech business communication professors Rich Sorenson, Grace De Bord, and Ida Ramirez, we establish relationships along two primary dimensions: dominate–subordinate and cold–warm. In the process of communicating, we attempt to *dominate* or *subordinate*. When we dominate, we attempt to control communication. When we subordinate, we attempt to yield control, or think first of the wishes and needs of the other person. Dominators expect the receiver of messages to submit to them; subordinate people send a signal that they expect the other person to dominate.[2]

We indicate whether we want to dominate or subordinate by the way we speak or write, or by the nonverbal signals we send. The dominator might speak loudly or enthusiastically, write forceful messages filled with exclamation points, or gesture with exaggerated, rapid hand movements. He or she might write a harsh e-mail message, such as, "It's about time you started taking your job seriously and put in some real effort."

In the subordinate mode, we might speak quietly and hesitantly, in a meek tone, being apologetic. A subordinate person might ask, "I know you have better things on your mind than to worry about me, but I was wondering when I can expect my reimbursement for travel expenses?" In a work setting we ordinarily expect people with more formal authority to have the dominant role in conversations. However, in more democratic, informal companies, workers with more authority are less likely to feel the need to dominate conversations.

The *cold–warm dimension* also shapes communication because we invite the same behavior that we send. Cold, impersonal, negative messages evoke similar messages from others. In contrast, warm verbal and nonverbal messages evoke similar behavior from others. Getting back to the inquiry about the travel-expense check, here is a colder-versus-warmer response by the manager:

Colder: Travel vouchers really aren't my responsibility. You'll just have to wait like everybody else.

Warmer: I understand your problem. Not getting reimbursed on time is a bummer. I'll follow up on the status of your expense check sometime today or tomorrow.

The combination of dominant and cold communication sends the signal that the sender of the message wants to control and to limit, or even withdraw from, a personal relationship. A team leader might say that she cannot attend a Saturday morning meeting because she has to go out of town for her brother's wedding. A dominant and cold manager might say, "I don't want to hear about your personal life. Everyone in this department has to attend our Saturday meeting."

Subordinate actions combined with warm communication signal a desire to maintain or build the relationship while yielding to the other person. A manager communicating in a warm and subordinate manner in relation to the wedding request might say, "We'll miss you on Saturday morning because you are a key player in our department, but I recognize that major events in personal life sometimes take priority over a business meeting."

Figure 7-2 summarizes how the dual dimensions of dominate–subordinate and cold–warm influence the relationship-building aspects of communication. Rather than

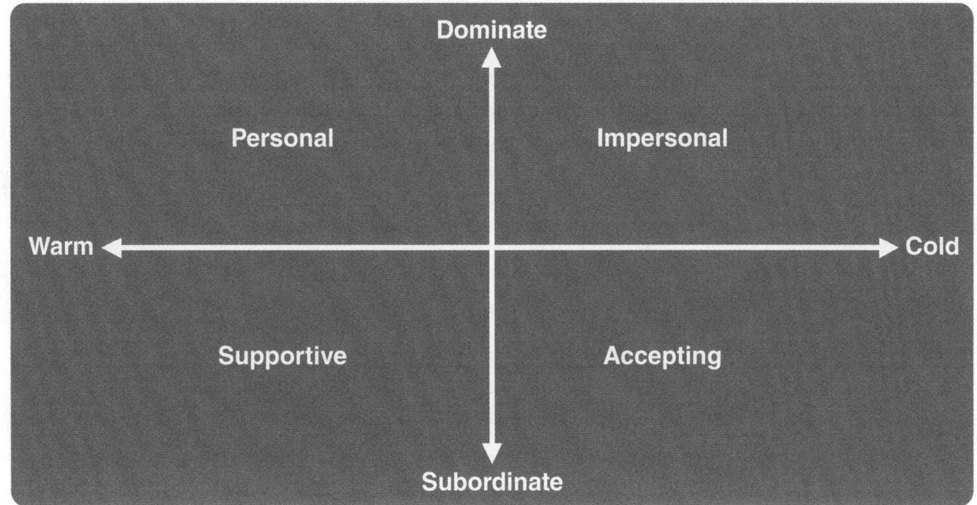

FIGURE 7-2

COMMUNICATION DIMENSIONS OF ESTABLISHING A RELATIONSHIP

Source: Adapted with permission from Rich Sorenson, Grace De Bord, and Ida Ramirez, *Business and Management Communication: A Guide Book*, 4th ed. (Upper Saddle River, NJ: Prentice Hall, 2001), p. 7.

regarding these four quadrants of relationships as good or bad, think of your purposes. In some situations you might want to dominate and be cold, yet in most situations you might want to submit a little and be warm in order to build a relationship. For example, being dominant and cold might be necessary for a security officer who is trying to control an unruly crowd at a sporting event.

Observe that the person in the quadrant *dominate-cold* has an impersonal relationship with the receiver, and the person in the *warm-subordinate* quadrant has a supportive relationship with the receiver. Being *dominant and warm* leads to a personal relationship, whereas being *subordinate and cold* leads to an accepting relationship. The combinations of *dominate-cold* and *warm-subordinate* are more likely to produce the results indicated.

What Is Nonverbal Communication (Sending and Receiving Silent Messages)?

◀ Learning Objective 3 ◀

Except for the introductory case, so far we have been considering mostly spoken communication. But much of the communication among people includes nonspoken and nonwritten messages. These nonverbal signals are a critical part of everyday communication. As a case in point, *how* you say "thank you" makes a big difference in the extent to which your sense of appreciation registers. In **nonverbal communication**, we use our body, voice, or environment in numerous ways to help put a message across. Sometimes we are not aware how much our true feelings color our spoken message.

Nonverbal communication
using the body, voice, or environment in numerous ways to help get a message across

An important use of nonverbal communication in the workplace is to detect **mixed messages**, or a discrepancy between what a person says and how he or she acts.[3] An extreme example would be when a coworker says that she would like to join you on a special project. While expressing her agreement her nostrils dilate, she looks down at the floor, her face twitches, and she twists her hair with her thumb and two fingers. Duh! This coworker really does not want to join your project, and you should question her about her sincerity.

Mixed messages
a discrepancy between what a person says and how he or she acts

One problem of paying attention to nonverbal signals is that they can be taken too seriously. Just because some nonverbal signals (such as yawning or looking away from a person) might reflect a person's real feelings, not every signal can be reliably connected with a particular attitude. Jason may put his hand over his mouth because he is shocked. Lucille may put her hand over her mouth because she is trying to control her laughter about the message, and Ken may put his hand over his mouth as a signal that he is pondering the consequences of the message. Here we look at seven categories of nonverbal communication that are generally reliable indicators of a person's attitude and feelings. We then describe briefly two applied uses of nonverbal communication: airport security and lie detection.

ENVIRONMENT OR SETTING

Where you choose to deliver your message indicates what you think of its importance. Assume that your supervisor invites you over for dinner to discuss something with you. You will think it is a more important topic under these circumstances than if it were brought up when the two of you met in the supermarket. Other important environmental cues include room color, temperature, lighting, and furniture arrangement. A person who sits behind an uncluttered large desk, for example, appears more powerful than a person who sits behind a small, cluttered desk.

Few people in an organization have the authority to control the physical factors of room color, temperature, and lighting, but there are exceptions. An office or building painted gray in the interior might suggest an impersonal, strictly business atmosphere. A business owner who keeps the temperature at 62°F during cold months or 75°F during warm months communicates a message of frugality.

DISTANCE FROM THE OTHER PERSON

How close you place your body relative to another person's also conveys meaning when you send a message. If, for instance, you want to convey a positive attitude toward another person, get physically close to him or her. Putting your arm around someone to express interest and warmth is another obvious nonverbal signal. However, many people in a work setting abstain from all forms of touching (except for handshakes) because of concern that touching might be interpreted as sexual harassment. Cultural differences must be kept in mind in interpreting nonverbal cues. A French male is likely to stand closer to you than a British male, even if they had equally positive attitudes toward you. A set of useful guidelines has been developed for estimating how close to stand to another person (at least in many cultures).[4] They are described here and diagrammed in Figure 7-3.

Intimate distance covers actual physical contact to about eighteen inches. Usually, it is reserved for close friends and loved ones or other people you feel affectionate toward. Physical intimacy is usually not called for on the job, but there are exceptions. For one, confidential information might be whispered within the intimate distance zone.

Personal distance covers from about one-and-a-half to four feet. In this zone it is natural to carry on friendly conversations and discussions. When people engage in a heated argument, they sometimes enter the personal distance zone. One example is a baseball coach getting up close to an umpire and shouting in his face.

Social distance covers from four to twelve feet and in general is reserved for interaction that is businesslike and impersonal. We usually maintain this amount of distance between ourselves and strangers, such as retail sales associates.

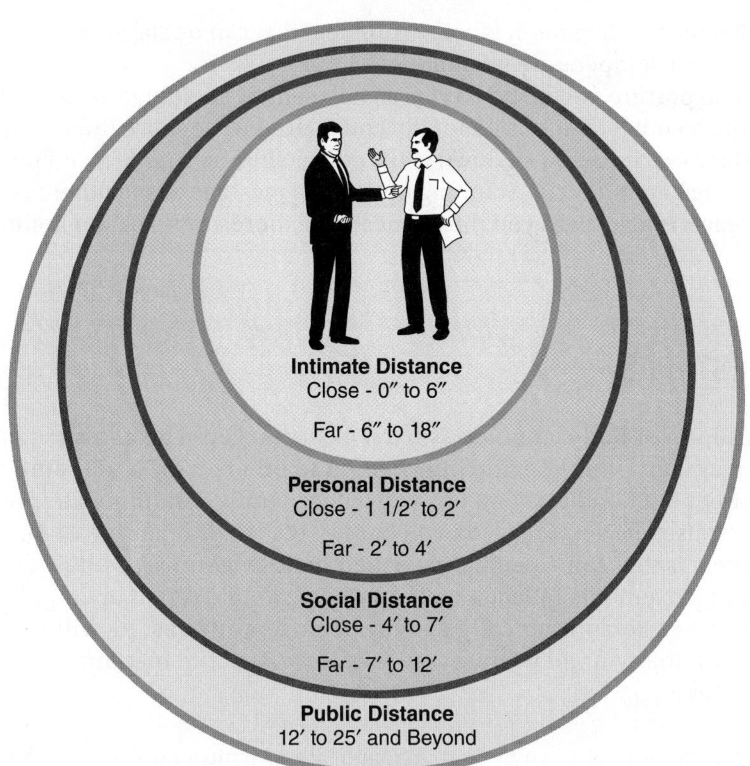

FIGURE 7-3
FOUR CIRCLES OF INTIMACY

Public distance covers from twelve feet to the outer limit of being heard. This zone is typically used in speaking to an audience at a large meeting or in a classroom, but a few insensitive individuals might send ordinary messages by shouting across a room. The unstated message suggested by such an action is that the receiver of the message does not merit the effort of walking across the room.

People sometimes manipulate personal space in order to dominate a situation. A sales representative might move into the personal or intimate circle of a customer simply to intimidate him or her. Many people become upset when you move into a closer circle than that for which a situation calls. They consider it an invasion of their personal space, or their "territorial rights."

POSTURE

Certain aspects of your posture communicate a message. Leaning toward another individual suggests that you are favorably disposed toward his or her message. Leaning backward communicates the opposite. For example, leaning back in your chair with your arms crossed is often interpreted as negatively toned and "stand-offish."[5] Openness of the arms or legs serves as an indicator of liking or caring. In general, people establish closed postures (arms folded and legs crossed) when speaking to people they dislike. Standing up straight generally indicates high self-confidence. Stooping and slouching could mean a poor self-image. In any event, there is almost no disadvantage to standing up straight.

A well-accepted component of nonverbal communication related to posture is defensive positions that make people feel more protected, such as crossing their arms over their chests. During a group meeting, an indicator that the presenter's ideas are being rejected is when several participants cross their arms simultaneously. An exception might be that the meeting room is cold, a problem that can be clarified by the presenter asking if the room temperature is comfortable.[6]

Related to posture are the nonverbal signals sent by standing versus sitting. Sitting down during a conversation is generally considered to be more intimate and informal than standing. If you do sit down while conversing, be sure to stand up when you wish the conversation to end. Standing up sends a message to the other person that it is time to leave. It also gives you the chance to be more attentive and polite in saying good-bye.

HAND GESTURES

An obvious form of body language is hand gestures. Hand gestures are universally recognized as conveying specific information to others within the same culture. If you make frequent hand movements, you will generally communicate a positive attitude. If you use few gestures, you will convey dislike or disinterest. An important exception here is that some people wave their hands vigorously while arguing. Some of their hand movements reflect anger. Another example is that open-palm gestures toward the other person typically convey positive attitudes. As will be described in Chapter 13, many hand gestures have culture-specific meanings. An off-color example follows:

> In many cultures holding your hand in front of you as if pushing something away tells the other person to stop—you have had enough. In West Africa, the same gesture means "There are different men who could be your father," thereby insulting the receiver's mother.[7]

It is often said that gestures speak louder than words, because if there is a discrepancy between words and gestures, the receiver will usually take your gestures more seriously. In general more weight is given to nonverbal cues than verbal cues when a discrepancy exists between the two.[8] Hand gestures are not unique in this regard. Nonverbal behaviors must match the spoken language or else people tend to believe what is expressed nonverbally rather than verbally.[9]

> *Imagine that you have been interviewed for a job you really want. At the close of the interview, the interviewer looks at you with a solemn face, and his arms are crossed with his hands tucked under his armpits. He says in a monotone, "We will get back to you soon." Most likely, you will continue your job search.*

FACIAL EXPRESSIONS AND EYE CONTACT

When used in combination, the head, face, and eyes provide the clearest indications of attitudes toward other people. Lowering your head and peering over your glasses, for instance, is the nonverbal equivalent of the expression "You're putting me on." As is well known, maintaining eye contact with another person improves communication with that person. To maintain eye contact, it is usually necessary to correspondingly move your head and face. Moving your head, face, and eyes away from another person is often interpreted as a defensive gesture or one suggesting a lack of self-confidence. Would you hire a job candidate who didn't look at you directly? Yet again, cultural differences can influence the meaning of eye contact. In some Asian cultures, looking down rather than maintaining eye contact is a sign of respect.

The face is often used as a primary source of information about how we feel. We look for facial clues when we want to determine another person's attitude. You can often judge someone's current state of happiness by looking at his or her face. The expression *sourpuss* attests to this observation. Happiness, apprehension, anger, resentment, sadness, contempt, enthusiasm, and embarrassment are but a few of the emotions that can be expressed through the face.

VOICE QUALITY

More significance is often attached to the *way* something is said than to *what* is said. A forceful voice, which includes a consistent tone without vocalized pauses, connotes power and control. Closely related to voice tone are volume, pitch, and rate of speaking. Anger, boredom, and joy can often be interpreted from voice quality. Anger is noted when the person speaks loudly with a high pitch and at a fast rate, with irregular inflection. Boredom is indicated by a monotone. Joy is often indicated by loud volume, high pitch, fast rate, upward inflection, and regular rhythm.

Avoiding an annoying voice quality can make a positive impact on others. The research of Jeffrey Jacobi, voice coach and founder of Jacobi Voice, provides some useful suggestions. A while back he surveyed a nationwide sample of 1,000 men and women and asked, "Which irritating or unpleasant voice annoys you the most?" His results are still valid today. The most irritating quality was a whining, complaining, or nagging tone.

Jacobi notes that we are judged by the way we sound. He also contends that careers can be damaged by voice problems, such as those indicated in the survey. "We think about how we look and dress. And that gets most of the attention. But people judge our intelligence much more by how we sound than how we dress."[10]

PERSONAL APPEARANCE

Your external image plays an important role in communicating messages to others. Job seekers show recognition of this aspect of nonverbal communication when they carefully groom for a job interview. People pay more respect and grant more privileges to people they perceive as being well dressed and attractive. The meaning of being well dressed depends heavily on the situation and the culture of the organization. In an information technology firm, neatly pressed jeans, a stylish T-shirt, and clean sport shoes might qualify as being well dressed. The same attire worn in a financial services firm would qualify as being poorly dressed. In recent years, more formal business attire has made a comeback, as reflected in more space in department stores being devoted to suits for men and women.

Tattoos and body piercing represent another aspect of personal appearance that sends a strong nonverbal message. The message that tattoos and body piercing send, however, depends to a large extent on the values and preferences of the receiver. A positive message sent by visible tattoos and piercing is that the individual is cool, modern, fashionable, and youthful in outlook. A negative message is the person with visible tattoos and piercing is immature, daring, and non-conscientious. As the percentage of people wearing visible tattoos and body piercing continues to increase, less significance will probably be attached to them. For example, about thirty years ago when a man appeared in the office wearing a pierced earring, it was considered shocking. Today, the same behavior is unremarkable—at least to many people.

Common sense and research indicate that a favorable personal appearance leads to higher starting salaries and, later, salary increases. One study showed that people perceived to be physically attractive tend to receive salaries 8 to 10 percent higher. A possible explanation offered for the results is that employers might attribute other positive attributes to employees they perceive as physically attractive.[11]

LIE DETECTION THROUGH NONVERBAL COMMUNICATION

As described in the case introduction to this chapter, effort has been directed toward detecting workplace lies via the target's nonverbal communication. A conservative approach is to regard certain indicators to suggest that a person might by lying, and then to investigate further the truthfulness of certain statements. For example, an employee suspected of selling employee Social Security numbers to an outside party might respond to any questioning about this theft with a quick, seemingly rehearsed answer. Further investigation, perhaps using a private detective, might be warranted.

It is important to recognize that surefire behavioral indicators of deception do not exist—that the behavior of liars is not consistently revealing. A team of three researchers who reviewed the evidence about human behavior and deception detection concluded that no researcher has documented a "Pinocchio response." (The nose of the fairy tale character Pinocchio grew when he told a lie.) The finding means that there is no behavior or pattern of behavior that in all people, in all situations indicates deception.

What is known with reasonable certainty is that lying requires extra mental effort. The liar must think quite hard to cover up and create events that have not happened. The extra effort will show up in the nonverbal form: longer pauses between thoughts, and the use of hand and head movements that accompany speech will be less frequent. With respect to emotions, liars do appear to be more nervous than truth tellers. The facial expressions of liars tend to be less pleasant, their voices are pitched higher and more tense, their pupils are more dilated, and they fidget more.[12]

The scientific evidence about nonverbal indicators of lying therefore supports the generally accepted belief that liars touch their face more, twitch more, avoid eye contact, and fidget considerably.[13]

NONVERBAL COMMUNICATION AND AIRPORT SECURITY

An advanced workplace application of nonverbal communication is to help combat drug trafficking and terrorism. The art of spotting nervous or threatening behavior has gained respect among airport security officials. Since the terrorist attacks on September 11, 2001, the Federal Bureau of Investigation (FBI) started teaching nonverbal behavior analysis to all new FBI recruits. In the past, passengers were selected to be interrogated mostly on the basis of what they looked like, such as a negative ethnic stereotype.

The nonverbal indicators of lying are incorporated into airport security procedures for detecting drug traffickers and terrorists. Customs agents are now trained to observe what people do and to ask pointed questions when suspicious nonverbal behavior surfaces. Among the indicators of suspicious behavior are darting eyes, hand tremors, a fleeting style, and an enlarged carotid artery (indicating the rapid blood flow associated with anxiety). Failure to make eye contact with the customs official is a strong red flag.[14]

Behavior detection officer is the term given to airport security officers who specialize in detecting nonverbal signs of stress, fear, and deception. Part of the officer's responsibility is to roam a major airport and watch for anyone who seems nervous or out of place, or is acting suspiciously. Particularly suspicious are passengers traveling without bags, sweating, and constantly checking people passing by, especially those with badges and guns. Facial movements detecting a lie, such as rapid eye movements, are also regarded as suspicious.

Other suspicious nonverbal communication cues are passengers avoiding eye contact or veering away when police approach. Suspicious-appearing people are routinely brought in for questioning, but suspicious nonverbal behavior alone is not sufficient evidence to be charged with attempting a crime.[15]

The American Civil Liberties Union objects to nonverbal behavior detection because it is easy to find these negative nonverbal behaviors if you look for them. The many flight cancellations and delays, for example, trigger many passengers into looking stressed and "suspicious."

An important human relations perspective on nonverbal communication and airport security is expressed by Mark Frank, a lie-detection expert at the University of Buffalo: He contends that the airport screening is usually carried out by police officers and security officers who have high motivation and considerable experience in lie detection. As a result these specialists tend to be effective.[16]

How Do I Use Social Media to Enhance My Communication Effectiveness?

Learning Objective 4

Social media have become integrated into personal communication in personal life, and to some extent on the job. Many large companies have established their own social media sites for employee use. At one extreme, at the online retailer, Zappos Inc., employees are encouraged to send tweets and Facebook postings all during the workday so they can be connected and be happy. At the other extreme, using social media on the job, except for a specific business purpose, can result in being disciplined, including being terminated. In Chapter 8 we explore the misuse of electronic communication including overdependence.

The most frequent job use of social media is much like e-mail. Workers send brief messages to each other by making posts on the Web site, and top-level management might distribute a message to hundreds of workers simultaneously. Almost infinite knowledge exists about social networking, including its technology, application for building a personal network, and marketing. Included in this abundance of information are claims that Twitter and Facebook have completely transformed the way we live, and have made e-mail obsolete.[17] Our aim here is to simply list a few of the positive and negative communication skills associated with the use of social networking sites, including company social media sites.

POSITIVE COMMUNICATION SKILLS AND SOCIAL NETWORKING

The use of Twitter, Facebook, and the like provides the serious worker with several opportunities for displaying positive communication and interpersonal skills:

1. **Demonstrate your loyalty by posting gracious comments about your employer.** Social networking sites include a heavy component of being mini-blogs, and therefore present an open forum for your ideas about the company. You can demonstrate empathy and compassion for the mission of your company by commenting on an action taken by the company that you perceive as positive. An example: "I'm proud to work for the Jeep division of Fiat/Chrysler. My wife and our three children were caught in a snow storm. I put my Cherokee into 4-wheel drive and made it through the storm until we could find a motel. There were dozens of overturned vehicles, but we made it to safety. The vehicle stabilization feature is really functional."

2. **Demonstrate professional-level communication skills.** When making entries on Twitter in particular, many people feel compelled to write carelessly, foolishly, and viciously. Demonstrate your professionalism by writing in a style suited for a printed newspaper or a term paper. Remember that many influential people regard written communication skills as a subset of interpersonal skills.

3. **Pay deserved compliments to company personnel.** The ability to compliment others in a sensible way is an advanced interpersonal skill. Complimenting a person in private may be useful, but public compliments are welcome also. An example of a Facebook post of this nature: "I want everybody to know that Tom Barnes, our facilities manager, spearheaded the planting of a garden on the office building roof. We are saving the planet, one petunia at a time."

4. **Establish meaningful contact with workers far and wide.** The major purpose of social networking is to develop valuable contacts with many people with whom it would be difficult to maintain person-to-person or phone contact. Selective use of the social networking sites enables you to relate, at least on a written level, to a variety of people in your field. You might be able to enhance your cross-cultural skills by interacting with professionals in different countries. (LinkedIn is particularly good for this purpose because so many of its members have a professional intent.)

5. **Display a desire to help others grow and develop.** Social networking sites afford an easy opportunity to point others toward helpful information, such as referring friends to useful Web sites and books. You can also alert people to dangers, such as a new scam related to the sale of gold. Although the same type of alerts can be accomplished by e-mail, social networking sites do not require long distribution lists. By pointing people in the direction of useful information you will be demonstrating part of a useful interpersonal and communication skill of helping others grow and develop. Instead of just writing about yourself on your post, include information that will help others.

NEGATIVE COMMUNICATION SKILLS AND SOCIAL NETWORKING

Social networking provides a setting for displaying negative as well as positive communication and interpersonal skills. In general, all of the positive opportunities mentioned above could be reversed to become negative. For example, instead of helping others grow and develop with postings on your site or their site, you slam and demean these people. Several adolescent suicides have been reported that appear to have been triggered by being insulted on a teen-oriented social networking site. The following list presents a few ways in which negative communication and interpersonal skills are sometimes displayed on social networking sites.

1. **Using social networking sites to eliminate face-to-face interactions with work associates.** As with e-mail, social networking sites provide an opportunity to avoid face-to-face interaction with coworkers, managers, and customers. However, the temptation is even greater with social networking sites because they tout the concept of being "friends" with people on your list of electronic contacts. A person might think consciously or subconsciously, "If my customer is already my friend, why should I have to talk to or personally visit him? Our relationship is already good." If all relationships could be built and maintained electronically, you would not need to be studying human relations.

Human Relations in Practice

Companies See the Relationship-Building Value of Business Travel

Cynthia is the CEO of a company that manufactures and sells industrial uniforms for a wide variety of companies including security firms, banks, hospitals, and chain restaurants. During a meeting with her top-level managers, she pointed out that sales had declined about 20 percent during the recent year. She has been so concerned about this trend that she had asked Jeremy, the director of marketing, to investigate possible reasons for the decline, and how the problem might be resolved.

Jeremy told the group, as he had told Cynthia, that the company may have gone too far in cutting some expenses that had actually helped boost profits. He focused on the cutback in business travel as a factor that may have hurt sales. "We cannot forget," said Jeremy, "that ours is a business built on relationships. Other companies, including overseas competitors, can provide our customers with uniforms that work just fine. People do business with people they like.

"And the best way to get someone to like you is to have an in-person meeting, over a meal with wine included. Let me show you a few facts. Look at this slide." (Jeremy then flashed a PowerPoint slide on a screen, showing the following facts and observations.)

Business travel is related to corporate profit because in-person meetings help promote business.

For every dollar spent on business travel, the average company experiences a $15 increase in profit resulting from increased sales.

The most profitable types of business travel are client meetings, participation in conventions and exhibitions, and vacation trips as rewards for outstanding performance.

Approximately 40 percent of prospective customers are converted to new customers with an in-person meeting, compared to 16 percent without such a meeting.

Despite the contribution of business travel to profits, a point of diminishing returns arrives when too much money is spent on travel.

Cynthia then made a comment that was well received by the group. "Okay, let's take an experimental approach. Let's up our travel budget by 25 percent for the upcoming fiscal year. Jeremy can work with the sales representatives to prudently invest in business travel. But no sending customers to the Super Bowl or Mardi Gras just to sell a handful of uniforms."

Question: What really is it about an in-person meeting that is more effective for sales than electronic messages and even videoconferencing (technologies such as Skype included)?

Source: Original story based on facts contained in the following: Alice Lesch Kelly, "Finding Value in Business Travel," *About .com. Business Travel* (http://businesstravel.about.com), accessed January 29, 2012, pp. 1; Tanya Mohn, "Some Rediscover the Benefits of Business Travel," *The New York Times* (www.nytimes.com), pp. 1–3; "Studies Show Clear Benefits of Business Travel," *Best in Travel* (www.breakingtravelnews.com), September 17, 2009, pp. 1–7; "Business Travel ROI" (www.ustravel .org), September 2008, pp. 1–2.

2. **Posting confidential or derogatory information about your employer.** In the words of technology writer Bridget Carey, "Employees need to realize some conversations are privileged. Just because you're in a meeting about a new product, or worse, layoffs, doesn't mean you should be broadcasting to the world."[18] Posting negative information and insults about your employer demonstrates even lower emotional intelligence. Nasty comments about the employer, even if deserved, are often made out of uncontrolled anger. Hundreds of employees have been fired because of making inflammatory comments on social networking sites about their employers. Poor interpersonal skill is also displayed by joining a social networking group dedicated to destroying the reputation of your employer.
3. **Posting derogatory information and photos about a coworker.** Social networking site administrators generally do not edit posts, so anybody registered on the site can post dreadful comments about another person as a mean prank or a deliberate effort to ruin the target's reputation. YouTube can serve a similar evil purpose. Some of these negative posts reflect backstabbing because another person encourages you to engage in embarrassing behavior. He or she then quotes you, or posts a photo or video of you engaged in outrageous behavior.
4. **Engaging in social networking at inappropriate times.** Many social networkers, "tweeters" in particular, are so habituated to visiting their favorite social networking site that they do so at inappropriate times, such as during work. Several NFL teams, including the Miami Dolphins, had to clamp down on players tweeting during practice. Many office workers access their social networking sites during meetings. The interpersonal skill deficiency of accessing a social network site for non-business purposes during working hours is that it reflects insensitivity and immaturity. (Print-related distractions would also be unwelcome, such as doing crossword puzzles during football practice or in a meeting.)

Despite all the emphasis on social media and other electronic forms of communication, many companies still see the value of face-to-face, in-person communication. The debate over the value of business travel, as described in the accompanying Human Relations in Practice box, focuses on the importance of building relationships in person.

Learning Objective 5

What Are Some Frequent Barriers to Communication?

Communication rarely proceeds as effectively as we would like. Many different factors filter out a message on its way to the intended receiver, shown as potential barriers in Figure 7-1. In this section we look at some of the human barriers to communication. If you are aware of their presence, you will be better able to overcome them.

Routine or neutral messages are the easiest to communicate. Communication roadblocks are most likely to occur when a message is complex, is emotionally arousing, or clashes with the receiver's mental set. An emotionally arousing message would deal with such topics as job security or money. A message that clashes with a receiver's mental set requires that person to change his or her familiar pattern of receiving messages. The next time you order a meal in a restaurant, order dessert first and an entrée second. The server will probably not "hear" your dessert order because it deviates from the normal ordering sequence. The barriers described here are as follows:

1. Limited understanding of people
2. One-way communication
3. Different interpretation of words (semantics)

4. Credibility of the sender and mixed signals
5. Distortion of information
6. Different perspectives and experiences
7. Emotions and attitudes
8. Communication overload
9. Improper timing
10. Poor communication skills
11. Cultural and language barriers

LIMITED UNDERSTANDING OF PEOPLE

If you do not understand people very well, your communication effectiveness will be limited. To take a basic example, if you frame your message in terms of what can be done for you, you may be in trouble. It's much more effective to frame your message in terms of what you can do for the other person. Suppose a person in need of money wants to sell food supplements to a friend. Mentioning financial need is a very self-centered message. It could be made less self-centered:

Very self-centered. "You've got to buy a few food supplements from me. I can't meet my credit card payments."

Less self-centered. "Would you be interested in purchasing a few food supplements that would bring you more energy and help you live longer? If your answer is yes, I can help you."

Limited understanding of people can also take the form of making false assumptions about the receiver. The false assumption serves as a communication barrier. A supervisor might say to a telemarketer (a person who sells over the phone), "If you increase sales by 15 percent, we will promote you to lead telemarketer." When the telemarketer does not work any harder, the supervisor thinks the message did not get across. The false assumption the supervisor made was that the telemarketer wanted a position with supervisory responsibility. What false assumptions have you made lately when trying to communicate with another person?

ONE-WAY COMMUNICATION

Effective communication proceeds back and forth. An exchange of information or a transaction takes place between two or more people. Person A may send messages to person B to initiate communication, but B must react to A to complete the communication loop. One reason written messages sometimes fail to achieve their purpose is that the person who writes the message cannot be sure how it will be interpreted. One written message that is subject to many interpretations is, "Your idea is of some interest to me." (How much is *some*?) Face-to-face communication helps clarify meanings.

Instant messaging helps overcome the one-way barrier because the receiver reacts immediately to your message. An example: "You said ship the first batch only to good customers. Who do you consider to be a *good* customer?" Ten seconds later comes the reply: "A good customer bought at least $4,000 worth of goods last year and is up-to-date on payments." Three seconds later, the first person writes, "Got it." E-mail is also widely used to clarify messages and engage in two-way communication.

A quick way to bring about the exchange of information necessary for two-way communication is to ask a question. An example here would be, "Are you clear on what I mean by a *good customer*?"

DIFFERENT INTERPRETATION OF WORDS (SEMANTICS)

Semantics
the study of the meaning and changes in the meaning of words or symbols

Semantics is the study of the meaning and changes in the meaning of words or symbols. These different meanings can create communication barriers. Often the problem is trivial and humorous; at other times, semantic problems can create substantial communication barriers. Consider first an example of trivial consequence.

An older supervisor told a new hire to the unit that her work so far was "good as gold." The young worker looked perplexed, and frowned. The supervisor then asked, "Don't you like your work to be good as gold?" The new employee said, "I thought you were giving me negative feedback. Gold goes up and down in price so often that I've been told it's not so good."

Of greater consequence is the use of a word or term without thorough explanation that could cause people to act in an unintended direction. An example is for a manager to use the term *restructure* when speaking to employees or outsiders. Four common interpretations of the word are the following: (1) refinance the company debt, (2) declare bankruptcy, (3) change the organization structure, or (4) lay off many workers. A negative consequence of not knowing the true meaning of the term would be for a competent employee to seek employment elsewhere because he or she feared being laid off.

A contributing factor to most problems of semantics is that a word or expression with multiple possible meanings is used without clarification and explanation. Language scholar Kees van Deemter observes that most words have fuzzy boundaries, so it is helpful to clarify key words for the target.[19] For example, when referring to our "wealthy customers," it is good to clarify what is meant by a *wealthy* customer. Perhaps the reference is to those customers in the top 2 percent income bracket. Or the reference might be to the top 1 percent, or even 50 percent.

CREDIBILITY OF THE SENDER AND MIXED SIGNALS

Mixed signals
type of message in which the sender might recommend one thing to others yet behave in another way

The more trustworthy the source or sender of the message the greater the probability that the message will get through clearly. In contrast, when the sender of the message has low credibility, many times it will be ignored. Communications can also break down for a subtle variation of low credibility. The disconnect occurs from **mixed signals,** a type of message in which the sender might recommend one thing to others yet behave in another way himself or herself. (Observe that *mixed message* as described earlier has a different meaning.) A team leader might tell others that a tidy worker is a productive worker. However, his or her own cubicle contains a four-month supply of empty soft-drink cans, and old papers consume virtually every square inch of his or her desk.

Mixed signals also refers to sending different messages about the same topic to different audiences. For example, company representatives might brag about the high quality of the company's products in public statements. Yet, on the shop floor and in the office, the company tells its employees to cut costs whenever possible to lower costs.

DISTORTION OF INFORMATION

A great problem in sending messages is that people receiving them often hear what they want to hear. Without malicious intent, people modify your message to bolster their self-esteem or improve their situation. An incident that occurred between Danielle and her supervisor is fairly typical of this type of communication barrier. Danielle asked her supervisor when she would be receiving a salary increase. Regarding the request as far-fetched and beyond the budget at the time, Danielle's supervisor replied, "Why should the company give you a raise when you are often late for work?"

Danielle *heard* her supervisor say, "If you come to work on time regularly, you will receive a salary increase." One month later, Danielle said to her supervisor that she had not been late for work in a month and should now be eligible for a raise. Her supervisor replied, "I never said that. Where did you get that idea?"

DIFFERENT PERSPECTIVES AND EXPERIENCES

People perceive words and concepts differently because their experiences and vantage points differ. On the basis of their perception of what they have heard, most people believe that all homeless people live in the street, parks, or public buildings such as libraries. In reality, many homeless people live in temporary housing such as shelters provided by the community.

Cultural differences create different perspectives and experiences, such as workers from Eastern cultures tending to have high respect for authority. A worker from India might more readily accept a message from the boss than would his or her counterpart from California or Sweden. In the last two places, workers have a more casual attitude toward authority.

EMOTIONS AND ATTITUDES

Have you ever tried to communicate a message to another person while that person is emotionally aroused? Your message was probably distorted considerably. Another problem is that people tend to say things when emotionally aroused that they would not say when calm. Similarly, a person who has strong attitudes about a particular topic may become emotional when that topic is introduced. The underlying message here is try to avoid letting strong emotions and attitudes interfere with the sending or receiving of messages. If you are angry with someone, for example, you might miss the merit in what that person has to say. Calm down before proceeding with your discussion or attempting to resolve the conflict. Emotional intelligence makes a key contribution in this situation.

COMMUNICATION OVERLOAD

A major communication barrier facing literate people is being bombarded with information. **Communication overload** occurs when people are so overloaded with information that they cannot respond effectively to messages. As a result, they experience work stress. Workers at many levels are exposed to so much electronic, printed, and spoken information that their capacity to absorb it is taxed. The problem is worsened when low-quality information is competing for your attention. An example is a flashing pop-up ad informing you that you have just won a free laptop computer, and all you have to do is follow a link to claim your prize. The human mind is capable of processing only a limited quantity of information at a time. Workers who intentionally multitask, such as reading instant messages and filling in a spreadsheet at the same time, aggravate the problem of communication overload. More information about this problem is in Chapter 8, about communication in the workplace and Chapter 16 about developing good work habits.

Communication overload phenomenon that occurs when people are so overloaded with information that they cannot respond effectively to messages

IMPROPER TIMING

Many messages do not get through to people because they are poorly timed. You have to know how to deliver a message, but you must also know *when* to deliver it. Sending a message when the receiver is distracted with other concerns or is rushing to get somewhere is a waste of time. A specific example is that your message might be wasted when you contact someone who getting set to leave for a lunch break at the moment. Furthermore, the receiver may become discouraged and therefore will not repeat the message later.

The art of timing messages suggests not to ask for a raise when your boss is in a bad mood or to ask a new acquaintance for a date when he or she is preoccupied. However, do ask your boss for a raise when business has been good, and do ask someone for a date when you have just done something nice for that person and have been thanked.

POOR COMMUNICATION SKILLS

A message may fail to register because the sender lacks effective communication skills. The sender might garble a written or spoken message so severely that the receiver finds it impossible to understand. Also, the sender may deliver the message so poorly that the receiver does not take it seriously. A common deficiency in sending messages is to communicate with low conviction by using *wimpy* words, backpedaling, and qualifying. Part of the same idea is to use affirmative language, such as saying "when" instead of "if." Also, do not use phrases that call your integrity into question, such as "to be perfectly honest" (implying that you usually do not tell the truth).[20] To illustrate, here are three statements that send a message of low conviction to the receiver: "I think I might be able to finish this project by the end of the week." "It's possible that I could handle the assignment you have in mind." "I'll do what I can."

Another communication skill deficiency that can serve as a communication barrier is to have a regional accent so strong that it detracts from your message. Your regional accent is part of who you are, so you may not want to modify how you speak. Nevertheless, many public personalities, business executives, and salespeople seek out speech training or speech therapy to avoid having an accent that detracts from their message.[21] Also, at high-level positions people typically want to be universal in their appeal. You may notice that commentators on national television usually speak in a universal, rather than regional, manner.

"You can have brilliant ideas; but if you can't get them across, your ideas won't get you anywhere."
Lee Iacocca
Former Chrysler chairman and Ford CEO

Communication barriers can result from deficiencies within the receiver. A common barrier is a receiver who is a poor listener. Improving listening skills is such a major strategy for improving communication skills that it receives separate mention later in this chapter.

CULTURAL AND LANGUAGE BARRIERS

Communication barriers in work and personal life can be created when the sender and receiver come from different cultures and are not fluent in each other's language. Quite often cultural differences and language differences exist at the same time. A cultural difference creating a barrier to communication often takes this form: A supervisor from a culture that emphasizes empowering (giving power to) employees is giving instructions to an employee from a culture that believes the boss should make all the decisions. In response to a question from the subordinate, the supervisor says, "Do what you think is best." The subordinate has a difficult time understanding the message because he or she is waiting for a firm directive from the boss.

Limited understanding of another person can sometimes be attributed to cultural differences. For example, a supervisor might send a message to Kim, a South Korean American in her group, that she can win an Employee of the Month award if she increases her productivity by 5 percent. Kim does not receive the message well because according to her cultural beliefs, it is negative behavior to stand out from the group. (After Kim assimilates more into the American culture, she will most likely receive the message more clearly.)

A language communication barrier is sometimes amusing, such as an American worker complimenting another by saying "You have been working like a dog" on this project. The second person might interpret the comment as suggesting he or she must be punished to work hard. At other times language barriers cause accidents. Many foreign-language-speaking construction workers in the United States encounter accidents because they do not clearly understand the instructions about danger.

A notable problem with language barriers has stemmed from the practice of *offshoring* (sending overseas) customer service and call center positions to India, as well as Mexico and the Philippines. For Mexicans and Filipinos, English is usually their second language so they have an accent unfamiliar to many Americans. Although English might be the primary or strong second language of Indian workers, it is not a type of English familiar to many Americans. As a result, many Americans who are not familiar with the accents of English-speaking Indians will say, "I can't understand the person who is trying to help me." Many of these people hang up in frustration. Several U.S.-based telecommunication companies have therefore reestablished customer service centers in the United States.

To help overcome cultural and language barriers, many companies invest considerable time and money in cross-cultural training, as will be explained in Chapter 14.

What Are Some Ways to Build Bridges to Communication?

Learning Objective 6

With determination and awareness that communication roadblocks and barriers do exist, you can become a more effective communicator. It would be impossible to remove all barriers, but they can be minimized. The following ten techniques are helpful in building better bridges to communication.

1. Appeal to human needs, and time your messages.
2. Repeat your message, using more than one channel.
3. Have an empowered attitude, and be persuasive.
4. Discuss differences in frames of reference.
5. Check for comprehension and feelings through feedback.
6. Minimize defensive communication.
7. Combat communication overload.
8. Use mirroring to establish rapport.
9. Engage in small talk and positive gossip.
10. Solicit feedback on your communication effectiveness.

APPEAL TO HUMAN NEEDS, AND TIME YOUR MESSAGES

People are more receptive to messages that promise to do something for them. In other words, if a message promises to satisfy a need that is less than fully satisfied, you are likely to listen. The person in search of additional money who ordinarily does not hear low tones readily hears the whispered message, "How would you like to earn $500 in one weekend?"

Timing a message properly is related to appealing to human needs. If you deliver a message at the right time, you are taking into account the person's mental condition at the moment. A general principle is to deliver your message when the person might be in the right frame of mind to listen. The right frame of mind includes such factors as not being preoccupied with other thoughts, not being frustrated, being in a good mood, and not being stressed out. (Of course, all this severely limits your opportunity to send a message!)

REPEAT YOUR MESSAGE, USING MORE THAN ONE CHANNEL

You can overcome many communication barriers by repeating your message several times. It is usually advisable not to say the same thing so as to avoid annoying the listener with straight repetition. Repeating the message in a different form is effective in another way: The receiver may not have understood the message the way in which it was first delivered. Repetition, like any other means of overcoming communication roadblocks, does not work for all people. Many people who repeatedly hear the message "text messaging while driving is dangerous" are not moved by it. It is helpful to use several methods of overcoming roadblocks or barriers to communication.

A generally effective way of repeating a message is to use more than one communication channel. For example, follow up a face-to-face discussion with an e-mail message or phone call or both. Your body can be another channel or medium to help impart your message. If you agree with someone about a spoken message, state your agreement and also shake hands over the agreement. Can you think of another channel by which to transmit a message?

HAVE AN EMPOWERED ATTITUDE, AND BE PERSUASIVE

A positive attitude helps a person communicate better in speaking, writing, and nonverbally. Being positive is a major factor in being persuasive, as mentioned previously in avoiding wimpy words. *Empowerment* here refers to the idea that the person takes charge of his or her own attitude.[22] Developing a positive attitude is not always easy. A starting point is to see things from a positive perspective, including looking for the good in people and their work. If your work is intrinsically motivating, you are likely to have a positive attitude. You would then be able to communicate about your work with the enthusiasm necessary.

Figure 7-4 summarizes key ideas about persuasive communication, a topic most readers have most likely studied in the past.[23] If you can learn to implement most of the ten suggestions, you are on your way toward becoming a persuasive communicator. In addition, you will need solid facts behind you, and you will need to make skillful use of nonverbal communication.

DISCUSS DIFFERENCES IN FRAMES OF REFERENCE

Frame of reference
model, viewpoint, or perspective

Another way of understanding differences in perspectives and experiences is to recognize that people often have different frames of reference that influence how they interpret events. A **frame of reference** is a model, viewpoint, or perspective. When two people with different frameworks look at a situation, a communication problem may occur. For instance, one person may say, "I have just found the *ideal* potential mate." To this person, an *ideal* mate would be a person who was kind, caring, considerate, in good health, gainfully employed, and highly ethical. The listener may have a perception of an *ideal* potential mate as someone who has a superior physical appearance and is wealthy (a traditional stereotype). Until the two people understand each other's frame of reference, meaningful communication about the prospective mate is unlikely. The solution to this communication clash is to discuss the frame of reference by each side defining the perception of an *ideal* mate.

FIGURE 7-4 KEY PRINCIPLES OF PERSUASIVE COMMUNICATION

1. *Know exactly what you want.* First clarify ideas in your mind.
2. *Never suggest an action without describing its end benefit.* Explain how your message will benefit the receiver. *Reciprocity* is a key principle of persuasion. If you want another person to do something, be clear about how you will reciprocate, which could mean the benefit the other person will receive.
3. *Get a yes response early on.* It is helpful to give the persuading session a positive tone by establishing a yes pattern at the outset.
4. *Use powerful words.* Sprinkle your speech with phrases like "bonding with customers," and "vaporizing the competition."
5. *When you speak, begin with your headline—the most important point.* After the headline, provide more information as needed. To come up with the right headline, imagine what you would say if you had only ten minutes to deliver your message. An environmental specialist might begin a message to management with, "My new program will help us save the planet."
6. *Minimize raising your pitch at the end of sentences.* Part of being persuasive is not to sound unsure and apologetic.
7. *Back up conclusions with data.* You will be more persuasive if you support your spoken and written presentations with solid data, but do not become an annoyance by overdoing it.
8. *Minimize "wimp" phrases.* See discussion under "Poor Communication Skills" in this chapter.
9. *Avoid or minimize common language errors.* Do not say "could care less," when you mean "couldn't care less," or "orientated" when you mean "oriented."
10. *Avoid overuse of jargon and clichés.* To feel "in" and cool, many workers rely heavily on jargon and clichés, such as referring to their "fave" (for *favorite*) product or that "At the end of the day," something counts. It is also helpful to minimize the use of catchphrases like *bottom line*, *quantum leap*, and *cutting edge*. It is best to avoid or minimize unprofessional expressions such as "you guys," "like," and "awesome." The problem is that if you make frequent use of overused expressions, you may give the impression of not thinking critically.
11. *Frame your position in the direction you want.* Describe in a positive way the option you want the receiver to choose, or describe in a negative way the option you don't want the receiver to choose. For example, if you want to convince others of the advantages of global outsourcing, you might refer to it as *seeking wage rates that will make us competitive.* If you want to convince others of the disadvantages of global outsourcing, you might refer to it as *shipping jobs from our country overseas.*
12. *Explain that there is limited opportunity to capitalize on your offer.* According to persuasion principle of *scarcity*, people desire what is rare. If you make statements such as "there is only one left in stock," or "we have only one position left on our team," you will often be persuasive.

CHECK FOR COMPREHENSION AND FEELINGS THROUGH FEEDBACK

Don't be a hit-and-run communicator. Such a person drops a message and leaves the scene before he or she is sure the message has been received as intended. It is preferable to ask for feedback. Ask receivers for their understanding or interpretation of what you said. For example, you might say after delivering a message, "What is your understanding of our agreement?" Also use nonverbal indicators to gauge how well you delivered your message.

A blank expression on the receiver's face might indicate no comprehension. A disturbed, agitated expression might mean that the receiver's emotions are blocking the message.

A comprehension check increases in importance when possible cultural and language barriers exist. A simple direct inquiry about comprehension is often effective, such as, "Is what I said okay with you" or "Tell me what I said." A friendly facial expression should accompany such feedback checks; otherwise your inquiry will come across like a challenge.

In addition to looking for verbal comprehension and emotions when you have delivered a message, check for feelings after you have received a message. When a person speaks, we too often listen to the facts and ignore the feelings. If feelings are ignored, the true meaning and intent of the message are likely to be missed, thus creating a communication barrier. Your boss might say to you, "You never seem to take work home." To clarify what your boss means by this statement, you might ask, "Is that good or bad?" Your boss's response will give you feedback on his or her feelings about getting all your work done during regular working hours.

When you send a message, it is also helpful to express your feelings in addition to conveying the facts. For example, "Our customer returns are up by 12 percent [fact], and I'm quite disappointed about those results [feelings]." Because feelings contribute strongly to comprehension, you will help overcome a potential communication barrier.

MINIMIZE DEFENSIVE COMMUNICATION

Defensive communication
tendency to receive messages in such a way that one's self-esteem is protected

Denial
the suppression of information one finds uncomfortable

Distortion of information was described previously as a communication barrier. Such distortion can also be regarded as **defensive communication**, the tendency to receive messages in such a way that our self-esteem is protected. Defensive communication is also responsible for people sending messages to look good. For example, when criticized for achieving below-average sales, a store manager might shift the blame to the sales associates in her store. Overcoming the barrier of defensive communication requires two steps. First, people have to acknowledge the existence of defensive communication. Second, they have to try not to be defensive when questioned or criticized. Such behavior is not easy because of **denial**, the suppression of information we find uncomfortable. For example, the store manager previously cited would find it uncomfortable to think of herself as being responsible for below-average performance.

COMBAT COMMUNICATION OVERLOAD

You can decrease the chances of suffering from communication overload by such measures as carefully organizing and sorting information before plunging ahead with reading. Speed-reading may help, provided that you stop to read carefully the most relevant information. Or you can scan through hard-copy reports, magazines, and Web sites looking for key titles and words that are important to you. Recognize, however, that many subjects have to be studied carefully to derive benefit. It is often better to read thoroughly a few topics than to skim through lots of information.

Being selective about your e-mail and Internet reading goes a long way toward preventing information overload. Suppose you see an e-mail message titled "Car Lights Left on in Parking Lot." Do not retrieve the message if you distinctly remember having turned off your lights or you did not drive to work. E-mail programs and Internet search software are available to help users sort messages according to their needs. You can help prevent others from suffering from communication overload by being merciful in the frequency and length of your messages. Also, do not join the ranks of pranksters who send loads of jokes via e-mail and who widely distribute their personal blogs.

USE MIRRORING TO ESTABLISH RAPPORT

Another approach to overcoming communication barriers is to improve rapport with another person. A form of nonverbal communication, called **mirroring**, can be used to establish such rapport. To mirror someone is to subtly imitate that individual. The most successful mirroring technique for establishing rapport is to imitate the breathing pattern of another person. If you adjust your own breathing rate to someone else's, you will soon establish rapport with that person. Mirroring sometimes takes the form of imitating the boss in order to communicate better and win favor. Many job seekers now use mirroring to get in sync with the interviewer. Is this a technique you would be willing to try?

Mirroring
form of nonverbal communication to overcome communication barriers by subtly imitating another; used to improve rapport with another person

Mirroring takes practice to contribute to overcoming communication barriers. It is a subtle technique that requires a moderate skill level. If you mirror (or match) another person in a rigid, mechanical way, you will appear to be mocking that person. And mocking, of course, erects rather than tears down a communication barrier.

ENGAGE IN SMALL TALK AND POSITIVE GOSSIP

The terms *small talk* and *gossip* have negative connotations for the career-minded person with a professional attitude. Negative gossip can badly damage a person's reputation, such a spreading the story that the company's chief security officer was recently arrested for shoplifting.[24] Nevertheless, the effective use of small talk and gossip can help a person melt communication barriers. Small talk is important because it contributes to conversational skills, and having good conversational skills enhances interpersonal communication. Trainer Randi Fredeig says, "Small talk helps build rapport and eventually trust. It helps people find common ground on which to build conversation."[25] A helpful technique is to collect tidbits of information to use as small talk to facilitate work-related or heavy-topic conversation in personal life. Keeping informed about current events, including sports, television, and films, provides useful content for small talk.

Being a source of *positive gossip* brings a person power and credibility. (*Positive gossip* is the passing along of information of a constructive nature that does not harm or demean another individual.) Workmates are eager to communicate with a person who is a source of not-yet-verified developments. Having such inside knowledge enhances your status and makes you a more interesting communicator. Positive gossip would include such tidbits as mentioning that the company will be looking for workers who would want a one-year assignment in Europe or that more employees will soon be eligible for profit-sharing bonuses. In contrast, spreading negative gossip will often erode your attractiveness to other people.[26]

SOLICIT FEEDBACK ON YOUR COMMUNICATION EFFECTIVENESS

It may require courage and a strong desire to improve, but soliciting feedback on your communication effectiveness can help overcome barriers. Asking a question electronically rather than in person is often effective because the other person has more time to reflect on the answer and perhaps give you a couple examples of your communication effectiveness or ineffectiveness. Here are a couple of candid answers in response to the question, "How well am I communicating with you?"

> I'd say quite well both in the way you speak, and in your written messages.
>
> When you're nervous you're not so good at communicating. You put your hand over your mouth, and you look down at the floor.

As with most forms of feedback about the self, the same comment made by more than one person is more reliable than one random comment. If three or four people make a similar comment about a communication error you are making, you know you have an area for improvement.

▶ Learning Objective 7 ▶

How Do You Overcome Gender Barriers to Communication?

Another strategy for overcoming communication barriers is to deal effectively with potential cultural differences. Two types of cultural differences are those related to gender (male versus female role) and those related to geographic differences. Of course, not everybody agrees that men and women are from different cultures. Here we describe gender differences, whereas cultural differences are a separate topic.

Despite the movement toward equality of sexes in the workplace, substantial interest exists in identifying differences in communication style between men and women. The basic difference between women and men, according to the research of Deborah Tannen, professor of sociolinguistics at Georgetown University, is that men emphasize and reinforce their status when they talk, whereas women downplay their status. As part of this difference, women are more concerned about building social connections.[27] People who are aware of these differences face fewer communication problems between themselves and members of the opposite sex.

As we describe these differences, recognize that they are group stereotypes. Individual differences in communication style are usually more important than group styles (men versus women). Here we will describe the major findings of gender differences in communication patterns.[28]

1. Women prefer to use conversation for rapport building. For most women, the intent of conversation is to build rapport and connections with people. It has been said that men are driven by transactions, whereas women are driven by relations. Women are therefore more likely to emphasize similarities, to listen intently, and to be supportive.

2. Men prefer to use talk primarily as a means to preserve independence and status by displaying knowledge and skill. When most men talk, they want to receive positive evaluations from others and maintain their hierarchical status within the group. Men are, therefore, more oriented to giving a *report*, whereas women are more interested in establishing *rapport*.

3. Women want empathy, not solutions. When women share feelings of being stressed out, they seek empathy and understanding. If they feel they have been listened to carefully, they begin to relax. When listening to the woman, the man may feel blamed for her problems or that he has failed the woman in some way. To feel useful, the man might offer solutions to the woman's problem.

4. Men prefer to work out their problems by themselves, whereas women prefer to talk out solutions with another person. Women look on having and sharing problems as an opportunity to build and deepen relationships. Men are more likely to look on problems as challenges they must meet on their own. Similarly men are more hesitant to ask questions when faced with a problem, and women gather information by asking questions. The communication consequence of these differences is that men may become uncommunicative when they have a problem.

5. Men tend to be more directive and less apologetic in their conversation, whereas women are more polite and apologetic. Women are therefore more likely to frequently use the phrases "I'm sorry" and "thank you," even when there is no need to express apology or gratitude. Men less frequently say they are sorry, because they perceive communications as competition, and they do not want to appear vulnerable.

6. Women tend to be more conciliatory when facing differences, whereas men become more intimidating. Again, women are more interested in building relationships, whereas men are more concerned about coming out ahead.

7. Men are more interested than women in calling attention to their accomplishments or hogging recognition. One consequence of this difference is that men are more likely to dominate discussions during meetings. Another consequence is that women are more likely to help a coworker perform well. In one instance, a sales representative who had already made her sales quota for the month turned over an excellent prospect to a coworker. She reasoned, "It's somebody else's turn. I've received more than my fair share of bonuses for the month."

8. Women are more likely to use a gentle expletive, whereas men tend to be harsher. For example, if a woman locks herself out of the car, she is likely to say, "Oh dear." In the same situation, a man is likely to say, "Oh ______." (Do you think this difference really exists?)

(Here we could be dealing with both a sex and generational difference, with recent generations of women being more likely to swear than previous generations.)

The use of expletives is more consequential than simply a difference in communication style. Many people feel uncomfortable, and even harassed, when hearing expletives in the workplace. A constructive counterapproach to the expletive user is to express your discomfort and politely ask for the person to refrain from swearing in your presence.

9. Women use the words "I," "me," and "mine" more frequently. It is generally thought that men use "I" more, because men are more narcissistic and self-congratulatory. Yet, recent research from several studies, and across cultures, indicates that women make more frequent use of "I," "me," and "mine." The reason appears to be that women are more aware of their internal state. In contrast, men use more articles such as "a," "an," and "the." The implication is that men talk more frequently about objects and things. Women also make more frequent use of then third-person pronouns, "he," "she," and "they" because women talk more about people and relationships.[29]

How can the information just presented help overcome communication problems on the job? As a starting point, remember that gender differences often exist. Understanding these differences will help you interpret the communication behavior of people. For example, if a male coworker is not as polite as you would like, remember that he is simply engaging in gender-typical behavior. Do not take it personally.

A woman can remind herself to speak up more in meetings because her natural tendency might be toward holding back. She might say to herself, "I must watch out to avoid gender-typical behavior in this situation." A man might remind himself to be more polite and supportive toward coworkers. The problem is that, although such behavior is important, his natural tendency might be to skip saying "thank you."

Men and women should recognize that when women talk over problems, they might not be seeking hard-hitting advice. Instead, they may simply be searching for a sympathetic ear so they can deal with the emotional aspects of the problem.

A general suggestion for overcoming gender-related communication barriers is for men to improve communication by listening with more empathy. Women can improve communication by becoming more direct.

▶ Learning Objective 8 ▶

How Can You Enhance Your Listening Skills?

Improving your receiving of messages is another part of developing better face-to-face and telephone communication skills. Unless you receive messages as they are intended, you cannot perform your job properly or be a good companion. Listening is a particularly important skill for anybody whose job involves solving problems for others because you need to gather information to understand the nature of the problem. Improving employee listening skills is important because insufficient listening is extraordinarily costly. Listening mistakes lead to reprocessing letters and e-mail messages, rescheduling appointments, reshipping orders, and recalling defective products. Effective listening also improves interpersonal relationships because people like to feel understood and respected.

A fundamental reason so many people do not listen well is because of the difference between the average speed of talking and the average speed of processing information. Humans speak at an average pace of 110 to 200 words per minute. In contrast, they can understand or process information in the range of 400 to 3,000 words per minute.[30] As a result, the mind tends to wander while listening to the slow pace of the sender talking. Human Relations Self-Assessment Quiz 7-2 is designed to help you think about your listening effectiveness.

Human Relations Self-Assessment Quiz 7-2

Common Listening Mistakes

Number	Statement About Listening	Not a Problem	Need Improvement
1.	I often finish people's sentences for them to save time.	❑	❑
2.	When another person talks to me I usually attempt to do something else such as glancing at my smart phone or looking at what's on my television screen.	❑	❑
3.	I change the subject quickly and frequently when someone is talking to me.	❑	❑
4.	I tune out right away when someone is telling me something I strongly disagree with.	❑	❑
5.	I make the statement "What did you say?" a few times in every conversation even though my hearing is okay.	❑	❑
6.	As soon as I disagree with something somebody tells me, I laugh at him or her.	❑	❑
7.	I become bored quickly when I am not the person doing the talking in a conversation.	❑	❑
8.	I often answer my own questions with a statement such as, "How are you today? You seem fine."	❑	❑
9.	I rarely remember a person's name after hearing it once.	❑	❑
10.	I never recall somebody saying to me, "Thanks for listening."	❑	❑

Scoring and Interpretation:

Assuming that you have enough self-insight to respond accurately to the ten statements, if you answered "Not a Problem" to at least eight of the statements you are a good listener. If you responded "Needs Improvement" to eight or more of the statements, you are advised to work on your listening skills.

ACTIVE LISTENING

A major component of effective listening is to be an **active listener**. The active listener listens intensely, with the goal of empathizing with the speaker. **Empathy** means understanding another person's point of view. If you understand the other person's paradigm, you will be a better receiver and sender of messages. Empathy does not necessarily mean that you sympathize with the other person. For example, you may understand why some people are forced to beg in the streets, but you may have very little sympathy for their plight.

Active listener
person who listens intensely, with the goal of empathizing with the speaker

Empathy
understanding another person's point of view

Accepting the Sender's Figure of Speech

A useful way of showing empathy is to accept the sender's figure of speech. By so doing, the sender feels understood and accepted. Also, if you reject the person's figure of speech by rewording it, the sender may become defensive. Many people use the figure of speech "I'm stuck" when they cannot accomplish a task. You can facilitate smooth communication by a response such as, "What can I do to help you get unstuck?" If you respond with something like, "What can I do to help you think more clearly?" the person is forced to change mental channels and may become defensive.[31]

Feedback and Paraphrasing

As a result of listening actively, the listener can feed back to the speaker what he or she thinks the speaker meant. Feedback of this type relies on both verbal and non-verbal communication. Feedback is also important because it facilitates two-way communication. To be an active listener, it is also important to **paraphrase**, or repeat in your own words what the sender says, feels, and means. In your paraphrasing, avoid rewording a person's figure of speech so long as that phrase is acceptable to you. You might feel awkward the first several times you paraphrase. Therefore, try it with a person with whom you feel comfortable. With some practice, it will become a natural part of your communication skill kit. Here is an example of how you might use paraphrasing:

Paraphrase
repeating in one's own words what a sender says, feels, and means

Other Person: I'm getting ticked off at working so hard around here. I wish somebody else would pitch in and do a fair day's work.

You: You're saying that you do more than your fair share of the tough work in our department, and it's ticking you off.

Other Person: You bet. Here's what I think we should be doing about it . . . .

Life coach Sophronia Scott advises that, after you have paraphrased, it is sometimes helpful to ask the person you listened to whether your impression of what he or she said is correct. Your goal is not to make others repeat themselves but to extend the conversation so you can obtain more useful details.[32]

Minimize Distractions

If feasible, keep your phone and your computer screen out of sight when listening to somebody else. Having distractions in sight creates the temptation to glance away from the message sender. At the start of your conversation, notice the other person's eye color to help you establish eye contact. (But don't keep staring at his or her eyes!) A major technique of active listening is to ask questions rather than making conclusive statements. Asking questions provides more useful information. Suppose a teammate is late with data you need to complete your analysis. Instead of saying, "I must have your input by Thursday afternoon," try, "When will I get your input?"

Allow Sender to Finish His or Her Sentence

Be sure to let others speak until they have finished. Do not interrupt by talking about you, jumping in with advice, or offering solutions unless requested. Equally bad for careful listening is to finish the sentence of a receiver. Almost all people prefer to complete their own thoughts, even though there are two curious traditions that run counter to this idea. One is that business partners who have been working together for many years, and understand each other well, have a tendency to finish the other partner's sentence. Couples in personal life behave similarly. Also, have you noticed how when you start to enter a phrase into a major search engine, suddenly you are given about ten choices that are not necessarily what you are planning to write? (Of course, this is responding to writing and not really listening, but the overtaking of your thinking is the same.)

Minimize Words That Shut Down Discussion

A key part of listening is to keep the conversation flowing. According to executive coach Marshall Goldsmith, an especially useful approach to keep conversation going in most work situations is for the listener to minimize certain negatively toned words that frequently shut down conversation. When you say, "no," "but," or "however," you effectively shut down or limit the conversation. No matter what words follow, the sender receives a message to the effect, "You are wrong and I am right." Even if you say, "I agree, but . . . " the shut-down message still comes through. The other person is likely to get into the defensive mode.

After the person has finished talking, there are times it will be appropriate to say, "no," "but," or "however."[33] Assume, for example, that a worker says to the business owner that the company should donate one-third of its profits to charity each year. The owner might then reply, "I hear you, but if we give away all that money, our profits will be too slim to grow the business."

Another way to block the free flow of communication is to make a shut-down response when someone asks, "Do you have the time to discuss something important?" The shut-down response is, "I'm busy right now, but go ahead anyway." The person who approached you is likely to feel slighted and might even leave the message unsaid.

PERSONAL COMMUNICATION STYLE

Personal communication style verbal and nonverbal communication style for a unique approach to sending and receiving information

In this chapter we have described many aspects of how people communicate, including gender-specific tendencies. How you combine verbal and nonverbal communication becomes part of your **personal communication style,** or your unique approach to sending and receiving information. Your personal communication style is a major component of your personality because it differentiates you from others. Hundreds of styles are possible, including the following:

- Katherine speaks loudly, smiles frequently, and moves close to people when speaking. Her communication style might be described as aggressive.
- Oscar speaks softly, partially covers his mouth with his hand while talking, and looks away from others. His communication style might be defined as passive or wimpy.
- Tim speaks rapidly, uses a colorful vocabulary, smiles frequently, and makes sweeping gestures. His communication style might be defined as flamboyant.

Key Terms

Communication, 182
Encoding, 182
Decoding, 183
Barriers to communication (or noise), 183
Nonverbal communication, 185
Mixed messages, 185
Semantics, 196
Mixed signals, 196
Communication overload, 197
Frame of reference, 200
Defensive communication, 202
Denial, 202
Mirroring, 203
Active listener, 207
Empathy, 207
Paraphrase, 207
Personal communication style, 208

Summary and Review

Communication is the sending and receiving of messages. Therefore, almost anything that takes place in work and personal life involves communication. The steps involved in communication are sending, transmission over a channel, and decoding.

Communication is a vehicle for building relationships. We establish relationships along two primary dimensions: dominate–subordinate and cold–warm.

- In the process of communicating, we attempt to dominate or subordinate.
- We indicate whether we want to dominate or subordinate by the way we speak or write or by nonverbal signals we send.
- The four combinations of dominate–subordinate and cold–warm lead to different types of relationships—impersonal, accepting, supportive, or personal.

Nonverbal communication, or silent messages, is an important part of everyday communication. Nonverbal communication includes the following:

- Environment or setting in which the message is sent
- Distance from the other person
- Posture
- Hand gestures
- Facial expressions and eye contact
- Voice quality
- Personal appearance

An advanced application of nonverbal communication is to help combat drug trafficking and terrorism by spotting nervous or threatening behavior.

Positive interpersonal and communication skills associated with social networking include (1) demonstrating your loyalty by making gracious comments about your employer, (2) demonstrating professional-level communication skills, (3) paying deserved compliments to company personnel, (4) establishing meaningful contact with workers far and wide, and (5) displaying a desire to help others grow and develop.

Negative communication and interpersonal skills associated with networking include (1) using social networking sites to eliminate face-to-face interactions with work associates, (2) posting confidential or derogatory information about your employer, (3) posting derogatory information and photos about a coworker, and (4) engaging social networking at inappropriate times.

Barriers to communication are most likely to occur when messages are complex or emotional or clash with the receiver's mental set. Communication roadblocks include the following:

- Limited understanding of people
- One-way communication
- Semantics
- Credibility of the sender and mixed signals
- Distortion of information
- Different perspectives and experiences
- Emotions and attitudes
- Communication overload
- Improper timing
- Poor communication skills
- Cultural and language barriers

Strategies to overcome communication roadblocks include these:

- Appealing to human need and timing your messages
- Repeating your message using more than one channel
- Having an empowered attitude and being persuasive
- Discussing differences in paradigms
- Checking for comprehension and feelings

- Minimizing defensive communication
- Combating communication overload
- Using mirroring to establish rapport
- Engaging in small talk and positive gossip
- Solicit feedback on your communication effectiveness

Some opinion and evidence exists about gender differences in communication style. For example, women prefer to use conversation for rapport building, and men prefer to use talk primarily as a means to preserve independence and status by displaying knowledge and skill. Understanding gender differences will help you interpret the communication behavior of people.

Improving your receiving of messages is another part of developing better communication skills. Unless you receive messages as intended, you cannot perform your job properly or be a good companion. A major component of effective listening is to be an active listener. The active listener uses empathy and can feed back to the speaker what he or she thinks the speaker meant.

Active listening also involves:

- Accepting the sender's figure of speech
- Feedback and paraphrasing
- Minimizing distractions
- Allowing the sender to finish his or her sentences
- Minimizing words that shut down discussion

How you combine verbal and nonverbal communication becomes your personal communication style.

Check Your Understanding

1. Based on Figure 7-1, describe one way in which you could use interpersonal communication to build a better relationship.
2. Many people contend they communicate much more formally when on the job and much more informally (including using a more limited vocabulary) when among family members and friends. What do you see as the potential advantages and disadvantages of using two communication styles?
3. Why is nonverbal communication so important for the effectiveness of a manager or sales representative?
4. What nonverbal meaning is sent by using a fist-bump instead of a handshake when meeting another person in a job-related setting?
5. Assume that a person who is intent on a career in business chooses to have several tattoos. Which type of tattoo is likely to send the most positive message about his or her maturity and seriousness?
6. Most social media Web sites do not include a spell check or a grammar check. To what extent does this mean that you don't have to be concerned with spelling and grammar when posting messages on these Web sites?
7. Assume that a coworker had been fired from the company. How good an idea would it be to send that coworker a tweet to express sympathy about the firing?
8. Based on your own observations, identify a term or phrase in the workplace that creates semantic problems.
9. So what if differences in communication patterns between men and women have been identified? What impact will this information have on your communication with men and women?
10. How would you rate the persuasive communication skills of the current president of the United States? Have you any suggestions as to how the president could improve?

Web Corner

Effective listening:
www.womensmedia.com/seminar-listening.html

Exploring nonverbal communication:
http://nonverbal.ucsc.edu/

INTERNET SKILL BUILDER

Improving Listening Skills

Infoplease offers some practical suggestions for improving your listening skills that both support and supplement the ideas offered in this chapter. Infoplease divides listening into three basic steps: hearing, understanding, and judging. Visit the site at www.infoplease.com/homework/listeningskills1.html. The Web site includes a video of a person offering a service that will enable you to earn money as a public speaker. What is your opinion of this man's persuasiveness and credibility? What is you opinion of the effectiveness of his nonverbal communication?

Developing Your Human Relations Skills

Human Relations Application Exercises

Applying Human Relations Exercise 7-1

I Want This Position

The purpose of this exercise is to practice your persuasive skills using a topic of interest to many people—being hired for an attractive position. One by one, students make a presentation in front of the class, presenting a persuasive argument as to why they merit the attractive position they have applied for. The instructor will decide whether to use a handful of volunteers or the entire class. The audience represents the hiring manager. The student will first explain the nature of the position. (Use your imagination here.) Next, make a three-minute convincing argument as to why you merit a job offer. You will probably have about fifteen minutes to prepare, inside or outside of class.

After the presentations, volunteers will offer feedback on the effectiveness of selected presentations. During the presentations of the other students, make a few notes about the presenter's effectiveness. You may need a couple of minutes between presenters to make your notes. Consider these factors:

- Overall, how convincing was the presenter? If you were the hiring manager, would you give him or her a favorable recommendation for being hired?
- Which techniques of persuasion did he or she use?
- What aspect of the presentation was unconvincing or negative?

What lessons did you take away from this exercise about persuasive communication?

Applying Human Relations Exercise 7-2

Active Listening

Before conducting the following role-plays, review the suggestions for active listening in this chapter. The suggestion about paraphrasing the message is particularly relevant because the role-plays involve emotional topics.

The Cost-Cutting Coworker

One student plays the role of a coworker who has just been appointed as the cost-cutting coordinator for the department. The cost cutter has decided to explain his or her new responsibilities to coworkers one at a time before calling a group meeting. He or she wants to emphasize how everybody has an important role in saving the company money, even in such minor initiatives as copying on two sides of a sheet of paper and not throwing out pencils until they are less than three inches long. The second worker decides to listen intently to the first worker. Other class members will rate the second student on his or her listening ability.

The Failed Nurse

One student plays the role of a coworker who has just been notified that she has failed her licensing exam to become a registered nurse (RN). She now faces being dismissed from the hospital because she has failed to obtain her license for the second time. She worries about what she will be able to do to earn a living. Another student plays the role of a coworker she corners to discuss her problems. The second worker decided to listen intently to her problems but is pressed for time. Other class members will rate the second student on his or her listening ability.

When evaluating the active listening skills of the role-players, consider using the following evaluating factors, on a scale of 1 (low) to 5 (high):

Evaluation Factor	Rating 1 2 3 4 5
1. Maintained eye contact	
2. Showed empathy	
3. Paraphrased what the other person said	
4. Focused on other person instead of being distracted	
5. Asked questions	
6. Let other person speak until he or she was finished	

Total Points: _____

Human Relations Class Activity

How Good Should Our Communication Skills Be?

"How good do my communication skills have to be to succeed in the workplace?" is a question on the minds of many career-oriented people. The purpose of this exercise is to observe the verbal and nonverbal communication skills of people who appear to have succeeded in their careers. The class in its entirety will observe a business leader or sports leader, such as a coach or an athletic director, being interviewed on television. Business channels and sports channels might be a good source of material, as might YouTube. CNBC is another potential source of useful interviews. The transmission can be real time or previously recorded, and it should last approximately five to ten minutes.

As you observe the leader (or perhaps two leaders) on television or on the Internet, grade the person or persons on two dimensions: verbal communication skills and nonverbal communication skills. Use a standard A though F system. Back up your grading with a few written comments, such as "Great eye contact with the interviewer," or "Dull, unanimated person. Put me to sleep." Also, attempt to answer the following questions:

1. What kind of impact is the presenter having on your classmates? To answer this question, take a few quick peeks around the room during the presentation, and observe the nonverbal communication of your classmates.
2. To what extent would this person be a good communications role model for me?
3. What, if any, communication tips did I learn from the person or persons in the interview(s)?

A couple of minutes after the grading and written observations are completed the class will discuss some of the student observations. Be alert to whether consensus exists about the quality of the communications skills observed.

Human Relations Case Study 7-1

Totally Connected Alan

Alan is an operations supervisor at a regional distribution center for a large online consumer-goods shopping Web site. He enjoys his position, and sees it as an important job on the path to attaining his long-range goal of becoming the vice president of logistics (the movement of goods) at his present company or another one. Alan perceives himself to be a high-tech professional who relies on constant communication to get his job done. "You won't find me using dinosaur technologies around the office," says Alan. "I'm totally connected."

A few of Alan's coworkers and his boss wonder sometimes if Alan isn't pushing his fascination with communication technology too far. When Alan attends a physical meeting with his group he keeps his smart phone at hand and his laptop open. He usually begins the meeting with a statement to the effect, "As I tweeted you folks early this morning, here is what we need to accomplish today."

Kim, one of the logistics specialists in Alan's group, commented to a friend, "Yesterday, Alan was walking down the hall, and was about twenty feet from my cubicle. He had something important to tell me about a misplaced shipment. So he sends me a text message instead of just entering my cubicle. I received his text message about two hours later because of a delay on the server. Alan was upset that I didn't respond more quickly to his message."

Alan believes the workers should receive frequent feedback on performance rather than wait for the year-end review. To provide feedback to the members of his department, Alan relies mostly on posting messages on Facebook and sending tweets. A recent Facebook post to one worker was, "Good job on verifying the identity of the mysterious customer, but why did it take you so long?" A recent tweet to another worker was, "U updated address database gr8. U r totally Superwoman."

Questions

1. To what extent are the people criticizing Alan simply out of touch with modern technology?
2. What suggestions might you have for Alan to improve his use of communication technology in the office?
3. How might Alan improve his written communication skills in order to qualify for the position of vice president of logistics?

Human Relations Role-Playing Exercise 7-1

Feedback About Feedback

One student plays the role of Juan, the worker who received the Facebook posting from Alan about taking so long on the assignment. Juan sends Alan a text message requesting a five-minute, face-to-face meeting about the Facebook posting. Juan is a private person who objects to receiving feedback in a public space such as a social media site. Another student plays the role of Alan who thinks that giving feedback about job performance on Facebook is entirely appropriate.

Observers rate the role-players on two dimensions, using a 1 to 5 scale from very poor to very good. One dimension is "effective use of human relations techniques." The second dimension is "acting ability." A few observers might voluntarily provide feedback to the role-players in terms of sharing their ratings and observations. The course instructor might also provide feedback.

Human Relations Case Study 7-2

The Financial Services Coach

Kristine Florentine is an account representative (stockbroker) at a branch office of a financial services firm. Her manager, Chad Olsen, is concerned that Kristine is 25 percent below quota in sales of a new hedge mutual fund offered by the company. (In the past, hedge funds were only for the wealthiest investors.) Chad sets up an appointment with Kristine to spur her to achieve quota. The conversation proceeds, in part, in this manner:

Chad: My most important responsibility is to help team members work up to their potential. I wanted to get together with you today to see if there is any way I can help you. During the past quarter you were 25 percent below quota in your sales of the new hedge fund.

Kristine: I know that I am under quota, but I can't help it. It's tough pushing a hedge fund these days. Our clients are becoming conservative, and they don't want to jump into an investment they don't understand well and is associated with taking a high risk.

Chad: Why don't your clients understand the hedge fund?

Kristine: It's a fund that the average investor does not understand. The information I send them is pretty complicated for a layperson.

Chad: What steps could you take to make this hedge fund easier for our clients and prospects to understand?

Kristine: Maybe I could work up a thirty-second presentation that would give a nice overview of the hedge fund. This would enable me to make a quick pitch over the telephone. I could get back with more details by e-mail.

Chad: Now you're making good sense. But I'm disappointed that an intelligent person like you didn't think of that before. Do you have a self-confidence problem when it comes to making quota on a new product?

Kristine: Most people would have a self-confidence problem if they were going through what I am these days. It's not that easy concentrating on my work.

Chad: I don't like to hear excuses, but I'll make an exception this time. What are you going through that makes it difficult for you to concentrate on your work, Kristine?

Kristine: My sister and I are pretty close, and she's in big trouble. I mean *big* trouble. She was down on her luck, so she started dealing drugs. I warned her. My folks warned her, but she wouldn't listen. She got busted recently and faces a ten-year prison term.

Chad: Sorry to hear about your sister. But can't you keep things in perspective? You weren't involved in her drug dealing, were you?

Kristine: What's really dragging me down is that my sister used to tell me that I was her role model. Some role model. Her life is ruined.

Chad: Now I understand why you are so down. However, let's meet again real soon to talk about your sales on the hedge fund.

Questions

1. Identify the strengths in Chad's listening technique.
2. Identify the areas for improvement in Chad's listening technique.
3. How effective is Chad as a coaching style of manager?

Human Relations Role-Playing Exercise 7-2

Listening to Kristine's Tale of Woe

The case about the financial services coach serves as the scenario and the story line for this role-play. One student plays the role of Kristine, who believes that her distress about her sister's personal problem is a valid reason for her below-average performance. Her hope is that her boss, Chad, will listen carefully to her tale of woe and be empathetic. She will try to get Chad to listen more attentively to her. Another person plays the role of Chad, who is quite work oriented. He is willing to listen to an employee's personal problems, but he believes that his most important role is to focus on business results.

For both scenarios, observers rate the role-players on two dimensions, using a 1 to 5 scale from very poor to very good. One dimension is "effective use of human relations techniques." The second dimension is "acting ability." A few observers might voluntarily provide feedback to the role-players in terms of sharing their ratings and observations. The course instructor might also provide feedback.

REFERENCES

1. Original story based on facts reported in the following sources: Kyle Stock, "Wary Investors Turn to Lie Pros," *The Wall Street Journal*, December 29, 2010, p. C3; Courtney Comstock, "Wall Street Firms Keep Begging Me to Screen Interviewers, Says Deception Detector," *Business Insider* (http://articles.businessinsider.com), December 30, 2010, pp. 1–3; "Lie Detector Tests for Investment Banking Jobs?" pp. 1–3, retrieved January 30, 2012 from: (http://investment-banking.jobsearchdigest.com; "Insite Security Rolls Out Human Factor Integrity Assurance Practice," *Insite Advanced Security Management* (www.insitesecurity.com), October 14, 2009, pp. 1–6.
2. Rich Sorenson, Grace De Bord, and Ida Ramirez, *Business and Management Communication: A Guide Book,* 4th ed. (Upper Saddle River, NJ: Prentice Hall, 2001), pp. 6–10.
3. Linda Talley, "Body Language: Read It or Weep," *HR Magazine*, July 2010, p. 64.
4. Edward T. Hall, "Proxemics—A Study of Man's Spatial Relationships," in *Man's Image in Medicine and Anthropology* (New York: International Universities Press, 1963); Pauline E. Henderson, "Communication without Words," *Personnel Journal,* January 1989, pp. 28–29.
5. William A. Gentry, Book review in *Personnel Psychology*, Summer 2010, p. 500.
6. Talley, "Body Language," pp. 64–65.
7. Brochure for Executive Advantage program, Washington, DC, offered by Letitia Baldrige, 1997, p. 6.
8. Carol Kinsey Gorman, *The Nonverbal Advantage: Secrets and Science of Body Language at Work* (San Francisco: Berrett-Koehler, 2008),
9. Nick Morgan, "How to Become an Authentic Speaker," *Harvard Business Review,* November 2008, p. 116.
10. Jeffrey Jacobi, *The Vocal Advantage* (Upper Saddle River, NJ: Prentice Hall, 1996).
11. Geneviève Coutu-Bouchard, "L'effet Pygmalion," *Montréal Campus,* April 24, 2002, p. 11.
12. Mark G. Frank, Melissa A. Menasco, and Maureen O'Sullivan, "Human Behavior and Deception Detection," in John G. Voeller, editor,*Handbook of Science and Technology Security, Volume 5* (New York: John Wiley, 2008), pp. 2–3.
13. Ericv Benac, "Nonverbal Ways to Tell Someone Is Lying," retrieved February 2, 2012, from: www.ehow.com.
14. Ann Davis, Joseph Pereira, and William M. Bulkeley, "Silent Signals: Security Concerns Bring New Focus on Body Language," *The Wall Street Journal,* August 15, 2002, pp. A1, A6.
15. Del Quentin Wilber and Ellen Nakashima, "They Don't Like Your Looks," *Washington Post,* September 19, 2007, p. DO1.
16. Cited in Sharon Weinberger, "Airport Security: Intent to Deceive?" *Nature News* (www.nature.com), May 26, 2010, p. 4.
17. For a useful perspective on how social networking is changing society, see Steven Johnson, "How Twitter Will Change the Way We Live," *Time,* June 15, 2009, pp. 32–27, and Sherry Turkle, *Along Together* (New York: Basic Books, 2011).
18. Bridget Carey, "Bosses Should Set Social Networking Rules," *The Miami Herald* (www.miamiherald.com), August 11, 2009, p. 1.
19. Kees van Deemter, *Not Exactly: In Praise of Vagueness* (New York: Oxford University Press, 2010).
20. "Weed Out Wimpy Words," *WorkingSMART,* March 2000, p. 2; George Walther cited in "Power Up Your Persuasiveness," *Executive Leadership,* July 2003, p. 1.
21. Joe Neumaier, "Sweet Sounds of Success: Dialect Coach Sam Chwat Accents Hollywood's Best," *USA Weekend,* July 12–14, 2002, p. 12; "Do You Want to Improve Your Speech?" Sankin Speech Improvement (www.sankingspeechimprovement.com), 2011.
22. Sharon Lund O'Neill, "An Empowered Attitude Can Enhance Communication Skills," *Business Education Forum,* April 1998, pp. 28–30.
23. Several of the ideas are from "Six Ways to Be More Persuasive," *Manager's Edge,* November 2008, p. 3; Charles Harrington Elster, "Cubicle Conversation," *The Wall Street Journal,* July 23, 2008, p. A15; "Talk in Headlines," *Manager's Edge,* April 2008, p. 8. For more details about point 9 in Figure 7-4, see Brian Fugere, Chelsea Hardaway, and Jon Warshawsky, *Why Business People Speak Like Idiots* (New York: Free Press, 2005); Jessica E. Vascellaro, "Yahoo Chief to Deliver More Straight Talk," *The Wall Street Journal,* January 26, 2009, p. A2; Statements 2 and 12 are based on the principles of persuasion developed by Robert Cialdini, as summarized in Michael Price, "Tapping Our Powers of Persuasion," *Monitor On Psychology*, February 2011, p.
24. Jeremy Smerd, "Gossip's Toll on the Workplace," *Workforce Management*, March 2010, p. 3. The example is original.
25. Quoted in Jacquelyn Lynn, "Small Talk, Big Results," *Entrepreneur,* August 1999, p. 30.
26. Nancy B. Kurland and Lisa Hope Pelled, "Passing the Word: Toward a Model of Gossip and Power in the Workplace," *Academy of Management Review,* April 2000, pp. 428–438.
27. Deborah Tannen, *Talking From Nine to Five* (New York: William Morrow, 1994).
28. John Gray, *Men Are From Mars, Women Are From Venus* (New York: HarperCollins, 1992); Deborah Tannen, "The Power of Talk: Who Gets Heard and Why," *Harvard Business Review,* September–October 1995, pp. 138–148; Laurie Arliss, *Gender Communication* (Englewood Cliffs, NJ: Prentice Hall, 2005).
29. James W. Pennebaker, "Your Use of Pronouns Reveals Your Personality," *Harvard Business Review*, December 2011, p. 33.
30. One source of this widely quoted statistic is Jared Sandberg, "Bad at Complying? You Might Just Be a Very Bad Listener," *The Wall Street Journal,* September 25, 2007, p. D1.
31. Daniel Araoz, "Right-Brain Management (RBM): Part 2," *Human Resources Forum,* September 1989, p. 4.
32. Cited in "Five Keys to Effective Listening," *Black Enterprise,* March 2005, p. 113.
33. Ideas from Marshall Goldsmith cited in "Eliminate Bad Words," *Manager's Edge,* special issue, 2008, p. 5.

8 Communication in the Workplace

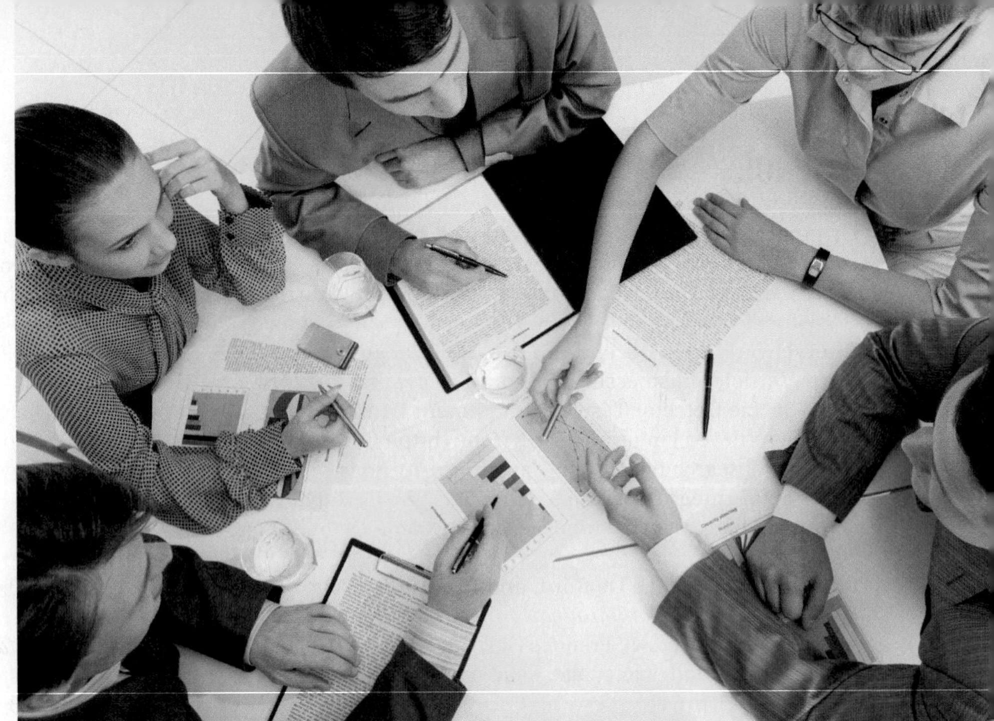

Outline

Sabre, the company that runs the majority of the world's airline flight reservation systems and also owns Travelocity, is also one of the leaders in employee social networking. Over seven years ago, Sabre management saw the value in social networking such as Facebook and Twitter for people connecting with each other, yet they were concerned that such sites waste considerable time. The company response was to build its own social media site based on intranet 2.0 (an advanced company-specific Internet.) The social networking system is called Sabre Town, and its primary purpose is to build more connections among the 9,000 Sabre employees worldwide.

Sabre Town has three main features: a Q&A section which enables users to search for users with certain technical expertise; employee profiles that highlight their skills, experience, and customer contacts; and job function groups such as project managers.

Sabre Town users can post a question to the entire organization, which triggers the site's relevant engine to send the question automatically to the fifteen most relevant employees. "Relevance" is based on information employees have entered into their profile, blog postings, and other questions and answers that have been previously posted. (An example of a question might be, "I have an 80-year-old client who wants to travel to Jakarta. She wants to know if the natives would be friendly toward a senior citizen who speaks only English.") Approximately 60 percent of questions are answered within one hour, and each question receives an average of nine responses.

Sabre Town also includes Mom2Mom and other groups formed for personal life reasons. Women employees throughout the company use the group to seek advice about pediatricians, childcare centers, and chat about personal and work problems. Senior executive Tony Brice explains that "Solving their problems pays off in the long run in terms of employee satisfaction and productivity."

Sabre Town has been judged to be a huge success. Over 90 percent of Sabre employees have joined the social networking site and actively participate. The quick response to questions has resulted in many cost savings for the company, such as making a quick sale because of an answer to a customer problem.[1]

The story about Sabre use of social networking illustrates the importance that companies place on exchanging information between and among interested parties. Effective communication contributes to organization success in many ways, such as keeping employees informed as to what needs to be accomplished and identifying problems before they cripple a company. For example, a lab technician might quickly warn his or her manager that a new food supplement being sold by the company had an unacceptably high level of mercury, thereby avoiding a recall and lawsuits. Another example of the benefit of effective communication is that workers kept up-to-date about key issues that affect them are much more likely to stay on the job. In this chapter we study communication in organizations from several perspectives: formal and informal communication channels, the communication challenges created by information technology, and dealing effectively with meetings.

Learning Objectives ▸

After studying the information and doing the exercises in this chapter, you should be able to:

1. Describe the formal channels of communication within organizations.
2. Describe the informal channels of communication within organizations.
3. Identify the challenges to interpersonal communication created by communication technology.
4. Be ready to do an effective job of conducting or participating in a business meeting.

▶ Learning Objective 1 ▶

What Are the Formal Channels of Communication Within Organizations?

Formal communication channels
the official pathways for sending information inside and outside an organization

Messages in organizations are sent over both formal (official) and informal (unofficial) channels. **Formal communication channels** are the official pathways for sending information inside and outside an organization. The primary source of information about formal channels is the organization chart. It indicates the channels the messages are supposed to follow. By carefully following an organization chart, an entry-level worker would know how to transmit a message to someone in the executive suite. Formal communication channels are often bypassed through information technology. Using e-mail, instant messaging, and company blogs, anybody can send a message to anybody else in the organization. During an emergency, workers are also likely to bypass formal channels, such as a technician telephoning the plant manager directly about a chemical spill.

Relatively recent formal channels of communication include company blogs, social networks, intranets, and webinars, as well as procedures for crisis management. We also look at communication directions.

Web sites have now become the premier formal crisis communication channel. Formal channels during a crisis are necessary for informing employees about a disaster, work assignments, health services and grief counseling, and assistance in returning to work. Other formal communication channels during a crisis include television or radio.

COMPANY BLOGS AS FORMAL CHANNELS

The company blog is a widely used formal mode of communication, paralleling the use of blogs in private life. Many companies have abandoned their own blogs in favor of using the public blogs of Facebook and Twitter to communicate with the public. Quite often a posting on Facebook or Twitter leads directly to a company Web site, so the posting is simply a link to the Web site itself or a blog. However, the Web site might contain a blog.

Blogs originated by consumers are often used to complain about products or services and less often to compliment a company. At the same time, the company can use an external blog to defend its reputation when under attack. For example, the company might have received a large number of negative Facebook and Twitter posts because the company reduced the healthcare benefits of retirees. The blog might explain that although company management wants to provide the best it can for retirees, it still needs enough cash to stay in business.

Blogs were first used by business to communicate with customers in a personal, direct manner and perhaps form a bond with them. The blog can provide customers with a behind-the-scenes look at the company. Blogs can be useful in bringing a company and its company together through the open sharing of ideas, issues, events, and feedback.[2] Today, the vast majority of business corporations have entered the *blogosphere* if you include Facebook, Twitter, and LinkedIn as blogs.

The blog communicates business information but with a soft, human touch. For example, the McDonald's blog explains some of the ways in which it gives back to the community such as sponsoring athletic teams for children, and engaging in neighborhood clean-up campaigns. The company blog can also be used to communicate with employees in a relaxed, casual tone. Employees, as well as customers, can interact through a blog by providing comments that can be a source of valuable feedback to management and communicated directly to other visitors to the site, external blogs are useful.

An individual who establishes a blog on his or her own to chat about the employer creates an *informal* rather than a formal channel—when the blog is not authorized by the company. Bloggers who publish negative information about their employer, or publish unprofessional photos of themselves, run the risk of being fired. The rationale behind these firings is that the employee is making unwarranted use of his or her association with the company. To prevent problems of negativity appearing on personal blogs by employees, many companies now establish guidelines, such as "no disclosure of negative information about the company," "no nude photos," or "no profanity."

A general guideline for the use of offensive blogs is that a person's First Amendment right to free speech is not protected if it defames a company or divulges trade secrets on a Web posting. As explained by Nancy Flynn, executive director of the ePolicy Institute, "You could find yourself on the wrong side of a civil lawsuit."[3]

SOCIAL NETWORKING WEB SITES, INTRANETS, AND WEBINARS

Formal communication channels in the workplace have kept pace with Internet-based communication technology. An important implication of this development is that workers at all levels are expected to use these channels to send and receive messages and to work collaboratively with each other. Here we describe three key Internet-based workplace communication channels: social networking Web sites, intranets, and webinars.

Social Networking Web sites

As a majority of workers have become members of social networking Web sites such as Facebook, LinkedIn, and Twitter, these sites have become natural channels for members of the same company to communicate. As is well-known, Twitter is used for brief messages of up to 140 characters, such as "Jogged today. Feel great." Because of their more widespread membership, Facebook, Twitter, and LinkedIn are more likely to be used as official workplace communication channels. Also, these social media sites have networks dedicated to companies or coworkers.

A major purpose of company social networking sites is to satisfy employee preferences for being connected to each other electronically. Many employers recognize that social networks are a platform for connecting to others preferred by many young employees, and many older ones as well. Many employees would prefer to communicate with coworkers by posting a message on a social networking site than speaking to the coworker or even sending him or her an e-mail.[4]

Social networking technologies on the job are quite similar to their use in personal life. Members are allowed to create profiles of themselves and link up with others in a virtual community.[5] The focus on the workplace site, however, is to communicate work-related messages. The sites are also useful for workers offering support to each other, such as encouraging another Facebook member when he or she is facing a challenging problem. Another official use of social networking by corporations is for recruiting workers, with many companies posting positions on these sites. Also, site members can pass along recruiting information to their network friends.

Yet, another business application of social networks is to connect workers looking for mentors with more experienced workers who are available for mentoring. Members create profiles, ask questions of potential mentors, and arrange for in-person meetings. The same software has a "praise" tab, enabling site members to write quick notes of appreciation to each other.

Social networking sites also have an application that rests at the border between a formal and informal communication channel. For example, all employees might be encouraged to join Facebook so they can network with each and build their working relationships. Facebook becomes a virtual watercooler. In the words of Jeremy Burton, CEO of Serena Software Inc., "Social networking tools like Facebook can bring us back together, help us to get to know each other as people, help us understand our business and our products, and help us better serve our customers."[6]

A concern about social networking sites in the workplace is that they facilitate spending time on nonwork matters, such as pausing to watch a coworker's surfing video instead of reviewing his or her input. Nestlé USA has created a social network with its own firewall. Employees can post content related to nutrition and health but are prohibited from using the site for dating or selling products or services.[7] Another problem is that the same social networking site that displays a professional presence might present unprofessional images and content.

Assume that your vice president of finance sends you a finance message from her Facebook page. Will you take her seriously when her page also includes photos of her mud wrestling in a bikini? (This is the reason that many companies implement a company-specific social networking site rather than a public site.)

Intranets

Intranet
a company version of the Internet with the basic purpose of giving employees a central place to find what they need amidst a sea of digital information

An **intranet** is essentially a company version of the Internet with the basic purpose of giving employees a central place to find what they need amidst a sea of digital information.[8] The intranet serves as a useful communication channel because updated information is readily available to workers, and the information is centralized, current, and correct. For example, an employee might want to know the company's per diem allowance for meals while traveling. Instead of having to send an e-mail to the boss or human resources department, the employee can search the intranet.

The intranet is also used for much more than a file for routine information. More advanced uses include posting a video displaying a new product or service, describing the company's stand on a particular environmental issue, or posting a motivational message from the CEO. The company might also post a vision statement focusing on its exciting plans for the future. Another useful purpose is to use the intranet as a storage place for the minutes of meetings.

An intranet can also have a wiki feature in which workers are encouraged to add information of their own to certain content, similar to Wikipedia. Employee interaction of this type is helpful when those adding input are well informed and serious. The wiki approach facilitates worker collaboration, including the modification of documents as needed. The on-the-spot modification replaces sending hundreds of e-mails with attachments back and forth. To guard against misinformation being circulated, the company restricts which content allows for employee interaction. For example, the company cannot allow employees to modify per diem meal allowances.

Some company intranets have added a human touch by adding such features as a phone book, menus from the company cafeteria, a classified ad section, and a dating site. Again, we see how a formal communication channel can also serve an informal, social purpose.

Webinars

Webinar
a web-based method of holding a seminar

Another formal communication channel is a Web-based method of holding a seminar, referred to as a **webinar**. The speaker sends information to participants, who can interact with the conference presenter by computer. Collaboration is possible through such means as asking and answering questions. A telephone hookup is also typically used, including a speakerphone so many people at the same time can tune in on the information flow. Slides are displayed throughout the presentation.

The participants in the webinar often are working alone, yet they can be gathered in groups at one or more locations. The meetings can include PowerPoint presentations and streaming videos. Chat is another possible feature, so participants can react to the points raised by other participants.

Webinars as a formal communication channel are efficient and save travel costs and time, but, as with some other forms of communication technology, they have a limited human touch. For example, it is more difficult to inspire a worker with a message to his or her computer screen than an in-person message complete with many nonverbal cues.

"We realize the line is disappearing between personal and business."
Ton Brice, Blair Holdings Corp., quoted in *Workforce Management*, September 2010, p. 20.

COMMUNICATION CHANNELS FOR MANAGING CRISES

Many companies have developed formal communication channels for managing crises, such as fires and explosions, massive product recalls, financial scandals, and terrorist attacks. One of the most crucial parts of a disaster plan is how to communicate with the company's workforce during a crisis. A key part of the challenge is to locate and reestablish contact with employees who may be scattered in the streets or stranded in airports around the world. Aon Corporation, an international insurance, risk-management, and consulting company, improvised to use its Web site as an official communication channel during the crisis of September 11, 2001. A company official said, "With everything else down, we decided to use the company Web site. That seemed like the only option we had."[9]

A more subtle type of crisis is widespread employee fear that the company might lay off large numbers of workers or go out of business. An effective communication strategy is for top management to quickly allay fear if the company is not truly in danger. A few years ago the bankruptcy of Lehman Brothers Holdings created fear for employees at the Navy Federal Credit Union in Vienna, Virginia. The credit union responded with a letter from the president that presented a realistic but positive assessment of the company. He emphasized that the credit union is conservative and never entered into subprime (high-risk) lending.[10]

During more recent crises, such as the earthquake in Japan in 2011, multinational companies made extensive use of intranets and social media to disseminate messages about whether or not company employees were accounted for. Calming messages about the search for the missing were also sent via social media.

COMMUNICATION DIRECTIONS

Another aspect of formal communications is the directions messages follow in the organization. Messages in organizations travel in four primary directions: downward, upward, horizontally, and diagonally, as illustrated in Figure 8-1.

Downward Communication

Downward communication is the flow of messages from one level to a lower level. It is typified by a middle manager giving orders to a lower-level supervisor or by top management sending announcements to employees. Information is sometimes transmitted from a higher level to a lower one without the sender inviting a response. When this occurs, the feedback built into two-way communication is lost.

Downward communication the transmission of messages from higher to lower levels in an organization

FIGURE 8-1

COMMUNICATION DIRECTIONS IN ORGANIZATIONS

Communication in organizations can take place in four directions: downward, upward, horizontal, and diagonal.

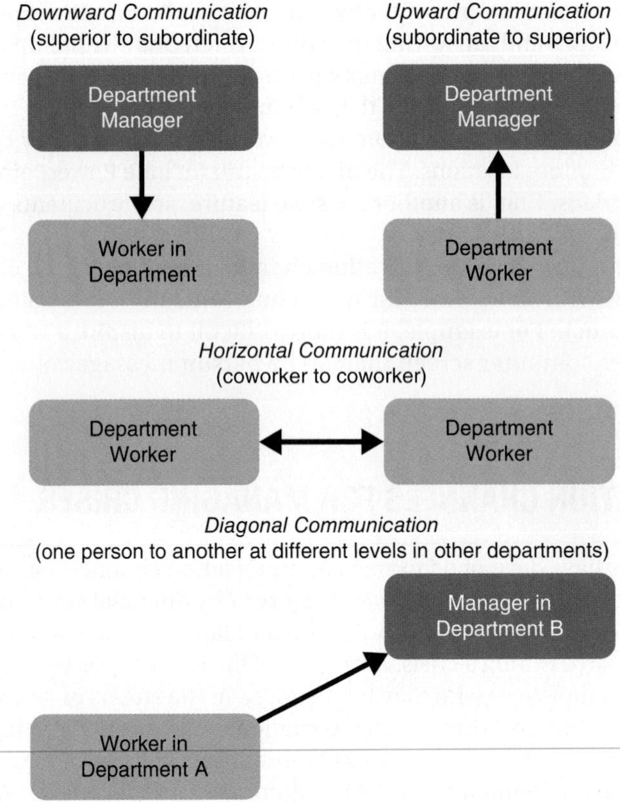

Upward Communication

Upward communication the transmission of messages from lower to higher levels in an organization

Open-door policy communication channel that is structured upward that allows employees to bring a gripe to top management's attention without first checking with the employee's manager

Upward communication is the transmission of messages from lower to higher levels in an organization. It is the most important channel for keeping management informed about problems within the organization. Simply talking regularly to employees improves upward communication. An **open-door policy** is a more structured upward communication channel that allows employees to bring a complaint to top management's attention without first checking with their manager. Managers who are willing to listen to bad news without becoming upset at the messenger are more likely to receive upward communication. Upward communication is more widely used in less bureaucratic firms than in highly bureaucratic firms. Almost all executives contend that they value upward communication, regardless of whether the majority of employees agree.

Horizontal Communication

Horizontal communication sending messages among people at the same organization level

Horizontal communication is sending messages among people at the same organization level. It often takes the form of coworkers from the same department talking to one another. Horizontal communication is the basis for cooperation and collaboration. When coworkers are not sharing information with and responding to one another, they are likely to fall behind schedule. Also, efforts are duplicated and quality suffers. Another type of horizontal communication takes place when managers communicate with other managers at the same level.

Diagonal Communication

Diagonal communication is the transmission of messages to higher or lower organizational levels in different departments. Because these pathways are infrequently spelled out on the organization chart, diagonal communication is usually an *informal* channel. A typical diagonal communication event occurs when a manager from one department contacts a lower-ranking person from a department outside of his or her chain of command. Diagonal communication becomes an *informal* pathway.

Diagonal communication
the transmission of messages to higher or lower organizational levels in different departments

What Are the Informal Channels of Communication Within Organizations?

Learning Objective 2

Informal communication channels are the unofficial network of channels that supplement the formal channels. Most of these informal channels arise out of necessity. For example, people will sometimes depart from the official communication channels to consult with a person with specialized knowledge. Suppose an administrative professional in the hospital admissions department spoke and wrote fluent German. Employees from other departments would regularly consult him or her when they were dealing with a patient from Germany. Here we study several aspects of informal communication channels: communities of practice, networks of contacts, the grapevine, rumors, chance encounters, and management by walking around.

Informal communication channels
unofficial networks of channels that supplement the formal channels

NETWORKS OF CONTACTS

Perhaps the most useful aspect of informal communication channels is that they enable workers to accomplish many tasks they would not be able to if they relied exclusively on formal channels. The network of contacts often means in practice that an individual worker might be in touch with people in his or her formal and informal channels to get work accomplished. However, the emphasis is on the informal communication channels. Here we describe several variations of networks of contacts that are primarily informal.

Communities of Practice

Two professors at the Warwick Business School, Richard McDermott and Douglas Archibald, have studied how work gets accomplished at many technical companies. A key conclusion they reached is that informal employee networks, or **communities of practice,** are an inexpensive and efficient vehicle for specialists to share knowledge and ideas. Effective communities of practice often assume responsibility for key problems. The communities of practice deliberately seek to expand the network of contacts so difficult technical problems can be conquered. A pharmaceutical specialist might ask, "Who can I consult to help me figure out how to stop the spread of fungus infections in people that continue to spread and eat skin." At Pfizer these informal employee networks are responsible for helping drug developers make difficult decisions on drug-safety issues.

Communities of practice
Informal employee networks

A key feature of these communities of practice is that experts from different parts of the company would share tidbits of knowledge, such as scattered information about drug safety. As such, they worked under an informal structure. Yet, these networks were so effective, that some companies, now consider them to be part of the formal structure.[11]

The Shadow Organization and Social Network Analysis

Shadow organizations
where much of the real work gets accomplished, the shadow organization is revealed by network analysis, which traces who talks to whom

Social network analysis
the mapping and measuring of relationships and links between and among people groups, and organizations that reveals the shadow organization

Some observers believe that the network of contacts explains how work really gets accomplished. According to this viewpoint, all companies have hidden **shadow organizations** where much of the real work gets accomplished.[12] For example, in most firms there are "tech fixers" who supplement—but do not replace—the technical support center. Suppose a worker is stuck with an information technology problem, such as being unable to access the e-mail system with his or her desktop computer. The worker might get in immediate contact with a tech fixer (whose formal job responsibilities do not include solving technical problems outside his or her department) for help with the problem.

The shadow organization is revealed by **social network analysis**, the mapping and measuring of relationships and links between and among people, groups, and organizations.[13]

The nodes in the network are the people, and the links show relationships or flow between and among the nodes as shown inFigure 8-2. Social network analysis helps explain how work gets accomplished in a given unit, such as shown in the interactions among Susan, Tim, and Tara on the right side of Figure 8-1. Perhaps the three of them mutually discuss credit risks. The interrelations can become quite complicated, because of the many number of people and interactions among them.

Social network analysis helps management survey the informal interactions among employees that can lead to innovative ideas. At the same time, the maps can point to areas where workers should be collaborating but are not. In this way, the maps help facilitate knowledge sharing. The maps can also be used to pinpoint the interactions one manager has so he or she can give the information to a successor.

Another insight gleaned for social network analysis is that the line indicates who trusts whom because they exchange ideas and go to each other for advice. According to corporate anthropologist Karen Stephenson, knowing who trusts whom is as important as knowing who reports to whom. Finding out who trusts whom is part of the social network analysis and is revealed by asking employees questions such as the following:[14]

- Whom do you go to for a quick decision?
- Whom do you hang out with socially?

FIGURE 8-2

A BASIC UNIT OF A SOCIAL NETWORK ANALYSIS

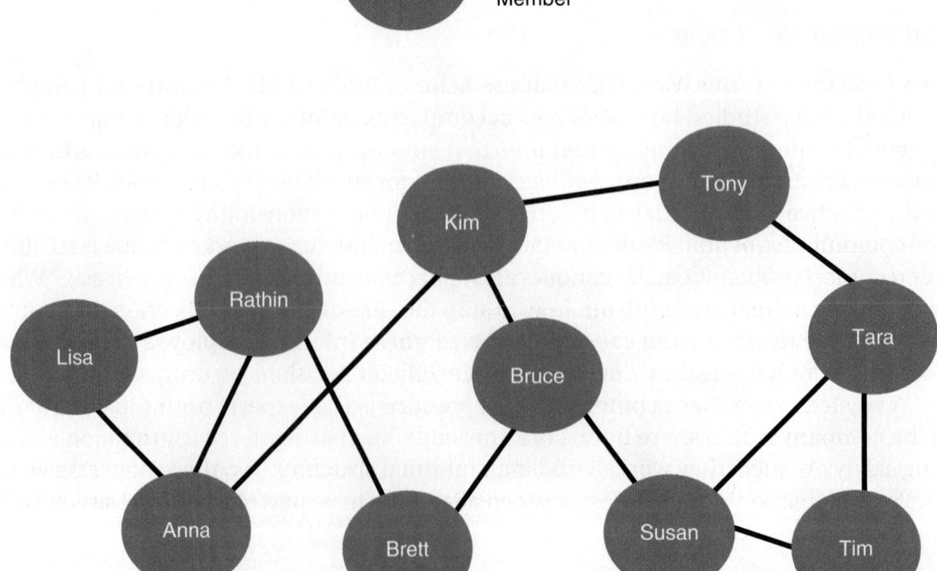

Human Relations Self-Assessment Quiz 8-1

The Strength of My Network of Contacts

To help you think through the effectiveness of your network of contacts, respond "Mostly Yes" or "Mostly No" to the following statements.

Statement About Contacts	Mostly Yes	Mostly No
1. I know at least ten people I could contact to give me advice about solving a work problem.	❑	❑
2. At least 95 percent of the people I am in touch with in the social media are people I have never met in person or talked to on the phone.	❑	❑
3. I am in touch with the majority of people in my network at least once a month.	❑	❑
4. The majority of my network members are doing well in their careers, or are good students.	❑	❑
5. Most of the people I follow on Facebook, Twitter, or other social media sites are celebrities I have never met or will never meet.	❑	❑
6. I almost never bother telephoning or seeing someone in person who I can contact through a social media website.	❑	❑
7. I would take advantage of the opportunity to attend a professional networking event, such as a face-to-face meeting of "tweeters."	❑	❑
8. I have a few people in my network who hold positions that I aspire to.	❑	❑
9. I am much more concerned about the quality of people in my network than the quantity.	❑	❑
10. When I encounter a person who holds a good position, or who appears to have the potential to be influential, I invite him or her to become a member of my social media network.	❑	❑

Scoring and Interpretation:

Give yourself 1 point for the following answers: Mostly Yes to questions 1, 3, 4, 7, 8, 9, and 10; Mostly No to questions 2, 5, and 6. If you scored 7 or more points, it appears that have established or are establishing a strong professional network. If you scored between 0 and 6, you may not be establishing a strong professional network. Furthermore, you might be wasting time on social media sites that you could be investing in career advancement.

- Whom do you turn to for advice?
- Whom do you go to with a good idea?
- Whom do you go to for career advice?

Your network of contacts can also extend outside the organization. A real estate developer, for example, might have contacts inside a bank who inform him of upcoming foreclosures. In this way the developer can make an early appraisal of the property to be ready with an effective bid on the foreclosed property. The mortgage specialist in the bank is part of the real estate developer's network of contacts.

A subtle perspective about social network analysis maps is that more connections aren't necessarily the best for the organization. If one person is too connected, he or she could be a bottleneck. Also, it is okay for some workers who spend a lot of time with customers or have expertise in highly specialized areas to show up on the outside of the web of interactions.

Human Relations Self-Assessment Quiz 8-1 gives you an opportunity to think about the quality of the contacts in your network.

THE GRAPEVINE

Grapevine
major informal communication channel in organizations; the grapevine refers to the tangled pathways that can distort information

The **grapevine** is the major informal communication channel in organizations. The *grapevine* refers to the tangled pathways that can distort information. The term referred originally to the snarled telegraph lines on the battlefield during the U.S. Civil War. The grapevine is often thought to be used primarily for passing along negative rumors and negative gossip. Gossips sometimes use the Internet and e-mail as channels for transmitting negative gossip. Facebook and Twitter are increasingly used to pass along gossip, often in the form of a question, such as "Is it true that one of our vice presidents was caught speeding in a company car?" When left to fester, gossip can cause individuals chagrin and also lead to turnover, conflict, and lawsuits. Gossip often increases when workers are bored or lack ample information about company events.

Managers can often stop negative gossip by confronting the source of the gossip, demanding that he or she stop. Positive gossip, however, makes a contribution to the organization because trading information strengthens ties among workers and humanizes the workplace. Gossip can be viewed as the glue that binds social groups together.[15] An example of positive gossip would be, "I heard management is considering adding a paid holiday next year. Everyone with five or more service years gets his or her birthday off from work."

Another contribution of gossip is that it makes workers feel good, a situation that will sometimes enhance productivity. As long as gossip does not consume too much of the workday, the results may be positive. Marty Kotis, the CEO of a commercial real estate development firm, explains that she wants employees to enjoy coming to work. Being happy and productive are not mutually exclusive. Assuming that workers attain the goals she has established, a little relaxation in the form of gossip does not hurt.[16]

The grapevine is sometimes used purposely to disseminate information along informal lines. For example, top management might want to hint to employees that certain work will be outsourced (sent to another company or outside the country) unless the employees become more productive. Although the plans are still tentative, feeding them into the grapevine may result in improved motivation and productivity.

Rumors

Rumors are an important informal communication force within organizations, and they tend to thrive in organizations with poor corporate communication, such as a penitentiary. Respondents to a worldwide survey agreed that rumors are an important early source of information. To ensure that rumors are more helpful than harmful, management might promote healthy, accurate communication. Consultant and author Tom E. Jones reinforces the importance of open communication to combat rumors. He recommends that unless the company is bound by some legal restriction, top-level management should tell everyone what they know about the facts. "Don't wait until you have all the details. Just get the truth out there fast."[17]

A problem with inaccurate rumors is that they can distract workers, create anxiety, and decrease productivity. A frequent byproduct of false rumors about company relocation or a pending merger is that some of the more talented workers leave in the hopes of more stable employment.

CHANCE ENCOUNTERS AND MANAGEMENT BY WALKING AROUND

Chance encounter
unscheduled informal contact between managers and employees

Another informal channel of significance is the **chance encounter**. Unscheduled informal contact between managers and employees can be an efficient and effective communication channel. Many years ago John P. Kotter, professor of leadership at Harvard Business School, found that effective managers do not confine their communication to formal meetings.[18] Instead, they collect valuable information during chance encounters. Spontaneous communication events may occur in the cafeteria, near the water fountain, in the halls, and on the elevator. In only two minutes, the manager might obtain the information that would typically be solicited in a thirty-minute meeting or through a series of e-mail or text-messaging exchanges. A representative question might be, "What seems to be the buzz on our newest product?"

One important communication channel can be classified as either formal or informal. **Management by walking around** involves managers intermingling freely with workers on the shop floor or in the office, as well as with customers. By spending time in personal contact with employees, the manager enhances open communication. During contacts with employees the manager will often ask questions such as, "How are you enjoying your work?" or "What bottlenecks have you encountered today?" Because management by walking around is systematic, it could be considered formal. However, a manager who circulates throughout the company is not following the formal paths prescribed by the organization chart. Management by walking around differs from chance encounters in that the latter are unplanned events; the former occur intentionally.

Management by walking around
managers intermingle freely with workers on the shop floor or in the office, as well as with customers; enhances open communication

Another perspective on management by walking around is that it is similar to a physician making rounds to visit his or her hospital patients. Instead of visiting patients, the manager drops by to see employees and engages in brief, informal conversations. Sample questions to ask on rounds include, "What is working well today?" "Do you have the tools and equipment you need to do your job?" "Is there anything I could do better?"[19] Recognizing the nature of the rounds, the employees are likely to respond with brief, spontaneous, and useful feedback—assuming the manager making the rounds is trusted!

What Are the Challenges to Interpersonal Communication Created by Communication Technology?

Learning Objective 3

Rapid advances in information (or communication) technology may enable workers to communicate more easily and quickly than they could even a few years ago. Although social media, including social networking, blogs, and photo sharing Web sites receive the most attention, other forms of communication technology are influential. Quite often the influence has been positive, but at other times the effectiveness of interpersonal communication has decreased. Six developments that illustrate the impact of information technology on interpersonal communication are e-mail, presentation technology, telephones and voice mail, telecommuting, multitasking, and overconfidence in computer-generated data. (The author realizes that traditional telephones are not usually considered part of communication or information technology, but they, too, are electronic devices that create communication challenges.)

E-MAIL AND COMMUNICATION AMONG PEOPLE

E-mail, including instant messaging and text messaging, is the information technology system with the most dramatic impact on interpersonal communication in the current era. The major impact of e-mail on interpersonal communication is that written messages replace many telephone and in-person exchanges. Team members often keep in regular contact with each other without having lengthy meetings or phone conversations.

E-mail including attachments of graphics and videos has become the dominant form of communication on the job. Several potential communication problems that e-mail and instant messaging create should be kept in mind to minimize these problems.

Indiscriminate Message Sending

A major problem with e-mail is that it encourages indiscriminate sending of messages. Some professional workers receive an average of three hundred e-mail messages per day, and some workers check their e-mail over thirty times an hour. Some of these workers make cynical comments such as, "My job is answering e-mail" or "I answer e-mail during the day and do my work at night and on weekends."

Donna Rawady, an executive coach, hints at a factor generating so much e-mail. The system has created unreasonable expectations on worker's time.[20] Many employees have become programmed to check their e-mail around the clock. The mental set becomes, "So long as I am checking e-mail, why not send a few messages?" Some workers conduct virtual joke-telling contests over e-mail, with some of the jokes being perceived as offensive by many other workers. The proliferation of electronic junk mail (spam) has prompted most company officials to take corrective action, such as the installation of spam filters.

To discourage excessive use of e-mails, several companies have experimented with prohibiting the use of e-mail on Fridays or on weekends. The purpose is to both ease the e-mail overload and encourage workers to interact with each other in person or by phone. Many workers hide behind e-mail instead of dealing directly with coworkers. Although the bans typically allow sending e-mails to customers and clients or responding to urgent matters, the usual flow of e-mail is halted. Many workers have complained about such limits to e-mail because it disrupts their work routine too severely. Another problem is that banning e-mail messages on Friday results in many workers stockpiling their e-mails and sending them on Monday morning or over the weekend.[21]

To minimize feeling overwhelmed by e-mail, it is best to schedule blocks of time for sending and answering e-mail—assuming you have the type of work that allows you to limit e-mail. One time-management software firm estimates that on average, office workers check their e-mail 50 times per day. Checking about once per hour would leave more time for other work activities. It is also useful to disable all the buzzes, beeps, and other alerts built into the e-mail system.[22] Consider also that sometimes a brief telephone conversation will help clarify an issue that might otherwise require a dozen e-mail exchanges. A representative example would be a human resources specialist involved in an e-mail exchange to explain a complicated benefit.

Many successful people control e-mail, rather than letting it control them. Excessive use of e-mail drains company productivity because workers who receive an e-mail typically spend about four minutes reading it and recovering from the interruption before they can return to other work. But for workers such as an online customer service representative, dealing with e-mail is their entire job.

Too Much Informality

The informal style of many e-mail exchanges can lead a person to believe that incorrect spelling, poor grammar, and disconnected thoughts are acceptable in all forms of business communication. The opposite is true. To appear professional and intelligent, writers of business e-mail messages should use correct spelling, grammar, capitalization, and punctuation. A conflict here, however, is that some professional people have begun to incorporate the informal writing style into their e-mails, including the lowercase *i* instead of *I*. Furthermore, some book titles from prestigious publishing companies use all lowercase.

E-mail has become a tool for office politicians who search for ways to look good themselves and make others look bad. Many office politicians use e-mail to give credit to themselves for their contributions to a project, perhaps using a companywide distribution list. When something goes wrong, such as a failed project, the office politician will inform hundreds of people that it was not his or her fault.

Avoidance of In-Person Reprimands

Many supervisors and other workers use e-mail to reprimand others because, by sending a message over the computer, they can avoid face-to-face confrontation. E-mail is well suited for managers who would prefer to avoid face-to-face contact with group members. Harsh messages sent over e-mail create several problems. First, it is shocking to be reprimanded or insulted in writing. Second, the person cannot offer a defense except by writing back an e-mail message explaining his or her position. Third, the recipient, not knowing what to do about the harsh message, may brood and become anxious.

Alternatives to E-mail

Some business firms have counterattacked the problems associated with e-mail by shifting to related technologies, as mentioned in relation to social networking sites and intranets. The major problem counterattacked is the time drain of sending and responding to e-mail messages. Among the e-mail replacements are private workplace wikis, blogs, instant messaging, RSS, and more elaborate forms of groupware that allow workers to create Web sites for the team's use on a specific project. A wiki is a site that allows a group of people to comment on and edit each other's work. As a result, a wiki can be a useful tool for sharing knowledge as well as publically displaying which workers are willing to publically display their bright ideas. *RSS* is the abbreviation for really simple syndication, which enables people to subscribe to the information they need. E-mail will probably remain strong for one-to-one communication, but the tools just mentioned will be relied on more heavily for collaboration.[23]

The shift away from e-mail to other methods of transmitting electronic messages may reduce the volume of messages but considerable exchange of information remains. For example, the French information technology company, Atos, shifted away from e-mail but then used social media tools such as a wiki which enables employees to communicate by contributing or modifying online content. The company also uses an online chat system which can lead to extensive back-and-forth communication.[24]

Figure 8-3 presents suggestions for good etiquette when using e-mail, including messaging. The good etiquette leads to more productive use of e-mail.

USE PRESENTATION TECHNOLOGY TO YOUR ADVANTAGE

Speakers in all types of organizations supplement their talk with computer slides, such as those created with PowerPoint, and often organize their presentation around them. Many people want presentations reduced to bulleted items and eye-catching graphics. (Have you noticed this tendency among students?) The communication challenge here is that during an oral presentation the predominant means of connection between sender and receiver is eye contact. When an audience is constantly distracted from the presenter by movement on the screen, sounds from the computer, or lavish colors, eye contact suffers, as does the message.

FIGURE 8-3 E-MAIL AND MESSAGING ETIQUETTE

Observing the following tips will enhance your e-mail etiquette and electronic communication effectiveness.

Keep it simple. Each message should have only one piece of information or request for action, so that it's easier for the receiver to respond. But avoid sending an e-mail with an attachment without some type of greeting or explanation. Do not allow e-mail threads longer than a couple of pages. E-mail messages longer than one screen often are filed instead of read.

Include an action step. Clearly outline what type of reply you're looking for as well as any applicable deadlines. *Use the subject line to your advantage.* Generic terms such as *details* or *reminder* do not describe the contents of your message or whether it's time sensitive. So the receiver may delay opening it. "Came in Under Budget" illustrates a specific (and joyful) title. "You Won the Sales Contest" is another winner. Do not forward a long chain of e-mails without changing the subject.

Take care in writing e-mails. Clearly organize your thoughts to avoid sending e-mails with confusing, incomplete, or missing information. Use business writing style, and check carefully for grammatical and typographical errors. (Also, generally avoid the trend to set I in lowercase.) When in doubt, use traditional formatting rather than bright colors and unusual fonts, because many people prefer standard formatting.

Inform receivers when sending e-mails from a wireless device. If you use a smart phone, include a tagline informing people that you are using such a device, which will help explain your terseness. Without explanation, you might project an image of rudeness or limited writing skill.

Be considerate. Use "please" and "thank you" even in brief messages. Part of being considerate, or at least polite, is to begin your e-mail with a warm salutation, such "Hello, Gina," rather than jumping into the subject with no greeting. Avoid profane or harsh language. Another way of being considerate is to send e-mails only when necessary, to help combat information overload. Sending copies only to recipients who need or want the information is part of being considerate.

Don't include confidential information. The problem is that e-mail is occasionally forwarded to unintended recipients. If your message is in any way sensitive or confidential, set up a meeting or leave a voice mail in which you request confidentially.

Do not use e-mail to blast a coworker and send copies to others. Criticizing another person with e-mail and copying others is equivalent to blasting him or her during a large meeting.

Ask before sending huge attachments. Do not clog e-mail systems without permission.

Encourage questions and demands for clarification. E-mail functions best when it is interactive, so ask receivers to send along questions they might have about your message, including any requests for clarification.

Consider the timing of e-mail messages. An e-mail that makes a major request should be sent earlier in the day so the person has time to process the request. Good news can be sent almost anytime. For some recipients, bad news is best sent early in the day so they can ask for your support in dealing with the problem. But very bad news (such as being laid off) is best delivered in person. Some people prefer to receive bad news later in the day so it will not interrupt their entire workday.

Use emoticons sparingly. Emoticons were considered creative and cute during their first several years, but have lost much of their positive impact. Sending smiles, frowns, and winks via punctuation marks is more acceptable for social than workplace messages. If you would not wink at a boss in person, it might not be acceptable in an e-mail.

Be cautious about using personal e-mail for work purposes. Especially if you work for a government agency, there could be legal complications in using personal e-mail for work purposes. The idea is that work-related e-mails should be part of the public record, and private firms may want to be able to review all messages exchanged among employees.

Avoid nasty messages, pornography, and other insensitivities. Many workers including executives continue to send insensitive e-mail messages containing pornography and harassing statements that lead to their suspension or even firing. Just because it is relatively easy to attach an offensive photo or video to a widely distributed video, does not make it sensible.

Instant messaging requires a few additional considerations for practicing good electronic etiquette:

Don't be Big Brother. Some bosses use instant messaging to check up on others, to make sure they are seated at their computer. Never intrude on workers unless it is urgent.

(continued)

Lay down the instant-messaging law. Make sure your message has some real value to the recipient before jumping right in front of someone's face. Instant messaging is much like walking into someone's office or cubicle without an appointment or without knocking.

Take it offline. When someone on your buddy list becomes too chatty, don't vent your frustration. By phone, in-person, or through regular e-mail, explain tactfully that you do not have time for processing so many instant messages. Suggest that the two of you get together for lunch or coffee soon.

Set limits to avoid frustration. To avoid constant interruptions, use a polite custom status message, such as "I will be dealing with customers today until 4:40."

Source: "Communicating Electronically: What Every Manager Needs to Know," *Communication Solutions*, Sample Issue, 2008, p. 2; Monte Enbysk, "Bosses: 10 Tips for Better E-mails," *Microsoft Small Business Center*, www.microsoft.com/smallbusiness/resources/technology/communications/bosses-10-tips-for-better-emails.aspx; Heinz Tschabitscher, "The Ten Most Important Rules of Email Etiquette." Accessed September 9, 2003, at: http://email.about.com/cs/netiquettetips/tp/core_netiquette.htm; Erich Schwartzel, "Use Emoticons Carefully in E-Mails with Boss, Others," *The Detroit News* (www.detnews.com), October 4, 2010, pp. 1–2; Mike DeBonis, "Personal E-Mail Used for City Work," *The Washington Post*, December 8, 2011, p. B3.

One of the biggest challenges is to learn how to handle equipment and maintain frequent eye and voice contact at all times. Several professionals in the field of business communication offer these sensible suggestions for overcoming the potential communication barrier of using presentation technology inappropriately:[25]

- **Reveal points only as needed.** Project the computer slides only when needed, and use a cursor, laser pointer, or metal pointer for emphasis.
- **Talk to the audience, not the screen.** A major problem with computer slides is that the presenter as well as the audience is likely to focus continually on the slide. If the presenter minimizes looking at the slide and spends considerable time looking at the audience, it will be easier to maintain contact with the audience. A related problem is when the speaker simply reads the slides to the audience without adding other content.
- **Keep the slide in view until the audience gets the point.** A presenter will often flash a slide or transparency without giving the audience enough time to comprehend the meaning of the slide. It is also important for presenters to synchronize the slides with their comments.
- **Reduce the text on each page of your PowerPoint presentation to a bare minimum.** Few people can really listen to you and read your slides at the same time, even if they think they are effective at multitasking. For many audiences, using the text as an outline of your talk, or talking points, is the most effective use of the slides.
- **Make sure to triple-check your presentation for spelling errors.** A spelling error projected on a screen can quickly become a joke passed around the room.

The point again is not to avoid the new technologies for communication but to use them to your advantage skillfully.

IMPROVE YOUR TELEPHONE, VOICE MAIL, AND SPEAKERPHONE COMMUNICATION SKILLS

A direct way of overcoming communication barriers is to use effective telephone and voice mail communication skills, because these two communication media often create communication problems. Also, many businesses attract and hold on to customers because their representatives interact positively with people through the telephone and voice mail. Many other firms lose money, and nonprofit organizations irritate the public because their employees have poor communication and voice mail skills. Furthermore, despite the widespread use of computer networks, a substantial amount of work among employees is still conducted via telephone and voice mail. For example, investment firms, such as Merrill Lynch, do not send sensitive financial information by e-mail but instead rely on telephone conversations.

Speakerphones present some of their own communication challenges. Small noises, such as crumpling paper, eating crunchy food, and placing a handset on a hard desk, magnify when broadcast over a speakerphone. If other people are present in the office, advise the person you are telephoning at the beginning of the conversation.[26] Doing so may save a lot of embarrassment, such as the caller making negative comments about your boss or coworker. Most of the previous comments about overcoming communication barriers apply to telephone communications, including speakerphones. Keep in mind these four representative suggestions for improving telephone effectiveness:

"Say your phone number slowly. I can't tell you how many people have zipped through it."
—Michael Shepley, owner of a public relations firm in New York City

- Vary your voice tone and inflection to avoid sounding bored or uninterested in your job and the company.
- Smile while speaking on the phone—somehow a smile gets transmitted over the telephone wires or optic fibers!
- Although multitasking has become the mode, when speaking on a telephone do not conduct a conversation with another person simultaneously, do not read e-mails, and do not have a television or radio playing in the background. (The last point is a challenge for people who work from home.) Business callers expect your undivided attention.
- Do not eat while talking on the phone, even though it is widely practiced. Many people are repelled by the sound of a person eating while talking—much like talking with food in your mouth in a restaurant. Loudly slurping a beverage is also objectionable to most people.
- Avoid offending customers by inappropriate use of smart phones. As a face-to-face sales representative, if you are going to use the phone to access information or take notes, explain your intention to customers in advance. Then return full attention to the meeting without stopping to check for messages.[27]

TELECOMMUTING AND THE REMOTE WORKFORCE

Telecommuter
employee who works at home or other offsite location full-time or part-time and sends output electronically to a central office

A **telecommuter** is an employee who works at home or other offsite location full-time or part-time and sends output electronically to a central office. An estimated 45 million people in the United States work at home, out of their cars, or as corporate employees working on the premises of the corporation's customer. Collectively, they are referred to as the remote (or distributed) workforce.[28] Information technology companies rely the most heavily on the distributed workforce. The majority of people who work at home do so only a day or two per week at their residence. Also, millions of people work from their homes in self-employment. Concerns about lengthy commutes, contagious diseases, and the high cost of gasoline have made working at home even more attractive for many workers in recent years. Some people believe that the pollutants from driving a gasoline-powered vehicle contribute to global warming. Furthermore, some people find workplaces to have too many interruptions and distractions, such as conversations with coworkers, superiors, and meetings.

Advantages of Telecommuting

An analysis of forty-six studies involving close to 13,000 employees found many important advantages of telecommuting. Remote workers tend to be more productive, are less likely to quit, and have higher job satisfaction than those who spend the entire workweek in the office. Employees gained the most benefits from telecommuting when managers granted them flexibility on when and how they worked from home or another remote location. (Some telecommuters work mostly from cafés like Starbucks.) An example of flexibility would be letting teleworkers be on the job outside the confines of a rigid schedule, such as from 9 a.m. until 5 p.m.[29]

For the advantages of remote work to materialize, workers have to be judged on measured output rather than the time invested. An example of measured output for a teleworker would be the number of medical claims applications produced in a week.

Interpersonal Communication Problems

Telecommuters can communicate abundantly via electronic devices, but they miss out on the face-to-face interactions so vital for dealing with complex problems. Another communication problem telecommuters face is feeling isolated from activities at the main office and missing out on the encouragement and recognition that take place in face-to-face encounters. (Of course, many telecommuters prefer to avoid such contact.) Many telecommuters have another communications problem: Because they have very little face-to-face communication with key people in the organization, they believe they are passed over for promotion. Most telecommuters spend some time in the traditional office, yet they miss the day-by-day contact. During a recession many would-be telecommuters fear that limited in-person contact with key people could leave them vulnerable to being laid off.[30]

Another communication problem with telecommuting is that it lacks a solid human connection. As one telecommuting marketing consultant put it, face time is critical for building empathy. "It's a human connection. It takes time, and human beings need visual cues, the symbols of being together and caring for one another."[31] To combat the problem of isolation, most companies schedule some face time with remote workers, perhaps every few months. At a minimum, a supervisor might phone the teleworkers at least once a week or hold a monthly videoconference.

Characteristics of Successful Telecommuters

A worker needs the right personality characteristics and work habits to be successful as a remote worker. Successful telecommuters should be able to work well without supervision and be highly self-disciplined to avoid falling to the many distractions at home or another remote location. You also need to be able to work well in isolation and not be dependent on frequent interaction with coworkers or a supervisor. High-maintenance employees who need frequent praise and attention are much better suited for working in a traditional office than telework.[32]

THE MULTITASKING MOVEMENT

A major consequence of electronic communication devices is that they encourage multitasking, for good or for bad. It has become standard communication practice for many workers to read e-mail while speaking on the phone, to surf the Internet while in a business meeting, and to check text messages while listening to a presentation. Some customer-contact workers even conduct cell phone conversations with friends while serving customers. Many workers are now using two or three computer monitors so they can write reports while attending to e-mail. Multitasking has become a way of life for many members of Generation Y, who grew up studying while watching television and chatting with their friends on a cell phone.

The Benefits of Multitasking

Advocates of multitasking contend that it increases productivity, such as accomplishing two or more tasks at once. A prime example is Marissa Mayer, the former Google executive, and now the CEO of Yahoo! Earlier in her career, when describing the "secrets of her greatness" she said that she does not feel overwhelmed with information, although she was receiving 700 to 800 e-mails a day. Mayer said she would work ten to fourteen hours straight on a weekend just to catch up.[33]

Cognitive Problems Associated with Multitasking

Although many workers can multitask successfully, the bulk of scientific evidence suggests that performing more than one demanding cognitive activity at once lowers accuracy and productivity, because you can devote 100 percent of your attention to only one task at a time. Would you want a brain surgeon to operate on a loved one while he or she chatted on the phone with an investment consultant? Or, to take a less than life-and-death situation, would you want your tax accountant to e-file your return while making calculations on someone else's return? Two dramatic examples from transportation accidents in recent years illustrate the potential disadvantages of multitasking and the advantages of concentrating on one task at a time.

The operator of a tugboat was towing a sludge barge in the Delaware River when it rammed into the stern of a duck boat on July 7, 2010. Two Hungarian tourists drowned as a result of the collision. The National Transportation Safety Board concluded that tugboat operator failed "to maintain the proper lookout" because of "distraction and inattentiveness as a result of his repeated personal use of his cell phone and the company laptop computer while he was solely responsible for navigating the vessel." Devlin's defense was that he was making the calls in response to a life-threatening emergency facing his son.[34]

On January 15, 2009, Captain Chesley "Sully" Sullenberger and his crew on US Airways flight 1549 made a spectacular landing in the Hudson River, New York City, saving the lives of 150 people on board. Sullenberger and his crew, consisting of a copilot and three flight attendants, concentrated on the task at hand.[35] No evidence was found that Sullenberger was engaged in any activity not directly related to avoiding the major potential catastrophe of an airline crash in New York. The captain and the crew obviously had loads of information to process, but all relating to the same survival task.

Decades of research indicate that the quality of mental output and depth of thought deteriorate as a person attends to more than one task simultaneously. One of the problems is that the brain does not handle multitasking well. The brain rapidly toggles (an on-and-off switch effect) among tasks rather than performing true simultaneous processing. The problem is more acute for complex and demanding tasks that require action planning, such as deciding how to respond to a customer complaint or solving an accounting problem. Highly practiced and routine tasks, such as sealing an envelope, suffer less from multitasking.

According to Basex, an IT research and consulting firm, the average worker dealing with information loses 2.1 hours of productivity every day to electronic interruptions and distractions. The primary productivity drainers are e-mail alerts, instant messages, buzzing smart phones, and cell phones. (Yet, used properly these productivity drainers can be productivity enhancers, as explained in Chapter 16.) A contributing problem is that the more you multitask by checking your messages, the more you feel the need to check them.[36]

Message from religious official performing the wedding ceremony

Response from multitasking professional (and groom)

FIGURE 8-4

MULTITASKING CAN BLUR THE DISTINCTION BETWEEN WORK AND PERSONAL LIFE

Interpersonal Consequences of Multitasking

Another byproduct of the multitasking movement with implications for interpersonal relationships is that electronic devices have facilitated breaking down the distinction between work and personal life. While out of the office, including vacations, is easy to be in frequent contact with the office digitally. A study conducted at Brigham Young University found that 60 percent of U.S. executives do not take a vacation without staying in touch with the office.[37] On the positive side, the wired worker can be more productive, such as providing input on an important work issue at any time. Also, if you take care of a few work problems while away from the office, you will be less overwhelmed with work when you return. On the negative side, interpersonal relationships may become impoverished because the wired worker concentrates less on friends and family even during leisure time, as illustrated in Figure 8-4.

Digital connectivity in the form of multitasking can weaken human connections in another way. When talking to people face-to-face it is more polite to focus on them rather than paying attention to your smart phone or computer screen. We caution, however, that some people in the workplace regard multitasking while talking to them as acceptable and typical behavior.

Whether communication in the workplace is formal or informal, electronic or printed, the human touch should be included for the highest level of effectiveness. Many of the points already made about informal communication illustrate this point.

OVERCONFIDENCE IN COMPUTER-GENERATED DATA

A subtle communication problem from heavy reliance on computers is that many people regard computerized data as infallible. Neglected in this assumption is the reality that humans, with all their possible shortcomings, entered the data into the computer. Communication problems occur because somebody acts on the computer-generated data and neglects to challenge or double-check the data. The same person might be unwilling to listen to a plea that the information is incorrect. As a result, the computer-generated data create a barrier to listening. Two examples follow of the phenomenon in question, and you can probably provide a personal example.

- A woman named Beatrice applied for a position as a front-desk clerk at a hotel. It appeared to the woman that she would be hired, but she was turned down at the last moment. She was told that a Google check revealed that she had been involved in an armed robbery of a convenience store several years ago. Beatrice explained that the Beatrice from the robbery had the same name, but they were not the same person. The hiring manager said, "Sorry, we rely heavily on Google results." (The error here was not validating the Google entry about the criminal Beatrice.)

- Your bank statement indicates that you are overdrawn by $251. You review your statement three times and are convinced that you have a positive balance of $85. The bank officer shuts you off by saying, "All our calculations are done by computer, so they are correct." (The error here is a classic case of assuming that the computer must be right and you must be wrong.)

The message from these examples is not that communication technology was in error but that somebody neglected to prevent a communication problem by verifying that the information was correct.

Learning Objective 4

How Does One Do an Effective Job of Conducting or Participating in a Business Meeting?

Much of workplace communication, including group decision making, takes place in meetings. Among the many purposes of meetings are disseminating information, training, building team spirit, and problem solving, including brainstorming. When conducted properly, meetings accomplish the purpose. Yet, when conducted poorly, meetings represent a substantial productivity drain. The following suggestions apply to those who conduct physical and electronic meetings, and some are also relevant for participants. Videoconferencing is sometimes used to conduct meetings with people in dispersed locations, as is teleconferencing. The globalization of business, as well as interest in reducing travel costs, has increased the demand for videoconferencing. By following these nine suggestions, you increase the meeting's effectiveness as a communication vehicle.

The accompanying Human Relations in Practice illustrates the point that business organizations look toward ways to enhance the productivity of meetings.

1. **Start with a key meeting outcome.** Before the meeting is called, the meeting leader defines the one thing that must be accomplished to consider the meeting a success. The outcome in mind is best framed even before establishing the agenda, because knowing what should be accomplished will help establish the agenda.[38] To illustrate, a hospital administrator establishes the key meeting outcome of "find new ways to shorten waiting time in the emergency room." The agenda might then include discussing what other hospitals have done to shorten waiting times in the emergency room.
2. **Meet only for valid reasons.** Many meetings lead to no decisions because they lacked a valid purpose in the first place. Having an agenda for the meeting is a valid reason because the agenda is an important purpose for getting together. Meetings are necessary only in situations that require coordinated effort and group decision making. E-mails and intranet exchanges can be substituted for meetings when factual information needs to be disseminated and discussion is unimportant. When looking to meet for valid reasons, be aware of possible cultural differences in the motives for having a meeting. In many cultures, meetings are conducted to build relationships. For example, a key to doing business in Asia is to get to know work associates on a personal level before getting down to problem solving, buying, or selling. So for an Asian manager, conducting a meeting to build personal relationships *is* a valid

Human Relations in Practice

Software Developer Atomic Object Holds Standup Meetings

When employees attend a staff meeting at software developer Atomic Object in Grand Rapids, Michigan, they don't dare be late or get too comfortable. The challenge is that the meetings rarely last longer than five minutes, and no sitting is allowed unless you are injured, physically challenged, or pregnant. The rules for the meeting state that attendance is mandatory, nonwork small talk is minimized, and standing up is required.

The object of these tightly focused meetings is to eliminate long-winded discussions where participants pontificate, play Angry Birds on their smart phones, or tune out. Vice president Michael Marsiglia discourages the use of tables at meetings because "They make it too easy to lean or rest laptops." At the end of the meeting, employees typically take a brief stretch and then get on with the rest of the workday.

Standup meetings at Atomic Object and other firms have been prompted by the growing use of "Agile," an approach to developing software that requires compressing development projects into short pieces. Agile also demands standup meetings during which participants update their coworkers with three items: What they have accomplished since yesterday's meeting; what they plan to do today; and any barriers they see to getting work done.

Atomic Object meetings are quite focused. After the meeting begins, all topics relate back to relevant issues in the office, current practices, or the industry at large. Meetings are scheduled at 9 a.m. with attendance mandatory. Getting the tech people into the office facilitates the in-person exchange of ideas that often facilitates creativity.

Despite the brevity of the standup meetings, Marsiglia says that they help decrease mistakes. The sharing of information and lessons learned during the meetings help coworkers from repeating mistakes made by other staff members.

Questions: Under what circumstances do you think that managers at Atomic Object should let a meeting run well beyond five minutes?

Source: Original story based on facts in the following sources: Rachel Emma Silverman, "No More Angling for the Best Seat: More Meetings Are Stand-Ups Jobs," *The Wall Street Journal,* February 2, 2012, pp. A1, A10; Garret Ellison, "Atomic Object in Grand Rapids Gets National Attention for Keeping Employees on Their Toes," *All Michigan,* February 2, 2012, pp. 1–4; "Let's Stand and Meet," *Steve Boyd Presentations* (www.steveboyspresentations), February 4, 2012, pp. 1–2; Michael Marsiglia, "10 Reasons We Have Daily 'Stand Up' Meetings," *Atomic Object's Blog On Software Design & Development,* July 7, 2009, pp. 1–3.

reason. For many Americans, also, an important purpose of face-to-face meetings is to build relationships. In the words of business columnist Jared Sandberg, "We are, by nature, needy huddlers and cuddlers."[39]

3. **Start and stop on time, and offer refreshments.** Meetings appear more professional and action oriented when the leader starts and stops on time. If the leader waits for the last member to show up, much time is lost and late behavior is rewarded. Stopping the meeting on time shows respect for the members' time. Offering refreshments is another tactic for emphasizing the importance of the meeting and also enhances satisfaction with the meeting. Agree in advance on when and if there will be a break to reduce anxiety about when the break will occur.

4. **Keep comments brief and to the point.** A major challenge facing the meeting leader is to keep conversation on track. Verbal rambling by participants creates communication barriers because other people lose interest. An effective way for the leader to keep comments on target is to ask the contributor of a non sequitur, "In what way does your comment relate to the agenda?"
5. **Encourage critical feedback and commentary.** Meetings are more likely to be fully productive when participants are encouraged to be candid with criticism and negative feedback. Openness helps prevent groupthink and also brings important problems to the attention of management.
6. **Strive for wide participation.** One justification for conducting a meeting is to obtain a variety of input. Although not everybody is equally qualified to voice a sound opinion, everyone should be heard. A skillful leader may have to limit the contribution of domineering members and coax reticent members to voice their ideas. Asking participants to bring several questions to the meeting will often spur participation. The meeting leader should not play favorites by encouraging the participation of some members and ignoring others. If the meeting leader spends the entire time making a PowerPoint presentation, participation will be discouraged. The slides should supplement the meeting and be starting points for discussion.
7. **Solve small issues ahead of time with e-mail or other forms of electronic communication.** Meetings can be briefer and less mundane when small issues are resolved ahead of time. E-mail is particularly effective for resolving minor administrative issues and also for collecting agenda items in advance. Intranets and blogs can serve the same purpose.
8. **Consider "huddling" when quick action is needed.** A huddle is a fast-paced, action-oriented way to bring workers together into brief meetings to discuss critical performance issues. A department store manager might bring together five floor managers ten minutes before opening to say, "We have a line-up of about 500 customers waiting to get in because of our specials today. Is everybody ready for the rush of excitement? What problems do you anticipate?" The huddle is particularly important when it would be difficult for the workers to attend a long meeting. Huddles are often accomplished standing up, which helps keep the meetings brief.
9. **Ensure that all follow-up action is assigned and recorded.** All too often, even after a decision has been reached, a meeting lacks tangible output. Distribute a memo summarizing who is responsible for taking what action and by what date.
10. **Be prepared to think on your feet.** As described in the accompanying *Human Relations in Practice,* some meetings are held with people standing up rather than sitting down. In these situations you have to literally "think on your feet," meaning that you have to make your point quickly. Standup meetings are usually quite brief, so you do not have much time to reflect on what you are saying.
11. **Minimize distractions during the meeting.** The group should agree on whether meeting participants will be allowed to use laptop computers for purposes other than recording information in the meeting. Agree also on whether using phones and text messaging is acceptable during the meeting. For example, Tim Brown, CEO of design firm IDEO, believes that it is unacceptable to use a smart phone during a meeting because engaging with the people present is important.[40] If handouts are used, allow participants enough time to read them so one person is not presenting while the others are reading. Ensure beforehand that computer-related equipment, such as the projector, is working and that it is compatible with the presenter's software.

Key Terms

Formal communication channels, 218
Intranet, 220
Webinar, 220
Downward communication, 221
Upward communication, 222
Open-door policy, 222
Horizontal communication, 222
Diagonal communication, 223
Informal communication channels, 223
Communities of practice, 223
Shadow organizations, 224
Social network analysis, 224
Grapevine, 226
Chance encounter, 226
Management by walking around, 227
Telecommuter, 232

Summary and Review

Messages in organizations are sent over both formal (official) and informal (unofficial) channels. Three key aspects of the formal channels are as follows:

- The company blog is a rapidly growing type of formal communication that might also be placed on social networking Web sites. It communicates business information with a soft, human touch.
- Formal communication channels in the workplace have kept up with Internet-based communication technology. Four such channels are social networking sites (such as Facebook), intranets, wikis, and webinars.
- Many companies have developed formal communication channels for managing crises, such as fires and terrorist attacks.
- Messages in organizations travel in four primary directions: downward, upward, horizontally, and diagonally. An open-door policy facilitates upward communication.
- An informal communication channel supplements the formal channel.
- A major informal communication channel is the network of contacts that employees use to accomplish work, sometimes referred to as the shadow organization. Communities of practice are an informal channel that has slipped into often being a formal channel. Social networking analysis is used to map the shadow organization.
- The grapevine is the major informal communication channel, and it carries rumors and gossip.
- Chance encounters between managers and employees foster informal communication, as does management by walking around.
- Communication technology creates challenges for interpersonal communication, despite all its advantages, as follows.
- E-mail, including instant messaging and text messaging, has the most dramatic impact on interpersonal communication in organizations. Some workers are overwhelmed by e-mail, whereas others have the system under control.
- E-mail encourages informal, unprofessional communication, and the system is too often used to play office politics.
- E-mail should be used to supplement, not as a substitute for, face-to-face negotiations.
- Some business firms have counterattacked the problems associated with e-mail by shifting to related technologies.
- Presentation technology creates challenges of its own, including the need to learn how to handle equipment and maintain eye contact at the same time. It is important to talk to the audience and not the screen and reduce the text on each page to a bare minimum.
- Effective telephone and voice mail communication skills are helpful in overcoming communication problems. Remember to vary your voice tone and avoid multitasking while speaking.
- Telecommuters are now referred to as the remote or distributed workforce.
- Telecommuters may miss out on the face-to-face interactions necessary for dealing with complex problems.
- Telecommuting is also a challenge because it lacks a solid human connection.

- Electronic communication facilitates the multitasking that is so popular with Generation Y.
- Advocates of multitasking claim it enhances productivity.
- The bulk of scientific evidence suggests that performing more than one demanding cognitive activity at once lowers accuracy and productivity. Mental output and depth of thought deteriorate while multitasking.
- Multitasking has facilitated breaking down the distinction between work and personal life.
- A subtle communication problem from heavy reliance on computers is that many people regard computerized data as infallible. As a result, the user of the data might not listen to pleas that the information is incorrect.

Much of workplace communication takes place in meetings. Among the many suggestions for productive meetings are the following:

- Start with a key meeting outcome.
- Meet only for valid reasons.
- Start and stop on time, and offer refreshments.
- Solve small issues ahead of time with e-mail.
- Minimize distractions during the meeting.

Check Your Understanding

1. Suppose you thought that the CEO of your company was moving the company in the wrong direction, and you want to tell him or her. Explain which communication channel you would choose to deliver your message.
2. Why is it that virtually every medium-size or large organization still has traditional telephones and is listed in the telephone directory?
3. In what way might management by walking around undermine the authority of the supervisor?
4. Why do so many businesspeople object to receiving an e-mail or text message in all caps?
5. Carol Bartz, a well-known technology executive, complained that she was notified about being fired from her position as CEO of Yahoo! by e-mail. What's her problem?
6. What do you think would the advantages and disadvantages of having a "no e-mail on Friday" policy at a busy office?
7. Give three examples of business situations in which telephone conversations still play a key role.
8. Give an example from your own life in which multitasking has enhanced your performance.
9. Give an example from your own life in which multitasking has lowered your performance.
10. Why are face-to-face meetings still so popular even in high-technology companies?

Web Corner

Suggestions for writing better e-mails

http://www.mindtools.com/CommSkll/EmailCommunication.htm

How to run an effective business meeting

http://www.meetingwizard.org/meetings/effective-meetings.cfm

INTERNET SKILL BUILDER

Social Media and Productivity

Use your preferred search engine or engines to identify two business settings in which the use of social media resulted in higher worker productivity or increased sales. Identify what the company did correctly with social media that led to the good result.

Developing Your Human Relations Skills

Human Relations Application Exercises

Applying Human Relations Exercise 8-1

Designing an Office for a Virtual-Customer Agent

Work in a team to design a home office for a virtual-customer agent, a worker whose responsibilities are to fill orders for merchandise for three different companies. The agent receives calls through a toll-free number and then uses the computer to enter the order. He or she also processes orders online. The office in question will be placed somewhere in a three-bedroom house that also has a family room, kitchen, basement, and enclosed porch.

While designing the office, include such factors as the layout of the furniture and equipment, the equipment needed, and any decorations. Keep in mind ergonomic factors that focus on making the equipment easy to use and with low risk for physical problems such as carpal tunnel syndrome and backaches. Because the virtual agent will have to pay for the office setup, derive a tentative budget.

Draw your design on any convenient format, including a flip chart, whiteboard, blackboard, or computer screen. Your team leader might be asked to present the design to the rest of the class so class members can compare the effectiveness of each design. Class members evaluating the home office design might use the following evaluation factors in addition to whatever their intuition suggests:

- To what extent does the office design help reduce possible conflict with other people living in the same household?
- How might this design offer productivity advantages over a conventional office?
- When and if customers or company representatives call into this office, how professional will the setup sound?
- How will this office design contribute to job satisfaction?

Applying Human Relations Exercise 8-2

Evaluating a Business Meeting

The class organizes into teams of about six students to conduct a meeting to formulate plans for building temporary housing for homeless people downtown in your city or a nearby city. Three other students, or the entire class, will observe the meeting. This exercise should take about thirty-five minutes, and it can be done inside or outside of class. Each team takes on the assignment of formulating plans for building temporary shelters for the homeless. The dwellings you plan to build, for example, might be two-room cottages with electricity and indoor plumbing. During the time allotted to the task, formulate plans for going ahead with shelters for the homeless. Consider dividing up work by assigning certain tasks to each team member. Sketch out tentative answers to the following questions: (a) How will you obtain funding for your venture? (b) Which homeless people will you help? (c) Where will your shelters be? (d) Who will do the actual construction?

After the meeting is completed, the three observers will provide feedback to the team members about the effectiveness of the meeting, using the following criteria:

1. How effective was the teamwork? Support your conclusion with an example of specific behavior.
2. How well did group members stay on track in terms of focusing on their goal?
3. Did the team members make any introductory warm-up comments to help build rapport?
4. To what extent was the participation among team members balanced?
5. Did the team move toward any conclusions or action plans?
6. Choose another criterion you think might be relevant.

Human Relations Class Activity

Company Messages on Company Web Sites or YouTube

Each class member is asked to search company Web sites, YouTube, or Hulu for a serious message to employees or other stakeholders, such as customers and stockholders. If you choose YouTube or Hulu, the video you choose should appear to have been authentically prepared by a company representative, not the work of a prankster. Finding a serious message might take some digging because so many corporate messages posted on YouTube or Hulu are strictly for entertainment purposes. But it is also possible to find video messages on an occasional company Web site.

At some point the class meets in a setting where it is possible to project videos on a large screen. Even if the screen is a large monitor for a PC, the activity will work. Depending on how much class time is available for the project, about six volunteers project their chosen video on the screen. As class members watch the selection of videos, form an impression of the communication effectiveness of each video. Answer such questions as:

- What message is the business organization really getting across to its intended audience?
- How convincing is the video in sending its message?
- How sincere does the message appear to be?

After students have reflected on the videos, have a brief class discussion of the answers to the above questions.

Human Relations Case Study 8-1

I Want To Get into the Loop

Lisa, an order fulfillment specialist, was informed by her supervisor that many managers in the company were now using social network analysis, in an attempt to figure out which associates other workers were turning to for help and friendship. The results of the social network analysis were not yet being used directly for salary increases or performance reviews. However, a list was being compiled of the most influential employees based on the social network analysis.

Very concerned about the social network analysis, Lisa expressed her uneasiness to her best friend in the company, Dion, a technical support specialist. She said, "Dion, I feel that I am going to be shut out of promotional possibilities here. The way I understand this new social network analysis, if other workers don't contact you much, you score pretty low on the network analysis. My problem is not that I have enemies here. It's just that hardly anybody ever asks me anything. For example, the only question I received this week was whether or not it was still raining."

Dion asked Lisa, "What have you done lately to get more people to rely on you for advice and friendship?"

Lisa replied, "I want to get into the loop, but I don't know how. Maybe I could wear clothing that was a little more stylish. Maybe I could send out tweets telling everybody what a star I am. I really just don't know what to do to upgrade my number of contacts."

"Maybe we can set aside some time next week to figure out how to make you a network star," said Dion with a smile.

Questions

1. To what extent should Lisa be concerned about showing up frequently on the company social network analysis?
2. What advice might you offer Lisa and Dion to help make her a "network star"? (In addition to your own analysis, you might find some ideas in Chapter 9 about getting along with people.)

Human Relations Role-Playing Exercise 8-1

Lisa Builds Her Network

One student plays the role of Lisa, who wants to be part of the network of more people. She spots Clyde, a marketing associate, sitting alone in the company cafeteria. She decides to see if she can become part of Clyde's network because she has heard that Clyde is influential in the company. Another student plays the role of Clyde who likes to develop network members only if they have something to offer. Run the scenario for about five minutes.

Human Relations Case Study 8-2

Karl Walks Around

Karl Bennett, a supervisor in a call center located in Iowa, was urged by his manager to walk around the center from time to time to chat informally with the call center workers. His boss said to Karl, "It's always good to know what the call center specialists are feeling and thinking. You might pick up some good ideas." Bennett had studied the technique of *management by walking around* in a human relations course, so he was enthusiastic about the idea.

Karl chose a Tuesday evening to conduct his walk around and decided to stop by the cubicles of four call center operators to test the technique. If it worked well, he would walk around again in another week.

Karl first stopped by the cubicle of Mandi, making sure first that she was not on the telephone with a customer. "I just dropped by to say hello and see how things are going," said Karl. "I take it everything is going fine, and that you have no problems," he continued. "Am I right?"

Mandi answered, "Yes, no real problems. Thanks for stopping by."

Next, Karl stopped by the cubicle of Pete, a relatively new operator. "How's it going Pete?" asked Karl. "What kind of problems might you be facing?"

Pete answered, "I'm having trouble understanding the accent of some of my customers. And some of the customers say I talk too fast. Other than that, the job is going well."

"That's interesting," said Karl. "But I see I have a couple of e-mails waiting for me on my BlackBerry. Maybe you do talk too fast. I'll get back to you later."

Karl thought to himself that the walk around was going fine so far. He then dropped by Brittany's cubicle. "What's happening, Brittany?" asked Karl as Brittany was completing a customer inquiry about a defective piece of equipment. Brittany raised the palm of her right hand to signal that she was not quite finished with the call.

Karl then asked, "Are your wedding plans going along okay?"

Brittany replied, "Yes, Karl. Everything is fine. Thanks for stopping by."

A few minutes later, Karl completed his walk around by stopping to visit Derek, a rabid Chicago Bears fan. "Hey, Derek, how goes it?" said Karl. "I think the Bears are headed to the league championship this year. What do you think?"

Derek answered, "Oh, yes, the Bears are strong this season, and I'm optimistic. But as long as you have dropped by, I wanted to mention that our instruction manuals seem to be too complicated. People are calling in again and again with the most basic questions, like how to find the serial number."

"Don't worry too much about that. A lot of our customers can hardly read these days. I think the term is *functionally illiterate*," said Karl with a smile.

Questions

1. How successful is Karl in using his walk around to uncover useful information?
2. What can Karl do to increase his questioning effectiveness?

Human Relations Role-Playing Exercise 8-2

Derek Wants More from Karl

The case about Karl walking around serves as the scenario and story line for this role-play. One student plays the role of Karl, who is making the rounds. His last stop of the day is a visit with Derek, who is encountering some problems with customers who find the instruction manuals to be too complicated. Karl seems to want to dismiss the problem by blaming the lack of comprehension on the poor reading ability of some customers.

Another student plays the role of Derek, who is quite serious about serving the needs of customers and wants to discuss the situation further. He believes that a supervisor should give careful thought to any customer problem. Derek therefore wants to engage Karl in more of a problem-solving discussion.

REFERENCES

1. Original story created from facts in the following sources: John Samuel, "News on the Social Networking and Social Media Industry," *Social Networking Watch* (www.socialnetworkingwatch.com), January 31, 2009, pp. 1-2; Toby Ward, "Employee Social Networking—Sabre Town Case Study," (www.prescientdigital.com), pp. 1-3. Accessed February 5, 2012; Alex Manchester, "Aiming for a Cost Saving Staff Director that's As Popular as Facebook," Melcrum Connecting Communications (www.melcrum.com), July 2009, pp. 1-3; Susan Ladika, "Socially Evolved," *Workforce Management,* September 2010, pp. 20, 22.
2. Steven Snell, "Corporate Blog Design: Trends and Examples," *Smashing Magazine,* August 20, 2009, pp. 1-70 (www.smashingmagazine.com).
3. Cited in Erika D. Smith, "Web Opens Another Defensive Front for Companies," *Indianapolis Star Syndicated Story,* July 1, 2007.
4. Ladika, "Socially Evolved," *Workforce Management,* p. 19.
5. Ed Frauenhelm, "Social Revolution," *Workforce,* October 22, 2007, pp. 1, 28-37.
6. Bill Roberts, "Social Networking at the Office," *HR Magazine,* March 2008, pp. 81-83.
7. Roberts, "Social Networking at the Office," p. 82.
8. Vauhini Vaura, "The Winning Formula," *The Wall Street Journal,* May 14, 2007, p. R1.
9. Patrick Kiger, "Lessons from a Crisis: How Communication Kept a Company Together," *Workforce,* November 2001, p. 28.
10. Jeremy Smerd and Jessica Marquez, "Calming Worried Workers," *Workforce Management,* October 6, 2008, pp. 1-3.
11. Richard McDermott and Douglas Archibald, "Harnessing Your Staff's Informal Networks," *Harvard Business Review,* March 2010, pp. 82-89.
12. Mark Hendricks, "The Shadow Knows," *Entrepreneur,* January 2000, p. 110; Jennifer Reingold and Jia Lynn Yang, "What's Your OQ?" *Fortune,* July 23, 2007, pp. 98-106.
13. Valdis Krebs, "Social Network Analysis: A Brief Introduction." from www.orgnet.com. Copyright © 2000-2011, Valdis Krebs
14. Cited in Ethan Watters, "The Organization Woman," *Business Week,* April 10, 2006, pp. 106-110.
15. Samuel Greengard, "Gossip Poisons Business: HR Can Stop It," *Workforce,* July 2001, pp. 26-27; Lea Winerman, "Have Your Heard the Latest?" *Monitor on Psychology,* April 2006, pp. 56-57.
16. Quoted in Joyce Rosenberg, "Business Owners Should Welcome Small Talk," *Associated Press,* January 14, 2008.
17. Quoted in Anne Fisher, "Psst! Rumors Can Help at Work," *Fortune,* December 12, 2005, p. 202.
18. John P. Kotter, The General Managers (New York: Free Press, 1991).
19. "Making Rounds like a Physician," Manager's Edge, February 8, 2006. As adapted from Quint Studer, *Hardwiring Excellence* (Gulf Breeze, FL: Fire Starter Publishing, 2005).
20. Cited in Enid Abelo, "Don't Underrate Old-Fashioned Communication," *Democrat and Chronicle,* September 26, 2010, p. 3E.
21. Sue Shellenbarger, "A Day without Email Is Like . . ." *The Wall Street Journal,* October 11, 2007, p. D1.
22. Marsha Egan, "E-Mail Overload? Three Ways to Tame Your In Box," *Christian Science Monitor,* March 17, 2011, pp. 1-2.
23. Michelle Conlin, "E-Mail Is So Five Minutes Ago: It's Being Replaced by Software That Promotes Real-Time Collaboration,"*Business Week,* November 28, 2005, pp. 111-112; Luis Suarez, "I Freed Myself from E-mail's Grip," *New York Times* (nytimes.com), June 29, 2008.
24. "French IT Company Hopes to Be E-Mail Free Within a Year," *The Denver Post* (www.denverpost.com), December 8, 2011, p. 1.
25. Jean Mausehund and R. Neil Dortch, "Presentation Skills in the Digital Age," *Business Education Forum,* April 1999, pp. 30-32; Michael Patterson, "The Pitch Coach," *Business Week SmallBiz,* Fall 2005, p. 61.
26. John T. Adams, III, "When You're on a Speakerphone, Don't Make Noise," *HR Magazine,* March 2001, p. 12.
27. Alex Williams, "Mind Your BlackBerry or Mind Your Manners," *The New York Times* (www.nytimes.com), June 21, 2009, p. 2.
28. Ravi S. Gajendran and David A. Harrison, "The Good, the Bad and the Unknown about Telecommuting: Meta-Analysis of Psychological Mediators and Individual Consequences," Journal of Applied Psychology, November 2007, p. 1524; Martine Letarte, "Travailler de Chez Soi," lapresseaffaires, le 30 mai 2011, pp. 1-2. ("Working at one's home," May 30, 2011.)
29. Gajendran and Harrison, "The Good, the Bad and the Unknown," pp. 1524-1541.
30. Annys Shin, "As Cuts Loom, Will Working from Home Lead to a Layoff?" *The Washington Post* (www.wshingtonpost.com), March 23, 2009, p. 1.
31. "Work à la Modem," *Business Week,* October 4, 1999, p. 176.
32. "Telecommuting Tips," *Manager's Edge,* December 2007, p. 1.
33. "Secrets of Greatness: How I Work," *Fortune,* March 20, 2006, p. 68.
34. Regina Medina, "NTSB: 'Deadliness of Distraction' at Heart of Ducks Tragedy," (www.articles.philly.com), June 22, 2011, p. 1.
35. Laura Browne, "Captain 'Sully' Sullenberger Leadership Lessons for Business," *Women's Business Examiner,* February 9, 2009.
36. Findings reported in Joe Robinson, "E-Mail Is Making You Stupid," *Entrepreneur,* March 2010, pp. 61, 62; Stephanie Pappas, "Digital Overload: Is Your Computer Frying Your Brain?" Live Science (www.livescience.com), November 9, 2010, pp. 1-3.
37. Mike DeGiorgi, "How to Know When You're Way Too Plugged In," *Executive Leadership,* April 2007, p. 7.
38. "Never Hold Another Bad Meeting," *Manager's Edge,* October 2008, p. 6.
39. Jared Sandberg, "Another Meeting? Good. Another Chance to Hear Myself Talk," *The Wall Street Journal,* March 11, 2008, p. B1.
40. "Bringing Design to Blue Chips: Tim Brown, CEO, IDEO," *Fortune,* November 12, 2007, p. 32.

9

Specialized Tactics for Getting Along with Others in the Workplace

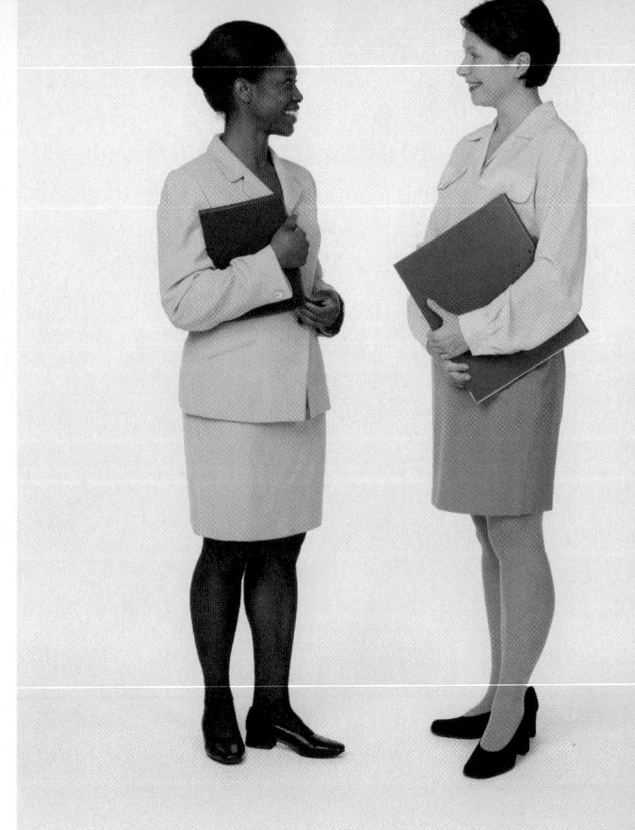

Outline

As comedian and sales consultant Burt Teplitzky views it, building a relationship with potential customers increases the probability of making a sale, and that building a relationship with employees leads to harmonious work relationships. He also believes that one of the best ways to build a relationship is through professionally-developed humor. By way of introduction, the sales consultant says, "My name is Burt Teplitzky, but you alrleady know my name—it's the bottom line on all eye charts. But perhaps more impressively, I'm also the former managing partner of the IMPROV Comedy Club's Education/Corporate Training Division." He was also a sales leader in a Beveryly Hills, California, real estate firm.

The focus of the Teplitzky approach to integrating humor into building workplace relationships (especially in selling) is the Punch-Point Benefit Formula. "Punch" refers to the joke's punchline, and the "point and benefit" refer to how the joke might facilitate the sale. Teplitzky gives an illustration of PPB related to dressing appropriately to do business in another culture. The humor gem proceeds as follows:

Tepliztky says that some investor friends and he have purchased a few properties in the Middle East. They decided to jointly travel to Egypt to learn more about the financial markets. One of the friends got lost in the desert, and developed a terrible thirst. He was approached by a camel rider who was selling ties. Later another camel rider approached him who was selling shirts. The traveler wanted only water, so he rejected both sales pitches. The shirt vendor cooperated enough to direct the visitor to a location where he could purchase water.

The thirsty visitor followed the directions and soon found himself facing a young man, and pleaded to purchase some water. "Plenty of water here," the young man says to the traveler who replies, "Thank goodness. Let me have some."

The punch: "I'm sorry sir," the young man said, "We don't serve anyone not wearing a shirt and tie." The point and benefit: You should always dress appropriately when you want something you value. The benefit is that you will now be more careful about your business attire. The point and benefit should take about 10 seconds to deliver.[1]

Learning Objectives

After reading the information and doing the exercises in this chapter, you should be able to:

1 Select several tactics for developing a good relationship with your manager or team leader.

2 Deal effectively with a problem manager.

3 Describe methods of getting along with coworkers.

4 Identify tactics that help a person become a good team player.

5 Pinpoint tactics for dealing effectively with difficult people.

6 Specify approaches to building good relationships with customers.

The story about the comedian turned business consultant illustrates a basic truth about success in business: It is helpful to build good relationships with potential customers in order to get them to cooperate with you. The same focus on relationship building is important when dealing with coworkers and superiors. In a sentiment shared by many observers, well-established executive coach Marshall Goldsmith says that a major factor in succeeding at high levels in an organization depends in part on simply getting along with others.[2]

This chapter presents information about developing productive relationships with three major groups of work associates: managers, coworkers, and customers. Along the way, we include information about coping with difficult bosses.

▶ Learning Objective 1 ▶

How Do You Develop a Good Relationship with Your Manager or Team Leader?

Getting along well with your manager is the most basic strategy of getting ahead in your career. If you cannot gain favor with the boss, it will be difficult to advance to higher positions or earn much more money. Obtaining good performance reviews and receiving favorable work assignments also depends on a good relationship with the person to whom you report. The boss might be more of a traditional boss, such as a person with the title of manager or supervisor. Or the boss might be a team leader who typically has less formal authority than a manager or supervisor. Your manager or team leader is always the person who is contacted first when someone wants to determine what kind of employee you are. Usually this information is sought when you are being considered for transfer, promotion, or a position with another firm.

Getting along with the boss is particularly important when the economy is sluggish or when the threat of outsourcing exists. Workers who have good relationships with their manager have more job security than those with poor relationships. In this section we present a variety of approaches that lead to constructive relationships with an immediate superior. The goal is to be legitimately perceived as a strong contributor to your work unit.

CREATE A POSITIVE FIRST IMPRESSION

A logical starting point in developing a good relationship with the person to whom you report is to create a positive first impression. Peter Stephens, a managing director of internships at the Washington Center for Internships and Academic Seminars, offers this advice: "Before setting foot in the office become a sponge. Exhaust your online resources and briefing materials to absorb anything you can about the organization. On the first day, show you are ready to work by walking in on time and exuding a can-do attitude." Equally important is to show that you are acclimating to the organizational culture by learning people's name and treat everyone with respect and civility.[3]

ACHIEVE GOOD JOB PERFORMANCE

Maintaining good job performance remains the most effective strategy for impressing your manager. When any rational manager evaluates a group member's performance, the first question asked is, "Is this employee getting the job done?" And you cannot get the job done if you are not competent. Many factors contribute to whether you can become a competent performer. Among them are your education, training, personality characteristics, job experience, and special skills, such as being able to organize your work. Factors external to you such as having a supportive boss and cooperative coworkers also contribute to good performance.

An advanced way of displaying good job performance is to assist your manager with a difficult problem he or she faces. Your manager, for example, might need to operate equipment outside his or her area of expertise. If you show the manager how to operate the equipment, he or she will think highly of your job performance.

An effective way of enhancing your job performance is to offer alternative solutions to complex problems. In this way you are more likely to follow a path favored by your boss, leading to good performance. The director of a senior living residence asked an administrator to find a way to reduce the number of falls by residents—a problem that plagues people of advanced age. Instead of suggesting one idea, the administrator offered several suggestions, as follows:

- Let's check to see if all our residents use footwear with appropriate treads.
- Instruct our health-care aides to coach all our residents about the proper use of canes.
- The entire staff should check periodically to see if our residents are making good use of handrails at the facility.

The director liked the idea of alternatives so much that she said, "Great ideas. Let's implement all three instead of just using one idea, as I had suggested."

A subtle issue about performing well to please your manager is that your manager has to be aware of your good performance and give you proper credit. One useful approach is to assist your boss by keeping him or her informed about exactly what work you are doing, the problems you are solving, and the successes you have attained.[4]

DISPLAY A STRONG WORK ETHIC

A strong **work ethic** is a firm belief in the dignity and value of work and therefore is important for favorably impressing a manager. An employee with a strong work ethic will sometimes be excused if his or her performance is not yet exceptional. This is true because the manager assumes that a strong work ethic will elevate performance eventually. Six suggestions follow for demonstrating a strong work ethic.

Work ethic
a firm belief in the dignity and value of work and, therefore, important for favorably impressing a manager

1. Work hard and enjoy the task. By definition, a person with a strong work ethic works diligently and has strong internal motivation. The person may appreciate external rewards yet appreciates the importance of any work that adds value to society.

2. Demonstrate competence even on minor tasks. Attack each assignment with the recognition that each task performed well, however minor, is one more career credit. A minor task performed well paves the way for your being given more consequential tasks.

3. Take the initiative by assuming personal responsibility for problems. An employee with a problem will often approach the manager and say, "We have a tough problem to deal with." The connotation is that the manager should be helping the employee with the problem. A better impression is created when the employee takes the initiative by saying, "I have a tough problem to deal with, and I would like your advice." This statement implies that you are willing to assume responsibility for the problem and for any mistake you may have made that led to the problem.

4. Assume responsibility for free-floating problems. A natural way to display a strong work ethic is to assume responsibility for free-floating (nonassigned) problems. Taking the initiative on even a minor task, such as ordering lunch for a meeting that is running late, can enhance the impression one makes on a manager.

5. Get your projects completed promptly. A byproduct of a strong work ethic is an eagerness to get projects completed promptly. People with a strong work ethic respect deadlines imposed by others. Furthermore, they typically set deadlines of their own more tightly than those imposed by their bosses.

"Don't' wait to be told what to do. . . . Pitch in when you have the time to do so."
—Joni Daniels, principal and founder of Daniels & Associates

6. Accept undesirable assignments willingly. Look for ways to express the attitude, "Whether this assignment is glamorous and fun is a secondary issue. What counts is that it is something that needs doing for the good of the company."

DEMONSTRATE GOOD EMOTIONAL INTELLIGENCE

Dealing effectively with feelings and emotions is a big challenge in the workplace. Demonstrating good emotional intelligence is impressive because it contributes to performing well in the difficult arena of dealing with feelings. A worker with good emotional intelligence would engage in such behaviors as (a) recognizing when a coworker needs help but is too embarrassed to ask for help, (b) dealing with the anger of a dissatisfied customer, (c) recognizing that the boss is also facing considerable pressure, and (d) being able to tell whether a customer's "maybe" means "yes" or "no."

Many of the competencies described throughout this chapter are facilitated by emotional intelligence. Nevertheless, being aware of strategies and tactics for dealing effectively with others helps you capitalize on your emotional intelligence.

BE DEPENDABLE AND HONEST

Dependability is a critical employee virtue. If an employee can be counted on to deliver as promised and to be at work regularly, that employee has gone a long way toward impressing the boss. A boss is uncomfortable not knowing whether an important assignment will be accomplished on time. If you are not dependable, you will probably not get your share of important assignments. Honesty is tied to dependability because a dependable employee is honest about when he or she will have an assignment completed. Dependability and honesty are important at all job levels. One of the highest compliments a manager can pay an employee is to describe the employee as dependable. Conversely, it is considered derogatory to call any employee undependable.

BE A GOOD ORGANIZATIONAL CITIZEN

An especially meritorious approach to impressing key people is to demonstrate organizational citizenship behavior. An effective way of being a good organizational citizen is to step outside your job description. Job descriptions are characteristic of a well-organized firm. If everybody knows what he or she is supposed to be doing, there will be much less confusion, and goals will be achieved. This logic sounds impressive, but job descriptions have a major downside. If people engage only in work included in their job description, an "it's not my job" mentality pervades. An effective way to impress your manager, therefore, is to demonstrate that you are not constrained by a job description. If something needs doing, you will get it done regardless of whether it is your formal responsibility.

An impressive way of stepping outside your job description is to anticipate problems, even when the manager had not planned to work on them. Anticipating problems is characteristic of a resourceful person who exercises initiative. Instead of working exclusively on problems that have been assigned, the worker is perceptive enough to look for future problems. Anticipating problems impresses most managers because it reflects an entrepreneurial, take-charge attitude. An example of anticipating a future problem took place at a large supermarket chain. A marketing specialist noted that dollar stores were growing at such a rapid pace, that sales would soon be hurt at the supermarket. In response, the chain soon developed a bottom-price section that helped stem the loss of sales to dollar stores.

CREATE A STRONG PRESENCE

A comprehensive approach to impressing your manager or team leader and other key people in the workplace is to create a strong presence, keeping yourself in the forefront. Such actions impress key people and simultaneously help advance your career. Stephanie Sherman, a career consultant, offers this advice for creating a strong presence:

- Get involved in high-visibility projects, such as launching a new product or redesigning work methods. Even an entry-level position on such a project can help a worker get noticed.
- Get involved in teams because they give you an opportunity to broaden your skills and knowledge.
- Get involved in social and community activities of interest to top management, such as those sponsored by the company. Behave professionally, and use your best manners.
- Create opportunities for yourself by making constructive suggestions about earning or saving money. Even if an idea is rejected, you will still be remembered for your initiative.
- Show a willingness to take on some of the tasks that your manager doesn't like to do but would be forced to do if you did not step in.[5]

A powerful way of creating a strong presence with a newly appointed manager is to take the initiative to state that you want to be part of his or her team. Instead of acting envious toward the new manager, approach the person with a statement of this effect: "I am experienced in my job, and I want to help. I may not be perfect, but I accept your goals for our unit."[6]

FIND OUT WHAT YOUR MANAGER EXPECTS OF YOU

You have little chance of doing a good job and impressing your manager unless you know what you are trying to accomplish. Work goals and performance standards represent the most direct ways of learning your manager's expectations. A **performance standard** is a statement of what constitutes acceptable performance. These standards can sometimes be inferred from a job description. Review your work goals and ask clarifying questions. An example would be, "You told me to visit our major customers who are sixty days or more delinquent on their accounts. Should I also visit the three of these customers who have declared bankruptcy?" In addition to having a clear statement of your goals, it is helpful to know the priorities attached to them. In this way you will know which task to execute first.

Performance standard a statement of what constitutes acceptable performance

A subtle aspect of understanding the expectations of your boss is adapting to his or her preferred style of work. Managers vary in terms of wanting written versus oral briefings. Some managers prefer to receive e-mail messages from you regularly, others once a week. In one situation, a manager asked his new CEO how he preferred to communicate. The CEO said he prefers a direct, collaborative style. As a result, the two agreed to get together in person frequently when both in town, from about 5:30 p.m. to 6 p.m.[7]

Many managers want to be treated informally, much like being a coworker. A minority of managers wanted to be treated as if they were royalty. Matching your work style to the work style of your boss can help build a strong relationship between the two of you.

MINIMIZE COMPLAINTS

Being open and honest in expressing your feelings and opinions is part of having good human relations skills. Nevertheless, this type of behavior, when carried to excess, could earn you a reputation as a whiner. Few managers want to have a group member around who constantly complains about working conditions, coworkers, working hours, pay, and so forth. An employee who complains too loudly and frequently quickly becomes labeled a pill or a pest.

Another important reason a boss usually dislikes having a direct report (subordinate) who complains too much is that listening to these complaints takes up considerable time. Most managers spend a disproportionate amount of time listening to the problems of a small number of ineffective or complaining employees. Consciously or unconsciously, a manager who has to listen to many of your complaints may find a way to seek revenge.

To make valid complaints to the manager, complain only when justified. And when you do offer a complaint, back it up with a recommended solution. Anyone can take potshots at something. The valuable employee is the person who supports these complaints with a constructive action plan. An example follows of a complaint, supported by action plans for its remedy.

> When a customer wants a refund of more than $50 we have to receive authorization from you. The problem is that you may be out of contact with us temporarily, even by your BlackBerry. The $50 rule was probably established twenty years ago and has not been adjusted for inflation. If authorization were required only for refunds of $100 or more, we could reduce a lot of bottlenecks.

One possibility for minimizing the need for complaints is to attempt to look at decisions from the boss's point of view. The company might decide to prohibit workers from using instant messaging for personal reasons during working hours. Instead of complaining that the prohibition on instant messages is unjust, the worker might attempt to understand why company management thinks instant messages lower productivity.

AVOID BYPASSING YOUR MANAGER

A way to embarrass and sometimes infuriate your manager is to repeatedly go to his or her superior with your problems, conflicts, and complaints. Such bypasses have at least three strongly negative connotations. One is that you don't believe your boss has the power to take care of your problem. Another is that you distrust his or her judgment in the matter at hand. A third is that you are secretly launching a complaint against your manager.

The boss bypass is looked on so negatively that most experienced managers will not listen to your problem unless you have already discussed it with your immediate superior. There *are* times, however, when running around your manager is necessary, such as when you have been unable to resolve a conflict directly with him or her (see the following section). Should your manager be involved in highly immoral or illegal actions, such as sexual harassments or taking kickbacks from vendors, a boss bypass might be warranted. But even under these circumstances, you should politely inform your manager that you are going to take up your problem with the next level of management.

In short, if you want to keep on the good side of your manager, bring all problems directly to him or her. If your boss is unable or unwilling to take care of the problem, you might consider contacting your boss's superior. Nonetheless, considerable tact and diplomacy are needed. Do not imply that your manager is incompetent but merely that you would like another opinion about the issues at stake. If an organization has a formal system for filing complaints, such as an open-door policy, it can be used to substitute for a boss bypass but should be used only when you are unable to resolve a problem with your boss.

ENGAGE IN FAVORABLE INTERACTIONS WITH YOUR MANAGER

The many techniques described previously support the goal of engaging in favorable interactions with your manager. Human Relations Self-Assessment Quiz 9-1 contains a list of behaviors used by employees to create positive interactions with their supervisors. Use these behaviors as a guide for skill building.

According to a synthesis of findings by organizational behavior professor Cecily D. Cooper at the University of Miami, an effective way of ingratiating yourself to your boss, as well as to others in the workplace, is to make effective use of humor. (The introductory case to this chapter supports this idea.) **Ingratiating** is an attempt to increase one's attractiveness to others, so as to influence their behavior. The most effective type

Ingratiating
an attempt to increase one's attractiveness to others to influence their behavior

Human Relations Self-Assessment Quiz 9-1

Manager Interaction Checklist

Use the following behaviors as a checklist for achieving favorable interactions with your present manager or a future one. The more of these actions you engage in, the higher the probability that you are building a favorable relationship with your manager.

1. Express agreement with manager's opinion whenever I truly agree.
2. Ask for assistance in areas in which I know that my manager enjoys giving assistance or providing an opinion.
3. Am polite toward my manager, including smiling frequently and expressing appreciation.
4. Avoid profanity in front of my boss, even if he or she uses profanity on the job.
5. Bring forth solutions to important problems facing the group or organization.
6. Contribute willingly to payroll deductions for charity such as United Way.
7. Put considerable effort into working on problems that I know are important to my manager.
8. Almost never miss or be late for a meeting called by my manager.
9. Almost always get a work assignment done on time.
10. Often volunteer to help my manager accomplish a significant task.
11. Compliment my manager when he or she has accomplished something substantial.
12. Occasionally take on work that is outside my job description and then explain to my manager what I did and why I did it.
13. Almost never complain about work or personal life to my manager.
14. In a meeting, I explain to the group why I think the manager's new idea will work.
15. Inform my boss should I hear that a customer or client enjoys our product or service.
16. Any social networking post I make about my manager or the company is positive.

of humor for building a relationship with the boss should be work related and hint at a strength of the boss, department, or company. If the humor is well received, it helps build a relationship with the manager (or other targets of the humor as well).[8] Here's an attempt at ego-building humor that worked well with one vice president. The department administrative assistant said, "Herb, we all know what a reputation you've developed in the company. When you are promoted to CEO, will you take the old gang for a ride in your corporate jet?"

Delivering Bad News

Although favorable interactions with a manager are valuable for relationship building, there are times when a group member has to deliver bad news. For example, you might have to inform the manager about a burst water pipe in the mainframe computer room or a bunch of customer complaints about a new product. You want to avoid being the messenger who is punished because he or she delivered bad news. Attempt to be calm and businesslike. Do not needlessly blame yourself for the problem. Mention that *we are* or *the company is* facing a serious challenge. If possible, suggest a possible solution, such as, "I have already investigated a backup computer service we can use until the damage is repaired."

Cross-Cultural Factors

When working to establish a good relationship with your manager, keep in mind that cultural factors could influence how a given tactic should be modified for best effectiveness. An example would be that displaying strong work ethic to a supervisor from Japan would be different from displaying the same ethic to a manager from France. The Japanese manager might think that working fifty-five hours a week indicates a strong work ethic, whereas the French manager might think that forty hours a week of hard work is exceptional. Another cultural factor in establishing a good relationship could be the amount of respect shown to the manager. A typical American manager might expect an informal, friendly relationship, with the two of you acting like equals. However, a manager from China might expect much more respect. In one situation a manager from China in charge of a chemistry lab in the United States became angry when workers addressed him by his first name. He expected to be addressed as "Dr." plus his last name.

Learning Objective 2

How Do You Cope with a Problem Manager?

Up to this point we have prescribed tactics for dealing with a reasonably rational boss. At some point in their careers, many people face the situation of dealing with a problem manager—one who makes it difficult for the subordinate to get the job done. At times, differences in values and goals could be creating the problem. The problem is sometimes attributed to the boss's personality or incompetence. A frequent personality problem is being a **bully**—a cruel and aggressive boss who intimidates and verbally abuses subordinates. Bullying bosses use frequently the techniques of berating the skills of a subordinate in front of coworkers, spreading rumors, disrupting the person's work, and screaming at him or her.[9]

bully
a cruel and aggressive boss who intimidates and verbally abuses subordinates

People who report to a bully often feel belittled and sapped of energy. Some bullies swear at group members, others insult them with statements such as, "Have you been stupid all your life, or is your stupidity something new?" A territory manager for a midsize technology company said that his toxic, bullying boss has temper tantrums, screams, and shouts obscenities at him on the phone. The boss also goes into long, useless tirades about customers, the industry, and colleagues. Rather than quitting the manager he invested effort in catering to the boss's needs.[10]

Our concern here is with constructive approaches to dealing with the delicate situation of working for a problem manager.

REEVALUATE YOUR MANAGER

Some employees think they have problem managers when those bosses simply have major role, goal, or value differences. (A role in this context is the expectations of the job.) The problem might also lie in conflicting personalities, such as being outgoing or shy. Another problem is conflicting perspectives, such as being detail oriented as opposed to taking an overall perspective. The differences just noted can be good or bad, depending on how they are viewed and used. For example, a combination of a detail-oriented group member with an "overall perspective" boss can be a winning combination.[11]

Another approach to being more cautious in evaluating your manager is to judge slowly and fairly. Many decisions your manager makes may prove to be worthwhile if you give the decisions time.[12] Top management at your company might issue an order that employees cannot surf the Internet for personal reasons on the job. You might think this rule is unfair and treats workers like adolescents. If you wait for the result of the decisions, you might find that productivity improves. Another benefit might be that many workers no longer have to work late because they save time by not surfing.

CONFRONT YOUR MANAGER ABOUT THE PROBLEM

A general-purpose way of dealing with a problem manager is to confront the problem and then look for a solution. Because your manager has more formal authority than you, the confrontation must be executed with the highest level of tact and sensitivity. A beginning point in confronting a manager is to gently ask for an explanation of the problem. Suppose, for example, you believed strongly that your team leader snubs you because he or she dislikes you. You might inquire gently, "What might I be doing wrong that is creating a problem between us?"

Another situation calling for confrontation would be outrageous behavior by the manager, such as swearing at and belittling group members. For example, a worker reported that in meetings his manager openly belittles his peers and the people higher in the organization. The worker was concerned that this behavior fosters poor morale and unprofessional attitudes among team members and hurts productivity.[13] Because several or all group members are involved in the example cited, a group discussion of the problem might be warranted. You and your coworkers might meet as a group to discuss the impact of the manager's style on group morale and productivity. This tactic runs the risk of backfiring if the manager becomes defensive and angry. Yet, confrontation is worth the risk because the problem of abuse will not go away without discussion.

Confrontation can also be helpful in dealing with the problem of **micromanagement**, the close monitoring of most aspects of group member activities by the manager. "Looking over your shoulder constantly" is an everyday phrase for micromanagement. If you feel that you are being supervised so closely that it is difficult to perform well, confront the situation. Say something of this nature: "I notice that you check almost all my work. Do you doubt my ability to perform my job correctly?" As a consequence, the manager might explain why he or she is micromanaging or begin to check on your work less frequently.

Micromanagement
the close monitoring of most aspects of group member activities by the manager

Despite the usefulness of confrontation about a problem with your manager, diplomacy is still important. Your confrontation should reflect a concern about performing well, not a need to strike back at your manager. Career coach Deb Koen writes that if your aim is to stay with your company, direct your energy at coming to an understanding so that the two of you can get along well enough to have a productive working relationship.[14]

OVERRESPOND TO THE MANAGER'S PET PEEVES

The territory manager mentioned earlier developed a tactic for dealing with his problem manager that is likely to work for you. If your boss has a pet peeve, cater to that demand. The manager in question knew that his boss likes orders to get processed immediately. (The boss's pet peeve is a delay in the processing of an order.) So the manager tried to process an order upon arrival. If he couldn't get to it immediately, he would send an e-mail stating that he is tied up on another project. Eight out of ten times, the boss would then do the order processing for the manager.[15] To be less manipulative, you might do an honest job of staying on top of any task that your boss deems to be extra important.

"If you're not looking at your work relationships as a resource, you should be. Relationships need to be nurtured and developed, like any other skill or asset. Assess the quality of your relationships, and make a concerted effort to improve the ones lower on the scale."

—Steve Arneson

Statement from this leadership coach appeared in his column, "Evaluate Your Work Relationships," *San Francisco Examiner* (www.examiner.com), January 8, 2009, p. 1.

LEARN FROM YOUR MANAGER'S MISTAKES

Just as you can learn from watching your manager do things right, you can also learn from watching him or her do things wrong. In the first instance, we are talking about using your manager as a positive model. Modeling of this type is an important source of learning on the job. Using a superior as a negative model can also be of some benefit. As an elementary example, if your manager criticized you in public and you felt humiliated, you would have learned a good lesson in effective supervision: Never criticize a subordinate publicly. By serving as a negative example, your manager has taught you a valuable lesson.

▶ **Learning Objective 3** ▶

How Do You Build Good Coworker Relationships?

Developing productive relationships with coworkers is a challenge for many workers. A CareerBuilder survey of more than 4,900 workers found that 39 percent of workers said they feel that they do not fit in with their coworkers. Based on these results, Rosemary Haefner, vice president of human resources at CareerBuilder, said that because today's workplace is so diversified, that sometimes behavior can come across as being inappropriate for the office.[16]

If you are unable to work cooperatively with others you are unlikely to be recommended for promotion to a supervisory position. It will also be difficult to hold on to your job. Poor relationships with coworkers can lead to frustration, stress, and decreased productivity, whereas getting along with them makes the workplace more satisfying. You need their cooperation and support, and they need yours. When workers need help in getting a job done, they will choose a coworker who is congenial over one who might have the edge in expertise.[17] Furthermore, the leading reason employees are terminated is not poor technical skills but rather inability or unwillingness to form satisfactory relationships with others on the job. In this section we describe basic

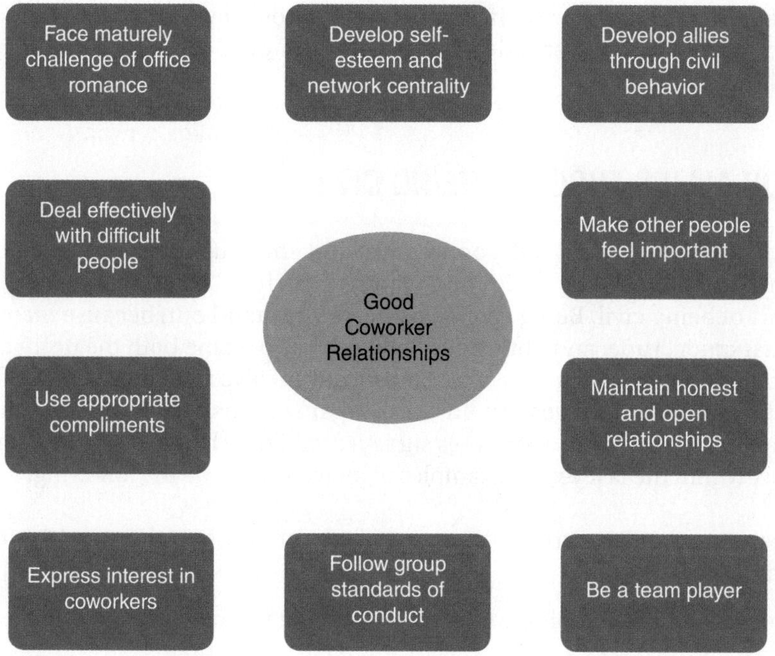

FIGURE 9-1

APPROACHES TO BUILDING COWORKER RELATIONSHIPS

tactics for developing and maintaining good coworker relationships, as outlined in Figure 9-1.

If your goal is to become part of the *in-crowd* in your work group, building coworker relationships is all the more important. According to clinical psychologist and author Judith Sills, the in-crowd is the group of cool kids at your office, those with access to the boss, power, and information.[18] A relevant point here is that to become part of the select, informal group you must work extra hard at cultivating members of that group.

HAVE HIGH SELF-ESTEEM AND BE AT THE CENTER OF A COMMUNICATION NETWORK

A starting point in building effective coworker relationships is to have the right personality structure and to be at the center of a communications network. Brent A. Scott, a professor of management at Michigan State University, and Timothy A. Judge, a professor of industrial/organizational psychology at Notre Dame University, conducted two studies to investigate what made workers popular, or generally accepted by one's peers.

The study with the most informative results involved 139 healthcare employees from 22 groups of a large hospital, with most of the work being conducted in teams. Popularity was measured in terms of how well the employee was liked by coworkers on a 1 to 5 scale. Self-esteem was measured by significant others of the study participants completing a core self-evaluation quiz about the participant. [You will recall having completed two different core self-evaluation quizzes in Chapters 2 and 4, both of which focus on self-esteem.] Work communication centrality was measured by asking each coworker to "check the names of people with whom you communicate as part of the job during a typical workweek."

The results showed that having a high core self-evaluation (including self-esteem) and being at the center of communications was related to popularity. The more popular employees also received more citizenship behavior from coworkers and less incidences of counterproductive, or disruptive, behavior—both of which reflect better coworker relationships.[19]

DEVELOP ALLIES THROUGH BEING CIVIL

People who are courteous, kind, cooperative, and cheerful develop allies and friends in the workplace. Practicing basic good manners, such as being pleasant and friendly, is also part of being civil. Being civil helps make you stand out, because many people believe that crude, rude, and obnoxious behavior has become both the norm and a national problem. Uncivil behaviors characteristically involve rudeness and discourteousness. A study of three Midwestern business organizations across different industries found that 86 percent of the employees surveyed said they had experienced some form of incivility within the last year.[20] Examples of incivility include the following:

- A salesperson makes sarcastic comments about another employee in front of a customer.
- A coworker initiates cell phone calls while listening to a presentation at a meeting.
- One worker continues responding to e-mail messages while another is talking to him in person.
- One worker gives a dirty look to another during a meeting.
- A person whistles or sings constantly in the office (an intensely annoying behavior for many people).[21]

Being civil also involves not snooping, not spreading malicious gossip, and not weaseling out of group presents, such as shower or retirement gifts. In addition, it is important to be available to coworkers who want your advice as well as your help in times of crisis.

Civility helps build workplace relationships and also helps prevent serious negative consequences to coworkers. Studies conducted with judicial court employees and municipal workers studied incivility in terms of being a personal target, or as part of the group atmosphere. It was found that experience with incivility had these harmful effects:

- Lower job satisfaction, leading to workers thinking about quitting
- A negative impact on mental health, which in turn damaged physical health[22]

Closely related to being civil is maintaining a positive outlook. Everyone knows that you gain more allies by being optimistic and positive than by being pessimistic and negative. Nevertheless, many people ignore this simple strategy for getting along well with others. Coworkers are more likely to solicit your opinion or offer you help when you are perceived as a cheerful person.

Human Relations Self-Assessment Quiz 9-2 provides an opportunity to think about the civility of your own behavior.

MAKE OTHER PEOPLE FEEL IMPORTANT

A fundamental principle of fostering good relationships with coworkers and others is to make them feel important. Making others feel important is honest because everybody in an organization has a contribution to make, including the CEO, payroll coordinator, and custodial worker.

Human Relations Self-Assessment Quiz 9-2

The Civil Behavior Checklist

To help you think through the civility of your behavior in relation to coworkers, respond "Mostly Yes" or "Mostly No" to the following statements.

Number	Statement about Behavior	Mostly Yes	Mostly No
1.	If a coworker says something that contains a factual error, I let the coworker finish the sentence before I explain the error.	______	______
2.	When a coworker and I walking together and approaching a door, I will typically open the door and let him or her go through the door first.	______	______
3.	When a coworker makes a small mistake, I will often say something to the effect, "What's wrong with you?"	______	______
4.	I frequently shout out vulgarities when in the presence of coworkers.	______	______
5.	When I learn about something outstanding a coworker has accomplished, I quickly compliment him or her in writing or in speaking.	______	______
6.	I ignore most e-mails and text messages coworkers send me unless the subject is urgent.	______	______
7.	I routinely check messages on my smart phone when a coworker is talking to me in person.	______	______
8.	I sometimes poke fun at coworkers who have a foreign accent.	______	______
9.	When I see a coworker for the first time at the beginning of a workday, I will smile even if I am in a bad mood.	______	______
10.	If a coworker asked me for help with a problem close to quitting time, I would gladly spend about fifteen minutes trying to help with the problem.	______	______

Scoring and Interpretation:

Give yourself 1 point for the following answers: Mostly Yes to questions 1, 2, 5, 9, and 10; Mostly No to questions 3, 4, 6, 7, and 8. If you scored 8 or more points, it appears that you behave civilly toward coworkers. If you scored between 0 and 7, you may be perceived as uncivil even in today's world. Furthermore, you might be developing the reputation of a person without good enough human relations skills to be promoted.

Although the leader has primary responsibility for satisfying this recognition need, coworkers also play a key role. One approach to making a coworker feel important would be to bring a notable accomplishment of his or hers to the attention of the group. Human Relations Self-Assessment Quiz 9-3 gives you an opportunity to think through your tendencies to make others feel important.

MAINTAIN HONEST AND OPEN RELATIONSHIPS

In human relations we attach considerable importance to maintaining honest and open relationships with other people. The mechanism underlying openness is **self-disclosure**, the process of revealing your inner self to others. (You will recall that self-disclosure was mentioned in Chapter 1 in relation to the Johari Window.) A person with a high degree of self-disclosure is open, whereas a person with a low degree of self-disclosure is closed. Nevertheless, you must be careful of excessive self-disclosure.

Self-disclosure the process of revealing one's inner self to others

Human Relations Self-Assessment Quiz 9-3

How Important Do I Make People Feel?

Indicate on a 1 to 5 scale how frequently you act (or would act if the situation presented itself) in the ways indicated: very infrequently (VI), infrequently (I), sometimes (S), frequently (F), very frequently (VF). Circle the number in the column that best fits your answer

	VI	I	S	F	VF
1. I do my best to correctly pronounce a coworker's name.	1	2	3	4	5
2. I avoid letting other people's egos get too big.	5	4	3	2	1
3. I brag to others about the accomplishments of my coworkers.	1	2	3	4	5
4. I recognize the birthdays of friends in a tangible way.	1	2	3	4	5
5. It makes me anxious to listen to others brag about their accomplishments.	5	4	3	2	1
6. After hearing that a friend has done something outstanding, I shake his or her hand.	1	2	3	4	5
7. If a friend or coworker recently received a degree or certificate, I would offer my congratulations.	1	2	3	4	5
8. If a friend or coworker finished second in a contest, I would inquire why he or she did not finish first.	5	4	3	2	1
9. If a coworker showed me how to do something, I would compliment that person's skill.	1	2	3	4	5
10. When a coworker starts bragging about a family member's accomplishments, I do not respond.	5	4	3	2	1

Total Score ________

Scoring and Interpretation:

Total the numbers corresponding to your answers.

40 to 50 points–Suggests that you typically make people feel important.

16 to 39 points–Suggests that you have a moderate tendency toward making others feel important.

10 to 15 points–Suggests that you need to develop skill in making others feel important. Study this chapter carefully.

Many people feel uneasy if another person is too self-revealing. The overly candid person risks being rejected. For instance, if you communicate all your negative feelings and doubts to another person, that person may become annoyed and pull away from you. It would be too open to tell an office mate, "I am ticked off that the manager has us sharing the same cubicle, but I'll put up with it until you quit or are fired."

Another aspect of being too revealing is to tell coworkers intimate details about your personal life, such as an intestinal disorder you might be suffering, a conflict you might be experiencing with a family member, and an overdraft dispute you might be having with a bank. According to relationship specialist, Elizabeth Bernstein, the TMI (too much information) phenomenon has invaded the workplace. Reality TV shows and social networking Web sites have contributed to creating a culture in which people are encouraged to share every intimate and boring detail of their lives. Many people have become desensitized to the reality that some aspects of personal life are best left private.[23]

Giving coworkers frank but tactful answers to their requests for your opinion is one useful way of developing open relationships. Assume that a coworker asks your opinion about a document he intends to send to his boss. As you read it, you find it somewhat incoherent and filled with spelling and grammatical errors. An honest response to this document might be, "I think your idea is a good one, but I think your memo needs more work before that idea comes across clearly."

Accurately expressing your feelings also leads to constructive relationships. If you arrive at work upset over a personal problem and appearing obviously fatigued, you can expect some reaction. A peer might say, "What seems to be the problem? Is everything all right?" A dishonest reply would be, "Everything is fine. What makes you think something is wrong?" In addition to making an obviously untrue statement, you would also be perceived as rejecting the person who asked the question.

If you prefer not to discuss your problem, an honest response on your part would be, "Thanks for your interest. I am facing some problems today. But I think things will work out." Such an answer would not involve you in a discussion of your personal problems. Also, you would not be perceived as rejecting your coworker. The same principle applies equally well to personal relationships.

BE A TEAM PLAYER

An essential strategy for developing good relationships with coworkers is to be a team player. A **team player** is one who emphasizes group accomplishment and cooperation rather than individual achievement and not helping others. Team play is important because of the emphasis on having teams of workers decide how to improve productivity and reduce costs. You will also have to be a team player if you reach the pinnacle of power in your organization. Executives are expected to be good team players as well as individual decision makers. But team play is even more important on the way to becoming an executive, because impatience and making unilateral decisions is more tolerated in the executive suite. Being an effective team player is important because without such capability collaborative effort is not possible.

Team player
one who emphasizes group accomplishment and cooperation rather than individual achievement and not helping others

Here we describe a representative group of behaviors that contribute to team play. In addition, engaging in such behavior helps you be perceived as a team player.

1. Share credit with coworkers. A direct method of promoting team play is to share credit for good deeds with other team members. Instead of focusing on yourself as the person responsible for a work achievement, point out that the achievement was a team effort. You will make a poor team player if you try to grab all the glory for ideas that work and distance yourself from ideas that do not work. An effective team member wants all other members to succeed. You will stand out by praising the people you work with rather than hogging any praise for the team.

2. Display a helpful, cooperative attitude. Working cooperatively with others is virtually synonymous with team play. Cooperation translates into such activities as helping another worker with a computer problem, covering for a teammate when he or she is absent, and making sure a coworker has the input required from you on time. A helpful cooperative attitude is the main component of organizational citizenship behavior.

3. To establish trust, keep confidential information private and give honest opinions. Trust is important for teamwork because trust is a major contributor to cooperation.[24] Confidential information a teammate shares with you should not be shared with others. Trust is exceedingly difficult to regain after a person has been betrayed. Giving honest opinions helps develop trust because the recipient of your honesty will regard you as a person of integrity. However, tact and diplomacy are still important. A dishonest opinion can often be detected through your nonverbal cues, such as discomfort in your voice tone.

Assume that a friend of yours is starting a business selling antique toys over the Internet. She asks you if you like her proposed domain name, www.OldjunkRus.com. You think the name is both ridiculous and an infringement on the Toys "R" Us name; yet you say, "Hey, terrific" with a sickened look on your face. You might lose some of your friend's trust.

4. Share information and opinions with coworkers. Teamwork is facilitated when group members share information and opinions. This is true because one of the benefits of group effort is that members can share ideas. The result is often a better solution to problems than would have been possible if people worked alone. The group thus achieves **synergy**, a product of group effort whereby the output of the group exceeds the output possible if the members worked alone.

Synergy
a product of group effort whereby the output of the group exceeds the output possible if the members worked alone

Another important aspect of sharing information and opinion with teammates is to provide technical expertise, or knowledge of the task. Most people are selected for a work team primarily because their specialized knowledge. To use your expertise to advantage, you must be willing to share it with teammates. Some experts perceive their specialized knowledge as a source of power. As a consequence, they are hesitant to let others share their knowledge for fear of losing power.

5. Provide emotional support to coworkers. Good team players offer each other emotional support. Such support can take the form of verbal encouragement for ideas expressed, listening to a group member's concerns, or complimenting achievement. An emotionally supportive comment to a coworker who appears to be experiencing stress might be, "This doesn't look like one of your better days. What can I do to help?" Figure 9-2 illustrates providing emotional support to a coworker.

6. Follow the Golden Rule. The ancient adage "Treat others the way you would like them to treat you" provides a firm foundation for effective teamwork. Although some may dismiss the Golden Rule as a syrupy platitude, it still works. For example, you would probably want someone to help you with a perplexing problem, so you take the initiative to help others when you have the expertise needed.

7. Avoid actions that could sabotage or undermine the group in any way. Frequently criticizing group members directly or complaining about them to outsiders works against the best interest of the group. Members within the group, as well as the team leader, will most likely hear that you criticized them to an outsider, thus doing severe damage to your ability to work cooperatively with them.

8. Attend company-sponsored social events. A worker's reputation as a team player is often judged both on the job and in company-sponsored social events, such as parties, picnics, and athletic events. If you attend these and participate fully, your reputation as a team player will be enhanced. Company-sponsored social events are also important because they provide an opportunity to build rapport with coworkers. Rapport, in turn, facilitates teamwork.

FIGURE 9-2

AN EXAMPLE OF PROVIDING EMOTIONAL SUPPORT TO A COWORKER

9. Avoid backstabbing. A special category of disliked behavior is **backstabbing,** an attempt to discredit by underhanded means, such as innuendo, accusation, and the like. A backstabber might drop hints to the boss, for example, that a coworker performs poorly under pressure or is looking for a new job. Sometimes the backstabber assertively gathers information to backstab a coworker. He or she might engage another worker in a derogatory discussion about the boss and then report the coworker's negative comments back to the boss. A person who develops a reputation as a backstabber will receive poor cooperation from coworkers. The person might also be considered untrustworthy by management, thus retarding his or her own career.

Backstabbing
an attempt to discredit by underhanded means such as innuendo, accusation, or the like

These nine points contribute specifically to effective team play. Recognize also that all other actions directed toward good coworker relationships will enhance team play. The accompanying Human Relations in Practice illustrates how a professional-level worker attempted to be an effective team player.

Human Relations in Practice Practice

Debt Collector Josephine Works at Being a Team Player

Josephine held a position as debt collector at a financial services company. She worked the phone, sent e-mail messages, and made in-person visits to collect money owed to the small business loan division of her company. Upon being hired, her manager, Spencer explained that although the five people in her group worked in separate cubicles and did most of their work independently, he welcomed teamwork. "I see us as a team that works together to improve the chances that our clients uphold their responsibilities of paying back their legitimate debts." Having played on the lacrosse team in high school and college, and having been assigned many team projects in college, Josephine bought into what Spencer was saying. After being on the job one week, she brought to the office a batch of home-baked cookies. She told her new teammates, "I know that we are all working hard to achieve a goal, so I wanted to spread a little cheer in the office."

When Josephine happened upon a technique that seem to be effective in settling on a debt, she sent an e-mail to Spencer and her teammates explaining what she did that went well. For example, she gave one restaurant owner some suggestions for cutting household expenses that would enable her to make progress on paying back the debt owed her company. As a result, the restaurant owner started sending the company $65 per week toward the debt.

Josephine also looked for opportunities to directly help her teammates. Her most effective approaches was to explain to her teammates that she was fascinated by conducting Internet searches, and that she would help anybody dig for information that could be useful in trying to get their job done. For example, a teammate needed some information about bankruptcy laws in the state of Maine, and Josephine dug up the information during lunch break.

Question: To what extent do you think Josephine is improving her standing in the company by her efforts at teamwork?

Source: Story contributed by Josephine Delgardio of Binghamton, New York.

FOLLOW GROUP STANDARDS OF CONDUCT

Group norms
unwritten set of expectations for group members—what people ought to do; basic principle to follow in getting along with coworkers

Organizational culture
values and beliefs of the firm that guide people's actions

The basic principle to follow in getting along with coworkers is to follow **group norms**. These refer to the unwritten set of expectations for group members—what people ought to do. Norms become a standard of what each person should do or not do within the group. Norms also provide general guidelines for reacting constructively to the behavior of coworkers. Norms are a major component of the **organizational culture**, or values and beliefs of the firm that guide people's actions. In one firm, the norms and culture may favor hard work and high quality. In another firm, the norms and culture may favor a weaker work ethic.

Group norms also influence the social aspects of behavior on the job. These aspects of behavior relate to such things as the people with whom to have lunch, getting together after work, joining a company team, and the type of clothing to wear to work. Sharing laughter, such as poking positive fun at coworkers, is another example of an important social behavior linked to a group norm.

Workers learn about norms through both observation and direct instruction from other group members. If you do not deviate too far from these norms, the group will accept much of your behavior. If you deviate too far, you will be subject to much rejection and feelings of isolation. In some instances, you might even be subjected to verbal abuse if you make the other employees look bad.

A confusing aspect of group norms for many people is how much physical contact of a friendly, nonsexual nature is acceptable and desirable in a given workplace. Concerns about being accused of sexual harassment tend to limit hugging and touching, yet many people do not want to be perceived as cold and distant by avoiding all physical contact. Among the many possible forms of physical contact acceptable in some workplaces are the following: handshake, light hug, back pat, high five, fist bump, chest bump, single-cheek kiss, double-cheek kiss, and bro-hug. (The bro-hug is a complicated maneuver that includes placing one arm over the other person's shoulder while shaking hands.)[25]

Clues to how much physical contact is permitted can be gleaned from observing others in the office. It is also important to recognize individual differences. For example, some people enjoy being hugged and receiving fist bumps, whereas others recoil when touched by a coworker. Another factor remains status differences. It is best to go light on initiating physical touching with higher-ranking workers, such as hugging the CEO when he or she visits your organizational unit. Cultural differences are also a factor with people from some cultures welcoming physical contact with coworkers. In contrast, people from some other cultures are offended by coworker touching. (See Chapter 13.)

Getting along too well with coworkers has its price as well. The risk of conforming too closely to group norms is that you lose your individuality. You become viewed by your superiors as "one of the office gang" rather than a person who aspires to move up in the organization. It is important to be a good team player, but to advance in your career you must also find a way to distinguish yourself, such as through creative thinking and outstanding performance.

EXPRESS AN INTEREST IN THE WORK AND PERSONAL LIVES OF COWORKERS

Almost everyone is self-centered to some extent. Thus, people favor topics closely related to themselves, such as their children, friends, hobbies, work, or possessions. Sales representatives rely heavily on this fact in cultivating relationships with established customers. They routinely ask the customer about his or her hobbies, family members, and work activities. You can capitalize on this simple strategy by asking coworkers and friends questions such as these:

How is your work going? (*highly recommended*)

How did you gain the knowledge necessary for your job?

How does the company use the output from your department?

How did your son enjoy computer camp?

Closely related to expressing interest in others is to investigate what you have in common, both professionally and personally, with peers. You might identify common interests, such as a focus on the company's market share, or a personal interest, such as hiking.

A danger in asking questions about other people's work and personal life is that some questions may not be perceived as well intentioned. There is a fine line between honest curiosity and snooping. You must stay alert to this subtle distinction.

USE APPROPRIATE COMPLIMENTS

An effective way of developing good relationships with coworkers and friends is to compliment something with which they closely identify, such as their children, spouses, hobbies, or pets. Compliments are also effective because they are a form of flattery. Paying a compliment is a form of positive reinforcement—rewarding somebody for doing something right. The right response is therefore strengthened or reinforced. A compliment is a useful multipurpose reward.

Another way of complimenting people is through recognition. The suggestions made earlier about making people feel important are ways of recognizing people and therefore compliments. Investing a small amount of time in recognizing a coworker can pay large dividends in terms of cultivating an ally. Recognition and compliments are more likely to create a favorable relationship when they are appropriate. *Appropriate* in this context means that the compliment fits the accomplishment. Praise that is too lavish may be interpreted as belittling and patronizing. Let's look at the difference between an appropriate and an exaggerated compliment over the same issue.

An executive secretary gets a printer operating that was temporarily not printing documents.

Appropriate compliment. Nice job, Stephanie. Fixing the printer took considerable skill. We can now resume making hard copies of documents.

Exaggerated compliment. Stephanie, I'm overwhelmed. You're a world-class printer specialist. Are there no limits to your talents?

Observe that the appropriate compliment is thoughtful and is proportionate to what Stephanie accomplished. The exaggerated compliment is probably wasted because it is way out of proportion to the magnitude of the accomplishment.

Cultural factors can mediate (influence) the most effective approach for getting along with coworkers. Although there is a strong tendency for people from another country to quickly adapt to the culture of your country, you still have to be sensitive to cultural differences for rapport building. An example would be for an American not to be disappointed when a British coworker offers modest, instead of effusive, compliments for a job well done. The American might have just won a sales contest and informs her British coworker of the feat. He responds, "Certainly, in the right direction." (Your disappointment might come across as a frown or some other subtle rejection.)

FACE MATURELY THE CHALLENGE OF THE OFFICE ROMANCE

A final aspect of getting along with coworkers to be considered here is dealing with the challenge of an office romance. The office has become a frequent meeting place, with more romances beginning at work than over the Internet. A survey indicated that over one-third of respondents had dated a coworker at least once during their career. Slightly over 30 percent indicated that the office romance eventually led to a marriage.[26]

People often work closely in teams and other joint projects, thus creating the conditions for romance to take place. Another basic reason why office romances are so frequent is that familiarity builds emotional and physical attraction. Based on research spanning twenty years, Cindy Hazan, an associate professor of human development at Cornell University, concludes that people need attachment. And proximity breeds attachment. "Proximity is really the core of attachment. Familiar people have a calming, soothing effect on us."[27]

Company Policies about Office Romances

Office romances can be disruptive to morale and productivity. Coworker romances are a more widespread potential problem because more romances take place between coworkers on the same level than between superiors and subordinates. The emphasis on *potential* is important because most coworker romances do not create problems. According to a study conducted by Ryerson University professor, Ann Cole, most coworkers are not disturbed by office romances if they do not have a negative impact on the workplace. The potential negative impacts include lowering productivity and demotivating coworkers. For example, it is discouraging for some workers to view public displays of affection among coworkers. Participants in the study also believed that higher management should intervene when there is an office romance between a manager and an employee in the same department.[28]

To help deal with the potential negative aspects of office romance, some companies have established policies covering such relationships, including written agreements. Either written, or implied, most companies are opposed to office romances between two people who are married to other people. At Cisco Systems, a dating policy does not encourage or discourage consensual relationships in the workplace, with some limits. Relationships between supervisors and subordinates are frowned upon, and may result in a transfer or reassignment.[29] Many companies have similar policies about breaking up the reporting relationship between a superior and subordinate who become romantically involved with each other.

The purpose of the consensual relationship contract (also referred to a *love contract*) is to avoid sexual harassment and retaliation lawsuits when the office romance terminates, especially when the two people are not at the same organizational level.[30] The contract is likely to emphasize that both parties must mutually and voluntarily consent to the social relationship. Furthermore, the policy states that the social relationship must not affect job performance or negatively impact the company's business. The contract will often specify what type of behavior is appropriate, such as eating lunch together in the company cafeteria. Inappropriate behavior, such as spending time together in a supply closet for purposes of romantic activity, is also specified.

Many companies are concerned about information leakage within their organization. If you date a person who has access to confidential information (such as trade secrets), management might be concerned that you are a security risk. You, therefore, might miss out on some opportunities for better assignments. Companies also worry about negative consequences stemming from office romances, such as sexual harassment claims, low morale of coworkers, lowered productivity from the couple involved in the romance, and an unprofessional atmosphere. Yet, an important positive consequence to employers of an office romance is that while the relationship is working well, the couple may have a heightened interest in coming to work. Also, romance can trigger energy that leads to enhanced productivity.

Be Discreet with the Office Romance

Sensitivity is required to conduct an office romance that does not detract from your professionalism. It is important not to abuse company tolerance of the coworker romance. Do not invite the person you are dating to meals at company expense, take him or her on nonessential business trips, or create projects to work on jointly. Strive to keep the relationship confidential and restricted to after hours. Minimize talking to coworkers about the relationship. Engaging in personal conversations during work time or holding hands in the company cafeteria is unprofessional and taboo. Such behavior as holding hands or kissing in public view is regarded as poor office etiquette.

Should your coworker romance terminate, you face a special challenge. You must now work together cooperatively with a person toward whom you may have angry feelings. Few people have the emotional detachment necessary to work smoothly with a former romantic involvement. Extra effort, therefore, will be required by both of you.

What should you do if you and your boss seem suited for a long-term commitment? Why walk away from Mr. or Ms. Right? My suggestion is that if you do become romantically involved, one of you should request a transfer to another department. Many office romances do lead to happy marriages and other long-term relationships. At the start of the relationship, however, use considerable discretion.

How Do You Build Good Relationships with Customers?

Learning Objective 4

Success on the job also requires building good relationships with both external and internal customers. Business success is built on good relationships, as emphasized again and again by business advisers. An employee whose thoughts and actions are geared toward helping customers has a **customer service orientation**. Good service is the primary factor that keeps customers coming back. This is important because profits jump considerably as the customer is retained over time. Customer loyalty is therefore a major goal for almost all business firms. Occasionally, a place of business does not want the same person back, such as a bankruptcy counseling service. Nevertheless, the financial counselor still wants loyalty in the form of referrals for other services.

Customer service orientation approach of employee whose thoughts and actions are geared toward helping customers

An overall approach to dealing effectively with customers is to be a good organizational citizen with respect to customer relationships. You gear a lot of your out-of-the-way effort into customer relationships. Specific behaviors of this type are presented in Figure 9-3. Time-tested suggestions for high-level customer service are presented next.[31] Taken together, these suggestions will help you bond with a customer, forming a close and valued ongoing relationship. You will be able to implement principles of good service more readily if you are treated well by your employer. When workers feel valued, and are adequately compensated, they usually spread the sunshine to customers. Satisfied employees create satisfied customers.

1. Establish customer satisfaction goals. Decide jointly with your manager how much you intend to help customers. Find answers to questions such as the following: "Is your company attempting to satisfy every customer within ten minutes of his or her request?" "Are you striving to provide the finest customer service in your field?" "Is your goal zero

FIGURE 9-3

SERVICE-ORIENTED ORGANIZATIONAL CITIZENSHIP BEHAVIORS

Source: Portion of a table from Lance A. Bettencourt, Kevin P. Gwinner, and Matthew L. Meuter, "A Comparison of Attitude, Personality, and Knowledge Predictors of Service-Oriented Organizational Citizenship Behaviors," *Journal of Applied Psychology*, February 2001, p. 32. Statements 17, 18, and 19 are based on "Is Your Service Attitude Up to Snuff?" *Communication Briefings*, September 2010, p. 4 (Adapted from Val and Jeff Gee, "Super Service," *www.mjlearning.com*).

1. Tells outsiders this is a good place to work.
2. Says good things about the organization to others.
3. Generates favorable goodwill for the company.
4. Encourages friends and family to use the firm's products and services.
5. Actively promotes the firm's products and services.
6. Follows customer service guidelines with extreme care.
7. Conscientiously follows guidelines for customer promotions.
8. Follows up in a timely manner to customer requests and problems.
9. Performs duties with unusually few mistakes.
10. Always has a positive attitude at work.
11. Regardless of circumstances, exceptionally courteous and respectful to customers.
12. Encourages coworkers to contribute ideas and suggestions for service improvement.
13. Contributes many ideas for customer promotions and communications.
14. Makes constructive suggestions for service improvement.
15. Frequently presents to others creative solutions to customer problems.
16. Takes home brochures to read up on products and services.
17. Does not require appreciation from customers so I can feel energized to serve them.
18. Believes that all customer complaints should be taken seriously.
19. Regards almost all customer expectations as realistic.

defections to competitors?" Your goals will dictate how much and the type of effort you put into pleasing customers.

2. Understand your customer's needs and place them first. The most basic principle of selling is to identify and satisfy customer needs. Many customers may not be able to express their needs clearly. Also, they may not be certain of their needs. To help identify customer needs, you may have to probe for more information. For example, an associate in a consumer electronics store may have to ask, "What uses do you have in mind for your television receiver aside from watching regular programs? Will you be using it to display digital photographs, videos, phone alerts, and the Internet?" Knowing such information will help the store associate identify which television receiver will satisfy the customer's needs.

After you have identified customer needs, focus on satisfying them rather than doing what is convenient for you or the firm. Assume, for example, that the customer says, "I would like to purchase nine reams of copier paper." The sales associate should not respond, "Sorry, the copying paper comes in boxes of ten, so it is not convenient to sell you nine reams." The associate might, however, offer a discount for the purchase of the full ten-ream box if such action fits company policy.

Customer needs also have to be understood when the customer has a problem. A large scale study of contact-center and self-service interactions revealed a simple truth about satisfying customers. What customers really want, and do not always receive, is just a satisfactory solution to their service issue.[32] For example, a customer who purchased a new SUV might want a windshield leak repaired. Sealing this leak means much more in terms of customer loyalty than giving him or her a free oil change and lubrication.

3. Show care and concern. A major customer complaint is that service providers did not care enough about their problems. For example, Delta Air Lines conducted customer feedback surveys indicating that customers write to the airline saying, "no one cared or apologized" when something went wrong, such as a canceled flight or lost baggage.[33]

During contacts with your customer, show concern for his or her welfare. Ask questions such as the following: "How have you enjoyed the television set you bought here a while back?" "How are you feeling today?" After asking the question, project a genuine interest in the answer. A strictly business approach to showing care and concern is to follow up on requests. A phone call or e-mail message to the requester of your service is usually sufficient follow-up. A follow-up is effective because it completes the communication loop between two people.

Another way to show care and concern is to stay in touch with key customers. Interact with them on a personal level by making reference to their personal concerns.[34] For example, a heating and air-conditioning sales rep might send an e-mail to a customer asking how the new system is working and how the customer's child was doing in her youth soccer league.

4. Communicate a positive attitude. A positive attitude is conveyed by factors such as appearance, friendly gestures, a warm voice tone, and good telephone communication skills. If a customer seems apologetic about making a heavy demand, respond, "No need to apologize. My job is to please you. I'm here to serve." One reason a positive attitude is important is that hostility by the customer contact person leads to customer dissatisfaction. Lorna Doucet, a professor of organizational behavior at the University of Illinois, conducted a study in the telephone service center for a large retail bank. She found that hostility by the service provider had the strongest negative effect on customers when it was combined with low technical performance (poor answers) by the call center representative. (Perceived hostility was measured by questionnaires.) Hostility was more tolerated if the customers received the answers they needed.[35]

5. Make the buyer feel good. A fundamental way of building a customer relationship is to make the buyer feel good. Also, make the buyer feel good because he or she has bought from you. Offer compliments about the customer's healthy glow or a report that specified vendor requirements (for an industrial customer). Explain how much you value the customer's business. An effective feel-good line is, "I enjoy doing business with you." Smiling is a useful technique for making the customer feel good. Also, smiling is a natural relationship builder and can help you bond with your customer. Smile several times during each customer contact, even if your customer is angry with your product or service. Yet, guard against smiling constantly or inappropriately because your smile then becomes meaningless. False smiling if carried out regularly is stressful, so look for opportunities to smile genuinely.

Another basic way of making the buyer feel good is to thank a major customer in writing, such as a handwritten note or even a post on Facebook or Twitter. Mention how much you appreciate the customer's continuing business.[36]

6. Strive for the "wow" experience. One of the most effective ways to please a customer is to provide him or her with an unusually sensitive and warm surprise, often referred to as a "wow" experience. A daily activity at every Ritz-Carlton hotel around the world, the staff meets to share "wow" stories. The stories accomplish two important ends. First, they offer workers local recognition in front of peers. Second, the wow stories reinforce the values each employee is expected to demonstrate as a Ritz-Carlton "ambassador" (being part of the hotel brand experience).[37]

Alan J. Fuerstman, the chief executive of Montage Hotels and Resorts, defines *wow* as a "spontaneous, personal gesture now." Employees at the chain attend training in how to deliver a wow experience to guests. Fuerstman cited the example of a server who brought a tray of crab cakes to the room of a guest who she knew was dying of cancer. The server found out in conversation with the woman that crab cakes were one of her favorite meals.[38]

7. Display strong business ethics. Ethical violations receive so much publicity that you can impress customers by being conspicuously ethical. Look for ways to show that you are so ethical that you would welcome making your sales tactics public knowledge. Also, treat the customer the same way you would treat a family member or a valued friend.

8. Be helpful rather than defensive when a customer complains. Take a complaint professionally rather than personally. Listen carefully and concentrate on being helpful. The upset customer cares primarily about having the problem resolved and does not care whether you are at fault. Use a statement such as, "I understand this mistake is a major inconvenience. I'll do what I can right now to solve the problem." Remember also that complaints that are taken care of quickly and satisfactorily will often create a more positive impression than mistake-free service. Another way of being helpful is to ask for enough details about what went wrong so that you can begin resolving the problem. Explain as soon as possible how you are going to fix the problem.

9. Invite the customer back. The southern U.S. expression "Y'all come back, now!" is well suited for good customer service. Specific invitations to return may help increase repeat business. The more focused and individualized the invitation, the more likely it will have an impact on customer behavior. ("Y'all come back, now!" is sometimes used too indiscriminately to be effective.) Pointing out why you enjoyed doing business with the customer and what future problems you could help with is an effective technique. Another way of encouraging the customer to return is to explain how much you value him or her.

10. Avoid rudeness. Although rudeness to customers is obviously a poor business practice, the problem is widespread. Rudeness by customer contact personnel is a major problem from the employer's standpoint. Be aware of subtle forms of rudeness, such as complaining about your job or working hours in front of customers. To elevate your awareness level about rudeness among customer contact personnel, do Human Relations Self-Assessment Quiz 9-4.

11. Engage in deep acting with respect to emotions. In many customer service situations it is helpful for the customer service provider to modify inner emotions in order to please the customer. For example, the manager of a pet cemetery might learn to feel truly sad when dealing with customers, and the manager of a sporting goods store might learn to experience true joy when selling children's trophies to parents. A group of researchers conducted a study in which restaurant servers who tended to use deep acting exceeded their customer's expectations and also earned higher tips.[39]

12. Keep electronic communications professional and polite. Many customer interactions take place by phone, e-mail, and Web site interactions. These electronic interactions are as important as those conducted face-to-face. The suggestions for proper e-mail etiquette and phone interactions described in Chapter 7 apply here. Above all, avoid the same informal breeziness that you might use in electronic interaction with friends. Be sure to check with company policy if it is acceptable to address customers by their first name only, as is widely practiced today.

13. Speak to the customer in his or her preferred language, even if you can speak his or her native language. In our multicultural world, a situation arises occasionally that gets at a subtle point in being sensitive and responsive to the needs of the client. The general point is to accept the customer's desire to speak in your language, even if you know his or her native language.

Assume that you are a tax preparer who is bilingual in English and German. A client, Gunther, enters your office. He speaks to you in English with a German accent, most likely because he has chosen to work on his English and is proud of his command of his second language. Because you can speak German fluently, you insist on communicating with him in German. You might think you are pleasing Gunther by speaking German, but if Gunther continues to speak in English that means he wants to speak English while having his taxes prepared. If you continue to speak in German with Gunther, you are likely to frustrate him and lose a repeat client.

Human Relations Self-Assessment Quiz 9-4

Am I Being Rude?

Following is a list of behaviors of customer contact workers that would be interpreted as rude by many customers. Indicate whether you have engaged in such behavior in your dealings with customers or whether you are likely to do so if your job did involve customer contact.

	Yes	No
1. I talk to a coworker while serving a customer.	______	______
2. I conduct a phone conversation with someone else while serving a customer.	______	______
3. I address customers by their first names without having their permission, or knowing if such informality is company policy.	______	______
4. I address customers as "you guys."	______	______
5. I chew gum or eat candy while dealing with a customer.	______	______
6. I laugh when customers describe an agonizing problem they are having with one of our company's products or services.	______	______
7. I minimize eye contact with customers.	______	______
8. I say the same thing to every customer, such as "Have a nice day," in a monotone.	______	______
9. I accuse customers of attempting to cheat the company before carefully investigating the situation.	______	______
10. I hurry customers when my break time approaches.	______	______
11. I comment on a customer's appearance in a flirtatious, sexually oriented way.	______	______
12. I sometimes complain about or make fun of other customers when I am serving another customer.	______	______

Interpretation:

The more of these behaviors you have engaged in, the ruder you are and the more apt you are to lose potential business for your company. If you have not engaged in any of these behaviors, even when faced with a rude customer, you are an asset to your employer. You are also tolerant.

The preceding thirteen points emphasize the importance of practicing good human relations with customers and having a customer service orientation. Good customer service stems naturally from practicing good human relations.

As you deal with customers in our culturally diverse and enriched workplace, remember also to be aware of possible cross-cultural differences. Be alert to customs that could make a difference in terms of the customer feeling good about his or her experience with you. An illustrative cultural difference is that in the typical Asian family, older family members accompany younger members when a major purchase, such as a home, is being contemplated. Although the older family members may stay in the background, they might be a major financial and emotional influence on the purchase. So the eager real estate agent should not act as if the older family members are simply along for the ride. Instead, the agent should show respect by presenting vital details to all the family members, not only the couple making the purchase.

Key Terms

Work ethic, 249
Performance standard, 251
Ingratiating, 253
Bully, 254
Micromanagement, 255
Self-disclosure, 259
Team player, 261
Synergy, 262
Backstabbing, 263
Group norms, 264
Organizational culture, 264
Customer service orientation, 267

Summary and Review

Adequate interpersonal skills are necessary for success in business. Developing a favorable relationship with your manager is the most basic strategy of getting ahead in your career. Specific tactics for developing a good relationship with your manager include the following:

- Create a positive first impression.
- Achieve good job performance.
- Display a strong work ethic. (Use such means as demonstrating competence on even minor tasks, assuming personal responsibility for problems, and completing projects promptly.)
- Demonstrate good emotional intelligence. (Deal effectively with the emotional responses of coworkers and customers.)
- Be dependable and honest.
- Be a good organizational citizen. (Be willing to work for the good of the organization even without the promise of a specific reward.)
- Create a strong presence. (Keep yourself in the forefront.)
- Find out what your manager expects of you.
- Minimize complaints.
- Avoid bypassing your manager.
- Engage in favorable interactions with your manager. (At times you may have to deliver bad news.)

Coping with a manager you perceive to be a problem is part of getting along with him or her. The bully is a frequent type of problem manager. Consider the following approaches:

- Reevaluate your manager to make sure you have not misperceived him or her.
- It is important to confront your manager about your problem. Often this problem is a case of being micromanaged.
- Overrespond to the manager's pet peeves.
- Learning from your problem manager's mistakes (even if he or she gets fired) is recommended.

Methods and tactics for building coworker relationships include the following:

- Have high self-esteem and be at the center of a communication network.
- Develop allies through being civil, including maintaining a positive outlook.
- Make other people feel important.
- Maintain honest and open relationships (including self-disclosure).
- Be a team player. (Observe the nine approaches reported here.)
- Follow group standards of conduct.
- Express an interest in the work and personal life of coworkers.
- Use appropriate (nonexaggerated) compliments.
- Face maturely the challenge of the office romance.

Team player approaches include sharing credit, maintaining a cooperative attitude, establishing trust, sharing information and opinions, providing emotional support, practicing the Golden Rule, avoiding sabotaging or undermining actions, sharing the glory, and avoiding backstabbing.

Job success also requires building good relationships with customers. Techniques for providing high-level customer service include:

- Establishing customer satisfaction goals
- Understanding your customer's needs and placing them first

- Showing care and concern
- Communicating a positive attitude
- Making the buyer feel good
- Striving for the "wow" experience
- Displaying strong business ethics
- Being helpful rather than defensive when a customer complains
- Inviting the customer back
- Avoiding rudeness
- Engaging in deep acting with respect to emotions
- Keeping electronic communications professional and polite
- Speak to the customer in his or her preferred language, even if you are can speak his or her native language.

Check Your Understanding

1. If team leaders don't have as much power as a regular manager, why is it still important to build a good relationship with your team leader?
2. How can a worker implement the tactic "engage in favorable interactions with your manager" without appearing to be "kissing up" to the boss?
3. Give an example of a Facebook post or tweet a person could write to make a coworker feel important.
4. If you were referred to as an "office politician" by a coworker Tweet, to what extent would you consider that to be a compliment?
5. Provide an example of a *group standard of conduct* in any place you have worked. What led you to conclude that the particular behavior was a group standard of conduct?
6. Many customer contact workers routinely say, "Have a nice day" when the customer's transaction has been completed. How effective is this expression in building customer relationships?
7. Suppose you thought the reason that a coworker of yours was a difficult person was because he or she had a true personality disorder. Would you recommend to that person directly that he or she seek mental health treatment? Explain your reasoning.
8. Considering that consumers post a lot of crazy comments on social networking sites, why should company management be concerned about these negative posts?
9. If rudeness is so widespread today, why bother being polite and considerate on the job?
10. Ask a person who has achieved job success what he or she thinks are two important ways of getting along with coworkers and customers. Compare notes with classmates.

Web Corner

Getting along with your boss and coworkers
http://careerplanning.about.com/od/bosscoworkers/

Managing relationships with the boss
www.howtoadvice.com/BossRelations

Creating the Wow experience for customers
http://terrybrock.com/creatingwow

INTERNET SKILL BUILDER

Workplace Relationships

Visit http://careers.homedepot.com, and proceed to Our Culture, Our Values, Living Our Values. Identify which skills mentioned relate to workplace relationships, including communication skills and self-understanding. Reflect back on any time you have visited a Home Depot or a competitor's store. How realistic is Home Depot about the interpersonal and personal skills required for a sales associate? If you happen to know a Home Depot employee, obtain his or her input in formulating your answer to the preceding question.

Developing Your Human Relations Skills

Human Relations Applications Exercises

Applying Human Relations Exercise 9-1

Giving Good Customer Service

Role-players in this exercise will demonstrate two related techniques for giving good customer service: Show care and concern and make the buyer feel good. The role-players will carry out the scenarios in front of the class. For both role-plays, the provider of customer service should think through before starting the role-play what specifically he or she is attempting to accomplish. For example, the role-player might ask himself or herself, "How am I going to show care and concern?" or "What am I going to do to make the buyer feel good?"

Scenario 1: Show care and concern. A sales representative meets with two company representatives to talk about installing a new information system for employee benefits. One of the company representatives is from the human resources department and the other is from the information technology department. The sales representative will attempt to show care and concern for both company representatives during the same meeting.

Scenario 2: Make the buyer feel good. A couple, played by two role-players, enters a new-car showroom to examine a model they have seen advertised on television. Although they are not in urgent need of a new car, they are strongly interested.

Customer Service Evaluation Factors	1 VP	2 P	3 A	4 G	5 VG
1. Maintained eye contact					
2. Was warm and supportive					
3. Smiled appropriately					
4. Displayed positive attitude					
5. Showed genuine concern					
6. Made buyer feel good					
Customer Evaluation Dimensions	**1 VP**	**2 P**	**3 A**	**4 G**	**5 VG**
1. Behaved realistically					
2. Showed respect for service provider					
3. Treated provider like a professional					
4. Showed appreciation for service provider's effort.					

The sales representative is behind quota for the month and would like to close a sale today. The rep decides to use the tactic "make the buyer feel good" to help form a bond.

The rest of the class will provide some constructive feedback, and perhaps compliments, to the role-players. Use the evaluation dimensions in the table to help you evaluate the effectiveness of the customer service providers and customers. Use a scale of 1 to 5 in making your ratings: 1 = very poor, 2 = poor, 3 = average, 4 = good, and 5 = very good.

Other comments about the role-players:

Applying Human Relations Exercise 9-2

The Thirty-Second Elevator Speech

A longstanding tip in career development and impressing higher-ups is to make a thirty-second impromptu presentation when you have a chance encounter with a key person in your organization. If you work in an office tower, the chance encounter is likely to take place on an elevator—and it is generally frowned on to have long conversations in an elevator. So the term *elevator speech* developed, describing a brief opportunity to impress a key person. Imagine that you have a chance encounter with a high-ranking executive in your area on the elevator or escalator, in the parking lot, during a company picnic, or at some other location. You then give that person a thirty-second pitch geared to make a positive impression. Because you must boil your pitch down to thirty seconds, you will need to prepare for a long time. (Credit President Abraham Lincoln for that insight.)

About six different pairs (impresser and person to be impressed) will carry out this role-play in front of the class. The evaluators will put themselves in the role of the target key person of the thirty-second evaluation. Consider using the following scale and answering the two questions:

__________ Wow, I was impressed. (5 points)

__________ I was kind of impressed with the person I ran into. (4 points)

__________ He or she left me with at least an average impression. (3 points)

__________ I found the person to be somewhat annoying. (2 points)

__________ That person I met left with a terrible impression. (1 point)

1. What I liked about person's thirty-second pitch:
2. What I saw as possible areas for improvement:

Find a mechanism to feed back some of your observations to the role-players. Volunteer to present the findings in class, give the person your comments on notepaper, or send him or her an e-mail.

Human Relations Class Activity

How We Got in Good with the Boss

The purpose of this class activity is to further understand what workers have actually done to develop a positive relationship with a present or former boss. This activity would require about forty-five minutes of class time for a class of approximately thirty students. The first step is for each person to think through, and write down, an effective tactic he or she has used in developing a good relationship with a manager, past or present. Any type of work experience counts. If you have no formal work experience, perhaps the experience can be related to sports or a club. Include in your analysis how the boss reacted to the tactic.

After about four minutes of class time have been invested in thinking through the tactic-and-result scenarios, students will come up in front of the class one by one to present their findings. Presentations should be about sixty seconds. After all students have presented, have a brief class discussion centering on these points:

1. Which two tactics appear to be the most frequently mentioned?
2. Which two tactics appeared to be the most creative?
3. Which one or two tactics gave you a useful idea for the future?
4. How closely do some of the tactics conform to the suggestions for developing a relationship with the manager or team leader presented in the text?

Human Relations Class Study 9-1

Sara Struggles to Be Liked

Sara was excited about her opportunity to become a production coordinator at Tractor Co., one of the few American businesses still manufacturing and selling tractors for commercial and residential markets. She also felt a sense of patriotism to work in manufacturing because only about 8 percent of the U.S. workforce was still making products. "I know that my grandparents are proud of me, because it was manufacturing that made this country great," said Sara.

Sara reported to Kelly, the production manager for domestic riding tractors, those used by homeowners and lawn care specialists. When Sara was first interviewed by Kelly, she thought she could work well enough with Kelly, but she didn't feel much spark between the two of them. Sara reasoned that a decent working relationship is all she would need with a boss. A close friendship would therefore not be so important.

As the weeks went by, Sara was eager to learn all she needed to be an outstanding production coordinator. She found that the production technicians were super-helpful in giving her hints about some of the real problems involved in getting the line of high-quality tractors ready for shipping to dealers.

Eager for feedback on how well she was performing her responsibilities, Sara would send the occasional progress report by e-mail to Kelly. Kelly typically did not respond to Sara's e-mails, but when she did her comment was something to the effect, "Message received. Thank you."

During a department meeting to discuss plans and problems, Sara thought she could do a better job of establishing rapport with Kelly. So she asked a question that she thought would delight Kelly: "Is it really true that we are one of the highest performing departments in Tractor Co. worldwide?" Kelly shrugged her shoulders and replied, "That would be news to me."

After the meeting, Sara thought that perhaps she was not being personal enough in building a better relationship with Kelly. So the following day when she saw Kelly for the first time in the morning, Sara said, "That's a sharp outfit you're wearing. You have given me a good idea for my own wardrobe." To which Kelly replied, "Thanks."

Questions

1. Is Sara trying too hard to get along better with Kelly?
2. Is Sara too worried about establishing better rapport with Kelly?
3. What recommendations can you offer Sara to improve her relationship with Kelly?
4. What suggestions might you offer Kelly to be a more effective manager from a human relations perspective?

Human Relations Role-Playing Exercise

Sara Attempts to Build Her Relationship with Kelly

The case study about Sara and Kelly serves as the background and the story line for this role-play. One person plays the role of Sara, who has been discouraged in her attempts to build a stronger relationship with her manager, Kelly. Sara decides that today she will use two specific tactics to improve her relationship with Kelly: "demonstrate a strong work ethic," and "find out what your manager expects of you." She plans to implement these tactics today when she will be discussing a new work assignment with Kelly. Another person plays the role of Kelly, who is expecting Sara to drop by her cubicle this morning to discuss the new work assignment. The person who plays the role of Kelly can act as she does in the case or can be more skilled at human relations.

For both scenarios, observers rate the role-players on two dimensions, using a 1 to 5 scale from very poor to very good. One dimension is "effective use of human relations techniques." The second dimension is "acting ability." A few observers might voluntarily provide feedback to the role-players in terms of sharing their ratings and observations. The course instructor might also provide feedback.

Human Relations Class Study 9-2

How Far Should Tom Go to Keep His Client Happy?

Tom is a sales consultant in the wealth management group at a well-established financial services firm. He manages the financial portfolios of many high-income professionals, and also has several institutions as clients. The institutions include a few colleges, hospitals, and nonprofit agencies. These institutions purchase some of their investments through Tom's firm.

Tom is an average performer as a sales consultant, which translates into an income in the top two percent of wage earners. He is satisfied with the nature of his work as well as his income. At the moment, one of Tom's biggest challenges is to decide how much time to invest in managing one client, a large hospital. Deborah, the pension fund manager, never seems to be quite satisfied. She sends Tom an e-mail almost every day, and telephones him almost every week with a question about how well or how poorly the investments placed through his firm are doing. (Tom's firm, as with other financial services firms, places very limited information in e-mail messages.)

Tom explained to his manager the challenges he was facing with Deborah in these words: "We both agree that keeping this hospital account is important. But how high-maintenance can a client get before we set a limit to how much service we can provide? When the few mutual funds we have placed with the hospital head down in value at the same time, she wants a fifteen-minute phone call to reassure her that the funds will rebound."

"When Deborah decides that the hospital should invest more money into one of our funds, she almost insists that I take her to lunch. The problem is that these lunches wind up taking about two-and-one-half hours out of my day, travel and time in the restaurant included. Another problem is that Deborah insists on so much documentation about her investments through us. She could really find some of this documentation on financial Web sites on her own."

"What have you told Deborah so far about the amount of time she is consuming in managing her account?" asked Tom's manager.

Tom said, "I have only given her the smallest hint so far. I said that our firm valued her account, and we will do what we can to satisfy her and the hospital, but that sometimes I need a little more time to get back to her."

Questions

1. To what extent is Tom neglecting the idea that client needs come first and that his goal is to please the client?
2. Should Tom be direct with Deborah and tell her that she is consuming too much time for the amount of business the hospital is giving his firm?
3. What advice might you offer Tom to maintain a good relationship with Deborah without the relationship being too disruptive to his own work schedule?

REFERENCES

1. Original story created from facts found in the following sources: Barbara Haislip, "Make 'Em Laugh: For Entrepreneurs, the Punch Line Can Be More Sales," *The Wall Street Journal,* May 16, 2011, p. R9; "Burt Teplitzky," Professional Speakers Bureau International (www.terrificspeakers.com), accessed February 10, 2012, pp. 1-3; Christine Lagorio, "Spicing Up That Sales Pitch," posted by 7 Christine lagorio@lagorio, accessed February 13, 2012; "Burt Teplitzky—Sell It With Humor," (http://sellitwithhuymor.com), Accessed February 12, 2012, p. 1.
2. Marshall Goldsmith (with Mark Reiter), *What Go You Here Won't Get You There: How Successful People Become Even More Successful* (New York: Hyperion, 2007).
3. Quoted in Heather Huhman, "Ten Ways to Impress Your Boss During the First Week," *Entry Level Careers Examiner* (www.examiner.com), December 4, 2008, p. 1.
4. Judith Sills, "How to Improve Your Credit Rating," *Psychology Today,* March/April 2008, p. 67.
5. Quoted in Anita Bruzzese, "Get the Boss to Take Notice of You," *Gannett News Service,* April 21, 1997.
6. Kevin P. Coyne and Edward J. Coyne Sr., "Surviving Your New CEO," *Harvard Business Review,* May 2007, p. 66.
7. Erin White, "How to Keep Your Job, or Decide to Leave, if New CEO Arrives," *The Wall Street Journal,* April 24, 2007, p. B5.
8. Cecily D. Cooper, "Just Joking Around? Employee Humor Expression as Ingratiatory Behavior," *Academy of Management Review,* October 2005, pp. 765–776.
9. Robert I. Sutton, cited in Ellen Simon, "Purge Jerks at Work, Says Author," Associated Press, March 18, 2007; Spencer Morgan, "Office Bullying," *Bloomberg Businessweek,* November 1–November 7, 2010, p. 76
10. Anonymous, "How to Live with the S.O.B." *Business Week,* August 25/September 1, 2008, pp. 48–50.
11. J. Kenneth Matejka and Richard Dunsing, "Managing the Baffling Boss," *Personnel,* February 1989, p. 50.
12. "So You're Smarter Than the Boss? Yeah, Right," *Executive Leadership,* June 2000, p. 5.
13. Cited in "Ask Annie," *Fortune,* April 1, 2002, p. 171.
14. Deb Koen, "Ways to Deal with Difficult Bosses," *Democrat and Chronicle,* October 11, 2009, p. 2E.
15. Anonymous, "How to Live with the S.O.B." pp. 48–49.
16. Data and quote from Heather Huhman, "Survey: Four-in-Ten Workers Feel They Don't Fit In with Their Colleagues," Examiner.com (www.examiner.com), January 26, 2010, p. 1.
17. Janet Banks and Diane Coutu, "How to Protect Your Job in a Recession," *Harvard Business Review,* September 2008, p. 113.
18. Judith Sills, "Hanging with the In-Crowd," *Psychology Today,* November/December 2007, pp. 65–66.
19. Brent A. Scott and Timothy A. Judge, "The Popularity Contest at Work: Who Wins, Why, and What Do They Receive?" *Journal of Applied Psychology,* January 2009, pp. 20–33.
20. Cited in Donna M. Owens, "Incivility Rising: Researchers Say Workers Might Not Have the Time to Be Civil," *Human Resource Management,* February 2012, p. 33; Christine M. Pearson and Christine L. Porath, "On the Nature, Consequences and Remedies of Workplace Incivility: No Time for 'Nice'? Think Again," *Academy of Management Executive,* February 2005, pp. 7–18.
21. Jared Sandberg, "Office Minstrels Drive the Rest of Us Nuts but Are Hard to Silence," *The Wall Street Journal,* February 14, 2006, p. B1.
22. Sandy Lim, Lilia M. Cortina, and Vicki J. Magley, "Personal and Workgroup Incivility: Impact of Work and Health Outcomes,"*Journal of Applied Psychology,* January 2008, pp. 95–107.
23. Elizabeth Bernstein, "You Did What? Spare the Office the Details," *The Wall Street Journal,* April 6, 2010, p. D1.
24. Andrew C. Wicks, Shawn L. Berman, and Thomas M. Jones, "The Structure of Optimal Trust: Moral and Strategic Implications,"*Academy of Management Review,* January 1999, p. 99.
25. Sue Shellenbarger, "Workplace Deals, Sealed With a Kiss?" *The Wall Street Journal,* November 9, 2011, p. D3.
26. Kaitlin Madden, "Flirting with Romance in the Office: Cube Mates Sometimes Find Soul Mates," *CareerBuilder,* February 12, 2012.
27. Quoted in Carlin Flora, "Close Quarters: Why We Fall in Love with the One Nearby," *Psychology Today,* January/February 2004, p. 15.
28. Nina Cole, "A Workplace Romance: A Justice Analysis," *Journal of Business and Psychology,* December 2009, pp. 363–372.
29. Sue Shellenbarger, "For Office Romance, the Secret's Out," *The Wall Street Journal,* February 10, 2010, pp. D1, D2.
30. Laura Tiffany, "How Useful Are Love Contracts?" *Entrepreneur,* October 2008, p. 84.
31. Some of the ideas in the list are from Linda Thornburg, "Companies Benefit from Emphasis on Superior Customer Service,"*HR Magazine,* October 1993, pp. 46–49, 3–22; Jena McGregor, "When Service Means Survival," *Businessweek,* March 2, 2009, pp. 26–33.
32. Matthew Dixon, Karen Freeman, and Nicholas Toman, "Stop Trying to Delight Your Customers," *Harvard Business Review,* July–August 2010, pp. 116–122.
33. Scott McCartney, "Delta Sends Its 11,000 Agents to Charm School," *The Wall Street Journal,* February 3, 2011, p. D3.
34. "The Art of the Schmooze," *Managing People at Work,* Sample Issue, 2006, p. 8.
35. Lorna Doucet, "Service Provider Hostility and Service Quality," *Academy of Management Journal,* October 2004, pp. 761–771.
36. "Wow Customers with Appreciation," *Communication Briefings,* October 2011, p. 1 (Adapted from Heidi Cohen, "How to Celebrate Your Customers," (http://heidicohen.com).
37. Carmine Gallo, "Wow Your Customers the Ritz-Carlton Way," *Executive Leadership,* April 2011, p. 4.
38. Perry Garfinkel, "A Hotel's Secret: Treat Guests like Guests," *New York Times* (nytimes.com), August 23, 2008.
39. Nai-Wen Chi, Alicia A. Grandey, Jennifer A. Diamond, and Kathleen Royer Krimmel, "Want a Tip? Service Performance as a Function of Emotion Regulation and Extraversion," *Journal of Applied Psychology,* November 2011, pp. 1337–1346.

10 Managing Conflict

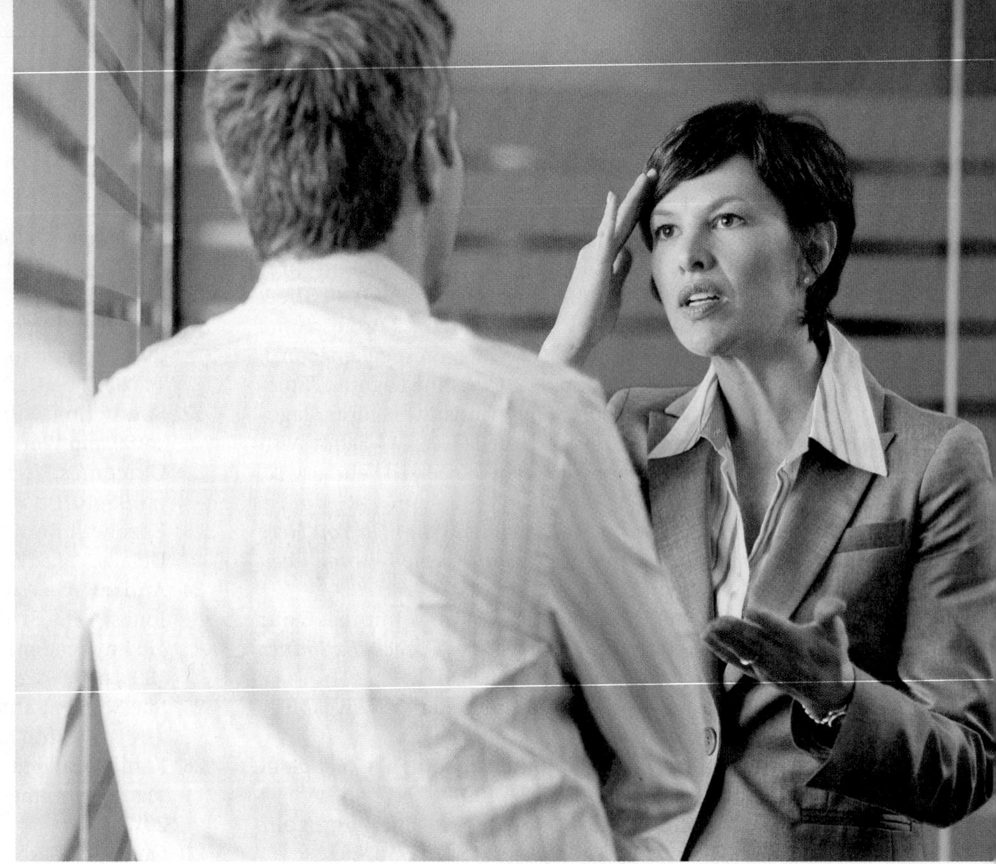

Outline

Jud, age 30, is quite happy with his job as a construction supervisor at a construction engineering firm. The work is exciting and challenging, and in Jud's opinion offers him the opportunity to contribute some value to society. In Jud's words, "When you help construct something like an apartment building, you do some good for the world."

Suddenly, the tranquility in Jud's life changed. On the positive side he and his wife, Shannon, had their first baby, Quentin. After a three-month maternity leave, Shannon returned to work as a medical secretary. Jud and Shannon took turns dropping off Quentin at the day-care center and then picking him up at night. On days Quentin was ill, the couple each took a half-day off from work or had a relative care for Quentin.

On the negative side, one day Jud was told by his manager that he would be sent on a six-month assignment to a construction site three hundred miles away. The company would pay the travel expenses for one weekend trip home per month. Jud thought, "What do I do now? This assignment will throw my home life into turmoil. The father of an infant can't work out of town. Yet, if I turn down this assignment I might either be fired or regarded as being too inflexible for a career in management with the firm."

In anguish, Jud planned to discuss his conflict with Shannon that evening.

Learning Objectives ▸

After studying the information and doing the exercises in this chapter, you should be able to:

1. Identify reasons why conflict between people takes place so often.
2. Pinpoint several helpful and harmful consequences of conflict.
3. Choose an effective method of resolving conflict.
4. Improve your assertion skills.
5. Improve your negotiating skill.
6. Pinpoint tactics for dealing effectively with difficult people.
7. Develop anger management skills.

The situation just described illustrates a reality about the workplace. Conflict takes place frequently, and being able to manage it successfully enables the workers involved to function more peacefully, and the company to get more work done. **Conflict** is a condition that exists when two sets of demands, goals, or motives are incompatible. For example, if a person wants a career in retailing yet also wants to work a predictable eight-hour day with weekends off, that person faces a conflict. He or she cannot achieve both goals. A conflict can also be considered a dispute, feud, or controversy.

Conflict
condition that exists when two sets of demands, goals, or motives are incompatible

Our approach to studying conflict includes explaining why so much conflict exists, constructive approaches to resolving conflict, dealing with difficult people, and the management of anger.

Learning Objective 1

Why Does So Much Conflict Exist?

Many reasons exist for the widespread presence of conflict in all aspects of life. All these reasons are related to the basic nature of conflict—the fact that not every person can have what he or she wants at the same time. As with other topics in this book, understanding conflict helps you develop a better understanding of why people act as they do. Here we describe nine key sources of conflict.

COMPETITION FOR LIMITED RESOURCES

A fundamental reason you might experience conflict with another person is that not everybody can get all the money, material, supplies, or human help they want. Conflict also ensues when employees are asked to compete for prizes, such as bonuses based on individual effort or company-paid vacation trips. Because the number of awards is so limited, the competition becomes intense enough to be regarded as conflict. Conflict stemming from limited resources has become prevalent as so many companies attempt to reduce expenses. Many units of the organization have to compete for the limited money available to hire new people or purchase new technology.

Another type of limited resource that leads to conflict is trade names. Several companies or individuals might believe that they have the right to use a particular trade name. Instead of being able to resolve the conflict themselves, they often resort to litigation. Imagine that a woman named Tiffany Horowitz wants to open a jewelry store called "Tiffany." Unfortunately, the lawyers for Tiffany & Co. will tell her to change the name on the storefront and Web site immediately or be sued for trademark infringement.

DIFFERENCES OF OPINION ON WORK-RELATED ISSUES AND RIGHTS

A natural source of conflict in the workplace centers on differences of opinion about work-related issues, including whose idea will work the best. One member of the design team for a luxury sports car might insist the paneling should be composed mostly of wood. Another might say that the car could get by with plastic paneling, saving the company considerable money. The two members might therefore be in conflict.

Conflict from differences of opinion can last a long time and can lead to dismissal from the employer. Sallie Krawcheck, the former head of Citigroup's wealth management unit, stepped down after months of conflict with the chief executive. One difference of opinion was that Krawcheck pushed Citigroup to reimburse clients whose investments were severely depleted. She argued that the reimbursement would be preferable to alienating highly profitable clients. Other managers resisted her position, contending that the clients should have recognized the risks associated with their investments.[1]

Conflict over rights will often take the form of one group or individual feeling that it has the right to engage in certain behavior despite a rule or custom denying that right. Smoking is forbidden in most workplaces, with some employers forbidding workers to smoke anywhere on the property—especially at a medical facility. The smokers who have to walk or drive about a half mile become quite upset with the nonsmokers who have blocked what they consider their right to smoke immediately outside of a building. A frequent conflict over custom is when some office workers believe they have the right to wear low-cut jeans and shirts that display their midriff to work, but the company officials say that such clothing is unacceptable.

INCIVILITY

In Chapter 9, incivility was described as a frequent problem in getting along with coworkers. Incivility toward work associates can also be regarded as a major contributor to workplace conflict. According to the research of Christine Porath of Georgetown University, after being a victim of workplace rudeness and hostility, two-thirds of employees said their performance declined. Four-fifths of employees indicated that they lost time worrying about the unpleasant incident, while two-thirds wasted time avoiding the offender. About one-eighth quit because of being treated uncivilly by a coworker.[2]

The relationship between incivility and conflict is twofold. First, being treated in an uncivil manner, such as being sworn at by a boss or coworker, usually leads to a dispute with that person. Second, conflict emerges because one cannot satisfy the goal of having a relatively calm workplace while at the same time being treated uncivilly. A frequently reported form of incivility leading to conflict is when one employee steals a coworker's lunch from the office refrigerator for himself or herself. The person whose lunch was stolen often goes into a rage.

PERSONALITY CLASHES AND DRAMA

Various value and personality differences among people contribute to workplace conflict. Many disagreements on the job stem from the fact that some people simply dislike each other. A **personality clash** is thus an antagonistic relationship between two people based on differences in personal attributes, preferences, interests, values, and styles. People involved in a personality clash often have difficulty specifying why they dislike each other. The end result, however, is that they cannot maintain an amiable work relationship. A strange fact about personality clashes is that people who get along well may begin to clash after working together for a number of years. Many business partnerships fold because the two partners eventually clash.

Personality clash
antagonistic relationship between two people based on differences in personal attributes, preferences, interests, values, and styles

You are probably familiar with "drama" in personal life such as the person who demands a "drama-free" relationship or says "I'm drama-free." Drama takes the form of an obstacle to what you want to attain, and often functions like a personality clash because the dramatic person does not get along with you.[3] Instead, he or she might blame you for a problem or be so preoccupied with personal problems that working smoothly with you is extremely difficult. A coworker who introduces drama might say, "I know that we are supposed to investigate these missing funds together, but I am facing a personal emergency today."

AGGRESSIVE PERSONALITIES AND WORKPLACE BULLIES

Coworkers naturally disagree about topics, issues, and ideas. Yet, some people convert disagreement into an attack that puts down other people and damages their self-esteem. As a result, conflict surfaces. **Aggressive personalities** are people who verbally and sometimes physically attack others frequently. Verbal aggression takes the form of insults, teasing, ridicule, and profanity. The aggression may also be expressed as attacks on the victim's character, competence, background, and physical appearance. When people are verbally abused, they are put on the defensive, making them feel uncomfortable.[4]

Aggressive personalities
people who verbally and sometimes physically attack others frequently

Aggressiveness can also take the extreme form of the shooting or knifing of a former boss or colleague by a mentally unstable worker recently dismissed from the company. Violence has become so widespread that homicide is currently the fourth leading cause of fatal occupational injuries in the United States, with approximately 500 workplace homicides annually.[5] Most of these deaths result from a robbery or commercial crime. Many of these killings, however, are perpetrated by a disgruntled worker or former employee harboring an unresolved conflict. As companies have continued to reduce their workforces despite being profitable, these incidents have increased in frequency.

Workplace bullying hurtful treatment of others in the workplace that malicious and typically repeated

Aggressive personalities are also referred to as *bullies.* **Workplace bullying** refers to hurtful treatment of others in the workplace that is malicious and typically repeated. Bullying includes tirades by managers as well as more subtle approaches to undermining employees, such as overloading them with responsibilities to facilitate their failing. Among their typical behaviors are interrupting others, ranting in a loud voice, and making threats. A typical attitude of a bullying boss is "My way or the highway," sending the message that the employee's suggestions are unwelcome. Bullying managers were described in Chapter 9.

During times of an economic slump, bullying and other forms of belligerent behavior tend to increase, particularly by supervisors. During the Great Recession that began in 2008 but really lingered into 2012, many employees reported that managers were increasingly using threats and intimidation tactics to cope with financial pressures. David Yamada, a law professor at Suffolk University, says that employees try to tune out abusive managers when a new position would be difficult to find.[6]

The best way to stand up to a bully, whether he or she is a boss or coworkers, is to document every incident and every detail, including who witnessed the bullying act. The documentation should then be shown to an objective authority such as the human resources manager. It is helpful for the documentation to include data about damaging effects, such as lost productivity and time from work.[7] An insurance claims specialist documented the fact that his boss kept harassing him about the clothing he wore to the office although he dressed in the same style as company managers. The specialist included in his documentation the fact that he had to visit his doctor for stress-related headaches because of the bullying.

PASSIVE-AGGRESSIVE PERSONALITIES

Passive-aggressive personality a person who appears to enthusiastically and readily respond to another person's request or demand while acting in ways that negatively and passively resist the request

Another form of aggressive behavior that contributes to job conflict is when someone creates problems by not doing something that needs to get accomplished. (Passive aggression is a deliberate and disguised way of expressing hidden anger.) A **passive aggressive personality** is a person who appears to enthusiastically and readily respond to another person's request or demand while acting in ways that negatively and passively resist the request.[8] For example, a passive-aggressive coworker might say that he will bring some key information to a meeting, yet when the meeting arrives he contends that he became too busy to gather the information. Human Relations Assessment Quiz 10-1 presents a checklist of common symptoms and behaviors of a passive-aggressive personality.

A key component of the passive-aggressiveness that creates problems in the workplace is that the person who is angry often has a pleasant exterior. His or her acts of forgetfulness and lack of follow through on assignments are driven by anger.

CULTURALLY DIVERSE TEAMS AND FACTIONAL GROUPS

Conflict often surfaces as people work in teams whose members vary in many ways. Ethnicity, religion, and gender are three of the major factors that lead to clashes in viewpoints. Differing educational backgrounds and work specialties can also lead to

Human Relations Self-Assessment Quiz 10-1

Am I Dealing with a Passive-Aggressive Personality?

At times you may be wondering why you are in so much conflict with a person who on the surface does not appear to be an angry, conflict-prone person. Your problem could be that you are dealing with a passive-aggressive personality. Carefully observe that person's behavior to look for certain telltale indictors of passive aggressiveness. Check the signs and symptoms that he or she has displayed at least several times.

1. Keeps forgetting to take care of problems ❑
2. Procrastinates on so many work-related matters ❑
3. Won't make a decision ❑
4. Says nothing when asked why a task was not completed ❑
5. Performs many tasks inefficiently ❑
6. Sulks rather than expressing anger directly ❑
7. Tends to blame other people and equipment for not getting an assignment accomplished ❑
8. Often has an excuse for not doing something important ❑
9. Makes frequent derogatory comments about coworkers and superiors when those people are not present ❑
10. Often expresses enthusiasm for an activity, but then fails to follow through ❑

Scoring and interpretation:

If the person you are evaluating receives a score of 8, 9, or 10, he or she will be a difficult person to work with, especially from the standpoint of dependability. He or she will probably be demoted or fired. In the meantime, attempt to implement some of the suggestions for dealing with difficult people presented later in this chapter.

conflict. Workers often shut out information that doesn't fit comfortably with their own beliefs, particularly if they do not like the person providing the information. When these conflicts are properly resolved, diversity lends strength to the organization because the various viewpoints make an important contribution to solving a problem. Groups that are reminded of the importance of effective communication and taught methods of conflict resolution usually can overcome the conflict stemming from mixed groups.[9]

Another form of diversity occurs when groups contain different factions, such as those representing two different companies that merged. Often the factional group consists of two subgroups, each with several representatives, such as a cost-cutting task force consisting of three representatives each from marketing, operations, and finance. The potential for conflict within factional groups increases when the subgroups differ substantially in demographic characteristics such as age, gender, and educational levels.[10]

COMPETING WORK AND FAMILY DEMANDS

Balancing the demands of work and family life is a major challenge facing workers at all levels. Yet, achieving this balance and resolving these conflicts is essential for being successful in career and personal life. The challenge of achieving balance is particularly intense for employees who are part of a two-wage-earner family. Currently, about two-thirds of women with children under age 18 work outside the home.[11] A heavy workload also intensifies the conflict because the person feels compelled to work long hours at the office, in addition to taking work home. Frequent business travel is another major contributor to work–family conflict.

Work–family conflict
conflict that occurs when an individual has to perform multiple roles: worker, spouse or partner, and often parent

Work–family conflict occurs when the individual has to perform multiple roles: worker, spouse or partner, and often parent. From the standpoint of the individual, this type of conflict can be regarded as work interfering with family life. From the standpoint of the employer, the same conflict might be regarded as family life interfering with work. Being a single parent can lead to even stronger work–family conflict when the other parent does not help manage unanticipated problems. An example would be managing the situation of a sick child not being able to attend school and refused from day care also because of the illness.

Incompatible Demands

Attempting to meet work and family demands is a frequent source of conflict because the demands are often incompatible. Imagine having to attend your child's championship soccer game and then being ordered at the last minute to attend a late-afternoon meeting. As revealed in a study with working adults, another complication of work–family conflict is that when family life interferes with work, the person will often feel guilty. Guilt will be experienced also by some people who feel that work interferes with family life.[12] Feelings of guilt arise because the person might feel that when one is being paid for doing a job, the job should have higher priority than taking care of personal issues. Or the person might feel guilty because he or she believes that family remains a higher priority than work.

The patterns of work–family conflict undergo subtle changes over time. The younger generation today expects fathers to contribute more to child care and women to contribute more to family income. Law professors Naomi Cohen and June Carbone observe that workers are becoming more flexible about gender roles and more interested in finding employers that strengthen their relationships with their children.[13]

Multitasking to Deal with the Conflict

Some people attempt to resolve their work–family conflict by doing some work at family and personal events. Watch any Little League baseball game, high school tennis match, or youth soccer match, and you will see parents at the sidelines busily engaged with their smart phones conducting work. Equally extreme is a recent trend for young people to do office work while on a date. A 36-year-old entrepreneur said that she and her date often both work by computer for a while after dinner. She insists on the right to bring along a laptop on a date.[14]

The Role of Work Group Support

The intensity of work–family conflict can sometimes be softened by a supportive work group. Other members of the work group might share experiences, offer suggestions, and perhaps even lend a hand such as taking care of a few errands for the coworker attempting to juggle work and family demands. A survey of over 2,400 faculty members was conducted at a Midwestern university, exploring how the work group might influence work–family conflict. A major finding of the study was that individuals who received high levels of social support from their work group reported lower levels of work–family conflict than those who received less social support.[15]

Cultural Differences

Cross-national differences based on culture can influence the extent to which workers experience work–family conflict. A study of 5,270 managers from twenty countries investigated how much work interfered with family life. Four clusters of countries were studied: the individualistic (Anglo) cluster versus three collectivistic (Asia, Eastern Europe, and Latin America). A collectivistic culture highly values the group. A finding was that work interfering with family life led to more dissatisfaction and intention to quit for people in individualistic than collectivistic societies. The researchers suggested that people in the collectivistic society might be more likely to remain loyal to the employer. Also, managers who value collectivism are more apt to respond to adverse conditions with greater affiliation toward coworkers.[16] A study with immigrant Latinos in the poultry-processing industry also suggested that workers with collectivistic beliefs experience less work–family conflict. For this group of Latinos, work is necessary and a vital method of ensuring family well-being.[17]

MICRO-INEQUITIES AS A SOURCE OF CONFLICT

Growing attention is being paid to snubbing, or ignoring, others as a source of conflict. A **micro-inequity** is a small, semiconscious message we send with a powerful impact on the receiver. A micro-inequity might also be considered a subtle slight. Conflict occurs because a person's feelings are hurt, and he or she feels trivialized. Two examples of workplace micro-inequities follow:

Micro-inequity
small, semiconscious message sent with a powerful impact on the receiver

- You check your messages on a phone or computer screen while a coworker is talking to you. (You are devaluing the other person's time and trivializing his or her importance.)
- A manager dismisses the first idea offered in a meeting by responding, "Okay, so who would like to get the ball rolling?" (The person who offered the idea feels like his or her suggestion is not even worth consideration and therefore has hurt feelings.)

Many companies, including IBM and Wells Fargo, offer training seminars to help managers avoid micro-inequities, including those already mentioned as well as such things as mispronouncing the names of subordinates and looking at a watch while someone else is talking.[18]

CROSS-GENERATIONAL CONFLICT

As explained in Chapter 5, differences in values across generations lead to differences in behavior. The following list presents three examples of potential work-related conflict across generations. The illustrations presented are stereotypes that apply to a *typical* member of each generation.

- **Preferred approach to communication.** Gen X members prefer to send text messages and use smart phones and IM. Gen Y members prefer e-mail, IM, and smart phones. Baby boomers prefer e-mail, cell phones, and face-to-face communication. A related source of conflict here is that older workers sometimes resent the amount of time younger workers appear to be wasting sending text messages. In some instances, however, the younger worker might be texting for a work purpose—unknown to the older worker.
- **Approach to problem solving.** Gen X members prefer to form a team to brainstorm a solution, as well as use the Internet and social networking for research. Gen Y

members prefer to think up a list of solutions on their own, then call a meeting to discuss the alternative solutions. Baby boomers like to think about what has worked in the past and how it can be replicated, then they call a meeting to discuss possible alternatives.

- **Requirement for being respected.** Gen X members want to have their ideas valued by co-workers. Gen Y members want to have their professionalism and growing knowledge valued. Baby boomers want to have their decades of work experience and input still valued.[19]

SEXUAL HARASSMENT: A SPECIAL TYPE OF CONFLICT

Sexual harassment
unwanted sexually oriented behavior in the workplace that results in discomfort or interference with the job

Many employees face conflict because they are sexually harassed by a supervisor, co-worker, or customers. **Sexual harassment** is an unwanted sexually oriented behavior in the workplace that results in discomfort or interference with the job. It can include an action as violent as rape or as subdued as telling a sexually toned joke. The word *unwanted* is important for understanding sexual harassment. When workers enjoy or welcome sexual behavior, such as joking and flirting, that behavior is not considered harassment.[20] Sexual harassment creates conflict because the harassed person has to make a choice between two incompatible motives. One motive is to get ahead, keep the job, or have an unthreatening work environment. But to satisfy this motive, the person is forced to sacrifice the motive of holding on to his or her moral values or preferences. For example, a person might say, "I want a raise, but to do this, must I submit to being fondled by my boss?" Here we focus on the types and frequency of sexual harassment and guidelines for dealing with the problem.

Types, Frequency, and Effects of Harassment

Two types of sexual harassment are legally recognized. Both are violations of the Civil Rights Acts of 1964 and 1991 and are, therefore, a violation of your rights. Union contracts also prohibit sexual harassment. In quid pro quo sexual harassment, the individual suffers loss (or threatened loss) of a job benefit as a result of his or her response to a request for sexual favors. The demands of a harasser can be blatant or implied. An implied form of quid pro quo harassment might take this form: A manager casually comments to one of his or her employees, "I've noticed that workers who become very close to me outside of the office get recommended for bigger raises."

The other form of sexual harassment is hostile-environment harassment. Another person in the workplace creates an intimidating, hostile, or offensive working environment. No tangible loss or psychological injury has to be suffered under this form of sexual harassment.

A major problem in controlling sexual harassment in the workplace is that most workers understand the meaning and nature of quid pro quo harassment but are confused about what constitutes the hostile-environment type. For example, some people might interpret the following behaviors to be harassing, whereas others would regard them as friendly initiatives: (a) calling a coworker "sweetie" and (b) saying to a subordinate, "I love your suit. You look fabulous." Judges, lawyers, and human resource specialists might also disagree on what constitutes hostile-environment harassment. Another confusing factor is that a plaintiff is likely to win a claim only if the employer failed to respond appropriately, such as counseling the perpetrator.[21]

Managers and human resource professionals are now responding to many sexual harassment claims related to sexually explicit photos sent via text messaging, a practice referred to as "sexting." In one case a Hooters waitress in Florida sued the restaurant, claiming her manager sexually harassed by sending her text messages with inappropriate photos of himself.[22]

Surveys as well as the opinions of human resource professionals suggest that somewhere between 50 and 60 percent of women are sexually harassed at least once in their careers. One study documented what has been observed in the past: Women in male-dominated organizations, such as a construction company, tend to be harassed more frequently than women in female-dominated organizations, such as a community service center. The same study found that women in male-dominated organizations who had relatively masculine personalities were sexually harassed the most. A "masculine" personality would include being highly aggressive and cold rather than warm.[23]

Aside from being an illegal and immoral act, sexual harassment has negative effects on the well-being of its victims. The negative effects of sexual harassment toward women were documented by University of Calgary psychology professors Chelsea R. Willness and Kibeom Lee and business professor Piers Steel. The researchers analyzed data from forty-one studies involving nearly 70,000 respondents. Sexual harassment experiences were associated with the negative outcomes of

- Decreased job satisfaction
- Lower commitment to the employer
- Withdrawing from work, such as being absent more frequently, escapist drinking, and a desire to quit
- Decreased productivity for both the individual and the work group
- Physical and mental health problems
- Symptoms of posttraumatic stress disorder

The negative effects in the list were more likely to occur when the climate (or culture) was more tolerant of sexual harassment.[24] For example, "flashing" women is considered to be part of the hazing ritual for recently hired women workers in certain male-dominated manufacturing settings.

Guidelines for Preventing and Dealing with Sexual Harassment

A starting point in dealing with sexual harassment is to develop an awareness of the types of behavior that are considered sexual harassment. Often the difference is subtle. Suppose, for example, you placed copies of two nudes painted by Renoir, the French painter, on a coworker's desk. Your coworker might call that harassment. Yet, if you took that same coworker to a museum to see the originals of the same nude paintings, your behavior would usually not be classified as harassment. This example illustrates that the setting of the words or behavior influences whether they are harassing. College courses in understanding and dealing with pornography often show adult (sexually explicit) films as part of the curriculum. If an accounting professor in a college of business showed the same films to accounting students, he or she would most likely be charged with sexual harassment.

Education about the meaning of sexual harassment is therefore a basic part of any company program to prevent sexual harassment. The situation and your tone of voice, as well as other nonverbal behavior, contribute to perceptions of harassment. For example, the statement "You look wonderful" might be perceived as good natured versus harassing, depending on the sender's voice tone and facial expression.

The easiest way to deal with sexual harassment is to speak up before it becomes serious. The first time it happens, respond with statements such as, "I won't tolerate that kind of talk," "I dislike sexually oriented jokes," or "Keep your hands off me." Write the harasser a stern letter shortly after the first incident. Confronting the harasser in writing dramatizes your seriousness of purpose in not wanting to be sexually harassed. If the problem persists, say something to the effect of, "You're practicing sexual harassment. If you don't stop, I'm going to exercise my right to report you to management."

Don't leave any room for doubt that the behavior or words you heard were unwelcome. Recurring incidents should be reported to the immediate manager, a higher-level manager, or a human resources official. When the harasser is the manager, of course, reporting the incident to him or her is ineffective. In the typical situation, the employer will keep the information it gathers as confidential as possible, consistent with state, provincial, and federal laws. Both the accused and the complainant will have a chance to present the case.

Whether you are the accused employee, the complaining one, or a potential witness, confidentiality is crucial in dealing with accusations of harassment. Two people have their reputations on the line, and you may not have all the facts.

A recommended approach to dealing with continuing harassment from the same person or persons is to maintain a dated log of the incidents. If the incidents are severe, such as unwanted groping or hugs, a copy of the log might be sent to a high-level manager in the company and a human resources professional. The principle here is that any type of documentation is better than none when dealing with a workplace issue of legal consequences.

Guidelines for Dealing with False Accusations of Sexual Harassment

Many workers, especially men, will be falsely charged with sexual harassment for such reasons as revenge related to another issue, a desire to get attention, or a misunderstanding of what constitutes sexual harassment. Next in frequency of false accusations of sexual harassment by women against men are false accusations by men against men. A remote third category is men falsely accusing women of harassment.

A strategy for a man defending against false accusations of sexual harassment is to establish the reputation of never engaging in sexual harassment. Among the possibilities here are (a) open no pornographic Web sites at work, (b) never touch women or men in the workplace except for a handshake, fist-bump or an occasional sideways hug in a group setting, (c) do not confer with a woman (or perhaps a man) face-to-face unless the door is open to an office or cubicle, and (d) don't make sexually toned comments or tell sexually oriented jokes.

When falsely charged of sexual harassment, the person should present a detailed account of his or her side of the story and point out that false accusations can be considered libel. The testimony of any witness to the alleged incident would also be helpful.

Learning Objective 2

What Are the Good and Bad Sides of Conflict?

Conflict over significant issues is a source of stress. We usually do not suffer stress over minor conflicts such as having to choose between wearing one sweater or another. Like stress in general, we need an optimum amount of conflict to keep us mentally and physically energetic. Handled properly, moderate doses of conflict can be beneficial. Some of the benefits that might arise from conflict can be summarized around the following key points. Figure 10-1 outlines the positive as well as the negative consequences of conflict.

1. Talents and abilities may emerge in response to conflict. When faced with a conflict, people often become more creative than they are in a tranquil situation. Assume that your employer told you that it would no longer pay for your advanced education unless you used the courses to improve your job performance. You would probably find

Interpersonal Conflict

Positive Consequences

- Talents and abilities emerge
- Need satisfaction leads to good feelings
- Unity after conflict
- Prevents premature agreement and poor decisions

Negative Consequences

- Poor well-being
- Wasted time and energy
- Financial and emotional costs
- Fatigue
- Self-interest dominates
- Workplace violence

FIGURE 10-1

THE GOOD AND BAD SIDES OF CONFLICT

Conflict between people and groups can have both positive and negative consequences.

ways to accomplish such an end. The late Steve Jobs of Apple Inc. was well-known for his tirades against engineers and designers when he disliked a product feature or product they suggested. As a result, the recipients of the tirade often came back with an improved product or product feature.

2. **Conflict can help you feel better because it satisfies a number of psychological needs.** By nature, many people like a good fight. As a socially acceptable substitute for attacking others, you might be content to argue over a dispute on the job or at home.

3. **As an aftermath of conflict, the parties in conflict may become united.** Two battling supervisors may become more cooperative toward each other in the aftermath of confrontation. A possible explanation is that the shared experience of being in conflict with each other *sometimes* brings the parties closer.

4. **Conflict helps prevent people in the organization from agreeing too readily with each other, thus making some very poor decisions.** Groupthink is the situation that occurs when group members strive so hard to get along that they fail to critically evaluate each other's ideas.

Despite the positive picture of conflict just painted, it can also have detrimental consequences to the individual, the organization, and society. These harmful consequences of conflict make it important for people to learn how to resolve conflict:

1. **Prolonged conflict can be detrimental to some people's emotional and physical well-being.** As a type of stress, prolonged conflict can lead to such problems as heart disease and chronic intestinal disorders. In one consultant firm, a woman age 52 suffered a stroke after prolonged work–family conflict. She struggled to balance long, intense working hours and the demands of two adolescent children.

2. **Relationships damaged by conflict can have consequences that impede individual, group, and organizational performance.** When coworkers have a falling out, the repercussions for the people in conflict as well as coworkers can include emotional strain, poor listening, reduced information processing, distraction from work tasks, and a lowering of commitment and satisfaction. As a result, performance suffers for the individual, group, and organization.[25]

3. People in conflict with each other often waste time and energy that could be put to useful purposes. Instead of fighting all evening with your roommate, the two of you might fix up your place. Instead of writing angry e-mail messages back and forth, two department heads might better invest that time in thinking up ideas to save the company money.

4. The aftermath of extreme conflict may have high financial and emotional costs. Sabotage—such as ruining machinery or destroying a company database—might be the financial consequence. At the same time, management may develop a permanent distrust of many people in the workforce, although only a few of them are saboteurs.

5. Too much conflict is fatiguing, even if it does not cause symptoms of emotional illness. People who work in high-conflict jobs often feel spent when they return home from work. When the battle-worn individual has limited energy left over for family responsibilities, the result is more conflict. (For instance, "What do you mean you are too tired to visit friends?" or "If your job is killing your interest in having friends, find another job.")

6. People in conflict will often be much more concerned with their own interests than with the good of the family, organization, or society. An employee in the shipping department who is in conflict with his supervisor might neglect to ship an order. And a gang in conflict with another might leave a park or beach strewn with broken glass.

"The credit crunch, bad economy, layoffs and mortgage crisis are contributing to severe stress and causing people to act out violently."
W. Barry Nixon, workplace violence consultant, quoted in Juliette Fairley, "Tasking Control of Anger Management," *Workforce Management*, October 2010, p. 10.

7. Workplace violence erupts, including the killing of managers, previous managers, coworkers, customers, as well as spouses and partners. Intense conflict can release anger, leading to aggressive behavior and violence. (As described earlier, an aggressive personality can lead to workplace violence.) Disgruntled employees, such as those recently fired, may attempt revenge by assassinating work associates. People involved in an unresolved domestic dispute sometimes storm into the partner's workplace to physically attack him or her. Unresolved conflict and frustration from financial, marital, or other domestic problems increase the odds of a person "going ballistic" at work.

Learning Objective 3

What Are Some Techniques for Resolving Conflicts?

Because of the inevitability of conflict, a successful and happy person must learn effective ways of resolving conflict. An important general consideration is to face conflict rather than letting conflict slide or smoothing over it. Ignoring or smoothing over conflict does little to resolve the real causes of conflict and seldom leads to an effective long-term solution. Here we concentrate on methods of conflict resolution that you can use on your own. Most of them emphasize a collaborative or win-win philosophy. Effective collaboration is regarded as vital to company success, in resolving conflict and other areas as well.[26] Several of the negotiating and bargaining tactics described may be close to the competitive orientation. Human Relations Self-Assessment Quiz 10-2 gives you the opportunity to think through your style of managing conflict.

BEING ASSERTIVE

Several of the techniques for resolving conflict described here require assertiveness. Learning to express your feelings to make your demands known is also an important aspect of becoming an effective individual in general. Expressing your feelings helps you establish good relationships with people. If you aren't sharing your feelings and attitudes with other people, you will never get close to them. Here we examine the nature of assertiveness and then describe several techniques for building assertiveness.

Human Relations Self-Assessment Quiz 10-2

Collaborative versus Competitive Styles of Conflict Management

Answer on a 1 to 5 scale how well you agree with each of the following statements: disagree strongly, disagree, neutral, agree, and agree strongly.

	Disagree Strongly	Disagree	Neutral	Agree	Agree Strongly
1. I like to see the other side squirm when I resolve a dispute.	5	4	3	2	1
2. Winning is everything when it comes to settling conflict.	5	4	3	2	1
3. After I have successfully negotiated a price, I like to see the seller smile.	1	2	3	4	5
4. I have a "smash-mouth" attitude toward resolving conflict.	5	4	3	2	1
5. In most conflict situations, one side is clearly right, and the other side is clearly wrong.	5	4	3	2	1
6. I think there are effective alternatives to strikes for settling union versus management disputes.	1	2	3	4	5
7. The winner should take all.	5	4	3	2	1
8. Conflict on the job is like a prize fight: The idea is to knock out the opponent.	5	4	3	2	1
9. I like the idea of tournaments in which first-round losers receive another opportunity to play.	1	2	3	4	5
10. Nice guys and gals usually finish first.	1	2	3	4	5

Scoring and Interpretation:

Add the point value of your scores to obtain your total. Scores of 40 and higher suggest that you prefer a *collaborative*, or *win–win*, approach to resolving conflict. You tend to be concerned about finding long-term solutions to conflict that will provide benefits to both sides. Scores of 39 and lower suggest that you prefer a *competitive* approach to resolving conflict. You want to maximize gain for yourself, with little concern about the welfare of the other side. In an organization that emphasizes collaboration, this approach to conflict resolution may not be welcome.

Assertive, Nonassertive, and Aggressive Behavior

As implied previously, **assertive people** state clearly what they want or how they feel in a given situation without being abusive, abrasive, or obnoxious. People who are assertive are open, honest, and up front because they believe that all people have an equal right to express themselves honestly. Assertive behavior can be understood more fully by comparing it to that shown by two other types of people. **Nonassertive people** let things happen to them without letting their feelings be known. They also prefer to avoid conflict. **Aggressive people** are obnoxious and overbearing. They push for what they want with almost no regard for the feelings of others, and are likely to create conflict.

Another representative assertive behavior is to ask for clarification rather than contradicting a person with whom you disagree. The assertive person asks for clarification when another person says something irritating, rather than hurling insults or telling the other person he or she is wrong. For example, assume someone says to you, "Your proposal is useless." Aggressively telling the person, "You have no right to make that judgment," shuts out any possible useful dialogue. You will probably learn more if you ask for clarification, such as "What is wrong with my proposal?"

Assertive
characteristic of people who state clearly what they want or how they feel in a given situation without being abusive, abrasive, or obnoxious; open, honest, and up-front people who believe that all people have an equal right to express themselves honestly

Nonassertive
characteristic of people who let things happen to them without letting their feelings be known

Aggressive
characteristic of people who are obnoxious and overbearing; they push for what they want with almost no regard for the feelings of others

FIGURE 10-2 ASSERTIVE, NONASSERTIVE, AND AGGRESSIVE GESTURES

Assertive	Nonassertive	Aggressive
Well balanced	Covering mouth with hand	Pounding fists
Straight posture	Excessive head nodding	Stiff and rigid posture
Hand gestures, emphasizing key words	Tinkering with clothing or jewelry	Finger waving or pointing
	Constant shifting of weight	Shaking head as if other person isn't to be believed
	Scratching or rubbing head or other parts of the body	
Moderately loud voice	Wooden body posture	Hands on hips
	Voice too soft with frequent pauses	Voice louder than needed, fast speech

Gestures as well as words can communicate whether the person is being assertive, nonassertive, or aggressive. Figure 10-2 illustrates these differences.

Becoming More Assertive and Less Shy

Shyness, or not being assertive, is widespread, and about 50 percent of the U.S. population is shyer than they want to be. The personality trait of shyness has positive aspects, such as leading a person to think more deeply and become involved in ideas and things. (Where would the world be today if Larry Page, the cofounder of Google, weren't shy as a youth?) But shyness can also create discomfort and lower self-esteem.[27]

An important distinction must be drawn between shyness and introversion. An introverted person, one who enjoys solitude and quiet reflection, is not necessarily shy. Shyness involves anxiety characterized by inhibited behavior and a fear of being judged in social situations. A shy person will avoid social situations out of fear, whereas an introvert will avoid social situations out of preference.[28]

There are a number of everyday actions a person can take to overcome being nonassertive or shy. Even if the actions described here do not elevate your assertiveness, they will not backfire and cause you discomfort. The suggestions for developing self-confidence presented in Chapter 2 are also relevant for overcoming shyness because part of being shy is not having adequate confidence in oneself. After reading the following five techniques, you might be able to think of others that will work for you.[29]

1. **Set a goal.** Clearly establish in your mind how you want to behave differently. Do you want to speak out more in meetings? Be able to express dissatisfaction to coworkers? You can overcome shyness only by behaving differently; feeling differently is not enough.

2. **Appear warm and friendly.** Shy people often communicate to others through their body language that they are not interested in reaching out to others. To overcome this impression, smile, lean forward, uncross your arms and legs, and unfold your hands.

3. **Conduct anonymous conversations.** Try starting a conversation with strangers in a safe setting, such as a sporting event, the waiting room of a medical office, at an airport, or a waiting line at the post office or supermarket. Begin the conversation with the common experience you are sharing at the time. Among them might be these:

"How many people do you estimate are in the audience?"

"How long does it usually take before you get to see the doctor?"

"What is your prediction about our plane arriving on time?"

"Where did you get that shopping bag? I've never seen one so sturdy before."

4. Greet strangers. For the next week or so, greet many of the people you pass. Smile and make a neutral comment such as "How ya doing?" or "Great day, isn't it?" Because most people are unaccustomed to being greeted by a stranger, you may get a few quizzical looks. Many other people may smile and return your greeting. A few of these greetings may turn into conversations. A few conversations may even turn into friendships. Even if the return on your investment in greetings is only a few pleasant responses, it will boost your confidence.

5. Practice being decisive. An assertive person is usually decisive, so it is important to practice being decisive. Some nonassertive people are even indecisive when asked to make a choice from a restaurant menu. They communicate their indecisiveness by asking their friend, "What are you going to have?" or asking the server, "Could you please suggest something for me?" or "What's good?" Practice quickly sizing up the alternatives in any situation and reaching a decision. This will help you be assertive and also project an image of assertiveness.

CONFRONTATION AND PROBLEM SOLVING LEADING TO WIN–WIN

The most highly recommended way of resolving conflict is **confrontation and problem solving**. It is a method of identifying the true source of conflict and resolving it systematically. The confrontation in this approach is gentle and tactful rather than combative and abusive. It is best to wait until your anger cools down before confronting the other person to avoid being unreasonable. Reasonableness is important because the person who takes the initiative in resolving the conflict wants to maintain a harmonious working relationship with the other party. Also, both parties should benefit from the resolution of the conflict.

Confrontation and problem solving
the most highly recommended way of resolving conflict; method of identifying the true source of conflict and resolving it systematically

Win–Win Conflict Resolution

Assume that Jason, the person working at the desk next to you, whistles loudly while he works. You find the whistling to be distracting and annoying; you think Jason is a noise polluter. If you don't bring the problem to Jason's attention, it will probably grow in proportion with time. Yet, you are hesitant to enter into an argument about something a person might regard as a civil liberty (the right to whistle in a public place). An effective alternative is for you to approach Jason directly in this manner:

You: Jason, may I talk to you about a little problem that is bugging me?

Jason: Go ahead. I don't mind listening to a problem.

You: My problem is that when you whistle it distracts me and grates on my nerves. It may be my problem, but the whistling does bother me.

Jason: I guess I could stop whistling when you're working next to me. It's probably simply a nervous habit.

An important advantage of confrontation and problem solving is that you deal directly with a sensitive problem without jeopardizing the chances of forming a constructive working relationship in the future. One reason that the method works so effectively is that the focus is on the problem at hand and not on the individual's personality.

The intent of confrontation and problem solving is to arrive at a collaborative solution to the conflict. The collaborative style reflects a desire to fully satisfy the desires of both parties. It is based on an underlying philosophy of **win–win,** the belief that after conflict has been resolved, both sides should gain something of value. The user of

Win–win
belief that after conflict has been resolved both sides should gain something of value

win–win approaches is genuinely concerned about arriving at a settlement that meets the needs of both parties or at least that does not badly damage the welfare of the other side. When collaborative approaches to resolving conflict are used, the relationships among the parties are built on and improved.

Here is an example of a win–win approach to resolving conflict. A manager granted an employee a few hours off on an occasional Friday afternoon because she was willing to be on call for emergency work on an occasional weekend. Both parties were satisfied with the outcome, and both accomplished their goals.

Another way of achieving win–win solutions to conflict is to address conflict productivity. Be prepared to discuss your differences with another person by completing statements such as the following:[30]

"What I would like to change about the current situation is . . ."

"What I am willing to do to bring about that change is . . ."

"The one issue I cannot give in on is . . ."

Following the win–win mindset, these three phrases reflect a willingness to work on the problem together. Even the nonnegotiable point about not giving in is expressed positively.

Win–Lose Conflict Resolution

The opposite approach to win–win conflict resolution is *win–lose,* in which one side attempts to maximize gain at the expense of the other side. Win–lose is also referred to as a *zero-sum game,* in which one side wins nothing and the other side wins everything. Many people believe that win–lose is the best approach to resolving conflict—and that is one reason so much conflict goes unresolved in the form of physical attacks on people and bankruptcies. A person with a competitive orientation is likely to engage in power struggles in which one side wins and the other loses. "My way or the highway" is a win–lose strategy. An extreme example of a win–lose strategy would be to bad-mouth a rival so he or she gets fired.

If faced with an adversary who has a win–lose orientation, a plausible defense is to keep on pointing out the benefits of finding a solution that fits both sides. A sales representative for a company that makes steel buildings (often used for warehousing) was about to be laid off because of poor business. He proposed to his boss, "Please give me one more chance. Give me just enough salary to pay my rent and feed our newborn child. All the rest of my income will come from commissions on the sales I make." The owner conceded, and the sales rep did earn his way, so a win–lose situation emerged into a win–win.

DISARM THE OPPOSITION

When in conflict, your criticizer may be armed with valid negative criticism of you. The criticizer is figuratively clobbering you with knowledge of what you did wrong. If you deny that you have made a mistake, the criticism intensifies. A simple technique has been developed to help you deal with this type of manipulative criticism. **Disarming the opposition** is a method of conflict resolution in which you disarm the criticizer by agreeing with his or her criticism of you. The technique assumes that you have done something wrong. Disarming the opposition generally works more effectively than counterattacking a person with whom you are in conflict.

Disarming the opposition method of conflict resolution in which you disarm the criticizer by agreeing with his or her criticism

Another reason disarming the opposition is effective is that it implies you are apologizing for a mistake or an error you have made. An apology often gets the other person on your side, or at least softens the animosity. By offering an apology and regretting your mistake, you are likely to gain sympathy from the person who disapproves of what you have done or who you have wronged.

Agreeing with criticism made of you by a manager or team leader is effective because, by so doing, you are in a position to ask that manager's help in improving your performance. Most managers and team leaders recognize that it is their responsibility to help employees overcome problems, not merely to criticize them. Imagine that you have been chronically late in submitting reports during the past six months. It is time for a performance review and you know you will be reprimanded for your tardiness. You also hope that your boss will not downgrade all other aspects of your performance because of your tardy reports. Here is how disarming the situation would work in this situation:

Your boss: Have a seat. It's time for your performance review, and we have a lot to talk about. I'm concerned about some things.

You: So am I. It appears that I'm having a difficult time getting my reports in on time. I wonder if I'm being a perfectionist. Do you have any suggestions?

Your boss: I like your attitude. I think you can improve on getting your reports in on time. Maybe you are trying to make your reports perfect before you turn them in. Try not to figure out everything to four decimal places. We need thoroughness around here, but we don't want to overdo it.

REFRAMING (INCLUDING COGNITIVE RESTRUCTURING AND ASKING QUESTIONS)

Another useful approach to resolving conflict is to reexamine or *reframe* the conflict situation by looking at in a different light. What follows are two practical approaches to reframing, one by searching for the positives in the situation and the other by asking questions.

Reframing through Cognitive Restructuring

An indirect way of resolving interpersonal conflict is to lessen the conflicting elements in a situation by viewing them more positively. According to the technique of **cognitive restructuring** you mentally convert negative aspects into positive ones by looking for the positive elements in a situation. How you frame or choose your thoughts can determine the outcome of a conflict situation. Your thoughts influence your actions. If you search for the beneficial elements in the situation, there will be less area for dispute. Although this technique might sound like a mind game to you, it can work effectively.

Cognitive restructuring
technique of mentally converting negative aspects into positive ones by looking for the positive elements in a situation

Imagine that a coworker of yours, Ted, has been asking you repeated questions about how to carry out a work procedure. You are about ready to tell Ted, "Go bother somebody else; I'm not paid to be a trainer." Instead, you look for the positive elements in the situation. You say to yourself, "Ted has been asking me a lot of questions. This does take time, but answering these questions is valuable experience. If I want to become a manager, I'll have to help group members with problems."

After having completed this cognitive restructuring, you can then deal with the conflict situation more positively. You might say to Ted, "I welcome the opportunity to help you, but we need to find a mutually convenient time. In that way, I can better concentrate on my own work." To get started with cognitive restructuring, do Applying Human Relations Exercise 10-1 at the end of the chapter.

Reframing by Asking Questions

Another way to use reframing is to step back, take a deep breath, and then ask all or some of the following questions about the conflict situation arising within the work group:

- Do I fully understand the situation?
- Am I sure what my coworker is really saying?
- Is the person really angry at me or just worried and anxious?
- Have I missed something important?
- Do I have all the facts?
- What is the real issue here?
- How do I want to react in this situation?
- How would I want to be treated if the situation were reversed?

By taking such an approach, you are more likely to communicate effectively and constructively with coworkers when conflict situations arise. You carefully talk through the issues rather than becoming explosive, defensive, and argumentative. A useful scenario for reframing through questioning would be when a coworker accuses you of not carrying your fair share of the workload.[31]

APPEAL TO A THIRD PARTY

Now and then you may be placed in a conflict situation in which the other party either holds most of the power or simply won't budge. Perhaps you have tried techniques such as confrontation and problem solving or disarming the opposition, yet you cannot resolve your conflict. In these situations you may have to enlist the help of a third party with power—more power than you or your adversary has. Among such third parties is your common boss, union stewards, or human resource managers. Filing a lawsuit against your adversary is another application of the third-party technique, such as filing an age-discrimination charge.

In some situations, simply implying that you will bring in a third party to help resolve the conflict situation is sufficient for you to gain advantage. One woman felt she was repeatedly passed over for promotion because of her sex. She hinted that if she were not given fairer consideration, she would speak to the Equal Employment Opportunity Commission (EEOC). She was given a small promotion shortly thereafter. Many conflicts about sexual harassment, as well as ethnic and racial harassment, are resolved through third-party appeal.

THE GRIEVANCE PROCEDURE

Grievance procedure
formal process of filing a complaint and resolving a dispute within an organization

The formal process of filing a complaint and resolving a dispute within an organization is the **grievance procedure**. It can also be regarded as a formal (officially sanctioned) method of resolving conflict, in which a series of third parties are brought into the picture. The third-party appeal described previously skips the step-by-step approach of a formal grievance procedure. In a unionized firm, the steps in the grievance procedure are specified in the written contract between management and labor. The grievance procedure is a key part of a labor agreement because one of the union's goals is to obtain

FIGURE 10-3 THE GRIEVANCE PROCEDURE

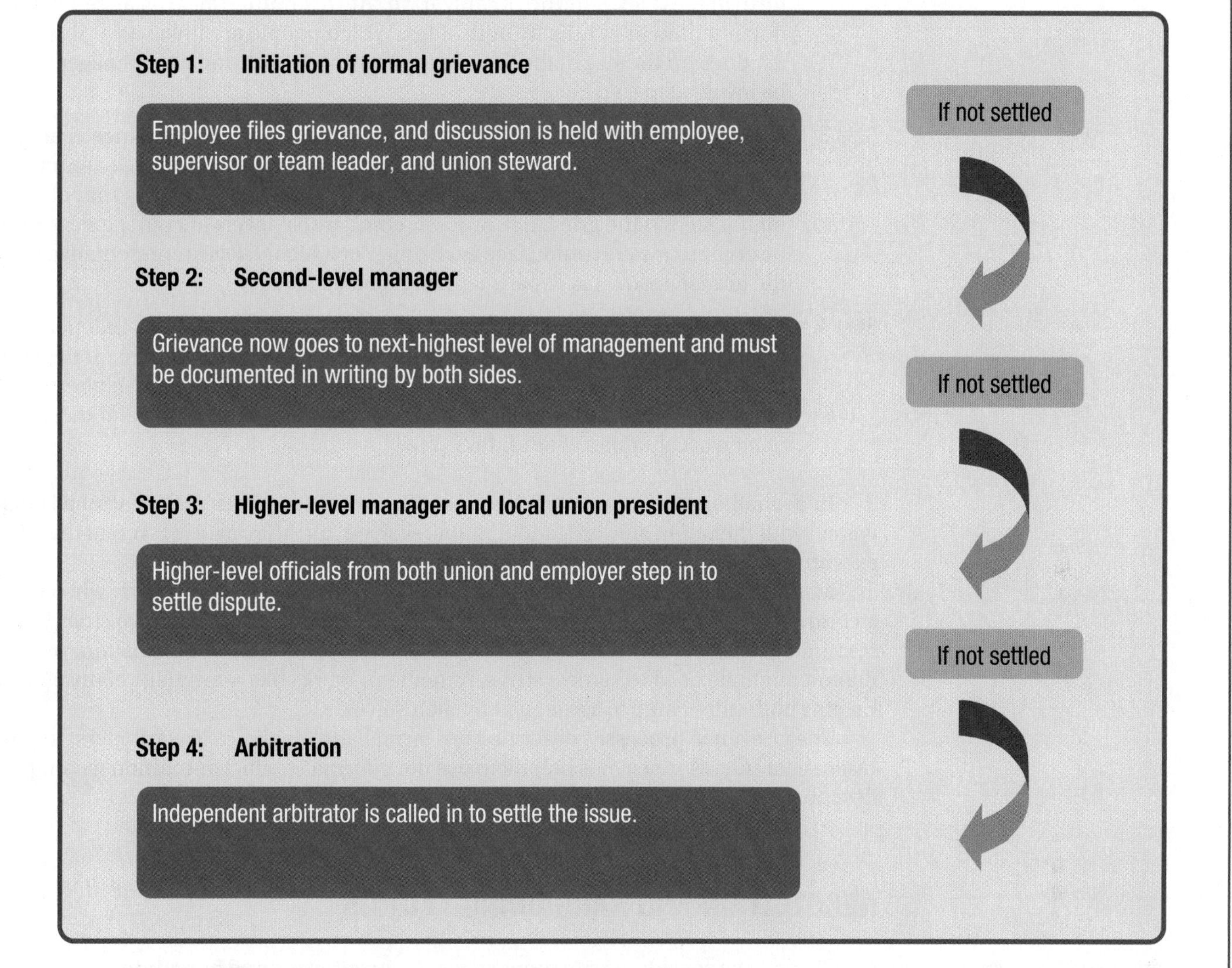

fair treatment for union members. An example of a grievance about favoritism would be, "I get the worst assignments because I'm not one of the boss's fishing buddies." An example of a grievance about discrimination would be, "I didn't get the transfer to the receptionist job because I'm fifty-five years old."

Step 1: Initiation of formal grievance
Employee files grievance, and discussion is held with employee, supervisor or team leader, and union steward.
If not settled
Step 2: Second-level manager
Grievance now goes to next-highest level of management and must be documented in writing by both sides.
If not settled
Step 3: Higher-level manager and local union president
Higher-level officials from both union and employer step in to settle dispute.
If not settled
Step 4: Arbitration
Independent arbitrator is called in to settle the issue.

The steps in the grievance procedure may vary from one to six, depending on the labor agreement or company procedures. A summary of four typical steps in a grievance procedure is presented next and outlined in Figure 10-3. If the company does not have a labor union, a specialist from the human resources department might serve as a third party.

Step 1 **Initiation of the formal grievance.** Suppose that an employee feels that he or she has been treated unfairly or that his or her rights have been violated in some way. The employee then files a grievance with the supervisor (or team leader). Most grievances end at step 1 by conversation among the employee, union steward, and the supervisor. At this stage, it makes sense to use some of the techniques for resolving conflict already described. (If the workforce is not represented by a union, another type of grievance procedure might be used.)

Step 2 **Second level of management.** If the steward, supervisor or team leader, and employee cannot reach a satisfactory solution to the conflict, it goes to the next-highest level in the organization. At this point, the grievance must be documented in writing by both sides. Which people are involved at this level depends on the size of the firm. In a small firm, a high-ranking manager might be involved in step 2.

Step 3 **A higher-level manager and the local union president.** If the grievance is not resolved at step 2, higher-level officials from both the union and the employer become involved in settling the dispute. A general principle is that at each higher step in the grievance process, comparable levels of management from both company and union face each other, or a higher-level representative from the human resources department might be involved.

Step 4 **Arbitration.** If the grievance cannot be settled at lower steps, an independent arbitrator may be called in to settle the issue. Only about 1 percent of grievances go all the way to arbitration. Arbitration is often used as an alternative to a strike. The arbitrator has the authority to settle the dispute and must be a person acceptable to both sides.

In a small organization, step 2 is sometimes omitted. After the grievance is discussed with the union steward, and it is not resolved, the grievance is taken to the chief executive or business owner, and then to arbitration if necessary.[32]

Mediation is often confused with arbitration. A mediator is a third party who enters a controversy but holds no power of decision. The mediator helps the two sides find a resolution to their conflict. Relatively few labor agreements allow for mediation, yet mediation might be used to settle a strike. A mediator works like a marriage counselor by helping both sides come to agreement by themselves.

The grievance processes described are formal and legalistic. Nevertheless, to represent your interests well, it is helpful to use the informal conflict-resolution techniques described earlier, such as confrontation and problem solving.

NEGOTIATION AND BARGAINING TACTICS

Negotiating and bargaining situation of conferring with another person to resolve a problem

Conflicts can be considered situations calling for **negotiating and bargaining,** conferring with another person to resolve a problem. When you are trying to negotiate a fair price for an automobile, you are also trying to resolve a conflict. At first the demands of both parties seem incompatible. After haggling for a while, you will probably reach a price that is satisfactory to both sides. Negotiation has many applications in the workplace, including buying, selling, arriving at a starting salary or raise, and deciding on a fair compensation for a contract worker. Negotiation may also take place with coworkers when you need their assistance. For example, you might need to strike a bargain with a coworker to handle some of your responsibilities if you are faced with a temporary overload.

A sampling of negotiating tactics to help you resolve conflict is presented next. As with other techniques of resolving conflict already presented, choose those that best fit your style and the situation. Many people feel awkward at the prospects of negotiating with a stranger, yet by learning and practicing new skills most people can become better negotiators.

Create a Positive Negotiating Climate

Negotiation proceeds much more swiftly if a positive tone surrounds the session, so it is helpful to initiate a positive outlook about the negotiation meeting. A good opening line in a negotiating session is, "Thanks for fitting this meeting into your hectic schedule." Nonverbal communication such as smiling and making friendly gestures helps create a positive climate. A calm voice helps build the trust necessary for creating a positive climate.

In negotiating with coworkers for assistance, a positive climate can often be achieved by phrasing demands as a request for help. Most people will be more accommodating if you say to them, "I have a problem, and I wonder if you could help me with it." The problem might be that you need the person's time and mental energy. By giving that person a choice of offering you help, you have established a much more positive climate than by demanding assistance.

Another way of creating a positive negotiating climate is to validate the other side's position by describing his or her position in your own words (a form of paraphrasing). Make a positive comment to the other person that emphasizes the value in the relationship.[33] Assume that you are renting a condominium, and the owner wants to raise the rent 10 percent for next year. You might state, "I recognize that your costs are rising. You are also a great landlord. But 10 percent more rent is a little beyond my budget."

Listen First to Investigate What the Other Side Wants

Listening skills are also part of effectiveness in negotiation. Negotiation professional Bobby Covie says, "There's a saying among negotiators that whoever talks the most during a negotiation loses." Being the first to listen helps establish trust. Listening also involves paying attention to what the other side is saying.[34] A person might begin a negotiating session claiming to want a bigger share of the division budget. Yet, careful listening might indicate that he really is looking for his department to receive more respect and attention. So the issue is not financial.

As shown in the example just presented, listening helps you dig for information as to why the other side wants what it does.[35] If the other side wants a bigger budget just to have more respect, there are less expensive ways to grant respect than granting a bigger share of the budget. Perhaps the manager can give the person a classier job title, rename the department, or appoint the person to head a task force. For example, the head of marketing is renamed "chief of brands," and her department "brand development."

Allow Room for Compromise, but Be Reasonable

The basic strategy of negotiation is to begin with a demand that allows room for compromise and concession. Anyone who has ever negotiated the price of an automobile, house, or used furniture recognizes this vital strategy. If you are a buyer, begin with a low bid. (You say, "I'll give you $160 for that painting" when you are prepared to pay $190.) If you are the seller, begin with a high demand. (You say, "You can have this painting for $230" when you are ready to sell it for as low as $150.) As negotiations proceed, the two of you will probably arrive at a mutually satisfactory price. This negotiating strategy can also be used for such purposes as obtaining a higher starting salary or purchasing excess inventory.

Common sense, and perhaps greed, propels many negotiators to allow *too much* room for compromise. They begin negotiations by asking way beyond what they expect to receive or offering far less than they expect to give. As a result of these implausible demands, the other side may become hostile, antagonistic, or walk away from the negotiations. Beginning with a plausible demand or offer is also important because it contributes to a positive negotiating climate.

Focus on Interests, Not Positions

Rather than clinging to specific negotiating points, keep your overall interests in mind and try to satisfy them. A negotiating point might be a certain amount of money or a concession that you must have. Remember that the true object of negotiation is to satisfy the underlying interests of both sides. Among the interests you and the other side might be trying to protect are money, lifestyle, power, and the status quo. For example, instead of negotiating for a particular starting salary, your true interests might be to afford a certain lifestyle. If the company pays all your medical and dental coverage, you can get by with a lower salary. Or your cost of living might be much lower in one city than in another. Therefore, you can accept a lower starting salary in the city with a lower cost of living.

Make a Last and Final Offer

In many circumstances, presenting a final offer will break a deadlock. You might frame your message something like this: "All I can possibly pay for your guitar is $250. You have my number. Call me when it is available at that price." Sometimes the strategy will be countered by a last and final offer from the other side: "Thanks for your interest. My absolute minimum price for this guitar is $300. Call us if that should seem okay to you." One of you will probably give in and accept the other person's last and final offer.

Role-Play to Predict What the Other Side Will Do

An advanced negotiating technique is to prepare in advance by forecasting what the other side will demand or offer. Two marketing professors from New Zealand, J. Scott Armstrong and Kesten Green, have discovered that when people role-play conflicts, their ability to predict outcomes jumps remarkably. The researchers presented 290 participants with descriptions of six actual conflicts and asked them to choose the most likely eventual decisions. The conflicts involved labor–management, commercial, and civil disputes. Five of these conflicts were chosen for role-playing. Without the use of role-playing, the participants did not do much better than chance, with a 27 percent success ratio. Next, the researchers asked twenty-one international game theorists (specialists in predicting outcomes of events) to forecast the conflict outcomes. The game theorists were correct only 28 percent of the time. (Chance here would be one-fifth, or 20 percent.)

Next, 352 students were instructed to role-play the conflicts in the six situations. The average correct decision was 61 percent versus 27 percent for the comparable group. The authors note that in more than forty years of studying forecasting, they have never seen a technique that led to such improvement in predictive accuracy.[36]

The implication for making you a better negotiator is to role-play with a friend in advance of the negotiating session you will be facing. The role-play should help you predict what the other side and you will do so you will be better prepared. For example, if your role-play suggests that the company would be willing to give you a 15 percent bonus for incredible performance, ask for a 15 percent bonus.

Allow for Saving Face

We have saved one of the most important negotiating and conflict resolution strategies for last. Negotiating does not mean that you should try to squash the other side. You should try to create circumstances that will enable you to continue working with that person if it is necessary. People prefer to avoid looking weak, foolish, or incompetent during negotiation or when the process is completed. If you do not give your opponent an opportunity to save face, you will probably create a long-term enemy.

Saving face could work in this way. A small-business owner winds up purchasing an intranet system for about twice what he originally budgeted. After the sale is completed, the sales rep says, "I know you bought a more professional intranet rig than you originally intended. Yet, I know you made the right decision. You will be able to boost productivity enough with the intranet to pay back the cost of the system in two years."

▶ Learning Objective 4 ▶

How Do You Deal with Difficult People?

Difficult people
a coworker is classified as difficult if he or she is uncooperative, disrespectful, touchy, defensive, hostile, or even very unfriendly

A major challenge in resolving conflict is dealing constructively with **difficult people**. A coworker is classified as difficult if he or she is uncooperative, disrespectful, touchy, defensive, hostile, or even very unfriendly. Difficult people are responsible for much of the conflict in the workplace. The difficult person often meets or exceeds performance standards yet annoys coworkers and superiors.[37] Other symptoms of being a difficult person include bullying and incivility.

A major problem with difficult people is that they can drag down the performance of the entire workgroup. A growing body of research indicates that the presence of a few nasty, lazy, or incompetent workers around can ruin the performance of a team or organization. It takes time to deal with the problems difficult people create, and their distracting behavior is often contagious.[38] Managers have the primary responsibility for keeping the office running smoothly, yet much of the day-by-day dealings with difficult people are coworker interactions.

Many companies take the problem of difficult people quite seriously, including office-wide bans on bad behavior. A leading example is the financial services firm, Robert W. Baird & Co. that has a "no jerks" rule. Paul Purcell, the top executive, estimates he has fired more than 25 offenders in a five-year period, including workers who hurt and belittle other people, and who put their own interests ahead of clients or the firm. Potential recruits for the firm are warned that jerks are not welcome.[39]

Four examples of difficult people follow:

- **The lone wolf.** Can't stand being part of anything: a team, a project, or group functions. Independent to a fault—makes no attempt to hide solitary preferences.
- **Chicken Little.** No matter how sunny things seem to be, he or she will always find a cloud to cast a shadow. ("What a great Web site we have. Twenty thousand visitors in the first week." "Yeah, but are more than 1 percent buying anything?")[40]
- **The high-maintenance person.** Requires so much assistance, special attention, and extra help that it wears you down. No matter what type of help you offer, they want a little more. If you bring a high-maintenance worker a soft drink, he or she is likely to say, "Didn't they have any decaffeinated soft drinks?"
- **The office magpie.** Always eager to chat and assumes that other workers want to do likewise. Whenever he or she is not faced with a pressing deadline barges into your workspace to shoot the breeze. Also known to send dozens of e-mails, along with chatty personal comments, over the same issue.[41]

In dealing with difficult coworkers, as well as difficult bosses, it is important to recognize that their problems could go much deeper than those of the types of individuals mentioned. Such individuals could be suffering from one or more of the personality disorders summarized in Figure 10-4. A **personality disorder** is a pervasive, persistent, inflexible, maladaptive pattern of behavior that deviates from expected cultural norms. The disorder is learned early in life and causes distress to the person and/or conflicts with others. Individuals with personality disorders range from harmless eccentrics to dangerous, aggressive individuals.[42]

Personality disorder
a pervasive, persistent, inflexible, maladaptive pattern of behavior that deviates from expected cultural norms

If your difficult coworker has a severe personality disorder, the techniques described in the following paragraphs will not work as well as they would with a difficult person who has a mild disorder. About 5 to 10 percent of the population suffer from a personality disorder, and the negative behavior is the most likely to be triggered by heavy stress.

Rather than attempt to list different tactics for dealing with specific types of difficult people, here we present eight widely applicable approaches for dealing with such individuals. Keep in mind that dealing with a difficult coworker requires grace and a firm grip on your own patience and temperament.[43]

Take Problems Professionally, Not Personally

A key principle in dealing with difficult people is to take what they do professionally, not personally. Difficult people are not necessarily out to get you. You may simply represent a stepping stone for them to get what they want.[44] For example, if a coworker insults you because you need his help Friday afternoon, he probably has nothing against you personally. He just prefers to become mentally disengaged from work that Friday afternoon. Your request distracts him from mentally phasing out of work as early as he would like.

FIGURE 10-4

TEN MAJOR PERSONALITY DISORDERS

Source: "Personality Disorders," in *Diagnostic and Statistical Manual* (IV-TR) (Washington, DC: American Psychiatric Association, 2000).

The ten personality disorders recognized by the American Psychiatric Association are grouped into three clusters. Many difficult people may in reality suffer from a personality disorder, such as the "control freak," who is experiencing an obsessive-compulsive disorder.

Cluster A: The Odd or Eccentric Group

1. *Paranoid Personality.* Pattern of distrust and suspiciousness with a tendency to attribute evil motives to others.
2. *Schizoid Personality.* Pervasive pattern of detachment from social relationships and restriction of emotion in interpersonal settings.
3. *Schizotypal behavior.* Appearance or thinking that is consistently strange or odd.

Cluster B: The Dramatic, Emotional, and Erratic Group

4. *Antisocial.* Chronic maladaptive behavior that disregards the rights of others.
5. *Borderline.* Instability of interpersonal relationships, self-image, and mood.
6. *Histrionic.* Excessive emotionality and attention-seeking behavior.
7. *Narcissistic.* Behavior includes grandiosity, need for admiration, and lack of empathy.

Cluster C: The Anxious and Fearful Group

8. *Avoidant.* Pattern of social inhibition, feelings of inadequacy, and hypersensitivity to negative evaluation.
9. *Dependent.* Predominantly dependent and submissive behavior.
10. *Obsessive-compulsive.* Preoccupation with orderliness, perfectionism, and control at the expense of flexibility and efficiency.

Give Ample Feedback

The primary technique for dealing with counterproductive behavior is to feed back to the difficult person how his or her behavior affects you. Focus on the person's behavior rather than on characteristics or values. If a Chicken Little type is annoying you by constantly pointing out potential disasters, say something to this effect: "I have difficulty maintaining my enthusiasm when you so often point out the possible negatives." Such a statement will engender less resentment than saying, "I find you to be a total pessimist, and it annoys me."

When the difficult person says something particularly hurtful, be explicit about its effect on you, as follows: "That remark sounded nasty, not funny," and ask "Were you intending to hurt my feelings?" or "Why did you make that sour expression?"[45]

Feedback can also be useful in dealing with a bully by pointing out how you recognize the bullying and how you find it to be unacceptable. For example, "You have insulted me three times this morning. Maybe you want to lower my self-confidence, but it is not working. I find most of your criticism to be pointless and mean spirited."

Listen and Respond

Closely related to giving feedback is listening and responding. Give the difficult person ample opportunity to express his or her concerns, doubts, anger, or other feelings. Face the person directly and maintain eye contact. Then acknowledge your awareness of the person's position.[46] An example: "Okay, you tell me that management is really against us and therefore we shouldn't work so hard." After listening, present your perspective in a way such as this: "Your viewpoint may be valid based on your experiences. Yet so far, I've found management here to be on my side." This exchange of viewpoints is less likely to lead to failed communication than if you are judgmental with a statement such as, "You really shouldn't think that way."

Use Tact and Diplomacy in Dealing with Annoying Behavior

Coworkers who irritate you rarely do annoying things on purpose. Tactful actions on your part can sometimes take care of these annoyances without your having to confront the problem. You might try one woman's method of getting rid of office pests: She keeps a file open on her computer screen and gestures to it apologetically when someone overstays a visit.

Sometimes subtlety doesn't work, and it may be necessary to diplomatically confront the coworker who is annoying you. A useful approach is to precede a criticism with a compliment. Here is an example of this approach: "You're one of the best people I've ever worked with, but one habit of yours drives me bananas. Do you think you could let me know when you're going to be late getting back to the office after lunch?"[47]

Use Nonhostile Humor

Nonhostile humor can often be used to help a difficult person understand how his or her behavior is blocking others. Also, the humor will help defuse conflict between you and that person. The humor should point to the person's unacceptable behavior yet not belittle him or her. Assume that you and a coworker are working jointly on a report. For each idea that you submit, your coworker gets into know-it-all mode and informs you of important facts that you neglected. An example of nonhostile humor that might jolt the coworker into realizing that his or her approach is annoying is as follows:

> If there is ever a contest to choose the human with a brain that can compete against a hard drive, I will nominate you. But even though my brain is limited to human capacity, I still think I can supply a few facts for our report.

Your humor may help the other person recognize that he or she is attempting to overwhelm you with facts at his or her disposal. You are being self-effacing and thereby drawing criticism away from your coworker. Self-effacement (self-criticism) is a proven humor tactic.

Avoid Creating a Dependency on You

A trap to avoid with many difficult people, and especially the high-maintenance person, is to let him or her become too dependent on you for solutions to problems. In your desire to be helpful and supportive to coworkers, you run the risk of creating a dependency. A difficult person might be pestering you to regularly help solve some of his or her most challenging work problems. The high-maintenance worker might ask you to look up a fact with a search engine, reboot a stalled computer, or help scrape ice from the windshield and windows of his or her car. You may want to be a good organizational citizen, yet you also need more time for your own work, and you do not want to make the person too dependent on you.[48] As an antidote to the problem, make frequent statements such as, "You know how to use Google," "I know you can reboot your computer," and "Perhaps you can scrape the ice yourself, because I have to do the same thing with my SUV."

Reinforce Civil Behavior and Good Moods

In the spirit of positive reinforcement, when a generally difficult person is behaving acceptably, recognize the behavior in some way. Reinforcing statements would include, "It's fun working with you today" and "I appreciate your professional attitude."

Play the Reverse Gossip Game

Difficult people often gossip quite negatively about others to purposely create conflict within the unit. When you hear negative gossip about a coworker, you can quiet

Human Relations in Practice

Telecommunications Manager Helps Jeff Overcome Obnoxious Behavior

Jessica, the CEO of a telecommunications company, was being distracted by the behavior of Jeff, the director of information technology (IT). The other key managers in the firm also suffered from Jeff's many moments of unpleasantness. Several times the director of finance suggested that Jessica just fire Jeff, and be done with the problem of his rude disruptive behavior. Jessica's response was consistent: "Losing Jeff might mean it would be more peaceful around here. But at the same time we would be losing a talented guy who has spearheaded the services that generate most of our revenue. I would prefer to see if I might be able to help Jeff understand what he is doing wrong, and perhaps change his approach."

At one meeting, Jessica said she wanted to spend about fifteen minutes talking about the tentative plans for a holiday party to celebrate a successful year. Jeff launched into a tirade about wasting company money on self-indulgence when so many people were being laid off at other companies. He also said that no company should hold a celebration when the city in which they were located had so many homeless people. The next day after the meeting Jeff sent an e-mail to every employee in the company explaining his position on the holiday party.

Following Jeff's latest outburst, Jessica took what she hoped would be constructive action to help him. First, she gathered feedback from the other key managers who attended the same meeting about how they negatively perceived Jeff's reaction to the planned holiday celebration. She shared the feedback with Jeff, and explained, "I just want you to know how much you can upset people." The second part of Jessica's improvement plan for Jeff was to send him appreciative e-mails and text messages congratulating him on anything he did out of the ordinary in a positive direction. She would also make casual reminders of Jeff's past accomplishments.

When asked how her plan of helping Jeff was proceeding, Jessica replied, "I think I hit the right formula. Jeff really knows how bad his behavior was, and how much he is loved and appreciated. The other managers and I have noted how much more relaxed and civil Jeff is now. But should he start being obnoxious again, he's going to get more feedback."

Questions What is your evaluation of Jessica's approach to dealing with the problems created by Jeff?

Source: The manager in question has chosen to remain anonymous.

the difficult person by engaging in *reverse gossip* through mentioning the coworker's strengths.[49] Here is an example:

> Suppose the difficult person says, "Jim sure does take a lot of time away from the office to take care of personal issues." You reply, "I'm not sure about that, but I have observed that Jim has given us a bunch of useful ideas this year."

The tactics for dealing with difficult people described require practice to be effective. Also, you may have to use a combination of the eight tactics described in this section to deal effectively with a difficult person. The point of these tactics is not to out-manipulate or subdue a difficult person but to establish a cordial and productive working relationship. The accompanying Human Relations in Practice illustrates a successful approach to dealing with a difficult person.

What Are Some Suggestions for Managing Anger?

Learning Objective 5

Limited ability to manage anger damages the careers and personal lives of many people. The ability to manage your anger, and the anger of others, is an important human relations skill now considered to be part of emotional intelligence. Managing anger is also part of dealing with bullies because they are usually angry people. A person who cannot manage anger well cannot take good advantage of his or her intellectual intelligence. As an extreme example, a genius who swears at the manager regularly will probably lose his or her job despite being so talented.

Although the emotion of anger is relatively easy to observe, it is more complicated than appears on the surface. Psychologist Raymond Novaco who developed the term *anger management* points out that anger does not occur by itself. Rather, it is embedded with many other emotions including sadness, grief, and shame. One implication of this finding is that you would have to manage a feeling such as sadness before you prevent your anger from surfacing frequently.[50]

Concerns about employees becoming violent have prompted many companies to offer employees training in anger management. Also, employees who become verbally abusive on the job are often sent to such training. Anger-management training is likely to encompass most of the suggestions presented next. Our concern here is with several tactics for managing your own anger and that of others effectively.

MANAGING YOUR OWN ANGER

A starting point in dealing with your anger is to recognize that at its best, anger can be an energizing force. Instead of letting it be destructive, channel your anger into exceptional performance. If you are angry because you did not get the raise you thought you deserved, get even by performing so well that there will be no question you deserve a raise next time. Develop the habit of expressing your anger before it reaches a high intensity. Tell your coworker that you do not appreciate his or her listening to an iPod while you are having dinner together the first time the act of rudeness occurs. If you wait too long, you may wind up grabbing the iPod and slamming it to the floor.

As you are about to express anger, *slow down.* (The old technique of counting to ten is still effective.) Slowing down gives you the opportunity to express your anger in a way that does not damage your relationship with the other person. Following your first impulse, you might say to the other person, "You're a stupid fool." If you slow down, this might translate into "You need training on this task."

Closely related to slowing down is a technique taught in anger-management programs: Think about the consequences of what you do when you are worked up. Say to yourself as soon as you feel angry, "Oops, I'm in anger mode now. I had better calm down before I say something or do something that I will regret later." To gauge how effectively you are expressing your anger, ask for feedback. Ask a friend, coworker, or manager, "Am I coming on too strong when I express my negative opinion?"[51]

Most anger management programs focus on emotional intelligence, especially understanding why you are frustrated, annoyed, or upset. You then learn to find a calm, constructive, means to get what you need, rather than lose your temper. Assume that you join a high-tech company, and that you are given no tech support to help you hook up your desktop computer to the company network. (The company does this on purpose because management assumes that anyone smart enough to get into the company should be able to hook up a computer.) If you have an anger problem, you would start swearing and perhaps throw a tantrum about the lack of support. A more emotionally intelligent approach to your problem would be to calmly ask one of your new coworkers for some technical assistance.

Here are a few additional suggestions from a variety of anger-management specialists for managing your own anger:[52]

- Reframe the situation as in the cognitive restructuring ideas presented earlier in this chapter. For example, "I won't go ballistic because the airline lost my baggage. Instead, I will look upon this as an opportunity in problem solving."
- Find a constructive solution to the problem at hand. For example, "So, I didn't get the big raise I anticipated. Instead, I will look for ways to cut my expenses 4 percent this year."
- Get a medical checkup and stay physically healthy if possible. Medical conditions such as diabetes, chronic pain, and low testosterone and low estrogen can make people irritable.
- Calculate the cost of your anger. For example, your reputation may suffer enormously blocking you from good career opportunities, or you might even get fired.
- Pay more attention to the important things in life rather than exploding over small incidents. Be aware that most frustrations, inconveniences, and insults are trivial and temporary.

MANAGING ANGER IN OTHER PEOPLE

A variation of confrontation and problem solving has developed specifically to resolve conflict with angry people: confront, contain, and connect. *Confront* in this context means that you jump right in and get agitated workers talking to prevent future blowups. The confrontation, however, is not aimed at arguing with the angry person. If the other person yells, you talk more softly. *Contain* refers to moving an angry worker out of sight and out of earshot. At the same time you remain impartial. The supervisor is advised not to choose sides or appear to be a friend.

You *connect* by asking open-ended questions such as "What would you like us to do about your concern?" to get at the real reasons behind an outburst. Using this approach, one worker revealed he was upset because a female coworker got to leave early to pick up her daughter at day care. The man also needed to leave early one day a week for personal reasons but felt awkward making the request. So instead of being assertive (explicit and direct) about his demands, he flared up.

An important feature of the confront–contain–connect technique is that it provides angry workers a place where they can vent their frustrations and report the outbursts of others. Mediator Nina Meierding says, "Workers need a safe outlet to talk through anger and not feel they will be minimized or put their job in jeopardy."[53]

CHOOSING A TACTIC FOR RESOLVING A CONFLICT OR MANAGING ANGER

How does a person know which of the tactics or strategies presented in this chapter will work best for a given problem? The best answer is to consider both your personality and the situation. With respect to your personality, or personal style, pick a tactic for resolving conflict that you would feel comfortable using. One person might say, "I would like the tactic of making a last and final offer because I like to control situations." Another person might say, "I prefer confrontation because I'm an open and up-front type of person." Still another person might say, "I'll avoid disarming the opposition for now. I don't yet have enough finesse to carry out this technique."

Human Relations Self-Assessment Quiz 10-3

How Much Am I Being Ostracized?

Indicate how frequently each of the statements below relates to you based on a particular work group. If a recent work group does not come to mind, use a student group, athletic team, or club. 1 = Never, 2 = Once in a while, 3 = Sometimes, 4 = Fairly often, 5 = Often, 6 = Constantly, 7 = Always.

Statement	Frequency (1–7)
1. Others ignored you at work.	________
2. Others left the area when you entered.	________
3. Your greetings have gone unanswered at work.	________
4. You involuntarily sat alone in a crowded lunchroom at work.	________
5. Others avoided you at work.	________
6. You noticed others would not look at you at work.	________
7. Others at work shut you out of the conversation.	________
8. Others refused to talk to you at work.	________
9. Others at work treated you like you weren't there.	________
10. Others at work did not invite you or ask you if you wanted anything when they went out for a coffee break.	________
Total Score	________

Although the authors of this scientifically developed quiz do not offer a scoring key, the higher the score, the more evident it is that you have been ostracized from the group. A score of 20 or lower would indicate almost no ostracism. Scores between 21 and 50 would indicate some ostracism. A score of 51 or higher would indicate substantial ostracism. If you believe that you are being ostracized too frequently, consider implementing some the suggestions for getting along with coworkers presented in Chapter 9.

Source: D. Lance Ferris, Douglas D. Brown, Joseph W. Berry, and Huiwen Lian, "The Development and Validation of the Workplace Ostracism Scale," *Journal of Applied Psychology*, November 2008, p. 1366.

In fitting the strategy to the situation, it is important to assess the gravity of the topic for negotiation or the conflict between people. A woman might say to herself, "My boss has committed such a blatant act of sexual harassment that I had best take this up with a higher authority immediately." Sizing up your opponent can also help you choose the best strategy. If she or he appears reasonably flexible, you might try to compromise. Or if your adversary is especially upset, give that person a chance to simmer down before trying to solve the problem.

Another perspective on conflict resolution and anger management is to ponder whether you too frequently need to resolve conflict and manage anger with coworkers (or other students). One indirect measure of being perceived as too conflict-prone, or too angry, is the extent to which you are ostracized (excluded) by other group members. Ostracism might also take place because a person is unpopular for other reasons, such as having a bland personality. Human Relations Self-Assessment Quiz 10-3 gives you an opportunity to think through whether you are being ostracized from a group of which you are a member.

Key Terms

Conflict, 279
Personality clash, 281
Aggressive personalities, 281
Workplace bullying, 282
Passive-aggressive personality, 282
Work–family conflict, 284
Micro-inequity, 285
Sexual harassment, 286
Assertive, 291
Nonassertive, 291
Aggressive, 291
Confrontation and problem solving, 293
Win–win, 293
Disarming the opposition, 294
Cognitive restructuring, 295
Grievance procedure, 296
Negotiating and bargaining, 298
Difficult people, 300
Personality disorder, 301

Summary and Review

Conflict occurs when two sets of demands, goals, or motives are incompatible. Such differences often lead to a hostile or antagonistic relationship between people. A conflict can also be considered a dispute, feud, or controversy. Among the reasons for widespread conflict are the following:

- Competition for limited resources
- Differences of opinion on work-related issues and rights
- Personality clashes and drama
- Aggressive personalities, including bullies
- Culturally diverse teams and factional groups
- Competing work and family demands
- Micro-inequities (semiconscious slights)
- Cross-generational conflict
- Sexual harassment

Sexual harassment is one of two types: quid pro quo (a demand for sexual favors in exchange for job benefits) and creating a hostile environment. It is important for workers to understand what actions and words constitute sexual harassment and how to deal with the problem.

The benefits of conflict include the emergence of talents and abilities, constructive innovation and change, and increased unity after the conflict is settled. Among the detrimental consequences of conflict are physical and mental health problems, wasted resources, the promotion of self-interest, and workplace violence.

Techniques for resolving conflicts with others include the following:

- Being assertive. To become more assertive, set a goal, appear warm and friendly, conduct anonymous conversations, greet strangers, and practice being decisive.
- Confrontation and problem solving leading to win–win. Get to the root of the problem and resolve it systematically. The intention of confrontation and problem solving is to arrive at a collaborative solution to the conflict. The opposite of win–win is win–lose, where each side attempts to maximize gain at the expense of the other.
- Disarm the opposition. Agree with the criticizer and enlist his or her help.
- Reframing. One approach is to use cognitive restructuring by mentally converting negative aspects into positive ones by looking for the positive elements in a situation. Also use reframing by asking questions such as, "Have I missed something important?"
- Appeal to a third party (such as a government agency).
- Use the grievance procedure (a formal organizational procedure for dispute resolution), used extensively in unionized companies.
- Use negotiation and bargaining tactics, including creating a positive negotiating climate; listening first to investigate what the other side wants; allowing room for compromise but being reasonable; focusing on interests, not positions; making a last and final offer; role-playing to predict what the other side will do; and allowing for face-saving.

Deal effectively with difficult people, including the following:

- Take problems professionally, not personally.
- Give ample feedback.
- Listen and respond.
- Use tact and diplomacy in dealing with annoying behavior.

- Use nonhostile humor.
- Avoid creating a dependency on you.
- Reinforce civil behavior and good moods.
- Play the reverse gossip game.

Limited ability to manage anger damages the careers and personal lives of many people. The ability to manage anger is part of emotional intelligence. In managing your own anger, remember that anger can be an energizing force.

- Express your anger before it reaches a high intensity.
- As you are about to express your anger, slow down.
- Ask for feedback on how you deal with anger.
- In dealing with the anger of others, use the confront, contain (move the angry worker out of sight), and connect (ask open-ended questions to get at the real reason behind the outburst) method.

In choosing a tactic for resolving conflict, consider both your personality or style and the nature of the situation facing you. The situation includes such factors as the gravity of the conflict and the type of person you are facing. Also, think through whether if you are so conflict-prone and angry that you are being ostracized from the group.

Check Your Understanding

1. Give an example from your life of how competition for limited resources can breed conflict.
2. Why are person-to-person meetings often better for resolving conflict than sending written messages back and forth?
3. Imagine that after two weeks on a new job that you want, your boss begins to treat you in a bullying, intimidating manner. What would you say to that boss?
4. Many male managers who confer with a female worker in their offices leave the door open to avoid any charges of sexual harassment. Are these managers using good judgment, or are they being overly cautious?
5. Assume that a worker is being sexually harassed by the owner of the business where he or she works. How should the harassed person deal with the problem?
6. Identify several occupations in which conflict resolution skills are particularly important.
7. Visualize a person taking the road test part of obtaining a driver's license. The candidate has done a poor job of parallel parking, and the examiner looks at him or her with a frown and says, "Not very impressive." How can this candidate make best use of the tactic "disarming the opposition"?
8. How might a person use cognitive restructuring to help deal with the conflict of having received a below-average raise while expecting an above-average raise?
9. What is your explanation of the research showing that role-playing a negotiation scenario helps people make more accurate predictions about the outcome of conflicts?
10. Suppose you thought the reason that a coworker was a difficult person was because he or she had a true personality disorder. Would you recommend to that person directly that he or she seek mental health treatment? Explain your reasoning.

Web Corner

Labor union approach to combating sexual harassment

www.ueunion.org Enter "sexual harassment" in the search slot, "Search UE."

Cognitive restructuring:

http://www.mindtools.com/stress/rt/CognitiveRestructuring.htm

Shyness

www.shyness.com (self-quizzes about shyness, plus the opportunity to participate in research about shyness)

Dealing with difficult people

http://humanresources.about.com/od/difficultpeople/tp/dealing_difficult.htm

INTERNET SKILL BUILDER

Conflict Resolution

Despite all the information available about resolving conflict in the workplace and in personal life, resolving conflict successfully remains difficult. Search the Internet to find a brief case history of successful conflict resolution in the workplace, in community life, or in personal life. Analyze the case to identify which approach or approaches to conflict resolution covered in this chapter were employed. Be prepared to share your findings with other class members.

Developing Your Human Relations Skills

Human Relations Application Exercises

Applying Human Relations Skill-Building Exercise 10-1

Win–Win Conflict Resolution

A few years ago, Family Dollar was attempting to build a new store in the town of Ridgway, Colorado, a town of 950 people. The discount retailer had purchased the property the company needed for the project. Family Dollar had obtained the necessary building permit. A citizen's group wanting to retain the small-town authenticity of Ridgway, decided to post a "Pledge to Boycott Family Dollar" online. The post asked consumers to boycott Family Dollar stores everywhere if the corporation does not respect the community's desire to remain "box-free." A company spokesperson said the store in Ridgway will be about 8,000 square feet. (A big-box store is usually a minimum of 50,000 square feet.)

Your task working as a group or individually is to find a resolution of the conflict between the community representatives of Ridgway and the representatives of Family Dollar. On your way to resolving the problem, express your opinion about the effectiveness of attempting a national boycott of Family Dollar as a solution to the problem. Your proposed solution to this conflict is important because the conflict frequently surfaces between retailers and town representatives. Compare your solution to the conflict with other members of the class, with an eye toward understanding what might be an effective win–win solution to the conflict between community representatives of Ridgway and leaders at Family Dollar.

Source: The facts supporting this exercise are found in Howard Pankratz, "Colorado Town Calling for a National Boycott of Family Dollar Stores," *The Denver Post* (www.denverpost.com/business), August 19, 2011, p. 1.

Applying Human Relations Exercise 10-1

Reframing through Cognitive Restructuring

The following are examples of negative statements about others in the workplace. In the space provided, cognitively restructure (reframe) each comment in a positive way.

Negative: Nancy is getting on my nerves. It takes her two weeks longer than anyone else on the team to complete her input.

Positive:

Negative: Rob is so obsessed with sports he is hurting my productivity. Where does it say in the employee handbook that I have to spend thirty minutes on Monday listening to Rob's comments on his team's weekend performance? Doesn't he know that I have a job to do and that I just don't care about his team?

Positive:

Negative: My boss is driving me crazy. He's forever telling me what I did wrong and making suggestions for improvement. He makes me feel like I'm in elementary school.

Positive:

Human Relations Class Activity

Negotiating for a Bigger Raise

During good times and bad times, most people would like to receive a bigger raise than the one the company or immediate manager has decided to grant. But it is not widely known which negotiating tactic or tactics is likely to be the most effective. The purpose of this class activity is to conduct a survey of written comments about the best way to negotiate for a bigger raise than management probably had in store for you (assuming that you worked for somebody else). In addition, the class will attempt to categorize the three most frequently occurring tactics. Following the text, the categories include "be the first to listen," "allow room for compromise, but be reasonable," "make a last and final offer," and so forth.

Method of data collection: Each class member sends an e-mail to two experienced working adults in your network, perhaps including yourself. Ask the person to complete the following sentence:

The best way to negotiate for a bigger raise for yourself is to ______________.

After collecting the responses, send them to a master e-mail or Web page for your class.

Method of analysis: After every class member has taken the opportunity to review the master file, each student compiles (a) what he or she considers the three most frequently used approaches to asking for a bigger raise and (b) which negotiating and bargaining tactics these approaches best fit. Here is an example for clarification: Suppose one of the most frequently used approaches is for the person wanting a bigger raise to state something to the effect of this: "Give me a bigger raise or I'll look elsewhere." This approach might be classified as "Make a last and final offer."

The analysis by individuals is then sent back to the master e-mail or Web site to prepare a final summary of the results. The class might then hold a discussion as to any takeaway lessons from this exercise.

Human Relations Class Study 10-1

The Apprehensive Sales Trainee

Maria was ecstatic about the position she just landed as a sales representative for a company that provides payroll and human resources services for small companies throughout the country. She was to be assigned a sales territory in Madison, Wisconsin, where she lived with her husband and three young children. Before working her territory, Maria had to attend ten days of training and orientation at company headquarters in Boston.

One of the key trainers in the program was the national sales manager, Todd, an energetic and successful man in his early forties. During a beverage break at the first morning of the training program, Todd approached Maria and complimented her on her "great tan," and "fabulous appearance." Maria was not particularly comfortable with the comments, but she let them pass.

Before the dinner meeting on the second night of the program, Todd came over to Maria and engaged her in a brief conversation about how she was enjoying the sales training. He then handed her a business card and said, "I imagine you might get lonely being away from home for so long, so here is my business card. Please get in touch if you would just like to hang out a little with me." Maria thought that Todd was stepping over the line of good business judgment, but she just smiled politely and said, "Thanks anyway, but I am so overwhelmed with all this great information I am receiving, I have no spare time."

The following morning, Maria received a text message from Todd on her BlackBerry that said, "Your beauty is devastating. Get back."

Maria later phoned her best friend in Madison and said, "Todd carries a lot of weight being the national sales manager. But I think his behavior toward me borders on sexual harassment. Yet, five days into my job, I guess I shouldn't attempt to rat on a company executive."

Maria's friend replied, "You have got to do something. That sales manager is a predator."

Questions

1. To what extent is Todd engaging in sexual harassment toward Maria?
2. If Todd is guilty, what type of sexual harassment is he committing?
3. What steps should Maria take so she can stop the harassment yet still maintain a good working relationship with Todd?
4. What would be the positives and negatives of Maria filing a complaint about Todd with the company?

Human Relations Role-Playing Exercise

Maria Tries to Fend Off Todd

The case about Maria, the sales trainee, provides the background information and story line for this role-play. One person plays the role of serious-minded Maria, who wants to receive high ratings in her sales training. She does not want to create problems at the company, yet she recognizes she has the right to a harassment-free environment. Another student plays the role of Todd, who is infatuated with Maria and also believes that he is powerful and somewhat irresistible to women. Todd corners Maria during a cocktail hour prior to dinner on the third night of the sales training program. He once again starts to hit on her, and Maria wants to avoid being hit on. At a least, a few sets of role-players should perform in front of the class for about seven minutes.

Observers rate the role-players on two dimensions, using a 1 to 5 scale from very poor to very good. One dimension is "effective use of human relations techniques." Focus on Maria's ability to effectively deal with sexual harassment. The second dimension is "acting ability." A few observers might voluntarily provide feedback to the role players in terms of sharing their ratings and observations. The course instructor might also provide feedback.

Human Relations Class Study 10-2

Ashley Uses Passion as an Excuse

Ashley works as a price estimator in the division of a large electronics company that manufactures and sells security systems to business firms. She holds a degree in electronics technology, and has extensive knowledge about security systems. In recent years her company has prospered because of heightened concerns about security. However, the market for security systems in her area has become saturated because virtually every firm has a security system. New business for the division comes mostly from getting companies to switch to her company, or from security system upgrades with existing customers.

As a result of the security business having stabilized in the geographic area, the atmosphere in the office has become tense. Workers have become less calm and pleasant than previously. Ashley, who has had a volatile personality since early childhood, has become tenser than her coworkers. During a recent project to upgrade the security system at a pharmaceutical warehouse, the sales representative accused Ashley of providing a cost estimate too high to clinch the deal. Ashley replied, "You are a sad (expletive) sales person. You will tell a prospective client anything just to bag a sale. So long as you get your commission, you don't care if the company loses money on the project." Ashley offered no apology for her outburst.

A week later at a department meeting to discuss goals for the year, Ashley said to the group, including the manager, "Goal setting for me is a dumb (expletive) idea. I will have no work to do unless this time-wasting, expense-account-hogging sales group gets off its butt and make some sales."

Horrified, the manager said to Ashley, "You are being totally unprofessional. Please apologize to the sales group."

Ashley said, "Okay, maybe I shouldn't be so truthful in what I say. I can't help it. I'm a passionate person who wants results for the company."

Questions

1. To what extent does Ashley being "passionate" justify her expression of anger toward coworkers?
2. What do you recommend that Ashley's manager and coworkers do to make her a less difficult person in the office?
3. What career advice might you offer Ashley? (Or, does she need any advice?)

Human Relations Role-Playing Exercise

Ashley Lashes Out

One student plays the role of the sales representative who accuses Ashley of providing a cost estimate too high to clinch the deal with the pharmaceutical warehouse. Another student plays the role of Ashley who lashes back at the sales rep. The goal of the sales representative is to be treated in a more civil manner by Ashley. The rep also wants Ashley to get more into a problem-solving mode. Ashley, in turn, thinks that the rep is more interested in bagging a sale than making money for the company.

Observers rate the role-players on two dimensions, using a 1 to 5 scale from very poor to very good. One dimension is "effective use of human relations techniques." Focus on the rep's ability to effectively deal with Ashley's anger and hostility. The second dimension is "acting ability." A few observers might voluntarily provide feedback to the role players in terms of sharing their ratings and observations. The course instructor might also provide feedback.

REFERENCES

1. David Enrich, "Krawcheck Is Leaving Citigroup," *The Wall Street Journal,* September 23, 2008, p. C8.
2. Susan G. Hauser, "The Degeneration of Decorum," *Workforce Management,* January 2011, pp. 16–21.
3. Marlene Chism, "Drop the Curtain on Workplace Drama," *Communication Briefings,* June 2011, p. 5.
4. Siobhan Leftwich, "Hey, You Can't Say That! How to Cope with Verbally Abusive People," *Black Enterprise,* January 2006, p. 95.
5. "Workplace Violence," *Occupational Safety & Health Administration,* (www.osha.gov), pp. 1–2. Accessed February 17, 2012.
6. Research and opinion reported in Ed Frauenheim, "Recession Unleashes Bossy Bullying," *Workforce Management,* April 2010, p. 22.
7. Cindy Krischer Goodman, "Workplace Bullies Bearing Down," *McClatchy Newspapers* (www.detnews.com), July 11, 2011, pp. 1–2.
8. Diane A. Safer, "Passive-Aggressive Behavior," *NYU Langone Medical Center* (www.med.nyu), pp. 1–2. Copyright © 2012 EBSCO Publishing; Signe Whitson, "Checking Passive Aggression: Refuse to Be a Victim of Such Behavior, *HR Magazine,* June 2010, pp. 115–116.
9. Angela Pirisi, "Teamwork: The Downside of Diversity," *Psychology Today,* November/December 1999, p. 18.
10. Jiatao Li and Donald C. Hambrick, "Factional Groups: A New Vantage on Demographic Faultlines, Conflict, and Disintegration in Work Teams," *Academy of Management Journal,* October 2005, pp. 794–813.
11. Kathy Gurchiek, "Not a 'Mommy' Issue," *HR Magazine,* April 2011, p. 41.
12. Beth A. Livingston and Timothy A. Judge, "Emotional Responses to Work–Family Conflict: An Examination of Gender Role Orientation among Working Men and Women," *Journal of Applied Psychology,* January 2008, pp. 207–216.
13. Cited in Gurchiek, "Not a 'Mommy' Issue," p. 41.
14. Adapted from Sue Shellenbarger, "Dinner and a PowerPoint," *The Wall Street Journal,* June 28, 2007, p. D1.
15. Devasheesh P. Bhave, Amit Kramer, and Theresa M. Glomb, "Work–Family Conflict in Work Groups: Social Information Processing, Support, and Demographic Dissimilarity," *Journal of Applied Psychology,* January 2010, pp. 145–158.
16. Paul E. Spector et al. (consisting of 22 researchers), "Cross-National Differences in Relationships of Work Demands, Job Satisfaction, and Turnover Intentions with Work–Family Conflict," *Personnel Psychology,* Winter 2007, pp. 805–835.
17. Joseph G. Gryzwacz et al., "Work–Family Conflict: Experiences and Health Implications among Immigrant Latinos," *Journal of Applied Psychology,* July 2007, pp. 1119–1130.
18. The examples, but not the interpretations, are from Julie Fawe, "Why Your Boss May Start Sweating the Small Stuff," *Time,* March 20, 2006, p. 80. See also Joann S. Lublin, "How to Stop the Snubs That Demoralize You and Your Colleagues," *The Wall Street Journal,* December 7, 2004, p. B1.
19. Chris Penttila, "Talking about My Generation," *Entrepreneur,* March 2009, p. 55.
20. Jennifer L. Berdahl and Karl Aquino, "Sexual Behavior at Work: Fun or Folly?" *Journal of Applied Psychology,* January 2009, p. 34.
21. Curt Levey, "Sexual Harassment's Legal Morass," *The Wall Street Journal,* November 7, 2011, p. A19.
22. "'Sexting' Causes Growing Harassment Risk," *The HR Specialist,* December 2010, p. 8.
23. Jennifer Berdahl, "The Sexual Harassment of Uppity Women," *Journal of Applied Psychology,* March 2007, pp. 425–437.
24. Chelsea R. Willness, Piers Steel, and Kibeom Lee,"A Meta-Analysis of the Antecedents and Consequences of Workplace Sexual Harassment," *Personnel Psychology,* Spring 2007, pp. 127–162.
25. Data synthesized in Hong Ren and Barbara Gray, "Repairing Relationship Conflict: How Violation Types and Culture Influence the Effectiveness of Restoration Rituals, *Academy of Management Review,* January 2009, p. 105.
26. Peopleclick Authoria (company name), "Driving Workforce Collaboration to Achieve High Performance" *Workforce Management,* October 2010, p. S11.
27. Bernardo J. Carducci, *Shyness: A Bold Approach.* (New York: HarperCollins, 1999).
28. Bryan Walsh, "The Upside of Being an Introvert," *Time,* February 6, 2012, pp. 40–45.
29. Philip Zimbardo, *Shyness: What It Is, What to Do about It* (Reading, MA: Addison-Wesley, 1977), pp. 220–226; Mel Silberman with Freda Hansburg, *PeopleSmart* (San Francisco: Berrett-Koehler, 2000), pp. 75–76.
30. "Complete These to Control Conflict," *Communication Briefings,* May 2010, p. 2.
31. "Conquer Conflict with This Technique," *Manager's Edge,* September 7, 2005. As adapted from Maria Broomhower, "Dissolving Conflict through Reframing," http://www.conflict911.com.
32. Stephen P. Robbins and David A. DeCenzo, *Supervision Today!,* 4th ed. (Upper Saddle River, NJ: Pearson Prentice Hall, 2004), p. 438.
33. "To Agree or Disagree?" *Chicago Tribune Career Builder,* November 4, 2007, p. 1, Section 6.
34. Quoted in Brenda Goodman, "The Art of Negotiation," *Psychology Today,* January/February 2007, p. 65.
35. Deepak Malhotra and Max H. Bazerman, "Investigative Negotiation," *Harvard Business Review,* September 2007, pp. 72–78.
36. J. Scott Armstrong, "Forecasting in Conflicts: How to Predict What Your Opponents Will Do," *Knowledge@Wharton* (www.knowledge.wharton.upenn.edu), February 13, 2002, p. 1.
37. Jathan Janove, "Jerks at Work," *HR Magazine,* May 2007, p. 111.
38. Robert Sutton, "How a Few Bad Apples Ruin Everything," *The Wall Street Journal,* October 24, 2011, p. R5.
39. Sue Shellenbarger, "To Combat an Office Tyrant, Look at the Roots," *The Wall Street Journal,* April 28, 2010, p. D3.
40. The first two types are from a brochure for ETC w/Career Track, Boulder, CO.

41. Matt Villano, "How to Shush the Office Magpie," *New York Times*. Retrieved December 25, 2005, from: www.nytimes.com.
42. Michael S. Beeson, "Personality Disorders." Retrieved March 25, 2006, from: www.emedicine.com/emerg/topic418.htm.
43. Naomi Cossack, "Skills Data, Retirement Benefits, Difficult Employees," *HR Magazine*, January 2007, p. 49.
44. Dru Scott, *Customer Satisfaction: The Other Half of Your Job* (Los Altos, CA: Crisp Publications, 1991), p. 16.
45. "Handle the Toughest Personalities," *Manager's Edge*, October 2008, p. 1.
46. "Master Dealing with Difficult People," *Manager's Edge*, March 2009, p. 8.
47. Jane Michaels, "You Gotta Get Along to Get Ahead," *Woman's Day*, April 3, 1984, p. 58.
48. Lin Grensing-Pophal, "High-Maintenance Employees," *HR Magazine*, February 2001, p. 89.
49. "Tame Team Tigers: How to Handle Difficult Personalities," *Manager's Edge*, Special Issue, 2008, p. 8.
50. Cited in Melinda Beck, "When Anger Is An Illness," *The Wall Street Journal*, March 9, 2010, p. D6.
51. Fred Pryor, "Is Anger Really Healthy?" *Pryor Management Newsletter*, February 1996, p. 3.
52. Beck, "When Anger Is An Illness," p. D6.
53. The quote and technique are both from Kathleen Doheny, "It's a Mad, Mad Corporate World," *Working Woman*, April 2000, pp. 71–72.

11

Becoming an Effective Leader

Outline

For many years Virginia Rometty had been a leader in the technology industry, including holding the position at IBM as the senior vice president and group executive for sales, marketing,and strategy. Effective January 1, 2012, she was elected as president and chief executive officer of IBM. Upon her appointment, Sam Palmisano, her predecessor pointed out that Rometty had successfully led a few of IBM's key businesses during the past ten years. In addition to being an outstanding manager of internal operations, she has been successful in helping clients use many of IBM's capabilities at the same time. Palmisano believed that as the new CEO, Rometty would be a combination of vision, focus on customer needs, intense drive, and a passion for employees and the future of the company.

During Rometty's three decades at IBM, prior to 2012, she developed a reputation as a polished executive who can close a sale and expand relationships with companies in different fields. Rometty was particularly effective in dealing with IBM customers. Staff members who have reported to Rometty also admire her ability to build relationships and to listen to problems.Rometty has promoted the idea for a long time that she and her team members are on an important mission. IBM has been fascinating and compelling for her because of the company's passion to apply technology and the scientific method scientific to major societal issues. (These issues include reducing congestion and pollution in major cities.)

Rometty began her career at IBM in 1981 as a systems engineer two years after graduating from Northwestern University with a degree in computer science and electrical engineering. Her first position after college was an internship at General Motors in Detroit.[1]

Learning Objectives ▸

After studying the information and doing the exercises in this chapter, you should be able to:

1. Identify personal traits and characteristics of effective leaders.
2. Identify behaviors of effective leaders.
3. Understand the nature of leadership style and the importance of the leader adapting to the situation.
4. Know what needs to be done to get along well with group members.
5. Map out a tentative program for developing your leadership potential and skills.
6. Describe several challenges involved in being a first-time leader.

To become president and CEO of IBM, Virginia Rometty no doubt has many good leadership qualities, but on display here is one of the many leadership characteristics or behaviors described in this chapter—thinking in big ways and building relationships. **Leadership** is the process of bringing about positive changes and influencing others to achieve group goals and coordinating the pursuit of these goals.[2] The key words in understanding leadership are *change* and *influence.* A leader often challenges the status quo and brings about improvements. A leader also influences people to do things, such as achieve higher performance that they would not do otherwise. We therefore measure the effectiveness of leaders in terms of the results they attain, such as running a profitable medical clinic or a winning athletic team. In short, the leader makes a difference.

Leadership
the process of bringing about positive changes and influencing others to achieve worthwhile goals

The study of leadership warrants your attention because today people at all levels in the organization are expected to exert some leadership. Organizations seek people to exert leadership at all levels by giving many of them an opportunity to engage in such tasks as motivating others and setting goals. Even if your job title does not include the mention of management responsibility, you will often be called on to be a temporary leader, such as being appointed the head of a committee or project. Our approach to the vast topic of leadership encompasses the attributes and behaviors of leaders, leadership style, getting along with subordinates, and developing your leadership potential.

▶ Learning Objective 1 ▶

What Are Some Traits and Characteristics of Effective Leaders?

Leadership effectiveness inner quality of a leader who helps the group accomplish its objectives without neglecting satisfaction and morale

A major thrust to understanding leaders and leadership is to recognize that effective leaders have the "right stuff." In other words, certain inner qualities contribute to leadership effectiveness in a wide variety of situations. **Leadership effectiveness** in this situation means that the leader helps the group accomplish its objectives without neglecting satisfaction and morale. The characteristics that contribute to effectiveness depend somewhat on the situation. A supervisor in a meatpacking plant and one in an information technology department will need different sets of personal characteristics. The situation includes such factors as the people being supervised, the job being performed, the company, and the cultural background of employees.

Leadership effectiveness also usually depends on the right combination of personal characteristics in a given situation.[3] For example, the leader of a group of packaging design specialists might need to be open to new ideas. At the same time the leader might need to have a good sense of humor, because packing specialists are creative enough to appreciate what is funny.

In the next several pages, we describe some of the more important traits and characteristics of leaders. Many of these traits and characteristics can be developed and refined. Figure 11-1 outlines the seven key traits.

SELF-CONFIDENCE AND COURAGE

Self-confidence is necessary for leadership because it helps assure group members that activities are under control. The confidence centers on a belief that a person has the knowledge, skills, and abilities associated with leading others. Assume you are a manager in a company that is facing bankruptcy. At a meeting you attend, the chief executive

FIGURE 11-1
SEVEN KEY LEADERSHIP TRAITS

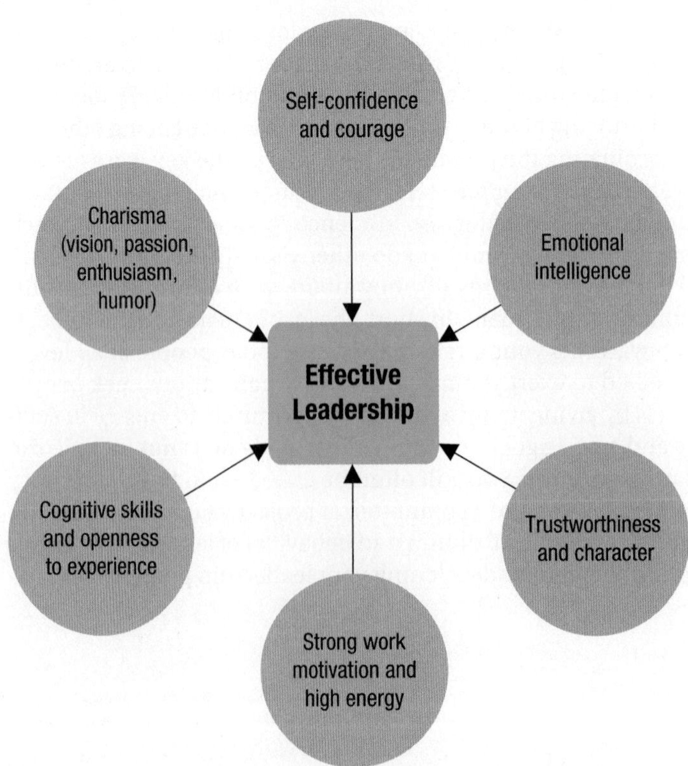

officer sobs, "I'm sorry, I'm just no good in a crisis. I don't know what's going to happen to the company. I don't think I can get us out of this mess. Maybe one of you would like to try your hand at turning around the company." You would probably prefer that the CEO behave in a confident, assured manner.

In other leadership situations as well, the leader who functions best is self-confident enough to reassure others and to appear in control. But if the leader is so self-confident that he so she will not admit errors, listen to criticism, or ask for advice, that too creates problems. Being too self-confident can lead to the person to ignore potential problems, thinking, "I can handle whatever comes my way."

One of many possible examples of a self-confident leader is Oprah Winfrey, who is well-known as a show business celebrity yet is also the head of an extensive business empire, including the multimedia conglomerate Harpo Inc. and the Oprah Winfrey Network (OWN). During staff meetings, Oprah is typically quite positive about the future of her company. "This is the foundation of greater things to come," she often told her managers as she developed an array of partnerships and spinoffs.[4]

Self-confidence often takes the form of the courage to face the challenges of taking prudent risks and taking initiative in general. Courage comes from the heart, as suggested by the French word for heart, *coeur*. Leaders must be able to face up to responsibility and be willing to put reputations on the line, even if this means taking a course of action others would not advise.

"As a leader, display a healthy level of humility. Humility is a different source of inner strength, meaning that you're open to input from others; admitting mistakes and most importantly, understanding your own limitations."
—Derica W. Rice, VP and CFO of Eli Lilly and Company. Quoted in Sonia Alleyne and Annya M. Lott, "The 100 Most Powerful Executives in Corporate America," *Black Enterprise*, February 2009, p. 116.

Being confident and courageous does not exclude a leader from also displaying humility. People who are too confident and courageous will often neglect to welcome input from others or listen to criticism. A leader with an appropriate degree of humility will also admit to having made a mistake and is therefore willing to change course. For example, a leader who decided against hiring experiencing store associates because they cost too much found that customer service suffered resulting in lower sales. The leader then added a few more experienced store associates, and customer service again improved.

EMOTIONAL INTELLIGENCE

Emotional intelligence is considered a major contributor to leadership effectiveness. Intelligence of this type can be developed through working on some of its components, such as learning to control your temper and developing empathy by listening to people carefully. It is also important to develop the habit of looking to understand the feelings and emotions of people around you. Also ask yourself, "How do I feel about what's going on here?" When you have a hunch about people's motives, look for feedback in the future to see if you were right. Here is an example of applying emotional intelligence:

Meg Whitman, the former eBay CEO was appointed to the chief position at Hewlett-Packard Co, after the company had just fired its second top executive within a year, and had faced several scandals. On her first day on the job, Whitman sought to reassure employees and calm the storm. She told employees at a town-hall meeting that HP needed to earn back their trust and respect following her predecessor's turbulent eleven months.[5]

A key point of this example is that Whitman could sense that company employees needed calming down at the moment more than they needed to hear about new business strategies or projected financial results.

TRUSTWORTHINESS AND CHARACTER

Considerable evidence exists that being trustworthy or honest contributes to being an effective leader. An effective leader is supposed to *walk the talk*, thereby showing a consistency between deeds (walking) and words (talking). Group members consistently believe that leaders must display honesty, integrity, and credibility. Leaders themselves believe that honesty and integrity make a difference in their effectiveness.[6] In this context, **trust** is defined as a person's confidence in another individual's intentions and motives and in the sincerity of that individual's words. Leaders must be trustworthy, and they must also trust the group members.

Trust
a person's confidence in another individual's intentions and motives and in the sincerity of that individual's words

It takes a leader a long time to build trust, yet one brief incident of untrustworthy behavior can destroy it. An example of untrustworthy behavior would be using company money for private purposes or sexually harassing a team member. Leaders are usually allowed a fair share of honest mistakes. In contrast, dishonest mistakes quickly erode leadership effectiveness. Having certain character traits contributes to being trustworthy and being perceived as a trustworthy person. **Character** in this context refers to doing the right things despite outside pressures to do the opposite. Being of good character also includes leaving enduring marks that set one apart from another.[7] To be of good character is to be moral. Three traits that contribute to good character are honesty, loyalty, and compassion.

Character
doing the right things despite outside pressures to do the opposite; includes leaving enduring marks that set one apart from another; being moral

Human Relations Self-Assessment Quiz 11-1 gives you the opportunity to think about your level of trustworthiness and honesty.

Human Relations Self-Assessment Quiz 11-1

The Trustworthiness and Honesty Checklist

Check whether each of actions and attitudes in the list below are generally true or generally false. Responding to this checklist is difficult because you are required to be objective and honest about your trustworthiness.

Number	Statement About Trustworthiness	Generally True	Generally False
1.	I do my best to tell the truth even it makes me look bad or appear to be guilty.	______	______
2.	More than one person has referred to me as a pathological liar.	______	______
3.	When I agree to a date for completing a project I am usually late anyway.	______	______
4.	I minimize telling people what they want to hear.	______	______
5.	My promises almost always match what I actually carry out.	______	______
6.	Many people have referred to me as being reliable.	______	______
7.	When (or if) I received too much change from a restaurant server of a store cashier, I gave (or would give) the extra money back.	______	______
8.	I give out lots of false compliments just to make friends.	______	______
9.	I am undependable.	______	______
10.	I admit to my faults and attempt to make the necessary improvements.	______	______

Scoring and Interpretation:

Give yourself one point for the following answers: Generally True to questions 1, 4, 5, 6, 7, and 10; generally false to questions 2, 3, 8, and 9. If you scored 8 or more points, you are most likely a trustworthy person, and these types of attitudes and behaviors would be an asset to you as a leader. If you scored between 0 and 7, you are likely to be perceived as untrustworthy by many people. Being perceived as untrustworthy could make it difficult for you to be promoted to a leadership position or be effective as a leader. A caution again is that it is quite difficult to be honest with oneself about one's honesty, so perhaps take this quiz again in one week.

STRONG WORK MOTIVATION AND HIGH ENERGY

Leadership positions tend to be both physically and mentally demanding. A successful leader must be willing to work hard and long to achieve success. Many business leaders often work seventy-hour weeks, as do a large number of business owners. Many leaders appear to be driven by a need for self-fulfillment. Another fundamental reason strong work motivation is required for effectiveness is that a person has to be willing to accept the heavy responsibility that being a supervisor entails. As one department manager said, "Whoever thought being a manager would mean that I would have to fire a single parent who has three children to feed and clothe?"

Working long and hard contributes to a leader being able to lead by personal example, or being a good role model for subordinates. More specifically if the leader shows good organizational citizenship behavior through extra hard work, group members are likely to model this behavior.[8]

COGNITIVE SKILLS

Cognitive skills, as well as personality, are important for leadership success. Problem-solving and intellectual skills are referred to collectively as **cognitive skills**. The term *cognition* refers to the mental process of faculty by which knowledge is gathered. To inspire people, bring about constructive changes, and solve problems creatively, leaders need to be mentally sharp. A synthesis of 151 different studies examining the relationship between intelligence and leadership performance found a slight positive relationship between the two variables. But when the leader's job emphasized playing an active role in making decisions about the work of the group (such as helping solve technical problems), intelligence showed a higher relationship with performance.[9]

Cognitive skills
problem-solving and intellectual skills

A cognitive skill of major importance is *knowledge of the business*, or technical competence. An effective leader has to be technically or professionally competent in some discipline, particularly when leading a group of specialists. It is difficult for the leader to establish rapport with group members when he or she does not know what they are doing. A related damper on leadership effectiveness is when the group does not respect the leader's technical skill. Good practical intelligence (*street smarts*) is also part of an effective leader's intellectual makeup. A leader with high practical intelligence could size up a good opportunity without spending an extensive amount of time analyzing what could possibly go wrong.

Knowledge of the business sometimes takes the form of a leader getting involved in small details about products. During Andrea Jung's tenure as CEO of Avon Products Inc. she once insisted on a redesign of Avon's lipstick case. Jung thought that the swivel mechanism was not sufficiently smooth.[10]

The accompanying Human Relations in Practice describes a leader whose technical skills are the basis for his leadership.

CHARISMA

An important quality for leaders at all levels is **charisma**, a type of charm and magnetism that inspires others and makes them loyal to the leader. Charismatic leaders are typically assertive because they are eager to reach out to others and express their feelings and thoughts. Not every leader has to be charismatic, yet to be an effective leader you often need some degree of this personality quality.

Charisma
type of charm and magnetism that inspires others; important quality for leaders at all levels

Being charismatic helps leaders form better relationships with workers, who might then work harder for them. A charismatic leader who inspires people therefore contributes to attaining results or being effective. One analysis suggests that the leader's

Human Relations in Practice

Apple Inc. Design Chief, Jonathan Ive, Relies Heavily on Technical Skills

London-born Jonathan Ive is the senior vice president of Industrial Design at Apple Inc., reporting directly to the CEO. Since 1996, he has led a design team, regarded by many as one of the best in the world. The late Steve Jobs played a major role in the design of Apple products. However, Ive is the chief creator behind many of the company's highly successful products, including the iMac, iBook, PowerBook G4, iPhone, and the iPod. Ive's emphasis on elegant and useful design has helped Apple products become consumer status symbols.

The modest, shy, and detail-obsessed Ive has the reputation of being one of the most brilliant designers of his generation. He has won numerous awards for his designs, such as Designer of the Year several times by the Design Museum. Based on his highly acclaimed designs, Ive was knighted by Queen Elizabeth II, age 85 at the time, and an iPod user. Several of the products he designed are part of the permanent collection in of museums worldwide including the Museum of Modern Art in New York, and the Pompidou in Paris.

It has been observed that Ive's design team is an intense version of a cult. His quiet nature combined with his design brilliance helps maintain a positive atmosphere for his team. From his early days as team leader, Ive believed in the group and encouraged them toward outstanding achievement. About twelve designers work together at an extremely high level both individually and as a group. The team is somewhat self-contained, and they rarely attend industry events or reward ceremonies.

Team members are culturally diverse, and they all focus on design excellence. The team is tight knit, having many dinners and taking field trips together. Team members work together in a large open studio, are rarely visited by others, even other Apple employees. However, design team members do step outside their physical isolation to interact with engineers, marketers, and manufacturing contractors in Asia.

Ive is a graduate of Newcastle Polytechnic (now Northumbria University), and also received an honorary doctorate from the same school. From the standpoint of appearance, Ive fits in readily with many of his male work associates at Apple, as well as other Silicon Valley firms. His head is shaven, his skin has an unshaven appearance, and he often wears a T-shirt and jeans to the office.

Question: How do Jonathan Ive's cognitive skills help him lead such a world class team of designers?

Source: Original story created from facts and observations in the following sources: John Letzing and Andrew Morse, "Apple's Ive Draws Design Spotlight," *The Wall Street Journal*, October 7, 2011, p. B4; "Jonathan Ive, Senior Vice President, Industrial Design," *Apple Press Info* (www.apple.com), accessed February 20, 2012; David Zilenlziger, "Jonathan Ive, Apple Design Chief, Knighted by iPod User Queen Elizabeth II, (www.ibtimes.com), December 31, 2011, pp. 1–3; "Who Is Jonathan Ive?" *Bloomberg Businessweek* (www.businessweek.com), September 215, 2008, pp. 1–5; "Jonathan Ive Biography," (www.askmen.com), pp. 1–14. Accessed February 20, 2012.

charisma spreads as the people most influenced by the leader say good things about him or her. The most influenced subordinates become third-party endorses spreading the word about the charismatic leader's effectiveness.[11]

A leader's charisma is determined by the subjective perception of him or her by other people. Therefore, it is impossible for even the most effective leaders to inspire and motivate everyone. Even popular business leaders are disliked by some of their employees. For example, the late Steve Jobs, cofounder of Apple Inc., was regarded as charismatic and inspirational by many employees and company outsiders. Yet, was also perceived to be arrogant, obnoxious, and tyrannical by many others who worked with him because of his explosive temper and second-guessing their decisions. Jobs admitted to being obnoxious on occasion, but he was so convinced that he was almost always right that such behavior was warranted. Charisma encompasses many traits and characteristics. Here we focus on vision, passion, enthusiasm, excitement, and humor.

Vision

Top-level leaders need a visual image of where the organization is headed and how it can get there. The person with vision can help the organization or group establish a vision. The progress of the organization depends on the executive having a vision, or an optimistic version of the future. Another essential part of having a vision is for leaders to make sure that others around them also understand the direction as well. Selling the vision is often attained by having vigorous discussions with many people about the proposed future. An example would be the CEO of JC Penny discussing with hundreds of people how he thinks the retailer will soon reestablish its prominence with middle-class shoppers.[12]

Effective leaders project ideas and images that excite people and therefore inspire employees to do their best. Leadership positions of lesser responsibility also call for some vision. Each work group in a progressive company might be expected to form its own vision, such as "We will become the best accounts receivable group in the entire auto replacement parts industry."

Vision, similar to other leadership characteristics, usually has the biggest impact when combined with one or more other characteristics. Marian Elena Lagomasino, the CEO of Asset Management Advisors LLC, has this to say about vision: "Leaders need a vision of what they want to have, then they need to have the courage to make it happen."[13]

Passion, Enthusiasm, and Excitement

Charismatic leaders are passionate about their work and their group members. Martha Stewart, the founder of Martha Stewart Living Omnimedia, is known for her passion. An observer said, "Anyone who knows Martha knows MSLO is the very purpose of her life. No two breaths are taken without thoughts of her business."[14] Part of the reason charismatic leaders can readily be passionate, enthusiastic, and excited is that they tend to be extraverted. The extraversion is most strongly associated with the type of charismatic leader who brings about major changes in the organization or an organizational unit.[15]

Because of their contagious excitement, charismatic leaders stimulate group members. Workers respond positively to enthusiasm, especially because enthusiasm may be perceived as a reward for good performance. Enthusiasm is also effective because it helps build good relationships with group members. Spoken expressions of enthusiasm include such statements as "great job" and "I love it." The leader can express enthusiasm nonverbally through gestures, nonsexual touching, and so forth.

An important positive consequence of the passion and enthusiasm of the leader is that they contribute to the emotional well-being of group members. A study with forty-eight groups of firefighters found that firefighters under the command of a charismatic officer were happier than those groups reporting to supervisors low in charisma. Both charisma and happiness were measured by questionnaires of known accuracy.[16]

The emotional state of followers (group members) is also significant for understanding how charisma works. When people are in a state of emotional arousal, such as facing a crisis or an unusual success, they are more ready to perceive a leader as being charismatic.[17] A historically important example is when Chrysler Corporation was facing bankruptcy in the late 1970s. Chairman Lee Iacocca spearheaded a federal government loan to save the company. In the process, the name Iacocca became almost synonymous with charisma. Chrysler employees, as well as suppliers and many others, were in dire need of a charismatic leader.

Sense of Humor

Humor is a component of charisma and a contributor to leadership effectiveness. Humor helps leaders influence people by reducing tension, relieving boredom, and defusing anger. The most effective form of humor by a leader is tied to the leadership situation. It is much less effective for the leader to tell rehearsed jokes. A key advantage of a witty, work-related comment is that it indicates mental alertness. A canned joke is much more likely to fall flat.

A sales manager was conducting a meeting about declining sales. He opened the meeting by saying, "Ladies and gentlemen, just yesterday I completed a spreadsheet analysis of our declining sales. If we continue our current trend, by the year 2019 we will have sales of negative $3,750,000. No company can support those figures. We've got to reverse the trend." The manager's humor helped dramatize the importance of reversing the sales decline.

A caution about charisma is that it is not entirely dependent on personal characteristics but also on what a person accomplishes. Achieving outstanding results may lead to being perceived as charismatic. An example would be if an almost-forgotten coach suddenly has an outstanding season and is then described as charismatic.

Although inherited characteristics, such as energy, contribute to charisma, most people can develop some charismatic qualities. Figure 11-2 presents suggestions for becoming more charismatic.

Learning Objective 2

What Are Some Behaviors and Skills of Effective Leaders?

The personal traits, skills, and characteristics just discussed help create the potential for effective leadership. A leader also has to *do* things that influence group members to achieve good performance. Workers want their leaders to be charismatic but also want competence and results.[18] The behaviors or skills of leaders described next contribute to productivity and morale in most situations. Before studying the behaviors and skills of effective leaders, do Human Relations Self-Assessment Quiz 11-2. The exercise will help you understand how ready you are to assume a leadership role. Taking the quiz will also give you insight into the type of thinking that is characteristic of leaders.

PRACTICE STRONG ETHICS

Being trustworthy facilitates a leader practicing strong (or good) ethics, the study of moral obligation, or separating right from wrong. Ethics deals with doing the right thing by employees, customers, the environment, and the law. Practicing good ethics contributes to effective leadership for several reasons. Workers are more likely to trust an ethical than an unethical leader, which helps the leader gain the support of the group. Good ethics

FIGURE 11-2 SUGGESTIONS FOR BECOMING MORE CHARISMATIC

Following are a number of suggestions for behaving charismatically, all based on characteristics and behaviors often found among charismatic leaders and other charismatic persons.

1. **Communicate a vision.** A charismatic leader offers an exciting image of where the organization is headed and how to get there. A vision is more than a forecast because it describes an ideal version of the future of an entire organization or an organizational unit, such as a department. The supervisor of paralegal services might communicate a vision such as, "Our paralegal group will become known as the most professional and helpful paralegal group in Arizona."
2. **Make frequent use of metaphors and analogies.** To inspire people, the charismatic leader uses colorful language and exciting metaphors and analogies. Develop metaphors to inspire people around you. To pick up the spirits of her maintenance group, a maintenance supervisor told the group, "We're a lot like the heating and cooling system in a house. A lot of people don't give us much thought, but without us their lives would be very uncomfortable."
3. **Inspire trust and confidence.** Make your deeds consistent with your promises. As mentioned earlier in this chapter, being trustworthy is a key leadership trait. Get people to believe in your competence by making your accomplishments known in a polite, tactful way.
4. **Be highly energetic and goal oriented.** Impress others with your energy and resourcefulness. To increase your energy supply, exercise frequently, eat well, and get ample rest. You can also add to an image of energy by raising and lowering your voice frequently and avoiding a slow pace.
5. **Be emotionally expressive and warm.** A key characteristic of charismatic leaders is the ability to express feelings openly. In dealing with team members, refer to your feelings at the time, such as "I'm excited because I know we are going to hit our year-end target by mid-October." Nonverbal emotional expressiveness, such as warm gestures and frequent touching (nonsexual) of group members, also exhibits charisma.
6. **Make ample use of true stories.** An excellent way of building rapport is to tell stories that deliver a message. Storytelling adds a touch of warmth to the teller and helps build connections among people who become familiar with the same story.
7. **Smile frequently, even if you are not in a happy mood.** A warm smile seems to indicate a confident, caring person, which contributes to a perception of charisma.
8. **Be candid.** Practice saying directly what you want rather than being indirect and evasive. If you want someone to help you, don't ask, "Are you busy?" Instead, ask, "Can you help me with a problem I'm having right now?"
9. **Make everybody you meet feel that he or she is quite important.** For example, at a company social gathering, shake the hand of every person you meet. Also, thank people frequently both orally and by written notes.
10. **Stand up straight and use other nonverbal signals of self-confidence.** Practice having good posture. Minimize fidgeting, scratching, foot tapping, and speaking in a monotone. Walk at a rapid pace without appearing to be panicked. Dress fashionably without going to the extreme that people notice your clothes more than they notice you. Shake hands firmly without creating pain, and make enough eye contact to notice the color of the other person's eyes. When you take that much trouble, you project care and concern.
11. **Be willing to take personal risks.** Charismatic leaders are typically risk takers, and risk taking adds to their charisma. Risks you might take include suggesting a bright but costly idea and recommending that a former felon be given a chance in your firm.
12. **Demonstrate to others that you are passionate about what you want others to accomplish.** Speak in an animated voice, use bold positive and negative facial expressions, and make ample use of gestures including making a fist.

Source: Point 12 is based on John Antonakis, Markika Fenley, and Sue Liechti, "Learning Charisma," *Harvard Business Review*, June 2012, p. 129.

serves as a positive model for group members, thus strengthening the organization. Also, ethical leaders help group members avoid common ethical pitfalls in the workplace. Many of these unethical practices, as listed next, can lead to lawsuits against the company. Three examples are (a) lying or misrepresenting facts, (b) suppressing grievances and complaints, and (c) covering up accidents and failing to report health and safety standards.

To simplify a complex issue, an effective leader practices the Golden Rule: *Do unto others as you would have others do unto you.*

A strategic way of behaving ethically as a leader according to psychologist Howard Gardner of the Harvard Graduate School of Education is to develop an *ethical mind.* It is mind-set that helps workers aspire to do good work that matters to their coworkers,

Human Relations Self-Assessment Quiz 11-2

Readiness for the Leadership Role

Indicate the extent to which you agree with each of the following statements. Use a 1 to 5 scale: (1) disagree strongly, (2) disagree, (3) neutral, (4) agree, (5) agree strongly. If you do not have leadership experience, imagine how you might react to the questions if you were a leader.

1.	It is enjoyable having people count on me for ideas and suggestions.	1	2	3	4	5
2.	It would be accurate to say that I have inspired other people.	1	2	3	4	5
3.	It's a good practice to ask people provocative questions about their work.	1	2	3	4	5
4.	It's easy for me to compliment others.	1	2	3	4	5
5.	I like to cheer up people even when my own spirits are down.	1	2	3	4	5
6.	What my team accomplishes is more important than my personal glory.	1	2	3	4	5
7.	Many people imitate my ideas.	1	2	3	4	5
8.	Building team spirit is important to me.	1	2	3	4	5
9.	I would enjoy coaching other members of the team.	1	2	3	4	5
10.	It is important to me to recognize others for their accomplishments.	1	2	3	4	5
11.	I would enjoy entertaining visitors to my firm even if it interfered with my completing a report.	1	2	3	4	5
12.	It would be fun for me to represent my team at gatherings outside our department.	1	2	3	4	5
13.	The problems of my teammates are my problems, too.	1	2	3	4	5
14.	Resolving conflict is an activity I enjoy.	1	2	3	4	5
15.	I would cooperate with another unit in the organization even if I disagreed with the position taken by its members.	1	2	3	4	5
16.	I am an idea generator on the job.	1	2	3	4	5
17.	It's fun for me to bargain whenever I have the opportunity.	1	2	3	4	5
18.	Team members listen to me when I speak.	1	2	3	4	5
19.	People have asked to me to assume the leadership of an activity several times in my life.	1	2	3	4	5
20.	I've always been a convincing person.	1	2	3	4	5

Total Score ___________________

Scoring and Interpretation:

Calculate your total score by adding the numbers circled. An interpretation of the scoring is as follows:

90–100 High readiness for the leadership role
60–89 Moderate readiness for the leadership role
40–59 Some uneasiness with the leadership role
39 or less Low readiness for carrying out the leadership role

If you are already a successful leader and you scored low on this questionnaire, ignore your score. If you scored surprisingly low and you are not yet a leader, or you are currently performing poorly as a leader, study the statements carefully. Consider changing your attitude or your behavior so that you can legitimately answer more of the questions with a 4 or 5. Studying the rest of this chapter will give you additional insight into the leader's role that may be helpful in your development as a leader.

employers, and society in general. You believe that maintaining an ethical compass is essential for the health of your employer. Gardner explains further:

> A person with an ethical mind asks herself, "What kind of person, worker, and citizen do I want to be? If all the workers in my profession adopted the mind-set I have, or if everyone did what I do, what would the world be like?"[19]

A leader with an ethical mind would avoid the unethical behaviors listed earlier, along with swindling investors with such schemes as selling them securities based on loans with very high—and undisclosed—default rates.

DIRECTION SETTING

Given that leaders are supposed to bring about change, they must point people in the right direction. Setting a direction includes the idea of establishing a vision for the organization or a smaller group. An example of direction setting by a top-level manager would be for the chief executive officer of a toy company to decide that the company should now diversify into the bicycle business. Direction setting by a team leader would include encouraging the group to strive toward error-free work from this point forward or to collaborate more with each other to form a true team. A specific example of direction setting is the initiatives taken by high-flying Delta Airlines executive Joanne Smith.

> A one-time flight attendant herself while in college, Smith pointed Delta in the direction of sprucing up its planes to attract passengers while the airline was still in bankruptcy-court protection. Among her initiatives were to replace faded carpets, replace worn-out fabric seats with leather upholstery, have flight attendants wear designer uniforms, and empower attendants to create their own passenger greetings.[20]

HELP GROUP MEMBERS REACH GOALS AND ACHIEVE SATISFACTION

Effective leaders help group members in their efforts to achieve goals according to the path-goal theory of leadership.[21] In a sense, they smooth out the path to reaching goals. One important way to do this is to provide the necessary resources to group members. An important aspect of a leader's job is to ensure that subordinates have the proper tools, equipment, and human resources to accomplish their objectives.

Another way of helping group members achieve goals is to reduce frustrating barriers to getting work accomplished. A leader who helps group members cut through minor rules and regulations would be engaging in such behavior. In a factory, a supervisory leader has a responsibility to replace faulty equipment, make sure unsafe conditions are corrected, and see that troublesome employees are either rehabilitated or replaced.

Another important general set of actions characteristic of an effective leader is looking out for the satisfaction of the group. Small things sometimes mean a lot in terms of personal satisfaction. One office manager fought for better beverage facilities for her subordinates. Her thoughtfulness contributed immensely to job satisfaction among them. Giving group members emotional support is another effective way of improving worker satisfaction. An emotionally supportive leader would engage in activities such as listening to group members' problems and offering them encouragement and praise. Encouragement can also take the form of asking group members to identify and fix whatever is holding them back.[22] For example, with encouragement from her head nurse, a new nurse admitted that her knowledge of calculating fractions and percentages was not good enough for dispensing certain medications. The newcomer nurse then set about to study the arithmetic she needed. (Again, basic human relations skills contribute to leadership effectiveness.)

Recent findings suggest that a powerful approach to enhancing job satisfaction is for leaders to help group members make progress in meaningful work. Even small steps forward boost the feeling that workers are on their way toward achieving something worthwhile.[23] Visualize a leader in shipyard directing hundreds of workers toward building a cruise ship—a meaningful task for many people. To enhance satisfaction, the leader might ask frequently what he or she could do to help overcome any barriers to getting work done, and also keep workers informed about how well they were progressing against schedule.

SET HIGH EXPECTATIONS

In addition to making expectations clear, it is important for leaders to set high expectations for group members. Effective leaders consistently hold group members to high standards of performance. The owner of a Kia dealership might say, "I see that our customer satisfaction ratings have been about 80 percent. From now on, I want to hear back from regional headquarters that our ratings average 95 percent. We'll figure out together how to do it." If you as a leader expect others to succeed, they are likely to live up to your expectations. This mysterious phenomenon has been labeled the **Pygmalion effect**. (In Chapter 3, we discussed the origins of this idea based on Greek mythology in relation to the Galatea effect, or setting high expectations for oneself.)

Pygmalion effect
leader's ability to elevate worker performance by the simple method of expecting them to perform well; the manager's high expectations become a self-fulfilling prophecy

The point of the Pygmalion effect is that the leader can elevate performance by the simple method of expecting others to perform well. The manager's high expectations become a self-fulfilling prophecy. Why high expectations lead to high performance could be linked to self-confidence. As the leader expresses faith in the group members' abilities to perform well they become more confident of their skills. Also, when a managerial leader believes that a group member will succeed, the manager communicates this belief without realizing it.

GIVE FREQUENT FEEDBACK ON PERFORMANCE

Effective leaders inform employees how they can improve and praise them for things done right. Often, a simple e-mail message can be effective feedback, such as, "Sue, the financial analysis you prepared for our client today was exactly the information he needed to purchase a $300,000 variable annuity. Thanks so much." Less effective leaders, in contrast, often avoid confrontation and give limited positive feedback. An exception is that some ineffective leaders become involved in many confrontations—they are masters at reprimanding people!

MANAGE A CRISIS EFFECTIVELY

When a crisis strikes, that's the time to have an effective leader around. When things are running very smoothly, you may not always notice whether your leader is present. Effectively managing a crisis means giving reassurance to the group that problems will soon be under control, specifying the alternative paths for getting out of the crisis and choosing one of the paths. Showing compassion for those directly affected by the crisis is also quite helpful. After Hurricane Katrina, for example, managers at McDonald's made a concentrated effort to be in touch with as many employees as possible to communicate concern about their welfare and to discuss their employment situation. As implied earlier, a crisis is a key opportunity for the leader to behave charismatically because group members are probably looking for charismatic leadership.

ASK THE RIGHT QUESTIONS

Leaders do not need to know all the answers. Instead, a major contribution can be to ask the right questions. Although being knowledgeable about the group task is important, there are many times when asking group members penetrating questions is more important. In today's complex and rapidly changing business environment, the collective intelligence of group members is needed to solve problems. Quite often a leader does not have the answer to a problem, so asking questions is important. Also, asking questions rather than giving answers is the natural method of helping group members become better problem solvers. Here are sample questions a leader might ask group members to help them meet their challenges:

- What are you going to do differently to reduce by 50 percent the time it takes to fill a customer order?
- Top management is thinking of getting rid of our group and subcontracting the work we do to outside vendors. What do you propose we do to make us more valuable to the company?
- Can you figure out why the competition is outperforming us?

BE A SERVANT LEADER

A humanitarian approach to leadership is to be a **servant leader**, one who serves group members by working on their behalf to help them achieve their goals, not the leader's goals. With confidence shaken in several well-publicized corrupt leaders, interest has increased in the development of leaders who set aside self-interest for the betterment of their followers and employers.[24]

Servant leader
one who serves group members by working on their behalf to help them achieve their goals, not the leader's goals

The idea behind servant leadership, as developed by Robert K. Greenleaf, is that leadership stems naturally from a commitment to service. Serving others, including employees, customers, and the community, is the primary motivation for the servant leader. The servant leader is passionate about the people he or she works with and for.[25] Servant leadership encompasses many different acts, all designed to make life easier or better for group members. Several acts or aspects of servant leadership are mentioned next.

- **Humble servant.** A good starting point is for the leader to see himself or herself as a humble servant. ("I'm here to serve you.") The leader downplays his or her ego to support the talents of others. Servant leaders also look for the opportunity to lend assistance directly to employees, such as a supermarket manager bagging groceries during an unanticipated rush of business. A servant leader would also provide the tools people needed to accomplish their work, such as fighting for enough money for the budget to purchase expensive new equipment.
- **Good listener.** A servant leader emphasizes listening to subordinates, because you cannot help people if you do not understand their concerns. Sam Palmisano, the former chairman and CEO of IBM, believes strongly in the listening aspect of servant leadership. He believes that effective leaders listen instead of making themselves the center of attention.[26]
- **Realistic about what can be done.** Although a servant leader is idealistic, he or she recognizes that one individual cannot accomplish everything. So the leader listens carefully to the array of problems facing group members and then concentrates on a few. As the head of a nurses' union told the group, "I know you are hurting in many ways. Yet, I think that the work overload issue is the biggest one, so we will head into negotiations working on obtaining sensible workloads. After that we will work on job security."
- **Development of subordinates.** Another important behavior of servant leaders is that they want subordinates to grow and succeed. They demonstrate genuine concern for the career growth of group members by providing emotional support and mentoring.[27] As such, a servant leader is likely to be perceived as a good coach.

A study with 71 teams in five banks indicated that servant leadership at the team level is associated with team effectiveness. Servant leadership was measured by team members rating their leader on a scale with items such as, "My manager seems to care more about my success than his or her own." Team performance was measured by member of upper-level management rating the team's performance on a 1 to 7 scale.[28]

▶ Learning Objective 3 ▶

What Is Leadership Style, and What Is Style Flexibility?

Leadership style
a leader's characteristic way of behaving in a variety of situations

Understanding the traits, behaviors, skills, and attitudes of leaders points to another major approach to explaining leadership. A **leadership style** is a leader's characteristic way of behaving in a variety of situations. Here we look at the classic dimensions of leadership style, participative leadership, and style flexibility or adaptability.

THE CLASSIC DIMENSIONS OF CONSIDERATION AND INITIATING STRUCTURE

Leadership styles have been characterized in many ways, beginning in the 1950s with studies at the Ohio State University conducted with factory supervisors and military personnel.[29] Most approaches to leadership style are variations, refinements, and expansions of this pioneering work. The researchers asked group members to describe their supervisors by responding to the questionnaires. Leaders were also asked to rate themselves on leadership dimensions (activities they performed). Two main dimensions were identified that accounted for the vast majority of a leader's activity: "consideration" and "initiating structure."

Consideration
the degree to which the leader creates an environment of emotional support, warmth, friendliness, and trust

Consideration is the degree to which the leader creates an environment of emotional support, warmth, friendliness, and trust. The leader creates this environment by being friendly and approachable and looking out for the welfare of the group. He or she also keeps the group informed about new developments and does small favors for the group, such as getting the break area repainted. In other words, the leader focuses on the human relations aspect of work.

Initiating structure
organizing and defining relationships in the group by engaging in such activities as assigning specific tasks, specifying procedures to be followed, scheduling work, and making expectations clear

Initiating structure means organizing and defining relationships in the group by engaging in such activities as assigning specific tasks, specifying procedures to be followed, scheduling work, and making expectations clear. In other words, the leader provides structure for the group and focuses on the work.

Leaders have been categorized with respect to how much emphasis they place on the two dimensions of consideration and initiating structure. As implied by Figure 11-3, the two dimensions are not mutually exclusive. A leader can achieve high or low status on both dimensions. For example, an effective leader might contribute to high productivity yet still place considerable emphasis on warm human relationships. A leader's style could be characterized in terms of which one of the four boxes he or she fits into in Figure 11-3.

THE PARTICIPATIVE (TEAM) LEADERSHIP STYLE

Participative leader
leader who shares decision-making authority with the group; motivates group members to work as a team toward high-level goals

For the past thirty-five years, the participative leadership style has received the most attention because this style enables the leader to share decisions with the group and capitalize on the talents of the group. By definition, a **participative leader** shares decision-making authority with the group. At his or her best, the participative leader motivates group members to work as a team toward high-level goals. Encouraging employees to participate in making decisions is the major approach to empowerment. Participative

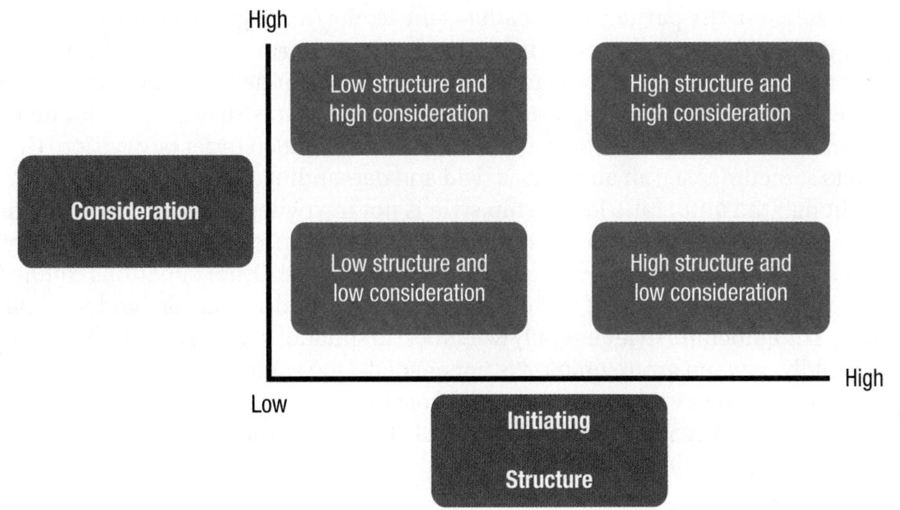

FIGURE 11-3

FOUR COMBINATIONS OF INITIATING STRUCTURE AND CONSIDERATION

A leader's behavior can be described in terms of four different combinations of consideration and initiating structure. For example, a leader who emphasizes both giving group members a high degree of structure and paying close attention to their needs would be characterized as "high structure and high consideration," the upper right box.

leadership is often favored because workers are more willing to implement decisions when they are involved in formulating the decisions. Participative leadership encompasses so many different behaviors that it is useful to divide it into three subtypes: consultative, consensus, and democratic.

Consultative Leaders

A **consultative leader** solicits opinions from the group before making a decision yet does not feel obliged to accept the group's thinking. Leaders of this type make it clear that they alone have authority to make the final decisions. A standard way to practice consultative leadership would be to call a group meeting and discuss an issue before making a decision. A positive example of a consultative leader is Tim Cook, the CEO of Apple Inc. He communicates freely with employees throughout the company, and solicits their opinion. Cook sends many e-mails to Apple employees, whom he addresses as "Team."[30]

Consultative leader leader who solicits opinions from the group before making a decision, yet does not feel obliged to accept the group's thinking; this type of leader makes it clear that he or she alone has the authority to make the final decisions

Consensus Leaders

A **consensus leader** encourages group discussion about an issue and then makes a decision that reflects the consensus of the group members. Consensus-style leaders thus turn over more authority to the group than do consultative leaders. The consensus style sometimes results in long delays in decision making because every party involved has to agree. The problem of delays can be minimized if group members are given a deadline to reach an agreement.

Consensus leader leader who encourages group discussion about an issue and then makes a decision that reflects the consensus of the group members

Democratic Leaders

A **democratic leader** confers final authority on the group. He or she functions as a collector of opinion and takes a vote before making a decision. The group usually achieves its goals when working under a democratic leader. Democratic leadership has more relevance for community activities than for most work settings.

When democratic leaders turn over too much authority to the group they are referred to as laissez-faire (or free rein) leaders. Laissez-faire leadership works only with highly motivated and self-sufficient individuals. Otherwise, group members left completely on their own may become dissatisfied and unproductive. A study with over 2,000 Norwegian workers found that workers managed with a laissez-faire style were likely to suffer from role ambiguity, or not knowing what is expected. As a result these workers were stressed and anxious, often guessing if they were focusing on the correct tasks and establishing the right priorities.[31]

Democratic leader leader who confers final authority on the group; functions as a collector of opinion and takes a vote before making a decision (in extreme sometimes referred to as a free-rein leader)

Autocratic leader
leader who attempts to retain most of the authority granted to the group; autocratic leaders make all the major decisions and assume subordinates will comply without question

In contrast to the participative leader is the leader/manager who makes decisions more independently. An **autocratic leader** attempts to retain most of the authority granted to the group. Autocratic leaders make all the major decisions and assume subordinates will comply without question. Leaders who use this style give minimum consideration to what group members are likely to think about an order or decision. Group members sometimes see an autocrat as rigid and demanding.

Although the autocratic leadership style is not in vogue, many successful leaders are autocratic. Among them are *turnaround managers*—those who specialize in turning around failing organizations or rescuing them from crises. Other situations calling for autocratic crisis management include earthquakes, product recalls, and workplace violence. The autocratic style generally works best in situations where decisions have to be made rapidly or when group opinion is not needed. One situation calling for autocratic leadership would be extinguishing an oil rig fire at sea.

Human Relations Self-Assessment Quiz 11-3 gives you the opportunity to measure your present or potential leadership style.

Adapting to the Various Styles as a Subordinate

Part of understanding leadership is being able to adapt to the style of your superior. To begin, the suggestions for getting along with your manager presented in Chapter 9 should work well for leaders of any style. In addition, keep these suggestions in mind for adapting to the three styles presented next.

1. **Participative style (consultative, consensus, and collaborative).** With a participative style of leader, it is important for you to play an active role as a subordinate. Above all, be prepared to offer suggestions for improving work processes and procedures. Offer constructive feedback for building on the suggestions of your leader. Demonstrate that you are a professional who wants to be considered a partner in the success of the organizational unit (such as a department or team).
2. **Autocratic style.** Be a good soldier. Expect to be given clear, precise, directions, and guidance. Provide input to your boss when asked, but keep in mind that even if you are quite talented, your manager has formal authority for running your organizational unit. When you become the boss, you can make the big decisions. An autocratic leader welcomes subordinates who readily accept assignments and follow through on time. Be brief and businesslike in your interactions with your boss, because he or she most likely does not like to spend lots of time in discussions with subordinates.
3. **Laissez-faire style.** Recognize that you are pretty much on your own in terms of receiving guidance, feedback, directions, and encouragement from your boss. Check in with your boss occasionally to make sure you are working on the right assignment or project. Do not hint that the lack of structure is intolerable for you. If you want guidance, consult a trusted coworker.

STYLE FLEXIBILITY AND ADAPTABILITY

Although leadership style refers to a person's characteristic approach to dealing with leadership tasks, effective leaders adapt their style to fit the situation. For example, a leader might typically use a consensus style, yet when managing a crisis he or she might become more authoritarian—giving subordinates directions in a hurry without waiting to achieve agreement among group members. A study of 3,000 executives revealed that leaders who get the best results do not rely on one style. Instead, they use several different styles in one week, such as being autocratic in some situations and democratic in others.[32] Furthermore, a more recent analysis of hundreds of studies suggests that leadership should be defined as "doing the right thing at the right time."[33] The leader makes the decision or chooses the action that fits the circumstances. An example might

Human Relations Self-Assessment Quiz 11-3

What Style of Leader Are You or Would You Be?

Answer the following questions, keeping in mind what you have done, or think you would do, regarding the scenarios and attitudes described.

Number		Mostly True	Mostly False
1.	I am more likely to take care of a high-impact assignment myself than turn it over to a group member.	______	______
2.	I would prefer the analytical aspects of a manager's job rather than working directly with group members.	______	______
3.	An important part of my approach to managing a group is to keep the members informed almost daily of any information that could affect their work.	______	______
4.	It's a good idea to give two people in the group the same problem and then choose what appears to be the best solution.	______	______
5.	It makes good sense for the leader or manager to stay somewhat aloof from the group, so he or she can make a tough decision when necessary.	______	______
6.	I look for opportunities to obtain group input before making a decision, even on straightforward issues.	______	______
7.	I would reverse a decision if several of the group members presented evidence that I was wrong.	______	______
8.	Differences of opinion in the work group are healthy.	______	______
9.	I think that an activity to build team spirit, such as the team fixing up a poor family's house on a Saturday, is an excellent investment of time.	______	______
10.	If my group were hiring a new member, I would like the person to be interviewed by the entire group.	______	______
11.	An effective team leader today uses e-mail for about 98 percent of communication with team members.	______	______
12.	Some of the best ideas are likely to come from the group members rather than the manager.	______	______
13.	If our group were going to have a banquet, I would get input from each member on what type of food should be served.	______	______
14.	I have never seen a statue of a committee in a museum or park, so why bother making decisions by a committee if you want to be recognized?	______	______
15.	I dislike it intensely when a group member challenges my position on an issue.	______	______
16.	I typically explain to group members what method they should use to accomplish an assigned task.	______	______
17.	If I were out of the office for a week, most of the important work in the department would get accomplished anyway.	______	______
18.	Delegation of important tasks is something that is very difficult for me.	______	______
19.	When a group member comes to me with a problem, I tend to jump right in with a proposed solution.	______	______
20.	When a group member comes to me with a problem, I typically ask that person something such as, "What alternative solutions have you thought of so far?"	______	______

(*continued*)

Scoring and Interpretation:

The answers in the participative/team-style leader direction are listed below. Give yourself one point for each answer that matches the scoring key.

1. Mostly false	**8.** Mostly true	**15.** Mostly false
2. Mostly false	**9.** Mostly true	**16.** Mostly false
3. Mostly true	**10.** Mostly true	**17.** Mostly true
4. Mostly false	**11.** Mostly false	**18.** Mostly false
5. Mostly false	**12.** Mostly true	**19.** Mostly false
6. Mostly true	**13.** Mostly true	**20.** Mostly true
7. Mostly true	**14.** Mostly false	

If your score is 15 or higher, you are most likely (or would be) a participative/team-style leader. If your score is 5 or lower, you are most likely (or would be) an authoritarian style leader.

Skill Development:

The quiz you just completed is also an opportunity for skill development. Review the twenty items and look for implied suggestions for engaging in participative leadership. For example, item 20 suggests that you encourage group members to work through their own solutions to problems. If your goal is to become an authoritarian leader (one who makes decisions primarily on his or her own) the items can also serve as useful guidelines. For example, item 19 suggests than an authoritarian leader looks first to solve problems for group members.

be transferring a valuable worker to a temporary assignment rather than firing him or her because of too little work for that individual at the moment.

Rule of Thumb for Style Flexibility

A rule of thumb for attaining style flexibility is to give considerable guidance, direction, and coaching to a worker who has low motivation or capability in terms of accomplishing the task. In contrast, give less guidance, direction, and coaching to a worker with high motivation and capability. The preceding is perhaps the best established finding about providing leadership to others.

Adapting Leadership Style to Cultural Values

Another way in which leadership style flexibility can be important is when it has to be adapted to fit cultural values. (Chapter 13 provides more information about these values.) Visualize an autocratic manager from France being sent to a Swedish subsidiary where Swedes strongly value democracy and status equality. The Swedish workers might not take too kindly to the French manager's autocratic behavior. And the French manager might dislike not being treated with great respect.

Learning Objective 4

How Does a Leader Get Along Well with Subordinates?

The concepts already mentioned in this chapter, as well as other information you have studied about getting along with people, apply to a leader getting along well with subordinates. We spotlight this topic by presenting a well-documented theory about leader–member relationships, as well as a few illustrative principles.

THE LEADER–MEMBER EXCHANGE MODEL

George Graen, a professor of organizational behavior at the University of Illinois, Champaign–Urbana, and his associates have developed a leadership model that focuses on the quality of leader–member relations. The **leader–member exchange (LMX) model** recognizes that leaders develop unique working relationships with each group member.[34] A leader might be considerate and compassionate toward one team member yet rigid and unfeeling toward another. Leaders usually face constraints on their time, so the number of high-quality relationships they can form with subordinates is limited. As a result, leaders might be selective about which group members with whom they develop close relationships.[35] Figure 11-4 illustrates the fact that a leader might have different quality exchanges with different group members.

Leader–member exchange (LMX) model
leadership model that focuses on the quality of leader–member relations; recognizes that leaders develop unique working relationships with each group member

Each relationship between the leader/manager and employees differs in quality. One subset of employees, the in-group, is given additional rewards, responsibility, and trust in exchange for their loyalty and performance. In contrast, another subset of employees (the out-group) is treated in accordance with a more formal understanding of the supervisor-subordinate relationship. The leader's first impression of a group member's competency heavily influences whether he or she becomes a member of the in-group or out-group.

In-group members have attitudes and values similar to the leader and interact frequently with the leader. Out-group members have less in common with the leader and operate somewhat detached from the leader. The one-to-one relationships have a major influence on the subordinate's behavior in the group. Members of the in-group become part of a smoothly functioning team headed by the formal leader. Out-group members are less likely to experience good teamwork. Being a member of the in-group facilitates achieving high productivity and satisfaction. Out-group members receive less challenging assignments and are more likely to quit because of job dissatisfaction.[36]

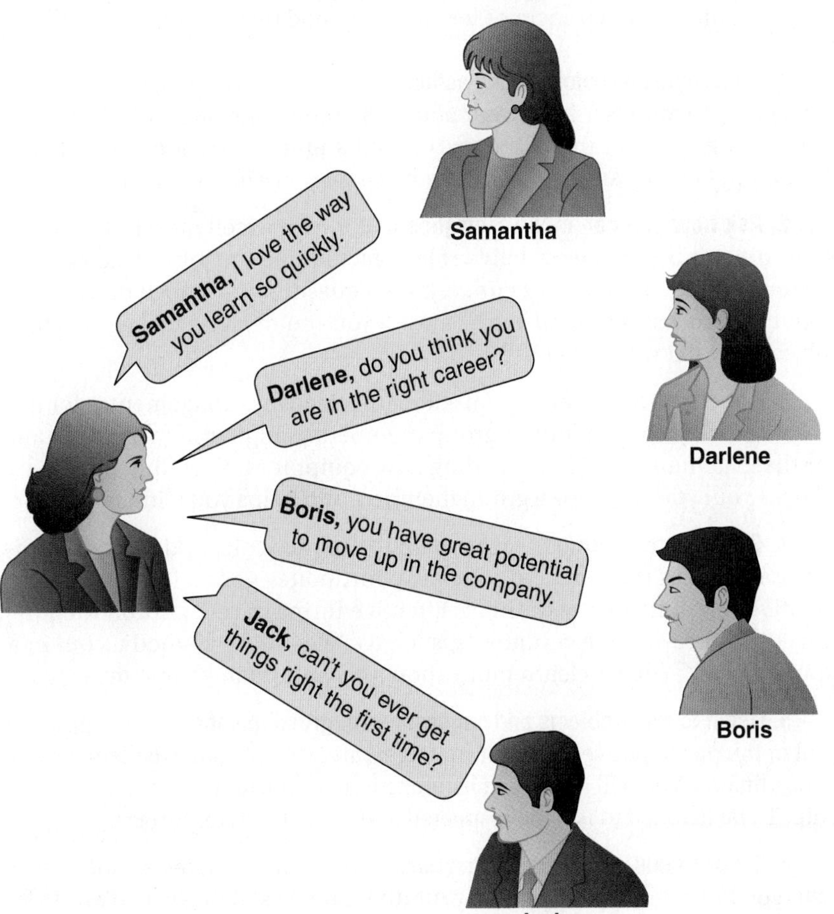

FIGURE 11-4

AN EXAMPLE OF THE LEADER-EXCHANGE MODEL IN ACTION

The leader has different quality relationship with each member in the group.

The specific relevance of the LMX model for getting along with group members is that if the leader establishes good relationships with group members, higher productivity and satisfaction is likely to occur. Here is an example of a good exchange between the leader and the manager can enhance productivity and satisfaction:

> Malcolm is a project manager at a company that makes modular (manufactured) housing. The project he heads is for the construction of patio homes for retirement communities. Beverly, one of the engineering technicians assigned to Malcolm's project, is just beginning her career. Malcolm recognizes that Beverly is talented and ambitious but that she needs guidance to get on the right track. He therefore sends her friendly text messages and e-mails from time to time commenting on her progress and the quality of her work. Malcolm also has positive face-to-face interactions with Beverly, offering her encouragement and suggestions. For example, one time Malcolm said to Beverly, "I know that you like perfection but we can't incorporate features into our patio homes that will jack up the price too high."

Because of the encouragement and mentoring Beverly received from Malcolm, she works extra hard and felt like she was growing professionally. As she told the company HR rep, "I'm so glad I joined this company. With Malcolm as my project manager, I'm growing professionally every day."

SUGGESTIONS FOR ATTAINING GOOD RELATIONSHIPS WITH SUBORDINATES

A key part of leadership is forming good relationships with people, so getting along with subordinates is essential. If you are a leader and your subordinates do not like you, it will be difficult for the group to achieve high productivity and satisfaction. A sampling follows of time-tested principles for attaining good relationships with subordinates.

1. Solicit opinions before taking action. In the spirit of participative leadership, find out what group members think of your potential action, even on relatively small matters such as selecting a restaurant for a department banquet. Subordinates will be pleased that their input matters, and they will be more cooperative in implementing your decision.

2. Ask how you can make their jobs better. An excellent relationship builder with subordinates is playing an active role in facilitating the jobs of subordinates running more smoothly. Toward this end, ask such questions as, "What drives you the craziest about the processes around here?" and "If you could have a fantasy tool that made your job easier, what would it be?"[37]

3. Fight for their demands. An axiom of effective management is for the supervisor to bring forth the demands of group members to higher management and then fight for these demands, such as needing new equipment. Carrying out this principle enhances your stature among group members and helps you win their support.

4. Give out recognition. Most people are recognition deprived, so being a boss who recognizes the contributions of subordinates goes a long way toward building positive relationships with them. Effective forms of recognition include thank-you notes and face-to-face comments, such as, "You really helped us out in a jam, and I appreciate it." You will learn more about recognition in your study of motivation.

5. Listen to the problems and suggestions of group members. Listening is an essential tool of the participative leader or manager, and it is also an excellent way of cultivating subordinates. You will recall that listening is an important component of servant leadership. To be listened to is to be respected and considered important.

6. Be courteous. Many managers are rude to subordinates, so showing courtesy will help you build relationships with your direct reports. Being courteous to subordinates would include such acts as responding quickly to e-mail messages, returning phone calls, not multitasking when subordinates are talking to you, not keeping people waiting for you, and not belittling them.

7. Look for opportunities to say yes to requests. Repeated refusals on requests can be demoralizing and demotivating for employees, especially when the request is feasible. Some requests, such as asking for a cash bar in the lunchroom, must be refused. But look for opportunities to say yes. A useful guideline is when a group member makes a request, avoid automatically replying, "We cannot do that." Instead, ask yourself, "Can we do that?"[38]

In short, getting along well with subordinates involves the practice of good human relations, in addition to recognizing that you need the support of your subordinates as much as they need you.

How Do You Develop Your Leadership Potential?

Learning Objective 5

How to improve your potential for becoming a leader is a topic without limits. Developing your leadership potential is possible because both nature and nurture contribute to leadership effectiveness. Just as in playing music or sports, you need certain talents to begin with, such as good eye–hand coordination, but with practice you can improve. The late John Wooden, perhaps the most successful college basketball coach in history, later became a leadership specialist. At age 93, Wooden offered his opinion that leadership can be taught, providing that you have qualities the command respect. Wooden also made clear that not everyone can become a leader.[39]

Almost anything you do to improve your individual effectiveness will have some impact on your ability to lead others. If you strengthen your self-confidence, improve your memory for names, study this book carefully, read studies about leadership, or improve your physical fitness (giving you more energy), you stand a good chance of improving your leadership potential. Eight modes of advancement might be kept in mind if you are seeking to improve your leadership potential:

1. General education and specific training. Almost any program of career training or education can be considered a program of leadership development. Courses in human relations, management, or applied psychology have obvious relevance for someone currently occupying or aspiring toward a leadership position. Many of today's leaders in profit and nonprofit organizations hold formal degrees in business. Specific training programs will also help you improve your leadership potential. Among them might be skill development programs in interviewing, employee selection, listening, cross-cultural training, budgeting, planning, improving work habits, resolving conflict, and communication skills. After acquiring knowledge through study, you then put the knowledge into practice as a leader.

Pioneering leadership scholar and University of Southern California professor Warren G. Bennis emphasizes that becoming a leader involves continual learning, development, and the reinvention of the self.[40] "Reinvention" in this sense could mean rethinking your assumptions about people or even changing careers into one you found that was a better fit with your values.

2. Leadership development programs. A focused way of improving your leadership potential is to attend development programs designed specifically to improve your ability to lead others and develop self-confidence. A popular type of leadership development program called *offsite training* places people in a challenging outdoor environment for a weekend or up to ten days. Participants are required to accomplish physical feats, such as climbing a mountain, whitewater canoeing, building a wall, or swinging between trees on a rope. Participants in these outdoor programs learn such important leadership skills and attitudes as teamwork and trusting others and gain confidence in their abilities to accomplish the seemingly impossible.

3. Acquire broad experience. Because leadership varies somewhat with the situation, a sound approach to improving leadership effectiveness is to attempt to gain supervisory experience in different settings. On-the-job experience remains a helpful way of improving leadership effectiveness, yet it can reach the point of diminishing returns.[41] Obtaining fresh ideas and insights from the study of leadership therefore remains important.

A person who wants to become an executive is well advised to gain supervisory experience in at least two different organizational functions, such as customer service and finance. Support for this viewpoint can be found from the work of Personnel Decisions International, a firm that specializes in leadership development. A long-term study found that first-level supervisors are more likely to succeed if they have cross-functional (having worked in different departments) experience.[42]

First-level supervisory jobs are an invaluable starting point for developing your leadership potential. It takes considerable skill to manage a fast-food restaurant effectively or to direct a public playground during the summer. First-level supervisors frequently face situations in which subordinates are poorly trained, poorly paid, and not well motivated to achieve company objectives. Taking a turn as a team leader is also valuable experience for developing leadership skills.

4. Modeling effective leaders. Carefully observe a capable leader in action and incorporate some of his or her approaches into your own behavior. You may not be able to or want to become that person's clone, but you can model (imitate) what the person does. For instance, most inexperienced leaders have a difficult time confronting others with bad news. Observe a good confronter handle the situation and try his or her approach the next time you have some unfavorable news to deliver. The biography or autobiography of a leader whom you admire is another source of ideas for modeling an effective leader.

5. Self-development of leadership characteristics and behavior. Study the leadership characteristics and behaviors described in this chapter. As a starting point, identify several attributes you think you could strengthen within yourself, given some self-determination. For example, you might decide that with effort you could improve your passion and enthusiasm. You might also believe that you could be more emotionally supportive of others. It is also helpful to obtain feedback from reliable sources, such as a trusted manager, about which traits and behaviors you particularly need to develop.

6. Practice a little leadership. An effective way to develop your leadership skills is to look for opportunities to exert a small amount of helpful leadership in contrast to waiting for opportunities to accomplish extraordinary deeds.[43] A "little leadership" might involve such behaviors as mentoring a struggling team member, coaching somebody about how to use a new high-tech device, or making a suggestion about improving a product.

Self-leadership
leading oneself; influencing oneself without waiting for an external leader to lead; all organizational members are capable of leading themselves to some extent

7. Practice self-leadership. One of the most effective ways of becoming a leader is to begin by leading yourself, or practicing **self-leadership.** According to this concept, all organizational members are capable of leading themselves to some extent. You influence yourself without waiting for an external leader to lead you, much like taking the initiative to accomplish something worthwhile or being a good organizational citizen. According to Charles C. Manz, a professor of business leadership at the University of Massachusetts, self-leadership extends as far as setting your own standards and objectives. "It addresses what should be done, and why it should be done, in addition to how to do it." Recognize, however, that you still have to accomplish what your leader wants you to accomplish, but you can go beyond the minimum required in your job.[44]

8. Become an integrated human being. A philosophical approach to leadership suggests that the model leader is first and foremost a fully functioning person. According to this belief, the type of person you are determines whether you will be an effective leader. According to consultant William D. Hitt, mastering the art of leadership comes with self-mastery. Leadership development is the process of self-development. As a result, the process of becoming a leader is similar to the process of becoming an integrated human being. For example, you need to develop values that guide your behavior before you can adequately guide the behavior of others, and you also need courage.[45]

What Are Several Key Challenges of Being a First-Time Leader?

▶ Learning Objective 6 ▶

Another way of preparing for becoming a leader for the first time is to think through some of the inevitable challenges in the first-time leader faces, as described next.

1. Uncertainty about how much time to spend leading versus doing individual tasks. From the first-level supervisor of entry-level workers to the chairperson of the board, leaders spend some time as individual contributors, including preparing budgets, thinking of ideas for new products, and making financial deals. As a new leader you have to work with your manager and perhaps your direct reports to find the right balance between doing and leading.

2. Assuming that you have the authority and freedom to do what you think is best. First-time leaders usually have much less authority and autonomy than they thought they would have. You are most likely to find yourself in a web of relationships with subordinates, bosses, coworkers, and perhaps customers. Many of these people make demands on you and question your judgment. "You are not really in control of anything," said one new manager.[46]

3. Overcoming the resentment of the people in the group who wanted your leadership position. If you are selected from among the group to be the new leader, you will have to deal with the resentment and envy of several direct reports who wanted your position. It can be helpful to deal openly with the issue with such statements as, "I know that other people would be equally qualified to be the leader of the group. Yet, management has chosen me for this position, at least for now. I respect your expertise and I need your contribution. I also want your respect for me in my job as the chosen leader."

4. Building relationships and fostering teamwork quickly enough. As a new leader, a high priority is to build constructive relationships with subordinates as quickly as possible, using many of the techniques described earlier in this chapter. Several direct reports who were your former coworkers may attempt to manipulate you and take advantage of prior friendships to receive special treatment. It is essential to build a professional, merit-based team climate as soon as possible. In the words of career coach Aya Fubara Eneli, "Friendships work best between equals. If you were already friends with some of the staff, expect those relationships to change. It's difficult to be a friend while giving orders and judging performance."[47]

5. Overcoming the need to be liked by everybody. The most admired leaders at every level are rarely liked by everybody. By the nature of their roles, leaders make decisions that not everybody agrees with. The changes you bring about may hurt the feelings of some people and jeopardize their positions. Your role is to establish and implement goals that will result in the greatest good.

Key Terms

Leadership, 317
Leadership effectiveness, 318
Trust, 320
Character, 320
Cognitive skills, 321
Charisma, 321
Pygmalion effect, 328
Servant leader, 329
Leadership style, 330
Consideration, 330
Initiating structure, 330
Participative leader, 330
Consultative leader, 331
Consensus leader, 331
Democratic leader, 331
Autocratic leader, 332
Leader–member exchange (LMX) model, 335
Self-leadership, 338

Summary and Review

Leadership is the process of bringing about positive changes and influencing others to achieve worthwhile goals and coordinating the pursuit of these goals. Effective leadership is needed at the top of organizations, but supervisors and team leaders also need to provide effective leadership. Effective leaders have the "right stuff." Certain traits and characteristics contribute to leadership effectiveness in many situations. Among them are the following:

- Self-confidence and courage
- Emotional intelligence
- Trustworthiness and character
- Strong work motivation and high energy
- Cognitive skills and openness to experience
- Charisma (vision, passion, enthusiasm, excitement, and humor)

Behaviors and skills of an effective leader (one who maintains high productivity and morale) include these:

- Practicing strong ethics
- Direction setting
- Helping group members reach goals and achieve satisfaction
- Setting high expectations (the Pygmalion effect)
- Giving frequent feedback on performance
- Managing a crisis effectively
- Asking the right questions
- Being a servant leader

Leadership style is a leader's characteristic way of behaving in a variety of situations. Most approaches to understanding leadership style stem from the two dimensions of consideration and initiating structure. Leaders can be characterized with respect to how much emphasis they place on these two dimensions.

Participative leaders share decisions with the group and capitalize on the talents of the group. The subtypes of participative leadership are consultative, consensus, and democratic. In contrast to the participative leader is the autocratic leader/manager who makes decisions more independently. Part of understanding leadership is being able to adapt to the style of your superior. For example, with a participative style of leader, play an active role as a subordinate, and be prepared to offer input into decisions.

Effective leaders tend to adapt their style to the situation, such as a consensus leader becoming authoritarian during a crisis. The effective leader does the right thing at the right time. In general, workers with low motivation and capability need more guidance, direction, and coaching. Cultural values, such as a belief in collectivism, can influence which style is best.

According to the leader–member exchange (LMX) model, leaders develop unique working relationships with each group member. If the leader establishes good relationships with group members, higher productivity and satisfaction are likely to occur.

Time-tested principles for attaining good relationships with subordinates include:

- Soliciting opinions before taking action
- Fighting for their demands
- Giving out recognition
- Listening to the problems and suggestions of group members

- Being courteous
- Looking for opportunities to say yes to requests

Many activities in life can in some way contribute to the development of a person's leadership potential. Eight recommended avenues for improving your leadership potential or leadership skills are as follows:

- General education and specific training
- Participating in leadership development programs
- Acquiring broad experience
- Modeling effective leaders
- Self-developing leadership characteristics and behavior
- Practicing a little leadership
- Practicing self-leadership
- Becoming an integrated human being

First-time leaders face key challenges, such as:

- Uncertainty about how much time to spend on leading versus doing individual tasks
- Assuming you have the authority and freedom to do what you think is best
- Overcoming the resentment of the people in the group who wanted your leadership position
- Building relationships and fostering teamwork quickly enough
- Overcoming the need to be liked by everybody

Check Your Understanding

1. Provide an example of something a leader motivated or inspired you to do that you would not have done without his or her presence.
2. If cognitive skills are really important for being an effective leader, what can a future leader do to enhance his or her cognitive skills?
3. Why does being charismatic often make a leader more effective?
4. What is your vision for yourself?
5. Provide an example of how you might use the Pygmalion effect in working with subordinates or with a child you have or might have.
6. In what way is the professor in this course a *servant leader* in his or her relationship with the students in the class?
7. Some organizational leaders continue to say, "I don't want to be loved. I just want to be respected." Why might respect for the leader be more important than love in many situations?
8. Give an example of a specific action taken by a present or former boss that helped cultivate good relationships with subordinates. Also identify an action that hurt relationships with subordinates.
9. Imagine yourself in either your present job or a job of your choice. How would you practice self-leadership in this job?
10. In what way does your program of study contribute to your development as a leader?

Web Corner

Overview of Leadership
www.ccl.org

Leadership Development Programs
www.academyleadership.com/

Servant Leadership
http://greenleaf.org

Internet Skill Builder
Charisma Development

You have already received suggestions in this chapter for developing your charisma. Visit www.core-edge.com to search for additional ideas for charisma development. Go to the section on charisma, and read a couple of case histories to uncover ideas you might try to enhance your charisma. Watch the video "A Conversation on Charisma." After digging through core-edge.com, list two concrete ideas you might implement to enhance your charisma.

Also answer these questions: (a) What is charismatology? and (b) What is your rating of the charisma of the presenter in the video?

Developing Your Human Relations Skills

Human Relations Application Exercises

Applying Human Relations Exercise 11-1

Developing Your Charisma

An effective way of developing your leadership potential is to project a more charismatic image, even if you do not truly make over your personality. If you appear more charismatic to others, they are more likely to respond to your leadership. Also, if you project a more charismatic image, you are more likely to be nominated for leadership positions and assignments. Following is a checklist of the suggestions for becoming more charismatic as presented in Figure 11-3. As you go through the list, select two or three ideas that you would be willing to try in the next two weeks. Note that some of the suggestions are much easier than others to implement in the short range.

Charisma Suggestions (see Figure 11-3 for explanations)	Yes, I Will Try It
1. Communicate a vision.	❑
2. Make frequent use of metaphors and analogies.	❑
3. Inspire trust and confidence.	❑
4. Be highly energetic and goal oriented.	❑
5. Be emotionally expressive and warm.	❑
6. Make ample use of true stories.	❑
7. Smile frequently, even if not in happy mood.	❑
8. Be candid.	❑
9. Make everybody you meet feel that he or she is important.	❑
10. Multiply the effectiveness of your handshake.	❑
11. Stand up straight and use other nonverbal signals of self-confidence.	❑
12. Be willing to take personal risks.	❑
13. Be self-promotional.	❑

Now that you have made your choice of suggestions, try them out with other people, including students, athletic team members, coworkers, or members of a community group. After your experience, answer the following questions:

1. How did people react to me when I attempted to be more charismatic?
2. How can I use this approach more effectively next time? (How should I fine-tune my approach?)
3. Are these approaches to charisma enhancement making any contribution to my development as a leader?

Applying Human Relations Exercise 11-2

My Personal Leadership Journal

A potentially important tool in your development as a leader is to maintain a journal or diary of your leadership experiences. Make a journal entry within twenty-four hours after you carried out a leadership action of any kind, or failed to do so when the opportunity arose. You will, therefore, have entries dealing with leadership opportunities both capitalized on and missed. An example: "A few of my neighbors were complaining about trash flying around the neighborhood on trash pick-up days, particularly when the wind was strong. I took the initiative to send e-mails and flyers to neighborhood residents discussing what could be done about the problem. I suggested that people pack their recycling boxes more tightly. I also suggested ever so politely that people should pick up their own flying trash. Soon the problem nearly disappeared."

Also include in your journal such entries as comments you receive on your leadership ability, leadership traits that you appear to be developing, and leadership ideas about which you learn. Also, keep a list of leadership articles and books you intend to read. You might also want to record observations about significant acts of leadership or leadership blunders that you have observed in others, either firsthand or through the media.

Review your journal monthly, and make note of any progress you think you have made in developing your leadership skills. Also consider preparing a graph of your progress in developing leadership skills. The vertical axis can represent skill level on a 1 to 100 scale, and the horizontal axis might be divided into time intervals, such as calendar quarters.

Applying Human Relations Exercise 11-3

Analyzing the Leadership Effectiveness of a Past or Present Supervisor

Visualize a current supervisor or one to whom you reported in the past. Analyze his or her approach to leadership based on your own observations and perhaps comments you heard from coworkers. Consider also the results the leader achieved. Your evaluation should be based on the supervisor's traits and characteristics including charisma, leadership style, and ability to get along with group members. Conclude your brief report with several suggestions for how the supervisor in question might become a more effective leader. Share your evaluation with your supervisor if you think it is positive and constructive.

Human Relations Class Activity

"Some Good Leadership Advice I Received."

Here is an opportunity for you to obtain some potentially useful information for your present or future career as a leader. Each class member contacts an experienced person in his or her network to get one brief piece of advice about his or her leadership development. Among the potential experienced people are business executives, business owners, human resource professionals, public officials, former instructors, athletic coaches, parents, or other family members. You might contact the person through an e-mail, text message, phone call, or social networking site. Try an approach of this nature: "I'm doing a class activity for a unit on leadership in a human relations course. Would you be willing to give me about two sentences of advice for helping me become a leader or develop my present leadership skills?" (You will most likely encounter a strong willingness to help by almost anybody you contact.)

Record the advice you receive in written form. During class, each student, or a number of volunteers, will make about a one-minute presentation sharing the leadership advice received. After all the presentations, hold a class discussion centering on these points:

- What was the most frequent advice offered?
- What was the most useful advice offered?
- What advice would most likely backfire?
- How helpful for my leadership development was this activity?

Human Relations Case Study 11-1

Charismatically Challenged Colleen

Twenty-seven-year-old Colleen worked as a merchandising specialist for ValuMart, one of the largest international retail chains. Based in the United States, ValuMart also has a strong presence in Canada, Europe, Japan, and Hong Kong. Colleen began her employment with ValuMart as a cashier and two years later was invited into the training program for merchandising specialists.

Colleen performed well as a merchandising trainee in the soft-goods line. Her specialty areas included linens and bedding, men's and women's jewelry, home decorations, and men's, women's and children's clothing. For several years in a row, Colleen received performance evaluation ratings of above average or outstanding. Among the write-in comments made by her supervisors were "diligent worker," "knows the tricks of merchandising," "good flair for buying the right products at the right price," and "fits right into the team."

Despite the positive performance evaluation ratings supported with positive comments, Colleen had a gnawing discontent about her career at ValuMart. Despite five years of good performance, she was still not invited to become a member of the group called "ValuTrackers." The ValuTrackers are a group of merchandising and operations specialists who are regarded as being on the fast track to become future ValuMart leaders. The leaders hold high-level positions such as head merchandiser, regional vice president, and store manager.

Several times when Colleen in quired as to why she was not invited to join the ValuTrackers, she was told something to the effect that she was not quite ready to be included in this elite group. She was also told not to be discouraged, because the company still valued her contribution.

One day Colleen thought, "I'm headed toward age 30, and I want a great future in the retail business now." So she convinced her boss, the merchandising supervisor (Evan), to set up a career conference with three people: Colleen, the boss, and her boss's boss (Heather), the area merchandising manager. She let Evan know in advance that she wanted to talk about her potential for promotion.

Evan started the meeting by saying, "Colleen, perhaps you can tell Heather and me again why you requested this meeting."

Colleen responded, "Thanks for asking, Evan. As I mentioned before, I'm wondering what you think is wrong with me. I receive a lot of positive feedback about my performance, but I'm not a ValuTracker. Also, you seem to change the subject when I talk about wanting to become a merchandising supervisor, and eventually a merchandising executive. What am I doing wrong?"

Heather responded, "Evan and I frequently talk about the performance and potential of all our merchandising specialists. You're a good performer, Colleen, but you lack that little spark that makes a person a leader. You go about your job efficiently and quietly, but that's not enough. We want future leaders of ValuMart to make an impact."

Evan added, "I go along with Heather's comments. Another point, Colleen, is that you rarely take the initiative to suggest ideas. I was a little shocked by your request for a three-way career interview, because it's one of the few initiatives you have taken. You're generally pretty laid-back."

"Then what do I have to do to convince you two that I should be a ValuTracker?" asked Colleen?

Heather replied, "Start acting more like a leader. Be more charismatic." Evan nodded in agreement.

Questions

1. What career advice can you offer Colleen?
2. What might Colleen do to develop more charisma?
3. What is your opinion of the fairness of the ValuTracker program?

Human Relations Role-Playing Exercise 11-1

Colleen Attempts to Project Charisma During a Videoconference

The case study about Colleen serves as the background and the story line for this role-play. One person plays the role of Colleen, who is serious about wanting to appear and act more charismatic in interactions with work associates. Suddenly, Colleen gets a bright idea. Key members of her store are scheduled for a videoconference with the corporate group about upcoming improvements in the stores, including both refurbishing the stores and upgrading the merchandise. Colleen recognizes that key people from corporate will be observing store employees who attend the conferences.

The student playing the role of Colleen, who will both listen to what is being presented, will also have the opportunity to interact with the corporate presenters. Colleen wants to impress the corporate group, all the time demonstrating that she has the kind of charisma that would make her a strong candidate for being a ValuTracker.

Another two students play the roles of two presenters from corporate, who react to the comments by Colleen between parts of their presentation about upgrading the stores. The presenters can make up their own suggestions for upgrading ValuMart, to give Colleen something specific to which she can react.

Observers rate the role-players on two dimensions, using a 1 to 5 scale from very poor to very good. One dimension is "effective use of human relations techniques." For Colleen, focus on how well she projects charisma. The second dimension is "acting ability." A few observers might voluntarily provide feedback to the role-players in terms of sharing their ratings and observations. The course instructor might also provide feedback.

Human Relations Case Study 11-2

What Kind of Leader Is Danny Wong?

Danny Wong, a claims supervisor at an insurance company, recently took a leadership development course sponsored by his company. The major thrust of the course was to teach supervisors how to implement participative leadership and management. The course leader said, "Today, almost all employees want to get involved. They want a say in important decisions affecting them. The era of the know-it-all manager has long passed."

Wong was mildly skeptical about the course leader's universal endorsement of participative leadership. Yet, he decided that if this is what the company wanted, he would adopt a more participative style. Six months after the leadership development program was completed, the human resources department attempted to evaluate its impact. One part of the program evaluation was to speak to employees about how the course influenced their boss's approach to supervision.

Rick Alluto, the company training director, conducted several of the interviews with employees. He spoke first with Amy Green, a claims analyst who reported to Danny. Rick told Amy that her answers would be confidential. He said that the purpose of these interviews was to evaluate the effectiveness of the leadership training program, not to evaluate the supervisor.

Amy responded, "It would be okay with me if Danny did hear my comments. I have nothing very critical to say. I think the leadership training program was useful. Danny is a much better manager now than in the past. He's much more aware that the people in his group have something useful to contribute. Danny asks our opinion on many issues.

"I'll give you an example. Danny was going to order a new office copier and printer. In the past he might have just ordered a new copier and printer and told us when it was going to be delivered. Instead, Danny held three meetings to decide on which brand of copier and printer would best meet our needs. Three of us chose a copier that everybody in the office, including the new office assistant, agreed would be best."

Rick then spoke to Kent Nelson, another claims analyst reporting to Danny. Kent said he appreciated the fact that the interviews would be confidential. However, he hoped that drift of his comments would get back to Danny so long as he was not identified. Kent offered this evaluation:

"Danny has gone downhill as a manager ever since he took your leadership development program. He has been lazier than ever. Danny always did have a tendency to pass off too much work to employees. Now, he's gone overboard. The recent copy of the photocopier and printer is a good example. Too many people spent too much time deciding on which machine to purchase. To make matters worse, a committee of three people was formed to research the possibilities. It seems to me that we can make better use of working time.

"If Danny keeps up his approach to supervision much longer, he won't have a job. We will be doing all his work. How can you justify a supervisor's salary if other people are doing his work?"

Rick thought to himself, "I wonder if Amy and Kent are talking about the same supervisor. Their comments make it difficult for me to know whether the development program is getting the job done."

Questions

1. How do you explain the different perceptions of Amy and Kent?
2. What suggestions can you offer Danny for making better use of the consensus leadership style?
3. What is the counterargument to Kent's point about Wong not justifying his pay?

Human Relations Role-Playing Exercise 11-2

Danny Wong Attempts to Practice Participative Leadership

One student plays the role of Danny Wong who has gathered his group to make recommendations for speeding up the processing of claims within the office. He has some ideas of his own, but wants to practice participative leadership and decision making. Several other students play the role of claims analysts within the group who are asked for their suggestions. At least one of the analysts within the group believes that Danny should be making the suggestions for improving the efficiency of processing claims.

Run the role play for about ten minutes. Observers will provide feedback on how well Danny implements participative decision making, yet still not exerting leadership.

REFERENCES

1. Original story created from facts and observations in the following sources: Spencer E. Ante and Joann S. Lublin, "IBM's Rometty Kept on Rising," *The Wall Street Journal,* October 27, 2011, pp. B1, B2; Ante and Lublin, "Rometty Replacing IBM's Palmisano, *The Wall Street Journal,* October 26, 2011, pp. B1, B5; Carol Hymowitz and Sarah Frier, "IBM's Rometty Breaks Ground as Company's First Female Leader,"*Bloomberg Businessweek* (www.businessweek.com), October 26, 2011, pp. 1–3; Eric Savitz, "IBM Names Virginia Rometty To Succeed Palmisano As CEO," *Forbes* (www.forbes.com), October 25, 2011, pp. 1–2; Pat Vaughan Tremmel, "Virginia Rometty Chosen for Top Job at IBM," (www.northwestern.edu/newscenter), October 26, 2001.
2. Mark Van Vugt, Robert Hogan, and Robert B. Kaiser, "Leadership, Followership, and Evolution," *American Psychologist,* April 2008, pp. 182–183.
3. Stephen J. Zaccaro, "Trait-Based Perspectives of Leadership," *American Psychologist,* January 2007, p. 6.
4. Sonia Alleyne, "Oprah Means Business," *Black Enterprise,* June 2008, p. 117.
5. Ben Worthen, "Whitman Takes Charge," *The Wall Street Journal,* September 24–25, 2011, p. B1.
6. Gareth R. Jones and Jennifer M. George, "The Experience and Evolution of Trust: Implications for Cooperation and Teamwork,"*Academy of Management Review,* July 1998, pp. 531–546; Jenny C. McCune, "That Elusive Thing Called Trust," *Management Review,* August 1998, pp. 10–16.
7. Cassie R. Barlow, Mark Jordan, and William H. Hendrix, "Character Assessment: An Examination of Leadership Levels," *Journal of Business and Psychology,* Summer 2003, p. 563.
8. TalYaffe and Ronit Kark, "Leading by Example: The Case of Leader OCB," *Journal of Applied Psychology,* July 2011, pp. 806–826.
9. Timothy A. Judge, Amy E. Colbert, and Remus Ilies, "Intelligence and Leadership: A Quantitative Review and Test of Theoretical Positions," *Journal of Applied Psychology,* June 2004, pp. 542–552.
10. Hannah Karp and Joann S. Lublin, "Avon's Jung Comes Under Fire," *The Wall Street Journal,* October 28, 2011, p. B2.
11. Benjamin M. Galvin, Prasad Balkundi, and David A. Waldman, "Spreading the Word: The Role of Surrogates in Charismatic Leadership Processes," *Academy of Management Review,* July 2010, pp. 477–494.
12. Herminia Ibarra and Otilia Obodaru, "Women and the Vision Thing," *Harvard Business Review,* January 2009, p. 65.
13. Luisa Beltran, "Standout Performer: Cuban-Born Maria Elena Lagomasino Managed to Ascend Wall Street without Blending In,"*Hispanic Business,* April 2007, p. 26.
14. Rick Weaver, "Five Essential Leadership Traits: The Story of Martha Stewart From Kmart to Macy's," *Ezine@rticles* (http://ezinearticles.com/?Five-Essential-Leadership-Traits:-The-Story-Of-Martha-Stewart-From-Kmart-To-Macys&id=461813) 2. Accessed January 2, 2011.
15. Joyce E. Bono and Timothy A. Judge, "Personality and Transformational and Transactional Leadership: A Meta-Analysis," *Journal of Applied Psychology,* October 2004, pp. 901–910.
16. Amir Erez et al., "Stirring the Hearts of Followers: Charismatic Leadership as the Transferal of Affect," *Journal of Applied Psychology,* May 2008, pp. 602–613.
17. Juan Carlos Pastor, Margarita Mayo, and Boas Shamir, "Adding Fuel to the Fire: The Impact of Followers' Arousal on Ratings of Charisma," *Journal of Applied Psychology,* November 2007, pp. 1584–1596.
18. Tom Bateman, "Leading for Results: Brief but Powerful Lessons from Katrina and Iraq," *Organizational Dynamics,* October–December 2008, p. 301.
19. "The Ethical Mind: A Conversation with Psychologist Howard Gardner," *Harvard Business Review,* March 2007, pp. 51–56.
20. Paulo Prada, "50: Joanne Smith: Senior Vice President of In-Flight Service and Global Product Development," *The Wall Street Journal,* November 10, 2008, p. R8.
21. Robert T. Keller, "A Test of the Path–Goal Theory of Leadership with Need for Clarity as a Moderator in Research and Development Organizations," *Journal of Applied Psychology,* April 1989, pp. 208–212.
22. "Carrot & Stick Failing? Try Encouragement," *Executive Leadership,* July 2007, p. 4.
23. Teresa Amabile and Steven Kramer, *The Progress Principle: Using Small Wins to Ignite Joy, Engagement, and Creativity at Work* (Boston: Harvard Business Review Press, 2011).
24. Robert C. Liden, Sandy J. Wayne, Hao Zhao, David Henderson, "Servant Leadership: Development of a Multidimensional Measure and Multi-Level Assessment," *Leadership Quarterly,* April 2008, pp. 161–177.
25. Robert K. Greenleaf, *The Power of Servant Leadership: A Journey into the Nature of Legitimate Power and Greatness* (San Francisco: Berrett-Koehler, 1998); James C. Hunter, *The World's Most Powerful Leadership Principle: How to Become a Servant Leader* (New York: Crown Business, 2004).
26. "The Best Advice I Ever Got," *Fortune,* May 12, 2008, p. 74.
27. Liden, et al, "Servant Leadership," p. 162.
28. Jia Hu and Robert C. Liden, "Antecedents of Team Potency and Team Effectiveness: An Examination of Goal and Process Clarity and Servant Leadership," *Journal of Applied Psychology,* July 2011, pp. 851–862.
29. Ralph M. Stogdill and Alvin E. Coons, eds., *Leader Behavior: Its Description and Mea surement* (Columbus: The Ohio State University Bureau of Business Research, 1957); Carroll L. Shartle, *Executive Performance and Leadership* (Upper Saddle River, NJ: Prentice Hall, 1956).
30. Jessica E. Vascellaro, "Apple in His Own Image," *The Wall Street Journal,* November 2, 2011, p. B1.
31. Anders Skogstad, Ståle Einarsen, Torbjorn Torscheim, Merethe Sschanke Assland, and Hilde Hetland, "The Destructiveness of Laissez-Faire Leadership Behavior," *Journal of Occupational Health Psychology,* Number 1, 2007, pp. 80–92.
32. Richard Pascale, "Change How You Define Leadership, and You Change How You Run a Company," *Fast Company,* April–May 1988, pp. 114–120.
33. Gary Yukl and Richard Lepsinger, *Flexible Leadership: Creating Value by Balancing Multiple Challenges and Choices* (San Francisco: Jossey-Bass, 2004).

34. George Graen and J. F. Cashman, "A Role-Making Model of Leadership in Formal Organizations: A Developmental Approach," in J. G. Hunt and L. I. Larson, eds., *Leadership Frontiers* (Kent, OH: Kent State University Press, 1975), pp. 143–165; Robert P. Vecchio, "Leader-Member Exchange, Objective Performance, Employment Duration, and Supervisor Ratings: Testing for Moderation and Mediation," *Journal of Business and Psychology,* Spring 1998, pp. 327–341.
35. Robert Eisenberger et al, "Leader-Member Exchange and Affective Organizational Commitment: The Contribution of Supervisor's Organizational Embodiment," *Journal of Applied Psychology,* November 2010, p. 1085.
36. Robert P. Vecchio, "Are You In or Out With Your Boss?" *Business Horizons,* vol. 29, 1987, pp. 76–78.
37. "Personalize Your Management Style," *Manager's Edge,* June 2007, p. 3.
38. "Motivate by Telling Staffers 'Yes,'" *Manager's Edge,* May 2007, p. 4.
39. Quoted in Casey Feldman, "Game Changers," *Fortune,* July 21, 2008, p. 54.
40. "Warren G. Bennis, Leadership Guru," in *Business: The Ultimate Resource* (Cambridge, MA: Perseus Publishing, 2002), p. 969.
41. D. Scott DeRue and Ned Wellman, "Developing Leaders via Experience: The Role of Developmental Challenge Learning Orientation, and Feedback Availability," *Journal of Applied Psychology,* July 2009, pp. 859–875.
42. Donna M. Owens, "Success Factors: The Right Experience Can Increase Your Leadership Potential," *HR Magazine,* August 2008, pp. 87–88.
43. Michael E. McGill and John W. Slocum Jr., "A Little Leadership Please?" *Organizational Dynamics,* Winter 1998, p. 48.
44. Craig L. Pearce and Charles C. Manz, "The New Silver Bullet of Leadership: The Importance of Self- and Shared Leadership in Knowledge Work," *Organizational Dynamics,* no. 2, 2005, p. 133. The quote is from the same source.
45. William D. Hitt, *The Model Leader: A Fully Functioning Person* (Columbus, OH: Battelle Press, 1993).
46. Linda Hill, "Becoming the Boss," *Harvard Business Review,* January 2007, pp. 51–52.
47. Quoted in Sonja D. Brown, "Congratulations, You're a Manager, Now What?" *Black Enterprise,* April 2006, p. 104.

12

Motivating Others and Developing Teamwork

Outline

Jessica Herrin is the CEO and founder of Stella & Dot, an at-home seller of jewelry and accessories with over $100 million in annual sales. She previously founded WeddingChannel.com, a successful virtual wedding registry, and worked for Dell Inc. in the global e-commerce group. Stella & Dot has 14,000 sales representatives referred to as stylists who sell their merchandise at other people's home from trunks.

Herrin believes strongly that motivated employees are the backbone of her enterprise. She says, "motivated missionaries change the world," and that there is no other way any other great company has been built. A major motivator for Stella & Dot sales representatives is the opportunity to earn a good living or side money yet still retaining the flexibility to take care of family responsibilities. Some team leaders even earn over $30,000 a month managing stylists all over the country. At the other end, some stylists earn just enough money to supplement the family income.

Another motivator for Stella & Dot stylists is that they are building something that doesn't have a ceiling blocking their promotion, and that has an endless runway. To help motivate her freelance workforce, Herrin treats them like professionals. "Recognition is the most powerful currency you have, and it costs you nothing," she says. The company hires managers who have a natural sense of gratitude, and who praise stylists for doing something right.

As part of her plan for motivating the stylists, Herrin personally sends e-mails and calls at least ten of these women every day, sends text messages, and places posts on Facebook. Part of Herrin's daily to-do list is to find and celebrate success. She emphasizes that saying "I appreciate you" goes a long way with people.[1]

The words of the CEO of a highly successful in-home seller illustrates the importance of appreciation and recognition for motivating a workforce. In this chapter we describe a variety of theories and practices for motivating others, including recognition. We also describe the closely related topic of developing teamwork because approaches to getting a team or group working well are essentially techniques of motivation. One of the biggest motivational challenges facing managers and team leaders is to get the team working together smoothly.

Learning Objectives ▸

After studying the information and doing the exercises in this chapter, you should be able to:

1. Understand how to diagnose what motivates people to perform well.
2. Recognize the contribution of two classical motivation theories to understanding work motivation.
3. Understand how to motivate others through empowerment and job design, including interesting work.
4. Understand how positive reinforcement, including financial incentives, recognition, and praise, are used for employee motivation.
5. Describe strategies and tactics for developing teamwork.
6. Understand group dynamics in terms of the development of groups and group roles.
7. Identify the characteristics of effective work groups, and be aware of the problem of groupthink.

▶ Learning Objective 1 ▶

How Do You Diagnose What Motivates Others Toward Good Performance?

Motivation
concept with two widely used meanings: (1) an internal state that leads to effort expended toward objectives and (2) an activity performed by one person to get another to accomplish work

An eternal challenge for people responsible for the work of others is to get them to perform at a high level. **Motivation** has two widely used meanings: (1) an internal state that leads to effort expended toward objectives and (2) an activity performed by one person to get another to accomplish work. Usually the manager is doing the motivating, yet many people in the workplace have a need to motivate others. To accomplish their work, people must motivate individuals who report to them, coworkers, supervisors, and customers. Understanding how to motivate others, therefore, is essential to your success. Keep in mind also that it is often important to motivate groups of people, such as a team, in addition to motivating people one at a time.

Knowledge of motivation is particularly important in the current era because so many workers do not feel identified with their work or their employers, as described in the discussion of worker engagement in Chapter 3. A starting point in being able to motivate people and groups is to understand what outcomes or payoffs they want from their work. If you know what a person wants—and the person knows what he or she wants—you are in a better position to motivate that person. Questions can be asked in person or through a survey.[2] Basic questions might include:

- What could this job offer you that would make you work at your best?
- What factors about this job would bring out your best?
- What might the company do to make you excited about your job?
- How can I (or we) make your job a wonderful experience for you?
- What would make you feel really good about your job?

A person's behavior is often more revealing than what he or she says. You might, therefore, also gain some diagnostic insights by observing what elements of the job or work situation strongly interest the subordinate. For example, one team member might display enthusiasm primarily when there is an opportunity to do exciting work. Another team member might be excited primarily when a weekend or holiday approaches. You could tentatively conclude that the first person is motivated by exciting work and the second by time off from work.

▶ Learning Objective 2 ▶

What Are Two Classic Theories of Work Motivation?

Two-factor theory of work motivation
two different sets of job factors—one set, the motivators, or satisfiers, can motivate and satisfy workers; the other set, dissatisfiers, or hygiene factors, can only prevent dissatisfaction

As described in Chapter 3, Maslow's hierarchy of needs arranges human needs into a pyramid-shaped model with basic physiological needs at the bottom and self-actualization needs at the top. Maslow's needs hierarchy provided an exciting beginning to recognizing the importance of understanding human needs to better motivate others. A practical application of the needs hierarchy is that when a manager wants to motivate a group member, he or she must offer the individual a reward that will satisfy an important need.

The study of the needs hierarchy led to the **two-factor theory of work motivation**. According to the research of late industrial psychologist Frederick Herzberg, there are two different sets of job factors.[3] One set, the motivators (or satisfiers), can motivate and satisfy workers. The other set, dissatisfiers (or hygiene factors), can only prevent dissatisfaction. Motivators relate to higher-order needs, whereas hygiene factors relate to lower-order needs.

The two-factor theory explains how to design jobs to make them motivational. The motivational elements are the intrinsic, or job content, factors that make a job exciting. Motivator factors include achievement, recognition, advancement, responsibility, the work itself, and personal growth possibilities. The extrinsic, or job context, factors are hygienic. Although they are health maintaining and desirable, they are not motivational. Examples of hygiene factors are pay, status, job security, working conditions, and quality of leadership. Herzberg believed that motivation increases when one combines pay with a motivator such as challenging work.

According to the two-factor theory, only the presence of motivator factors leads to more positive energized behavior. For example, challenging work will motivate many people to exert increased effort. If intrinsic factors, such as challenging work, are not present, the result is neutral rather than negative, and the worker will feel bland rather than angry or unhappy. Although the presence of hygiene (or extrinsic) factors is not motivational, their absence can cause dissatisfaction, as in the following illustration. A police captain reported that when officers were assigned old patrol cars, they complained frequently, but when assigned brand new patrol cars, they did not express much appreciation. Nor did they increase their productivity as measured by the number of citations issued.

The two-factor theory has made two lasting contributions to work motivation. First, it has helped managers realize that money is not always the primary motivator. Second, it has spurred much of the interest in designing jobs to make them more intrinsically satisfying, as described later in this chapter.

A Modern Look at the Two-Factor Theory

A major problem with the two-factor theory is that it de-emphasizes individual differences and glosses over the importance of hygiene factors in attracting and retaining workers. Hygiene factors such as good benefits and company management satisfy and motivate many people. Many working parents will work extra hard to keep their jobs at a company that offers on-site child care or flexible working hours. The case opener about women being motivated to work at a job they could fit conveniently into their lifestyle illustrates this point.

Furthermore, benefits such as company-subsidized health insurance, dental insurance, and a retirement pension would motivate many workers today to work hard and stay with a firm. The reason is that some private and public employers have drastically reduced benefits in recent years. Also, time off and flexible hours are particularly appealing to younger workers and will motivate them to work harder and stay with their employer.

Because of their historical importance, and the fact that the theories of Maslow and Herzberg still influence modern thinking, the two theories are compared in Figure 12-1.

How Do You Motivate through Empowerment, Job Design, and Various Forms of Positive Reinforcement?

◀ Learning Objective 3 ◀

Among the standard practices for employee motivation are empowerment, job design, and various forms of positive reinforcement, including financial incentives, recognition, and praise.

FIGURE 12-1 COMPARISON OF THE HIERARCHY OF NEEDS AND TWO-FACTOR THEORY

Maslow's Hierarchy of Needs	Herzberg's Two-Factor Theory *Satisfiers or Motivators*	Managerial Action
Self-actualization Self-esteem	Achievement Recognition Work itself Responsibility Advancement Growth	Allow these factors to be present to increase satisfaction and motivation.
	Dissatisfiers or Hygiene Factors	
Social (love, affection, or belonging) Safety and security Physiological	Company policy and administration Supervision Working conditions Salary Relationship with coworkers Personal life Status Job security	Keep these factors at adequate levels to prevent dissatisfaction and de-motivation.

EMPOWERMENT

A comprehensive strategy for employee motivation is to grant workers more power by enabling them to participate in decisions affecting themselves and their work. Empowerment basically involves passing decision-making authority and responsibility from managers to employees. A key point is that the leader shares power with group members. Because group members have some power, they can influence the manager, such as giving him or her guidance.

Empowerment
process by which a manager shares power with team members, thereby enhancing their feelings of self-efficacy

Workers experience a greater sense of self-efficacy and ownership of their jobs when they share power. According to this logic, **empowerment** is the process by which a manager shares power with team members, thereby enhancing their feelings of self-efficacy. Because the worker feels more effective, empowerment contributes to intrinsic motivation. The individual has a choice in initiating and regulating actions, such as in deciding how to perform a particular task.[4] Sharing power with team members enables them to feel better about themselves and perform at a higher level. Teams as well as individuals can be empowered. An example of empowering a team would be to give it responsibility for developing a new product.

Empowerment as Shared Leadership

Shared leadership
the leader granting group members authority to carry out some of the leadership activities

Another way of understanding empowerment is that it involves **shared leadership**, or the leader granting group members authority to carry out some of the leadership activities. Instead of relying exclusively on the designated head of the group for leadership, the group members guide and influence themselves. The shared leadership is particularly useful when group members have certain technical knowledge they need to accomplish the work and the leader lacks this knowledge. At any given period of time the group member with the key knowledge, skills, and abilities for the task at hand becomes the person in charge. As an extreme example, if a hurricane attacked the building the person who would take charge would be someone with experience in dealing with a hurricane. But the leader of the group plays an important role in coaching the team members in how to assume leadership responsibility.[5]

Visualize a group of environmental specialists seeking ways to make an existing office building environmentally friendly. All group members have specialized knowledge of their own that they want to share with coworkers and influence them with. The leader steps back to allow this shared leadership take place, such as one group member influencing others to plant a garden on the roof to help moderate temperature and absorb carbon dioxide.

Several Forms of Empowerment

Employee empowerment often takes the form of giving customer-contact employees more freedom in making decisions. At the same time, the employees are encouraged to exercise initiative and imagination (such as figuring how to satisfy an unusual customer demand), and they are rewarded for doing so.

Package carrier UPS empowers its managers to deal with crises at the local level so they can respond quickly. Immediately following the 9/11 terrorist attacks, UPS in lower Manhattan was left with thousands of undeliverable packages to World Trade Center addresses. The UPS managers decided on their own to first sort out all those packages containing medical and pharmaceutical supplies, so the supplies would be available immediately to treat the wounded. Decisions were made later about what to do with packages addressed to demolished addresses.

Although customer-contact employees are empowered, they are still given overall direction and limits to the extent of their authority. One limit is that a customer service worker cannot overturn a company rule, thereby creating a health or safety hazard. For example, a hotel receptionist would not be authorized to allow a guest to park in a fire safety zone just because a space close to the hotel was not available at the time.

An extreme form of empowerment is when workers establish their own priorities and choose which projects they would like to pursue. Although there may not be loads of workplaces that can grant so much freedom to employees, it can be done. For example, an advertising firm that guided other companies in social media advertising might be so overloaded with work that associates might be given leeway in which company they wanted to accept as a client at the moment.

MOTIVATION THROUGH JOB DESIGN AND INTERESTING WORK

Many management experts contend that if you make jobs more interesting there may be less need for motivating people with external rewards. Also, attempting to motivate people by external rewards may not be sufficient. Motivating people through interesting work is based on the principle of **intrinsic motivation**, which refers to a person's beliefs about the extent to which an activity can satisfy his or her needs for competence and self-determination. Instead of looking to somebody else for rewards, a person is motivated by the intrinsic, or internal, aspects of the task.

Intrinsic motivation
a person's beliefs about the extent to which an activity can satisfy his or her needs for competence and self-determination; instead of looking to somebody else for rewards, a person is motivated by the intrinsic, or internal, aspects of the task

Intrinsic motivation contributes even more to productivity when combined with **prosocial motivation**, the desire to expend effort to help other people. People who are agreeable by nature are more likely to have strong prosocial motivation. A study was conducted with fundraising callers whose task was to telephone alumni to raise money for the university. A major finding was that those callers who experienced both intrinsic

Prosocial motivation
the desire to expend effort to help other people

and prosocial motivation tended to have high productivity in terms of calls made and funds raised.[6]

Job enrichment
making a job more motivating and satisfying by adding variety and responsibility

Job enrichment refers to making a job more motivating and satisfying by adding variety and responsibility. A job is considered enriched to the extent that it demands more of an individual's talents and capabilities. As the job becomes more meaningful to you, you become better motivated and, it is hoped, more productive. Unless you want an enriched job, these positive results may not be forthcoming. Substantial research and practical experience has gone into enriching jobs. Three noteworthy characteristics of an enriched job are direct feedback, client relationships, and new learning.[7]

Direct feedback occurs when a worker receives immediate knowledge of the results he or she is achieving. This evaluation of performance can be built into the job (such as a highway patrol officer catching a speeder) or provided by a supervisor. *Client relationship* refers to an employee having a client or customer to serve, whether that client is inside or outside the organization. In this regard, both a customer service representative and a hairstylist have enriched jobs.

New learning takes place when a job incumbent feels that he or she is growing psychologically, including acquiring new skills. In contrast, an impoverished job allows for no new learning. The information technology component built into most jobs provides ample opportunity for new learning, as would learning a second language to relate better to customer in another country. Another perspective on new learning is that it has positive effects beyond immediate motivation. Margaret Hintz, a team manager at a staffing firm says, "When employees hear that management is willing to invest in their development, it sends a clear message that they are valued and have a future with the company. It creates a stronger company culture, which minimizes employee dissatisfaction and turnover."[8]

A basic example of job enrichment is as follows: Instead of simply putting an accounts payable specialist in charge of more accounts, put the person in charge of following up on the calls, talking with collection agencies, and redesigning the workflow.[9]

Going beyond the formal theory of job enrichment, interesting work also includes having a sense of purpose as you may have studied in relation to self-motivation and goal setting. The interesting work is often at the team level. Jack Welch, the former chairman of GE, and his wife, Suzy Welch, a former *Harvard Business Review* editor, say that a bold mission allows bosses to say, "There's the hill. Let's take it together."[10] An example of a bold mission leading to interesting work for most people would be working on a community redevelopment project or finding a cure for childhood leukemia.

MOTIVATION THROUGH POSITIVE REINFORCEMENT

Positive reinforcement
increasing the probability that behavior will be repeated by rewarding people for making the desired response; improves learning and motivation

Rewarding a worker for achieving a certain result or behaving in a particular way is a widely used motivational tactic, and has become ingrained into our culture in work and personal life. **Positive reinforcement** means increasing the probability that behavior will be repeated by rewarding people for making the desired response. The phrase *increasing the probability* means that positive reinforcement improves learning and motivation but is not 100 percent effective. The phrase *making the desired response* is also noteworthy. To use positive reinforcement properly, a reward must be contingent on doing something right. Simply paying somebody a compliment or giving the person something of value is not positive reinforcement. Because financial incentives, recognition, and praise are given for attaining a given goal, they function as positive reinforcement.

Positive reinforcement is easy to visualize with well-structured jobs, such as data entry or producing parts. Yet, positive reinforcement is also used to encourage desired behavior for those in highly paid, complex jobs. An accountant who developed a new method of the company getting paid faster might be rewarded with two extra days of vacation.

Rules for the Effective Use of Positive Reinforcement

Although using rewards to motivate people seems straightforward, positive reinforcement requires the systematic applicant of rules. The rules are specified from the standpoint of the person trying to motivate another individual, such as a group member, coworker, supervisor, or customer. The same rules also apply to motivating a work group.

Rule 1: State Clearly What Behavior Will Lead to a Reward. The nature of good performance, or the goals, must be agreed on by the manager and group member. Clarification might take this form: "We need to decrease by 40 percent the number of new credit card customers who have delinquent accounts of sixty days or more."

Rule 2: Choose an Appropriate Reward. An appropriate reward is effective in motivating a given person and feasible from the standpoint of the individual or the company. If one reward does not motivate the person, try another. One person might be motivated by time off from work, another by an interesting assignment, and a third by an e-mail note of praise with a copy to a high-ranking executive. Many employees are strongly motivated by the possibility of receiving a promotion, especially because promotions offer the prospect of more status and higher pay.[11] The importance of choosing the right reward underscores the fact that not all rewards are reinforcers. A reward is something of perceived value by the person receiving the reward, but if the reward does not strengthen the desired response (such as wearing safety goggles), it is not a true reinforcer.[12]

Rule 3: Supply Ample Feedback. Positive reinforcement cannot work without frequent feedback to individuals. Feedback can take the form of simply telling people they have done something right or wrong. Brief e-mail messages or handwritten notes are other forms of feedback. As described at the outset of the chapter, effective motivators make extensive use of handwritten thank-you notes.

Rule 4: Schedule Rewards Intermittently. Rewards should not be given on every occasion of good performance. **Intermittent rewards** sustain desired behaviors longer and also slow down the process of behaviors fading away when they are not rewarded. If each correct performance results in a reward, the behavior will stop shortly after a performance in which the reward is not received. Another problem is that a reward given continuously may lose its impact. A practical value of intermittent reinforcement is that it saves time. Few managers or team leaders have enough time to dispense rewards for every correct action by group members.

Intermittent rewards sustaining desired behaviors longer and slowing down the process of behaviors fading away when they are not rewarded

Rule 5: Make the Rewards Follow the Observed Behavior Closely in Time. For maximum effectiveness, people should be rewarded soon after doing something right. A built-in, or intrinsic, feedback system, such as software working or not working, capitalizes on this principle. E-mail and instant messaging are again useful here because it would be difficult for the manager or team leader to congratulate in person team members who work in another location.

Rule 6: Make the Reward Fit the Behavior. People who are inexperienced in applying positive reinforcement often overdo the intensity of spoken rewards. When an employee does something of an ordinary nature correctly, a simple word of praise such as "Good job" is preferable to something like "Fantastic performance." A related idea is that the magnitude of the reward should vary with the magnitude of the accomplishment.

Rule 7: Make the Rewards Visible. Another important characteristic of an effective reward is the extent to which it is visible, or noticeable, to other employees. When other workers notice the reward, its impact multiplies because other people observe what kind of behavior is rewarded.[13] Rewards should also be visible, or noticeable, to the employee. A reward of $5 per week added to a person's paycheck might be hardly noticeable, after payroll deductions. However, a bonus check for $200 might be very noticeable. A dramatic technique for making rewards visible is to offer workers something luxurious, exotic, or self-indulgent they would most likely not purchase for themselves even if they could afford it. Examples include a luxury vacation, or gift certificates for a series of massages.[14]

Rule 8: Change the Reward Periodically. Rewards do not retain their effectiveness indefinitely. Employees and customers lose interest in striving for a reward they have received many times in the past. This is particularly true of a repetitive statement such as "Nice job" or "Congratulations." It is helpful for the person giving out the rewards to compile a list of potential rewards and try different ones from time to time.

Positive reinforcement has a long history of improving productivity on the job, including the control of absenteeism. Dollar General invited the performance management company, Aubrey Daniels International, to help control absenteeism when it reached 16 percent at the company's distribution center. Dollar General developed a point system, and organized workers into teams. A racetrack was drawn on the wall with each team represented by its own race car. Following basic positive reinforcement principles, team members were able to earn points by arriving on time. If they arrived late, they could earn points for their teams in other ways such as by returning from breaks on time. Each day, the race cars advanced according to the number of points earned.

Jeff Sims, the Dollar General senior vice president, says that the positive reinforcement program facilitated supervisors no longer yelling at workers if they were late. Company managers began thanking employees for coming to work. We said, "We really need your help to get those points tomorrow morning." After completion of a specified number of laps, the team with the most points was authorized to choose the food served at the distribution center. Within two weeks of the program's introduction, attendance had moved up to 95 percent (from 84 percent).[15]

You may think the Dollar General motivational approach is hokey, but there is a message. With even modest rewards, positive reinforcement can help a company attain key goals.

FINANCIAL INCENTIVES AS POSITIVE REINFORCEMENT

Money is a natural motivator, and no program of motivation can exclude the role of financial compensation. Even the most ardent critics of the motivational power of money recognize that nonfinancial motivators are effective only when compensation is considered to be fair and adequate. When workers are preoccupied with not being paid fairly, they are less likely to respond to other approaches to motivation. When money is used as a motivator, it becomes a positive reinforcer because a person receives more money for performing well.

A challenge in understanding the role of money and other forms of compensation is that they are not pure concepts. High pay is also closely associated with other outcomes such as status and recognition. Thus, a person may work hard to earn more money as a way of achieving more status and recognition. Here we describe programs making pay partially contingent on performance, individual factors that influence the effectiveness of financial incentives, and problems with financial incentives.

Linking Compensation to Performance

Variable pay
incentive plan that intentionally pays good performers more money than poor performers

Many employers make a systematic effort to link some portion of pay to performance to make pay more motivational. **Variable pay** (or *merit* pay) is an incentive plan that intentionally pays good performers more money than poor performers. Employees receive more money by excelling on performance measures such as number of sales or number of computer programs completed. Whatever the specific plan, employees receive a base level of pay along with a bonus related to performance. The better your performance as measured by your employer, the higher your pay. Linking salary increases to good performance helps employers spare the cost of giving too many workers a pay boost. At the same time such plans are perceived to be useful in retaining valuable employees.

Another approach to relating pay to performance is to link bonuses to results obtained by the work group or the entire company. A companywide bonus plan ties individual merit pay to overall company or division performance, such as a year-end bonus based on company profits. The financial results on which the bonuses are determined can be measured at the division, group, business unit, or company level. Sometimes the bonus is based on a combination of the levels mentioned.Here is a successful example of using a bonus plan to motivate employees:

> David Hayes, the founder and CEO of Skyline Construction in San Francisco, offered his employees a bonus plan. Seventy-five percent of the eligible workers opted for the lowest salary combined with the highest bonus. After two years, sales grew from $36 million to $71 million, while costs as a percentage of sales shrank.The original plan was successful enough to be converted into an employee stock ownership plan which is still in use.[16]

Personal Factors Influencing the Power of Financial Incentives

Individual differences profoundly influence the motivational power of financial incentives. Workers who attach a high value to financial incentives will be more motivated by money than those who attach a low value. A major influencing factor is that money is a good motivator when you need it badly enough. Money has a motivational pull for most people who think that they need more money. Once people have enough money to pay for all those things they think are important in life, money may lose its effectiveness. There are tremendous individual differences in what people classify as necessities. If, for example, somebody thinks owning three cars and having two residences is a necessity, that person will be motivated by money for a long time.

Problems Created by Financial Incentives

Despite their effectiveness as motivators, financial incentives also create human problems. A major concern is that financial rewards can lead a person to focus on rewards rather than the joy built into exciting work. Another problem is that after people receive several increases based on performance, merit pay comes to be perceived as a right or entitlement. A person who does not receive a merit increase one quarter often feels that he or she has been punished. Another problem with cash awards is that they sometimes interfere with teamwork as employees concentrate on individual financial rewards.

Also, pay-for-performance plans can prompt executives, corporate professionals, and sales representatives to focus on achieving exceptional financial results, sometimes by unethical means. The problems sometimes associated with goals, such as not caring how you reach your goal, are closely linked to the pursuit of financial rewards. Many of the Wall Street financial scandals in recent years came about because investment specialists invented complex investment instruments to sell to the public. Often these instruments, such as "collateralized debt obligations," were derived from very high-risk loans.

MOTIVATION THROUGH RECOGNITION AND PRAISE

The workplace provides a natural opportunity to satisfy the **recognition need**—the desire to be acknowledged for one's contributions and efforts and to feel important. A manager can thus motivate many employees by making them feel important. Employee needs for recognition can be satisfied both through informal recognition and by establishing formal recognition programs. If the recognition prize is made contingent on achievement, the recognition program functions like positive reinforcement.

Recognition need
the desire to be acknowledged for one's contributions and efforts and to feel important

Praise as Recognition

Praising workers for good performance is closely related to informal recognition. An effective form of praise describes the worker's performance rather than merely making an evaluation. Describing good performance might take this form: "You turned an angry customer into an ally who referred new business to us." A more general evaluation would be "You are great with angry customers."

Although praise costs no money and requires only a few minutes of time, many workers rarely receive praise. (You may recall that the entrepreneur in the opening commented about how much workers want to be appreciated.) According to the American Psychological Association Stress in America survey, only 46 percent of respondents agree or strongly agreed with the statement, "Overall, I am satisfied with the employee recognition practices of my employer."[17] Data from a decade-long study suggest that 79 percent of employees who quit their job contend that a key reason they left was lack of appreciation.[18] Managers and team leaders therefore have a good opportunity to increase motivation by the simple act of praising good deeds. Other informal approaches to recognizing good performance include taking an employee to lunch, a handshake from the manager or team leader, and putting flowers on an employee's desk.

Tailor Praise to Individual Preferences

An advanced use of praise is to tailor the praise to the needs of the person being praised, much like the diagnostic approach to motivation. A study with 103 working adults found that people who perceived themselves to be technically oriented have a more negative attitude toward being flattered (a strong form of praise). Instead, they prefer a laid-back, factual statement of how they made a contribution. (An example: "Your solution to the problem saved us 30 percent in raw material costs.") Conversely, people who perceived themselves to be less technically oriented were more positively disposed toward being flattered. (An example: "I love it. What a fantastic solution to our problem.") Also, women had a more positive attitude toward being flattered than did men.[19] So it would appear that nontechnically oriented women would be the most receptive to praise and flattery!

Another example of differences in response to recognition and praise is that not every employee wants to receive the accolade of "employee of the month" or to receive public recognition. A cultural difference is that many Asian workers prefer that praise be given privately or shared with the team publicly.[20] Team recognition rather than individual recognition is often more effective in Japan. Another cultural difference is that recognition of individuals is preferred in Bangalore, India.[21]

Company Recognition Programs

Formal recognition programs are more popular than ever as companies attempt to retain the right employees and keep workers productive who worry about losing their jobs or having no private work area. Recognition programs are also regarded as one of the best ways to drive employee engagement.[22] The reason could be that employees become more emotionally attached to an employer who appreciates them.

Company recognition programs include awarding watches and jewelry for good service, plaques for good performance, and on-the-spot cash awards (about $25 to $50) for good performance. On-the-spot small bonuses for doing something exceptional sometimes take the form of a gift certificate for out-of-the-ordinary performance such as having identified a major safety hazard before it became a problem.

To enhance the impact of recognition programs, some companies customize awards to fit local and individual preferences. At the Everett Clinic, a healthcare provider in Washington state, supervisor and peers are authorized to send out "HeroGrams" for exceptional performance. Based on the number of HeroGrams they receive, employees can choose among such rewards as gift certificates and paid days off—depending on their preferences.[23]

Because so many workers are not in face-to-face contact with their managers, managers often deliver verbal recognition by e-mail or telephone. Furthermore, some recognition programs are administered through Web sites in which the employee can choose from among a list of possible awards.[24]

Human Relations in Practice

Sports Medicine Center Motivates Its Employees through Recognition

Lynn Fraser is the director of the physical therapy unit within the Center of Sports Medicine at a large private hospital. Sports injuries have surged in recent years as more students and full-time workers alike participate in sports. For example, there is a long waiting list for men and women and boys and girls who want treatment for a torn anterior cruciate ligament (ACL). Fraser says, "There is a boom in demand for physical therapy for sports injuries. Our group is under continuous pressure. We could easily find productive work for another five physical therapists and aides, but budget restrictions have placed a lid on hiring for now. Yet even with a bigger budget for staffing it would be difficult to hire five new therapists because there is such a shortage of these people."

To help deal with the problem of an overworked staff, all of whom could find employment elsewhere, Fraser decided to start an employee recognition program. She enlisted the services of a human resources specialist within the hospital to help launch the program. Both Fraser and the HR specialist, Alex Garcia, agreed that the physical therapy group needed a recognition program more sophisticated than a plaque celebrating the employee of the month.

The data for giving recognition awards stem from three sources. First are comment cards given to patients of the physical therapy unit as they leave the facility, asking them questions about their experience at the unit. A second, and related, source of data are e-mail inquiries sent to a random sample of patients. Both sources of information invite patients to explain what they liked and disliked about their experiences, including the opportunity to identify the names of staff members who were particularly helpful.

A third source of data is spontaneous comments about staff members made to the receptionists at the desk. The receptionists are invited to record, by computer, any positive comments made about therapists and other staff members. For example, a patient might comment while paying the bill, "That Holly [one of the physical therapists] is a miracle worker."

The recognition committee consists of Fraser, Garcia, and the chief sports medicine physician. The committee meets once a month to evaluate the three sources of data to see which two staff members—professional workers and support workers included—merit a recognition award. The recognition rewards consist of (a) a written statement of appreciation that is included in the staff member's human resource filed, (b) gift certificates for two to an upscale restaurant, and (c) a two-year subscription to a health magazine.

When asked how the recognition program was working, Fraser replied, "The subjective results are that our professionals and support staff make quite positive comments about the program. The objective results are that after two years our turnover of the professional and support staff is much lower than the national and regional averages."

Source: Case history collected at a large private hospital in the northeastern United States.

The accompanying Human Relations in Practice insert illustrates the effective use of a company recognition program. Human Relations Self-Assessment Quiz 12-1 gives you an opportunity to think about how some of the motivators described in this chapter might apply to you.

Human Relations Self-Assessment Quiz 12-1

My Own Motivators

Listed below are ten job factors that are motivators for many workers. Check the factors or motivators that apply to you.

Number	Job Factor or Motivator	Would Motivate Me	Would Not Motivate Me
1.	Promise of a 10 percent salary increase for good performance	______	______
2.	Opportunity to do work on an exciting assignment	______	______
3.	Threat of being fired if I do not meet performance standards	______	______
4.	A fancy new job title with no pay increase	______	______
5.	Promise of two extra weeks of vacation per year	______	______
6.	Promise of one-step promotion for good performance	______	______
7.	Time off from job to do volunteer work in community	______	______
8.	Recognition placed on company Web site	______	______
9.	Opportunity to mentor other workers if I perform well	______	______
10.	Opportunity to work on project of my choosing if I perform well.	______	______

Scoring and Interpretation

The more of the ten factors that you said would motivate you the more readily you are or will be a motivated worker. Checking the following job factors suggests that you are more motivated by external factors: 1, 3, 4, 5. 6, and 8. Checking the following job factors suggests that that you are motivated by internal factors: 2, 7, 9, and 10.

▶ Learning Objective 4 ▶

What Are Some Strategies and Tactics for Building Teamwork?

Teamwork
work done with an understanding and commitment to group goals on the part of all team members

Team
a small number of people who are committed to common goals and approaches to which they hold themselves mutually accountable

Group
a collection of people who interact with one another, and are working toward some common purpose; a team approaches being a supergroup

So far in this chapter we have studied how leaders and managers can influence subordinates by direct use of motivational techniques. Team leaders, as well as other managers, also need to use techniques that influence subordinates to work well together in a team. Influencing others is similar to motivating them. In this section we describe methods for building **teamwork**—work done with an understanding and commitment to group goals on the part of all team members.[25]

The term *team* is used frequently in human relations, yet it merits a formal definition. A **team** is a small number of people who are committed to common goals and approaches to which they hold themselves mutually accountable. A **group** is slightly different because it has less emphasis on teamwork. It is a collection of people who interact with one another, and are working toward some common purpose. All teams are groups, but not all groups are teams—a team approaches being a supergroup.

In the following sections we describe more about how groups function because such knowledge can indirectly help the manager or leader do a better job of developing teamwork. An analogy is that if a professor understands how people learn, he or she can be more effective at teaching.

Good teamwork enhances, but does not guarantee, a successful team. For example, a group with excellent teamwork might be working on improving a product or service no longer valued by the company or customers. No matter what the output of the team, it will probably be ignored. A list of strategies and tactics for building teamwork follows.

"Teamwork is the ability to work together toward a common vision; the ability to direct individual accomplishments toward organizational objectives. It is the fuel that allows common people to attain uncommon results."
—Andrew Carnegie, steel manufacturer and philanthropist, 1835–1919

1. Get qualified members. A starting point in developing good teamwork is to select members for the team who are interested in and qualified to be strong team members. The hiring manager or team leader should look for individuals who have enjoyed and performed well on teams in the past, both on and off the job. A study conducted in a manufacturing organization with highly interdependent teams found that being conscientious, extraverted, and having knowledge about teamwork were positively related to good job performance as a team member.[26]

2. Be well motivated yourself. A basic strategy for motivating the team toward teamwork or another worthwhile purpose is for the team leader to be well motivated, thereby being a good role model. The importance of the group leader being well motivated was demonstrated in a study with customer service representatives at a large travel agency franchise. The specific finding of the study was that when team leaders had strong motivation to adapt a new technology, the motivation to adapt increased for the representatives. Modeling took place because when the team leaders adapted the new technology, so did the customer service representatives. Charismatic team leaders were the most successful in motivating the workers to adapt the new technology.[27]

3. Have urgent, constructive purpose. Another early step is to help team members believe they have an urgent, constructive purpose. An example would be, "If we don't patch this software problem, we will get 95 percent returns." A demanding performance challenge helps create and sustain the team. Rewards should stem from meeting the challenge. The urgent, constructive purpose often stems from the team's mission, such as "eliminating or reducing environmental hazards while manufacturing our HD television screens."

4. Compete against common enemy. Competing against a common enemy is one of the best-known methods of building team spirit. It is preferable that the adversary is external, such as an independent diner competing against franchised family restaurants.

5. Have a culture of teamwork. A primary strategy for teamwork promotes the attitude that working together effectively is an expected norm. Developing such a culture of teamwork generally proves difficult when a strong culture of individualism exists within the firm. The team leader can communicate the norm of team work by making frequent use of words and phrases that support teamwork. Emphasizing the words *team members* or *teammates*, and de-emphasizing the words *subordinates* and *employees*, helps communicate the teamwork norm. The norm of teamwork is also fostered by having a code of conduct to which members agree. Provisions of the code might include, "Never abandon a teammate" and "Never humiliate a teammate."

As a team leader, you can contribute to a culture of teamwork by remembering to share credit with teammates whenever you receive a compliment for what the group has accomplished. Tell the group directly about the praise. Or if the praise is given publicly, make a statement in front of the team, such as, "I appreciate the compliment, but I could not have done it without Gus, Jennifer, Fred, and Hillary." Although, this sentiment is widely expressed, it still has a positive impact on teamwork.

6. Use the consensus decision-making style. Using the consensus decision-making style provides another way to reinforce teamwork. A sophisticated approach to enhancing teamwork, it feeds team members valid facts and information that motivate them to work together. New information prompts the team to redefine and enrich its understanding of the challenge it is facing, thereby focusing on a common purpose.

The consensus decision-making style helps develop teamwork also because the team members feel empowered because they feel involved in decision making. As the team members share in decision making, they are likely to develop a cooperative spirit.

7. Use teamwork language. A subtle yet potent method of building teamwork emphasizes the use of language that fosters cohesion and commitment. In-group jargon bonds a team and sets the group apart from others. At one business process outsourcing firm, when an associate wants a PowerPoint presentation, he or she is likely to say, "Send me a deck." The culture at Microsoft heavily emphasizes using hip jargon to build teamwork. Using the term *bandwidth* as a synonym for *intelligence* appears to have been invented by former CEO and chairman Bill Gates.

8. Minimize micromanagement. To foster teamwork, the manager should minimize micromanagement, or supervising group members too closely and second-guessing their decisions. Micromanagement can hamper a spirit of teamwork because team members do not feel in control of their own work. A relatively frequent example of a team leader being a micromanager (or *control freak*) is dictating which font should be used on team reports.

9. Reward the team as well as individuals. One high-impact strategy for encouraging teamwork rewards the team as well as individuals. The most convincing team incentive is to calculate compensation partially on the basis of team results. For a more general reward strategy, managers apply positive reinforcement whenever the group or individuals engage in behavior that supports teamwork. For example, team members who took the initiative to have an information-sharing session can be singled out and praised for this activity. The use of team-based incentives began in manufacturing, but it has spread to hospitals and health systems. Rewards are typically tied to specific goals, such as increased patient satisfaction or a reduction in accounts receivables.[28]

10. Publish a team book or Web site. To enhance team spirit, the manager can publish a team book containing a one-page biography of each team member. The same type of information might be posted on a Web site dedicated to team information, or a social media Web site such as Facebook. The biography can include a photo, a list of hobbies, personal interests, and family information. As team members look through the book, they become better acquainted with each other, leading to feelings of closeness.

11. Show respect for team members. Showing respect for team members is a general technique for building teamwork. Respect can be demonstrated in such ways as asking rather than demanding something be done—for example, "Jason, would you investigate developing a Web site for the team?" Giving team members your undivided attention when they come to you with a problem is another demonstration of respect, as are making positive comments about other team members and not talking behind their backs.

12. Send members to offsite training. Another option available to organizations for enhancing teamwork comes through experiential learning, such as sending members to offsite (or outdoor) training. Participants acquire teamwork skills by confronting physical challenges and exceeding their self-imposed limitations. (As mentioned in Chapter 11, offsite training is also used for leadership development.) In rope activities, which are typical of outdoor training, participants attached to a secure pulley with ropes climb ladders and jump off to another spot.

A day at an auto-racing track, another form of outdoor training for elite teams, provides team members with an opportunity to drive at racecar speeds in some kind of cooperative venture. Getting the team to work together in doing a social good, such as repairing a rundown house in a poor neighborhood, is another popular form of team building. Gourmet cooking as a team is now popular for teamwork development because so much cooperation is required to get the meal prepared correctly.

All of these challenges require teamwork rather than individual effort, hence their contribution to team development. Offsite training generally offers the most favorable outcomes when the trainer helps the team members comprehend the link between such training and on-the-job behavior.

13. Encourage communication among virtual team members. A special challenge in developing good teamwork is when the members are geographically dispersed, as in a virtual team. Because the members communicate with each other mostly by e-mail and group software, they lose out on the face to-face interaction useful for building teamwork. A technologically advanced approach is for the virtual team members to use online team rooms where everyone can see the state of work in progress and interact with each other simultaneously.[29] (The setup is much like a blog for team member use.) Bringing the group together for an occasional face-to-face meeting is also helpful in building teamwork.

A study showed that virtual teams profit from norms that describe how communication technology will be used. After these norms are accepted, trust—and therefore teamwork—is likely to be enhanced. These norms include such actions as how often to check the team's knowledge repository (for example, the team intranet) and how to use the repository for useful discussions rather than as a place to store documents. Norms also need to be established regarding what information should be posted, when to post it, and how to comment. Rules of etiquette should also be established, such as only using all capitals to communicate urgent messages.[30]

14. Make appropriate use of a team slogan, logo, and clothing. Many teams and groups in the workplace will develop closer ties among each other when they identify with a team logo and slogan that might be emblazoned on T-shirts, coffee mugs, pencils, and pens. The purpose of the symbols is to remind the group that they are part of a greater whole.[31] For some work situations, such as a group of financial planners or tax consultants, such gimmicks might be inappropriate. Yet for many groups, such as manufacturing employees, call center workers, and distribution center specialists, the team slogan, logo, and clothing might work well. The team members should be encouraged to develop the slogan and logo. For example, a group of dog and cat groomers might label themselves the Proud Pet Champions and use a logo of a cartoon dog and cat next to "PPC." in large letters.

15. Step in to resolve conflict. Conflict often arises in teams, especially when team members believe that they have the authority to decide on which work procedure or process to use.[32] Based on this freedom, the team members might squabble about which procedure or process is the most effective. Too much conflict lowers the team spirit, so the team leader should encourage the team members to resolve the conflict themselves or step in to facilitate conflict resolution. The techniques described in Chapter 10 should work well for resolving conflict within the team.

Effective managers and team leaders pick and choose from strategies as appropriate to build teamwork. Relying too heavily on one tactic, such as establishing a mission statement or outdoor training, limits the development of sustained teamwork.

16. Maintain a positive mood. Another application of thinking positively is that when team leaders typically display a positive mood, team performance is likely to be enhanced. A study conducted in Taiwan with 85 retail sales teams involving 365 team members found that leaders' positive mood enhanced various aspects of team performance. Objective measures of team performance included commissions and premiums, whereas subjective measures consisted of team leaders' evaluations.[33] The inspirational message from this study is that people tend to perform better when their leader is a happy person rather than a grouch.

▶ Learning Objective 5 ▶

How Does Understanding Group Dynamics Contribute to Teamwork Development and Motivation?

Group dynamics
the forces operating in groups that affect how members work together

An indirect way of a leader being effective at developing teamwork and motivating team members is to be knowledgeable about how groups operate. **Group dynamics** refers to the forces operating in groups that affect how members work together. To help zero in on this vast body of knowledge, we feature three practical topics: the stages of group development, team member roles, and the characteristics of an effective work group, including the problem of groupthink.

STAGES OF GROUP DEVELOPMENT

Key to understanding the nature of work groups is to know what the group does (the content) and how it proceeds (the process). A key group process is the group's development over time. To make this information more meaningful, relate it to any group to which you have belonged for at least one month. Understanding the stages of group development can lead to more effective group leadership or membership. The five group stages are shown in Figure 12-2 and described next.[34]

Stage 1. **Forming.** At the outset, members are eager to learn what tasks they will be performing, how they can benefit from group membership, and what constitutes acceptable behavior. Members often inquire about rules they must follow. Confusion, caution, and communality are typical during the initial phase of group development.

Stage 2. **Storming.** During this "shakedown" period, individual styles often come into conflict. Hostility, infighting, tension, and confrontation are typical. Members may argue to clarify expectations of their contributions. Coalitions and cliques may form within the group, and one or two members may be targeted for exclusion. Subgroups may form to push for an agenda of interest to them. (Despite the frequency of storming, many workplace groups work willingly with one another from the outset, thus skipping stage 2.)

Stage 3. **Norming.** After storming comes the quieter stage of overcoming resistance and establishing group standards of conduct (norms). Cohesiveness and commitment begin to develop. The group starts to come together as a coordinated unit, and harmony prevails. Norms stem from three sources. First, the group itself quickly establishes limits for members, often by effective use of glares and nods. For example, the team member who swears at the leader might receive angry glances from other

FIGURE 12-2
THE STAGES OF GROUP DEVELOPMENT
Most Groups Follow a Predictable Sequence of Stages

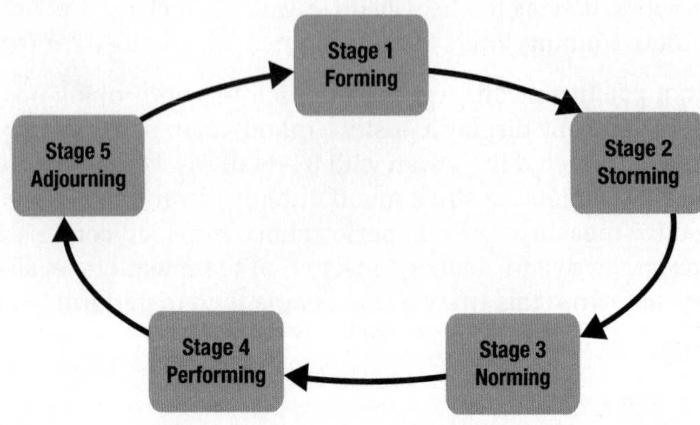

members. Second, norms may also be imposed that are derived from the larger organization and from professional codes of conduct. A third source of norms might be an influential team member who inspires the group to elevate its performance or behavior. The head of an audit team might say, "Let's develop the reputation of an audit team that is the most professional and objective in the industry."

Stage 4. Performing. When the group reaches the performing stage, it is ready to focus on accomplishing its key tasks. Issues concerning interpersonal relations and task assignment are put aside as the group becomes a well-functioning unit. Intrinsic motivation and creativity are likely to emerge as the group performs. At their best, members feel they are working "for the cause," much like a political campaign team or a team bringing a breakthrough product to market.

Stage 5. Adjourning. Temporary work groups are abandoned after their task has been accomplished, much like a project team to erect an office tower. The same group members, however, have developed important relationships and understandings they can bring with them should they be teammates in the future. The link between adjourning and forming shown in Figure 12-2 is that many groups do reassemble after one project is completed. The link between stages 1 and 5 would not apply for a group that disbanded and never worked together again.

A key managerial challenge is to help the group move past the first three stages into performing. At times, group members may have to be notified that they are spending too much time on process issues and not enough on the task at hand.

TEAM MEMBER ROLES

A major challenge in learning to become an effective team member is to choose the right roles to occupy. A **role** is a tendency to behave, contribute, and relate to others in a particular way. It is helpful for the leader to understand these roles as he or she attempts to get the group working together smoothly. For example, the leader might want to make sure that all positive roles are filled. If you carry out positive roles, you will be perceived as a contributor to team effort. If you neglect carrying out these roles, you will be perceived as a poor contributor. Human Relations Self-Assessment Quiz 12-2 will help you evaluate your present inclinations toward occupying effective roles as a team member. In this section we describe a number of the most frequently observed positive roles played by team members. We also mention a group of negative roles.

Role
tendency to behave, contribute, and relate to others in a particular way

According to the role theory developed by Meredith Belbin and his group of researchers at Belbin Associates, there are nine frequent roles occupied by team members.[35] All of these roles are influenced to some extent by an individual's personality.

1. **Creative problem solver.** The creative problem solver is creative, imaginative, and unorthodox. Such a person solves difficult problems. A potential weakness of this role is that the person tends to ignore fine details and becomes too immersed in the problem to communicate effectively.
2. **Resource investigator.** The resource investigator is extroverted, enthusiastic, and communicates freely with other team members. He or she will explore opportunities and develop valuable contacts. A potential weakness of this role is that the person can be overly optimistic and may lose interest after the initial enthusiasm wanes.
3. **Coordinator.** The coordinator is mature, confident, and a natural team leader. He or she clarifies goals, promotes decision making, and delegates effectively. A downside to occupying this role is that the person might be seen as manipulative and controlling. Some coordinators delegate too much by asking others to do some of the work they (the coordinators) should be doing.

Human Relations Self-Assessment Quiz 12-2

Team Player Roles

For each of the following statements about team activity, check mostly agree or mostly disagree. If you have not experienced such a situation, imagine how you would act or think if placed in that situation. In responding to the statements, assume that you are taking the questionnaire with the intent of learning something about yourself.

	Mostly Agree	Mostly Disagree
1. It is rare that I ever miss a team meeting.	_____	_____
2. I regularly compliment team members when they do something exceptional.	_____	_____
3. Whenever I can, I avoid being the note taker at a team meeting.	_____	_____
4. From time to time, other team members come to me for advice on technical matters.	_____	_____
5. I like to hide some information from other team members so I can be in control.	_____	_____
6. I welcome new team members coming to me for advice and learning the ropes.	_____	_____
7. My priorities come first, which leaves me with very little time to help other team members.	_____	_____
8. During a team meeting, it is not unusual for several other people at a time to look toward me for my opinion.	_____	_____
9. If I think the team is moving in an unethical direction, I will say so explicitly.	_____	_____
10. Rarely will I criticize the progress of the team even if I think such criticism is deserved.	_____	_____
11. It is not unusual for me to summarize the progress in a team meeting, even if not asked.	_____	_____
12. To conserve time, I attempt to minimize contact with my teammates outside of our meetings.	_____	_____
13. I intensely dislike going along with a consensus decision if the decision runs contrary to my thoughts on the issue.	_____	_____
14. I rarely remind teammates of our mission statement as we go about our work.	_____	_____
15. Once I have made up my mind on an issue facing the team, I am unlikely to be persuaded in another direction.	_____	_____
16. I am willing to accept negative feedback from team members.	_____	_____
17. Simply to get a new member of the team involved, I will ask his or her opinion.	_____	_____
18. Even if the team has decided on a course of action, I am not hesitant to bring in new information that supports another position.	_____	_____
19. Quite often I talk negatively about one team member to another.	_____	_____
20. My teammates are almost a family to me because I am truly concerned about their welfare.	_____	_____
21. When it seems appropriate, I joke and kid with teammates.	_____	_____
22. My contribution to team tasks is as important to me as my individual work.	_____	_____
23. From time to time I have pointed out to the team how we can all improve in reaching our goals.	_____	_____
24. I will fight to the last when the team does not support my viewpoint and wants to move toward consensus.	_____	_____
25. I will confront the team if I believe that the members are thinking too much alike.	_____	_____
	Total Score	_____

Scoring and Interpretation

Give yourself one point (+1) for each statement you gave in agreement with the keyed answer. The keyed answer indicates carrying out a positive, as opposed to a negative, role.

1. Mostly agree
2. Mostly agree
3. Mostly disagree
4. Mostly agree
5. Mostly disagree
6. Mostly agree
7. Mostly disagree
8. Mostly agree
9. Mostly agree
10. Mostly disagree
11. Mostly agree
12. Mostly disagree
13. Mostly disagree
14. Mostly disagree
15. Mostly disagree
16. Mostly agree
17. Mostly agree
18. Mostly agree
19. Mostly disagree
20. Mostly agree
21. Mostly agree
22. Mostly agree
23. Mostly agree
24. Mostly disagree
25. Mostly agree

20–25 You carry out a well above average number of positive team roles. Behavior of this type contributes substantially to being an effective team player. Study the roles in this chapter to further build your effectiveness as a team member.

10–19 You carry out an average number of positive team roles. Study carefully the roles described in this chapter to search for ways to carry out a greater number of positive roles.

0–9 You carry out a substantially above average number of negative team roles. If becoming an effective team player is important to you, you will have to diligently search for ways to play positive team roles. Study the information about roles in this chapter carefully.

4. **Shaper.** The shaper is challenging, dynamic, and thrives under pressure. He or she will use determination and courage to overcome obstacles. A potential weakness of the shaper is that he or she can be easily provoked and may ignore the feelings of others.
5. **Monitor–evaluator.** The monitor–evaluator is even tempered, engages in strategic (big picture and long-term) thinking, and makes accurate judgments. He or she sees all the options and judges accurately. A potential weakness of this role occupant is that he or she might lack drive and the ability to inspire others.
6. **Team worker.** The team worker is cooperative, focuses on relationships, and is sensitive and diplomatic. He or she is a good listener who builds relationships, dislikes confrontation, and averts friction. A potential weakness is that the team worker can be indecisive in a crunch situation or crisis.
7. **Implementer.** The implementer is disciplined, reliable, conservative, and efficient. He or she will act quickly on ideas and convert them into practical actions. A potential weakness is that the implementer can be inflexible and slow to see new opportunities.
8. **Completer–finisher.** The completer–finisher is conscientious and eager to get the job done. He or she has a good eye for detail and is effective at searching out errors. He or she can be counted on for finishing a project and delivering on time. A potential weakness is that he or she can be a worrier and reluctant to delegate.
9. **Specialist.** The specialist is a single-minded self-starter. He or she is dedicated and provides knowledge and skill in rare supply. A potential weakness of the specialist is that he or she can be stuck in a niche with little interest in other knowledge and may dwell on technicalities.

The weaknesses in the roles point to problems the team leader or manager can expect to emerge, and therefore allowances should be made. Belbin refers to these potential problems as *allowable weaknesses*, because allowances should be made for them. To illustrate, if a team worker has a tendency to be indecisive in a crisis, the team should not have high expectations of the team worker when faced with a crisis. Team workers will be the most satisfied if the crisis is predicted and decisions involving them are made before the pressure mounts.[36]

Another perspective on team roles is that team members will sometimes engage in *self-oriented roles.* Members will sometimes focus on their own needs rather than those of the group. The individual might be overly aggressive because of a personal need, such as wanting a bigger budget on his or her project. The individual might hunger for recognition or power. Similarly, the person might attempt to dominate the meeting, block others from contributing, or serve as a distraction. One of the ploys used by distracters recently is to engage in cell phone conversations during a meeting and blaming it on "those people who keep calling me."

The many roles just presented overlap somewhat. For example, the implementer might engage in specialist activities. Do not be concerned about the overlap. Instead, pick and choose from the many roles as the situation dictates—regardless of whether overlap exists.

The behavior associated with the roles just described is more important than remembering the labels. For example, remembering to be creative and imaginative is more important than remembering the specific label *creative problem solver*.

THE PROBLEM OF GROUPTHINK (TOO MUCH CONSENSUS)

Groupthink
a deterioration of mental efficiency, reality testing, and moral judgment in the interest of group solidarity; extreme form of consensus

For a team to be truly effective, somebody has to step forth and say, "The emperor has no clothes" when the group is making an outrageously bad decision. Often the shaper or monitor–evaluator plays this role. **Groupthink** is a deterioration of mental efficiency, reality testing, and moral judgment in the interest of group solidarity. Simply put, groupthink is an extreme form of consensus. The group atmosphere values getting along more than getting things done.[37] The group thinks as a unit, believes it is impervious to outside criticism, and begins to have illusions about its own invincibility. As a consequence, the group loses its powers of critical analysis.

One historically important example of groupthink took place in relation to the explosion of the space shuttle *Challenger*. According to several analyses of the incident, NASA managers were so committed to reaching space program objectives that they ignored safety warnings from people both within and outside the agency. As reported in an internal NASA briefing paper dated July 20, 1986, both astronauts and engineers expressed concern that the agency's management had a groupthink mentality. Of related significance, the management style of NASA managers is characterized by a tendency not to reverse decisions and not to heed the advice of people outside the management group. The analysis of their styles was conducted by a series of management-style tests administered several years prior to the *Challenger* explosion.[38]

Groupthink appears to have contributed to several of the major financial scandals of several years ago involving major investment banks. The investment banks in questions offered mortgage-backed securities to the public without informing their clients that the mortgages behind these securities were high risk. When homeowners defaulted on their mortgages, the securities lost considerable value or became worthless. Groupthink was probably involved because highly-paid intelligent individual financial executives most likely would have attempted frauds of this magnitude.

The negative aspects of groupthink can often be prevented if the team leader, or a member, encourages all team members to express doubts and criticisms of proposed solutions to the problem or suggested courses of action. It is also helpful to periodically invite qualified outsiders to meet with the group and provide suggestions.

What Are the Characteristics of an Effective Work Group?

Learning Objective 6

Groups, like individuals, have characteristics that contribute to their uniqueness and effectiveness. Effectiveness includes such factors as objective measures of production (for example, units produced), favorable evaluations by the manager, and worker satisfaction. In understanding how groups can be effective, keep in mind that a justification for forming groups and teams is that they can produce more than the sum of the individual members, or have synergy. As the late Stephen Covey explained, to synergize is to combine the efforts, power, and positive energy of people who come together in order to accomplish a goal. The process of synergizing also multiplies the value all participants bring to the interaction.[39]

For a group to be effective, the members must strive to act like a group or team. Also, the task given to the group or team should require collective effort instead of being a task that could be better performed by individuals. For example, many customers would prefer to be called on by an individual sales representative rather than by a sales team, so for some customers the rep should work individually rather than in a team effort. As shown in Figure 12-3, and based on dozens of different studies, effective work group and team characteristics can be grouped into twelve characteristics or factors.

FIGURE 12-3 KEY CHARACTERISTICS OF EFFECTIVE TEAMS AND WORK GROUPS

1. The team has clear-cut goals linked to organizational goals so that group members feel connected to the entire organization. Group members are empowered so they learn to think for themselves rather than expecting a supervisor to solve all the difficult problems. At the same time, the group believes it has the authority to solve a variety of problems without first obtaining approval from management.
2. Group members are assigned work they perceive to be challenging, exciting, and rewarding. As a consequence, the work is self-rewarding.
3. Members depend on one another to accomplish tasks and work toward a common goal. At the same time, the group believes in itself and that it can accomplish an interdependent task. Group members who engage in *social loafing* (not doing their fair share) are advised by other group members and the team leader that the must perform at an acceptable level.
4. Members learn to think "outside the box" (are creative).
5. Members receive extensive training in technical knowledge, problem-solving skills, and interpersonal skills. Also, the team develops *team cognition* in which knowledge important to the group is organized and distributed within the group, allowing for appropriate action.
6. Group size is generally about six people, rather than ten or more.
7. Team members have good intelligence and personality factors, such as conscientiousness and pride, that contribute to good performance.
8. There is honest and open communication among group members and with other groups in the organization.
9. Members have the philosophy of working as a team—twenty-five brains, not only fifty hands.
10. Members are familiar with their jobs, coworkers, and the work environment. This experience adds to their expertise. The beneficial effects of experience may diminish after a while because the team needs fresh ideas and approaches.
11. The team has emotional intelligence in the sense that it builds relationships both inside and outside the team. Included in emotional intelligence are norms that establish mutual trust among members, a feeling of group identity, and group efficacy.
12. Stronger performing group members assist weaker performing group members accomplish their task, particularly when the performance of the "weakest link" in the group is key for group performance.

Sources: Michael A. Campion, Ellen M. Papper, and Gina Medsker, "Relations Between Work Team Characteristics and Effectiveness: A Replication and Extension," *Personnel Psychology*, Summer 1996, p. 431; Vanessa Urch Druskat and Steven B. Wolff, "Building the Emotional Intelligence of Groups," *Harvard Business Review*, March 2001, pp. 80–90; Claus W. Langred, "Too Much of a Good Thing? Negative Effects of High Trust and Individual Autonomy in Self-Managing Work Teams, "*Academy of Management Journal*, June 2004, pp. 385–399; Leslie A. DeChurch and Jessica R. Mesmer-Magnus, "The Cognitive Underpinnings of Effective Teamwork: A Meta-Analysis," *Journal of Applied Psychology*, January 2010, pp. 32–53; Avan Jassawalla, Hemant Sashittal, and Avinash Malshe, "Students' Perceptions of Social Loafing: Its Antecedents and Consequences in Undergraduate Business Classroom Teams," *Academy of Management Learning & Education*, March 2009, pp. 42–54.

Key Terms

Motivation, 350
Two-factor theory of work motivation, 350
Empowerment, 352
Shared leadership, 352
Intrinsic motivation, 353
Prosocial motivation, 353
Job enrichment, 354
Positive reinforcement, 354
Intermittent rewards, 355
Variable pay, 356
Recognition need, 357
Teamwork, 360
Team, 360
Group, 360
Group dynamics, 364
Role, 365
Groupthink, 368

Summary and Review

Motivating others toward good performance begins with the diagnosis of motivation. Diagnostic questions might include, "What could this job offer you that would make you work at your best?" Diagnosis should also include observing the subordinate's behavior in terms of what interests him or her.

Two classic theories of worker motivation are Maslow's hierarchy of needs and Herzberg's two-factor theory of motivation.

- A practical application of the needs hierarchy is that when a manager wants to motivate a group member, he or she must offer the individual a reward that must satisfy an important need.
- According to the two-factor theory of work motivation, one set of factors, the motivators or satisfiers, can motivate and satisfy workers. The other set, dissatisfiers, or hygiene factors, can only prevent dissatisfaction.

Empowerment is a comprehensive motivational strategy that grants workers more power by enabling them to participate in decisions affecting them and their work.

- Empowerment contributes to intrinsic motivation.
- Empowerment is commonplace in the service industry.
- Empowered employees must still be given overall direction and limits to the extent of their authority.

Motivation can take place through job design and interesting work, based on the principle of intrinsic motivation. Job enrichment makes a job more motivating and satisfying through means such as the following:

- Direct feedback to the job incumbent
- The opportunity for client relationships
- New learning

Rules for effectively using positive reinforcement to motivate employees include the following:

- State clearly what behavior will lead to a reward.
- Choose an appropriate reward.
- Supply ample feedback.
- Schedule rewards intermittently.
- Make the rewards follow the observed behavior closely in time.
- Make the reward fit the behavior.
- Make the rewards visible.
- Change the reward periodically.

Financial incentives are a natural motivator and are a form of positive reinforcement. Such incentives have multiplied in importance as companies struggle to stay afloat in worldwide competition. Money is also tied in with recognition. Key issues about financial incentives include the following:

- To make pay more motivational, many employers link pay to performance such as in variable pay and financial bonuses.
- Personal factors influence the power of financial incentives, including the value the worker attaches to money and the need for money.
- Financial incentives can cause problems, including a focus more on rewards than the joy built into exciting work and workers attaining good financial results by unethical means.

Motivation through recognition and praise is an important motivational strategy because the workplace provides a natural opportunity to satisfy the recognition need. Praising workers for good performance is closely related to informal recognition. Many workers rarely receive praise. An advanced use of praise is to tailor the praise to the needs of the person. Formal recognition programs are important for employee retention as well as motivation.

Team leaders as well as other managers need to use techniques that influence subordinates to work well together as a team. Among the many suggestions presented in the chapter for building teamwork are the following:

- Select members for the team who are interested in being and qualified to be strong team members.
- Help team members believe they have an urgent, constructive purpose.
- Use the consensus decision-making style.
- Reward the team as well as individuals.
- Show respect for team members.
- Maintain a positive mood.

Understanding how groups operate (group dynamics) helps a leader effectively build teamwork. One useful concept is the stages of group development: forming, storming, norming, performing, and adjourning. Team members occupy various roles, including the following:

- Resource investigator
- Coordinator
- Monitor–evaluator
- Completer–finisher
- Specialist

A key potential problem with group effort is groupthink, or extreme consensus. The problem can be lessened by team members occupying a critical role.

An effective work group has characteristics that contribute to its uniqueness and effectiveness, as outlined in Figure 12-3. For a group to be effective, the members must strive to be a team and work on a task that requires collective effort.

Check Your Understanding

1. How could diagnosing the motivational wishes and needs of employees save a company a lot of money when launching motivational programs?
2. What objection might some employees have to being empowered?
3. In what way does job enrichment appeal to the pride some people have in their work?
4. Give an explanation from motivation theory as to why do so many people from the film industry who are already well-off financially still want to win an Academy Award.
5. What type of recognition on the job would be motivational for you? How do you know?
6. Assume that Jennifer from the tech support center gets rid of a nasty virus in your desktop computer. What is likely to be an effective statement of praise for her?
7. Assume that your employer sent you to an offsite team-building exercise that you feared doing, such as climbing a wall. How would you deal with the situation?
8. Reflect on any group you currently belong to or were a member of in the past. Describe how the group went through the stages of group development.
9. Give an example of one or two group norms that a team of firefighters might have.
10. Identify several of the characteristics of an effective work group that one of your favorite athletic team possesses. Justify your reasoning the best you can.

Web Corner

Tips for motivating a cleaning crew (or other basic workers)
www.custodian.info/crew.html

Gourmet cooking as a team building exercise
www.recipeforsuccess.com/team-cuisine

Teamwork quotes and proverbs
www.heartquotes.net/teamwork-quotes.html

INTERNET SKILL BUILDER

Motivating Employees

Visit www.nelson-motivation.com to watch a five-minute video clip of one of Bob Nelson's talks. After watching the video, answer the following questions:

1. What have I learned that I could translate into a skill for motivating employees?
2. Which theory, or approach, to motivation does Nelson emphasize in his presentation?

Developing Your Human Relations Skills

Human Relations Application Exercises

Applying Human Relations Exercise 12-1

The Job Enrichment Squad

Work individually or in small groups to develop skill in enriching several standard jobs by making them more interesting, challenging, and responsibility oriented. As part of your analysis, see if you can find someone who has held such a job (either you or a group member), and interview the job incumbent for some ideas. You might use e-mail or instant messaging as an alternative or supplement to telephone or face-to-face interviews. Choose three from among the following positions:

- Supermarket cashier
- Highway toll collector
- Custodial worker at an educational institution
- Home health aide
- Car wash attendant
- Call center operator for service with mobile phones

In your problem-solving activity and in your interviews, seek answers to these basic questions: (1) What is the most boring part of this job? (2) What is the most exciting part of this job? (3) What is the most de-motivating part of the job? (4) What is the most motivating part of the job? (5) Find an answer to any other questions or issues you think are relevant.

After you have completed your analysis, prepare a report of about two brief paragraphs as to how the specific job can be more motivational through job design.

Applying Human Relations Exercise 12-2

Team Member Roles

A team of approximately six people is formed to conduct a twenty-minute meeting on a significant topic of their choosing. The possible scenarios follow:

Scenario A: Management Team. A group of managers is pondering whether to lay off one-third of the workforce to increase profits. The company has had a tradition of caring for employees and regarding them as the company's most precious asset. But the CEO has said privately that times have changed in our competitive world, and the company must do whatever possible to enhance profits. The group wants to think through the advisability of laying off one-third the workforce and explore other alternatives.

Scenario B: Group of Sports Fans. A group of fans has volunteered to find a new team name to replace "Redskins" for the local basketball team. One person among the group of volunteers believes that the name "Redskins" should be retained because it is a compliment, rather than an insult, to Native Americans. The other members of the group believe that a name change is in order, but they lack any good ideas for replacing a mascot team name that has endured for more than fifty years.

Scenario C: Community Group. A community group is attempting to launch an initiative to help battered adults and children. Opinions differ strongly as to what initiative would be truly helpful to these people. Among the alternatives are establishing a shelter for battered people, giving workshops on preventing violence, and self-defense training. Each group member with an idea strongly believes that he or she has come up with a workable possibility for helping with the problem of battered people.

While the team members are conducting their heated discussion, other class members make notes on which team members carry out which roles. Watching for the nine different roles, as well as the self-oriented roles, can be divided among class members. For example, the people in the first row might look for examples of the creative problem solver. Use the role worksheet that follows to help make your observations. Summarize the comment that is indicative of the role. An example would be noting in the shaper category: "Linda said naming the team the 'Washington Rainbows' seems like too much of an attempt to be politically correct."

Creative problem solver ______________________

Teamworker ______________________

Resource investigator ______________________

Implementer ______________________

Coordinator ______________________

Completer–finisher ______________________

Shaper ______________________

Specialist ______________________

Monitor–evaluator ______________________

Self-oriented roles ______________________

Human Relations Class Activity

A Survey of Positive Motivators

As explained in Chapter 12, positive reinforcement only works well as a motivational technique when the right (effective) motivators (or reinforcers) are used. Plenty of written information is available about what constitutes effective motivators, including recognition. For this class activity, you will collect fresh data about effective motivators. The steps are as follows:

1. Each student completes the following sentence: "The most effective form of positive reinforcement I ever received on the job (or in school, sports, or community activity) was ____________________."
2. Each student submits his or her answer to a class database. If the class has a Web site, intranet, or similar centralized method of collecting input, simply submit your answer using that medium. If you do not have such a system, simply send an e-mail or instant message to every class member with your answer.
3. Each student, or a few volunteers, will them compile a list of the five most effective motivators, based on how frequently the motivator was mentioned. For example, perhaps four class members completed the sentence with a response such as, "I was given a gift certificate for having been an outstanding performer."
4. If the class size is large enough, look for possible sex differences in preference for motivators.
5. Hold a class discussion of (a) how well you think the class findings might fit many different work settings and (b) how useful this activity has been in giving you ideas for motivating workers.

Human Relations Case Study 12-1

The Car Wash Blues

Pedro Ramirez was so proud. After years of saving money and building up his credit rating, Ramirez bought a car wash in St. Paul, Minnesota, that had been closed for several months. After redecorating and repainting the shop, Pedro renamed the car wash Sparkle Car Wash. Pedro reasoned that his car wash had an above-average opportunity to be successful because the many snowy fall and winter days in St. Paul helped keep autos and small trucks in need of washing.

Before opening, Pedro decided to staff the car wash. He hired an uncle as a part-time bookkeeper, along with five car wash attendants. To help promote business at Sparkle Car Wash, Pedro placed thousands of flyers tucked under the windshield wipers of cars parked in mall parking lots and on the street. The flyers along with the fact that the neighborhood needed another car wash helped bring business to an acceptable level. Pedro's uncle told him that if the present volume of car washes held up and labor costs remained stable, the car wash business would be a financial success.

Within two months, Pedro began to experience some labor problems. Three of the car wash attendants quit, with two just not coming back after they were paid. These two car wash attendants who quit were replaced, but one had to be fired. Instead of paying attention to customers, he remained distracted by his iPod and often ignored customer requests. These included customers asking for help closing a vehicle window or asking about how to operate the auto vacuum cleaners.

Two weeks later, two more car wash attendants quit, both offering the excuse that they had found a "real job" somewhere else. One of the attendants said customers were making crude remarks toward her. The other attendant complained that almost nobody gave him a tip.

Pedro developed a motivational program to help keep his attendants on the job, as well as playing more careful attention to customers. He would allow them one free car wash a week, along with a paid-for lunch at McDonald's if they performed well for the entire week. Two weeks later, one more car wash attendant quit, and more careful attention was not being paid to customer requests.

Questions

1. How effective do you think the rewards of a weekly car wash and a meal at McDonald's will be in motivating the car wash attendants to stay on the job and treat customers better?
2. What other approach to employee motivation might work for reducing turnover and providing better customer service?
3. To what extent do you think it might be hopeless to motivate car wash attendants to stay on the job longer and provide better customer service?

Human Relations Role-Playing Exercise

Pedro Conducts a Motivational Interview with Bubba

The case, "The Car Wash Blues," provides the setting for this role-play but takes the storyline further. One student plays the role of Pedro, who decides he must be more professional in his attempt to motivate the car wash attendants. He decides to conduct a diagnostic interview with Bubba, one of the newly hired car wash attendants. Among the questions he will ask Bubba are:

- What can management at Sparkle Car Wash offer you that would make you want to stick around as well as do your best to make our customers happy?
- How important is money to you?
- What are your career plans?

Another student plays the role of Bubba, who was not expecting a diagnostic interview. In fact, no boss in previous jobs has paid serious attention to him other than to reprimand him for poor performance. But because the interview is being conducted on company time, Bubba welcomes the change of pace from wiping down cars with a chamois cloth. (If a woman plays the role of Pedro or Bubba, she is free to use a name other than Pedro or Bubba.)

Observers rate the role-players on two dimensions, using a 1 to 5 scale from very poor to very good. One dimension is "effective use of human relations techniques." For Pedro, focus on how well he shows a sincere interest in attempting to motivate Bubba. The second dimension is "acting ability." A few observers might voluntarily provide feedback to the role-players in terms of sharing their ratings and observations. The course instructor might also provide feedback.

Human Relations Case Study 12-2

Ruth Waves a Red Flag

Carlos is the team leader of a cost-reduction team within a baked-goods company that produces bakery products under its own label, as well as private labels for grocery-store chains such as Giant and Winn-Dixie. Top-level management formed the team to arrive at suggestions for reducing costs throughout the organization. A transcript of one of the meetings is presented next.

Carlos: We've been gathering information for a month now. It's about time we heard some specific suggestions.

Jack: At the top of my list is cutting pension benefits. Our pension payments are higher than the minimum required by law. Our medical benefits are way above average. If we cut back on pension benefits, no current employees would be adversely affected.

Melissa: I like your analysis, Jack. No sense risking laying off employees just to keep retirees happy.

Jordan: We should make absolutely certain there are no legal complications here. Then we can sharpen our cost-cutting knives and dig right in.

Gunther: I'd support cutting pension benefits. It would probably reduce expenses more dramatically than the ways I have uncovered.

Carlos: There seems to be consensus so far that we should considered making recommendations about cutting pension benefits. Ruth, what do you think?

Ruth: I think it is much too early to reach consensus on such a sensitive issue. Cutting pension benefits would create panic among our retirees. Our older employees would be screaming as well. We'll have an avalanche of negative publicity in the media.

Jordan: Hold on, Ruth. I said the team should first check out this idea with the legal department.

Ruth: Just because cutting pension benefits could squeeze by legally doesn't mean that it's a good idea. We haven't examined the negative ramifications of cutting pension benefits. Let's study this issue further before word leaks out that we're taking away the golden egg.

Carlos: Maybe Ruth has a point. Let's investigate this issue further before making a recommendation.

Questions

1. What role, or roles, is Ruth occupying on the cost-reduction team?
2. How effective does Ruth appear to be in her role?
3. What role, or roles, is Jack occupying on the cost-reduction team?
4. How effective does Jack appear to be in his role?
5. How effective is Carlos in his role as a team leader?

REFERENCES

1. Original story created from facts and observations presented in the following sources: Beth Kowitt, "Full-Time Motivation for Part-Time Employees," *Fortune*, October 17, 2011, p. 58; "Jessica Herrin," *Mommy Tracked* (www. momytracked .com), © 2011 Mom Inc., pp. 1–2; Jessica Herrin, "Make Your Employees Motivated Missionaries," *Inc.* (www.inc.com), January 31, 2012, pp. 1–2; Tamara Schweitzer, "Balancing a Start-up and a Baby," *Inc.* (www.inc.com/magazine), September 1, 2010, pp. 1–3.
2. John Sullivan, "Personalizing Motivation," *Workforce Management,* March 27, 2006, p. 50.
3. Frederick Herzberg, Bernard Mausner, and Barbara Synderman, *The Motivation to Work,* 2nd ed. (New York: Wiley, 1959); Herzberg, *Work and the Nature of Man* (Cleveland: World Publishing, 1966).
4. Gretchen M. Spreitzer, "Psychological Empowerment in the Workplace: Dimensions, Measurement, and Validation," *Academy of Management Journal,* October 1995, pp. 1443–1444.
5. Jay B. Carson, Paul. E. Tesluk, and Jennifer A. Marrone, "Shared Leadership in Teams: An Investigation of Antecedent Conditions and Performance," *Academy of Management Journal,* October 2007, pp. 1217–1234; Craig L. Pearce, Charles C. Manz, and Henry P. Sims Jr., "Is Shared Leadership the Key to Team Success?" *Organizational Dynamics,* July–September 2009, pp. 238.
6. Adam M. Grant, "Does Intrinsic Motivation Fuel the Prosocial Fire? Motivational Synergy in Predicting Persistence, Performance, and Productivity," *Journal of Applied Psychology,* January 2008, pp. 48–58.
7. Frederick Herzberg, "The Wise Old Turk," *Harvard Business Review,* September–October 1974, pp. 70–80.
8. Quoted in Laura Raines, "Don't Neglect Performance Management in Tough Times," *AJC* (www.ajc.com/business), September 7, 2010, p. 2.
9. David Javitch, "Getting Your Employees Excited Again," *Entrepreneur,* August 7, 2006.
10. Jack and Suzy Welch, "Keeping Your People Pumped," *Business Week,* March 27, 2006, p. 122.
11. Philip Moss, Harold Salzman, and Chris Tilly, "Under Construction: The Continuing Evolution of Job Structures in Call Centers,"*Industrial Relations,* Vol. 47, 2008, pp. 173–208.
12. Fred Luthans and Alexander Stajkovic, "Reinforce for Performance: The Need to Go Beyond Pay and Even Rewards," *Academy of Management Executive,* May 1999, p. 52.
13. Steven Kerr, *Ultimate Rewards: What Really Motivates People to Achieve* (Boston: Harvard Business School Publishing, 1997).
14. Mark Henricks, "Start Their Engines," *Entrepreneur,* January 2008, p. 85.
15. Todd Henneman, "Daniels' Scientific Method," *Workforce Management,* October 10, 2005, p. 46.
16. Mark Henricks, "Pay for Performance," *Entrepreneur,* November 2008, pp. 77–78; "Skyline Construction Employee Stock Ownership Plan, 2010 Form 5500," *Bright Scope* (www .brightscope.com), accessed March 2, 2012.
17. Reported in "Employees Want More Recognition, Growth Opportunity," *Monitor on Psychology,* May 2011, p. 12.
18. Charlotte Huff, "Risk of Creating 'Soft' Employees," *Workforce Management,* September 24, 2007, p. 28.
19. Andrew J. DuBrin, "Self-Perceived Technical Orientation and Attitudes Toward Being Flattered," *Psychological Reports,* Vol. 96, 2005, pp. 852–854.
20. Charlotte Garvey, "Meaningful Tokens of Appreciation: Cash Awards Aren't the Only Way to Motivate Your Workforce," *HR Magazine,* August 2004, p. 103.
21. Charlotte Huff, "Motivating the World," *Workforce Management,* September 24, 2007, p. 31.
22. Julie Bos, "Beating the Burnout: Six Top Strategies for Effective Employee Rewards and Recognition," *Workforce Management,* October 2010, p. 40.
23. Leah Shepherd, "Getting Personal," *Workforce Management,* September 2010, p. 28.
24. Bob Nelson, "Long-Distance Recognition," *Workforce,* August 2000, pp. 50–52.
25. Many of the suggestions are from Jon R. Katzenbach and Douglas K. Smith, "The Discipline of Teams," *Harvard Business Review,* March–April 1993, p. 112; Gilad Chen et al., "A Multilevel Study of Leadership, Empowerment, and Performance in Teams," *Journal of Applied Psychology,* March 2007, pp. 331–346; "Improve Teamwork With a 'Code of Conduct,'" *Manager's Edge,* February 2005, p. 1.
26. Frederick P. Morgeson, Matthew H. Reider, and Michael A. Campion, "Selecting Individuals in Team Settings: The Importance of Social Skills, Personality Characteristics, and Teamwork Knowledge," *Personnel Psychology,* Autumn 2005, pp. 583–611.
27. Jean-Francois Coget, "Does Managerial Motivation Spill Over to Subordinates?" *Academy of Management Perspectives,* November 2011, pp. 84–85; Jan Wieseke et al., "How Leaders' Motivation Transfers to Customer Service Representatives," *Journal of Service Research,* November, 2011, pp. 214–233.
28. Matt Bolch, "Rewarding the Team" *HR Magazine,* February 2007, p. 92.
29. Ann Majchrzak, Arvind Malhotra, Jeffrey Stamps, and Jessica Lipnack, "Can Absence Make a Team Grow Stronger?" *Harvard Business School,* May 2004, pp. 131–137.
30. Arvind Malhotra, Ann Majchrzak, and Benson Rosen, "Leading Virtual Teams," *Academy of Management Perspectives,* February 2007, pp. 61–62.
31. "5 Ways to Create Team Motivation," *Manager's Edge,* November 2007, p. 4.
32. Claus W. Langfred, "The Downside of Self-Management: A Longitudinal Study of the Effects of Conflict on Trust, Autonomy, and Task Interdependence in Self-Managing Teams," *Academy of Management Journal,* August 2007, pp. 885–900.
33. Joseph C. Santora, "Do Happy Leaders Make for Better Team Performance?" *Academy of Management Perspectives,* November 2011, pp. 88–90; Nai-Wen Chi, Yen-Yi Chung, and Wei-Chi Tsai, "How Do Happy Leaders Enhance Team Success? The Mediating Role of Transformational Leadership, Group Affective Tone, and Team Processes," *Journal of Applied Social Psychology,* June 2011, pp. 1421–1454.

34. J. Steven Heinen and Eugene Jacobsen, "A Model of Task Group Development in Complex Organizations and a Strategy of Implementation," *Academy of Management Review,* October 1976, pp. 98–111.

35. "R. Meredith Belbin," in *Business: The Ultimate Resource* (Cambridge, MA: Perseus Publishing, 2002), pp. 966–967; Belbin Team-Roles. Retrieved March 12, 2005, from http://www.belbin.com/belbin-teamroles.htm.

36. From a review of Meredith Belbin, *Management Teams: Why They Succeed or Fail,* 2nd ed. (London: Butterworth Heinemann, 2004), by Colin Thomson appearing at http://www.accountingweb.co.uk. Retrieved March 13, 2005.

37. Irving L. Janis, *Victims of Groupthink: A Psychological Study of Foreign Policy Decisions and Fiascos* (Boston: Houghton Mifflin, 1972), 39–40; Glenn Whyte, "Groupthink Reconsidered," *Academy of Management Review,* January 1989, pp. 40–56.

38. Kenneth A. Kovach and Barry Bender, "NASA Managers and Challenger: A Profile of Possible Explanations," *Personnel,* April 1987, p. 40.

39. Stephen R. Covey, *The Seven Habits of Highly Effective People* (New York: Simon & Schuster, 1989)

13

Diversity and Cross-Cultural Competence

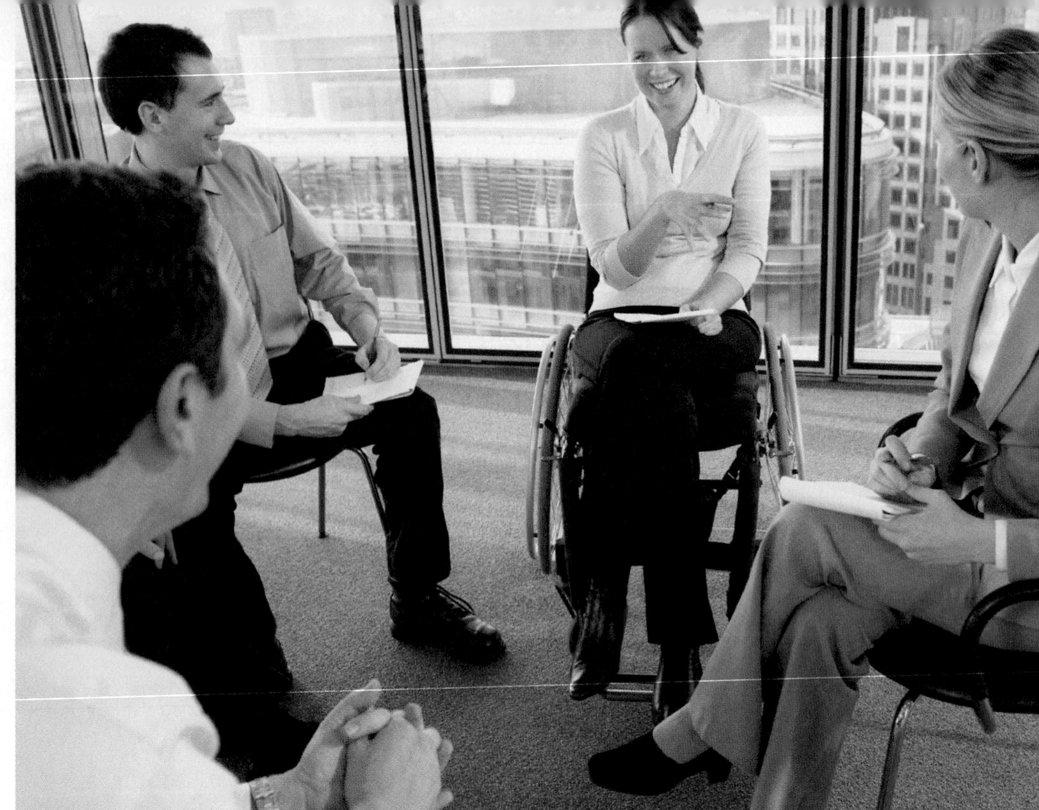

Outline

PepsiCo does far more than produce and sell Pepsi-Cola. The company offers nineteen different product lines that generate more than $1 billion annual retail sales. The company's main product lines are Quaker, Tropicana, Gatorade, and Pepsi-Cola, each of which makes other food or beverages. Besides offering well-known consumer products for a long time, PepsiCo has been a leader in diversity and inclusion long before equal opportunity in the workplace was widely practiced.

In 1947, PepsiCo hired an all-black marketing team to increase slowing sales in the African American community. Today, a portion of executive bonuses is linked to their recruitment and retention of diverse employees, plus how well they support diversity and inclusion among their staff. Other diversity-related bonus factors include how well PepsiCo products are selling to multicultural consumers, and how much of the bench (people with potential for moving up the ladder) is composed of women and people of color.

A core belief of upper management at PepsiCo is that making optimum use of diverse strengths and talents helps make the company successful. The company is careful to weave diversity and inclusion into the fabric of its culture.

Jennifer Owens, director of the Working Mother Research Institute, reports that PepsiCo has been honored five times on Working Mother's Best Companies for Multicultural Women in part for its programs that inspire women to advocate for themselves as professionals.

Pamela Culpepper, senior vice president, Global Diversity and Inclusion Officer at PepsiCo said that attracting, retaining, and promoting women and multicultural leaders around the world is a competitive advantage aligned with the company's purpose. "Across the organization we have embraced diversity and the idea that by harnessing the diverse strengths backgrounds, and perspectives, we win."[1]

Learning Objectives ▸

After studying the information and doing the exercises in this chapter, you should be able to:

1. Explain some of the major ways in which cultures differ from one another.
2. Pinpoint barriers to cross-cultural relations.
3. Describe techniques for improving cross-cultural relations.
4. Be sensitive to potential cultural bloopers.
5. Be prepared to overcome cross-cultural communication barriers.
6. Recognize and understand gender differences in leadership style.
7. Be aware of additional ways in which organizations use diversity to advantage
8. Be aware of some of the legal aspects of working in a culturally diverse environment.

The story about PepsiCo illustrates the point that welcoming diversity has become an established practice in large, successful organizations. As a result, being able to work well with people from diverse groups, including other cultures both outside and inside your own country is important for career success. To work well with diverse groups, it is helpful to make a distinction between two types of diversity. *Surface-level diversity* is about differences in visible characteristics such as gender, race, and ethnicity. *Deep-level diversity* is about differences in underlying psychological characteristics such as personality, attitudes, values, and sexual orientation.[2] For example, as a team member you might encounter surface-level diversity, but you will almost always encounter deep-level diversity.

Being able to relate to a culturally diverse customer base is also necessary for success. Not only is the workforce becoming more diverse, but also business has become increasingly international or globalized. Small-and medium-size firms, as well as corporate giants, are increasingly dependent on trade with other countries. Furthermore, with the large number of jobs sent overseas, more U.S. workers will have contact with personnel in foreign countries.

Customers often take a careful look at the diversity of their supplier. Melissa Donaldson, the senior manager of inclusion practices at the technology supplier, CDW, says that more customers ask for the company's approach to diversity and inclusion.[3] Retailers are also involved in globalization because so many store customers are immigrants. Many companies are using bilingual Web sites to convert online browsers into in-store customers. Similarly, other retailers are hiring store associates with foreign language skills and updating store signs and displays to appeal to immigrants.[4] The globalization of business therefore increases the relevance of cross-cultural skills.

This chapter presents ideas and techniques you can use to sharpen your ability to work effectively with people from diverse backgrounds. The buzzword for this activity is to be *inclusive* in your relationships with people. We also include a discussion of antidiscrimination legislation that protects the rights of workers, as well as specific company initiatives dealing with diversity.

Learning Objective 1

What Are the Major Dimensions of Differences in Cultural Values?

Everything we do in work and personal life is influenced by a combination of heredity and culture, or nature and nurture. You might be thirsty at this moment because a genetically produced mechanism in your brain tells you it is time to ingest fluid. But if you choose to drink a Diet Pepsi or papaya juice with a coworker, you are engaging in culturally learned behavior. **Culture** is a learned and shared system of knowledge, beliefs, values, attitudes, and norms. As such, culture includes an enormous amount of behavior. Here we describe eight dimensions (or facets) of cultural values that help us understand how cultures differ from each other.[5] In other words, various cultures value different types of behavior.

Culture
a learned and shared system of knowledge, beliefs, values, attitudes, and norms

Recognize that these dimensions are stereotypes, representing a typical value for a person in a given culture. You might find, for example, that most Chinese people are oriented more toward the group than seeking individual recognition, but you might meet some Chinese people who are egotistical and self-centered.

1. Individualism versus collectivism. At one end of the continuum is individualism, a mental set in which people see themselves first as individuals and believe that their own interests take priority. Members of a society who value individualism are more concerned with their careers than with the good of the firm. Members of a society who value collectivism, in contrast, are typically more concerned with the organization or the work group than with themselves. An example of individualistic behavior would be to want to win an "employee of the month" award; an example of collectivistic behavior would be to want to win an award for the team. Highly individualistic cultures include the United States, Canada, and the Netherlands. Japan and Mexico are among the countries that strongly value collectivism. But with the increasing emphasis on teamwork in American culture, more U.S. workers are becoming collectivistic.

2. Acceptance of power and authority. People from some cultures accept the idea that members of an organization have different levels of power and authority. In a culture that believes in concentration of power and authority, the boss makes many decisions simply because he or she is the boss. Group members readily comply because they have a positive orientation toward authority, including high respect for elders. In a culture with less acceptance of power and authority, employees do not recognize a power hierarchy. They accept directions only when they think the boss is right or when they feel threatened. Cultures that readily accept power and authority include France, China, Malaysia, and India. Countries that have much less acceptance of power and authority are the United States and, particularly, the Scandinavian countries (for example, Sweden).

3. Materialism versus concern for others. In this context, materialism refers to an emphasis on assertiveness and the acquisition of money and material objects. It also means de-emphasizing caring for others. At the other end of the continuum is concern for others, an emphasis on personal relations, and a concern for the welfare of others. Materialistic countries include Japan and Italy. The United States is considered to be moderately materialistic. For example, the high participation rates in charities suggest that Americans are somewhat interested in the welfare of others, and therefore not totally materialistic. Scandinavian countries all emphasize caring as a national value.

4. Formality versus informality. A country that values formality attaches considerable importance to tradition, ceremony, social rules, and rank. At the other extreme, informality refers to a casual attitude toward these same aspects of culture. Workers in Latin American countries highly value formality, such as lavish public receptions and processions. Americans, Canadians, and Scandinavians are much more informal. Casual observation suggests that most of the industrialized world is becoming more informal through such practices as an emphasis on using the first name only during business introductions and talking with customers over the phone.

5. Urgent time orientation versus casual time orientation. Individuals and nations attach different importance to time. People with an urgent time orientation perceive time as a scarce resource and tend to be impatient. People with a casual time orientation view time as an unlimited and unending resource and tend to be patient. Americans are noted for their urgent time orientation. They frequently impose deadlines and are eager to get started doing business. Asians and Middle Easterners, in contrast, are patient negotiators. Many corporate workers and entrepreneurs engaged in international business recognize the importance of building relationships slowly overseas.

6. Work orientation versus leisure orientation. A major cultural difference is the number of hours per week and weeks per year people expect to invest in work versus leisure or other nonwork activities. American corporate professionals typically work about fifty-five hours per week, take forty-five-minute lunch breaks, and take two weeks of vacation. Japanese workers share similar values with respect to time invested in work. In contrast, many European countries have a shorter workweek with longer vacations. As European governments have accumulated enormous debt, there has been a move by several governments to lengthen work weeks.

7. High-context versus low-context cultures. Cultures differ in how much importance they attach to the surrounding circumstances, or context, of an event. People from a high-context culture place more emphasis on *how* something is said rather than *what* is said. (They emphasize nonverbal communication.) For example, a person from a high-context culture is not likely to take you seriously if you smile when you say that you do not like his or her service.

High-context cultures make more extensive use of body language as part of their emphasis on nonverbal communication. Some cultures, such as the Hispanic and African American cultures, are high context. In contrast, Northern European cultures are low context and make less use of body language. The Anglo American culture is considered to be medium-low context. People in low-context cultures seldom take time in business dealings to build relationships and establish trust.

8. Social support seeking. This dimension refers to the degree to which people seek out others to help them with difficult problems through such means as listening, offering sympathy, and giving advice. Asians and Asian Americans are more reluctant to explicitly request support from close others than are European Americans. The hesitancy comes about because the Asians and Asian Americans are more concerned about negative relationship consequences, such as disrupting group harmony or receiving criticism from the other person. Another possible reason for the hesitancy is that Asians and Asian Americans expect social support without having to ask.[6]

The eight cultural values mentioned contribute to understanding how cultural differences contribute to diversity, but many other factors also lead to cultural differences.

Among these factors would be the region of the country in which a person was raised and whether the person lived in a large city, a small city, or a rural area. Socioeconomic class is a major contributor to cultural differences. For example, people from a higher socioeconomic class are likely to place more value on physical exercise and fitness, leading to better health.[7] One possible explanation is that people with higher disposable income can afford to invest in physical health.

An example of how cultural values can influence workplace behavior can be found in how McDonald's restaurants are operated around the world. In the United States, a manager is more likely to arrive at a solution to a workplace issue. In China, the manager might be quicker to seek approval from a supervisor based on the value of collectivism.[8]

MULTICULTURAL IDENTITIES AND THE CULTURAL MOSAIC

Multicultural identities individuals who incorporate the values of two or more cultures because they identify with both their primary culture and another culture or cultures

Another complexity about understanding cultural differences is that many people have **multicultural identities** because they identify with both their primary culture and another culture or cultures. As a consequence, these people may incorporate the values of two cultures. Being bilingual contributes to having two cultural identities because it is easier to identify with a foreign culture when one speaks the language of that culture.[9]

Young people develop a global identity that gives them a feeling of belonging to a worldwide culture. The feeling of belongingness enables them to communicate with people from diverse places when they travel, when others travel to where they live, and when they communicate globally using e-mail, social media, and the telephone. Television and movies also help us develop a global identity.

Further, according to this theory, people retain a local identity along with their global identity. Young people in India provide an apt example. The country has a rapidly growing high-tech sector led mostly by young people. Yet most of these well-educated young people still cling to local traditions, such as a marriage arranged by the parents and the expectation that they will care for their parents in old age.[10]

Another complexity of culture is that a person's country is but one cultural influence. For example, people from the upper socioeconomic group within one country or ethnic group might value education and the use of grammatically correct speech more than people from a lower socioeconomic group.

The Cultural Mosaic

Cultural mosaic an individual's unique mixture of multiple cultural identities that yields a complex picture of the cultural influences on that person

The fact of multicultural identities and different values among people from the same country and ethnic groups has been labeled the cultural mosaic by management professors Georgia T. Chao from Michigan State University and Henry Moon of Emory University. The **cultural mosaic** refers to an individual's unique mixture of multiple cultural identities that yields a complex picture of the cultural influences on that person. Rather than choosing a particular "tile" such as race, gender, or country of origin, people develop an identity based on a mix of smaller tiles.[11] Every reader of this book is probably an example of a cultural mosaic. One of thousands of possible examples is that one person could derive a cultural identity from being a (1) U.S. citizen, (2) African American, (3) Baptist, (4) male, (5) musician, (6) football player, (7) accountant, and (8) Southerner.

Religious Values

The religious value part of the cultural mosaic often affects when people are willing to work or not work. One potential cultural clash is that the rights of an individual to freely practice and observe religious beliefs sometimes collide with company goals. Differences in religious practices must be recognized because the number of religions in the workplace has increased substantially.

Religious diversity can create problems as more companies move to 24/7 (around-the-clock, seven-days-per-week) schedules. Employers therefore need more flexibility from employees, yet religious beliefs often limit times at which employees are willing to work. The message for improved understanding is that employers must recognize workers' religious beliefs. At the same time, workers must understand the importance of a company meeting the demands of the marketplace, such as having twenty-four-hour customer service support. Workers, for example, can trade off working on each others' religious holidays.

APPLYING KNOWLEDGE OF CULTURAL DIFFERENCES IN VALUES

How might you use this information about cultural differences to improve interpersonal relationships on the job? A starting point would be to recognize that a person's national values might influence his or her behavior. Assume that you wanted to establish a good working relationship with a person from a high-context culture. Make sure your facial expression fits the content of your words. For example, do not smile when, as a supervisor, you say, "No, you cannot take off tomorrow afternoon to have your French poodle groomed." You would also want to emphasize body language when communicating with that individual. A related point is that people from high-context cultures are more likely to touch and kiss strangers. As Fernando, who was raised in the Dominican Republic and is studying in the United States, said, "In my country, I hug people I meet for the first time. When I do it here, they think I'm very rude."

The accompanying Human Relations in Practice describes how one of the world's best-known companies improved its business results by understanding cultural differences.

What Are Some Approaches to Improving Cross-Cultural Relations?

◀ Learning Objective 2 ◀

By now you are probably aware of how to improve cross-cultural relations by avoiding some of the mistakes already mentioned or implied, such as relying too heavily on group stereotypes. In this section, we take a systematic look at approaches you can use on your own along with training programs designed to improve cross-cultural relations.[12] The methods and techniques for such improvement are outlined in Figure 13-1. Self-Assessment Quiz 13-1 provides an opportunity to think about your cross-cultural skills and attitudes that could influence your ability to develop good cross-cultural relations.

Methods and techniques

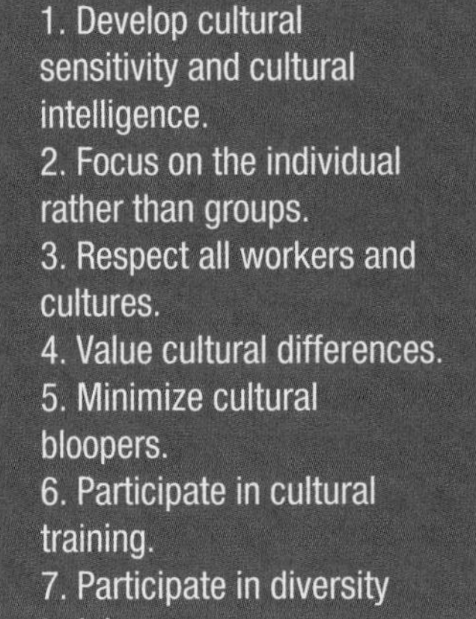

1. Develop cultural sensitivity and cultural intelligence.
2. Focus on the individual rather than groups.
3. Respect all workers and cultures.
4. Value cultural differences.
5. Minimize cultural bloopers.
6. Participate in cultural training.
7. Participate in diversity training.

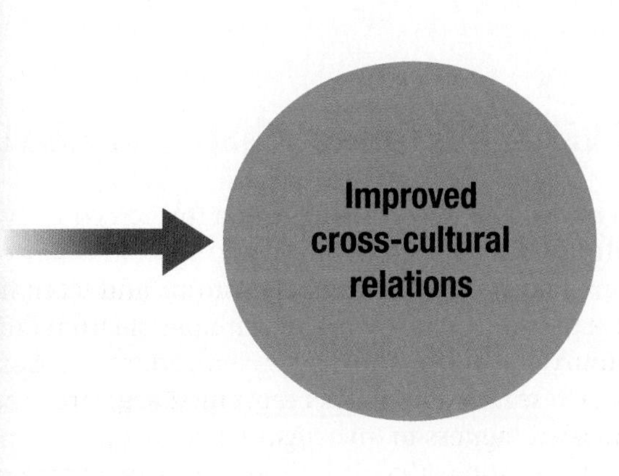

FIGURE 13-1
IMPROVING CROSS-CULTURAL RELATIONS

Human Relations in Action

McDonald's Adapts to Cultural Differences in France

In 1999, McDonald's was under severe attack in France. A political group bulldozed a McDonald's restaurant in Millau, France, to protest against U.S. trade restrictions on French dairy products. With bullhorn in hand, José Bové an agricultural unionist, declared to the television news reporters, "We attacked this McDonald's because it is a symbol of multinationals that want to stuff us with junk food and ruin our farmers." Five years later McDonald's was declared in the French media to be the epitome of *malbouffe*, or "junk food" and deemed partly to blame for the nation's rising obesity rate.

Today, France is McDonald's second most profitable market in the world among restaurants in 123 countries. The chain has 1,200 restaurants in France—all locally owned franchises. Much of this surprising growth can be attributed to McDonald's adapting to the French culture and customs.

In 1995, McDonald's started using French cheeses as well as French mustard sauce. McDonald's also demonstrated the power of understanding the cultural peculiarities of consumers across national boundaries. In France, barely 10 percent of meals are eaten outside the home, compared to nearly 40 percent in the U.S. and U.K. Another difference is that French consumers rarely snack between breakfast, lunch, and dinner.

McDonald's has capitalized on the French cultural preference for longer meals by using surplus labor to provide table-side service, particularly in taking orders from lingering diners inclined to order an additional coffee or dessert item. Thanks to such initiatives, the average French consumer spends about US $15 per visit to McDonald's—four times what the American counterparts spends. To further cater to French tastes, the restaurant chain offers the baguette bread roll.

McDonald's franchisees have invested heavily in their ambiance, including a welcoming interior to create an environment where customers linger. The décor includes sleek modern tables with plush comfortable chairs, fireplaces, flat-screen TVs, and high-impact wall graphics. Outside, instead of high golden arches, the store's visual profile is subdued.

Question:. What evidence have you seen that McDonald's adapts to cultural differences and preferences *within* the United States (or Canada)?

Source: Adapted from "Born in the USA, Made in France: How McDonald's Succeeds in the Land of Michelin Stars," *Knowledge@Wharton*, (www.knowledge.wharton.upenn.edu), January 3, 2012, pp. 1–3.

DEVELOP CULTURAL SENSITIVITY AND CULTURAL INTELLIGENCE

To relate well to someone from a foreign country, a person must be alert to possible cultural differences. When working in another country, one must be willing to acquire knowledge about local customs and learn how to speak the native language, at least passably. When working with people from different cultures, even from one's own country, the person must be patient, adaptable, flexible, and willing to listen and learn.

Cultural sensitivity
an awareness of and a willingness to investigate the reasons why people of another culture act as they do

These characteristics mentioned are part of **cultural sensitivity**, an awareness of and a willingness to investigate the reasons why people of another culture act as they do.[13] A person with cultural sensitivity will recognize certain nuances in customs that will help build better relationships with people from cultural backgrounds other than

Human Relations Self-Assessment Quiz 13-1

Cross-Cultural Skills and Attitudes

Following are skills and attitudes that various employers and cross-cultural experts think are important for relating effectively to coworkers in a culturally diverse environment.

	Applies to Me Now	Not There Yet
1. I have spent some time in another country.	______	______
2. At least one of my friends is deaf or blind or uses a wheelchair.	______	______
3. Currency from other countries is as real as the currency from my own country.	______	______
4. I can read in a language other than my own.	______	______
5. I can speak in a language other than my own.	______	______
6. I can write in a language other than my own.	______	______
7. I can understand people speaking in a language other than my own.	______	______
8. I use my second language regularly.	______	______
9. My friends include people of races different from my own.	______	______
10. My friends include people of different ages.	______	______
11. I feel (or would feel) comfortable having a friend with a sexual orientation different from mine.	______	______
12. My attitude is that although another culture may be very different from mine, that culture is equally good.	______	______
13. I would be willing to (or already do) hang art from different countries in my home.	______	______
14. I would accept (or have already accepted) a work assignment of more than several months in another country.	______	______
15. I have a passport.	______	______

Interpretation

If you checked "Applies to Me Now" for ten or more of the preceding items, you most likely function well in a multicultural work environment. If you answered "Not There Yet" to ten or more of the preceding items, you need to develop more cross-cultural awareness and skills to work effectively in a multicultural work environment. You will notice that being bilingual gives you at least five points on this quiz.

Source: Several ideas for statements on this quiz are derived from Ruthann Dirks and Janet Buzzard, "What CEOs Expect of Employees Hired for International Work," *Business Education Forum,* April 1997, pp. 3–7; Gunnar Beeth, "Multicultural Managers Wanted," *Management Review,* May 1997, pp. 17–21.

his or her own. A culturally sensitive person will also recognize that humor does not easily translate from one culture to another and that some types of humor might be offensive in another culture. Assume, for example, you are having lunch with a group of Japanese workers on a trip to Japan. You begin your joke with, "This old guy walks into a bar . . . ." The Japanese workers might take offense because older people are highly respected in Japan.

Cultural sensitivity is sometimes referred to as *multicultural savvy* because you are smart enough to work well in different cultures. An example would be sizing up quickly whether the people you are visiting in a work context are task focused or relationship focused.[14] To draw another cultural stereotype, suppose Jan, a Northerner is visiting a plant in the Deep South of the United States on a mission to help them install a new cloud-computing system. Using her multicultural savvy, Jan observes that the IT (information technology) staff at the plant want to get to know her a little before jumping into the complexities of cloud computing (the group has a relationship focus for the moment). So at lunch Jan does not talk about cloud computing until she senses that the group is ready to focus on the task.

One approach to enhancing cultural sensitivity is to keep in mind the types of cultural differences mentioned throughout this chapter, even down to such details as holding a fork in your left hand when dining in England and India. Another approach is to raise your antenna and observe carefully what others are doing. Suppose you are on a business trip to a different region of your country and are invited to have dinner at the plant general manager's house. You notice that she takes off her street shoes on entering the house. You do likewise to establish better rapport, even if your host says, "Oh, please don't bother." It is obvious from your host's behavior that she observes a "shoe code" in her house.

An advanced aspect of cultural sensitivity is to be able to fit in comfortably with people of another culture by observing the subtle cues they give about how a person should act in their presence. **Cultural intelligence**, or **CQ**, is an outsider's ability to interpret someone's unfamiliar and ambiguous behavior the same way that person's compatriots would.[15] (CQ refers to a cultural quotient.) With high cultural intelligence a person would be able to figure out what behavior would be true of all people and all groups, such as rapid shaking of a clenched fist to communicate anger. Also, the person with a high CQ could figure out what is peculiar to this group and those aspects of behavior that are neither universal nor peculiar to the group. These ideas are abstract, so an example will help clarify.

Cultural intelligence (CQ) an outsider's ability to interpret someone's unfamiliar and ambiguous behavior the same way that person's compatriots would

An American expatriate manager served on a design team that included two German engineers. As other team members floated their ideas, the engineers condemned them as incomplete or underdeveloped. The manager concluded that the Germans in general are rude and aggressive.

With average cultural intelligence, the American would have realized he was mistakenly equating the merit of an idea with the merit of the person presenting it. The Germans, however, were able to make a sharp distinction between the two. A manager with more advanced cultural intelligence might have tried to figure out how much of the two German's behavior was typically German and how much was explained by the fact that they were engineers.

Similar to emotional intelligence, cultural intelligence encompasses several different aspects of behavior. The three sources of cultural intelligence relate to the cognitive, emotional/motivational, and the physical, explained as follows:[16]

1. **Cognitive (the head).** The cognitive part of CQ refers to what a person knows and how he or she can acquire new knowledge. Here you acquire facts about people from another culture, such as their passion for football (soccer in North America), their business practices, and their promptness in paying bills. Another aspect of this source of cultural intelligence is figuring out how you can learn more about the other culture.
2. **Emotional/motivational (the heart).** The emotional/motivational aspect of CQ refers to energizing one's actions and building personal confidence. You need both confidence and motivation to adapt to another culture. A man on a business trip to the Ivory Coast in Africa might say to himself, "When I greet a work associate in a restaurant, can I really pull off kissing him on both cheeks. What if he thinks I'm weird?" With strong motivation, the same person might say, "I'll give it a try. I kind of greet my grandfather the same way back in the United States."
3. **The body (physical).** The body aspect of CQ is the action component. The body is the element for translating intentions into actions and desires. Kissing the same-sex African work associate on both cheeks is the *physical* aspect previously mentioned. We often have an idea of what we should do, but implementation is not so easy. You might know, for example, that when entering an Asian person's home you should take off your shoes, yet you might not actually remove them—thereby offending your Asian work (or personal life) associate.

To practice high cultural intelligence, the mind, heart, and body have to work together. You have to figure out how you have to act with people from another culture, you need motivation and confidence to change, and you have to translate your knowledge and motivation into action. So when you are on a business trip to South Korea, go ahead and bow when you are introduced to the plant manager.

An advanced example of cultural sensitivity and perhaps cultural intelligence would be understanding what behavior qualifies something as being racist. Cultural anthropologists Thomas Kochman and Jean Mavrelis explain that for the majority of Americans, motive and intent have to be present. For African Americans, inconsistent treatment along racial lines characterizes an action as being racist. An example follows:

In one workplace, black workers asked their white male supervisor, "Why did the white workers get all the good vacation times?" The supervisor said that vacation times were given on a "first come, first served basis." Blacks then asked, "Why did the white workers know to come in first?" It turned out that the posting of vacation times was done on the first shift, which had most white workers.[17]

A study conducted with 305 real estate agents at 26 real estate firms in the United States indicated that cultural intelligence really does translate into business results. Agents with higher cultural intelligence, as measured by a questionnaire, tended to have more sales with customers from cultures different than their own. The effects of good cultural intelligence were even stronger (more sales) when the firm was perceived to be culturally intelligent and had a positive climate with respect to diversity.[18]

FOCUS ON INDIVIDUALS RATHER THAN GROUPS

Understanding broad cultural differences is a good starting point in building relationships with people from other cultures. Nevertheless, it is even more important to get to know the individual rather than relying exclusively on an understanding of his or her cultural group. Instead of generalizing about the other person's characteristics and values (such as assuming that your Mexican American coworker chooses to be late for meetings), get to know his or her personal style. You might find that this particular Mexican American values promptness and becomes anxious when others are late for a meeting. A consultant in the area of cross-cultural relations suggests that the best way to know individuals is to build personal relationships with people and not to generalize.[19]

Focusing on individuals rather than groups is sometimes difficult because people tend to hold on strongly to cultural stereotypes. Evidence that these stereotypes are strong comes from an experiment with college students who were purposely presented with stereotype-busting strangers. One of these stereotype busters was a young Asian American woman with a thick Southern drawl. (She was really a hired actress trained by a voice coach to learn an accent specific to Charleston, South Carolina.) Students worked in pairs with either a stereotype buster or a person whose behavior was consistent with the stereotype. Students paired with a stereotype buster performed less well on a word-finding game, showed more physical signs of stress, and smiled less frequently. Watching a participant's initial meeting with one of the surprising partners was revealing according to the experimenter, Wendy Berry Mendes of Harvard University: "She'd begin the introduction with, 'Hi, I'm Jenny and I'm from Charleston, South Carolina,' and our participants just froze and stared at this truly surprising person. Their body posture stayed closed and more defensive during the interaction."[20]

One lesson for cross-cultural relations to be learned from this experiment is to focus on the individual's characteristics and try not to be upset because the person's behavior is not consistent with your stereotype of how he or she is supposed to behave. For example, many Americans find it strange when they meet a black businessperson with an English or French accent. As one American tourist said when visiting Paris, "I didn't know black people spoke French." (The same tourist never took her study of geography seriously.)

RESPECT ALL WORKERS AND CULTURES

An effective strategy for achieving cross-cultural understanding is to simply respect all others in the workplace, including their cultures. An important component of respect is to believe that although another person's culture is different from yours, it is equally good. Respect comes from valuing differences, such as one person speaking Standard English and the other favoring American Sign Language. Respecting other people's customs can translate into specific attitudes, such as respecting one coworker for wearing a yarmulke on Friday or another for wearing an African outfit to celebrate Kwanzaa. Another way of being respectful would be to listen carefully to the opinion of a senior worker who says the company should never have converted to voice mail in place of assistants answering the phone (even though you disagree). An aspect of respecting all workers is the importance of respecting the rights of majorities, including white males.

Another way of showing respect for all workers and cultures is to develop supportive peer relations in the workplace with people from different cultural groups. A supportive relationship includes a feeling of closeness and trust, the sharing of thoughts and feelings, and the feeling that one is able to seek assistance from another. Such respect in the form of support doubles in importance because the creativity advantage of a diverse group is more likely to surface when there is a supportive relationship among coworkers who differ demographically.

Sexual equity
parity among heterosexual, gay, lesbian, bisexual, and transgender employees

Another way of respecting all workers and cultures is to practice **sexual equity**—parity among heterosexual, gay, lesbian, bisexual, and transgender employees. The last four groups have come to be referred to collectively as GLBT. Sexual equity most frequently takes the form of an employer offering health-care coverage for same-sex domestic partners.[21] Less typical is the initiative of IBM, which has developed an accreditation program for GLBT suppliers to help GLBT-friendly companies identify accommodating companies as business partners.

True respect of any group goes beyond company policies and extends to informal social behavior. A group of workers who invited a transgender coworker (one who had switched sexes) would be showing total respect by inviting him or her to join them for an after-work drink. (For some people, however, religious beliefs would make showing such respect difficult.)

VALUE CULTURAL DIFFERENCES

Multicultural worker
one who can work effectively with people of different cultures

Recognizing cultural differences is an excellent starting point in becoming a **multicultural worker**—one who can work effectively with people of different cultures. More important, however, is to *value* cultural differences. The distinction goes well beyond semantics. If you place a high value on cultural differences, you will perceive people from other cultures to be different but equally good. Gunnar Beeth, an executive placement specialist in Europe, noted many years ago that you cannot motivate anyone, especially someone of another culture, until that person first accepts you. A multilingual sales representative has the ability to explain the advantages of a product in other languages. In contrast, a multicultural sales rep can motivate foreigners to make the purchase. The difference is substantial.[22]

A challenge in showing respect for other cultures is not to act revolted or shocked when a member of another culture eats something that lies outside your area of what is acceptable as food. Some Westerners are shocked and repelled to find that some Easterners eat insects, cats, dogs, sheep's eyeballs, chicken soup containing the feet, and rattlesnakes. Some Easterners are shocked and repelled to find that Westerners eat a sacred animal such as cow and are surprised about popcorn.[23]

Other cross-cultural differences in customs also represent a challenge when trying to respect another culture. An American might find it difficult to respect the Pakistani practice of having young children work in factories. In contrast, the Pakistani might find it difficult to respect the American practice of putting old relatives in nursing homes and hospices. Sometimes it takes careful reflection on one's own culture to be able to respect another culture.

A well-documented advantage stemming from valuing cultural differences is creative problem solving. The diversity of viewpoints within the group can enhance group creativity. Another perspective on the contribution of cultural differences to creativity is that multicultural experience helps us become more creative.[24] In practice, this finding could mean that working with different cultural groups within the same company, or outside the company, would facilitate workers becoming more creative problem solvers. Broadening your perspective helps develop your flexible thinking. A more specific advantage is that exposure to different cultures might trigger a profitable idea that you could transport to your own culture. For example, cottages of about 500 square feet found in many cultures outside the United States now have a small but growing market in the United States.

Recognize Own Cultural Biases

A potential barrier to working smoothly with people from cultures other than our own is an almost unconscious tendency to react positively or negatively toward those people for a particular culture or demographic group. Let us begin with a seemingly harmless example. Your positive bias toward Indians is that they are careful and methodical in executing work tasks. Consequently, when you are in a busy department store, without thinking why you go to the checkout line with an Indian cashier. A negative bias would be a person rejecting a job offer because his or her supervisor would be a person of about age 70. The bias might be that the applicant perceives an older person as intellectually slow, living in the past, and technology-challenged.

Daryl Dixon chief diversity and equity officer for Multnomah County in Oregon points out that having bias is human nature. A challenge is therefore learning how to manage those biases appropriately, such as asking yourself whether you prejudge anybody lately based on his or her culture.

Human Relations Self-Assessment Quiz 13-2 offers you an opportunity to think candidly about cultural biases you might have.

Human Relations Self-Assessment Quiz 13-2

The Personal Biases and Prejudices Checklist

Check whether each of the attitudes, beliefs, and actions in the list below are generally true or generally false. Responding to this checklist is difficult because you are required to be objective and honest about your biases and prejudices.

Number	Statement about Biases and Prejudices in Relation to People	Generally True	Generally False
1.	I can imagine a woman being an effective president of the United States.	_______	_______
2.	I would feel comfortable if my boss were a midget.	_______	_______
3.	I would be fearful of any woman wearing a covering over her face in an airport.	_______	_______
4.	It makes sense to charge higher interest rates for loans and mortgages to minority group members even if their credit rating is above average.	_______	_______

(Continued)

Number	Statement about Biases and Prejudices in Relation to People	Generally True	Generally False
5.	If I or a loved one needed brain surgery, I would want the surgery performed only by a male, Caucasian brain surgeon.	______	______
6.	During a major athletic contest, such as a basketball or soccer game, I would want a black person to take the game-deciding shot.	______	______
7.	I would prefer not to be a passenger on an airplane if the pilot were older than age 50.	______	______
8.	My like or dislike for President Barack Obama had (or has) nothing to do with his being African American (or mixed race).	______	______
9.	When I am uncertain about a person's race or ethnic background, I often ask "What are you?"	______	______
10.	If I needed a financial planner, I would never hire one who was under age 35.	______	______

Scoring and Interpretation

Give yourself one point for the following answers: Generally True to questions 3, 4, 5, 6, 7, 9, and 10; generally false to questions 1, 2, and 8. If you scored 5 or more points, you most likely have biases and prejudices that hold you back a little from having strong cross-cultural relations. If you scored between 0 and 4, you are likely to be perceived as an unbiased person, and one whose biases and prejudices create very few problems in interpersonal relationships. Being perceived as unbiased and unprejudiced could facilitate you getting along well with coworkers, and being selected for a leadership position. A caution is that it is quite difficult to be honest with oneself about one's level of bias and prejudice, so perhaps take this quiz again in one week.

MINIMIZE CULTURAL BLOOPERS

An effective way of being culturally sensitive is to minimize actions that are likely to offend people from another culture based on their values and customs. Cultural bloopers are most likely to take place when you are visiting another country. The same bloopers, however, can also be committed with people from a different culture within your own country. To avoid these bloopers, you must carefully observe persons from other cultures. Studying another culture through reading is also helpful. Even small behaviors, such as asking for ketchup to accompany an omelet while in France, can strain a business relationship.

E-commerce and other forms of Internet communication have created new opportunities for creating cultural bloopers. Web site developers and the workers responsible for adding content must have good cross-cultural literacy, including an awareness of how the information might be misinterpreted. Here is a sampling of potential problems:

- Numerical date formats can be readily misinterpreted. To an American, 4/9/15 would be interpreted as April 9, 2015 (or 1915!). But many Europeans would interpret the same numerical expression as September 4, 2015.
- Colors on Web sites must be chosen carefully. For example, in some cultures purple is the color of royalty, whereas in Brazil purple is associated with death.
- Be careful of metaphors that may not make sense to a person for whom your language is a second language. Examples include "We've encountered an ethical meltdown" and "Our biggest competitor is over the hill."

Communicating your message directly in your customer's mother tongue provides a competitive advantage. Consumers are more likely to purchase from a Web site written in their native language. The translator, of course, must have good knowledge of the subtleties of the language to avoid a blooper. An English-to-French translator used the verb *baiser* instead of *baisser* to describe a program of lowering prices. *Baisser* is the French verb "to lower," whereas *baiser* is the verb "to kiss." Worse, in everyday language, *baiser* is a verb that refers to having an intimate physical relationship! Much of translation is done with software these days, but the translator program can make many embarrassing errors, such as recognizing "fall" as meaning a tumble instead of a season.

Keep two key facts in mind when attempting to avoid cultural mistakes. One is that members of any cultural group show individual differences. What one member of the group might regard as an insensitive act another might welcome. Recognize also that one or two cultural mistakes will not peg you permanently as a boor. Figure 13-2 will help you minimize certain cultural bloopers.

FIGURE 13-2 CULTURAL MISTAKES TO AVOID WITH SELECTED CULTURAL GROUPS

Western Europe	
Great Britain	• Asking personal questions. The British protect their privacy. • Thinking that a businessperson from England is unenthusiastic when he or she says, "Not bad at all." English people understate positive emotion. • Gossiping about royalty.
France	• Expecting to complete work during the French two-hour lunch. • Attempting to conduct significant business during August—*les vacances* (vacation time). • Greeting a French person for the first time and not using a title such as *sir* or *madam* (or *monsieur, madame*, or *mademoiselle)*
Italy	• Eating too much pasta, as it is not the main course. • Handing out business cards freely. Italians use them infrequently.
Spain	• Expecting punctuality. Your appointments will usually arrive twenty to thirty minutes late. • Make the American sign for "okay" with your thumb and forefinger. In Spain (and many other countries) this is vulgar.
Scandinavia (Denmark, Sweden, Norway)	• Being overly conscious of rank in these countries. Scandinavians pay relatively little attention to a person's place in the hierarchy. • Introducing conflict among Swedish work associates. Swedes go out of their way to avoid conflict.
Greece	• Saying good-bye by using the American handshake. Greeks regard this practice to be an insult.
Asia	
All Asian countries	• Pressuring an Asian job applicant or employee to brag about his or her accomplishments. Asians feel self-conscious when boasting about individual accomplishments and prefer to let the record speak for itself. In addition, they prefer to talk about group rather than individual accomplishments. • Giving gifts with four items such as four dollars or four boxes of candy because the number four connotes death in many Asian countries.
Japan	• Shaking hands or hugging Japanese (as well as other Asians) in public. Japanese consider the practices to be offensive. • Looking directly in the eye of a business acquaintance for more than a few seconds. • Not interpreting "We'll consider it" as "no" when spoken by a Japanese businessperson. Japanese negotiators mean "no" when they say, "We'll consider it."

(*Continued*)

FIGURE 13-2 (*Continued*)

	• Not giving small gifts to Japanese when conducting business. Japanese are offended by not receiving these gifts.
	• Giving your business card to a Japanese businessperson more than once. Japanese prefer to give and receive business cards only once.
China	• Not taking a business card presented to you seriously, such as quickly stuffing it in your pocket.
	• Using a strong handshake instead of a limp one. Insisting on a handshake rather than a polite bow.
	• Giving expensive gifts, because this may obligate the person to reciprocate with something of equal value to you. Giving a clock can backfire because the Mandarin word for "to give clocks" resembles "to attend to a dying relative."
	• Making cold calls on Chinese business executives. An appropriate introduction is required for a first-time meeting with a Chinese official.
Korea	• Saying no. Koreans feel it is important to have visitors leave with good feelings.
India	• Telling Indians you prefer not to eat with your hands. If the Indians are not using cutlery when eating, they expect you to do likewise.
Thailand	• Pointing the soles of your shoes toward another person. Be aware of this potential mistake when sitting.
Mexico and Latin America	
Mexico	• Flying into a Mexican city in the morning and expecting to close a deal by lunch. Mexicans build business relationships slowly.
Most Latin American countries	• Attempting to impress Brazilians by speaking a few words of Spanish. Portuguese is the official language of Brazil.
	• Wearing elegant and expensive jewelry during a business meeting. Most Latin Americans think people should appear more conservative during a business meeting.

Note: A cultural mistake for Americans to avoid when conducting business in most countries outside the United States and Canada is to insist on getting down to business quickly. Other stereotyped American traits to avoid are aggressiveness, impatience, and frequent interruptions to get your point across. North Americans in small towns also like to build a relationship before getting down to business. Another general mistake for Americans is to use a familiar, laid-back style in locales where "business casual" is unacceptable and first names are reserved for family and friends.

Source: Two of the items about China are from Eric Spitsnagel, "Impress Your Chinese Boss," *Bloomberg Businessweek*, January 15, 2012, pp. 80–81.

Avoiding cultural bloopers might also be framed as being *politically correct.* The point of political correctness is to avoid offending anybody. As an American when visiting India, you would therefore not say to your hosts that "Eating with your hands is disgusting." Nor would you say to an Inuit (aka Eskimo), "Killing seals is barbaric."

PARTICIPATE IN CULTURAL TRAINING

Cultural training
set of learning experiences designed to help employees understand the customs, traditions, and beliefs of another culture

For many years companies and government agencies have prepared their workers for overseas assignments. The method most frequently chosen is **cultural training**, a set of learning experiences designed to help employees understand the customs, traditions, and beliefs of another culture. In today's diverse business environment and international marketplace, learning about individuals raised in different cultural backgrounds has become more important. Many industries therefore train employees in cross-cultural relations. Cultural training is considered essential for international workers involved with people from other cultures because negotiating styles differ across cultures. For example, the Japanese prefer an exchange of information to confrontation. Russians, in contrast, enjoy combat in negotiations.[25] (Again, we are dealing with cultural stereotypes.)

Much of the information presented in this chapter, such as understanding cultural values and bloopers, is often incorporated into cultural training. Here we look at two perspectives on cultural training: training for domestic employees, and foreign language training.

Cultural Training for Domestic Employees

Many employees who never leave the country work with people from around the globe, so cultural training has been extended also to domestic employees. "Whether a multinational or a start-up business out of a garage, everybody is global these days," says Dean Foster the head of an international consultancy in New York. A specific example is that managers at a mining and exploration company in Britain sought cross-cultural training because the company was unsuccessful in winning business from an American company. During the training, the company learned that the proposal turned off Americans because it started with ten pages listing all the risks inherent in the venture and how much money would be lost if it failed.

The cultural training consultant pointed out that Americans often perceive failure to be a learning experience, so the American company considered the proposal to be negative. The British, however, were following their cultural value of being risk averse. When the British company rewrote the proposal with a positive spin, they received a signed contract the next day. "Differences got overlooked because we both speak English," said the consultant.[26]

Foreign Language Training

Learning a foreign language is often part of cultural training or can also be a separate activity. Knowledge of a second language is important because it builds better connections with people from other cultures than does relying on a translator. Many workers aside from international business specialists also choose to develop skills in a target language. Speaking another language can help build rapport with customers and employees who speak that language. Almost all language training has elements similar to taking a course in another language or self-study. Companies invest heavily in helping employees learn a target language because it facilitates conducting business in other countries. Medical specialists, police workers, and firefighters also find second-language skills to be quite helpful. Clients under stress, such as an injured person, are likely to revert to their native tongue.

Many multinational companies have downplayed the importance of American workers being fluent in a second language because English has become the standard language of commerce. Despite the merits of this observation, speaking and writing well in the language of your target can help establish rapport. Furthermore, from the standpoint of career management it is worth noting that more and more highly placed managers in large companies are bilingual. Another value of foreign-language training is to better communicate with subordinates, coworkers, and customers. For example, it is estimated that in the United States, nearly two-thirds of construction workers do not speak English as their primary language. Construction supervisors who speak Spanish can prevent many accidents.[27]

As with any other skill training, these investments can only pay off if the trainee is willing to work hard developing the new skill outside the training session. It is unlikely that almost anyone can develop conversational skills in another language by listening to foreign language CDs or taking classes for thirty days. A couple of the better-known foreign language programs brag that you do not have to engage in "useless memorization" or "conjugate verbs" with their program. Yet it is impossible to know even your native language without remembering words or knowing which tense to use in speaking or writing. The quick training program, however, helps you develop a base for further learning. Allowing even ten days to pass without practicing your target language will result in a sharp decline in your ability to use that language.

PARTICIPATE IN DIVERSITY TRAINING

Diversity training
program that attempts to bring about workplace harmony by teaching people how to get along with diverse work associates; often aimed at minimizing open expressions of racism and sexism

The general purpose of cultural training is to help workers understand people from other cultures. Understanding can lead to dealing more effectively with them as work associates or customers. **Diversity training** has a slightly different purpose. It attempts to bring about workplace harmony by teaching people how to get along with diverse work associates. Quite often the program is aimed at minimizing open expressions of racism and sexism. Diversity training takes a number of forms. Nevertheless, all training programs center on increasing awareness of and empathy for people who are different in some noticeable way from oneself. Many diversity programs also emphasize awareness and empathy for people who are not visibly different from oneself, such as having a different sexual orientation, different religious beliefs, or being autistic.

Recognizing Differences

A starting point in diversity training is to emphasize that everybody is different in some way and that all these differences should be appreciated. The subtle point here is that cultural diversity does not refer exclusively to differences in race, ethnicity, age, and sex. As the United States Office of Civil Rights explains, "Diversity is a term used broadly to refer to many demographic variables, including but not limited to race, religion, color, gender, national origin, disability, sexual orientation, age, education, geographic origin, and skill characteristics."[28]

Diversity training emphasizes *inclusion*, or including everybody when appreciating diversity. Figure 13-3 presents a broad sampling of the ways in which workplace associates can differ from one another. All these differences are tucked under the welcoming *diversity umbrella.* Studying this list can help you anticipate the type of differences to understand and appreciate in a diverse workplace. The differences include cultural as well as individual factors. Individual factors are also important because people can be discriminated against for personal characteristics as well as group characteristics. Many people who are disfigured, for example, believe they are held back from obtaining a higher-level job because of their disfigurement, such as a facial birthmark.

Another important part of diversity training is to develop empathy for diverse viewpoints. To help training participants develop empathy, representatives of various groups explain their feelings related to workplace issues. In one segment of such a program, a minority group member was seated in the middle of a circle. The other participants sat at the periphery of the circle. First, the coworkers listened to a Vietnamese woman explain how she felt excluded from the in-group composed of whites and African Americans in her department. "I feel like you simply tolerate me. You do not make me feel that I am somebody important. You make me feel that because I am Vietnamese I don't count." The next person to sit in the middle of the circle was Muslim. He complained about people wishing him Merry Christmas. "I would much prefer that my coworkers would stop to think that I do not celebrate Christian holidays. I respect your religion, but it is not my religion."

Another approach used in diversity training to recognize differences is for workers to simulate having a specific disability. Two such approaches are to walk around the office or training room blindfolded and using a cane to simulate blindness, or to navigate around the property using a wheelchair.[29] By simulating a specific disability, the worker might develop a better appreciation of the hurdles the disabled worker faces.

FIGURE 13-3 THE DIVERSITY UMBRELLA

- Race
- Sex or gender
- Religion
- Age (young, middle aged, and old)
- Generation differences, including attitudes (e.g., baby boomers versus the generation Y)
- Ethnicity (country of origin)
- Education
- Abilities
- Mental disabilities (including attention deficit disorder)
- Physical status (including hearing status, visual status, being able-bodied, wheelchair user)
- Values and motivation
- Sexual orientation (heterosexual, homosexual, bisexual, transsexual)
- Marital status (married, single, cohabitating, widow, widower)
- Family status (children, no children, two-parent family, single parent, grandparent, opposite-sex parents, same-sex parents)
- Personality traits
- Functional background (area of specialization, such as marketing, manufacturing)
- Technology interest (high tech, low tech, technophobe)
- Weight status (average, obese, underweight, anorexic)
- Hair status (full head of hair, bald, wild hair, tame hair, long hair, short hair)
- Style of clothing and appearance (dress up, dress down, professional appearance, casual appearance, tattoos, body piercing including multiple earrings, nose rings, lip rings)
- Tobacco status (smoker versus nonsmoker, chewer versus non-chewer)
- Your creative suggestion

Diversity training sometimes includes providing guidelines for dealing with different groups and individuals to help create a positive work environment. A segment of a diversity program geared toward creating a positive environment for people with physical disabilities is likely to suggest things you should not say to or behave toward these individuals:

- "What's wrong? What happened?" or "Were you born that way?"
- Speaking slowly or loudly to a wheelchair user.
- "I don't even think of you as a person with a disability."
- "But you look so good."[30]

Concerns about Diversity Training

A criticism of many diversity training programs is that too many angry feelings are expressed and that negative stereotypes are reinforced, leading to strained relationships. Another criticism is that the program might be considered patronizing because the majority of participants are already respectful of people different from themselves and know how to work harmoniously with a wide variety of people.

Even when diversity training attains its goal of enhanced cross-cultural understanding, the training may not lead to enhanced promotional opportunities for women and minorities. An analysis of decades of federal employment statistics provided by business firms found no real change in the number of women and minority managers after diversity training began. In contrast, mentoring programs did facilitate the promotion of women and minorities.[31]

▶ Learning Objective 3 ▶

How Do You Overcome Cross-Cultural Communication Barriers?

A key part of developing good cross-cultural relations is to overcome or prevent communication barriers stemming from cultural differences. Personal life, too, is often culturally diverse leading to culturally based communication problems. The information about avoiding cultural bloopers presented in this chapter might also be interpreted as a way to prevent communication barriers. Here we describe ten additional strategies and tactics to help overcome cross-cultural communication barriers.

1. Be alert to cultural differences in customs and behavior. To minimize cross-cultural communication barriers, recognize that many subtle job-related differences in customs and behavior may exist. For example, people from many Asian cultures typically feel uncomfortable when asked to brag about themselves in the presence of others. From their perspective, calling attention to oneself at the expense of another person is rude and unprofessional.

2. Use straightforward language and speak slowly and clearly. When working with people who do not speak your language fluently, speak in an easy-to-understand manner. Be patient for many reasons, including the fact that your accent in your native tongue may not be the same as the person from whom your target learned your language. (For example, English as learned in India is quite different from English as learned in Ohio.) Minimize the use of idioms and analogies specific to your language. For example, in North America the term *over the hill* means outdated or past one's prime. A person from another culture may not understand this phrase yet be hesitant to ask for clarification. Speaking slowly is also important because even people who read and write a second language at an expert level may have difficulty catching the nuances of conversation. Facing the person from another culture directly also improves communication because your facial expressions and lips contribute to comprehension.

Speaking slowly and clearly is more effective at overcoming communication barriers than shouting at a person who does not understand your language well. For example, some Americans visiting other countries will shout at a restaurant server, "DON'T YOU SPEAK ENGLISH?" Shouting makes people defensive, including shouting at blind people to enhance comprehension. (Because the blind person cannot see a person's lips to enhance understanding, speaking clearly and not murmuring is helpful.) Also, a deaf person who reads lips will usually not understand words better when the speaker shouts. The vibrations given off by the shouting might be considered offensive.

3. When the situation is appropriate, speak in the language of the people from another culture. Americans who can speak another language are at a competitive advantage when dealing with businesspeople who speak that language. The language skill, however, must be more advanced than speaking a few words and phrases. A new twist in speaking another language has surged recently: As more deaf people have been integrated into the workforce, knowing American Sign Language can be a real advantage to a worker when some of his or her coworkers or customers are deaf.

4. Observe cultural differences in etiquette. Violating rules of etiquette without explanation can erect immediate communication barriers. A major rule of etiquette is that in most countries people in high-status positions expect to be treated with respect. Formality is important, unless invited to act otherwise. When visiting a company in Japan, for example, it is best to be deferent to (appeal to the authority of) company dignitaries. Visualize yourself as a company representative of a high-tech American firm that manufactures equipment for legally downloading music over the Internet. You visit Sony Corporation in Japan to speak about a joint venture. On meeting the marketing vice president, bow slightly and say something to the effect of, "Mr. __________, it is my honor to discuss doing business with Sony." Do not commit the etiquette mistake of saying something to the effect of, "Hi, Charlie. How's the wife and kids?" (An American actually said this at a Japanese company shortly before being escorted out the door.)

5. Be sensitive to differences in nonverbal communication. Stay alert to the possibility that a person from another culture may misinterpret your nonverbal signal. To use positive reinforcement, some managers will give a sideways hug to an employee or will touch an employee's arm. People from some cultures resent touching from workmates and will be offended. Koreans in particular dislike being touched or touching others in a work setting. (Refer to the discussion of cultural bloopers.) Another example of a potential nonverbal communication problem is "thumbs up" indicator used frequently in North America to convey the thought "Good job." Yet in some geographic areas such as Australia and Nigeria, the gesture is considered offensive.[32]

6. Do not be diverted by style, accent, grammar, or personal appearance. Although all these superficial factors are related to business success, they are difficult to interpret when judging a person from another culture. It is therefore better to judge the merits of the statement or behavior. A brilliant individual from another culture may still be learning your language and thus make basic mistakes in speaking your language. He or she might also not have developed a sensitivity to dress style in your culture.

7. Listen for understanding, not agreement. When working with diverse teammates, the differences in viewpoints can lead to conflict. To help overcome such conflict, follow the LUNA rule: Listen for Understanding, Not Agreement. In this way you gear yourself to consider the viewpoints of others as a first resort. For example, some older workers may express some intense loyalty to the organization, whereas their younger teammates may speak in more critical terms. By everyone listening to understand, they can begin to appreciate each others' paradigms and accept differences of opinion.[33] Listening is a powerful tool for overcoming cross-cultural communication barriers.

8. Be attentive to individual differences in appearance. A major cross-cultural insult is to confuse the identity of people because they are members of the same race or ethnic group. Research suggests that people have difficulty seeing individual differences among people of another race because they code race first, such as thinking, "He has the nose of an African American." However, people can learn to search for more distinguishing features, such as a dimple or eye color.[34]

9. Ask lots of questions to clarify potential misunderstandings. Many cross-cultural communication barriers can be avoided by asking questions to clarify potential misunderstandings. Even when speaking the same language, cultural traditions might lead to misunderstanding. For example, a representative from a foreign company might say that he or she "would be honored to try your product." However, "being honored" might imply that the person wants to try the products for free.

10. Do not misinterpret a formal communication style during a multicultural team meeting. Business consultant Sangeeta Gupta reminds us that workers from many Asian, Middle Eastern, and Latin countries, as well as those from the American South, will often use a formal communication style during a meeting. Formal communicators are likely to take their turn to speak and will often wait to hear what their manager has to say before expressing an opinion. In a U.S. environment, this formality might be interpreted as the team member not having much to contribute.[35] To overcome the barrier, encourage the more formal communicators to contribute in a polite, nonintimidating manner.

A major cross-cultural communication problem arises when the American who called cannot understand the version of English spoken by the customer service or technical support representative at a call center. Americans who can understand people well only from their own geographic region are likely to have the most difficulty in understanding the overseas technical support or customer service representative. The problem has been particularly acute with customers seeking technical assistance for prepaid cell phones. For example, the rep from the Philippines might ask the American to enter a long series of numerals—a challenging task even if you are familiar with the other person's accent.

In recognition of the potential cross-cultural communication barriers that occur with overseas call centers, the trend toward such outsourcing is slowing down. One compromise is to offer technical support and customer service from American centers during daytime working hours and overseas service during the night.

▶ Learning Objective 4 ▶

What Are Several Additional Ways in Which Organizations Use Diversity to Advantage?

To both make possible and capitalize upon diversity, organizations take many initiatives as already implied or mentioned in this chapter. Here we describe briefly five specific programs and processes aimed at capitalizing upon workplace diversity: creating diverse teams; matching organization diversity with community diversity; physical accommodations for workers with physical disabilities; work versus personal life accommodations; and employee network groups.

DIVERSE TEAMS

A building block for diversity is to staff teams, as well as other work groups, with members who are different from each other in some important respect. As mentioned previously, diversity within the group can enhance creativity. Diversity within the group can be among many factors including ethnic background, race, gender, income level, educational background, and field of specialty.

Educational background and specialty field are emphasized here because many people are not aware that there is more to diversity than race, ethnicity, and gender. Consultant Ann Evangelista explains that race and gender is only the tip of the diversity iceberg. Diversity also stems from an individual's personal and professional background, personal interests, geographic upbringing, personality traits, and approach to problem solving.[36]

An example of diversity based personality-traits and problem-solving style is that a work team can benefit from members who are detail-oriented as well as those who prefer to look at the big picture. One member might have a creative idea, such as "We would satisfy customers better if our waiting lines were shorter." Another member with good skill in detailed thinking might develop a revised process that would decrease the time customers spent waiting in line for service.

MATCHING ORGANIZATIONAL DIVERSITY WITH COMMUNITY DIVERSITY

A standard practice for many business, education, and government organizations is to approximately match diversity within the organization to that of diversity within the community. Home Depot is a good example because the mix of store associates approximately matches the cultural diversity within the community, such as one-third of the associates being Latino in a section of Chicago that is about one-third Latino.

In some companies, matching organizational diversity with community diversity is practiced at the executive level as well as throughout the organization. *Hispanic Business* magazine develops an annual list of twenty-five companies who have one or more Latinos occupying executive positions. Among the highest ranking Latino executives are Armando J. Olivera, the CEO of Florida Power & Light, and Grace Lieblein, the president and managing director of GM of Brazil (*do Brasil*).[37]

ACCOMMODATIONS FOR PEOPLE WITH PHYSICAL DISABILITIES

Many organizations practice diversity by making special accommodations for people with physical disabilities. These accommodations include making it easier for wheelchair users to navigate the workplace, and providing software that makes it possible for the visually impaired and blind workers to perform their tasks. The Canadian bank, CIBC, has been at the forefront of hiring people with physical disabilities, with about 4 percent of CIBC's 40,000 plus Canadian employees having a physical disability. A specific example is Martha Johnson, an IT specialist who has cerebral palsy. In recent years she needed a walker to get around. Management at her bank installed an automatic door on her floor to facilitate her getting around.[38]

Another representative example of a company making appropriate accommodations for employees with physical disabilities is the Integrated Defense Division of Boeing Company. James Harper, a professional worker with polio, enjoyed minor accommodations when he began with as an accountant with Boeing many years ago. He was given a close parking space and hourly rest breaks to ease the pain in his legs. His leg brace, extending from his foot to his thigh, often restricts blood flow causing cramping and discomfort. Today, Harper has a foot rest and a desk that adjusts in height so he can work standing or sitting.[39]

WORK VERSUS PERSONAL LIFE ACCOMMODATIONS

As mentioned in Chapter 10 in relation to work versus personal life conflict, employers often make accommodations to employees so they can fulfill their family and personal life obligations while still performing their job well. The link to diversity is that diversity includes such factors as having a young family, being responsible for parents in need, being a single parent, and having a prominent position in the community such as being a Girl Scout or Boy Scout leader.

Work and personal life integration programs can include allowing a parent to work at home on days when personal life demands are overwhelming. The ability of employees to stay in touch with the office electronically has facilitated making accommodations to employees who cannot be at work on a particular day. However, if enough employees abuse the privilege, this emergency form of accommodation is likely to be removed.

A survey by wireless network provider iPass Inc. points to the importance of making accommodations to employees who prefer not to work from a traditional office all the time. Of more than 3,100 mobile employees surveyed, approximately 80 percent said that "work shifting" makes them more productive and efficient, even when they worked more hours. Also, 90 percent of those surveyed indicated that without a flexible work arrangement, they would be far less satisfied or conducting a job search.[40]

EMPLOYEE NETWORK (AFFINITY) GROUPS

Another company initiative toward recognizing diversity is to permit and encourage employees to form **employee network (or affinity) groups**. The network group is

Employee network (or affinity) groups
network group of employees throughout the company who affiliate on the basis of a group characteristic such as face, ethnicity, sex, sexual orientation, or physical ability status

composed of employees throughout the company who affiliate on the basis of a group characteristic such as race, ethnicity, sex, sexual orientation, or physical ability status. Group members typically have similar interests and look to the groups as a way of sharing information about succeeding in the organization.

Allstate has at least seven employee network groups running at any given time. Two examples are 3AN (Allstate Asian American Network), and ANGLES (Allstate Network of Gay and Lesbian Employees and Supporters). The mission statement of 3AN is "3AN develops leaders of tomorrow through professional development, networking, cultural awareness, and knowledge sharing." The group's vision statement is "Leverage the diverse experiences of Asian Americans at Allstate to create value that supports Allstate."[41]

Employee network groups sometimes play a functional role in the organization in addition to the social role. A prime example is The Latino Employee Network (called Adelante) at Frito-Lay, the snack food division of PepsiCo. The group made a major contribution during the development of Doritos Guacamole Flavored Tortilla Chips. Adelante members provided feedback on taste and packaging to help ensure the authenticity of the product in the Latino community. The network members' insight helped make the guacamole-flavored Doritos into one of the most dramatically successful new-product launches in the history of Frito-Lay.[42] Olé!

A caution about employee network groups is that they can result in employee segregating rather than integrating themselves into the workforce, thereby defeated the purpose of diversity initiatives. A relevant example here is that as an organization has no concern about an employee's sexual orientation with respect to hiring or promotion, why should gay and lesbian workers single themselves out by joining a network group for gay, lesbian, and transgender employees?

A notable conclusion to this section as well as to information about diversity initiatives mentioned elsewhere in the chapter is that promoting diversity can be a good financial investment. A thorough study supporting this conclusion was conducted across 654 store units of a major U.S. retail organization. The survey participants were 56,000 store associates and 3,500 managers working in a variety of departments. Diversity climate (or atmosphere and attitudes related to diversity) was measured by a questionnaire, and sales results over a few years were measured using objective data. The highest sales growth was found in stores in which both store associates and managers perceived highly pro-diversity climates. In contrast, the lowest sales growth was evident for stores in which both associates and managers reported less hospitable diversity climates.[43]

▶ Learning Objective 5 ▶

What Are Some of the Legal Aspects of Working in a Culturally Diverse Environment?

In this chapter we have emphasized the interpersonal aspects of building good relationships with work associates who are demographically and culturally diverse. The legal side of diversity focuses on such matters as protecting workers from being discriminated against, such as not being denied a job you are qualified for because of race, gender, age, or physical disability. A major purpose of these laws is to help all workers be treated fairly. According to one analysis, the groups disadvantaged in the U.S. workplace are women, people of color, sexual minorities, and people with disabilities.[44] Note that not all members of these groups are disadvantaged, including the reality that in 2013 the CEO of American Express was an African American man, and the CEO of Xerox Corp. was an African American woman.

Legislation may help advance the rights of many workers, but it does not require workers to develop constructive relationships with each other or to develop cultural intelligence. Here we look briefly at relevant employment legislation, as well as affirmative action.

FEDERAL LAWS PROHIBITING JOB DISCRIMINATION

Workers are protected by a series of federal laws that prohibit job discrimination. In addition, states, provinces (Canada), and municipalities have their own laws governing fair treatment of employees. Furthermore, many employment lawyers bring forth lawsuits for discrimination not specifically mentioned in federal laws. For example, a job candidate might claim that he or she was denied a position for which he or she was qualified because he or she was obese. A state or local judge could then decide whether the claim was justified. The general purpose of job discrimination laws is to protect individuals who have been disadvantaged in the past because of demographic (not cultural) characteristics. Employment legislations began with prohibiting employment discrimination based on race, color, religion, sex, or national origin. Figure 13-4 summarizes Federal Equal Employment Opportunity (EEO) laws. These laws apply to all private employers, state and local governments, and educational institutions that employ fifteen or more individuals.

An effective way of understanding how these laws might affect the individual is to specify the discriminatory practices prohibited by these laws. Under Title VII, the Americans with Disabilities Act (ADA) and the Age Discrimination in Employment Act (ADEA), it is illegal to discriminate in any aspect of employment, including hiring and firing; compensation, assignment, or classification of employees; transfer, promotion, layoff, or recall; job advertisements; recruitment; testing; use of company facilities; training and apprenticeship programs; fringe benefits; pay, retirement plans, and disability leave; or other terms and conditions of employment. Discriminatory practices under these laws also include the following:

1. Harassment on the basis of race, color, religion, sex, national origin, disability, or age.
2. Retaliation against an individual for filing a charge of discrimination, participating in an investigation, or opposing discriminatory practices.

- Title VII of the Civil Rights Act of 1964 (Title VII) prohibits employment discrimination based on race, color, religion, sex, or national origin.
- The Equal Pay Act of 1963 (EPA) protects men and women who perform substantially equal work in the same establishment from sex-based wage discrimination.
- The Age Discrimination in Employment Act of 1967 (ADEA) protects individuals who are 40 years of age or older.
- Title I and Title V of the Americans with Disabilities Act of 1990 (ADA) prohibits employment discrimination against qualified individuals with disabilities in the private sector and in state and local governments.
- Sections 501 and 505 of the Rehabilitation Act of 1973 prohibit discrimination against qualified individuals with disabilities who work in the federal government.
- The Civil Rights Act of 1991 provides, among other things, monetary damages in cases of intentional employment discrimination.
- Title II of the Genetic Information Nondiscrimination Title II of the Genetic Nondiscrimination Act of 2008 makes it illegal for companies to discriminate against employees for insurance purposes, based upon genetic testing. The employee cannot be discriminated against due to family medical history, either. The employer is not allowed to ask for genetic testing to be done nor ask for genetic testing results of a fetus either being carried by the employee or a family member of the employee.

The U.S. EEOC enforces all of these laws. EEOC also provides oversight and coordination of all federal equal employment opportunity regulations, practices, and policies.

Source: Available at www.eeoc.gov/facts/ganda.html.

FIGURE 13-4
FEDERAL LAWS PROHIBITING JOB DISCRIMINATION

3. Employment decisions based on stereotypes or assumptions about the abilities, traits, or performance of individuals of a certain sex, race, age, religion, or ethnic group or individuals with disabilities.
4. Denying employment opportunities to a person because of marriage to, or association with, an individual of a particular race, religion, national origin, or an individual with a disability. Title VII also prohibits discrimination because of participation in schools or places of worship associated with a particular racial, ethnic, or religious group.

Although all of these forms of discrimination may appear clear-cut, a good deal of interpretation is required to decide whether a given employee is the subject of discrimination. For example, assume that a woman files a charge of sexual harassment. Later, she is bypassed for promotion. She claims she is now the victim of discrimination, yet the company claims that she did not have the appropriate interpersonal skills to be promoted to a supervisory position.

Among the remedies awarded to individuals judged to be discriminated against are back pay, promotion, reinstatement, and the employer paying attorney's fees and court costs. Compensatory and punitive damages are also possible.

ADDITIONAL EXAMPLES OF LEGISLATION AND COURT RULINGS TO ENSURE EQUAL RIGHTS

The federal legislation described earlier set the stage for a wide variety of laws and judicial rulings to prevent employment discrimination and thereby protect the rights of workers. Similar legislation is found in Canada, as well as European and some Asian countries. Here we highlight a few representative examples of how the rights of workers against discrimination are protected beyond major federal legislation summarized in Figure 13-4.[45]

- **Unconscious bias.** Several court rulings have recognized that unconscious prejudice and bias can prevent women and people of color from achievement and advancement after they have joined an employer. One example is a class-action suit against Wal-Mart involving more than 2 million women (*Dukes et al. v. Wal-Mart Stores Inc.*, 2004).
- **Protection for people with disabilities.** The Ticket to Work and Work Incentives Improvement Act of 1999 and the Workforce Investment Act of 1998 both focus on increased workforce participation for people with disabilities. For example, the 1998 act mandates state attention to developing employment programs, including career centers to help the disabled. (A problem remains in implementing disability legislation in unambiguously defining the meaning of *disability*. For example, one worker was fired for downloading pornography on his desktop computer. He sued, claiming he had a *disability* of pornography addiction. The judge supported the company.)
- **State laws protecting the employment rights of gay, lesbian, bisexual, or transgender (GLBT) workers.** Connecticut is among the many states protecting the rights of GLBT workers. Employers of more than three employees are forbidden from refusing to hire, discharge, or discriminate against the person in compensation, or in terms, conditions, or privileges of employment because of sexual orientation. The law covers most significant job actions such as hiring, firing, failure to promote, demotion, excessive discipline, harassment, and different treatment of the employee. In addition, employment agencies may not participate in discrimination by refusing to properly classify or refer people for employment, or otherwise discrimination because of sexual orientation. Labor unions also are forbidden from denying membership based on sexual orientation.

AFFIRMATIVE ACTION

Affirmative action programs that comply with antidiscrimination laws and attempt to correct past discriminatory practices

A key aspect of implementing the spirit and letter of antidiscrimination law in the United States has been affirmative action programs. **Affirmative action** consists of complying with antidiscrimination laws and correcting past discriminatory practices. During 1965, President Lyndon Johnson signed an executive order prohibiting federal contractors from discriminating in employment decisions on the basis of race, color, religion, sex, or national origin. Government contractors are also required to take affirmative action to ensure that all individuals have an equal opportunity for employment.

Under an affirmative action program, employers actively recruit, employ, train, and promote minorities and women, groups who have been discriminated against by an employer in the past. As a result, women and minority group members have been underrepresented in certain positions. Part of an affirmative action plan might be to actively recruit Latino business graduates to place them in a company management training program.

Affirmative action has been the subject of continuing debate. Proponents of affirmative action believe that it provides the opportunity many people need to prove their capability and earn just rewards. Opponents of affirmative action believe that it provides preferential treatment for certain groups and winds up discriminating against workers who are qualified but do not fit an affirmative action category. Frederick Lynch, an associate professor government at Claremont McKenna College in California contends that diversity programs promote the idea of hiring people because of their skin color, gender, or other demographic characteristics. He considers these actions to be tokenism.[46] What is your opinion about the merits of affirmative action?

Key Terms

Summary and Review

Being able to work well with people from other cultures, both outside and inside your own country, is important for career success. Eight dimensions of cultural values that help us understand how cultures differ from one another are as follows:

- Individualism versus collectivism
- Acceptance of power and authority
- Materialism versus concern for others
- Formality versus informality
- Urgent time orientation versus casual time orientation
- Work orientation versus leisure orientation
- High-context versus low-context cultures (with an emphasis on body language)
- Social support seeking

Many people have multicultural identities because they identify with their own culture as well as other cultures. Similarly, according to the cultural mosaic, people have a rich mixture of cultural identities. The religious value part of the cultural mosaic often affects when people are willing to work or not work. It is important to be alert to possible cultural differences.

Seven specific methods and techniques for improving cross-cultural relations are as follows:

- Develop cultural sensitivity (be aware of differences) and cultural intelligence (cognitive, emotional, and body components).
- Focus on individuals rather than groups.
- Respect all workers and cultures (including practicing sexual equity).
- Value cultural differences (this also involves showing respect).
- Minimize cultural bloopers (embarrassing mistakes).
- Participate in cultural training, including language training. (The skill dimensions of cross-cultural training are interpersonal, information, analytic, action, and adaptive.)
- Participate in diversity training, or learning to get along with diverse work associates.

Cross-cultural communication barriers can often be overcome by the following:

- Being alert to cultural differences in customs and behavior.
- Using straightforward language and speaking slowly and clearly.
- Speaking in the language of the other group.
- Observing cultural differences in etiquette.
- Being sensitive to differences in nonverbal communication.
- Not being diverted by style, accent, grammar, or personal appearance.
- Listening for understanding, not agreement.
- Being attentive to individual differences in appearance.
- Asking lots of questions to clarify potential misunderstandings.
- Correctly interpreting a formal communication style during a multicultural team meeting.

Additional ways in which organizations use diversity to advantage are as follows:

- Diverse teams
- Matching organizational diversity with community diversity

- Accommodations for people with physical disabilities
- Work versus personal life accommodations
- Employee network (or affinity) groups
- Research suggests that a positive diversity climate contributes to business success.

The legal side of diversity focuses on such matters as protecting workers from discrimination, but it is not part of developing cross-cultural competence. Workers are protected by a series of federal, state, and municipal laws that govern fair treatment of employees. It is illegal to discriminate in any aspect of employment including hiring and firing, compensation, and recruitment. Legislation and court rulings continue to emerge to ensure the equal rights of workers. Affirmative action programs consist of complying with antidiscrimination laws and correcting past discriminatory practices.

Check Your Understanding

1. In what way might having a high acceptance for power and authority make it difficult for a person to work well on a team that has very little supervision?
2. Identify three positive stereotypes about cultural groups that are related to job behavior. (An example would be the observation that Mexican laborers are known for their hard work and dependability.)
3. When you meet someone from another culture, what can you do to demonstrate that you respect that person's culture?
4. Provide an example of cultural insensitivity of any kind that you have seen, read about, or could imagine.
5. In an era of welcoming cultural diversity, does a company have the right to exclude employees with visible body piercings from any type of positions?
6. Suppose a company wants to promote cross-cultural understanding. Should the executives then discourage employees from one racial or ethnic group from forming a club or sitting together in the company cafeteria? Explain your position.
7. Should a business firm reach out to same-sex couples in the company and encourage them to bring their partners or same-sex dates to the holiday party? Explain your reasoning.
8. Suppose that Joe a coworker of yours takes a one-month leave of absence for a transgender transformation, and returns to the group as Josie, dressed in women's clothing. How comfortable would you be in now addressing this coworker as "Josie"?
9. It has been often observed that many automobile sales representatives are biased against women customers. How might this bias (if true) be evident on the sales floor of the dealer?
10. How might you be able to convert cross-cultural skills into higher income and job status for yourself?

Web Corner

Cultural training

www.slrobbins.com (Contains video of S. L. Robbins conducting a cultural-awareness training session.)

Cultural diversity

www.diversityinc.com

INTERNET SKILL BUILDER

Developing Your Multicultural Skills

A useful way of developing skills in a second language and learning more about another culture is to use as a home page (the page that appears when you open the Internet) a page written in your target language. In this way, each time you go the Internet on your own computer, your home page will contain fresh information in the language you want to develop.

Assume that your target language is French. Enter a phrase such as "French language newspaper" or "French current events" in the search box. Once you find a suitable choice, insert that newspaper as your cover page. The search engine might have brought you to www.france2.fr or www.cyberpresse.ca. These Web sites keep you abreast of French and French Canadian international news, sports, and cultural events—written in French. Now every time you access the Internet, you can spend a few minutes becoming multicultural. The foreign language site is also likely to have a few brief videos featuring native speakers, not only news commentators. You can save lot of travel costs and time using the Internet to help you become multicultural.

Developing Your Human Relations Skills

Human Relations Application Exercises

Applying Human Relations Exercise 13-1

Avoiding Cultural Mistakes

Refer to Figure 13-2, Cultural Mistakes to Avoid with Selected Cultural Groups. Review the list of cultural groups listed. After you have chosen one or two cultural groups, imagine how and where you might have an opportunity to relate to someone from one of these culture groups. During the next thirty days, look for an opportunity to relate to a person from another culture in the way described in these suggestions. You may have to be creative to find a target with whom you can practice your cross-cultural skills. Before approaching your target, answer these questions:

1. What would be my usual approach to dealing with a person from that culture? (An example here would be as follows: "Usually when I visit the neighborhood convenience store operated by a Korean family, I attempt to place the money for purchases directly in the hands of the cashier.")
2. What will I do differently after studying the suggestions in Figure 13-2? (Because touching a Korean's hand might be uncomfortable for him or her, I will lay the money on the counter and let the cashier pick it up.)

Observe the reaction of the other person for feedback on your cross-cultural effectiveness. Then assess whether your approach to improving cross-cultural relations had any effect on your target.

Applying Human Relations Exercise 13-2

Developing Empathy for Differences

Class members go up to the front of the room one by one and give a brief presentation (perhaps two or three minutes) of any way in which they have been perceived as different and how they felt about this perception. The difference can be of any kind, relating to characteristics such as ethnicity, race, field of study, physical appearance, height, weight, hair color, or body piercing. Here is an example repeatedly heard from very tall people: "I am so tired of the same old stupid comment, 'How's the weather up there?' It also annoys me that so many people ask me to change a lightbulb in a highly placed fixture. Even worse, because I'm tall, people think I would want to help them move furniture." An example heard frequently from information technology students is as follows: "When I'm out socially, people are forever asking me about some software problem they are facing. They think I know all about every software package ever written. Even worse, they think I have no life outside of computers. Why should I want to talk about computer problems when I'm partying?"

After each member of the class has presented (perhaps even the instructor), class members discuss what they learned from the exercise. Points to look for include the following:

- What pattern do you see in the ways people perceive themselves to be different?
- What is the most frequent difference reported by class members?
- What kind of perceptions by others seem to hurt the most?

It is also important to discuss how this exercise can improve relationships on the job. What would be at least one takeaway from the exercise?

Human Relations Class Activity

Cultural Gaffes in Both Directions

Many analyses of cross-cultural relations emphasize the mistakes American make in dealing with people from other cultures, as described in Figure 13-2. But people from non-American cultures also make mistakes in dealing with Americans. An example would be an Iranian businessperson who did not take an American company manager seriously because she was a woman.

The class assignment here is for students to collect two cross-cultural gaffes (or mistakes): one made by an American in relation to a person from another culture and one made by a foreigner in relation to an American. Use any method of gaffe collection you want, including conversations with people you know, your own observations, e-mails, blogs, or Internet search engines.

At a time designated by the instructor, each student or a number of volunteers present their gaffes in front of class. The gaffes can be presented in about two minutes. As class members listen to the gaffes, look for (a) frequently occurring gaffes and (b) lessons to be learned from these gaffes. An example of a lesson would be how to use this information about gaffes to improve cross-cultural relations.

Human Relations Case Study 13-1

Chantal Struggles with a Big Sale in Mexico City

Chantal is a key sales representative at her company that sells and installs large-scale heating and air-conditioning systems in new buildings as well as those undergoing renovation. Chantal often makes an initial visit to a potential customer, and she is then backed up a sales engineer as well as several technicians. Chantal was sent down to Mexico City to meet with the executive team that was converting a beautiful old church into condominium units.

Chantal knew that the sale and service on this potential contract was worth several million U.S. dollars (or about 35 million Mexican pesos). Chantal met with the executive team at the hospital on Friday morning for an all-day discussion of her company's services. All was going well, and Chantal could picture a big commission and loads of exciting work coming her way. The executive team then invited Chantal to stay over on Saturday and Sunday, attend a big soccer game, dine at a couple of restaurants, and tour the city.

Chantal thought the invitation was excessive in terms of her personal time, so she attempted to tactfully decline the invitation. The representative of the team seemed taken back, but he said that he understood that she had a busy schedule.

When Chantal returned to her office on Monday morning she found an e-mail message from the lead executive on the condominium development team. He said that he liked what her company had to offer but that they would need much more time to study her proposal. He also pointed out that in Mexico developing a good relationship comes first before signing a contract.

Chantal was horrified, and wondered what she did wrong. She was wondering what to do next to nail down this giant contract.

Questions

1. What might have the executive been referring to in terms of "developing a good relationship before signing a contract"?
2. What significance might the weekend stay offered to Chantal have had for the condominium development team?
3. What advice can you offer to Chantal from a cross-cultural value standpoint to attempt to salvage this giant contract?

Human Relations Role-Playing Exercise

Chantal Tries to Win Back Those Potential Pesos

One student plays the role of Chantal who pleads on the phone with the condominium representative to have another chance to win the contract for her firm. She decides that she wants to demonstrate how important relationship building is to her and to her firm. Another person plays the role of Hugo, the lead executive on the condominium development project. He dislikes the American attitude of getting down to business so quickly, but he has some sympathy for Chantal's sincerity.

Observers rate the role-players on two dimensions, using a 1 to 5 scale from very poor to very good. One dimension is "effective use of human relations techniques." For Chantal, focus on how well she demonstrates a sincere interest in developing a good relationship with the Mexican team. The second dimension is "acting ability." A few observers might voluntarily provide feedback to the role-players in terms of sharing their ratings and observations. The course instructor might also provide feedback.

Human Relations Case Study 13-2

Dennis Decides to Capitalize on His Spinal Cord Problem

Dennis, a middle-aged man, works for a data storage company as a quality assurance engineer. He has received average ratings on his last few performance reviews. Six months ago he was diagnosed as having the early stages of spinal stenosis. The condition is a narrowing of the space around the spinal cord which puts pressure on the spinal canal and nerve roots. The condition is painful, but most days Dennis can walk well, although he sometimes uses a cane.

The industry involved in the manufacture of data-storage devices has been growing recently, boosted by the spreading use of cloud computing in which data are stored and software downloaded from the Internet. However, the company Dennis works for is in a downturn because so many data storage devices are now being manufactured in low-wage countries. Dennis is becoming fearful that he could become part of a company downsizing. With his present physical condition, he would find it particularly uncomfortable for him and his family to go through the process of relocating geographically.

Dennis then develops a plan for minimizing the chances that he might be part of a company downsizing. He has heard and observed that the company is making an effort to be more culturally diverse, including having more physically challenged workers on the payroll. Dennis purchases a wheelchair that he finds helpful on days when his spinal stenosis is the most painful. He now begins to use the wheelchair two days a week on the job. As Dennis explained to his wife and a few close friends, "The company will never lay off an engineer in a wheelchair."

One day Dennis receives an e-mail from the manager of human resources asking him if he would be able to provide medical documentation of his need for the use of a wheelchair at work. Dennis thought to himself, "No problem here. I can find a doctor to document the severity of my spinal stenosis."

Questions

1. To what extent do you think Dennis is exploiting the company's interest in having a culturally diverse workforce?
2. What do you think of the ethics of Dennis coming to work in a wheelchair although he is usually able to walk, even with the assist of a cane?
3. If you were an executive at the company in which Dennis works, how would his wheelchair user status influence your decision to retain him as an employee?

Human Relations Role-Playing Exercise

Meg Confronts Dennis, the Part-time Wheelchair User

One student plays the role of Meg, the quality assurance supervisor. She is becoming suspicious about Dennis' use of a wheelchair thinking that perhaps he is looking for sympathy. Meg recognizes that this is a very delicate topic, but she decides to confront Dennis about his motivation and need for using a wheelchair at work a couple of times per week. Another student plays the role of Dennis who resents that Meg would question his integrity. Dennis wheels into Meg's cubicle for his meeting today.

Other students provide feedback, and perhaps also offer their opinion whether a role play of this nature is appropriate for the study of human relations. For example, is it acceptable to touch the topic that somebody might exaggerate a disability just to avoid being laid off?

REFERENCES

1. Original story created from facts and observations in the following sources: "PepsiCo honored by Working Mother Magazine as a Best Company for Multicultural Women for Fifth Consecutive Year," *PR Newswire* (www.prnewswire.com), May 24, 2011, pp. 1–2; "PepsiCo Diversity & Inclusion," (www.pepsico.com), accessed March 6, 2012, pp. 1–2; Amy George, "PepsiCo," *Executive Diversity Services, Inc.* (www.executivediversity.com), © Copyright 2010 Executive Diversity Services, Inc., pp. 1–2; The Editors, "Top Executives in Diversity," *Black Enterprise*, May 2011, p. 92; Laura Egodigwe, "Staying Focused on Best Practices," *Black Enterprise*, May 2009, p. 44.
2. Kristen M. Klein and Mo Wang, "Deep-Level Diversity and Leadership," *American Psychologist*, December 2010, pp. 932–933.
3. Melissa Donaldson, "The Bottom Line on Diversity," *Workforce Management*, May 18, 2009, p. 8.
4. Tiffany Hsu, "Retailers Catch On to the Buying Power of Immigrants," *Los Angeles Times* (www.latimes.com), December 24, 2008.
5. Geert Hofstede, *Culture's Consequences: International Differences in Work-Related Values* (Beverly Hills, CA: Sage, 1980). Updated and expanded in "A Conversation With Geert Hofstede," *Organizational Dynamics*, Spring 1993, pp. 53–61; Harry Triandis, "The Many Dimensions of Culture," *Academy of Management Executive*, February 2004, pp. 88–93; Manasour Javidan, Peter W. Dorfman, May Sully de Luque, and Robert J. House, "In the Eye of the Beholder: Cross-Cultural Lessons in Leadership from Project GLOBE," *Academy of Management Perspectives*, February 2006, pp. 69–70.
6. Heejung S. Kim, David K. Sherman, and Shelley E. Taylor, "Culture and Social Support," *American Psychologist*, September 2008, pp. 518–526.
7. Adam P. Cohen, "Many Forms of Culture," *American Psychologist*, April 2009, p. 197.
8. Janet Wiscombe, "McDonald's Corp.," *Workforce Management*, November 2010, p. 38.
9. Carlin Flora, "Double Talk," *Psychology Today*, September–October 2010, p. 75.
10. Jeffrey Jensen Arnett, "The Psychology of Globalization," *American Psychologist*, October 2002, pp. 777–778.
11. Georgia T. Chao and Henry Moon, "The Cultural Mosaic: A Methodology for Understanding the Complexity of Culture," *Journal of Applied Psychology*, November 2005, pp. 1128–1140.
12. Based on the contribution of Terri Geerinck in Andrew J. DuBrin and Terri Geerinck, *Human Relations for Career and Personal Success*, 2nd Canadian ed. (Toronto: Prentice Hall, 2001), p. 201. Geerinck also contributed the idea of a separate chapter on cross-cultural competency.
13. Arvind V. Phatak, *International Dimensions of Management* (Boston: Kent, 1983), p. 167.
14. Kathryn Tyler, "Global Ease," *HR Magazine*, May 2011, pp. 41–42.
15. P. Christopher Earley and Elaine Mosakowski, "Cultural Intelligence," *Harvard Business Review*, October 2004, p. 140. The example is from the same source, same page.
16. Earley and Mosakowski, "Toward Cultural Intelligence: Turning Cultural Differences into Workplace Advantage," *Academy of Management Executive*, August 2004, pp. 154–155.
17. Cited and quoted in Annya M. Lott, "The Truth About Our Differences," *Black Enterprise*, July 2010, p. 59.
18. Xiao-Ping Chen, Dong Liu, and Rebecca Portnoy, "A Multi-Level Investigation of Motivational Cultural Intelligence, Organizational Diversity Climate, and Cultural Sales: Evidence from U.S. Real Estate Firms," *Journal of Applied Psychology*, January 2012, pp. 93–106.
19. Todd Raphael, "Savvy Companies Build Bonds With Hispanic Employees," *Workforce*, September 2001, p. 19.
20. Experiment reported in Christopher Munsey, "Stereotype-Busting Can Spur Stress, Reduce Cognitive Performance," *Monitor on Psychology*, June 2007, p. 11.
21. Diane Cadrain, "Sexual Equity in the Workplace," *HR Magazine*, September 2008, pp. 44–50.
22. Gunnar Beeth, "Multicultural Managers Wanted," *Management Review*, May 1997, p. 17.
23. A few of these tasty morsels are from Lillian H. Chaney and Jeanette S. Martin, *Interpersonal Business Communication*, 3rd ed. (Upper Saddle River, NJ: Pearson Prentice Hall, 2004), p. 190.
24. Angela Ka-yee Leung, William W. Maddux, Adam G. Galinsky, and Chi-yue Chiu, "Multicultural Experience Enhances Creativity: The When and How," *American Psychologist*, April 2008, pp. 169–181.
25. Marc Diener, "Culture Shock," *Entrepreneur*, July 2003, p. 77.
26. The quotes in this section as well as the general idea are from Tanya Mohn, "Learning to Work With a Culture, Even From a Distance," *The New York Times* (www.nytimes.com), March 8, 2010, pp, 1–4.
27. Donna M. Owens, "Multilingual Workforces," *HR Magazine*, September 2005, p. 127.
28. Definition from the U.S. Department of the Interior, Office of Civil Rights, as quoted in Janet Perez, "Diversity Inside-Out,"*Hispanic Business*, April 2006, p. 64.
29. Todd Henneman, "Making the Pieces Fit," *Workforce Management*, August 2011, pp. 12–18.
30. "7 Things Never to Say to People With Disabilities," (www.diversityinc.com/things-not-to-say), May 27, 2008, pp. 1–2.
31. Study reported in Lisa Takeuchi Cullen, "The Diversity Delusion," *Time*, May 7, 2007, p. 74.
32. "Escape These Cross-Cultural Traps," *Communication Briefings*, Volume XXII, Number 1, Condensed Issue, 2008.
33. "Use Team's Diversity to Best Advantage," *Executive Strategies*, April 2000, p. 2.
34. Siri Carpenter, "Why Do 'They All Look Alike'?" *Monitor on Psychology*, December 2000, p. 44.
35. Sangeeta Gupta, "Mine the Potential of Multicultural Teams," *HR Magazine*, October 2008, p. 80.
36. Cited in "All Inclusive: Bringing Workplace Diversity to Higher Level," *Chicago Tribune Career Builder*, March 11, 2012, p. 16.
37. Richard Larson, "Making Inroads," *Hispanic Business*, January–February 2012, pp. 18–19.

38. Terrence Belford, "Opening Doors for Employees With Disabilities," *The Toronto Star* (www.thestar.com), June 13, 2008.
39. LaToya M. Smith, "Breaking Barriers in the Workplace," *Black Enterprise*, February 2009, p. 60.
40. Survey reported in Henry G. Jackson, "Flexible Workplaces: A Business Imperative," October 2011, p. 10.
41. "Allstate Diversity," Retrieved March 14, 2012, from www.allstate.com/diversity.
42. Robert Rodriguez, "Diversity Finds Its Place," *HR Magazine*, August 2006, p. 56
43. Patrick F. McKay, Derek R. Avery, and Mark A. Morris, "A Tale of Two Climates: Diversity Climate From Subordinates, and Managers' Perspectives and Their Role in Store Unit Sales Performance," *Personnel Psychology*, Winter 2009, pp. 767–791.
44. Ruth E. Fassinger, "Workplace Diversity and Public Policy," *American Psychologist*, May–June 2008, p. 252.
45. Fassinger, "Workplace Diversity," pp. 262–265; "Bush Signs Genetic Anti-Discrimination Bill," *Associated Press*, May 21, 2008.
46. Cited in Henneman, "Making the Pieces Fit," p. 18.

14

Getting Ahead in Your Career

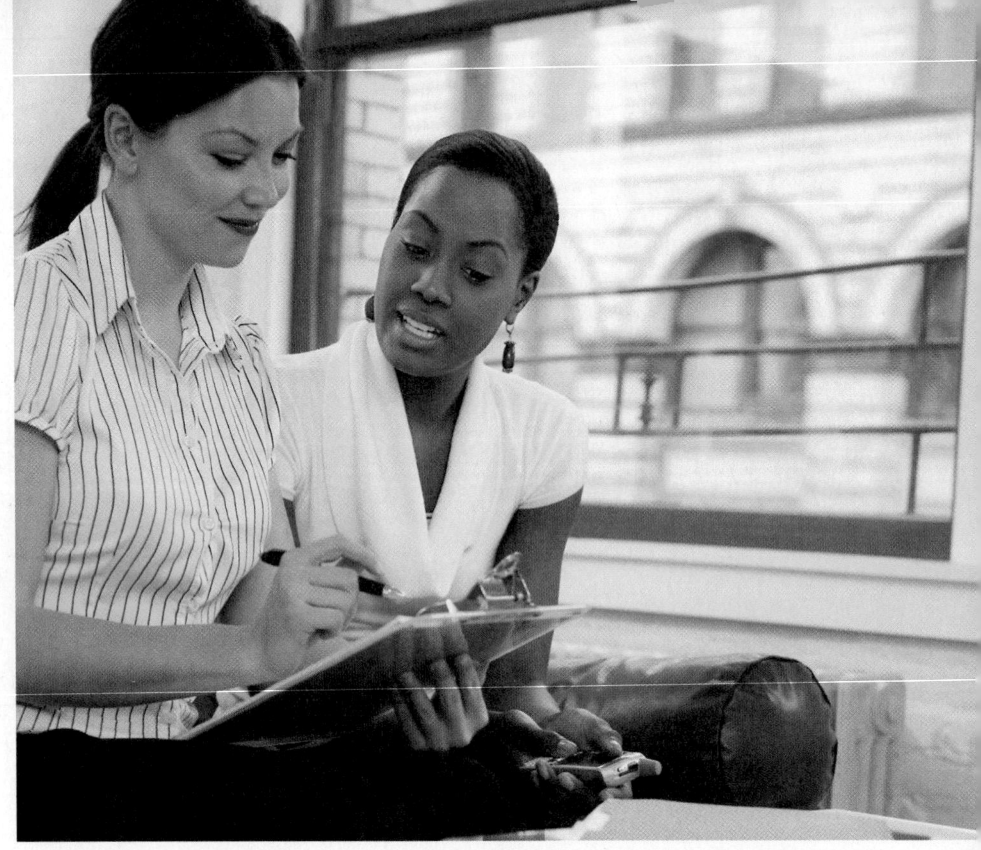

Outline

Linda Hudson does not wear a cape to work, but she does qualify as a Superwoman. She is the president and CEO of BAE Systems, Inc. Hudson leads more than 40,000 workers across more than 130 sites in the United States, United Kingdom, Sweden, Israel, Mexico, and South Africa. Before joining BAE Systems, She served for seven years as an officer and vice president of General Dynamics Corp, and was president of a key division of the company. Hudson earned a bachelor's degree with honors in systems engineering from the University of Florida where all her classmates were men.

Hudson has also received considerable recognition and awards from several groups for her professional accomplishments and philanthropic activities. Based on her leadership roles, work experience, and education, Linda Hudson has plenty of career advice to offer.

Hudson says it is profoundly important to realize that relationships with people define everything that we do. It is the quality of those relationships that make an organization function well.

According to Hudson, many people have professional credentials, but they lack the passion and people connection that will propel their careers by setting them apart from others. Many business school graduates have a good theoretical knowledge of business but they don't have a clue of what it's like with respect to people skill, she contends. Often, they also lack knowledge of learning how to deal with disappointment and failure. Other people fall short because they lack a can-do attitude and capability.

Hudson emphasizes projecting your voice, because a squeaky, soft voice does not suggest an aura of importance or authority when making a presentation to a group or in a one-on-one situation. Early in her career, she took lessons from a voice coach to learn how to better project and develop a lower pitch, thereby helping her make better presentations to large groups.

Hudson recommends that you work within the system rather than fight it. Years ago, she was a manager at a company that had no maternity-leave policies in place for her job level when she was pregnant. Rather than demanding that the company come up with the necessary changes, she helped write the policies and practices for maternity leave for high-level workers.[1]

Learning Objectives ▸

After studying the information and doing the exercises in this chapter, you should be able to:

1. Identify job-finding methods and use the Internet to assist you in your job search.
2. Prepare an effective cover letter and job résumé, and prepare for the job interview.
3. Select several strategies and tactics for getting ahead in your career by taking control of your own behavior.
4. Select several strategies and tactics for advancing your career by exerting control over your environment.
5. Understand networking techniques and be ready to implement them.

The career advice offered by the senior executive just described, if implemented successfully, will help you advance in your career. This chapter offers many useful approaches to career advancement, but our discussion of career advancement is preceded by the necessary first step of conducting a job campaign.

We have divided the vast information about career advancement into three sections. The first section deals with approaches to managing or taking control of your own behavior to advance or retain a good position. The second section deals with approaches to exerting control over your environment to improve your chances for success. The third section deals with networking, the most widely accepted career advancement strategy. To begin relating career development to yourself, do Human Relations Self-Assessment Quiz 14-1.

Human Relations Self-Assessment Quiz 14-1

The Career Development Inventory

Career development activities inevitably include answering some penetrating questions about yourself, such as the twelve questions that follow. You may need several hours to do a competent job answering these questions. After individuals have answered these questions by themselves, it may be profitable to hold a class discussion about the relevance of the specific questions. A strongly recommended procedure is for you to date your completed inventory and put it away for safekeeping. Examine your answers in several years to see (a) how well you are doing in advancing your career and (b) how much you have changed.

Keep the following information in mind in answering this inventory: People are generous in their self-evaluations when they answer career development inventories, so you might want to discuss some of your answers with somebody who knows you well.

1. How would you describe yourself as a person?
2. What are you best at doing? Worst?
3. What are your two biggest strengths or assets?
4. What skills and knowledge will you need to acquire to reach your goals?
5. What are your two biggest accomplishments?
6. Write your obituary as you would like it to appear.
7. What would be the ideal job for you?
8. What career advice can you give yourself?
9. Describe the two peak work-related experiences in your life.
10. What are your five most important values (the things in life most important to you)?
11. What goals in life are you trying to achieve?
12. What do you see as your niche (spot where you best fit) in the modern world?

Learning Objective 1

What Are the Basics of Conducting a Job Search?

The purpose of this section is to provide a review of a few key ideas you need to conduct a successful job search, including sources of job leads, preparation of a cover letter and job résumé, and performing well in a job interview. Recognizing that few people stay with one employer for an entire career, conducting a job search is an important part of career development. Although job search knowledge is readily available, this concise information can be used as a refresher and a reminder to be systematic in finding a new position. We also present a few fine points to help give you an edge over those who do the minimum necessary to find a new position.

TARGET YOUR JOB SEARCH

A job search begins with a reasonably flexible description of the type of job or jobs for which you are looking. Flexibility is called for because, with so many different jobs available, it is difficult to be too specific. Also, flexibility with respect to the type of employer is important. For example, many job seekers overlook the possibilities of working for the

U.S. government. The federal government hires graduates in dozens of fields, and the starting pay is competitive with similar private-sector jobs.

Your chances of finding suitable employment are directly proportional to the number of positions that will satisfy your job objectives. One person with a degree in information technology might be interested exclusively in working in the information systems division of a major corporation. Another person with the same background is willing to work in the information technology field for a large company, a small company, a high-tech start-up, a government agency, a hospital, or an educational institution. The second person has a better chance than the first of finding a job in a geographic location he or she wants.

Closely tied in with the type of work you are seeking is the type of organization in which you would prefer to work. You are much more likely to be successful in your new job and your career when you find a good **person–organization fit**—the compatibility of the individual and the organization. In other words, what type of organizational culture (or atmosphere) would fit you best? Your job satisfaction will be higher, and you are likely to stay longer with an employer, when there is a good person–organization fit. In addition to fitting in well with the organization, it is also important to fit your job, group, and supervisor.[2]

Person–organization fit
the compatibility of the individual and the organization

Unless you have had exposure to different types of organizations, you may have only tentative ideas about a good person–organization fit for you. Questioning people who work at different places can provide you with some useful clues. A vital source of input about a prospective employer is present and past employees. Further, plant tours open to the public can provide valuable tips about what it is like to work in a particular firm.

Visits to stores, restaurants, and government agencies will provide informal information about the general nature of working conditions in those places. Using the Internet to find facts about a company has become standard practice. The Internet search includes the firm's Web site as well as news stories about the company. Also, the time spent talking to your prospective supervisor and coworkers is time well spent.

BE AWARE OF QUALIFICATIONS EMPLOYERS ARE SEEKING

A constructive early stage of conducting a job search is to be aware of what qualifications many employers are seeking. What you are looking for in an employer must be matched against what an employer is looking for in an employee. If you are aware of what employers are seeking, you can emphasize those aspects of yourself when applying for a position. For example, applicants for almost any type of position should emphasize their information technology skills. Job interviewers and hiring managers do not all agree on the qualifications they seek in employees. Nevertheless, a number of traits, characteristics, skills, and accomplishments are important to many employers. Human Relations Self-Assessment Quiz 14-2 summarizes these qualifications in a way that you can apply to yourself as you think about your job hunt.

FINDING JOBS THROUGH NETWORKING AND THE INTERNET

Two cornerstone principles of conducting a job campaign are to use several different methods and keep trying. These two principles should be applied because most approaches to job finding are inefficient yet effective. *Inefficient* refers to the fact that a person might have to make many contacts to find only one job. Yet the system is *effective* because it does lead to a desired outcome—finding a suitable position. Here we look at two of dozens of possible routes for conducting a job search—networking and the Internet.

Human Relations Self-Assessment Quiz 14-2

Qualifications Sought by Employers

Directions: Following is a list of qualifications widely sought by prospective employers. After reading each qualification, rate yourself on a 1 to 5 scale by circling the appropriate number: 1 = very low, 2 = low, 3 = average, 4 = high, 5 = very high.

1.	Appropriate education for the position under consideration and satisfactory grades	1	2	3	4	5
2.	Relevant work experience	1	2	3	4	5
3.	Communication and other interpersonal skills	1	2	3	4	5
4.	Motivation and energy	1	2	3	4	5
5.	Problem-solving ability (intelligence) and creativity	1	2	3	4	5
6.	Judgment and common sense	1	2	3	4	5
7.	Adaptability to change including ability to take on tasks not directly part of your field of expertise	1	2	3	4	5
8.	Emotional maturity (acting professionally and responsibly)	1	2	3	4	5
9.	Teamwork (ability and interest in working in a team effort)	1	2	3	4	5
10.	Positive attitude (enthusiasm about work and initiative)	1	2	3	4	5
11.	Emotional intelligence (ability to deal with own feelings and those of others)	1	2	3	4	5
12.	Customer service orientation (wanting to meet customer needs)	1	2	3	4	5
13.	Up-to-date information technology skills	1	2	3	4	5
14.	Willingness to continue to study and learn about the job, company, and industry	1	2	3	4	5
15.	Likableness and sense of humor	1	2	3	4	5
16.	Dependability, responsibility, and conscientiousness (including good work habits and time management)	1	2	3	4	5
17.	Willingness and ability to work well with coworkers and customers from different cultures	1	2	3	4	5
18.	Behaves ethically toward customers and company employees and obeys laws and regulations	1	2	3	4	5
19.	Can relate well to customers (even if not in formal customer contact position)	1	2	3	4	5
20.	Able to use social networking sites for business purposes	1	2	3	4	5

Interpretation

Consider engaging in some serious self-development, training, and education for items on which you rated yourself low or very low. If you accurately rated yourself as 4 or 5 on all the dimensions, you are an exceptional job candidate.

Networking (Contacts and Referrals)

Networking
the process of establishing a group of contacts who can help you in your career

The most effective method of finding a job is through personal contacts who might then refer you to a potential employer. **Networking** is the process of establishing a group of contacts who can help you in your career. Networking is particularly helpful because it taps you into the *internal job market.* This market is the large array of jobs that haven't been advertised and are usually filled by word of mouth or through friends and acquaintances of employees. More jobs are found by a referral from a personal contact than through any other more formal sources such as recruitment sites on the Internet or print advertising. A Right Management survey found that 42 percent of job seekers found their job through a networking contact.[3] Furthermore, the most consistent piece of advice about conducting a job search is to use networking extensively.[4]

Networking has become a confusing term because it refers to in-person networking as well as to establishing contacts by use of social networking Web sites. Whether the source of your contact is in-person or online, the result is the same for job-hunting purposes as long as the contact is valuable. For example, a social media "friend" or "follower" who lives 6,000 miles away from you probably is not worth much for job-hunting in your town.

The best way to reach the jobs in the internal market is by getting someone to recommend you for one. When looking for a job, it is therefore important to tell every potential contact of your job search. Be able to tell your story briefly, in terms of your experience, strengths, and the type of work you are seeking.[5] The more influential the person, the better. Be specific about the type of job you are seeking. When workers are in short supply, some companies give cash bonuses and prizes to employees for referring job candidates to them. To use networking effectively, it may be necessary to create contacts aside from those you already have. Networking is time-consuming yet is usually well worth the effort.

Potential sources of contacts for your network include the following: friends, family members, faculty and staff, athletic team members, professional associations, and career and job fairs. Attending job fairs also illustrates the point that every feasible method of job finding should be attempted. Recruiters who are looking to fill specific positions might be present at the job fair, along with those recruiters who are looking only to build relationships for the future.

Joining online networking sites, such as Facebook.com, Twitter.com, and LinkedIn.com has become standard practice for conducting a job search. A major purpose of these sites is for members to help each other find jobs. Some sites emphasize professional contacts, whereas others focus on developing friendships. The contacts you might develop through social media sites can lead to information about job openings, sometimes by using an advanced search function.

Many employers recruit directly through these sites, such as a company having a Facebook site. The usefulness of online networking increases when you meet face-to-face a few of the most promising contacts. Another benefit of being active with social networking sites is that recruiters often search these sites for possible candidates to fill a position. A representative example is that Waste Management Inc., the environmental services company, has recruiters and other employees find user groups and join discussions on social media sites.[6]

Another contribution of social networking Web sites to job finding is that hiring managers frequently look through these Web sites to find potential candidates. The best candidates are invited to submit a résumé or be interviewed by telephone. However, this process works better for Web site members who are experienced and have unusual expertise. The reason that recruiters are more likely to peruse LinkedIn is because so many of its members are experienced professionals.[7]

An important caution about networking: Too many people are consuming too much of other people's time to help them with their job searches. Keep your request for assistance brief and pointed. Ask to reciprocate in any way you can. For example, you might prepare a chart or conduct research for a manager who gave you a job lead. Bothering influential network members too frequently can lead to your being ignored as a pest or high-maintenance person.

Web Sites for Job Finding

Using the Internet, for little or no cost, the job seeker can post a résumé or scroll through hundreds of job opportunities. Web sites such as CareerBuilder and Monster are job boards (or résumé database services) that give employers access to résumés submitted by job hunters. It is also helpful to look for job Web sites for a specific field, such as information technology, finance, or sales. Employment consultant Peter Weddle writes that A-level performers tend to focus on niche sites when conducting a job search.[8]

The employment section of company Web sites can be as effective as general job boards in finding job leads. Another Internet approach to finding jobs is to simply insert the position you are seeking, such as "accounts payable specialist," "banquet manager," or "surgical technician" into a search engine. You are likely to find recruiters and employers claiming to have such a position open.[9]

Job hunting on the Internet can lead to a false sense of security. Using the Internet, a résumé is cast over a wide net, and hundreds of job postings can be explored. As a consequence, the job seeker may think that he or she can sit back and wait for a job offer to come through e-mail, your niche on a social networking site, or into your Web site. In reality, the Internet is only one source of leads that should be used in conjunction with other job-finding methods. Thousands of other job seekers can access the same job openings, and many of the positions listed have already been filled.

A major challenge of job hunting through the Internet is finding a way to speak to a company representative about your application. Telephoning the human resources department of a large company usually leads to a voice mail system with a lengthy menu and rarely a return call. A plausible approach to making a personal contact is to call the main number of your target company and get connected to the operator. Ask for the department where you hope to work, and you may be able to establish a personal contact—provided that you do not encounter another lengthy menu.

Although online networking is standard practice, building relationships face-to-face is a key component of the job search. Lauren Milligan, the founder of a career coaching service says that technology tools have not changed the fact that people prefer to hire somebody they like. Meeting face-to-face will often enhance your likeableness.[10]

THE JOB RÉSUMÉ AND COVER LETTER

The job résumé and job interview remain an essential part of the job search. A review of the basics of the two job-finding methods is essential for most job seekers.

Preparing an Effective Job Résumé

The major purpose of a résumé is to market yourself to a prospective employer. The résumé therefore presents a targeted message that will help you obtain a job interview, not a job. You need a résumé both as an outside candidate and often when seeking a transfer within a large firm. Effective résumés are straightforward, factual presentations of a person's experiences, education, skills, and accomplishments. The word *factual* is important because employers frequently verify facts presented on résumés, and gross inaccuracies lead to immediate rejection of the candidate. A challenge in preparing an effective résumé is to suit many different preferences—for example, some people spell *résumé* with the acute accents (*résumé* is a French word) and some without. Searching through job-search books and Web sites, you will find hundreds of different opinions as to what constitutes an effective job résumé. Résumé preparation is a broad topic, yet many of the major points are described in the following list.

1. Length. Résumé length illustrates how employers hold different opinions about the best résumé format. For people of limited job experience, a one-page résumé is usually sufficient. For candidates with more experience, two pages may suffice. A *curriculum vitae* (CV) is used to provide a more comprehensive work and education history of the sender and can easily run to more than six pages. A CV is used primarily by professors and scientists and would include such detailed information as publications, patents, and committee experience.

2. General construction. Information about résumé construction is readily available. For example, Microsoft Word includes job résumé templates under File/New/Other Documents. You will find there templates for contemporary, elegant, and professional résumés, plus a résumé wizard that helps you construct an individualized résumé. Using the search engine term, *sample job résumé*, you will find dozens of potential models to consider. Done properly, a résumé can lead to an interview with a prospective employer. Done poorly, it will block you from further consideration. *Poorly* refers to such features as misspellings, misuse of words, disorganization, lack of accurate contact information, too many abbreviations and acronyms, and too many unaccounted-for blocks of time. Job candidates who are found to have misrepresented facts (such as pretending to have graduated from a particular school) on a résumé are immediately disqualified. According to the Society for Human Resource Management, approximately 75 percent of employers reject applicants if their résumés contain spelling errors or contain major grammatical errors.[11]

Figure 14-1 presents a representative job résumé for a recent college graduate. The sample illustrates the reality that almost all potential employers expect to find on your résumé, information about your skills, education, experience, and contact information. We mention this basic observation because some people think a résumé is obsolete and should be replaced with a biographical story, or a statement of how you can bring about change in an organization.

Note that the traditional sections of the "job objective" and "references upon request" have been intentionally omitted from this sample résumé. The reason is that these two sections are considered old-fashioned by many job search specialists.[12] Your

FIGURE 14-1 A SAMPLE JOB RÉSUMÉ FOR A RECENT COLLEGE GRADUATE

Maria Gravista

622 Reynolds Avenue, Lexington, KY 40502 mgravista@yahoo.com 502-617-8278 Facebook, Twitter, and LinkedIn pages under my name. Personal Web site: www.MariaGravista.com.

Profile

Sales and customer service specialist with solid basic business skills, eager to help her employer and customers, and advance in responsibilities. Good work experience for my age, including teamwork. Speak and write fluently in English and Spanish.

Key Accomplishments and Skills

Spearheaded department store inventory liquidation of $50,000, and introduced new line of merchandise at the same time. Helped recruit and select ten part-time store associates in one-month time frame.

Work well with Windows and Macintosh operating systems, Microsoft and Apple office suites. Set up and conduct marketing on social media sites including Facebook, Twitter, and LinkedIn. Work well with Adobe Photoshop, Picasa, and PowerPoint. Web site development. Prepare thorough reports, and analyze quantitative and qualitative data well. Can converse with work associates and customers in English and Spanish.

Formal Education

2011–2013: Western Kentucky Valley College: Associates degree in business and marketing, with information technology minor. 3.25 GPA. Captain of soccer team. Vice president of marketing club.

2007–2011: Benjamin Franklin High School, Lexington, KY. Graduated with high honors, and class president. Captain of soccer team, played shooting guard on basketball team for three seasons.

Retail and Customer Experience

2008–2013: Majestic Department Store, Lexington, KY: Began as shelf-stocking clerk, then worked as store associate in women's clothing, jewelry, TV, and consumer electronics. Assigned to projects on inventory liquidation and merchandising. Received outstanding performance reviews.

2004–2007: Newspaper delivery girl for Kentucky Gazette. Well-liked by customers, and complimented for making my deliveries on time even during inclement weather. Received four awards as Gazette Carrier of the Month.

2009–present: Work with family eBay store to purchase goods from dollar stores and Wal-Mart, and resell in European markets.

job objective will be implied by the position you are applying for or in the cover letter, and references will be asked for, most likely during the interview. Also note that the résumé has substituted "retail and customer experience" for the more general "work experience."

3. Keyword importance. Keywords are an essential part of résumé construction because prospective employers screen for these words both visually and electronically. **Keywords** are terms for skills, certifications, job activities, and other qualifications sought for a particular job.[13] Although keywords vary according to the position in question, here is a sampling: *cost reduction, revenue enhancement, customer satisfaction, social media marketing, Google optimization, business process improvement, diversity skills, Mandarin Chinese.* Another use of key words is to match them the best possible to the position applied for, such as using the word *maintenance* several times in the résumé when applying for a position as a maintenance supervisor at a factory.

Keywords
terms for skills, certifications, job activities, and other qualifications sought for a particular job

Keywords must be chosen carefully because so many job searchers use the same buzzwords to describe themselves, such as *creative, effective, communication skills, outstanding, motivated, and dynamic.*[14] "Creative" is the most-used adjective in LinkedIn profiles, according to a review of millions of user pages on the site. As a result, describing yourself as "creative" may appear to be noncreative.

4. Customization. Your résumé should be customized somewhat to fit the position under consideration, rather than sending a generic version to all prospective employers. The cover letter, as mentioned later, makes the major contribution to customization. Customizing your résumé could mean emphasizing your sales accomplishments of any type if you were applying for a sales position or highlighting your community activities when applying for a position as an administrator at a nonprofit organization. Career consultant Louise Kursmark notes that any element in your résumé can be omitted, expanded, or shortened in response to a specific job opening. It is preferable to omit irrelevant information than to appear that you are not focused in your job search.[15]

5. Skills and accomplishments. Whichever style of résumé you choose, it should include a section about your job-related skills and accomplishments. A *skill* is an activity, such as preparing a PowerPoint presentation, compiling a research report on consumer preferences, or translating documents from Spanish to English. Most employers hire for skills, so being specific about your skills in a résumé is essential. (Skill description is also quite important during a job interview.) Skills can be based on academic pursuits, paid work, volunteer work, and sometimes sports, such as a team captain mentioning "activity scheduling" as a skill. Remember, though, that a skill is something you can do now and does not refer to a course you once took, unless you have practiced the skill learned in the course. The skills mentioned on your résumé might be incorporated into the profile section.

The importance of listing key skills has increased dramatically in recent years because, according to an expert on employment software at IBM, about 90 percent of large companies use applicant tracking systems to search résumés for the right skills and experience.[16]

Quantifying accomplishments and making objective statements is helpful in making a positive self-presentation, yet it is not always feasible to do so. Two examples of making your accomplishments more tangible would be, as follows:

Reduced home invasions by 28 percent during my three years in my precinct (police captain).

Revised medical billing process resulting in 37 percent fewer patient complaints about errors in medical bills (business administration analyst in hospital).

6. The video résumé. Another challenge when job hunting is whether to send a video résumé. Done professionally, a video résumé can be an asset, but some employers do not want to bother downloading and watching a video. Also, some employers are concerned that a video clearly reveals demographic factors about the candidate, such as sex, race, and approximate age. Rejecting the candidate might therefore lead to charges of discrimination. A sensible approach is to ask whether the employer would like to receive your video résumé in addition to the traditional version. Many job candidates post a video on their social media blog site or personal Web site, and make note of its availability. However, attaching a copy of the video will often be more welcome than expecting the employer representative to track down your video on the Internet.

7. Additional information about you. To provide prospective employers with information about yourself beyond the résumé, you might provide a link to your personal Web site or page on LinkedIn or similar social networking site. The site becomes a permanent online home for your credentials. In this way, the employer has a choice about obtaining additional information, but you are not forcing the representative to obtain the information to review your credentials. Take care to assure that your social media profiles match your résumé. If the job descriptions on your profile do not match the ones on your résumé, it could arouse suspicion by the prospective employer.[17]

The Cover Letter

A résumé should be accompanied by a cover letter explaining who you are and why you are applying for a particular position. Many companies now require a cover letter as part of the application process, as do many city and county governments. The cover letter customizes your approach to a particular employer, whereas the résumé is a more general approach. (Be aware, however, that it is often recommended to modify your résumé to suit a particular position or similar positions.) The cover letter can be as influential as a résumé in deciding who receives an interview offer.

Sometimes it is helpful to prepare an attention-getting cover letter in which you make an assertive statement about how you intend to help the employer deal with an important problem. A person applying for a credit manager position might state, "Let me help you improve your cash flow by using the latest methods for getting customers to pay on time, or even early."

The cover letter should contain a few short paragraphs and should focus on the skills and background you'll bring to the job. Follow this with a brief bullet-point list of your accomplishments. If possible mention a company insider in your network, and then close the cover letter with appreciation for any consideration your qualifications might be given. If you do not have the name of the contact person, use an approach such as, "Dear Purchasing Manager." The ubiquitous "Hi" or "Hey" are best used for e-mails, text messages, and social networking sites.

Figure 14-2 presents a traditional, yet brief, cover letter. Use this approach if you are concerned about being too bold in your cover letter, or if you are applying to a highly traditional business firm. Modify any sample letter to fit the particular circumstance and your individuality to avoid making it appear that you are using a template, and therefore not thinking independently.

THE SUCCESSFUL JOB INTERVIEW

A successful job campaign results in one or more employment interviews. Screening interviews are often conducted by phone, particularly for customer service positions requiring telephone skills. An effective way of preparing for a telephone interview is to prepare a thirty-second presentation of yourself including your name, your schooling, job experience, and the type of job you want. Keep working at your presentation until you reduce it to thirty seconds of clear, useful information.

More extensive interviews are usually conducted in person. Being interviewed by one person at a time is still standard practice. Many firms, however, also conduct panel

FIGURE 14-2

A TRADITIONAL COVER LETTER

27 Running Brook Road Baton Rouge, Louisiana 70801 (507) 825-6742 swooden@aol.com
Ms. Melissa Flowers Director of Human Resources Medical Supplies Corporation 7385 South Clinton Avenue New Orleans, Louisiana 70130

Dear Ms. Flowers:

Please accept my application for the position of purchasing assistant, posted on your company Web site, and also in the *Times Picayune,* March 27.

My company, Wentworth Industries, is currently sending its manufacturing operations to Malaysia, and my position will be terminated on April 30. I am strongly interested in being considered a candidate for the position of purchasing assistant. As shown in my résumé, I have the following key qualifications:

- Two years of experience in a purchasing department including one year as an office assistant, and one as a purchasing assistant
- An appropriate academic background with a major in business administration
- Courses in purchasing and inventory management, and computer applications

Thank you for considering my application.

Cordially,

Sara Wooden

Sara Wooden

(or group) interviews in which the job candidates speak to several prospective work associates at the same time. Often the group interview is conducted in a casual environment, such as a restaurant or company cafeteria. The candidate may not be aware that meeting with the group is actually an interview and that he or she is being judged.

A list of key observations about the employment interview follows. A general guide for performing well in a job interview is to present a positive but accurate self-picture. As with the job résumé, there is more written and filmed about the job interview than one person could process in a lifetime.

1. **Practice the job interview, as well as prepare.** Becoming a skillful interviewee requires practice. You can acquire this practice as you go through the job-finding process. In addition, you can rehearse simulated job interviews with friends and other students. Practice answering the questions posed in Figure 14-3. You might also think of several questions you would not like to be asked and develop answers for them. Think through how you have handled difficult job situations, such as dealing with a tight deadline or resolving conflict with a customer, so you can describe these situations during an interview.

   Preparing a video of the practice interviews is especially helpful because it provides feedback on how you presented yourself. In watching the playback, pay particular attention to your spoken and nonverbal communication skills. Then make adjustments as needed. Many colleges of business and career schools require students to be videotaped before they go out on job interviews.

   As is well known, preparing for the interview means knowing relevant facts about the potential employer as gleaned from its Web site, articles about the company, and speaking with anybody you know affiliated with the company. The suggestions made about finding a good person–organization fit is also relevant for interview preparation. Explaining why you are a good fit for the organization, such as when applying for a position with United Airlines describing your love for airplane travel, and how often you and your family have flown United.

FIGURE 14-3
TWELVE QUESTIONS FREQUENTLY ASKED OF JOB CANDIDATES

The following questions are of the same basic type and content encountered in most employment interviews. Practice answering them in front of a friend, camcorder, or mirror.

1. Why did you apply for this job?
2. What are your short-term and long-term goals?
3. What are your strengths?
4. What are your areas for improvement? (Or, what are your weaknesses?)
5. Why should we hire you?
6. What do you know about our firm?
7. Describe how well you work under pressure.
8. Here's a sample job problem. How would you handle it?
9. Why did you leave your last job?
10. What negative information about you is likely to show up when we conduct a background check of you?
11. Why would hiring you make us more profitable (or stay within budget)?
12. What are your accomplishments?
13. Give me an example of a time in which you took the initiative on the job.
14. What is your opinion of your online presence?
15. Do you have any questions?

Note: Questions 7 and 8 are often asked as part of a behavioral interview.

Another useful aspect of preparing for an interview is to inquire as to the most appropriate attire. Professional style dress, such as a suit is usually best, yet some companies prefer that job candidates wear business casual. A word of caution is that even if the CEO wears a hoodie to work, such as at Facebook, you still want to appear more professional at your interview.

2. **Explain how you can help the prospective employer.** Your chances of performing well in a job increase if you are suited for the job. An effective job-getting tactic is to explain to a prospective employer what you think you can do to help the company. Look for opportunities to make **skill-benefit statements**—brief explanations of how your skills can benefit the company. If you were applying for a billing specialist position in a company that you knew was having trouble billing customers correctly, you might make this skill-benefit statement: "Here is how I would apply my skill and experience in setting up billing systems to help develop a billing system with as few glitches as possible." Or you might state that your previous employer had a billing problem and then explain how you helped solve the problem.

   Telling a story about an accomplishment will help explain how you can help the company, and also humanize your presentation. For example, a person applying for a position as a supervisor of collection agents might tell a story about her experiences as a collection agent when she one time rowed a boat out to a person's yacht to talk about a repayment schedule. The accompanying Human Relations in Practice illustrates the use of storytelling during a job interview.

Skill-benefit statements brief explanations of how an individual's skills can benefit the company

3. **Respond well to a behavioral interview.** Another approach to employment interviewing is the **behavioral interview,** in which a candidate is asked how he or she handled a particular problem in the past. Such an interview is essentially a job sample because the interviewee is asked how a previous problem was dealt with. An example of a behavioral interview questions is as follows: "Tell me how you dealt with an angry customer. What was the problem, and what was the outcome?" Behavioral interviews are used frequently because they seem more related to job behavior than

Behavioral interview a candidate is asked how he or she handled a particular problem in the past

Human Relations in Practice

Job Candidate Dion Tells a True Story

Twenty-seven-year-old Dion was conducting a job search to find a position as a project manager on a construction site. He knew that his education and work experience qualified him for such a position despite being younger than most people who aspire to such responsibility. As part of his Internet research, Dion came upon a newspaper article that encouraged readers to create true stories that would give you an edge over the competition. (The article in question is Laura Raines, "Stories Can Power Up Your Career or Job Search," *Atlanta Journal Constitution* (www.ajc.com), December 21, 2011.)

Dion moved past the preliminary screening to obtain an interview for a construction site manager at company that specialized in constructing office buildings. When Dion was asked, "Why should we hire you?" he decided to present the story he created for his job hunt. Dion thought he could back up his story with details of his background after he broke the ice with his story. Dion looked directly at the two interviewers and presented the following anecdote: "Let me share with you how I helped a previous employer out of a mess. I was a construction supervisor on a site that was building a hospital on a tight deadline. If the project didn't come in on time, we would lose about $100,000 in bonus money for having the building completed on time. One day, ten members of our skilled construction team quit en masse because a competitor stole them away by offering much higher hourly pay than my company could afford."

"I told my boss, the project manager, to give me 48 hours to find some really good replacements. One of the people in my network, Miguel, had some key contacts in the Mexican community in town. Working together, we rounded up a bunch of skilled Mexican guys and gals who had either had good construction skills, or were eager to learn. I thought of Miguel because Mexican construction workers have such a great work ethic."

"Within one week, we hired ten replacements, and they all proved to be capable workers. Our company met the deadline for putting up the hospital, and management was very pleased with my recruiting initiative."

Dion did receive the job offer he wanted, and he thinks that his story contributed heavily to his being chosen among several other candidates.

Question: What kind of story could you create to display your credentials, should you be in the job market?

personal characteristics, general interview impressions, or test scores. Of course, this assertion neglects the important fact that a person with strong potential may never have handled the type of job situation presented yet could do so in the future.

4. **Be prepared to discuss your strengths and weaknesses (developmental opportunities).** Most interviewers will ask you to discuss your strengths and developmental opportunities. (These and other frequently asked questions are presented in Figure 14-3.) Knowledge of strengths hints at how good your potential job performance will be. If you deny having areas for improvement, you will appear un-insightful or defensive. When describing your weaknesses, it is helpful to also describe how you overcame

a problem or your action plan for dealing with the problem. For example, "Two people told me that my people skills were not nearly as good as my technical skills. I then invested time and money into strengthening my people skills. I took an interpersonal skills course that really helped me."

Some candidates describe developmental opportunities that could be interpreted as strengths. A case in point: "I have been criticized for expecting too much from myself and others." Do you think this approach is unethical?

5. **Ask a few good questions.** Many interviewers expect the job candidate to ask a few questions that relate to the heart of the job or the nature of the organization. Two such questions are (a) What would I have to accomplish in this position that would make me an outstanding performer? (b) What kind of organizational culture do you have? Having a couple of questions to ask in advance is also helpful because many interviewers ask, "What questions do you have?"

6. **Smooth out rough spots in your background.** Problems and concerns about your background will often be expressed during a job interview, although they will often prevent you from receiving an interview. About 95 percent of employers routinely conduct background investigations of prospective employees. A background investigation by a firm hired for the purpose could include speaking to neighbors and coworkers about your reputation. In addition, the investigator may delve into your driving record, check for criminal charges or convictions, survey your credit record, and find out whether you have had disputes with the government about taxes. Using a candidate's credit record to help make hiring decisions has come under legal challenge, yet is still practiced.[18]

   Any job seeker who has severe negative factors in his or her background cannot readily change the past. Yet the job seeker can receive copies of a credit bureau report to make sure it is fair and accurate. If inaccuracies exist, or certain credit problems have been resolved, the credit report might be changed in the applicant's favor. Or, bring up the negative credit rating during an interview to present your side of the story. Perhaps you had cosigned a loan for a friend who fell behind on his or her payments. It might also be possible to obtain a more favorable reference from an employer by making a polite request.

7. **Be ready for a camcorder interview.** To save time and travel money, some employers are using camcorders to conduct job interviews, or to use such interviews as a screening interview before inviting a candidate to visit the company. Skype is often the technology of choice. If you are interviewed from home take precautions to create a professional setting. Eliminate clutter from view. Decrease or eliminate background noises such as a television set playing, people talking, and traffic sounds heard through an open window. Dress as you would for an in-person interview, and avoid a light shining on your face that would wash out your features. If possible avoid using older technology that provides a weak image or poor audio.

   Steve Langerud, director of professional opportunities, recommends that during a Skype interview you look at the camera, not the screen. Looking at the camera makes it appear that you are looking at the interviewer. It is also important to sit still and not gesture excessively because it can present a distracting picture.[19]

8. **Send a thank-you note.** The thank-you note, whether by e-mail or handwritten, should briefly mention your interest in the position and perhaps reinforce an important point, such as your confidence in your ability to make a contribution. Because so many managers and human resource professionals are inundated with e-mail messages, a hand-written note stands out better. Sending the note within forty-eight hours is recommended and suggests that you are on top of your game.[20] If necessary, follow up again, but avoid being perceived as desperate or as a pest by making repeated follow-ups.

JOB HUNTING DURING DIFFICULT ECONOMIC TIMES

Difficult economic times surface about every ten years, so it is likely that during one of these downturns you will be conducting a job search. During difficult economic times the probability increases that the job seeker will be unemployed. The most important general principle to keep in mind is to be even more conscientious in following standard job-hunting suggestions when jobs are in short supply. You might have to attempt more approaches to finding a job, and the hunt could take longer. Also, be prepared to tolerate frustration because so many people are competing for the same jobs. For example, recruiters at career fairs may appear physically and emotionally exhausted. Five more specific guidelines are presented next.

1. **Go where the jobs are.** When a person is between positions and when times are bad, there are still some jobs available. At times a job seeker may have to be willing to relocate to a more prosperous region to find a job. Another approach is to look for industries that are expanding and to apply for a position within your area of expertise or preference within those industries. At present, skilled workers and professionals will be in high demand in the sciences, technology, businesses, information technology, and healthcare. The term *business* is enormously broad, and specific occupations in demand in the business sector are sales representatives for wholesalers and manufacturers, management information systems specialists, and supply-chain management specialists. Expanding fields within business include automobile manufacturing, food processing, and energy companies (especially oil in North Dakota).[21]
2. **If you have been laid off, get over the emotional hurdle before plunging into the job search.** A reality of conducting a job search during a recession is that the person may have been laid off. Before starting a search for new employment, the person has to overcome the emotional shock of having been laid off—essentially fired. The person should spend about two days ruminating about the problem and describing his or her hurt feelings to friends and family members. The danger of not getting past the emotional shock is that the person will engage in self-pity and bitterness during interviews or contact with network members.[22] People angered about job loss have also been known to write angry blogs that will be perceived negatively by prospective employers and network members who might want to help with the job search.
3. **Minimize defensiveness about having been laid off during a downsizing.** Many job seekers during a business downturn are those who have been laid off because their employer has downsized. Many recruiters and hiring managers recognize that having been laid off is therefore not necessarily related to poor job performance. Consequently, you can make matter-of-fact statements such as, "I am job hunting because our entire unit was downsized due to a drop in business," or "Our CEO decided to eliminate the marketing department as a survival measure."
4. **Intensify your efforts at meeting people face-to-face and maintain a positive attitude.** When fewer jobs are available, personal contact with people who might be able to help you multiplies in value. Perhaps working online can help you arrange a few contacts to meet in person, but spending too much time online can be self-defeating. Although it may be difficult, it is important for the unemployed or underemployed personal to maintain a positive attitude. Network members are more likely to want to help a person with a positive attitude. Of more importance, prospective employers are more likely to hire a candidate with a positive attitude rather than one who appears demoralized and discouraged.
5. **Stay active professionally while unemployed.** Employers are often biased against unemployed workers, particularly when they are not recent graduates. To help counteract this bias it is helpful to engage in some professional-level activities while conducting a job search. Among the possibilities are doing volunteer work in your field, such

as helping poor people complete their income tax forms or helping a small business develop a social media presence. Joining an association in your field, such as the American Marketing Association, indicates you have a professional outlook. Building your own Web site indicates a willingness to apply your communication technology skills, and to be modern. Part-time or temporary work, such as doing a subcontracting project, also indicates a desire to remain professionally active.[23]

6. **Be quite flexible when you do receive an offer.** An unemployed person has very little bargaining power, so do not attempt to negotiate for a higher starting salary or additional benefits when you receive an offer. Instead, perform so well in the new position that higher compensation will be forthcoming.[24]

YOUR ONLINE REPUTATION AND THE JOB SEARCH

A person's online reputation, or online presence, can have a significant impact on the job search. A person's social media postings can have a powerful impact on an employment decision.

It is essential to not have embarrassing information about or photographs of you accessible through search engines. Furthermore unprofessional posts that include many mistakes in grammar and spelling, as well as vulgarities and rants against others can create a negative image.

Negative information about oneself on the Internet can sometimes be removed by asking or hiring a service for such purposes. Many social media posts can be readily removed if you have an account with the Web site. Another aspect of your online reputation is that you might need to distance yourself from others who share your name. If you have a LinkedIn profile, insert a clear photo of yourself. When you send your résumé, by either a hard copy or online, provide a link to your profile.

Another way to learn about what public information exists about you is to place your own name into a couple of search engines. Sometimes another person with the same name as yours—particularly if many people have the same name as you—might have been involved in criminal activity, so be prepared to defend yourself! "Googling" candidates has become standard practice to uncover both positive and negative information about job applicants. Going one step further, many employers search social Web sites like MySpace and Facebook to see if the candidate has engaged in outrageous behavior such as swimming in a public fountain while under the influence of alcohol—and then bragged about the episode on the social media site. Sometimes this negative information can be hidden by adjusting privacy options—if you have the right skill.

What Are Some Effective Career Advancement Strategies and Tactics?

◀ Learning Objective 2 ◀

As you look to advance your career, it is helpful to divide your approach into developing your personal qualities and developing qualities that focus more on your interaction with the environment.

TAKING CONTROL OF YOURSELF

The unifying theme to the strategies, tactics, and attitudes described in this section is that you must attempt to control your own behavior. You can advance your career by harnessing the forces under your control. Such a perspective is important because individuals have the primary responsibility for managing their own careers. Some companies have career development programs, but the individual is still responsible for achieving his or her goals.

Develop Expertise, Passion, and Pride

A starting point in getting ahead is to develop a useful job skill. This tactic is obvious if you are working as a specialist, such as an insurance underwriter. Being skilled at the task performed by the group is also a requirement for being promoted to a supervisory position. After being promoted to a supervisory position or another managerial job, expertise is still important for further advancement. It helps a manager's reputation to be skilled in such things as developing business strategy, social media applications, preparing a budget, and interviewing job candidates.

The subject of expertise has received considerable attention in recent years. Two major conclusions of these studies are that expertise takes a long time to develop and that hard work combined with coaching is more important than raw talent in attaining expertise. *Long time* refers to about ten years in a complex endeavor such as research, writing, music, or charismatic leadership.[25] The hard work should focus on overcoming a specific problem, such as not being able to make presentations.

Although it may take a long time to develop expertise, it does not mean that all people with high levels of expertise are chronologically old. Two unusual examples of people exerting high-level leadership while young are Clara Shih who became a director of Starbucks at age 30, and Vadim Perelman who became a director of Tix and Unilens Vision at age 29.[26]

Although expertise is highly recommended, the workplace also demands that a person perform a variety of tasks such as those required in working on a team. A finance specialist assigned to a product development team would also be expected to know something about marketing, such as how to analyze a marketing survey. A recommended approach is to have depth in your primary field but also have breadth by having several lesser areas of expertise. A widespread example is that no matter what your specialty field, you are also expected to have information technology skills.

Passion goes hand in hand with expertise; it contributes to problem solving and is a major requirement for being an effective leader. It is difficult to sustain expertise if you are not passionate about your specialty field. The phrase "following your passion" often refers to turning a hobby or intense interest into a career, but corporate employees can also be passionate about work. A work-passionate person, for example, would regularly read information about his or her specialty. Developing expertise and being passionate about your work leads naturally to being proud of what you produce. People who take pride in their work are likely to achieve higher quality and a good reputation. From the standpoint of management, proud workers are major contributors because their pride motivates them to excel.

Develop a Code of Professional Ethics

Another solid foundation for developing a career is to establish a personal ethical code. An ethical code determines what behavior is right or wrong, good or bad, based on values. The values stem from cultural upbringing, religious teachings, peer influences, and professional or industry standards. A code of professional ethics helps a worker deal with such issues as accepting bribes, backstabbing coworkers, and sexually harassing a work associate.

Perform Well, Including Going Beyond Your Job Description

Good job performance is the bedrock of a person's career. In rare instances, a person is promoted on the basis of favoritism alone. In all other situations, an employee must have received a favorable performance evaluation to be promoted. Before an employee is promoted, the prospective new boss asks, "How well did this person perform for you?" To be an outstanding performer, it is also necessary to go outside your job description by occasionally taking on tasks not expected of you. Going beyond your job description is part of being a good organizational citizen. During a prolonged business downturn, workers at all levels are likely to work harder, thereby raising the bar on what constitutes good performance. A paralegal who performed well by doing the preparation work for three house closings in one day might now get four accomplished.

Performing well on all your assignments is also important because it contributes to the **success syndrome,** a pattern in which the worker performs one assignment well and then has the confidence to take on an even more difficult assignment. Each new assignment contributes to more self-confidence and more success. As you succeed in new and more challenging assignments, your reputation grows within the firm.

Success syndrome pattern in which the worker performs one assignment well and then has the confidence to take on an even more difficult assignment

Continue to Hone Your Interpersonal Skills

Interpersonal skills, such as those you have been studying in this book, help propel you forward in most careers. To take an extreme example, most people do not think that morticians need good interpersonal skills. But funeral directors insist that an effective mortician must be able to project empathy and compassion without appearing artificial.

Among the many ways in which interpersonal skills help advance your career is to gain you the cooperation of coworkers. A study by Brent A. Scott of Michigan State University and Timothy A. Judge of the University of Florida found that popular workers (those with good interpersonal skills) drew more coworker support regardless of their place on the organization chart.[27] Getting along well with coworkers, in turn, will often facilitate being promoted. Furthermore, building a strong relationship with your boss is essential for advancing your career, as explained in Chapter 9.

Develop a Proactive Personality

If you are an active agent in taking control of the forces around you, you stand a better chance of capitalizing on opportunities. Also, you will seek out opportunities, such as seeing problems that need fixing. A **proactive personality** is a person relatively unconstrained by forces in the situation and who brings about environmental change. Steven Covey classifies proactivity as one of the seven habits of highly successful people because proactive people take responsibility for their own lives, rather than waiting for fate to help them.[28]

Proactive personality characteristic of a person who is relatively unconstrained by forces in a situation and who brings about environmental change; highly proactive people identify opportunities and act on them, showing initiative, and keep trying until they bring about meaningful change

People who are highly proactive identify opportunities and act on them, showing initiative, and keep trying until they bring about meaningful change. Jeffery A. Thompson, a professor of organizational behavior at Brigham Young University, found that one reason proactive personalities perform better is that they develop the social networks they need to help them achieve their goals. For example, the person with a proactive personality would know who to contact for help with a specific business or technical problem.[29]

A health and safety specialist with a proactive personality might identify a health hazard others had missed. He or she would identify the nature of the problem and urge management for funding to control the problem, making use of his or her network. Ultimately, his or her efforts in preventing major health problems would be recognized. Having a proactive personality makes it easier for a person to be a good organizational citizen because such behavior is "built into your DNA." A study conducted with 200 Chinese employees in 54 work groups found that having a proactive personality led to better relationships with the superior. The better relationship then led to more organizational citizenship behavior.[30]

Managers prefer workers with a proactive personality because these workers become proactive employees, or those who take the initiative to take care of problems. Today's employee is supposed to be enterprising. Instead of relying solely on the manager

Human Relations Self-Assessment Quiz 14-3

Tendencies Toward Being a Proactive Personality

Indicate on a 1 to 5 scale the extent of your agreement with the statements below: agree strongly (AS), agree (A), neutral (N), disagree (D), disagree strongly (DS).

Number	Statement	AS	A	N	D	DS
1.	I plan carefully for things that might go wrong.	5	4	3	2	1
2.	I don't worry about problems until after they have taken place.	1	2	3	4	5
3.	If I see something that is broken, I fix it.	5	4	3	2	1
4.	I have been told several times that I am good at taking the initiative.	5	4	3	2	1
5.	I often let things like a computer password expire without making the necessary changes.	1	2	3	4	5
6.	When something important needs doing, I wait for somebody else to take the initiative.	1	2	3	4	5
7.	I think that having a home security system is a good investment in money.	5	4	3	2	1
8.	I look around for good opportunities that would help me in my career or personal life.	5	4	3	2	1
9.	I don't give much thought to the future because there is not much I can do about it.	1	2	3	4	5
10.	It is a good idea to start saving or investing for retirement at the beginning of your career.	5	4	3	2	1

Scoring and Interpretation

Total the numbers corresponding to your answers, and make these probable interpretations:

40–50 You have strong tendencies toward being a proactive personality. Such proactivity should be (or already is) an asset to you in your career and personal life.

28–39 You have about average tendencies toward being proactive. To enhance your success and have more fun in life, you might attempt to become more proactive.

10–27 You have a problem with proactivity. Both your work and personal life would probably be enhanced if you became more proactive.

Source: The idea for this scale and several of its statements stem from Thomas S. Bateman and J. Michael Crant, "The Proactive Component of Organizational Behavior: A Measure and Correlates," *Journal of Organizational Behavior*, March 1993, p. 112.

to figure out what work needs to be accomplished, he or she looks for projects to undertake. It may not be easy to develop a proactive personality, but a person can get started by taking more initiative to fix problems and attempt to be more self-starting.

Human Relations Self-Assessment Quiz 14-3 gives you an opportunity to think about your own tendencies toward having a proactive personality.

Create Good First Impressions and a Favorable Appearance

Each time you interact with a new person inside or outside your company, you create a first impression. Fair or not, these first impressions have a big impact on your career. If your first impression is favorable you will often be invited back by a customer. Your first impression also creates a halo that may influence perceptions about the quality of your work in the future. If your first impression is negative, you will have to work extra hard to be perceived as competent later on.

Looking Successful. Looking successful contributes to a positive first impression. Your clothing, your desk and cubicle or office, and your speech should project the image of a successful, but not necessarily flamboyant, person. Appearing physically fit is also part of the success image. Your standard of dress should be appropriate to your particular career stage and work environment. The best guideline for dressing successfully is to carefully observe the dress code of your firm. Another guideline to consider is to dress for the job you want next, not the job you have now.

Many salespeople and managers today maintain a flexible clothing style by such means as keeping a jacket and extra jewelry in the car or office. When an unanticipated meeting with a customer or some other special occasion arises, a quick modification of clothing style is possible.

Looking successful does not always mean sinking considerable money into clothing and accessories. Many discount stores offer stylish clothing, and physical fitness can be attained without belonging to an athletic club.

Appearing to Be in Control. Projecting a sense of control is another key factor contributing to a positive first impression. Show that you are in control of yourself and the environment and that you can handle job pressures. Avoid letting your body language betray you—fidgeting or rubbing your face sends negative nonverbal messages. Make your gestures project self-assurance and purpose. A verbal method of appearing in control is to make a positive assertion such as, "This is a demanding assignment, and I welcome the challenge."

Tattoos and Body Piercing. Body art in the form of tattoos and piercing often figures into physical appearance. More companies today accept such decorations as a fact of modern culture. Despite this general acceptance of body art, excessive decoration in visible places could be a career deterrent, particularly in more traditional business firms.[31] One of many examples is that the accounting firm KPMG advises their own employees with piercings other than in their ears to "Please leave the metal at home."[32]

Document Your Accomplishments and Be Visible

Keeping an accurate record of your job accomplishments can be valuable when you are being considered for promotion, transfer, or assignment to a team or project. Documenting your accomplishments can also be used to verify new learning. In addition, a record of accomplishments is useful when your performance is being evaluated. You can show your manager what you have done for the company lately. Many professional-level workers maintain a portfolio of their accomplishments, such as samples of work accomplished. The portfolio is much like that used by photographers, artists, and models when applying for a job. Here are two examples of documented accomplishments from different types of jobs:

1. A bank teller suggested that at least one person in the bank should be fluent in American Sign Language to facilitate serving deaf customers. After implementing the idea, the bank attracted many more deaf customers.
2. A maintenance supervisor decreased fuel costs in the office by 27 percent in one year by installing ceiling fans.

After documenting your accomplishments, it pays to advertise, therefore being visible to key people. A key part of being visible is to get others to appreciate your good work.[33] Let key people know in a tasteful way of your tangible accomplishments, and focus on how these accomplishments helped the organization. You might request an opportunity to make a presentation to your boss to review the status of one of your successful projects. Or you could use e-mail for the same purpose if it would be presumptuous for you to request a special meeting to discuss your accomplishments.

Keep Growing through Continuous Learning and Self-Development

Many employers expect employees to keep learning, either through company-sponsored programs or on their own. It is particularly important to engage in new learning in areas of interest to the company, such as developing proficiency in a second language if the company has customers and employees in other countries. Continuous learning can take many forms, including formal schooling, attending training programs and seminars, and self-study. To engage in continuous learning, it is essential to remain open to new viewpoints on your established beliefs. A belief (or stereotype) that has been true for a long time may no longer hold true. A person might think, for example, that almost all workers older than sixty are simply putting in time until they reach the traditional retirement age of sixty-five. In reality, many workers plan to continue to work well into their seventies and eighties.

A useful perspective on continuous learning and self-development is to enhance complementary skills that will enable you to make fuller use of your strengths. A key example is that technical skills can be more effective when communication skills improve, making the person's expertise more apparent and more accessible.[34] With the improved communication skills the tech whiz might be able to better explain his or her ideas to others, leading to better use of knowledge about technology.

Observe Proper Etiquette

Business etiquette
special code of behavior required in work situations

Proper etiquette is important for career advancement because such behavior is considered part of acting professionally. **Business etiquette** is a special code of behavior required in work situations. Both *etiquette* and *manners* refer to behaving in an acceptable and refined way. The steady decline of civility in the workplace has created a renewed interest in the study and practice of business etiquette.[35]

In the digital era, etiquette is just as important as ever because of the new challenges that high-tech devices bring. For example, is it good etiquette to read the information on a coworker's computer screen when visiting his or her cubicle? Or should you multitask when on the phone with your boss or coworker? The globalization of business also creates challenges, such as figuring out when visiting another country whether handshakes are acceptable.

Deciphering what constitutes proper etiquette and business manners requires investigation. One approach is to use successful people as models of behavior and sources of information. Another approach is to consult a current book about business etiquette. The basic rules of etiquette are to make the other person feel comfortable in your presence, be considerate, and strive not to embarrass anyone. Also, be cordial to all, remembering that everyone deserves our respect. Specific guidelines for practicing etiquette stem from these basic rules. Figure 14-4 presents examples of good business etiquette and manners.

FIGURE 14-4 BUSINESS ETIQUETTE AND MANNERS

Following are sixteen specific suggestions about business etiquette and manners that should be considered in the context of a specific job situation. For example, "Make appointments with high-ranking people" is not so relevant in a small, informal company when the company places less emphasis on formality.

1. *Be polite to people in person.* Say "good morning" and "good evening" to work associates at all job levels. Smile frequently. Offer to bring coffee or another beverage for a coworker if you are going outside to get some for yourself. When somebody shakes your hand, stand up instead of remaining in your chair.
2. *Write polite letters and e-mail messages.* An important occasion for practicing good etiquette is the writing of business and personal letters and e-mail messages. Include the person's job title in the inside address and spell the person's name correctly. Use supportive rather than harsh statements. (For example, say "It would be helpful if you could" rather than "You must.") When writing a hard-copy letter, avoid block writing because it is much harsher than indented lines.
3. *Practice good table manners.* Avoid smacking your lips or sucking your fingers. If someone else is paying the bill, do not order the most expensive item on the menu (such as a bottle of very expensive champagne). Offer to cut bread for the other person, and do not look at the check if the other person is paying. A pet peeve of many people is dining with others who chew with their mouths open.

4. *Names should be remembered.* It is good manners and good etiquette to remember the names of work associates, even if you see them only occasionally. If you forget the name of a person, it is better to admit this rather than guessing and coming up with the wrong name. Just say, "I apologize, but I have forgotten your name. Tell me once more, and I will not forget it again."
5. *Men and women should receive equal treatment.* Amenities extended to women by men in a social setting are minimized in business settings. During a meeting, a man is not expected to hold a chair or a door for a woman, nor does he jump to walk on the outside when the two of them are walking down the street. Many women resent being treated differently from men with respect to minor social customs. In general, common courtesies should be extended by both sexes to one another. A handshake and a smile are a better greeting than a kiss on the cheek of the opposite-sex person. Yet if a client or customer initiates the light kiss, it is acceptable to follow suit.
6. *Shouting is out.* Emotional control is an important way of impressing superiors. Following the same principle, shouting in most work situations is said to detract from your image.
7. *The host or hostess pays the bill (and also gives a good tip).* An area of considerable confusion about etiquette surrounds business lunches and who should pay the check—the man or the woman. The rule of etiquette is that the person who extends the invitation pays the bill. After the meal is completed it is good etiquette to leave a tip of 15 percent to 20 percent, and poor etiquette to leave a smaller one.
8. *Introduce the higher-ranking person to the lower-ranking person.* Your boss's name will be mentioned before a coworker's, you introduce the older person to the younger person, and a client is introduced first to coworkers. ("Ms. CEO, I would like you to meet our new custodial assistant.")
9. *Address superiors and visitors in their preferred way.* As the modern business world has become informal, a natural tendency has developed to address people at all levels by their first names. It is safer to first address people by a title and their last names and then wait for them to correct you if they desire. You will probably find that over 90 percent of people want to be addressed by their first name. But important exceptions exist. For example, many Asian executives prefer to be referred to by a title such as Mr., Mrs., Ms., or Dr.
10. *Make appointments with high-ranking people rather than dropping in.* Although the business world has become increasingly informal, it is taboo in most firms for lower-ranking employees to casually drop in to the office of an executive. Use e-mail instead to contact higher-ranking managers directly.
11. *When another person is opening a door to exit a room or building, do not jump in ahead of him or her.* Many people have developed the curious habit of quickly jumping in past another person (moving in the opposite direction) who is exiting. Not only is this practice rude, but it can also lead to an uncomfortable collision.
12. *Minimize annoying, irritating, and interrupting work associates with your cell phone.* It is best to stick with a standard ringtone, rather than a bizarre noise or parts of a song. Do not yell into the phone. In most organizations, it is best to put your phone away during a meeting and turn it off, including vibration mode. Check your phone before the meeting. If you are expecting a medical or another emergency call during the meeting, inform others of your problem before the meeting. Minimize receiving or making phone calls and text messages while talking to a work associate.
13. *Follow company etiquette about using laptop computers during a meeting.* Managers at some companies encourage the use of laptop and tablet computers at meetings because participants can readily take notes and access data that contribute to the meeting. Managers at other companies might find the use of laptop computers during meetings to be rude and discourteous behavior. The major reason is that the laptop user often focuses on matters that are not related to the meeting, such as reading e-mail and doing other work.
14. *Be sensitive to cross-cultural differences in etiquette.* When dealing with people from different cultures, regularly investigate possible major differences in etiquette, as described in Chapters 7 and 13.
15. *Minimize social kissing in an American workplace, but welcome it in Europe.* Kissing in business is generally regarded as rude except among close acquaintances, yet it is more frequent in Europe. However, European kissing amounts to pecks on both cheeks or the top of the hand, never on the lips.
16. *Avoid inappropriate dress.* Several image consultants and office fashion experts regard the following as the most common workplace style sins: "Hooker" earrings (long and dangly); chest hair exposed because of unbuttoned shirt; exposed bra straps; open-toe shoes; and exposed tattoos.

Caution: Although all the above points could have some bearing on the image you project, violation of any one of them would not necessarily have a negative impact on your career. It is the overall image you project that counts the most. Therefore, the general principle of being considerate of work associates is much more important than any one act of etiquette or manners.

Sources: Jim Rucker and Jean Anna Sellers, "Changes in Business Etiquette," *Business Education Forum,* February 1998, p. 45; Andrea Sachs, "Learn How to Behave," *Time,* August 2005, p. A5; Dean Hachamovitch, "Minding the Meeting, or Your Computer?" *New York Times* (www.nytimes.com), August 26, 2007; Louise Lee, "Cell? Well . . . Use Your Phone for Good, Not Evil," *Business Week Small Biz,* February/March 2009, p. 22; Peggy Post, "A Recession Etiquette, " *Time,* January 26, 2009, p. 55; "The Top Five Office Fashion Faux Pas," *Bloomberg Businessweek,* October 11–October 17, 2010, p. 95.

Develop Your Personal Brand

Personal brand your distinctive set of strengths, including skills and values

Another important component of career development is to develop your **personal brand,** or your distinctive set of strengths, including skills and values. (Your expertise usually represents your distinctive set of strengths.) Your personal brand makes you unique, thereby distinguishing you from the competition. Although the analogy of each person becoming a recognizable brand name, such as Nike or Tiffany, is far-fetched, the idea of becoming a trusted person of value is sound. Your identity as shown on the Internet, including on social networking sites or your personal blog, is also part of your personal brand. Digital media present a good opportunity for explaining who you are.[36] A common practice is to provide a link on a Twitter account that has a one-paragraph summary of your identity. A major value that contributes to your brand is your consistency, because an employer wants employees to consistently deliver results.

Your personal brand will be more effective if it is authentic in the sense of accurately reflecting who you are. You might add a little drama to your strengths, but the strengths should still be true. For example, if Mike regularly volunteers to feed people at a mission for the homeless, he might describe himself as having "enduring humanitarian values." Yet it would be a stretch for him to say he is "committed to ending world hunger." Notice that Mike's personal brand would include a deep concern for human welfare.

You begin developing your personal brand by identifying the qualities or characteristics that distinguish you from coworkers. What have you done recently to make you stand out? What benefits do you offer? Do you deliver high-quality work on time? Are you a creative problem solver? Next, you would make yourself visible so you can cash in your uniqueness (your brand). Almost all the ideas in this chapter will help you develop your personal brand. Three useful questions to ask in formulating your personal brand are as follows:[37]

- What am I passionate about—what do I really love?
- What are my greatest strengths?
- How can I use my strengths to fuel my passion?

Developing a personal brand statement requires considerable work and might require some professional coaching. Here is the personal brand statement Mike developed:

> I am a hard-hitting package of strengths who can be a real asset to an employer. Few people combine superb analytical, information technology, and people skills the way I do. The help I give the homeless shows that I really care about the welfare of others. In school, as well as on the job, I have established a record of high performance and dependability.

EXERTING CONTROL OVER THE OUTSIDE WORLD

In this section we emphasize approaches that require you to exert some control over the outside environment. If you do not control it, at least you can try to juggle it to your advantage. For example, the "Find a Mentor" section suggests that you search out a friendly and supportive person in your field who can help you advance in your career.

Develop Career Goals

Career path sequence of positions necessary to achieve a goal

Planning your career inevitably involves some form of goal setting. Your career goals should have the same characteristics as other goals, as described in Chapter 3. Because organizations change so frequently, along with positions, today it may be better to establish general goals that focus on the type of work you want to do in the future. For example, "Within five years I plan to be leading a group of people toward improving the supply-chain management in a business firm,

Before establishing career goals, it is helpful to clarify your values, as described in Chapter 5. These are probably the same values that enabled you to choose a career in the first place. While sketching out a career, you should also list your personal goals. They should mesh with your work plans to help avoid major conflicts in your life. Some lifestyles, for example, are incompatible with some career goals. You might find it difficult to develop a stable home life (spouse, children, friends, community activities, garden) if you aspire to hold a field position in international marketing.

Most career goals should include an approximate time element, which is crucial to sound career management. Your long-range goal might be clearly established in your mind (such as owner and operator of a health spa). At the same time you must establish short-range goals (get any kind of job in health spa) and intermediate-range goals. Goals set too far in the future that are not supported with more immediate goals may lose their motivational value.

Achieve Broad Experience

Most people who land high-ranking positions usually have broad experience. Therefore, a widely accepted strategy for advancing in responsibility is to strengthen your credentials by broadening your experience. It is best to achieve breadth early in your career because it is easier to transfer when an individual's compensation is not too high. Broadening can come about by performing a variety of jobs or sometimes by performing essentially the same job in different organizations. You can also achieve breadth by working on committees and special assignments.

Breadth can also be attained through self-nomination. Have the courage and assertiveness to ask for a promotion or a transfer. Your manager or team leader may not know that you are actually seeking more responsibility. An effective method of convincing him or her is to volunteer for specific job openings or for challenging assignments. A boss may need convincing because many more people will be seeking advancement than are actually willing to handle more responsibility.

A major benefit of broad experience is that you achieve more career portability, allowing you to move to another employer should the need exist. The employability derives from being a more flexible person with a broader perspective. For example, a person who has worked in both the underwriting (setting rates for risks) and the claims aspects of insurance would be well regarded by insurance companies.

Tony Bates, now the president of the Skype division of Microsoft Corp., illustrates how breadth of experience can help position a person for a major job. Before being recruited by Skype, Bates was in charge of the enterprise, commercial and small-business division of Cisco Systems. By age 43, he had extensive experience in managing technology and operations (such as manufacturing).[38]

Find a Mentor

The vast majority of successful people have had one or more mentors during their careers. A **mentor** is a more experienced person who guides, teaches, and coaches another individual. In years past, mentors were almost always higher-ranking people. Today mentors can be peers and even lower-ranking individuals. A lower-ranking individual, for example, can educate you on how other parts of the organization work—something you may need to know to advance. Being mentored by a young person, usually for purposes of learning new technology, is often referred to as *reverse mentoring.* Under a **buddy system,** the company assigns a new employee a coworker who looks out for his or her welfare, such as explaining company etiquette.[39] The buddy acts somewhat like a mentor, yet the relationship with the buddy may be for a shorter term.

Mentor
a more experienced person who guides, teaches, and coaches another individual

Buddy system
the company assigns a new employee a coworker who looks out for his or her welfare, such as explaining company etiquette

Many organizations assign a mentor to a company newcomer, yet you might want to supplement company-assigned mentoring with a mentor you find on your own. It is particularly helpful to find a mentor who has the skills or characteristics you would like to develop.[40] For example, if you think that you need to develop your charisma, attempt to find a charismatic mentor. Sometimes you are able to develop a mentor from the contacts you make on the Internet. After the person becomes your mentor, much of the mentoring can take place through e-mail and messaging. (Busier mentors may prefer e-mail and text messages because they can respond at their leisure.) E-mentoring will sometimes increase the pool of potential mentors and allow relationships to develop without social bias, such as people being suspicious of the nature of a mentoring relationship between a middle-age man and a young woman.[41]

A recent development in e-mentoring is to provide frequent, brief feedback to workers being mentored in a Twitter-like format. The brief, frequent, electronic feedback fits the preferences of millennials who want constant feedback and information on their career progress, explains Susan Hutt, an executive at a Toronto software company. An example, "Hey, it's Joe your manager. Ask for more feedback from other members of your team."[42]

Mentorship is an important development process in many occupations: master–apprentice, physician–intern, teacher–student, and executive–junior executive. An emotional tie exists between the less experienced person (the protégé) and the mentor. The mentor serves as a positive model and a trusted friend. A mentor can also offer candid advice, not otherwise available.

A variation of traditional one-on-one mentoring is to establish a group of mentors who might help you with different types of problems. Having multiple mentors is often necessary because an individual mentor may not have all the skills, or time, to provide all the guidance you need. One mentor might be quite good at helping you deal with human relations problems, another with communication technology problems, and another with the financial aspects of your job. Having multiple mentors is asking to have a personal board of directors, or a small group of people who serve as your advisers.[43]

In return, the person being mentored expresses appreciation, gives positive feedback to the mentor, and shares victories. It is also important to offer a concrete service in return for the mentor's advice. Possibilities include offering to collect information, prepare computer graphics, or run a few errands. Many mentors believe that they have much to learn from their protégés. Finding a mentor involves the same process as networking. You might ask people in your network if they could think of a possible mentor for you. With e-mentoring, geographic distance does not create a substantial barrier. With any prospective mentor, it is best to begin gradually by asking for some advice and then see how the relationship develops.

Deal Constructively with Having a Subordinate Older Than You or a Younger Boss

In the modern workplace, chronological age does not govern who is likely to be the subordinate or the boss. Two challenges that must be dealt with effectively to help advance one's career are dealing with a subordinate older than you or having a boss younger than you.

Older Subordinate. A tricky workplace issue is developing a constructive relationship with a subordinate considerably older than you. An effective starting point in building the relationship is to show respect for the subordinate's experience and wisdom. Ask for his or her input based on experience, but avoid phrases such as, "As an old-timer, you must know . . ." Listening carefully to the older subordinate will help develop a good working relationship.

If the subordinate brings up the problem of age differences, point out that the company appointed you to the position of administrative boss despite the age difference and that you did not create the situation. Working to create teamwork, as described in Chapter 12, will help break down age barriers because the focus will be on team accomplishment rather than a boss–subordinate rivalry. Include the older subordinate when asking for input about topics often thought to be of more interest to younger workers, such as communication technology.[44]

Younger Boss. Many workers face an ego problem when reporting to a person younger in age, even if the age difference is slight. A starting point in building a constructive relationship is to recognize that having a younger boss is part of the modern world, just like having a doctor or lawyer younger than you. Do not assume that because your boss is younger, he or she is not qualified for the position. Take the initiative to communicate frequently with your boss in an open way that focuses on work issues rather than the age difference. Communicate with your boss as readily as you would with a boss older than you, and you will quickly break down communication barriers.

Look for the learning opportunities that working for a younger boss might bring, such as new ideas based on his or her recent education and fascination with technology. Express your interest in learning new technologies and business processes. Perhaps the younger boss can help you bring other young people into your network, thereby expanding your learning opportunities. Take the opportunity to show that you embrace change, because the negative stereotype about older workers is that they resist change. Unless absolutely necessary, avoid statements such as, "We tried that in the past, and it won't work." Show that you are willing to challenge the status quo by making statements such as, "So far our process has worked, but maybe it can work better if we make some changes."

Express enthusiasm for being part of the team, because the majority of younger bosses believe that teamwork is a major contributor to success. But be willing to express disagreement, but in a diplomatic, collaborative way. A quick way to irritate a younger boss is for you to act in the role of a finger-wagging parent.[45]

Balance Your Life

Balancing your life among the competing demands of work, social life, and personal interests can help you advance your career. Having balance gives you additional energy and vitality that will help you in your career. Having something exciting to look forward to outside of work can sometimes provide a spark that will help you perform well. Also, outside interests, including raising a family, are expensive, giving you another incentive to be an outstanding performer.

Without balance, a career person runs the risk of burnout and feeling that work is not worthwhile. The late Stephen Covey wrote, "Always being the last to leave the office does not make you an indispensable employee. In fact, those who work long hours for extended periods are prone to burnout. The trick is to have your priorities clear, honor your commitments, and keep a balance in life."[46]

Developing Your Networking Skills

Learning Objective 3

As a career advancement tactic, networking serves several purposes. The contacts you establish can offer you a promotion, help you find a better position, become a customer, become a valuable supplier, help you solve difficult problems, or find a mentor. People in your network can also offer you emotional support during periods of adversity.

A recommended approach to networking is to keep a list of at least twenty-five people whom you contact at least once a month. The contact can be as extensive as a luncheon meeting or as brief as an e-mail or text message. Many networkers use social media to both develop and maintain contacts. The starting point in networking is to obtain an ample supply of business cards, and introduce yourself to as many potentially valuable network members as feasible. Some small business owners spend a lot of time in airports and on airplanes primarily for the purpose of developing contacts. You then give a card to any person you meet who might be able to help you now or in the future.

While first developing your network, be inclusive. Later, as your network develops, you can strive to include a greater number of influential and successful people. People in your network can include relatives, classmates, and people you meet while traveling, vacationing, or attending trade shows. Develop both depth and breadth to your network, meaning that some of your network members are truly friends and valuable contacts, whereby others are you know less well and may be able to help you only occasionally. At times you can tap into the networks of your network members, thereby multiplying your own network. However, not everybody wants to give out the names in their network.

Community activities and religious organizations can also be a source of contacts. Golf is still considered the number one sport for networking because of the high-level contacts the sport generates. The range of potential people in your network is much greater over the Internet than if networking is done locally and in person. Some of the people in these groups can become valuable business contacts, although many relationships with your "friends" or "followers" are weak associations. Online networking includes newsgroups, mailing lists, chat rooms, and e-mail. Figure 14-5 offers some additional networking suggestions, and Exercise 14-1 provides a worksheet for networking.

FIGURE 14-5
NETWORKING SUGGESTIONS

The following networking suggestions are gathered from a number of career counselors and business writers. Select and choose from among the list those ideas that appear to best fit your personality and circumstances.

- *Expand and diversify your network.* Everyone you come in contact with is a potential resource to help you in your career. Even someone whose sole purpose is to cheer you on during downturns can be a valuable ally. Keep filling your network with new contacts, because older contacts may fade away. Retired people who have had successful careers can be a valuable source of contacts, and they typically enjoy assisting people at earlier stages in their careers.
- *Add value as well while asking for assistance.* Consider how you can help the other person, and listen as much as talk.
- *When networking by e-mail, include your telephone number and address.* The other person may want to contact you by means other than an e-mail. Don't give up—e-mail messages may get deleted by accident or disappear because of technical problems.
- *Join groups whose purpose and members fit your field of interest*, such as groups of accountants, health-care professionals, or automobile and truck dealers.
- *When approaching someone to be part of your network, explain how you received his or her name,* or refresh the person's mind as to how you met previously.
- *If you attend a formal networking event (such as a professional meeting), "work the room."* Engage in professional conversations with as many people as feasible. Being the first to say "hello" can pay dividends. Greet people with a smile and a firm handshake, and deliver a twenty-five-word or so self-introduction. In the introduction explain who you are, what you do, and how you can be helpful.
- *Create good relationships with your peers and fellow students.* Some of them may occupy influential positions in the future.
- *Strive to develop a personal relationship with at least two people at higher levels in your place of work.* Keep these people informed of what you are doing, and ask for their advice.
- *Be memorable for positive reasons.* Making a lasting positive impression is a promising way of keeping a network alive.

- *When you have a change of status, such as accepting a new position, notify network members.* Notify everyone when your contact information changes, and monitor your contacts to keep their information current. Social networking sites are particularly useful for this task.
- *Pursue further possible network members you encounter on social networking Web sites.* Having a "follower" or a "friend" on such a site does not necessarily mean that he or she is a valuable professional contact. Especially with LinkedIn, communicate with people you know. Do not send invitations to people who do not know you. LinkedIn is supposed to be a vehicle for strengthening relationships with people you already know. (Also, LinkedIn members are typically busy professionals.)

Sources: Anita Bruzzese, "Restrain Yourself and Think When Networking by E-Mail," *Gannett News Service,* June 30, 2003; Heather Huhman, "Getting the Net Worth Out of Your Network," *San Francisco Examiner* (www.examiner.com), December 22, 2008; Julia Angwin, "How to Twitter," *The Wall Street Journal,* March 7–9, 2009, p. W3; Niala Boodhoo and Bridget Carey, "LinkedIn CEO Shares Advice on Social Network, Careers," *Miami Herald* (www.miamiherald.com), May 12, 2009; Tina Smagala, "Tips to Improve In-Person Networking," *Democrat and Chronicle Business,* May 10, 2011, p. 5B; Chris Brogan, "The Network Is Everything," *Entrepreneur,* October 2010, p. 36.

Networking is obviously beneficial in a field such as direct selling, in which you contact people you know to purchase your goods or services. For example, if you sell products such as financial services, Avon, or Tupperware, you are expected to capitalize on personal contacts. Almost any successful businessperson you meet uses networking, at least to some extent. A study conducted in Germany over a three-year period with over 200 workers in several fields demonstrates that networking really does enhance career success. Networking was shown to enhance current salary as well as growth of salary over time. Furthermore, workers who engaged in more networking had higher job satisfaction. The researchers concluded that networking has a good return on investment.[46] We caution again to be selective about your networking. Overreliance on networking, such as contacting people who probably have no interest in hearing from you, can be annoying to the recipient.

Key Terms

Person–organization fit, 415
Networking, 416
Keywords, 420
Skill-benefit statements, 423
Behavioral interview, 423
Success syndrome, 429
Proactive personality, 429
Business etiquette, 432
Personal brand, 434
Career path, 434
Mentor, 435
Buddy system, 435

Summary and Review

Major components of the job search are as follows:

- Target your job search including a reasonably flexible statement of the type of job you are seeking (your job objective). Knowing what type of organization you would prefer to work for will help focus your job search.
- Be aware of the qualifications employers are seeking.
- Finding jobs through networking and the Internet. The most effective method of finding a job is through personal contacts, or networking. Getting someone on the inside to recommend you for a job is the best way to reach the internal job market. Job hunting on the Internet can be done through social networking sites, job boards, company Web sites, and direct entry into a search engine of the job you are seeking. Despite using the Internet, it is important to speak to a person to conduct your job search.
- Preparing an effective job résumé. The major purpose of a résumé is to market yourself to a prospective employer. Effective résumés are straightforward, factual presentations of a person's experiences, skills, and accomplishments. Avoid making untrue statements on your résumé. There is no one best way to prepare a résumé, but keywords are important, and so is customizing your résumé for a specific position. A résumé should include a section about your job-related skills and accomplishments.
- A cover letter should accompany the résumé, and should explain who you are and why you are applying for a particular position.
- The successful job interview includes various tactics, including practice and preparation, explaining how you can help the employer, and responding well to a behavioral interview. Also, be prepared to discuss your strengths and weaknesses, ask a few questions, and smooth out rough spots in your background, and be ready for a camcorder interview.
- Job hunting during difficult economic times includes such considerations as (a) going where the jobs are, (b) getting over the emotional hurdle of having been laid off, (c) minimizing defensiveness about having been laid off, (d) intensifying your efforts at meeting people face-to-face, (e) staying active professionally while unemployed, and (f) being quite flexible when you do receive an offer.
- Your online reputation is important for the job search.

One set of strategies and tactics for getting ahead can be classified as taking control of your own behavior. Included are these approaches:

- Develop expertise, passion, and pride.
- Develop a code of professional ethics.
- Perform well, including going beyond your job description.
- Develop a proactive personality.
- Create good first impressions and a favorable appearance.
- Document your accomplishments.
- Keep growing through continuous learning and self-development.
- Observe proper etiquette.
- Develop your personal brand.

Another set of strategies and tactics for career advancement centers on taking control of your environment, or at least adapting it to your advantage. Included are the following:

- Develop career goals.
- Achieve broad experience.
- Find a mentor (also use the buddy system if offered by the company).
- Deal constructively with having a subordinate older than you or a younger boss.
- Balance your life.

Developing networking skills is a major career advancement tactic that can help you find a new position, become a customer, become a valuable supplier, solve difficult problems, find a mentor, and receive emotional support. Keep a list of at least twenty-five people whom you contact monthly. With mentors, add value while asking for assistance. Social networking sites can be useful in building your network.

Check Your Understanding

1. During times when there is a shortage of skilled workers, why is it still important to study how to conduct a job campaign?
2. What do you think might be the reason that many job applicants find it so difficult to put away their cell phones during a job interview?
3. What can you do today to help you develop a contact that could someday lead to a job?
4. Make up a behavioral interview question that you might be asked, and develop a good answer.
5. Bill Gates and the late Steve Jobs dropped out of college, so why does completing your degree enhance your chances for career success?
6. Which expertise would you like to have that would probably take ten years to develop?
7. What is the most important fact about you that is already in, or should be in, your personal brand?
8. If you were a *reverse mentor,* what kind of help do you think you could offer a mentor much chronologically older than you?
9. How might a person go about networking for career advancement in an airport or on an airplane?
10. Which criteria are you using, or will you use, to know if your career is successful?

Web Corner

Personal brand building
www.personalbrandcoaching.com

Career advice, including job search and salaries
www.vault.com.

***Career advancement suggestions from* The Wall Street Journal**
www.careerjournal.com.

Find a mentor
www.advancementoring.com

INTERNET SKILL BUILDER

So many job boards exist on the Internet that conducting an Internet-based job search can be baffling. A direct approach is to visit Monster+Hot Jobs (on the front page of www.yahoo.com) and enter three specific job titles of interest to you. You will be directed to lots of job opportunities closely matching the job titles you entered. It may be helpful to enter variations of the same job title, such as both "administrative assistant" and "executive assistant." Your assignment is to identify five jobs for which you appear to be qualified. Even if you have no interest in conducting a job search, it is informative to be aware of job opportunities in your field. Seek answers to the following questions:

1. Do I appear to have the qualifications for the type of job I am seeking?
2. Is there a particular geographic area where the job or jobs I want are available?
3. How good are opportunities in my chosen field?

Developing Your Human Relations Skills

Human Relations Application Exercises

Applying Human Relations Exercise 14-1

Building Your Network

Networking can be regarded as the process of building a team that works with you to achieve success. You can start the following exercise now, but it will probably take your entire career to implement it completely. To start networking or make your present networking more systematic, take the following steps:

Step 1: Jot down your top three goals or objectives for the following three months, such as obtaining a new job or promotion, starting a small business, or doing a field research study.

1. ______________________________
____

2. ______________________________
____

3. ______________________________
____

Step 2: List family members, friends, and acquaintances who could assist you in meeting your goals or objectives. Prepare a contact card or database entry for each person on your list, including as many details as you can about the person and the person's family, friends, employers, and contacts. Include in your contacts members of your online network, assuming they are more than people who do not really know you but simply list you as a "friend" or "favorite."

Step 3: Identify what assistance you will request of your contact or contacts. Be realistic in light of your prior investment in the relationship. Remember, you have to be a friend to have a friend.

Step 4: Identify how you will meet your contact or contacts during the next month. Could it be for lunch or at an athletic field, nightclub, sports club, recreational facility on campus, cafeteria, and so forth? Learn more about your contacts during your face-to-face meetings. In some cases you may have to use the telephone or e-mail to substitute for an in-person meeting. Look for ways to mutually benefit from the relationship. At the beginning of each week, verify that you have made a small investment in building these relationships.

Step 5: Ask for the help you need. A network must benefit you. Thank the contact for any help given. Jot down on your planner a reminder to make a follow-up call, letter, or e-mail message to your contacts. In this way, you will have less work to do before you make another request for help.

Step 6: For each person in your network, think of a favor, however small, that you can return to him or her. Without reciprocity, a network fades rapidly.

Applying Human Relations Exercise 14-2

Strategies and Action Plans for Career Success

If implemented effectively, the activity described next could bring you enormous career satisfaction and success even if you have already made progress in your career. The activity lists the strategies and tactics presented in this chapter, along with a space for an action plan to accompany the strategy or tactic. Choose about six of the strategies and tactics you think will be the most useful for you, and sketch the basics of the action plan you intend to use to implement the strategy or tactic. Here is an example: Suppose you choose the strategy "Develop a Proactive Personality." Your action plan might be, "Will stay on the alert for opportunities to take the initiative. Will look for potential problems, and then recommend solutions to my boss."

Number	Career Strategy or Tactic	Action Plan to Implement Strategy or Tactic
1.	Develop expertise, passion, and pride	
2.	Develop a code of professional ethics	
3.	Perform well, including going beyond your job description	
4.	Continue to hone your interpersonal skills	
5.	Develop a proactive personality	
6.	Create good first impressions and a favorable appearance	
7.	Document your accomplishments and be visible	
8.	Keep growing through continuous learning and self-development	
9.	Observe proper etiquette	
10.	Develop your personal brand	
11.	Establish career goals	
12.	Find a mentor	
13.	Deal constructively with having a subordinate older than you or a younger boss	
14.	Balance your life	
15.	Develop your networking skills	

Human Relations Class Activity

Overcoming Barriers to Career Success

To assist in achieving your career goals, answer the following questions. Keep in mind, however, that you might want to confine your answers to information that you would be willing to share with fellow students:

1. What is the biggest potential barrier to my career success?
2. How do I plan to overcome or deal with this barrier?

Possible answers to these two questions are almost unlimited, yet here is a sample answer: "My biggest barrier to career success is that I want to become a certified financial planner, but I don't have a big enough family or network of friends to develop a client base. My plan is to get started networking now, including becoming much more active in online networking."

Each class member, or a group of volunteers, will address the class one by one with answers to the two questions. Perhaps answers to the questions can be distributed electronically to all class members before the day of presentations. After the presentations, hold a brief class discussion about (a) the barriers most commonly cited and (b) the most likely effectiveness of the plans for overcoming the barriers.

Human Relations Role-Playing Exercise

Cheryl Seeks a Mentor

Marketing assistant Cheryl works for a large pharmaceutical company. She would like to advance her career, perhaps someday becoming a marketing executive. Cheryl has read and heard frequently that one of the best ways to advance one's career in a large company is to find a successful mentor, but the company she works for does not have a formal mentoring program. Cheryl therefore decides to find a mentor on her own. She sends an e-mail to Meg Aspen, the director of marketing for health products (such as vitamins and food supplements), wanting to know if Meg would be interested in becoming her mentor. Already overloaded with work, Aspen responds that she will give Cheryl a fifteen-minute interview next Thursday at 4:45 p.m. to discuss her request.

One student plays the role of eager Cheryl, who wants to make a good connection with Meg immediately. Another student plays the role of Meg Aspen, who is not thrilled about taking on additional responsibility, but she wants to be at least a little helpful. Run the role-play for about eight minutes.

Observers rate the role-players on two dimensions, using a 1 to 5 scale from very poor to very good. One dimension is "effective use of human relations techniques." For Cheryl, focus on how well she projects a genuine interest in learning from a mentor. The second dimension is "acting ability." A few observers might voluntarily provide feedback to the role-players in terms of sharing their ratings and observations. The course instructor might also provide feedback.

Human Relations Class Study 14-1

Pamela Develops a Brand Called Pam Peters

Pamela is doing well in her career as a hotel front office manager. Among her varied duties are greeting hotel guests, handling customer service and complaints, and scheduling housekeeping and the custodial staff. Pamela began working in the hotel field as a high school student when an uncle helped her obtain a position on the wait staff of a local Hilton Hotel. While attending career school, Pamela had worked her way up to an assistant manager at a Holiday Inn Express.

Pamela believes that she has the potential to advance into the executive ranks of a big hotel chain. She is so earnest about advancing in her career that she attended a two-day workshop about building a personal brand. Inspired by what she heard, and the written instructions she received, Pamela decided to build a personal brand. The workshop leader, Baxter, told Pamela, "Pam Peters, you are unique, and almost a brand already. Just look at some of your assets. Your education is fine, your work experience is terrific, and as a six foot-tall woman, you certainly do stand out."

That evening Pamela began working on her brand statement on her laptop, and uploaded into her smart phone so she could tweak it a bit during the day, when so inspired during breaks from her manager position at the hotel. The fifth version of Pamela's brand statement read as follows:

Pam Peters is a total package. She is super-skilled, six feet tall, with a winning smile backed up by an engaging warm personality. Got a hotel problem? Who else are you going to call but the dynamic Pam Peters who will jump on the problem with wisdom, experience, and outstanding problem solving ability? She can convert angry customers into loyal customers, and disgruntled hotel employees into superior performers.

Pam can inspire the housekeeping staff into cleaning windows and she is an expert in Windows. Pam is up to date on the latest in communication technology, and she will always be an early user on the next hot technology. Pam Peters is the person to lead your workers to higher levels of teamwork, and your hotel to higher profitability.

Questions

1. What is your evaluation of the effectiveness of Pamela's personal brand statement?
2. What suggestions might you offer to Pamela to improve her brand statement?
3. To what extent do you think Pamela should even bother having a personal brand?

Human Relations Role-Playing Exercise

The HR Manager Reviews "The Brand Called Pam Peters"

Pamela, described earlier, has an opportunity to meet with the corporate HR (human resources) manager Luke Watkins to discuss her career at the hotel. One student plays the role of Pamela, who about five minutes into the interview, requests that the HR manager visit her Web site to read her brand statement. Another student plays the role of Luke, who being a bit traditional is lukewarm toward the idea of a professional person presenting herself as a brand. Pamela is so excited about her personal brand statement, but she quickly learns that she will have to convince Luke of its relevance.

Run the role play for about seven minutes, and observers will note if Pam is making any progress in using her brand statement to sell her credentials for promotion to Luke Watkins.

Human Relations Class Study 14-2

Jim Works the Airports and the Flights

Jim is a co-owner of a firm that supplies tech support to companies that are either not big enough to have their own tech support staff or choose to outsource all or part of such support. As Jim sees it, his number of potential customers is almost unlimited. In addition to being on the lookout for new customers, Jim says, "If the right job offer came along, I might sell my half of the firm to my partner and collect a great salary for the foreseeable future."

Several years ago, Jim developed a few contacts during a seven-hour layover at Chicago O'Hare Airport who shortly thereafter became major customers. His early good luck at the airport in developing contacts gave him the idea of visiting airports and taking flights purposely for business development, and perhaps finding the ideal job.

Jim searches a few travel Web sites to find low-price flights to major cities. When he can fly business class at a reasonable price, Jim dresses in his best business attire and carries a luxurious briefcase and a flashy BlackBerry. He also carries dozens of impressive-looking business cards. Jim arrives a few hours before flight time and then clears the security gate. He believes that the best contacts are made in the seating areas near the boarding gates. In Jim's words, "You get the serious types near the gates. Even the restaurants and bars near the gates are a better source of contacts than the areas outside the security area."

When Jim spots a person who looks prosperous seated near the boarding gate, he looks to sit down near the person. If his prospect is on the cell phone or reading a newspaper, Jim waits for a logical pause before making his approach. One of his most effective approaches is to smile and then say, "Hi, I'm Jim Baxter, and my firm does tech support. I sure hope the flight leaves on time." If the stranger shows no interest in starting a conversation, Jim tries another attempt a few minutes later. If still no interest on the stranger's part, Jim gets up from his seat, and says, "Have a nice flight."

During a flight, Jim approaches only a person seated next to him. With a flight of even one hour, Jim has plenty of time to make a soft sales pitch or discuss possible job openings in tech-support management at the prospect's firm.

Jim notes that his approach to developing contacts and new business is much less expensive than advertising in trade magazines or on Web sites. "And besides," he says, "my method is much more personal."

Questions

1. What is your evaluation of the effectiveness of using airports and flights as a method of prospecting for customers and a possible new position?
2. What is your evaluation of the ethics of Jim's approach to developing customers and looking for a new position?
3. How would you react to Jim if he approached you while you were seated next to him in flight or in the waiting area?

REFERENCES

1. Original story created from facts and observations reported in the following sources: Beth Kowitt, "Linda Hudson, Tips for Climbing the Corporate Ladder," *Fortune,* March 21, 2011, p. 42; "Remarks by Linda P. Hudson, CEO, BAE Systems, NCMA World Congress, Denver, Colorado, July 11, 2011," www.aia-aerospeace.org; Adam Bryant, "Fitting In, and Rising to the Top," *The New York Times* (www.nytimes.com), September 19, 2009, pp. 1–5; "Linda Hudson," *Our People-BAE Systems* (www.baesystems.com), accessed March 14, 2012.
2. Amy L. Kristof-Brown, Ryan D. Zimmerman, and Erin C. Johnson, "Consequences of Individuals' Fit at Work: A Meta-Analysis of Person–Job, Person–Organization, Person–Group, and Person–Supervisor Fit," *Personnel Psychology,* Summer 2005, p. 310.
3. Survey cited in Toddi Gutner, "Dealing With Job Search When You Least Expect It," *The Wall Street Journal,* September 16, 2008, p. D6.
4. "Why the Job Search Is Like 'Throwing Paper Airplanes Into the Galaxy'," *Knowledge@Wharton* (http://knowledge.wharton.upenn.edu), February 20, 2011, p. 4.
5. Alina Tugend, "When Job Hunting, Be Your Own Salesman," *New York Times* (www.nytimes.com), October 11, 2008, p. 2.
6. Joe Light, "Recruiters Troll Facebook for Candidates They Like," *The Wall Street Journal,* August 8, 2011, p. B8.
7. Tira Pyrillis, "The Bait Debate," *Workforce Management,* February 2011, p. 19.
8. Quoted in Deborah Silver, "Niche Sites Gain Monster-Sized Following," *Workforce Management,* March 2011, p. 10.
9. Sarah E. Needleman, "Recruiters Use Search Engines to Lure Job Hunters," *The Wall Street Journal,* March 9, 2009, p. B4.
10. Quoted in Kaitlin Madden, "Job Search Tactics That Still Work: Face-to-Face Networking, Mentors Prove Effective," *Career Builder,* December 18, 2011, p.2F.
11. Survey reported in Tiffany Hau, "Crafting a Résumé That Will Grab Recruiters," *Los Angeles Times* (www.latimes.com), March 29, 2009.
12. Kelly Eggers, "The Ten Worst Things to Put on Your Résumé," *FINS Finance* (www.fins.com), March 16, 2011, p. 4.
13. Laura Smith-Proulx, "Who (or What) Is Really Reading Your Résumé—and Why Should You Care?" *San Francisco Examiner* (www.examiner.com), March 17, 2009.
14. Beth Braccio Hering, "Words to Use, Lose On Résumé," *Career Builder,* June 26, 2011; Diane Stafford, "Take These Buzzwords Off Your '12 Résumé," *McClatchy Newspapers,* December 26, 2011, p. 1.
15. Quoted in Anthony Balderrama, "Create a Semi-Reusable Résumé: Simplify the Job Application Process," *Career Builder,* September 11, 2011.
16. Cited in Lauren Weber, "Your Résumé vs. Oblivion," *The Wall Street Journal,* January 24, 2012, p. B1.
17. Sara Murray, "Credit Checks on Job Seekers by Employers Attract Scrutiny," *The Wall Street Journal,* October 21, 2010, p. A5.
18. Cited in Katlin Madden, "10 Must-Dos for Skype Interviews," *Career Builder,* October 2, 2011.
19. Debra Auerbach, "Job Search Follow-Up Do's and Don'ts," *Career Builder,* February 5, 2012.
20. "Growing Industries In Need of Workers in 2012," *Forbes* (www.forbes.com), February 14, 2012, pp. 1–4. (*Investopedia* contributor).
21. Sara E. Needleman, "The Interview That'll Bag a Job," *The Wall Street Journal,* April 14, 2009, p. D4.
22. Debra Auerbach, "Résumé Boosters for Job Seekers," *Career Builder,* March 4, 2012.
23. Martha I. Finney, *Rebound* (Upper Saddle River, NJ: FT Press, 2009).
24. K. Anders Ericsson, Michael J. Prietula, and Edward T. Cokely, "The Making of an Expert," *Harvard Business Review,* July–August 2007, pp. 114–121; Geoff Colvin, *Talent Is Overrated* (New York: Portfolio, 2008).
25. Joann S. Lublin, "Directors Show Youth, Too," *The Wall Street Journal,* February 7, 2012, p. B6.
26. Brent A. Scott and Timothy A. Judge, "The Popularity Contest at Work: Who Wins, Why, and What Do They Receive?" *Journal of Applied Psychology,* January 2009, pp. 20–33.
27. Stephen R. Covey, *The 7 Habits of Highly Successful People* (New York: HarperCollins, 1989).
28. Jeffery A. Thompson, "Proactive Personality and Job Performance: A Social Capital Perspective," *Journal of Applied Psychology,* September 2005, pp. 1011–1017.
29. Ning Li, Jian Liang, and J. Michael Crant, "The Role of Proactive Personality in Job Satisfaction and Organizational Citizenship Behavior: A Relational Perspective," *Journal of Applied Psychology,* March 2010, pp. 395–404.
30. Tim Grant, "Tattoos, Piercings Bad Sign for Job," *Scripps Howard News Service,* August 19, 2010.
31. Cited in Rita Pyrillis, "Body of Work," *Workforce Management,* November 2010, p. 24.
32. Beth Kowitt, "Tips for Keeping Your Job," *Fortune,* December 8, 2008, p. 14.
33. John H. Zenger, Joseph R. Folkman, and Scott K. Edinger, "Making Yourself Indispensable," *Harvard Business Review,* October 2011, pp. 84–92.
34. "Etiquette School," *Bloomberg Businessweek,* October 10–October 24, 2010, p. 90.
35. Dorie Clark, "Reinventing Your Personal Brand," *Harvard Business Review,* March 2011, p. 81.
36. Judy Martin, "Aligning Your Passion With Your Personal Brand," *San Francisco Examiner* (www.examiner.com), March 7, 2009.
37. Roger Cheng and Andrew Morse, "Skype Hires New Chief From Cisco Before IPO," *The Wall Street Journal,* October 5, 2010, p. B7.
38. Vicki Neal, "What Is the Advantage of a Buddy System?" *HR Magazine,* March 2009, p. 27.
39. Jeff Wuorio, "How to Find the Perfect Mentor," *USA Weekend,* December 9–11, p. 5.
40. Betti A. Hamilton and Terri A. Scandura, "E-Mentoring: Implications for Organizational Learning and Development in a Wired World," *Organizational Dynamics,* 32, no. 4, 2003, p. 388; Donna M. Owens, "Virtual Mentoring," *HR Magazine,* March 2006, pp. 105–107.
41. Jeanne C. Mesiter and Karie Willyerd, "Mentoring Millennials," *Harvard Business Review,* May 2010, pp. 68–72.

42. Kathy E. Kram and Monica C. Higgins, "A New Approach to Mentoring," *The Wall Street Journal,* September 22, 2008, p. R10.
43. A few of the ideas are based on "Managing a Staff of Older Employees," *All Business.* Retrieved April 5, 2009, from www.allbusiness.com © 1999–2009.
44. "Is Your Boss Younger Than You? Tricks to Make It Work," www.preretirementlife.com, January 7, 2008; "Dealing With a Younger Boss," www.abclocal.go.com, January 8, 2009.
45. Stephen Covey, "How to Succeed in Today's Workplace," *USA Weekend,* August 29–31, 1997, pp. 4–5.
46. Hans-Georg Wolff and Klaus Moser, "Effects of Networking on Career Success: A Longitudinal Study," *Journal of Applied Psychology,* January 2009, pp. 196–206.

15

Learning Strategies, Perception, and Life Span Changes

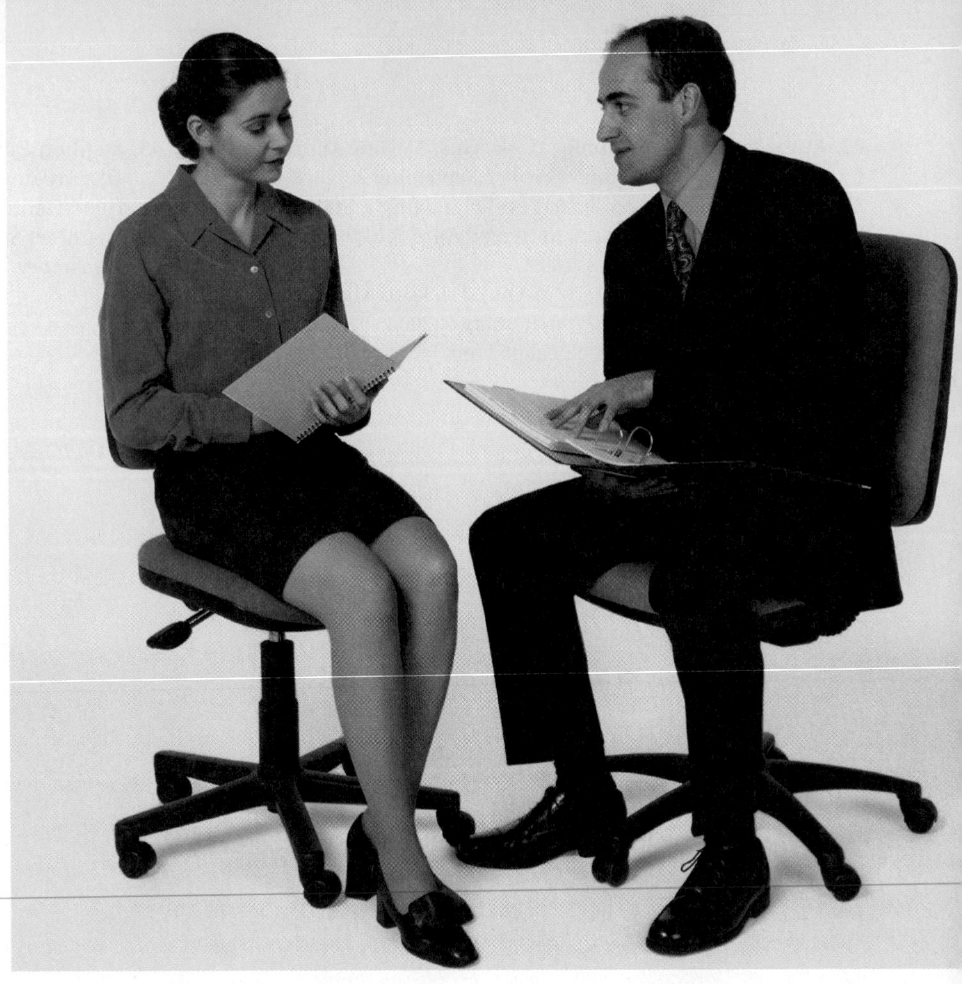

Outline

David Heitner grew up in New Jersey, the son of a radiologist. His professional career began as a business analyst at Dun & Bradstreet. Short on cash, he began cleaning floors at a few Pizza Huts to supplement his income, which was the start of a booming side business. He sold the business when he joined the investment firm Merrill Lynch in 1996.

The tech bust in the early 2000s reduced Heitner's earnings as a broker, so he decided to make a dramatic career shift based on full-time and part-time experiences. His major idea was to apply the financial, marketing, and management savvy he had picked up at the two financial firms and apply it to the somewhat disorganized commercial cleaning industry. Most of his colleagues at Merrill laughed, and many invited him to drop by and clean their toilets.

His company, Heits Building Services, sells master franchises to business operators. The operators of the master franchises, in turn, sell franchises to people trained in how to properly clean all kinds of workplaces. Heits is a professional green cleaning company that also offers services such as painting, power washing, and granite restoration. His company emphasizes that green cleaning products can improve indoor air quality, and are less toxic than other cleaners. The Heits system helps prevent the spread of diseases in the workplace, and cleans up transfer points for germs such as doorknobs, faucets and sinkers, lockers, showers, desktops, chairs, and sports equipment.

Heitner advises the person who switches careers from a corporation to self-employment to never look back after making up your mind. Focus totally on developing your business, and do not listen to people who tell you that your idea will not work. He says, "These are the people who are jealous that you decided to make a change in your life. Once you get the fire in your gut, there is no turning back."[1]

Perhaps few readers of this book want to open a commercial cleaning business, but David Heitner's story illustrates an important point about the world of work. It is possible that at any stage of our life cycle that we may be required to make major adaptations and changes. In this chapter we deal with a series of issues and topics that enable a person to develop career thrust and stay on track: how people learn, how perception influences their behavior, and the major challenges people face at different stages of their life, including a career change.

Learning Objectives ▸

After studying the information and doing the exercises in this chapter, you should be able to:

1. Understand the basic learning processes, three advanced learning processes, and e-learning.
2. Explain the meaning of learning styles, and develop insight into your own style.
3. Explain the importance of continuous learning.
4. Explain how perception influences behavior.
5. Identify the stages of the life cycle.
6. Understand the challenges of responding to changes in adolescence, adulthood, and late adulthood.
7. Describe the impact of the life span on life and job satisfaction.
8. Recognize the realities of dealing with a career change.
9. Be better prepared to cope with change.

Learning Objective 1

What Are the Major Learning Strategies and Processes?

Learning
generally considered a lasting change in behavior based on practice and experience

Much learning takes place on the job simply because people spend such a large proportion of their lives at work. Furthermore, workers at all levels are expected to learn new job skills and technology continuously. **Learning** is generally considered to be a lasting change in behavior based on practice and experience. Yet it is possible to learn something and store it in your mind without changing your behavior.[2] For example, you read that if you press "F12" in Windows 2010 you open the "Save As" function. You keep it in your mind but do not use the command yet. The new knowledge is stored in your upper brain but is not yet put into action.

Here we describe several different methods of learning, beginning with classical conditioning, the simplest type. Then we describe learning of intermediate complexity, operant conditioning, followed by two ways in which more complicated skills are learned: modeling and informal learning. We conclude with e-learning because of its widespread use in delivering content for learning. Although we describe different methods of learning, most learning depends on several methods. For example, in learning to operate a new vehicle you might need to develop simple reflexes to adjust to getting into the car. You would also use higher-level learning to understand how to use a GPS.

CLASSICAL CONDITIONING: LEARNING SIMPLE HABITS AND REFLEXES

Classical conditioning
principles stemming from Ivan Pavlov's digestion experiments that help people understand the most elementary type of learning—how people acquire uncomplicated habits and reflexes

In the late 1890s, Russian physiologist Ivan Pavlov conducted a long series of experiments about digestion. While studying a dog, he noticed that the dog salivated not only with the presence of food in the mouth but also at the sight of the food, the sound of the food trays, and even the footsteps of the experimenter. The principles of **classical conditioning** stemming from his experiments help us to understand the most elementary type of learning—how people acquire uncomplicated habits and reflexes. The basic principles and concepts are included in more complicated forms of learning.

How Classical Conditioning Takes Place

Classical conditioning works in this manner. Kurt takes an entry-level, unskilled job in a factory. His first day on the job a bell rings in his department at 11:34 a.m. Suddenly, every other worker stops working and opens a lunchbox or heads out to the company cafeteria. Kurt says to himself, "The bell must mean it's time for lunch." By the third day on the job, Kurt develops stomach pangs and begins to salivate as soon as the bell rings. Prior to this job, Kurt was in the habit of eating lunch at 1 p.m. and did not begin to have stomach pangs until that time.

Classical conditioning helps explain such elementary job behavior as how people learn to avoid being conked on the head by cranes and low-hanging pipes. With classical conditioning, people also learn to avoid being burned twice by a hot pipe or not turning off a computer before saving a file.

Habits in Everyday Life

Although habits may appear to be simple mechanisms, they are a major part of everyday life on and off the job. According to several studies, as much as 45 percent of what we do every day is habitual. In this sense, *habitual* refers to performing the same act almost without thinking in the same location or at the same time each day, based on subtle cues.[3] Among these many habits might be locking your car doors as you exit the car, putting one hand on your head each time you are asked a question, and checking your smart phone every time you exit a building. Another habit, the e-mail urge, often occurs after a person has finished reading a document, completed a certain type of task, or returned to his or her cubicle after some other activity.

OPERANT CONDITIONING: LEARNING THROUGH THE CONSEQUENCES OF OUR BEHAVIOR

Operant conditioning is learning that takes place as a consequence of behavior. In other words, a person's actions are instrumental in determining whether learning takes place. Operant conditioning is the cornerstone of behaviorism, as reflected first in the work of John B. Watson and then later by B. F. Skinner. The process by which a person learns the correct way to make an overseas phone call illustrates operant conditioning. At first the instructions may seem confusing, such as whether to first enter 1 or 9 before entering the other numbers. After a few tries, the person chooses the proper sequence of numbers and then has learned how to enter an overseas number.

Operant conditioning
learning that takes place as a consequence of behavior; a person's actions are instrumental in determining whether learning takes place

Reinforcement Strategies

The term *reinforcement* in general refers to the means by which behaviors are selected and retained. It gets at the idea that a response, such as shifting your weight on a snowboard to make a turn, is strengthened. A confusing factor here is that reinforcement strategies apply both to learning and motivation (see Chapter 3). Learning typically precedes motivation because if you have not learned to do something, motivation alone will not get the job done. The four reinforcement strategies are positive reinforcement, negative reinforcement (avoidance learning or motivation), punishment, and extinction.

Positive Reinforcement and Negative Reinforcement. The distinction between positive and negative reinforcement is very important. Positive reinforcement adds something rewarding to a situation, such as praise or a gift certificate. Positive reinforcement is thus receiving a reward for making a desired response. **Negative reinforcement** is effective because it takes away something unpleasant from a situation. It is a form of avoidance learning or motivation. Negative reinforcement is thus being rewarded by being relieved of discomfort. The international telephone call described above included negative reinforcement. Getting the sequence of numbers correct avoided the unpleasant situation of hearing a voice say "The number that you entered is incorrect or is no longer in service."

Negative reinforcement
taking away something unpleasant from a situation; being rewarded by being relieved of discomfort; form of avoidance learning or motivation

Negative reinforcement is not the same thing as punishment. Negative reinforcement is pleasant and, therefore, a reward. Punishment, by definition, is something unpleasant, unless the person involved likes to be punished. With masochists, the reward is to be punished!

Punishment. Being punished for your mistakes can be an important part of learning. **Punishment** is the introduction of an unpleasant stimulus as a consequence of the learner having done something wrong (in the eyes of the person in control of the situation). Or the threat of punishment can be used instead of actually punishing people for the wrong response in a learning or motivational situation. Punishment assists the operant conditioning process because it weakens the particular response. You tend not to repeat a response because of its negative consequences.

Punishment
the introduction of an unpleasant stimulus as a consequence of the learner having done something wrong

Extinction. The purpose of punishment is to eliminate a response. The same result can often be achieved through the reinforcement strategy of **extinction.** It refers to the weakening or decreasing of the frequency of undesirable behavior by removing the

Extinction
the weakening or decreasing of the frequency of undesirable behavior by removing the reward for such behavior

reward for such behavior. It is the absence of reinforcement. One way to stop the office clown from acting up is for coworkers to ignore that person's antics. The clown's behavior is said to be *extinguished.*

Schedules of Reinforcement

An important issue in operant conditioning (and in motivation) is how frequently to reward people when they make the correct response. Two broad types of schedules of reinforcement are in use—continuous and intermittent.

Under a *continuous schedule,* behavior is reinforced each time it occurs, such as saying "good job" every time a bank teller has exactly the right amount of money in terms of withdrawals and deposits at the end of the day. Continuous schedules usually result in fastest learning, but the desired behavior quickly diminishes when the reinforcement stops. Under an *intermittent schedule* the learner receives a reward after some instances of engaging in the desired behavior but not after each instance. Intermittent reinforcement is particularly effective in sustaining behavior because the learner stays mentally alert and interested. At any point, the behavior might lead to the desired reward. Lottery tickets that occasionally pay small rewards, such as $7, operate on this principle.

MODELING AND INFORMAL LEARNING: LEARNING COMPLICATED SKILLS

Classical and operant conditioning provide only a partial explanation of how people learn on the job. When you acquire a complicated skill, such as speaking in front of a group, preparing a budget, or designing a store display, you learn much more than simply a single stimulus-response relationship. You learn a large number of these relationships, and you also learn how to put them together in a cohesive, smooth-flowing pattern. Two important processes that help in learning complicated skills are modeling and informal learning. Both are based on processes that are inferred to take place in the brain.

Modeling
learning a skill by observing another person perform the skill; considered a form of social learning because it is learned in the presence of others

Modeling occurs when you learn a skill by observing another person perform the skill. Modeling is considered a form of social learning because it is learned in the presence of others. Many apprentices learn part of their trade by modeling an experienced craftsperson who practices the trade. Modeling is widely used in teaching sports through DVDs that give the viewer an opportunity to observe the skill being performed correctly. Although modeling is an effective way of learning, the learner must also have the proper capabilities and motivation.

Informal learning
planned or unplanned learning that occurs without a formal classroom, lesson plan, instructor, or examination; a way of learning complex skills in the workplace

Informal learning is another way of learning complex skills in the workplace. It is planned or unplanned learning that occurs without a formal classroom, lesson plan, instructor, or examination. The central premise of such learning is that employees acquire important information outside of a formal learning situation. The learning can be spontaneous, such as getting a tip on retrieving information from the intranet while waiting in line at the cafeteria. Or the company might organize the work area to encourage such informal learning, such as having lounges where employees interact. The employees capitalize on a learning situation in an unstructured situation where the rewards stemming from the learning are not explicit.

Implicit learning
learning that takes place unconsciously and without an intention to learn

Informal learning can be regarded as a variation of **implicit learning,** or learning that takes place unconsciously and without an intention to learn.[4] Perhaps you have not been attempting to learn the Spanish word for *danger,* but after seeing the word *peligro* adjacent to the English word *danger* many times (such as near electric wires), you learn the Spanish word.

Human learning is a complex field of study, with interesting and useful research emerging regularly. For example, according to one study, when college and high school students were shown two paragraphs with different fonts, they recalled 14 percent more of the facts printed in the difficult-to-read font.[5] One interpretation of these findings is that if you have to concentrate harder to decipher something, you will remember it better. Which of the following will lead to better recall for you? (a) The original digital camera was invented in the United States. (b) The original digital camera was invented in the United States. Of course, without good enough vision to read the font, no learning will take place.

E-LEARNING

Important innovations in learning have taken place in both schools and industry through the use of e-learning or distance learning. Here, the learner studies independently outside of a classroom setting and interacts with a computer in addition to studying course material. **E-learning** is an Internet form of computer-based training. However, other forms of computer-based learning are sometimes included in the definition of e-learning. Some learning programs are computer based without being delivered over the Internet. For example, the tutorials included in some software packages are a form of computer-based training. An e-learning course usually is carefully structured, with specific lesson plans for the student. Videos and other graphics are usually incorporated into an e-learning course. E-learning is more of a method of delivering content than a method of learning, yet the process helps us understand more about learning.

E-learning
studying independently outside of a classroom setting and interacting with a computer in addition to studying course material; Internet form of computer-based training

A major impetus behind e-learning is that so many employees are geographically dispersed, making it difficult to gather them in one place for learning. Luxottica Group is an Italian company that holds a leading position in luxury and sports eyewear, with 7,000 optical and sunglass retail stores in North America and throughout the world. The company chain stores include LensCrafters, Pearle Vision, and Sunglass Hut. To standardize training of 38,000 employees worldwide, the HR group put training online. Luxottica associates now have instant access to information they need to accomplish their daily tasks, including new-product details, as well as continuing education to keep skills current.[6]

Although e-learning is technologically different from more traditional forms of learning, it still is based on basic methods of learning. For example, the learner will often need reinforcement to keep going. Trainers at GE Capital found that when managers gave reinforcement to employees on attendance, made them feel important, and tracked their progress, employees were more likely to complete the course.[7]

Traits and Attitudes of the Learner

Another relevant aspect of e-learning is that its success depends on self-motivation and self-discipline. Self-motivation is important because an assignment to take an e-learning course by the company often is not motivation enough to work independently. Self-discipline is necessary to create a regular time for performing class work, and it prevents distractions by work or home activities. In educational settings, successful distance learning also requires high motivation. Some students may not take e-learning seriously. Most students need the structure of a face-to-face instructor, a classroom, and other students to keep them focused on the course.[8] Other data suggest that workers are more likely to apply information acquired in an instructor-led program. One explanation offered is that a commitment will more probably develop between the instructor and the learner than between a computer and a learner.[9]

Strengths and Limitations of E-Learning

E-learning has gained momentum, yet most companies prefer to use blended learning (Internet and classroom) because it combines the personal nature of classroom training with the cost efficiencies of learning via the Internet. The cost efficiencies include decreases in travel and lodging costs and payments to classroom instructors. But classroom training provides the difficult-to-measure benefit of employees spontaneously exchanging ideas that could lead to a creativity breakthrough.

Human Relations in Practice

Blended Learning at Westinghouse Electric

Jim Ice, the director of talent management at Westinghouse Electric Co., says the company has invested tens of millions of dollars in a corporate university, officially called the Westinghouse University. Its purpose is to train new and current employees in key skills and knowledge. Because there had been almost no nuclear plant construction since the Three Mile accident in 1979, Ice said that the company was recruiting employees who had no previous experience in the nuclear industry.

The Westinghouse University uses online classes and simulation exercises. Employees take exams to demonstrate to their managers that they have mastered job-required skills such as analyzing air samples and conducting radiation surveys.

A representative example of company training is the Westinghouse Online Nuclear Instrumentation Course. The course incorporates a progressive, student-centered, interactive learning approach designed to enhance learning. By blending a variety of instructional methods and delivery options, including online learning and classroom instruction, Westinghouse hopes to engage students in the learning process and improve job performance.

Technical content in the course is delivered in the form of interactive, animated PowerPoint presentations, as well as threaded discussions in which students discuss technical aspects of the nuclear instrumentation system, maintenance as well as other information. Numerous student learning assessments are conducted within the online course.

Question: Why should a nuclear energy company be concerned about using advanced learning techniques for its employees?

Source: The account is based on facts and observations in Lauren Weber, "Fine-Tuning the Perfect Employee," *The Wall Street Journal*, December 5, 2011, p. B9; "Learning and Development at Westinghouse Electric Europe," *European Nuclear Society* (www.euronucleqar.org), e-news Issue 31, Winter 2011, pp. 1–6; "NIC 337 Online-Nuclear Instrumentation System" (www.training.westinghousenuclear.com), accessed March 20, 2012.

In general e-learning is most effective in delivering conceptual subject matter, such as product information, whereas classroom training is more effective for learning interpersonal skills.[10] Furthermore, when an organization wants to build a civil, welcoming workplace, frequent discussions are superior to computer-based lessons.[11] The human touch is important for learning human relations! E-learning does provide some guidance, but an instructor adds an extra touch, such as answering questions and clarifying concepts. Frequent e-mail exchanges between students and instructors help bring the human touch into e-learning.

The accompanying Human Relations in Practice illustrates that blending e-learning and classroom learning can be useful in learning technical skills.

GROUP LEARNING

Although true learning requires a brain, groups can learn in the sense that members come to adapt their behavior collectively in response to experience. How groups learn has been studied by three professors of organizational behavior: Jeanne M. Wilson of the College of William & Mary, Paul S. Goodman of Carnegie Mellon University, and Matthew A. Cronin of George Mason University. According to their definition, **group learning** is a change in the group's repertoire of potential behavior. For example, a group of hospital workers might rehearse how to deal with a major health attack such as poisoning of the water supply and then implement the learning should the attack occur. According to the same researchers, group learning has three basic features: sharing, storage, and retrieval.[12]

Group learning
A change in the group's repertoire of potential behavior

1. *Sharing* is the process by which new knowledge, routines, or behaviors becomes distributed among group members. At the same time, group members must understand that others in the group possess that learning. With our emergency response workers in the hospital, each person shares new insights with the others, such as where to house all the people that might need treatment.
2. *Storage* is the process of storing in memory what has been learned. Similar to learning at the individual level, the change in behavior must be recorded for it to be most useful. If you get stung by a hive of bees once when painting a house because you poked a beehive, you must remember not to make the same mistake again. The hospital emergency response team should remember what worked and what didn't work in handling one crisis so they can better deal with the next crisis. In addition to memory, a group could store knowledge in a database.
3. *Retrieval* is the ability of group members to find and access the knowledge for subsequent inspection and use. As with individual learning, the group has to be able to access the information when needed. An individual within the group might help the group retrieve the information by stating, "Here's how we dealt with hysterical people during the last emergency."

Social media is used by some companies to facilitate group learning. Group members might access the same Facebook page to quickly and frequently exchange information, such as the hospital emergency team in question updating each other on what works and what doesn't work in responding to emergencies.

What Are Several Different Learning Styles?

◀ Learning Objective 2 ◀

Another important concept in understanding learning is **learning style,** the idea that people learn best in different ways. For example, some people acquire new material best through passive learning. Such people quickly acquire information through studying texts, manuals, magazine articles, and Web sites. They can juggle images in their mind as they read about abstract concepts such as supply and demand, cultural diversity, or customer service. Others learn best by doing rather than by studying—for example, learning hands-on about customer service by dealing with customers in many situations.

Learning style
the idea that different people learn best in different ways

Another key dimension of learning styles is whether a person learns best by working alone or cooperatively, such as in a study group. Learning by oneself allows for more intense concentration, and one can proceed at one's own pace. Learning in groups and through classroom discussion allows people to exchange viewpoints and perspectives. Considerable evidence has been accumulated that peer tutoring and cooperative learning are effective for acquiring knowledge.[13] Another advantage of cooperative learning is that it is more likely to lead to changes in behavior. Assume that a manager holds group discussions about the importance of achieving high customer satisfaction. Employees participating in these group discussions are more likely to assertively pursue high customer satisfaction on the job than those who only read about the topic. Learning styles have also been studied more scientifically, and one such approach is described next.

LEARNING STYLES ASSOCIATED WITH PERSONALITY AS MEASURED BY THE GOLDEN PERSONALITY TYPE PROFILER

Another way of understanding learning styles is to recognize that your personality can influence your learning style. You may have observed, for example, that when an impulsive person needs to learn how to use an electronic device, that person will often grab the device and start hitting the various buttons. A more reflective person will often first read the manual or look over the device carefully before attempting to get it to function.

One of the best-known methods of measuring personality types is the Myers-Briggs Type Indicator (MBTI), a self-report questionnaire designed to make the theory of psychological types developed by psychoanalyst Carl Jung applicable to everyday life.[14] Another leading method of measuring types is the Golden Personality Type Profiler.[15] Jung developed the theory of psychological types, but he did not develop the two measuring instruments just mentioned. As measured by the Golden instrument, four separate dichotomies direct the typical use of perception and judgment by an individual.

1. **Energy flow: Extraversion versus introversion.** Extraverts direct their energy primarily toward the outer world of people and objects. In contrast, introverts direct their energy primarily toward the inner world of experiences and ideas.
2. **Information gathering: Sensation versus intuition.** People who rely on sensing focus primarily on what can be perceived by the five primary senses of vision, touch, sight, sound, and smell. People who rely on intuition focus primarily on perceiving patterns and interrelationships.
3. **Decision making: Thinking versus feeling.** People who rely primarily on thinking base conclusions on logical analysis and emphasize objectivity and detachment. People who rely on feelings base conclusions on personal or social values and focus on understanding and harmony.
4. **Lifestyle orientation: Judging versus perceiving.** Individuals who score high on judging tend to orient their lives in a deliberate and planned manner. Individuals who score high on perceiving tend to orient their lives in a spontaneous and open-ended manner.[16]

Combining the four types with each other results in sixteen personality types, such as the ESFP, or The Entertainer. ESFP refers to extraverted/sensing/feeling/perceiving. It is believed that approximately 13 percent of the population can be classified as the ESFP type. People of this type are optimistic and are skilled at living joyfully and entertaining others. ESFPs are effective at communicating their good-natured realism to others.

You might want to take the Golden Personality Type Profiler (see Appendix B in this book). Our concern here is with how your personality influences your learning style. Figure 15-1 presents four of the sixteen personality types along with the implications for each one with respect to learning style. You will observe that the learning styles are complex rather than focusing on specific factors, such as preferring observing over reading.

IMPROVING LEARNING AND BRAIN FUNCTIONING THROUGH REST

Interest has escalated in recent years for everyday approaches to improving a person's ability to learn and solve problems. We will return to this topic again in our discussion of cognitive challenges throughout the life span when we discuss the role of mental and physical activity to enhance learning later in this chapter. Here we look at the importance of *inactivity* to improve brain functioning and learning. Common wisdom

FIGURE 15-1 THE LEARNING STYLES ASSOCIATED WITH FOUR DIFFERENT GOLDEN PERSONALITY TYPES

Personality Type	Highlights of Type	Learning Style Features, Including Preference for Type of Instructor
ENFP (The Proponent) Extraverted/iNtuitive/ Feeling/Perceiving	Lives continually in the realm of the possible. When absorbed in his or her latest project, he or she thinks of little else. Filled with energy, he or she is tireless when in pursuit of goals. Has an almost magnetic quality that enables him or her to have fun in almost any setting. The combination of Extraversion, Intuition, and Perceiving is well suited for leadership.	• A preference for lessons that involve adventuresome and creative experiences • A need for time to explore possibilities, ask questions, and use imagination • Learning through a variety of methods: reading, writing, listening, observing, and interacting with others • A dislike of narrow structures or straight lectures • Excelling when the instructor takes a personal interest in him or her
ENFJ (The Communicator) Extraverted/iNtuitive/ Feeling/Judging	Chief concern is fostering harmony and cooperation between self and others. Has strong ideals and a potent sense of loyalty, whether to a mate, a school, a hometown, or a favorite cause. Usually good at organizing people to get things done while keeping everyone happy. At work, well armed to deal with both variety and action. Typically patient and conscientious, he or she makes a concerted effort of sticking with a job until finished.	• Performing best in a structured learning environment • Believing interaction with others and discussion of the lesson to be very important • Learning best when he or she understands how the material is connected to helping people • Liking theories and abstractions • Resisting instructors who are not warm and personable
INFP (The Advocate) Introverted/iNtuitive/ Feeling/Perceiving	Capable of immense sensitivity and has an enormous emotional capacity, which is guarded closely. Has to know people well before, letting down the guard, and displaying warmth. Interpersonal relationships are a crucial focus. Has powerful sense of faithfulness, duty, and commitment to the people and causes he or she is attracted to. Able to express emotion and move people through communication. A perfectionist on the job. Prefers a quiet working environment and, despite attraction for human companionship, will often work best alone. Will work at best only in job he or she truly believes in.	• A preference for flexible environments where he or she can use imagination and creativity • Learning best from lectures and written work rather than rote methods • Enjoyment of abstraction and the world of ideas • A preference for instructors who are personally interested in him or her
INFJ (The Foreseer) Introverted/iNtuitive/ Feeling/Judging	Imaginative, inspired, tenacious, creative, and inward looking. Also stubborn, easily bored by routine work, and often pays little attention to obstacles. Makes decisions easily. Lives in a world of ideas and will have a unique vision. Pours all own energy into achieving goals. Trusts own intuition. Can express emotion and move people through written communication. Although the companionship of people is cherished, prefers a quiet working environment and working alone. Perfectionist about quality. Creativity is his or her hallmark.	• A value for lifelong learning by interacting with others or through reading and writing • Preference for tools and materials that are organized • Enjoyment of future-oriented concepts, theories, abstractions, and ideas • Avoiding dictatorial educational settings, as well as either/or thinking

Source: Karen A. Deitz and John P. Golden, *Boundless Diversity: An Introduction to the Golden Personality Type Profiler* (San Antonio, TX: Pearson TalentLens, 2004).

Code: E = Extraverted, N = iNtuitive, F = Feeling, P = Perceiving, I = Introverted, J = Judging.

suggests that it is easier to learn when you are rested, and scientific evidence supports this contention. Resting the brain relates to style, because learning when rested is part of one's approach to learning.

The potential benefits of sleep include stronger memory and better attention spans. According to James B. Maas, a psychology professor at Cornell University, good sleep is a necessity rather than a luxury: "Your alertness, energy, performance, thinking, productivity, creativity, safety, and health will be affected by how much you sleep."[17] Besides enhancing alertness, sleep is a way for the brain to store new information into long-term memory. The benefits are most likely to take place from rapid eye movement (REM) sleep that usually takes place during the sixth and eighth hours of sleep, when people are most likely to dream.

During REM sleep the brain typically replenishes neurotransmitters, the chemical substances that transmit chemical impulses across synapses. The neurotransmitters are important because they organize the neural networks essential for remembering, learning, performance, and problem solving. So a catnap, or power nap, may boost productivity, but an ample amount of deep sleep is a bigger contributor to better learning and brain functioning. Sleep spindles—spikes of activity that surface during REM sleep—help people learn and remember how to perform physical tasks, such as playing golf, tennis, and basketball.

A simpler explanation for how sleep improves memory is that sleep contributes to a reduction in brain overload. During sleep, the synapses (connections between nerve cells) that were formed during the day's learning can relax a little.[18] A practical implication of this finding is that adequate sleep will do more for your memory than increasing your input of caffeine, because the caffeinated brain might become overcharged with information.

The various approaches to learning, including learning styles, help us understand how people learn. How *much* people learn is another important consideration in understanding learning in the workplace. In general, people with higher mental ability and personality traits that allow them to concentrate better (such as emotional stability and conscientiousness) acquire knowledge and skills more readily.

CONTINUOUS LEARNING DURING YOUR CAREER

A reality of almost all professional, technical, and sales occupations is that career success, and even survival, depends on continuous learning (as suggested at several places in this book). Continuous learning relates to learning style because learning throughout one's career is an approach to learning. A commonplace example is that we all have to keep learning how to use new software and hardware just to perform a job. The CEO may need to understand how enterprise-level software helps the different divisions in a firm work together, and the auto-supply store associate has to learn how to track parts by computer. Acquiring human relations skills, such as working well with coworkers from different cultures, is another area of continuous learning facing many workers.

▶ Learning Objective 3 ▶

How Does Perception Influence How People Interpret the World?

Understanding learning strategies helps us cope better with the world of work, and understanding how we interpret information we receive is also important. Most of us interpret what is going on in the world outside us as we perceive it, not as it really is. You do not usually experience a mass of colors; instead, you experience a color photograph.

You do not experience a thousand different vibrations in the air; instead, you hear a favorite CD. When we answer a question, we answer in terms of our interpretation of what we hear.

An everyday happening, such as a change in air temperature, helps to illustrate the nature of human perception. Assume that you live in Vermont. A temperature of 52°F (11.1°C) would seem warm in January. The same temperature would seem cold in July. Our perception of temperature depends on many things going on inside our mind and body.

Perceptions on the job are very important. Many studies, for example, have investigated the consequences of employee job perceptions. The results show that employees who perceive their job to be challenging and interesting have high job satisfaction and motivation. In addition, these favorable perceptions lead to better job performance.[19]

In summary, **perception** deals with the various ways in which people interpret things in the external world and how they act on the basis of these perceptions. The aspects of perception described here are (a) why perceptual problems exist, (b) agreement about perceived events, and (c) how people perceive the causes of behavior. Our discussion focuses on the social rather than the physical aspects of perception, such as taste, sound, and touch.

Perception
the various ways in which people interpret things in the external world and how they act on the basis of these perceptions

WHY PERCEPTUAL PROBLEMS EXIST

Under ideal circumstances, people perceive information as it is intended to be communicated or as it exists in reality. Suppose a company promotes a specialist to a team leader position because he or she is thought to have good potential for advancement. The manager offering the promotion hopes the specialist does not see the promotion as a plot to have the person work extra hours without being paid overtime. (Team leaders usually do not receive overtime pay.) Both characteristics of the stimulus (the idea or thing to be perceived) and the mental processes of people can lead to distorted perceptions. Figure 15-2 outlines why perceptual problems exist.

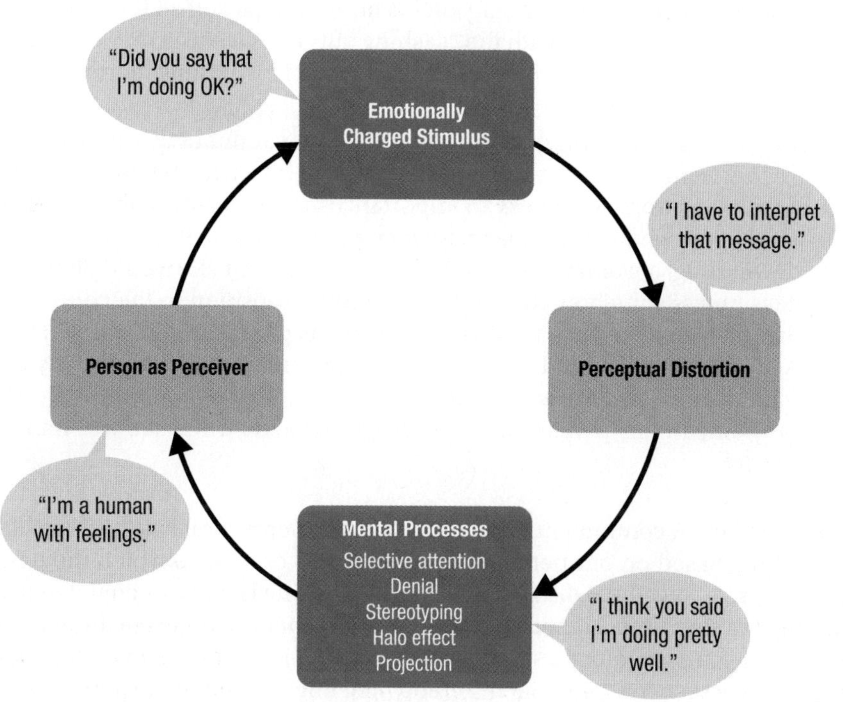

FIGURE 15-2
CONTRIBUTORS TO PERCEPTUAL PROBLEMS

Characteristics of the Stimulus

Perceptual problems are most likely to be encountered when the stimulus or cue to be perceived has an emotional meaning. Assume that Brian, an office supervisor, announces to his staff, "I would like you to meet Brenda. She's a temporary worker here to help us out this week." Announcing the presence of an office temporary could trigger several different perceptions. The specific perceptions would depend on many motives, needs, and the knowledge of department employees. Among the possible interpretations are these:

> "An office temp? I wonder if this means the company is going to cut down the regular workforce and use temps to help us through peak loads."
>
> "This seems to be a sure sign that business has picked up. The front office would never authorize extra help unless business was booming. Things look good for getting a decent raise this year."
>
> "I wonder if Brian has brought in a temporary worker to show us we had better get hustling or we could be replaced. I've heard a lot of these so-called temps usually wind up with full-time jobs if they like the temporary assignment."

To help reduce misperceptions, Brian should provide more complete information on why Brenda is being hired, such as pointing to a surge in orders. Reducing ambiguity helps minimize perceptual errors.

Mental Processes of People

The devices people use to deal with sensory information play a major role in creating perceptual problems. Several of these can also be classified as defensive behavior.

Selective attention
giving exclusive attention to something at the expense of other aspects of the environment

Selective Attention. The major contributor to perceptual distortions is the tendency for us to attend to the stimuli that are most relevant to our needs. Giving exclusive attention to something at the expense of other aspects of the environment is referred to as **selective attention.** If a stimulus fits our needs, desires, or interests we are likely to give it our attention. At the same time, we are likely to pay only minor attention to the surrounding stimuli. Thus, Joe Homeowner hears the wonderful news from the telemarketer that he is eligible to "cash out" on the equity on his home and pay off all those high-interest debts. Only after going forward with the "cashing out" does it sink in for Joe that he now has incurred a new long-term second mortgage on top of his existing mortgage.

Denial. If the sensory information is particularly painful to us—for example, if it hurts our self-esteem—we tend to go one step beyond selective attention. Denial is the process of excluding from awareness an important aspect of reality. This mental process is often found in the workplace, especially when people face such threats as job loss. As part of a downsizing, a woman was told by her manager that she would be terminated in thirty days unless somehow she could find another position in the company. That evening she informed her husband, "Our company is going through a downsizing, so it looks like I will be transferred to a different department in thirty days." By denying the reality of the message, the woman failed to search actively for another job within the company. She finally perceived the message correctly when she was handed her severance check.

Stereotyping. A common method of simplifying perception is to evaluate an individual or thing based on our perception of the group or class to which the person or object belongs. A perceptual disadvantage of stereotyping is that you do not look for the way in which somebody or something might be different from others in the same group. For example, a job seeker might say, "I won't look for a job in the retail field because retailing jobs have such low pay." Such stereotyping might result in the person's neglecting to investigate high-paying opportunities within the retail field based on the rapid promotions possible. Stereotypes can be positive as well as negative. For example, you might have the stereotype that all accountants are thorough and accurate. As a result, you fail to carefully review the tax return prepared by your accountant.

Halo Effect. We have a tendency to color everything that we know about a person because of one recognizable favorable or unfavorable trait. When a company does not insist on the use of objective measures of performance, it is not uncommon for a supervisor to give a favorable performance rating to people who dress well or smile frequently. The fine appearance or warm smile of these people has created a halo around them. Employees often create a negative halo about a supervisor simply because he or she is gruff or stern in manner or speech.

Projection. Another shortcut in the perceptual process is to project our own faults onto others instead of making an objective appraisal of the situation. Our feelings and thoughts are unacceptable to us, so we attribute them to another person. In this way we feel less anxious about ourselves. A manager who has a self-discipline problem himself might respond negatively to an employee's request to work at home one day per week. The manager might say, "Sorry, can't let you work at home. You would probably goof off half the day before you got down to work."

PERCEPTUAL CONGRUENCE

The discussion of perception so far has focused on perceptual errors. At times, most people in the organization perceive an event in the same way. **Perceptual congruence** refers to the degree to which people perceive things the same way. High congruence generally implies valid perception, but people can also agree on a distorted perception. For example, four members of a work team might have the authority to choose a fifth team member. All four might share the same inaccurate perception that a particular candidate is a good fit. After one month, they learn that the individual is a loner who functions poorly in a team environment.

Perceptual congruence the degree to which people perceive things the same way

Despite the reservation cited, high congruence generally leads to more positive consequences for the organization than low congruence. A case in point is that it is beneficial for managers and group members to perceive the group members' tasks in the same manner. If store associates and managers at LensCrafters agree that their mission is to help people see better—rather than optimizing sales—customers will be better off and the company will stay profitable based on a reputation of being ethical.

ATTRIBUTION THEORY: HOW WE PERCEIVE THE CAUSES OF BEHAVIOR

An important aspect of perception is our explanation for the causes of behavior. Stated differently, to what do we *attribute* a given behavior? **Attribution theory** is the study of the process by which people ascribe causes to the behavior they perceive. A major finding of attribution theory is that most people give relatively little weight to the circumstances in making judgments about a person's behavior. We are more likely to attribute a person's actions or results to personal characteristics than to outside forces. A supervisor who presses us to finish a project is more likely to be perceived as being impatient than as caught up in a highly competitive environment.

Attribution theory the study of the process by which people ascribe causes to the behaviors they perceive

Another finding of attribution theory is that people have a general tendency to attribute their achievements to good inner qualities, whereas they attribute failure to adverse factors within the environment. A manager would thus attribute increased productivity to his or her leadership skills but blame low productivity on poor support from the organization.

▶ Learning Objective 4 ▶

How Do We Respond to Life Span Changes and Challenges?

At different stages in life we face different challenges, beginning with the embryo struggling for enough oxygen and ending with the 100-year-old fretting about physical well-being and passing on his or her estate. (Did you know that sales of birthday cards celebrating a person's 100th birthday have surged in recent years?) Here we overview the stages of the life cycle and challenges associated with adolescence and beyond.

STAGES OF THE LIFE CYCLE

Several approaches have been developed over the years to explain the various stages of human development, or the tasks people face at different periods in life. Among the best known is the eight stages of human development formulated by psychiatrist Erik H. Erikson in the 1950s.[20] Figure 15-3 presents an outline of these stages and the associated primary crisis for each one. According to Erikson, the socialization process consists of the "eight stages of man," with each stage representing a psychosocial crisis. The crisis must be resolved at each stage before the next stage can be satisfactorily negotiated.

Satisfactory learning and resolution of each stage is necessary if the child is to manage the next and later stages successfully. The building of a skyscraper is an appropriate

FIGURE 15-3

ERIKSON'S EIGHT STAGES OF DEVELOPMENT AND ASSOCIATED CRISIS

Source: Erik H. Erikson, *Childhood and Society* (New York: Norton, 1963); Child Development Institute, "Stages of Social-Emotional Development in Children and Teenagers," retrieved May 10, 2006, from: www.childdevelpmentinfo.com.

Stages and Ages	The Primary Crisis and Related Comment
1. Infancy (0–1 year)	*Learning basic trust versus basic mistrust (hope)* A well-nurtured child develops trust and security.
2. Toddler (1–2 years)	*Learning autonomy versus shame (will)* The well-parented child emerges from this stage proud rather than feeling shamed.
3. Preschool (3–5 years)	*Learning initiative versus guilt (purpose)* Healthy children broaden their skills at this stage through active play.
4. Elementary school (6–12 years)	*Learning industry versus inferiority (competence)* Here the child learns the more formal life skills such as mastering reading and arithmetic, and some self-discipline.
5. Adolescence (13–19 years)	*Learning identity versus identity diffusion (fidelity)* The adolescent can now answer satisfactorily and happily the question, "Who am I?"
6. Young adulthood (20–40 years)	*Learning intimacy versus isolation (love)* The successful young adult experiences the type of intimacy that makes possible a good marriage or a genuine or enduring friendship.
7. Middle adulthood (40–65 years)	*Learning generativity (building a generation) versus self-absorption* In adulthood, the successful adult engages in a partnership and raises children.
8. Late adulthood (65 and over)	*Learning integrity versus despair (wisdom)* The mature adult has integrity, is independent, and enjoys people and work. If the earlier psychosocial crises have not been resolved, he or she may have a self-view of disgust and despair.

metaphor. Each floor, including the foundation and ground level, must be built correctly or the next floor will collapse. An example of this stage-by-stage development is that if the young adult cannot experience intimacy at stage 6, he or she will not be successful at the marriage or parenting that takes place at stage 7.

Erikson's stages of human development have prompted later investigation into how humans develop through different phases of their lives. Despite these analyses of life stages, there are huge cultural and individual differences in the successful development of an adult. For example, what about Russian males, whose life expectancy is only about 59 years? (The life expectancy of Russian women is about 73 years. Russian women consume less vodka than do their male counterparts.) Do Russian men never deal with stage 8, integrity versus despair? And is it not possible to be a successful, well-adjusted adult even if you are not in a committed relationship and have no children?

Next, we summarize briefly challenges people face in adolescence, adult life, and late life.[21] The first stage, infancy and childhood, is an important building block for later stages but lies outside the purview of our treatment of human relations.

RESPONDING TO CHALLENGES IN ADOLESCENCE

In its technical meaning **adolescence** is the period in life from approximately ages 13 to 20. From a biological standpoint, adolescence begins with puberty, the beginning of sexual maturation marked by rising levels of sex hormones and rapid growth. During adolescence many people start building work-related human skills, such as teamwork, and also engage in career choice and career preparation. Adolescents (or *teenagers*) vary considerably in their accomplishments, with some teenagers being successful entrepreneurs, information technology consultants, professional athletes, and movie stars. Industries such as retailing and food service depend on the adolescent workforce, suggesting that even average teenagers occupy an important work role in society.

Adolescence
the period in life from approximately age 13 to 20; from a biological standpoint, adolescence begins with puberty

Cognitive Challenges

Adolescents headed for a successful career must rise to the challenge of developing logic, abstract thought, and hypothetical reasoning. Many adolescents are studying five different subjects at once and feel compelled to think well enough to perform well in school and on college entrance exams. Adolescents must also deal with the development of moral reasoning in which they attempt to learn acceptable versus unacceptable codes of conduct. According to Lawrence Kohlberg, former moral education professor at Harvard University, adolescents begin to develop three levels of moral thought:[22]

- At the *preconventional level* moral dilemmas are resolved in a self-centered way. An act is moral if it enables someone to avoid punishment or obtain reward. Obeying safety rules or returning a lost wallet might fit this category of moral development.
- At the *conventional level* moral dilemmas are resolved in ways that reflect laws or norms set by parents and other influential adults. Making a complete stop at a stop sign on a country road when no one else is watching would fit the conventional level of moral development.
- At the *postconventional level* moral dilemmas are resolved by relating to abstract principles such as equality, justice, and the value of life. An adolescent at this level of moral development might start a food-and-clothing campaign for homeless people in the community.

One reason offered for the unethical behavior of many adults in executive positions in business is that they did not advance to the postconventional level of moral development.

Personality and Social Challenges

Identity crisis
adolescent struggle to establish a reliable self-concept, or personal identity, including concerns over ethnic identity, the need to keep close ties with the family or develop peer relations, sexuality, and body image

As an adolescent struggles to establish a reliable self-concept, or personal identity, he or she faces an **identity crisis.** In a multicultural world, the adolescent may need to establish an ethnic identity. Adolescents often struggle with whether to retain close ties with the family or invest more energy in developing peer relations. Adolescents struggle with sexuality, with some happily engaging in sex and others facing unintended negative consequences such as parenthood, paternity suits, dropping out of school, and sexually transmitted diseases. Another conflict many adolescents face is one of body image, with discontent possibly leading to anorexia and excessive body piercing.

Successfully Managing the Teenage Brain

Teenage brain
a stage of brain development in which people are easily influenced by their environment and more prone to impulsive behavior

A cognitive challenge of the adolescent years meriting separate mention is dealing successfully with the **teenage brain,** a stage of brain development in which people are easily influenced by their environment and more prone to impulsive behavior. Based on several research findings, the teenage brain differs from the adult brain in six primary ways:[23]

- Overproduction of dendrites, which leads to a greater propensity for learning new concepts and skills.
- Pruning, or loss of dendrites not being used, taking place more rapidly.
- Decision-making processes governed by the amygdala, leading to the propensity for teenagers being more emotionally driven in an impulsive sense.
- The medial prefrontal cortex, located in the front of the brain, is not developed to the same extent as in adults. As a result, the teenager will often have less empathy and guilt than adults.
- The frontal lobe, responsible for cognitive processes such as reasoning, planning, and judgment, is only about 80 percent developed in teenagers. The frontal lobe finally connects with the rest of the brain between ages 25 and 30.
- The reward centers of adolescent brains lead them to overestimate the value of rewards, more so than children or adults. Teenagers intensely want social rewards, especially respect of their peers.[24] As a result a teenager might engage in dangerous behavior, such as posting a racy photo of himself or herself on Facebook.

The heavy reliance on the amygdala often causes misunderstandings, incendiary language, and faulty decision making despite high cognitive capacity. This helps explain why a teenager might engage in such activity as mastering a complex calculus problem in class or building a robot and then run a red light after class "just for the excitement."

Another characteristic of teenage thinking governed by brain differences is that a teenager's judgment of what he or she would do in a given situation is driven by the question, "What would I do?" In contrast, adults tend to ask, "What would I do, given how I would feel and given how the people around me would feel as a result of my actions?"[25]

RESPONDING TO ADULT LIFE CHALLENGES

Adulthood is not marked by the same more predictable milestones as childhood and adolescence. Assuming that a person lives until about age 80, he or she spends more than half of life in the adult stage, so adults face an enormous number of challenges, including managing social life, work, and finances; raising children; keeping a blended family cooperating; staying current with technology; and investing for retirement.

Cognitive Challenges

Adults face the unique challenge of applying the many cognitive skills they have acquired during study. For example, some people who performed well in math exams have no clue how to calculate miles per gallon on a vehicle or balance a checkbook. To prosper in a career, the adult must often learn creative-thinking skills and apply wisdom. For example, the self-employed adult must find a way to convince bankers or venture capitalists on the merits of investing in his or her idea for the launch of a new product or service. An adult faces the challenge of learning to think more flexibly rather than finding the "correct" answer to a problem—the essence of creative thinking.

Recent research about the capacity of the middle-age adult brain is encouraging. Results suggest that the middle-aged brain not only retains many of the cognitive skills of youth but actually acquires new ones. For many people, the middle-age brain is calmer, more stable, and better able to sort through social situations. Memorization skills and perceptual speed begin to decline in young adulthood, whereas verbal abilities, spatial reasoning, simple math abilities, and abstract reasoning all improve in middle age.[26] All of these positive results are not surprising when you consider that middle-age people are at the top of many fields including business, sciences, medicine, and the arts.

Personality and Social Challenges

Adults must learn to become less self-centered and refine their interpersonal skills, including developing business etiquette. For some young people a major adjustment is to learn to take off their sports cap when eating at a restaurant or being interviewed for a job. Many adults in their forties face a **midlife crisis,** when they feel unfulfilled and search for a major shift in career or lifestyle. Adults facing a midlife crisis often wonder whether their choice of career or life partner was the right decision. During the more common **midlife transition,** adults may take stock of their life and formulate new goals, such as an engineer working for IBM deciding to teach high school math. (IBM encourages such transitions to foster math and science knowledge and skills.) Among the dozens of other personality and social challenges facing adults are the loss of a youthful appearance and a decreased reproductive or sexual capacity. Such challenges have spurred the development of plastic surgery, youth-enhancing cosmetics, and lifestyle drugs such as those designed to enhance sexual performance.

Midlife crisis
time that adults in their forties face when they feel unfulfilled and search for a major shift in career or lifestyle

Midlife transition
adults taking stock of their lives and formulating new goals; among dozens of other personality and social challenges facing adults are the loss of a youthful appearance and a decreased reproductive or sexual capacity

The Sandwich Generation Challenge

During the adult stage of life many people face the difficult challenge of being part of the **sandwich generation**—those placed in the middle between the needs of their own children and their aging relatives. According to one estimate, nearly two-thirds of baby boomers will be taking care of an elderly parent during the next ten years. Taking care of the parent sometimes translates into having an older relative live with the couple or person, along with the children, resulting in an intergenerational household. Such an arrangement was common in the United States in years past, and is now common throughout the world. During economic downturns intergenerational living increases in frequency. The sandwich generation challenge might be faced by a couple, or a single parent, and is often complicated by the person or couple needing to plan for their own retirement.[27]

Sandwich generation
those placed in the middle between the needs of their own children and their aging relatives

Successfully managing the challenge of being a member of the sandwich generation includes such steps as taking the time for oneself or each other to avoid neglecting marriage or personal life. Avoiding emotional, physical, and financial overload is also important. Getting help from community and government resources is another way of coping with the sandwich-generation challenge.[28]

RESPONDING TO LATE-LIFE CHALLENGES

The challenges of late life have increased because more people live longer beyond the traditional retirement age, and many remain active and in good health. Yet still many other people in late life are infirmed, impoverished, and dependent on family and government to maintain their well-being.

Cognitive Challenges

"Cognitive decline in late adulthood is becoming the No. 1 public health problem we face as a country, particularly as the baby boomers age," says psychologist Denise C. Park, director of the Center for Vital Longevity at the University of Texas at Dallas.[29] Although many people in late adulthood face cognitive decline, many others do not. The ability to learn rapidly and reason abstractly and logically may decline through adulthood, starting as early as age 30. Part of the problem is that there is a normal slowing down in cognitive functioning starting in the fifties and sixties. Neurotransmitters, the chemicals that enable nerve cells to communicate, diminish.[30] Another problem is that older people have some difficulty in concentrating when interrupted by extraneous sounds.[31] But wisdom and judgment based on the accumulation of knowledge may increase up into the eighties. The issue of the cognitive skills of late-life adults has been the subject of much opinion and research in recent years because the life span of people has increased, and so many old people hold responsible positions, drive cars, and even fly airplanes solo.

Common wisdom suggests that staying in shape mentally by such activities as doing crossword puzzles, surfing the Internet, or studying a foreign language can slow the decline of an aging brain. Brain-imaging studies support the idea that mental workouts help preserve **cognitive fitness,** a state of optimized ability to remember, learn, plan, and adapt to changing circumstances. Acquiring expertise in such diverse areas as playing a cello, juggling, speaking a foreign language, and driving a taxicab expands your neural systems and helps them communicate with one another. This means that learning new skills can alter the physical makeup of the brain even in later life. Engaging in play also enhances brain functioning, which helps explain the link between creativity and play.[32]

Cognitive fitness
a state of optimized ability to remember, learn, plan, and adapt to changing circumstances

Workouts are another way of maintaining cognitive fitness. Better blood flow to the brain takes place, as well as producing chemicals that encourages the growth of connectors between neurons, which are the key to learning and memory.[33] Furthermore, a study conducted at the University of Illinois with participants in their seventies found that six months of walking for about one hour three times weekly improved memory, attention, and decision making.[34]

A long-term study called Active trained 2,832 adults 65 to 94 years old in memory, reasoning, or visual attention and perception. The study is slightly less optimistic about the results of mental workouts. Although the trainees performed better on the skill they practiced, that training did not translate to improvement in the other skills. Many mentally active, late-life adults show smaller cognitive decline than their less mentally active counterparts. Yet, the mentally active people most likely had a stronger cognitive reserve (mental capacity) that led them to stay mentally active.[35] More recent research also suggests that fending off cognitive decline is difficult, and follows no simple solution such as doing a crossword puzzle every day, or eating loads of vegetables.[36]

Although this study did not support the "use it or lose it" hypothesis, it demonstrates that older adults can still master specific cognitive tasks with practice. So your grandmother who studies Mandarin Chinese may not then be able to decipher a manual for a smart phone easily, but at least she now knows Mandarin.

Staying physically healthy in general has a positive impact on preserving cognitive functioning. Part of staying healthy is obtaining physical exercise and managing stress. One reason that physical exercise helps brain functioning is that the exercise increases the amount of blood flow to the brain.

Personality and Social Challenges

A change noted in late adulthood is that people begin to value the present more because they correctly perceive that they have a shorter future than do younger adults. As a result, late-life adults are less concerned about activities that may have a payoff in the long run, such as networking. Instead, they look to spend time with good friends and family already available. Practical problems for those in the most advanced years are that many friends die and family members move away. Thus, the late-life adult may have to seek out new friends. Retirement communities, including assisted living, provide an opportunity for affluent older people to make new social contacts, to help compensate for the loss of friends and family members.

A challenge for some late-life adults is to engage in fulfilling physical activities to replace favored activities of previous years. For example, a 75-year-old with a hip and knee replacement may not be able to play tennis or golf any longer and may have to find satisfaction in a replacement activity such as light hiking.

An encouraging observation about career people at various life stages is that they often work together cooperatively to blend their talents and knowledge. The Silicon Valley business model has typically paired together young tech wizards with older counselors such as 22-year-old Stephanie Kaplan, a cofounder of hercampus.com, who meets with media executives with lengthy experience.[37]

LIFE AND JOB SATISFACTION THROUGHOUT THE LIFE SPAN

People at various stages of their life span often wonder what type of satisfaction and happiness awaits them at later stages. Typical self-questions are these: Will I enjoy my work more in late career? Will I be more (or less) happy in my later years? Although the research evidence about life and job satisfaction throughout the life span is not entirely consistent, some trends are notable.

Life Satisfaction and Age

Life satisfaction tends to increase throughout adulthood, partially because many of the major challenges in life are met as one reaches the fifties and sixties. For example, by middle age most people have completed their formal education, chosen a career, and reared children. According to a study by Daniel Mroczek, a psychology professor at Fordham University, life satisfaction for men tends to peak at age 65. His study synthesized more than twenty years of data from almost 2,000 men in the Veterans Affairs Normative Aging Study. The life satisfaction and personal traits of the subjects were measured over almost a thirty-year span.

After life satisfaction peaking around 65, the men around age 95 were about as happy as they were in their mid-forties. Nevertheless, there was considerable variation among individuals, with some people peaking in satisfaction early and then experiencing a permanent decline in happiness. In contrast, some of the men in the study continued to gain in happiness. Personality factors influenced the happiness and satisfaction curve. Highly extraverted people were more likely to have high levels of life satisfaction and more stability in life satisfaction. (One interpretation of these findings is that extraversion helps a person develop friends, and positive human contact contributes to life satisfaction.) Another finding was that life satisfaction dropped considerably during the last year of life—often because a person has poor physical health during his or her final year.[38]

Women also tend to gain in life satisfaction as they become older. Psychology students Brian Scott Ehrlich and Derek Isaacowitz, guided by their professors at the University of Pennsylvania, conducted a study of subjective well-being, including life satisfaction, among young, middle-aged, and older people. The sample consisted of

190 women and 90 men, ranging in age from 18 to 93. Young adults and middle-aged adults showed relatively the same degree of life satisfaction, and older adults tended to be the most satisfied with life. The findings about older people having higher life satisfaction were of modest magnitude, but they did support similar evidence from other studies.[39]

Not all researchers have found that life satisfaction increases with age. Yet the bulk of evidence is at least that the ratings of life satisfaction do not *decline* with age. Apparently, as long as people have a reasonable amount of love and satisfying work, they tend to stay happy.[40]

Job Satisfaction and Age

Job satisfaction also tends to increase with age, as would be predicted, because work satisfaction is such a major component of life satisfaction. A 2011 survey of 62,000 people conducted as part of the Gallup-Healthways Well-Being index found that seniors have the highest level of job satisfaction among U.S. workers. Close to 95 percent of seniors reported being satisfied with their jobs in contrast to 84 percent of workers age 18 to 29 indicating satisfaction.

A general explanation for the many studies indicating the increase in job satisfaction during a person's career is that by the time people reach their fifties, they have discovered in which field they perform the best. Good performance, in turn leads to respect, more autonomy on the job, and more income.[41]

Learning Objective 5

What Are Some Basic Concepts about Changing Careers?

The new type of career emphasizes doing work that fits your major values in life, so many people switch careers to find work that fits their values. And these values could include earning enough money to support a family well and pursue preferred leisure activities. People also switch careers for other factors, such as one's work becoming obsolete, or the need for a higher income. Human Relations Self-Assessment Quiz 15-1 provides you an opportunity to think through why you might need to change careers, including changing a field you intended to enter.

FACTORS INFLUENCING A SUCCESSFUL CAREER CHANGE

A successful career change begins with a clear goal in mind. Clarify what you want to do next and why, explains Cheryl Palmer the owner of a career coaching firm.[42] An example of widely expressed vague goal is "I want to change careers so I can help people." A more specific goal with an explanation would be "I want to change careers so I can be a financial planner and help people make better financial decisions. I think this is important because so many people are in trouble because of poor financial planning."

A major principle of career switching is to *be thorough.* Go through the same kind of thinking and planning that is recommended for finding a first career. Obtaining valid career information is essential, such as consulting www.bls.gov/oco, the online edition of the *Occupational Outlook Handbook.* The advantage for the career switcher, however, is that the experienced person often has a better understanding of the type of work he or she does not want to do. *Finding a mentor* who can help guide you through a career change is also helpful.

One of the first steps in making a career change is to *assess your likes and dislikes.* Career coach Randall S. Hansen advises that many people change careers because they

Human Relations Self-Assessment Quiz 15-1

Should I Be Thinking about a Career Change?

Listed below are ten factors or thoughts that prompt many people to change careers or majors. Check which ones apply to you.

Number	Reason for Career Changing	Yes	No
1.	I hate my field.		
2.	I doubt that my health will enable me to stay in my field for too much longer.		
3.	When I meet people in public or on the Internet, I feel uncomfortable telling them what I do (or will do) for a living.		
4.	I need more status than my current field would bring me.		
5.	About the only satisfaction I get from my line of work (or would get from my potential line of work) is to pay my living expenses.		
6.	My work (or contemplated work) is a poor fit with my personal values.		
7.	I envy people who are working in careers they enjoy.		
8.	I need much more independence than my career allows (or would allow).		
9.	I often calculate how many years there are before I can retire.		
10.	I am definitely unsuited for my field (or contemplated field).		

Scoring and interpretation

If you agreed with seven or more of the above statements, consider seriously speaking to a career counselor about what actions you should take to either find a more satisfying career or make your present career more satisfying. If you agreed with between two and six of the above statements, give some thought to whether you are in the right career. Also, think through what might be the most unsatisfactory parts of your line of work, with an eye toward making some positive changes. If you agreed with none or one of the above statements it could mean that you are in the right field in terms of your interests and values. If you also have the right talent and skills, you are headed for (or have already attained) career success.

dislike their job, their boss, and their company. Yet you also need to examine your likes. What work-related activities excite and energize you?[43] Many people learn more about their career preferences by taking a career assessment instrument combined with the guidance of a career counselor. Two of the most scientifically developed career inventories are as follows:

- Campbell Interest and Skill Survey (http://Keirseycampbell.com)
- 16PF Personal Career Development Profile Plus (www.careers-by-design.com)

A new career should be *built gradually.* Few people are able to leave one career abruptly and step into another. For most people who switch careers successfully, the switch is more of a transition than an abrupt change. A constructive approach would be to take on a few minor assignments in the proposed new field and then search for full-time work in that field after building skill. An electronics technician, for example, might request to visit customers with sales representatives to facilitate a switch to industrial selling. To prepare for your new career, you may need to acquire the necessary education and training, such as an accountant deciding to become a pharmacist.

Sometimes an interim assignment can offer a person useful ideas for a complete career change or at least a different emphasis. One possibility is filling in for someone who is on family leave because of the birth or adoption of a child. Filling in for the boss can give a person a firsthand sense of managerial work.

Another key factor in many career changes is to transfer useful skills from the present career to the new career so you are not starting from zero. Among the skills that transfer well from one career to another are problem-solving, interviewing people, persuasive skills, information technology skills, and resolving conflict.

CHANGING CAREERS WITHOUT CHANGING EMPLOYERS

A major concern many people have about changing careers is the loss of job security that they have already established with a large employer. If you stay with the same employer after a career switch, you are able to retain the same benefits, including retirement contribution. Your familiarity with the corporate culture will still be an asset. However, if the employee switches careers into a lower-rated position, a salary cut might occur. Only a select number of large employers offer the opportunity for a career change, yet it can happen:

> Christine Murphy had been a consultant for Accenture Ltd. for eight years. She then became a human resources professional without leaving the professional-services firm. Murphy arranged the move with the help of an Accenture program that supports internal career changes.
>
> Jill B. Smart, Accenture's chief human resources officer, says she developed the career-change initiative after reviewing exit interviews showing that many employees leave the company because they want to work in different fields. These employees almost always thought they had to look outside the company for a career switch.[44]

From the employer perspective, programs of internal career changes improve retention rates. From the standpoint of the employee, the same program satisfies his or her need to develop new skills and make a career change.

SELF-EMPLOYMENT AS A CAREER CHANGE

A major reason that many employees consider a new career is that they crave more independence. As a consequence, an increasingly popular path for the career switcher is to move from salaried employment to self-employment. The prospective self-employed person needs to decide on which particular business to enter. For many people, self-employment means continuing to perform similar work, such as the company cafeteria manager entering the food catering business. Other formerly employed workers go into competition with their former employers, such as a restaurant manager opening a restaurant of his or her own. Another approach to self-employment is to choose an enterprise that fits a passion of yours, such as a wine connoisseur opening a wine store or operating a wine-store franchise.

A major opportunity for self-employment is to purchase a franchise, thus lowering the risk of a start-up business. Currently, franchises account for about one-third of retail sales in the United States and Canada. Yet franchises require a substantial financial investment, ranging from about $6,000 to over $1 million. Furthermore, some of the big name franchisors, such as Dunkin' Donuts, require that the franchisee purchase multiple stores simply to get started. Another caution is that some franchise operators may work about seventy hours per week to earn about $18,000 per year.

Franchise opportunities continue to grow, with franchises available in many types of businesses and services, including the following:

- Business coaching and consulting
- Children's enrichment programs including reading, writing, and physical fitness
- Building siding systems
- Sports equipment and apparel
- Travel agencies for cruises
- Computer troubleshooting
- Cell phone and smart phone repair
- Child care
- Senior care

Anyone contemplating self-employment of any type should recognize that it offers potentially high rewards as well as risks. Wealth and personal satisfaction are possible. However, if the fledgling enterprise does not do well immediately, the owner may have to live for a couple of years without income.

What Are Some Tactics for Coping with Change?

Learning Objective 6

We have all heard that adapting to change is necessary for career success, and even survival. At the same time, a well-accepted proposition is that change is never easy.[45] Many people need help occasionally when changes at work present challenges. A fitting conclusion to this chapter is therefore to present a few tactics for coping with change. A useful strategy for coping with many changes is to *be proactive, not reactive*.[46] Think through the possible workplace changes that might take place, and get ready as soon as possible. For example, if it appears that your company will be getting rid of as much office space as feasible in the near future, begin preparing yourself for doing more work from remote locations. A few more specific tactics follow.

First, *look for the personal value that could be embedded in a forced change*.[47] If you are downsized, take the opportunity to assume responsibility for your own career rather than being dependent on the organization. Many downsizing victims find a new career for themselves that better fits their interests or try self-employment in search of more job security. Whether or not self-employment is truly more secure than working for a large employer, many people fear that a big company will lay them off during a corporate downsizing.

When faced with a significant change, *ask "What if?" questions*, such as What if my company is sold tomorrow? What if I went back to school for more education? and What if I did accept that one-year assignment in China? When confronting major change, *force yourself to enjoy at least some small aspect of the change*. Suppose the edict comes through the organization that purchases can now be made only over the Internet. This means you will no longer be able to interact with a few of the sales reps you considered to be buddies. With the time you save, however, you will have spare hours each week for leisure activities.

You are less likely to resist change if you *recognize that change is inevitable*. Dealing with change is an integral part of life, so why fight it? Keep in mind also to *change before you have to, which can lead to a better deal*. If your manager announces a new plan, get on board as a volunteer before you are forced to accept a lesser role. If your company has made the decision to start a Six Sigma (company wide quality improvement) program, study the subject early and ask for a role as a facilitator or team leader. Stop trying to be in control all the time, because you cannot control everything. Many changes will occur that you cannot control, so relax and enjoy the ride. Finally, recognize that change has an emotional impact, which will most likely cause some inner turmoil and discomfort. Even if the change is for the better, you might remain emotionally attached to your old system—or neighborhood, car, or desktop computer.

Continuing to acquire useful knowledge is also helpful in dealing with change because you have the new knowledge at hand to get past the change. When digital photography became dominant, the operators of many portrait studios felt threatened and were too slow to offer digital services to their customers. Many of these photographers who waited too long to offer digital services were forced out of business. In contrast, many other portrait photographers were early learners of digital technology and survived the transition well.

The bestseller *The World Is Flat: A Brief History of the Twenty-First Century* (2005)[48] by Thomas L. Friedman has made thousands of educators and individuals aware of the potential changes imposed on us by globalization and outsourcing. One key point of the book is that the global economic playing field has been leveled by information technology that enables people to collaborate regardless of their location. Another key point is that the success of individual workers will depend on the development of specialized skills. Furthermore, to cope with these changes workers must constantly upgrade their skills. At the same time, they should search for jobs that cannot be outsourced or that are anchored because they must be done at a specific location, such as calling on an industrial customer.

Many personal-service jobs cannot be outsourced or sent offshore, including hairdressers, massage therapists, custodial technicians, and auto mechanics. Yet even here, some personal-service workers in North America complain that residents from lower-wage countries are willing to perform these services at lower wages than the North American workers are. Some corporate professional jobs are more difficult to outsource than others. The positions less likely to be outsourced are those requiring the combination of technical (or discipline) skills plus connections with people. A real estate agent with hundreds of personal contacts cannot be replaced by a Web site. An information systems specialist who performs hands-on work with managers at his or her company cannot be replaced by an information technology specialist working 8,000 miles away in another country. The change-management lesson here is that building relationships with work associates helps ward off some of the threats of the "flat world."

Key Terms

Learning, 450
Classical conditioning, 450
Operant conditioning, 451
Negative reinforcement, 451
Punishment, 451
Extinction, 451
Modeling, 452
Informal learning, 452
Implicit learning, 452
E-learning, 453
Group learning, 455
Learning style, 455
Perception, 459
Selective attention, 460
Perceptual congruence, 461
Attribution theory, 461
Adolescence, 463
Identity crisis, 464
Teenage brain, 464
Midlife crisis, 465
Midlife transition, 465
Sandwich generation, 465
Cognitive fitness, 466

Summary and Review

In this chapter we have studied additional knowledge that helps a person attain career thrust.

- Classical conditioning is the most elementary form of learning. It occurs when a previously neutral stimulus is associated with a natural (unconditioned) stimulus. Eventually, the neutral stimulus brings forth the unconditioned response. For example, a factory whistle blown just prior to the lunch break induces employees to salivate and experience hunger pangs.
- Operant conditioning (or instrumental learning) occurs when a person's spontaneous actions are rewarded or punished, which results in an increase or a decrease in the behavior. Much of human learning occurs through operant conditioning. The four reinforcement strategies involved in such conditioning are positive reinforcement, negative reinforcement, punishment, and extinction. A continuous reinforcement schedule rewards behavior each time it occurs, whereas an intermittent schedule delivers rewards periodically.
- Two important processes that help in learning complicated skills are modeling and informal learning. Modeling occurs when you learn a skill by observing another person perform that skill. Informal learning is unplanned and occurs in a setting without a formal classroom, lesson plan, instructor, or examination. Informal learning can be spontaneous, or the company might organize the work area to encourage such learning. Informal learning can be regarded as a form of implicit learning.
- E-learning is an Internet form of computer-based training. The geographical dispersion of employees makes e-learning more important. Self-motivation and self-discipline are essential for the e-learner. Most companies continue to use blended learning (Web and classroom) to capitalize on the efficiencies of e-learning yet still rely on human contact.
- Groups can learn in the sense that members come to adapt their behavior collectively in response to experience. Group learning has the three basic features of sharing, storage (in the brain), and retrieval.
- People learn best in different ways—for example, some people acquire information best through passive learning. A preference for working alone versus cooperatively is another difference in learning style.
- According to the Golden Personality Type Profiler, two dimensions of psychological functioning are the basis for the relationship between personality and learning style. We judge through thinking (T) and feeling (F). We perceive through sensing (S) and intuition (N). The four mental processes of thinking, feeling, sensing, and intuition result in four learning styles, as shown in Figure 15-1.
- In general, people with higher mental ability and personality traits that allow them to concentrate better (for example, conscientiousness) acquire knowledge and skills more readily.
- A reality of almost all professional, technical, and sales occupations is that career success and survival depend on continuous learning.

- Perception, the organization of sensory information into meaningful experiences, influences job behavior. Perceptual problems stem from both a stimulus with an emotional meaning and the mental processes of people. These mental processes, or shortcuts, include selective attention, denial, stereotyping, the halo effect, and projection.
- Perceptual congruence refers to the degree to which people perceive things the same way. High congruence generally leads to more positive consequences for the organization than does low congruence.
- Attribution theory explains how people attribute the causes of behavior. People have a general tendency to attribute their achievements to good inner qualities, whereas they attribute failure to adverse factors within the environment.
- According to Erickson, the socialization process consists of the "eight stages of man," with each state representing a psychosocial crisis. The crisis must be resolved at each stage before the next stage can be successfully negotiated.
- The challenges of adolescence include the cognitive challenge of developing logic and abstract thought as well as developing moral reasoning. A key personality and social challenge is the identity crisis. Successfully managing the teenage brain is another challenge, with the brain being quite adept at new learning yet tending toward impulsiveness and lack of empathy.
- The challenges of adulthood include applying cognitive skills to real-life problems. Adults must also learn to become less self-centered and refine their interpersonal skills. Adults may also face a midlife crisis and a midlife transition, as well as being part of the sandwich generation.
- The challenges of late adulthood include cognitive decline, even though older people can be trained to learn new, complex tasks. A change facing late-life adults is more of a focus on the present.
- Life satisfaction tends to increase throughout adulthood but may peak for men at about age 65. Job satisfaction also tends to increase with age, partially because older adults have gravitated into positions for which they have skills, and are rewarded.
- A successful career change begins with a clear goal. A major principle of career switching is to be thorough. Obtain valid career information, and assess your likes and dislikes. A new career should be built gradually, often by phasing into the new career part-time. An increasingly popular path for the career switcher is to move from salaried employment to self-employment.
- Suggestions for managing change well include being proactive, searching for the personal value that could be embedded in forced change, asking "What if," forcing yourself to enjoy at least some small aspect of the change, recognizing that change is inevitable, and understanding that change has an emotional impact. To help cope with possible changes caused by outsourcing and offshoring of one's job is to incorporate building relationships into one's job.

Check Your Understanding

1. Why is it that so many employers believe that a valuable skill for their employees is to "learn how to learn"?
2. How might having a mentor contribute to your learning through modeling?
3. Provide an example of knowledge that you have acquired without a conscious intention to learn.
4. What steps can a company take to encourage informal learning among employees?
5. If e-learning is so effective, why haven't most schools of higher education converted completely to distance learning?
6. Give an example of where it *is* true that perception is more important than reality.
7. What evidence can you present that you now have, or ever had, a *teenage brain*? Or what evidence can you present that you do not have, or never have had, a *teenage brain*?
8. How does the widespread use of information and communication technology force most workers to be continuous learners?
9. What are the reasons that a 40-year-old college president would be regarded as *young* by so many people, yet a 40-year-old professional athlete would be regarded as *old*?
10. What is your strategy for dealing with the biggest change you will have to face during the next twelve months?

Web Corner

Changing a bad habit
www.changeonehabit.com
http://www.ehow.com/how_4530057_change-bad-habits.html

Insight into your learning style based on multiple intelligences
www.edutopia.org/your-learning-styles

Information about career changing
www.quintcareers.com

INTERNET SKILL BUILDER

Millennial Life Span Challenges

Although opinions vary as to the precise meaning of a *millennial,* the term generally refers to the last generation born in the twentieth century. Search the Internet to identify about ten life span challenges facing the millennials—in other words, challenges facing members of this generation attributed to their stage in life. You can probably supplement the list with reading you have done or personal observations. Did you find the World Wide Web useful for this type of search, or did you have better luck with a library database?

Developing Your Human Relations Skills

Human Relations Application Exercises

Applying Human Relations Exercise 15-1

Developing Your Brain and Learning Ability

The belief is widespread that the human brain can be developed through mental exercise. We found about 181 million entries using the Bing search engine entry "exercising the brain." Even when a given brain builder may work for many other people, you do not know if the technique will help you specifically. Here is an opportunity to try a brain exercise and see what the positive consequences might be for you. You will need a few minutes a day for at least ten days to determine whether the technique works. First, do one or both of the following exercises for ten to fourteen days:

1. Recite the alphabet backward until you are proficient. Perform the exercise a few times a day until you can do the backward version almost as easily as the forward version.
2. Learn a new word in your native language or your second language every day. Visualize the new words that you have learned during this time span.

After the ten days or two weeks are completed, reflect on your learning ability and memory. Compare your learning on new tasks today with your learning in the past. Is it easier for you to study? Do you grasp the meaning of news stories more quickly? Can you remember phone numbers or e-mail addresses more readily? If other classmates have done this exercise, ask them about their experiences. Have these exercises resulted in more brain power for them?

If these straightforward exercises really improve brain power, what are some of the implications for human relations?

Source: The core idea for the two games is credited to http://me.essortment.com/brainexercises_rcas.htm.

Applying Human Relations Exercise 15-2

Life Span Challenges Facing Seniors

The life span challenges described in this chapter that seniors face are certainly valid. Your role in this exercise is to find out directly what challenges advanced seniors face. We refer to people 70 years old and beyond. The older the people you can find for this study, the better. Do you have access to a person at least 100 years old? Conduct interviews with parents (if they qualify), grandparents, nursing home residents, friends, and neighbors. Obtain a sample of at least four people. Ask your interviewees about the challenges and problems they face now, those in the recent past, and those they anticipate in the future. After you have collected your interview data, answer these questions:

1. What are the physical and health problems facing these seniors?
2. What are the emotional and human relations problems facing these seniors?
3. What could other people do to help these seniors with some of their most pressing concerns?

Human Relations Class Activity

Capitalizing on the Halo Effect

The halo effect can work to a person's advantage or disadvantage in terms of job finding and career advancement, depending on how a person is perceived. The class assignment is to investigate which characteristics or behaviors of a professional or future professional will help or hurt him or her. Each student in the class communicates with an experienced worker in speaking or writing to obtain answers to the following two questions:

1. Give me an example of a characteristic or action of a worker that would make you think he or she either is worthy of hiring or has good potential to advance in his or her career.
2. Give me an example of a characteristic or action of a worker that would make you think he or she either is not worthy of hiring or has limited potential to advance in his or her career.

Next, individual students enter their survey findings into a shared database or class Web site or e-mail their findings to all other students. After looking through all the results, reach a conclusion about positive and negative halos held by participants in the survey. For example, two results might be (1) "It looks like having good oral communication skills creates a positive halo" and (2) "It looks like being rude creates a negative halo."

After students have reached their conclusions, a brief class discussion is held about frequent reasons for creating a positive or negative halo and how useful this information might be.

Human Relations Case Study 15-1

Julie's Bad Habit

Julie works as a market research analyst at a large business communications firm, a position she has held for close to one year. Her primary responsibility is to conduct research via the Internet on a variety of topics. Sometimes her research assignments are to provide information to be used in an advertising or public relations campaign conducted by her employer. At other times, she conducts research needed by a client instead of tracking down information to be used for an advertising or public relations campaign.

Julie's recent Internet researches have included finding answers to the following: (a) What percent of subcompact cars are bought by Latinos? (b) How much per year do people under 30 spend on vitamins and food supplements? (c) How many people age 65 and over purchase single-use cameras?

Julie's boss is satisfied with most of the results of Julie's Internet research but not with her speed. Julie has explained her predicament to her manager in these terms:

> I'm sorry that I don't get my Internet researches done faster. My problem is that I've developed some bad habits that have become part of how I work. About every ten minutes I check my e-mail. And on days the stock exchange is open, I check how the market is doing about every fifteen minutes. About six times a day I check to see if I have a LinkedIn message. Also, I sometimes take a quick peek at my cell phone to see if anybody has left me a tweet.
>
> My habit is that I check my e-mail, the stock market results, LinkedIn, or Twitter right after I've accomplished something, like having found a Web site that seems to have the information I need. When I do not to check my e-mail or the Web sites, I become so nervous that I cannot concentrate on my work. But I don't go outside for a cigarette like some of my coworkers do.

On more than one occasion, Julie's boss has explained to her that if she can't break her bad habit, she will have to find another job.

Questions

1. What do you recommend Julie do to break her "bad habit"?
2. What might Julie's manager do to help her get her Internet research accomplished more quickly?
3. How might Julie continue with her checking habit yet still get her work accomplished on time?

Human Relations Role-Playing Exercise

Julie's Boss Attempts to Break Her Bad Habit

The case study about Julie serves as the background and the story line for this role-play. One person plays the role of Julie, who feels that if she does not break, or lessen, her habit of checking her e-mail and Internet sites, she could lose her job. Her boss, Kim, will be visiting her cubicle right after lunch to see if she can help Julie.

Another person plays the role of Kim, who wants to help Julie but also recognizes that research has to get accomplished quickly to be most useful to the firm. Kim is not very sympathetic toward the idea that a bad habit is a valid excuse for not getting work accomplished on time. Kim attended parochial school, where the teachers were quite strict about students paying full attention to their work. She remembers clearly how laptop computers and cell phones were not allowed in the classroom unless they were needed for a class assignment.

Observers rate the role-players on two dimensions, using a 1 to 5 scale from very poor to very good. One dimension is "effective use of human relations techniques." For Kim, focus on how effective she is in helping Julie correct her bad habit. The second dimension is "acting ability." A few observers might voluntarily provide feedback to the role-players in terms of sharing their ratings and observations. The course instructor might also provide feedback.

Human Relations Case Study 15-2

Dental Marketing Specialist Brad

Brad, a former marketing and information technology major, at age 21, founded Dental Outreach. The purpose of his small firm was to establish a variety of Internet-based marketing programs for dental practices. His mother and father are both practicing dentists. Being part of a dental family has helped Brad understand the need for dentists to attract new patients, retain current patients, and also expand services including teeth whitening and restoration. Among the many initiatives taken by his firm was to electronically send birthday cards, reminders about dental appointments, and dental health tips.

Dental Outreach was off to a good start, as Brad sold his marketing program to six dental practices he knew through his family, as well as a couple of referrals. To expand his business, Brad used the phone and an e-mail campaign to line up a few prospects. He thought that as a young entrepreneur with a technology-based company, he should look the role of a tech savvy young person. So Brad would show up at offices of prospective customers with shaggy hair, stubble on his face, as well as wearing jeans and a tee shirt with Dental Outreach printed on the back.

Brad was successful in a few of these office calls to generate new business, but he encountered some resistance. One office receptionist and manager said to Brad, "Oh, I thought the owner was coming here to discuss Dental Outreach. Are you the tech support person?" One of the dentists who spoke to Brad said, "What you have to offer seems on target. But I am not going to leave the marketing of my practice to a teenager."

After ten sales calls, Brad became a little discouraged. He thought to himself, "Maybe it's too early in my career to operate a dental marketing service."

Questions

1. What does this case have to do with perception, as well as life stages?
2. To what extent is Brad being a victim of age discrimination?
3. What advice can you offer Brad to help him attain more success in obtaining more customers for Dental Outreach?

REFERENCES

1. Original story created from facts and observations in the following sources: Devesh Dwivedi, "Employee Turned Entrepreneur—David Heitner," pp. 1-9, retrieved March 20, 2012, from: www.entrepreneurinmaking.com/blog/; Al Lewis, "Former Lynch Broker Cleans Up with Career," *The Denver Post* (www.denverpost.com), November 17, 2009, pp. 1-3; "Your Quick Guide to Professional Cleaning" (http://heitsofcentrallnc.com), © 2010, Heits Building Services.
2. John W. Donahoe and David C. Palmer, *Learning and Complex Behavior* (Boston: Allyn & Bacon, 1994), p. 2.
3. Research reported in Charles Duhigg, "Warning: Habits May Be Good for You," *New York Times* (www.nytimes.com), July 13, 2008, p. 3.
4. Michael A. Stadlelr and Peter A. Frensch, eds., *Handbook of Implicit Learning* (Thousand Oaks, CA: Sage, 1998).
5. "Hard-to-Read Fonts Promote Better Recall," *Harvard Business Review*, March 2012, pp. 32–33.
6. Greg Wright, "Retailers Buy Into E-Learning," *HR Magazine*, December 2010, p. 87.
7. Karen Frankola, "Why Online Learners Drop Out," *Workforce*, October 2001, p. 54.
8. "Assessing Online Learning: Defining the Efficacy of Online Learning," *Keying In*, March 2001, p. 3.
9. "The Business Value of E-Learning," *Elearning!* (www.2elearning.com), December 18, 2007.
10. Joe Mullich, "A Second Act for E-Learning," *Workforce Management*, February 2004, p. 52.
11. Stephen Paskoff, "The Ethical Workplace," *Workforce Management*, October 2011, p. 49.
12. Jeanne M. Wilson, Paul S. Goodman, and Matthew A. Cronin, "Group Learning," *Academy of Management Review*, October 2007, pp. 1041–1059.
13. Wanda L. Stitt-Gohdes, "Teaching and Learning Styles: Implications for Business Teacher Education," in *The Twenty-First Century: Meeting the Challenges to Business Education* (Reston, VA: National Business Education Association, 1999), p. 10.
14. Isabel Briggs Myers, *Introduction to Type*, 6th ed. (Mountain View, CA: CPP, Inc., 1998), p. 10. Revised by Linda K. Kirby and Katharine D. Myers.
15. John Patrick Golden, *Golden Personality Type Profiler Technical Manual* (San Antonio, TX: Pearson TalentLens, 2005).
16. Golden, *Golden Personality Type Profiler*, p. 27.
17. The quote and the content in this section are from Mark Greer, "Strengthen Your Brain by Resting It," *Monitor on Psychology*, July/August 2004, p. 60.
18. Giulio Tononi, "Understanding the Function of Sleep Comes One Step Closer," *Medical News Today* (www.medicalnewstoday.com), May 4, 2007, p. 2.
19. Ricky W. Griffin, "Effects of Work Redesign on Employee Perceptions, Attitudes, and Behavior: A Long-Term Investigation,"*Academy of Management Journal*, June 1991, p. 42.
20. Erik H. Erikson, *Childhood and Society* (New York: Norton, 1963); Child Development Institute, "Stages of Social-Emotional Development in Children and Teenagers," retrieved May 6, 2006, from: www.childdevelpmentinfo.com.
21. Our discussion of the challenges of adolescence and adulthood follows closely Saul Kassin, *Psychology*, 3rd ed. (Upper Saddle River, NJ: Prentice Hall, 2001), pp. 406–440; and Charles G. Morris and Albert A. Maisto, *Psychology: An Introduction*, 11th ed. (Upper Saddle River, NJ: Prentice Hall, 2002), pp. 418–441.
22. Lawrence Kohlberg, *Essays on Moral Development: Vol. 2. The Psychology of Moral Development* (New York: Harper & Row, 1984).
23. Debra Bradley Ruder, "A Work in Progress: The Teen Brain," *Harvard Magazine* (http://harvardmagazine.com/2008/09/the-teen-brain.html); "Teaching the At-Risk Teenage Brain," *ASCD Inservice*.
24. Research reported in Alison Gopnik, "What's Wrong with the Teenage Mind?" *The Wall Street Journal*, January 28–29, 2012, p. C1.
25. Sara Goudarzi, "Study: Teenage Brain Lacks Empathy: Area of Brain Associated with Higher-Level Thinking Underused in Youths,"*LiveScience*, September 8, 2006, pp. 1–2.
26. Melissa Lee Phillips, "The Mind at Midlife," *Monitor on Psychology*, April 11, 2011, pp. 38–41.
27. Sheri Stritof and Bob Stritof, "Sandwich Generation: The Cluttered Nest Syndrome," retrieved April 7, 2009, from: www.about.com.marriage.
28. Stritof and Stritof, "Sandwich Generation."
29. Quoted in Amy Novotney, "What Works to Protect Cognition?" *Monitor on Psychology*, November 2010, p. 36.
30. Melinda Beck, "The Science Behind 'Senior Moments,' " *The Wall Street Journal*, May 27, 2008, p. D1.
31. Robert Lee Hotz, "Surveying the Brain for Origins of the Senior Moment," *The Wall Street Journal*, December 2, 2008, p. A14.
32. Roderick Gilkey and Clint Kitts, "Cognitive Fitness," *Harvard Business Review*, November 2007, pp. 53–66.
33. Research reported in Andrea Bartz, "Watered-Down Thinking," *Psychology Today*, January/February 2011, p. 37.
34. Research reported in Bonnie Rochman, "Workouts for Your Brain," *Time*, January 18, 2010, p. 60.
35. Research from the *New England Journal of Medicine* summarized in Sharon Begley, "Oops! Mental Training, Crosswords Fail to Slow Decline of Aging Brain," *The Wall Street Journal*, April 21, 2006, p. B1; Begley, "Studies on Dementia Often Confuse Causes with Consequences," *The Wall Street Journal*, April 28, 2006, p. B1.
36. Novotney, "What Works to Protect Cognition?" p. 38.
37. Debra Shigley, "Life's New Timeline," *Psychology Today*, November/December 2011, p. 67.
38. Research summarized in Karen Kersting, "Happiness in Men Usually Drops After Age 65, Study Finds," *Monitor on Psychology*, March 2005, p. 10.
39. Brian Scott Ehrlich and Derek Isaacowitz, "Does Subjective Well-Being Increase with Age?" *Perspectives in Psychology*, Spring 2002, pp. 20–26.
40. Kassin, *Psychology*, p. 435.
41. Study cited in Frances Burke, "What Is the Relationship Between Job Satisfaction and Age?" pp. 1–2, retrieved March 26, 2012, from: www.smallbusiness.chron.com.
42. Cited in Kaitlin Madden, "Plan a Successful Career Change," *Career Builder*, March 11, 2012.

43. Randall S. Hansen, "Quintessential Careers: The 10-Step Plan to Career Change," retrieved April 13, 2006, from: www.quintcareers.com.
44. Sarah E. Needleman, "New Career, Same Employer," *The Wall Street Journal,* April 21, 2008, p. B9.
45. "Dealing with Change in the Workplace" (Employee Assistance Program), p. 1, retrieved March 26, 2012, from: *Maine.gov.*
46. Tino Toskala, "Coping with Change in Your Workplace—Be Proactive, Not Reactive," *Ezine @rticles,* p. 1, retrieved March 26, 2012, from: www.ezinearticles.com.
47. This and the next item noted are from Fred Pryor, "What Have You Learned From Change?" *Manager's Edge,* September 1998, p. 2.
48. Thomas L. Friedman, *The World Is Flat: A Brief History of the Twenty-First Century* (New York: Farrar, Straus and Giroux, 2005).

16

Developing Good Work Habits

Outline

Adriana Cisneros De Griffin is loaded with responsibility as an executive, and also manages an active family and personal life. She is the chairwoman and director of strategy of the Cisneros Group of Companies, one of the largest privately held media, entertainment, and consumer product business firms in the world. The Cisneros Group wholly owns or controls companies ranging from broadcast television and television production to consumer products and real estate.

Cisneros is the granddaughter of the business empire's founder, Diego Cisneros, and the daughter of its recent chairman, Gustavo Cisneros. Cisneros has a BA from Columbia University, a master's degree in journalism from New York University, and a master's degree from Harvard Business School.

Cisnero's job is worldwide, but she lives in New York City. She says that when she is home, she rises early to jog along the West Side Highway. After returning home, she wakes up her two children, eats breakfast with them, and then heads to the office. She begins her workday by touching base with several teams located around the world. The balance of her day is spent in meetings and conference calls with strategic partners. When she can free up the time, she has lunch at a restaurant with colleagues or potential business partners.

After completing her day at the office, Cisneros heads home to have dinner with her children, bathe them, and read stories. After the children are asleep, she spends quality time with her husband.

While travelling on business, Cisneros spends considerable time in meetings, developing new relationships, and networking in the community with people who could have an impact on her business. Despite her heavy business travel, Cisneros makes it home for the weekend so she can spend time with her family. Her favorite hobby is climbing mountains with a peak of about 14,000 feet, and aspires to climb Kilimanjaro.[1]

Learning Objectives ▸

After studying the information and doing the exercises in this chapter, you should be able to:

1 Appreciate the importance of good work habits and time management.

2 Decrease any tendencies you might have toward procrastination.

3 Develop attitudes and values that will help you become more productive.

4 Develop skills and techniques that will help you become more productive.

5 Overcome time-wasting practices.

An important implication of the story about the international strategy executive is that you have to be well organized to hold down a major executive position, and still maintain a family life and pursue personal interests. Because good work habits and time management (including concentrating carefully on a major task) improve productivity, they contribute to success in business.

Work habits refer to a person's characteristic approach to work, including such things as organization, priority setting, and handling of e-mail and intranets. Good work habits and time management are more important than ever because of today's emphasis on **productivity,** which is the amount of useful work accomplished in relation to the resources consumed. Being more productive often translates into eliminating unnecessary steps and finding ways to get more accomplished in less time.

Work habits
a person's characteristic approach to work, including such things as organization, priority setting, and handling of paperwork and e-mail

Productivity
the amount of quality work accomplished in relation to the resources consumed

Also, because so many workers are expected to be productive without close supervision, including the telecommuter, good work habits increase in importance. Furthermore, a person is more likely to be fired from a job or flunk out of school because of poor work habits than because of poor aptitude.

People with good work habits tend to achieve higher career success and have more time to invest in their personal lives. They also enjoy their personal lives more because they are not preoccupied with unfinished tasks. Effective work habits are also beneficial because they eliminate a major stressor—the feeling of having very little or no control over your life. Being in control also leads to a relaxed, confident approach to work.

The goal of this chapter is to help you become a more productive person who is still flexible. Someone who develops good work habits is not someone who becomes so obsessed with time and is so rigid that he or she makes other people feel uncomfortable. Ideally, a person should be well organized yet still flexible.

Information about becoming more productive is organized here into four related categories. First is overcoming procrastination, a problem that plagues almost everybody to some extent. The second is developing attitudes and values that foster productivity. The third category is the lengthiest: developing skills and techniques that lead to personal productivity. The fourth category is overcoming time wasters.

▶ Learning Objective 1 ▶

How Does a Person Deal with Procrastination?

Procrastination
delaying a task for an invalid or weak reason

The leading cause of poor productivity and career self-sabotage is **procrastination**—delaying a task for an invalid or weak reason. Another way of understanding procrastination is that it is the gap between intention and action. We want to do something but we delay taking action, often because the immediate reward associated with delay is more important at the moment than the reward that will come later from completing a task.[2] Perhaps Melissa wants to start working on her income tax report because the tax deadline is soon approaching. However, she delays starting the tax project for an hour so she can get the immediate reward of checking the "status" of twenty-five of her Facebook friends. The reward Melissa is delaying is the satisfaction of getting her tax form completed, and perhaps a $2,500 refund.

Procrastination is the major work habit problem for most workers and students. Unproductive people are the biggest procrastinators, but even productive people have problems with procrastination at times. A business owner who does not ordinarily procrastinate might delay preparing a safety and health report, knowing that a few safety violations might be found on the premises.

WHY PEOPLE PROCRASTINATE

People procrastinate for many different reasons, as described in the following list.

1. **Unpleasant task or overwhelming task.** When we perceive the task to be done (such as quitting a job) as unpleasant, we tend to procrastinate. Similarly, we tend to procrastinate when we perceive the job facing us to be overwhelming, such as assembling a computer console that arrives in a large box. To avoid an overwhelming or taxing task, some people flood their workday with small, easy-to-do tasks. As a result, these people do not appear to be procrastinators on the surface.[3]
2. **Fear of consequences.** Another major cause of procrastination is a fear of the consequences of our actions. One possible negative consequence is a negative evaluation of your work. For example, if you delay preparing a report for your boss or instructor, that person cannot criticize its quality. Bad news is another negative consequence that procrastination can sometimes delay. If you think your smart phone may need to be replaced because it no longer works well, delaying a trip to the electronics store will avoid the verdict of "replacement needed."

Fear of success
belief that if one succeeds at an important task, one will be asked to take on more responsibility in the future; a reason some people procrastinate

3. **Fear of success.** Another reason some people procrastinate is the **fear of success.** People sometimes believe that if they succeed at an important task they will be asked to take on more responsibility in the future. They dread this possibility. Some

students have been known to procrastinate completing their degree requirements to avoid taking on the responsibility of a full-time position.

4. **Lack of meaningful reward.** People frequently put off tasks that do not appear to offer a meaningful reward. Suppose you decide that your résumé needs a thorough updating, including deleting not-so-relevant information. Even if you know this task should be done, the accomplishment of an updated résumé might not be a meaningful reward, particularly if you are not in the job market.
5. **Rebelling against control.** Many people procrastinate as a way of rebelling against being controlled. Procrastination, used in this way, is a means of defying unwarranted authority.[4] Rather than submit to authority, a person might tell himself, "Nobody is going to tell me when I should get a report done. I'll do it when I'm good and ready." Such people might be referred to as "anti-control freaks."
6. **Enjoying the rush.** A curious reason for procrastination is to achieve the stimulation and excitement that stems from rushing to meet a deadline. Some people, for example, enjoy fighting their way through traffic or running through an airline terminal so they can make an appointment or airplane flight barely on time. They appear to enjoy the rush of adrenaline, endorphins, and other hormones associated with hurrying.
7. **Perfectionism.** Finally, some people procrastinate because they are perfectionists. They attempt to perfect a project before being willing to admit the project is completed. As a result, the person procrastinates not about beginning a project but about letting go. When asked, "Have you finished that project?" the perfectionist replies, "No, there a few small details that still need to be worked out." Being a perfectionist can also block starting new projects because the perfectionist will often want to keep working on the present project. The perfectionist is often hesitant to take on the risk of a new project because trying something new is likely to result in mistakes. Also, perfectionists like order, and a new task may not be so easy to organize.[5] Perfectionism comes in degrees, with slight perfectionists simply being extremely conscientious and heavy-duty perfectionists almost stalled in their actions. Human Relations Self-Assessment Quiz 16-1 gives you an opportunity to measure your degree of perfectionism.

TECHNIQUES FOR REDUCING PROCRASTINATION

To overcome or at least minimize procrastination, we recommend a number of specific tactics. A general approach, however, is simply to be aware that procrastination is a major drain on productivity. Being aware of the problem will remind you to take corrective action in many situations. When your accomplishment level is low, you might ask yourself, "Am I procrastinating on anything of significance?"

Calculate the cost of procrastination. You can reduce procrastination by calculating its cost.[6] One example is that you might lose out on obtaining a high-paying job you really want by not having your résumé and cover letter ready on time. Your cost of procrastination would include the difference in salary between the job you do find and the one you really wanted. Another cost would be the loss of potential job satisfaction.

Counterattack. Forcing yourself to do something overwhelming, frightening, or uncomfortable helps to prove that the task was not as bad as initially perceived. Assume that you have accepted a new position but have not yet resigned from your present one because resigning seems so uncomfortable. Set up a specific time to call your manager or send an e-mail to schedule an appointment. Force yourself further to show up for the resignation appointment. After you break the ice with the statement "I have something important to tell you," the task will be much easier.

Human Relations Self-Assessment Quiz 16-1

Tendencies Toward Perfectionism

Many perfectionists hold some of the following behaviors and attitudes. To help understand your tendencies toward perfectionism, rate how strongly you agree with each of the statements below on a scale of 0 to 4: 0 = disagree strongly; 1 = disagree; 2 = neutral; 3 = agree; 4 = strongly agree.

	Statement					
1.	Many people have told me that I am a perfectionist.	0	1	2	3	4
2.	I often correct the speech of others.	0	1	2	3	4
3.	It takes me a long time to write an e-mail because I keep checking and rechecking my writing.	0	1	2	3	4
4.	I often criticize the color combinations my friends are wearing.	0	1	2	3	4
5.	When I purchase food at a supermarket, I usually look at the expiration date so I can purchase the freshest.	0	1	2	3	4
6.	I can't stand when people use the term *remote* instead of *remote control.*	0	1	2	3	4
7.	If a company representative asked me, "What is your *social*?" I would reply something like, "Do you mean my *Social Security number*?"	0	1	2	3	4
8.	Neatness is very important to me.	0	1	2	3	4
9.	I like the idea of having every decoration in my home just right.	0	1	2	3	4
10.	I never put a map back in the glove compartment until it is folded just right.	0	1	2	3	4
11.	Once an eraser on a pencil of mine becomes hard and useless, I throw the pencil away.	0	1	2	3	4
12.	I adjust all my watches and clocks so they show exactly the same time.	0	1	2	3	4
13.	It bothers me that all the clocks at an athletic club or college sometimes do not have the same exact time.	0	1	2	3	4
14.	I clean the keyboard on my computer at least once a week.	0	1	2	3	4
15.	I organize my e-mail messages and computer documents into many different, clearly labeled files.	0	1	2	3	4
16.	You won't find old coffee cups or soft-drink containers on my desk.	0	1	2	3	4
17.	I rarely start a new project or assignment until I have completed my present project or assignment.	0	1	2	3	4
18.	It is very difficult for me to concentrate when my work area is disorganized.	0	1	2	3	4
19.	Cobwebs in chandeliers and other lighting fixtures bug me.	0	1	2	3	4
20.	It takes me a long time to make a purchase such as a video camera because I keep studying the features on various models.	0	1	2	3	4
21.	When I balance my checkbook, it usually comes out right within a few dollars.	0	1	2	3	4
22.	I carry enough small coins and dollar bills with me so when I shop I can pay the exact amount without requiring change.	0	1	2	3	4
23.	I throw out any underwear or T-shirts that have even the smallest holes or tears.	0	1	2	3	4
24.	I become upset with myself if I make a mistake.	0	1	2	3	4
25.	When a fingernail of mine is broken or chipped, I fix it as soon as possible.	0	1	2	3	4
26.	I am carefully groomed whenever I leave my home.	0	1	2	3	4
27.	When I notice packaged goods or cans on the floor in a supermarket, I will often place them back on the shelf.	0	1	2	3	4

28.	I think that carrying around antibacterial cleaner for the hands is an excellent idea.	0	1	2	3	4
29.	If I am with a friend, and he or she has a loose hair on his or her shoulder, I will remove it without asking.	0	1	2	3	4
30.	I know that I am a perfectionist.	0	1	2	3	4

Scoring and Interpretation

91 or over You have strong perfectionist tendencies to the point that it could interfere with your taking quick action when necessary. Also, you may annoy many people with your perfectionism.

61–90 Moderate degree of perfectionism that could lead you to produce high-quality work and be a dependable person.

31–60 Mild degree of perfectionism. You might be a perfectionist in some situations quite important to you but not in others.

0–30 Not a perfectionist. You might be too casual about getting things done right, meeting deadlines, and being aware of details.

Jump-start yourself. You can often get momentum going on a project by giving yourself a tiny assignment simply to get started. One way to get momentum going on an unpleasant or overwhelming task is to set aside a specific time to work on it. If you have to write a report on a subject you dislike, you might set aside Saturday from 3 to 4 p.m. as your time to first attack the project. If your procrastination problem is particularly intense, giving yourself even a five-minute task, such as starting a new file, might help you gain momentum. After five minutes, decide if you choose to continue for another five minutes. The five-minute chunks will help you focus your energy.

Peck away at an overwhelming task. Assume that you have a major project to do that does not have to be accomplished in a hurry. A good way of minimizing procrastination is to peck away at the project in fifteen- to thirty-minute bits of time. Bit by bit, the project will get down to manageable size and therefore not seem so overwhelming. A related way of pecking away at an overwhelming task is to subdivide it into smaller units. For instance, you might break down moving into a series of tasks, such as filing change-of-address notices, locating a mover, and packaging books. Pecking away can sometimes be achieved by setting aside as little as five minutes to work on a seemingly overwhelming task. When the five minutes are up, either work five more minutes on the task or reschedule the activity for sometime soon.

Motivate yourself with rewards and punishments. Give yourself a pleasant reward soon after you accomplish a task about which you would ordinarily procrastinate. You might, for example, jog through the woods after having completed a tough take-home exam. The second part of this tactic is to punish yourself if you have engaged in serious procrastination. How about not visiting your favorite social networking site for one week?

Make a commitment to other people. Put pressure on yourself to get something done on time by making it a commitment to one or more other people. You might announce to coworkers that you are going to get a project of mutual concern completed by a certain date. If you fail to meet this date, you may feel embarrassed.

Express a more positive attitude about your intentions. Expressing a more positive attitude can often lead to changes in behavior. If you choose words that express a serious intention to complete an activity, you are more likely to follow through than if you choose more uncertain words. Imagine that a coworker says, "I *might* get you the information you need by next Friday." You probably will not be surprised if you do not receive the information by Friday. In contrast, if your coworker says,

"I *will* get you the information you need by next Friday," there is less likelihood the person will procrastinate. Psychologist Linda Sapadin believes that you are less likely to procrastinate if you change your "wish" to "will," your "like to" to "try to," and your "have to" to "want to."[7]

▶ Learning Objective 2 ▶

What Are Some Proper Attitudes and Values to Develop?

"Effective time management has become an urgent priority for both workplace performance and personal sanity."
—Fran Finn, organizational productivity expert, quoted in *Executive Focus*, February 2009, p. 17.

Developing good work habits and time-management practices is often a matter of developing proper attitudes toward work and time. For instance, if you think that your job is important and that time is valuable, you will be on your way toward developing good work habits. In this section we describe a group of attitudes and values that can help improve your productivity through better use of time and improved work habits.

DEVELOP A MISSION AND GOALS

A mission, or general purpose in life, propels you toward being productive. Assume that a person says, "My mission is to become an outstanding professional in my career and a loving, constructive parent." The mission serves as a compass to direct your activities, such as being well organized in order to attain a favorable performance appraisal.

Goals are more specific than a mission statement. The goals support the mission statement, but the effect is the same. Being committed to a goal also propels you toward good use of time. Imagine how efficient most employees would be if they were told, "Here is five days of work facing you. If you get finished in less than five days without sacrificing quality, you can have that time to yourself." If the saved time fit your mission, such as having more quality time with family members, the impact would be even stronger.

The late Stephen Covey, a popularizer of time-management techniques, expresses the importance of a mission of goals in his phrase, "Begin with the end in mind." He recommends you develop your mission statement by first thinking about what people who know you well would say at your funeral if you died three years from now. Also, list your various roles in life, such as spouse, child, family member, professional, and soccer player. For each role, think of one or two major lifetime goals you have in that area. Then develop a brief mission statement describing your life's purpose that incorporates these goals.[8]

A person might have the mission of becoming an outstanding professional person. Your goals to support that mission might include achieving advanced certification in your field, becoming an officer in a professional organization, and making large donations to charity. When you are deciding how to spend your time each day, give goals related to your mission top priority.

VALUE GOOD ATTENDANCE AND PUNCTUALITY

On the job, in school, or in personal life, good attendance and punctuality are essential for developing a good reputation. Also, you cannot contribute to a team effort unless you are present. Poor attendance and consistent lateness are the most frequent reasons for employee discipline. Furthermore, many managers interpret high absenteeism and lateness as signs of emotional immaturity. An important myth about attendance and punctuality—that a certain number of sick days are owed an employee—should be challenged early in a person's career. Some employees who have not used up their sick days will find reasons to be sick at the end of the year.

The causes of chronic lateness follow those of the causes of procrastination. Time-management specialist Diane DeLonzor says that the motivations are often unconscious, related to personality characteristics such as lack of self-control and a desire for thrill seeking. Some people are drawn to the adrenaline rush of that last-minute sprint to the meeting (or class), while others receive an ego boost from overscheduling and filling each moment with activity. Trying to get one more thing done before leaving for an appointment will often lead to being late. Keeping a time log (as described later in the chapter) can help control lateness because the result can be a more accurate estimation of the amount of time necessary to complete various activities. For example, if it takes a person forty-five minutes to commute to work, he or she must leave the residence about fifty-five minutes before an important meeting.[9]

VALUE YOUR TIME

People who place a high value on their time are propelled into making good use of time. If a person believes that his or her time is valuable, it will be difficult to engage that person in idle conversation during working hours. Valuing your time can also apply to personal life. The yield from clipping or gathering grocery coupons is an average of $9 per hour—assuming that purchasing national brands is important to you. Would a busy professional person, therefore, be better off clipping and gathering coupons or engaging in self-development for the same amount of time? Being committed to a mission and goals is an automatic way of making good use of time.

VALUE NEATNESS, ORDERLINESS, AND SPEED

Neatness, orderliness, and speed are important contributors to workplace productivity and therefore should be valued. An orderly desk or work area does not inevitably signify an orderly mind. Yet orderliness does help most people become more productive. Less time is wasted and less energy is expended if you do not have to hunt for missing information. Knowing where information is and what information you have available is a way of being in control of your job. When your job gets out of control, you are probably working at less than peak efficiency. Being neat and orderly helps you achieve good performance. Frequently breaking your concentration for such matters as finding an e-mail message you printed a month ago inhibits high performance.

Neatness is linked to working rapidly because clutter and searching for misplaced items consume time. Employers emphasize speed to remain competitive in such matters as serving customers promptly and bringing new products and services to the market. Speed is widely considered a competitive advantage, as in getting a product to market faster than others or delivering takeout lunches on time.

The best approach to maintaining a neat work area and to enhance speed is to convince yourself that neatness and speed are valuable. You will then search for ways to be neat and fast, such as putting back a reference book immediately after use or making phone conversations brief. The underlying principle is that an attitude leads to a change in behavior.

Clearing your mind of clutter can contribute more to personal productivity than clearing your work space. Time-management consultant Dorothy Madden notes that if there are too many thoughts swirling around in your mind, it is difficult to be organized.[10] Many of the techniques described in this chapter, such as creating to-do lists, are aimed at uncluttering the brain.

Although neatness and orderliness are usually an effective approach to accomplishing work, at times a little disorder can be beneficial. According to Eric Abrahamson and David H. Freedman, coauthors of *A Perfect Mess,* neatness has some disadvantages. A major disadvantage of being a *neat freak* is that so much time is spent on keeping a desk clutter-free that it takes time away from major activities such as dealing with customers or clients. Also, to get things done you may wind up making a mess, such as in painting or redecorating your work area. According to Abrahamson and Freedman, "Moderately disorganized people, institutions, and people turn out to be more efficient, more resilient, more creative, and in general more effective than highly organized ones.[11]

Keep in mind also that Albert Einstein had a messy work area, as do many successful scientists and professors. Einstein is frequently quoted as having said, "If a cluttered desk is a sign of a cluttered mind, of what, then, is an empty desk a sign?"

WORK SMARTER, NOT HARDER

People caught up in trying to accomplish a job often wind up working hard but not in an imaginative way that leads to good results. Much time and energy, therefore, are wasted. A working-smart approach also requires that you spend a few minutes carefully planning how to implement your task. An example of working smarter, not harder, is to invest a few minutes of critical thinking before launching an Internet search. Think through carefully what might be the keywords that will lead you to the information you need. In this way, you will minimize conducting your search with words and phrases that will lead to irrelevant information. For example, suppose you want to conduct research on back-stabbing as negative office politics. If you use only the term *back-stabbing,* the search engine will direct you to such topics as street crime and medical treatment for wounds. Working smarter is to try "back-stabbing in the office" or "backstabbing and office politics."

An advanced approach to working smarter is to avoid doing work that is already being accomplished in another part of the organization by using information technology designed to foster collaboration. Some programs make it easier to find out what co-workers in other parts of a far-flung company are working on, thus avoiding duplication. Company blogs and intranets can also be helpful in identifying other workers who are engaged in a similar project. For example, you might be mining data attempting to discover which customers are likely to buy a variety of products from your employer.[12] A page on the intranet might tell you that Sally in Madison, Wisconsin, is working on the same project. If you then collaborate, you will save lots of time—and work smarter.

APPRECIATE THE IMPORTANCE OF REST AND RELAXATION

A productive attitude to maintain is that overwork can be counterproductive and lead to negative stress and burnout. Proper physical rest contributes to mental alertness and improved ability to cope with frustration. David Volpi, director of the Manhattan Snoring and Sleep Center, says that insufficient sleep can cause daytime fatigue, poor concentration, irritability, and low energy. Memory and ability to pay attention may also suffer.[13]

Constant attention to work or study is often inefficient. It is a normal human requirement to take enough breaks to allow you to approach work or study with a fresh perspective. Napping during the day has gained in popularity as a productivity booster. Workers who have private offices might nap under the desk, while cubicle dwellers often nap with their head on the desk. Each person has to establish the right balance between work and leisure within the bounds of freedom granted by the situation.

Another widely used workplace refresher is browsing the Internet. Used in moderation surfing the Internet can serve an important restorative function, according to research conducted at the National University of Singapore. Cyberloafing can refresh workers mentally after long periods of concentrating on work. The research also found that surfing the Web enhanced productivity more than talking or texting with friends, or sending personal e-mail messages.[14] (Again, brief excursions on the Web can be refreshing but when done in excess, productivity diminishes.)

Neglecting the normal need for rest and relaxation can lead to **workaholism,** an addiction to work in which *not* working is an uncomfortable experience. (In some cases, therefore, workaholism leads to neglect of rest and relaxation.) Some types of workaholics are perfectionists who are never satisfied with their work and therefore find it difficult to leave work behind. Career counselor Janet Salyer notes, "Workaholics put the job before family, friends, and their own health. And even if they're spending time with their families, their minds are on work."[15] In addition, the workaholic who is a perfectionist may become heavily focused on control, leading to rigid behavior.

Workaholism
an addiction to work in which not working is an uncomfortable experience

However, some people who work long and hard are classified as happy workaholics who thrive on hard work and are usually highly productive. As executives, they encourage others to work hard to achieve company goals and also pursue what matters to them in their personal lives.[16] Furthermore, many people who work long and hard to be successful in their careers also intensely enjoy other activities. Warren Buffet, the legendary investor who is one of the world's richest people, carries an enormous workload, although he is more than 80 years old. But he is also a fanatic about bridge and regularly interrupts his workday to play bridge on the computer.

What Are Some Effective Time-Management Techniques?

Learning Objective 3

So far we have discussed improving productivity from the standpoints of dealing with procrastination and developing the right attitudes and values. Skills and techniques also contribute substantially to becoming more productive. Here we describe some well-established methods of work habit improvement along with several new ones. For these techniques to enhance productivity, most of them need to be incorporated into and practiced regularly in our daily lives. This is particularly true because many of these techniques are habits, and habits have to be programmed into the brain through repetition.

CLEAN UP AND GET ORGANIZED

An excellent starting point for improving work habits and time management is to clean up the work area and arrange things neatly. The starting point in the popular system of work habits and time management developed by David Allen is to unclutter your life. You begin by collecting everything you must do, or hope to do, or that is unfinished or undecided. All of these items are written on sheets of paper, a process referred to as a *mind sweep.*[17] You are likely to find that many of these tasks can be thrown out right away. An example would be a throwing out an expired discount coupon from an office supply store. Despite the contribution of a mind sweep, simply jotting down a key task will not remove it completely from your mind, particularly if it is a bothersome task. An example would be an item on a supervisor's to-do list about firing an employee.

Eliminate clutter by throwing out unnecessary paper and deleting computer files that will probably never be used again. The idea is to learn to simplify the work area so that there are fewer distractions and the brain can be more focused. In addition, finding important files becomes easier. Designate a specific time, such as one Saturday morning, for cleaning up your work area and getting rid of files that will not be needed again.

Desktop search software such as Google Desktop or Apple's Spotlight can help you find many missing documents. But there is still a productivity advantage to having fewer obsolete documents and files in your computer, including a desktop with dozens of icons with similar-sounding names. Conducting an electronic search to find your expense report is one more task on your to-do list.

Getting organized includes sorting out which tasks need doing, including assignments and projects not yet completed. Getting organized can also mean sorting through the many small paper notes attached to the computer and on the wall. A major cleanup principle is therefore to discard anything that is no longer valuable. A suggestion worth considering is to throw out at least one item every day from the office and home—even if the item thrown out is as humble as an empty ballpoint pen. Because new items come into the office and home almost daily, you will always have possessions left.

PLAN YOUR ACTIVITIES

Planning
primary principle of effective time management; deciding what to accomplish and the actions needed to make it happen

The primary principle of effective time management is **planning**—deciding what you want to accomplish and the actions needed to make it happen. The most elementary—and the most important—planning tool is a list of tasks that need doing. Almost every successful person works from a to-do list. These lists are essentially daily goals. Before you can compose a useful list, you need to set aside a few moments each day to sort out the tasks at hand. A good starting point in using to-do lists is to prepare such a list on Sunday for the rest of the week. The list can then be modified on Monday through Saturday. A list used by a working parent is presented in Figure 16-1.

Completing tasks on to-do lists is so essential for personal productivity as well as stress reduction that many people hire virtual assistants to tackle their tasks. The virtual assistants typically focus on online tasks such as shopping and resolving a problem with a bank.[18] However, some personal assistants take care of physical chores such as

FIGURE 16-1
A SAMPLE TO-DO LIST

Job

Make 10 calls to prospects for new listings.
Have "For Sale" signs put outside Hanover Blvd. house.
Set up mortgage appointment at 1st Federal for the Calhouns.
Update Web site listings.
Upgrade antivirus software.
Check for possible sales leads on Facebook, LinkedIn, and Twitter.
Meet with the Guptas at 5 p.m.
Set up time to show house to the Bowens.

Home

Buy running shoes for Todd.
Buy jeans for Linda.
Get icemaker fixed on refrigerator.
Write and send out monthly bills.
Clip cat's nails.
Check out problem with hot-water tank.
Make appointment with dentist to have chipped filling replaced.
Check Twitter and send out at least ten Tweets this evening.

FIRST REALTY CORPORATION

Jacksonville, Florida

jbartow@firstrealty.com

shopping in stores, getting automobiles repaired, and going to the drycleaner. The link between a personal gofer and work productivity is that when you have fewer unfinished personal tasks you can concentrate better on work.

Where do you put your to-do lists? Many people dislike having small to-do lists stuck in different places. One reason is that these lists are readily lost among other papers. Many people, therefore, put lists on desk calendars or printed forms called *planners,* which are also available for computers. Planners give you an opportunity to record your activities in intervals as small as fifteen minutes. Day-Timer Planner Pads include the categories of weekly lists of activities by category, daily things to do, appointments, notes/calls, and expenses. Many people place their to-do list in an appropriate place on their desktop computer or smart phone. Whether you use a paper or digital calendar, it is important to carry it with you so you can refer to it frequently.

Another useful approach for organizing your lists is to use a notebook small enough to be portable. The notebook becomes your master list to keep track of work tasks, errands, social engagements, and shopping items. Anything else requiring action might also be recorded—even a reminder to clean up the work area again. Some people have such clear focus that they register their to-do lists in their brain, thereby skipping paper or a computer.

No matter where you place your to-do list, its usefulness diminishes if the list is not consulted regularly, perhaps twice per day.

How do you set priorities? Faced with multiple tasks to do at the same time, it is possible to feel overwhelmed and freeze as a result. The time-tested solution is to establish a priority to each item on the to-do list. A typical system is to use A to signify critical or essential items, B to signify important items, and C for the least important ones. Although an item might be regarded as a C (for example, refilling your stapler), it still has a contribution to make to your productivity and sense of well-being. Many people obtain a sense of satisfaction from crossing an item, however trivial, off their list. Furthermore, if you are conscientious, small undone items will interfere with concentration.

To effectively set priorities, you have to recognize which tasks are critical or important. In general, those activities that deal directly with the major purposes of your job are critical, such as dealing with a major customer or completing your portion of a budget. Tasks your manager perceives to be urgent should also be classified as critical tasks. Emergency items, such as dealing with the effects of a tornado or a product recall, are also essential tasks.

How do you plan when you have to interact with people from different time zones? The globalization of business has created challenges in planning work with people in other time zones. Even within the United States there are four time zones in the contiguous United States plus different time zones for Alaska and Hawaii. (And add the Atlantic time zone for Canada.) One way to take time zone differences into account is to consult the international calling section of the phone book and then calculate. For example, when you are in Chicago it is seven hours later in Italy, and fifteen hours later in Japan. So if your work associate in Italy wants to speak to you at 8:30 a.m. her time, phone her at 1:30 a.m. your time. Or, to speak to your Japanese work associate at 8:30 a.m. his time, make the call at 6:30 p.m. your time. Your understanding of time-zone differences can also be used to send work via the Internet so it arrives by a particular time for a work associate.

If you prefer to avoid the calculations, consult a time zone converter such as www.timeanddate.com. These sites will also help you choose a reasonable time for a phone call between two different time zones, or a conference call or videoconference that involves people from several different countries. In general, if the meeting is held often, people from different time zones will have to take turns being inconvenienced.

How do you schedule and follow through? To be effective, a to-do list must be an action tool. To convert your list into action, prepare a schedule of when you are going to do each of the items on the list. Follow through by doing things according to your schedule, checking them off as you go along.

Time-and-activity charts (also referred to as Gantt charts) have been used in factories and offices for over a hundred years to keep track of projects. Many people find these basic charts useful in scheduling their own activities and keeping track of progress. Time-and-activity charts also reinforce the reality that much of work is calendar driven. A calendar anticipates all the dates, deadlines, and seasons essential to running a successful business firm. For example, many customers want shipments by a particular date, and bills are due at a specific time. Figure 16-2 presents a time-and-activity chart you might want to use as a personal productivity booster.

BOOST YOUR ENERGY

Many workers are not as productive as they or the company would like them to be largely because they lack enough energy for the demands of their work. According to Tony Schwartz, the founder of the Energy Project in New York City, increasing your energy is the best way to get more done faster and better. Becoming more energetic leads to more productivity gains than merely working longer hours.

Experience with many companies participating in the Energy Project suggests that workers perform at their peak when they alternate between periods of intense focus and taking appropriate rest pauses. Employees are able to increase their productivity by

FIGURE 16-2

A TIME-AND-ACTIVITY CHART FOR SCHEDULING ACTIVITIES

Charting key tasks and their deadlines, along with your performance on the task, can often get you focused and organized.

Deadlines for Task Accomplishment

Task to Be Accomplished	Feb. 1	Feb. 28	Mar. 15	Mar. 31	Apr. 15	Apr. 30
Expense reports	Did it					
Antivirus treatment for PC		Two days late				
Web site updated			Blew it			
Plan office party				Did it		
File federal and state tax reports					In the mail at midnight ☺☺	
Provide input to department budget						On time

practicing simple rituals that refuel their energy, such as a brief walk to take a breather, or turning off e-mail at specific times so they can concentrate better.[19] Proper rest, nutrition, and exercise also enhance physical and mental energy.

A study with 214 professional and clerical workers in a software development company provides additional insights into what works and what doesn't work for boosting energy. The participants completed questionnaires about their approaches to energy management as well as their perceived levels of vitality and fatigue (both aspects of energy).

A surprise finding of the study was that none of the five most common work-related strategies was significantly related to vitality or fatigue. The five strategies with little impact on increasing energy were (1) check e-mail, (2) switch tasks, (3) make a to-do list, (4) offer help to someone at work, and (5) talk to a coworker or supervisor. The micro-break energy-boosting strategies of having a snack and drinking a caffeinated beverage appeared to both decrease vitality and increase fatigue.

The energy-management strategies most positively related to vitality were all directly work related: (1) learn something new, (2) focus on what gives me joy in work, (3) set a new goal, (4) do something that will make a colleague happy, (5) make time to show gratitude to someone I work with, (6) seek feedback, (7) reflect on how I make a difference at work, and (8) reflect on the meaning of my work. The human relations message here is that all of these strategies are work related (not micro-breaks such as popping an energy drink). All of these strategies reflect thoughts about notions of learning, relationships, and meaning at work.[20] Note that the findings from the Energy Project indicated work pauses as contributing more to energy.

The accompanying Human Relations in Practice illustrates how a worker might boost his energy.

Human Relations in Practice

Distribution Center Manager Troy Refuels on the Job

Troy is a distribution center manager for a company that makes electronic components used for a wide variety of consumer appliances including washers and dryers, hair dryers, electronic shopping carts, and electronic scooters for the mobility challenged. In his thirties, Troy has had difficulty managing his anger, which he believes can disrupt his productivity and damage his relationships with subordinates and colleagues.

Troy was one of the first managers in his company to participate in an energy management program sponsored by his company, and conducted by a consulting firm specializing in workplace energy management. Troy was coached on how to manage his feelings more effectively. He learned to make it a practice to step away from frustrating situations and take walks around the distribution center lot when he felt that his frustration was reaching an uncomfortable level. During his brief walks, Troy would often count to ten and/or breathe deeply.

The walking ritual helped Troy relax, refocus, and then think through more clearly how he should best respond to the frustrating situation or person. As a result of these slight changes, Troy believes that he has more positive energy to invest in his job. He also believes that his job performance has improved.

Question: In your experience, does dealing better with frustration give you more energy?

Source: The program in question is based on the work of the Energy Project, as described in Tony Schwartz, "The Productivity Paradox: How Sony Pictures Gets More Out of People by Demanding Less," *Harvard Business Review*, June 2010, pp. 64–69.

GET OFF TO A GOOD START

Get off to a good beginning, and you are more likely to have a successful, productive day. Start poorly, and you will be behind most of the day. According to time-management specialist Merrill Douglass, people who get going early tend often to be in the right place at the right time more, thereby seeming to be lucky. "When you start early, you are lucky enough to get a good parking spot. You are lucky enough to avoid traffic jams. You are lucky enough to finish your job by the end of the day."[21] To get off to a good start regularly, it is important to start the day with the conscious intention of starting strong.

A current study with college students found that those whose performance peaks in the morning have a better chance at career success. (An example of proactivity would be investing time in identifying long-range goals for themselves.) The reason is that the morning people are more proactive than people who are at their best in the evening.[22] Maybe a person cannot completely overcome being a night person rather than a morning person, but he or she can strive to perform better at the start of the day. An effective way of getting off to a good start is to tackle the toughest task first because most people have their peak energy in the morning. (You will recall that a variation of this technique is useful in combating procrastination.) With a major task already completed, you are off to a running start on a busy workday.

MAKE GOOD USE OF OFFICE TECHNOLOGY

Companies now derive productivity increases from office automation. Used properly, most high-tech devices in the office improve productivity. How you use these ever-present devices is the key to increased productivity. Mobile workers, or those who conduct much of their work away from the office, quite often enhance their productivity by accessing intranets and staying in contact with coworkers. Many customer-contact workers are enhancing their productivity by using tablet computers to access vital information about a product or service, such as a pharmaceutical sales rep finding out immediately how a new drug might interact with other drugs.

Making good use of office technology also implies avoiding those aspects of office technology most likely to drain productivity. At the top of the list are those beeps and alerts (or "ghost alerts") that float on to your screen to announce new e-mails for the fact that somebody in your Skype network is now online.[23] An exception is that if your job requires paying immediate attention to incoming e-mail messages, the alerts will enhance productivity. How about a radiation leak technician being alert to news about radiation leaks?

A major consideration is that the time saved using office technology must be invested in productive activity to attain a true productivity advantage. Assume that you save two hours by ordering office equipment over the Internet. If you invest those two hours in activity such as finding ways to save the company money, you are more productive.

A helpful attitude about boosting personal productivity through office technology is to stay alert to new tools that would be useful in your situation. For example, a person who travels frequently for business might be able to use a portable scanner, which scans receipts, business cards, and documents and organizes the information into a database. This information saves time when submitting expense reports. The business owner could use this information for preparing income taxes.

A productivity error many workers make with respect to office technology is that they assume because they are using the technology they are being productive. Thus, the worker who checks a company intranet ten times per hour perceives himself or herself to be highly productive. Unless the person's job requires such frequent checking, he or she is being unproductive.

CONCENTRATE ON ONE KEY TASK AT A TIME

Effective people have a well-developed capacity to concentrate on the problem or person they face, however surrounded they are with potential distractions. The problems of being distracted by personal e-mail and social media Web sites are well known, with new types of distractions growing in impact. The placement firm of Challenger, Gray & Christmas estimates that American companies might be losing as much as $1.5 billion in productivity during the professional football season due to fantasy football leagues.[24] (Fantasy football is a game played on the Internet in which the players pretend they are owners of a professional football team, and compete against other owners.) Another reason it is difficult for many workers to concentrate is that they have so many electronic devices to choose from at the same time, including those they are carrying. All of these devices contain distractions such as social media sites and personal blogs.

The best results from concentration are achieved when you are so absorbed in your work that you are aware of virtually nothing else at the moment—referred to as the flow experience. Attaining flow requires uninterrupted concentration. Another useful byproduct of concentration is that it reduces absent-mindedness. If you really concentrate on what you are doing, the chances diminish that you will forget what you intended to do.

An extreme good example of concentration on one task at a time is Jack Dorsey, the cofounder of Twitter and CEO of payments platform Square. On average he spends eight hours at Twitter and then another eight at Square. "The only way to do this is to be very disciplined," says Dorsey. (You won't find him tweeting away his sixteen-hour workday!) Two examples of his concentration are that he devotes Monday to management meetings and running the company. Tuesday is devoted to product development.[25]

Conscious effort and self-discipline can strengthen concentration skills. An effective way to sharpen your concentration skills is to set aside ten minutes a day and focus on something repetitive, such as your breathing pattern or a small word. This is the same approach that is used in meditation to relieve stress. After practicing concentration in the manner just described, concentrate on an aspect of your work, such as preparing a report.

Some people have difficulty concentrating on important tasks, or almost any task, because they have attention deficit hyperactivity disorder (ADHD), formerly called attention deficit disorder (ADD). Workers with ADHD may find it difficult to focus, organize, and finish tasks and often forget to accomplish items on their to-do list. Before workers with ADHD can improve their concentration on important tasks, they may require professional help in terms of medicine, counseling, or cognitive behavior therapy.[26]

Note that the suggestion here is to concentrate on one *key* task at a time. As described later in this chapter, sometimes doing two or three minor tasks at the same time can help save time. In general, younger people are more effective at multitasking than much older people, yet being distracted can lower performance for both groups, as described in Chapter 8. The many electronic distractions in the office make it more difficult to concentrate on important tasks. Some of these distractions are self-imposed, such as the temptation to jump to e-mail, an instant message, or a Web site indicating today's stock market performance.

The key to concentrating on important tasks is to develop better self-discipline, following the model presented in Chapter 3. The self-disciplined person is, by definition, able to focus on the present without jumping to other tasks. According to Edward Hallowell, director of the Center for Cognitive and Emotional Health in Sudbury, Massachusetts, you need to set limits on the constant bombardment of information that surrounds you.[27] This could mean, for example, that while attempting to develop a new idea for reducing costs within your department, you eliminate any other activity for thirty minutes.

STREAMLINE YOUR WORK, AND EMPHASIZE IMPORTANT TASKS

As companies continue to operate with fewer workers than in the past even during good economic times, more nonproductive work must be eliminated. Getting rid of unproductive work is part of improving a business process. Every employee is expected to get rid of work that does not contribute to productivity or help customers. Another purpose of work streamlining is to get rid of work that does not add value for customers. Time-management guru David Allen says that you must constantly recalibrate your resources to attain the best results, and say "not now" to less important tasks.[28]

Here is a sampling of work that typically does not add value:

- Sending receipts and acknowledgments to people who do not need them
- Writing and sending e-mails and reports that nobody reads or needs
- Holding meetings that do not accomplish work, exchange important information, or improve team spirit
- Checking up frequently on the work of competent people

In general, to streamline your work, look for duplication of effort and waste. An example of duplication of effort would be to routinely send people e-mail three times with the same question. An example of waste would be to call a meeting for disseminating information that could easily be communicated by e-mail.

Important (value-contributing) tasks are those in which superior performance could have a large payoff. No matter how quickly you took care of making sure that your store paid its bills on time, for example, this effort would not make your store an outstanding success. If, however, you concentrated your efforts on bringing unique and desirable merchandise into the store, this action could greatly affect your business success.

Many people respond to suggestions about emphasizing important tasks by saying, "I don't think concentrating on important tasks applies to me. My job is so filled with routine that I have no chance to work on the big breakthrough ideas." True, most jobs are filled with routine requirements. What a person *can* do is spend some time, perhaps even one hour a week, concentrating on tasks of potentially major significance.

WORK AT A STEADY PACE

In most jobs, working at a steady clip pays dividends in efficiency. The spurt worker creates many problems for management. Some employees take pride in working rapidly, even when the result is a high error rate.

Another advantage of the steady-pace approach is that you accomplish much more than someone who puts out extra effort only once in a while. The completely steady worker would accomplish just as much the day before a holiday as on a given Monday. That extra hour or so of productivity adds up substantially by the end of the year. Despite the advantages of maintaining a steady pace, some peaks and valleys in your work may be inevitable. Tax accounting firms, for example, have busy seasons.

Working at a steady pace throughout the day is difficult because it counters a natural tendency to slow down toward the end of a workday. The staffing firm Accountemps polled 150 senior executives on employee productivity. A third of the executives said that from 4 to 6 p.m. is the least productive time of the day; another third cited the post-lunch period from noon to 2 p.m. as being the least productive. Suggestions for combating the productivity dip include napping, getting fresh air, taking a short walk, and tackling the most challenging tasks early in the day.[29]

CREATE SOME QUIET, UNINTERRUPTED TIME

Many office workers find their days hectic, fragmented, and frustrating. Incessant interruptions make it difficult to get things done. The constant start–stop–restart pattern lengthens the time needed to get jobs done. Quiet time can reduce the type of productivity drain previously described. To achieve quiet time, create an uninterrupted block of time, enabling you to concentrate on your work. This could mean turning off the telephone, not accessing your e-mail, and blocking drop-in visitors during certain times of the workday.

Quiet time is used for such essential activities as thinking, planning, getting organized, doing analytical work, writing reports, and doing creative tasks. Interruptions lower productivity more for mental than physical work. This is true because interruptions break the flow of thought, and it takes time to get back into a train of thought.

Quiet time is difficult to find in some jobs, such as those requiring customer contact. An agreement has to be worked out with the manager about when and where quiet time can be taken. Sometimes the quiet time can be taken at home early in the workday or in a vacated office or conference room.

MAKE USE OF BITS OF TIME, AND USE MULTITASKING FOR ROUTINE WORK

A truly productive person makes good use of miscellaneous bits of time both on and off the job. While waiting in line at a post office, you might update your to-do list; while waiting for an elevator, you might be able to read a brief report; and if you have finished your day's work ten minutes before quitting time, you can use that time to clean out a file. When traveling for business, bring as much work as you can comfortably carry. Many business travelers carry a laptop or tablet computer so they can perform work in transit. And many professionals use smart phones in place of a larger computer to access company information. Spare time at airports because you arrive early or because of flight delays provides a good opportunity to perform routine work. By the end of the year, your productivity will have increased much more than if you had squandered these bits of time.

Some forms of making use of bits of time, such as reviewing your to-do list as you ride the elevator, are a form of constructive multitasking. Doing two or more routine chores simultaneously can sometimes enhance personal productivity. While exercising on a stationary bike, you might read work-related information; while commuting, listen to the radio for information of potential relevance for your job. Also, while reading e-mail, you might clean the outside of your computer; while waiting for a file to download, you might arrange your work area or read a brief report.

Despite searching for productivity gains through multitasking, it is important to avoid rude or dangerous acts or a combination of the two. A rude practice is doing paperwork while on the telephone or sitting in class. Dangerous practices include engaging in an intense conversation or sending and receiving text messages while driving. Checking e-mail on a laptop or onboard computer while driving is more dangerous because you are forced to lose full eye contact with the road.

STAY IN CONTROL OF PAPERWORK, THE INBOX, AND E-MAIL

Despite the major shift to the use of electronic messages, the workplace is still overflowing with printed messages, including computer printouts. You will notice your local office supply store has enormous loads of printing paper in stock. Paperwork essentially involves taking care of administrative details, such as correspondence, expense account forms, and surveys. Responding to e-mail messages, instant messages, and text messages has created additional administrative details that require handling, even if they are actually *electronic work* rather than paperwork.

Unless you handle paperwork, e-mail, instant messages, and text messages efficiently, you may lose control of your job or home life, which could lead to substantial negative stress. Ideally, a small amount of time should be invested in paperwork and routine e-mail every day. Non–prime time (when you are at less than peak efficiency but not overly fatigued) is the best time to take care of administrative routine work.

A workable suggestion for most people intent on staying on top of e-mail and instant messages is to set aside some time to respond to every important message that you have not taken care of in the last two days. Move all other messages of potential future value to the archive folder. Whenever you receive a new e-mail or instant message, take action by responding, deleting, forwarding, or storing it. When an e-mail requires a complicated response, you are justified in leaving the e-mail in your inbox until you obtain the information necessary to respond intelligently.[30]

Learning Objective 4

How Does One Overcome Time Wasters?

Another basic thrust to improved personal productivity is to minimize wasting time. Workers wasting time is one of the most devastating problems facing work organizations of all types, probably far exceeding the cost from theft and fraud. According to a survey by America Online and Salary.com, the average worker admits to wasting 2.09 hours per 8-hour workday, aside from lunch and scheduled breaks.[31] Current less formal observations support these earlier findings, with the exception that during a recession workers tend to waste less time. One caution about this figure of two hours wasted is that many employees who waste time during the day will speed up their work toward the end of the workday or work at home to catch up on unfinished tasks.

Many of the techniques already described in this chapter help save time. The tactics and strategies described next, however, are directly aimed at overcoming the problem of wasted time.

Human Relations Self-Assessment Quiz 16-2 gives you an opportunity to think through how you waste or do not waste work-related time.

MINIMIZE DAYDREAMING

Allowing the mind to drift while on the job is a major productivity drain. Daydreaming is triggered when the individual perceives the task to be boring—such as reviewing another person's work for errors. Unresolved personal problems are an important source of daydreaming, thus blocking your productivity. This is especially true because effective time utilization requires good concentration. When you are preoccupied with a personal or business problem, it is difficult to give your full efforts to a task at hand.

The solution is to do something constructive about whatever problem is sapping your ability to concentrate. Sometimes a relatively minor problem, such as driving with an expired operator's license, can impair your work concentration. At other times, a major problem, such as how best to take care of a parent who has suffered a stroke, interferes with work. In either situation, your concentration will suffer until you take appropriate action.

Human Relations Self-Assessment Quiz 16-2

My Tendencies Toward Wasting or Not Wasting Time

Indicate the extent to which you engage in the time-wasting activities listed below on a three-point scale: 1 = never or rarely, 2 = sometimes, 3 = frequently or almost daily. Think of these activities in relation to the job, classroom, or while studying.

Number	Activity or Behavior	Rarely or Never	Sometimes	Frequently or Almost Daily
1.	I access my favorite social media site during the workday.	1	2	3
2.	I daydream about a variety of topics.	1	2	3
3.	I make phone calls related to social life.	1	2	3
4.	I surf the Web such as checking into sports sites, shopping sites, and YouTube.	1	2	3
5.	I run a personal errand.	1	2	3
6.	I look out the window or gaze at the ceiling.	1	2	3
7.	I send and receive text messages unrelated to work.	1	2	3
8.	I go for a brief walk just to relax.	1	2	3
9.	I go get a beverage or snack.	1	2	3
10.	I engage a coworker in conversation not related to the work or subject under study.	1	2	3

Scoring and Interpretation

Add the numbers you have circled or checked.

10–15 A score this low suggests that you waste very little time that could contribute to your productivity. However, your productivity might increase slightly if you took an occasional pause from your work to refresh you mind.

16–24 A score within this range suggests that you are about average with respect to wasting time on the job or in relation to study. You might look for ways to waste a little less time, particularly if your score is at the higher end of the average range (20–24).

25–30 A score this high suggests that you are wasting too much time with respect to work or study. As a result, you might be suffering a personal productivity drain. Concentrate more to reduce your time wasting. You might begin by eliminating one of your biggest time wasters, and move on to tackle another.

PREPARE A TIME LOG TO EVALUATE YOUR USE OF TIME

An advanced tool for becoming a more efficient time manager is to prepare a time log of how you are currently investing your time. For five full workdays or school days, write down everything you do, including such activities as responding to e-mail and taking rest breaks. A daily planner is the tool of choice for a time log. Some people use a spreadsheet for the same purpose, including many executives. Study your results, and look for patterns of lost time. A hospital administrative worker who used a log discovered that she was spending about twenty minutes at the start of each workday circling around the parking ramp look for a space. Her conclusion was that by arriving five minutes earlier to the hospital, she could find a space within a few minutes.

Time leak
anything you are doing or not doing that allows time to get away from you

One of the most important outputs of a time log is to uncover time leaks. A **time leak** is anything you are doing or not doing that allows time to get away from you. Among them are spending too much time for lunch by collecting people before finally leaving and walking to a coworker's cubicle rather than sending an e-mail. The process of streamlining your work will also identify time leaks.

AVOID UNPRODUCTIVE USE OF COMPUTERS

An unproductive use of computers is to tinker with them to the exclusion of useful work. Many people have become intrigued with computers to the point of diversion. They become habituated to creating new reports or exquisite graphics and making endless changes. It is easy to become diverted by the thousands of commands in a program such as Microsoft Word or PowerPoint. Some managers spend so much time with computers that they neglect leadership responsibilities, thus lowering their productivity. Using multiple open tabs on the screen should be done only when absolutely necessary because it invites distractions by jumping from one Web site to another.[32]

In addition to these problems, Internet surfing for purposes not strictly related to the job has become a major productivity drain. For example, many Internet shopping sites and sports sites have found that their peak number of visits is during traditional working hours. Social networking sites are also visited frequently during typical working hours.

The message is straightforward: To plug one more potential productivity drain, avoid using the computer for nonproductive purposes. Many companies block the use of recreational Web sites on company equipment so that workers have to resort to authorized sites, such as those selling equipment and supplies!

KEEP TRACK OF IMPORTANT NAMES, PLACES, AND THINGS

How much time have you wasted lately searching for such items as a phone number you jotted down somewhere, your keys, or an appointment book? Many managers and professionals store such information in a database, in their cell phones, or even in a word processing file. Such files are more difficult to misplace than a pocket directory, yet these files should be backed up to prevent lost data.

Two steps are recommended for remembering where you put things. First, have a parking place for everything. Put your keys, appointment book, or smart phone in the same place after each use. (This tactic supports the strategy of being neat and orderly to minimize wasting time.) Second, make visual associations. To have something register in your mind at the moment you are doing it, make up a visual association about that act. Thus, you might say, "Here I am putting my auto insurance policy in the back section of my canvas bag."

SET A TIME LIMIT FOR CERTAIN TASKS AND PROJECTS

Spending too much time on a task or project wastes time. As a person becomes experienced with certain projects, he or she is able to make accurate estimates of how long a project will take to complete. A paralegal might say, "Getting this ready for the lawyer's approval should take two hours." A good work habit to develop is to estimate how long a job should take and then proceed with strong determination to get that job completed within the estimated time period. A productive version of this technique is to decide that some low- and medium-priority items are worth only so much of your time. Invest that much time in the project but no more. Preparing a file on advertisements that come across your desk is one example.

SCHEDULE SIMILAR TASKS TOGETHER (CLUSTERING)

An efficient method of accomplishing small tasks is to group them together and perform them in one block of time. Clustering of this type has several applications. If you are visiting an office supply store, think of whatever you need there to avoid an unnecessary repeat visit. As long as you are visiting a particular search engine, look for some other information you will need soon. A basic way of scheduling similar tasks together is to make most of your phone calls in relation to your job from 11:00 to 11:30 each workday morning. Or you might reserve the last hour of every workday for e-mail and other correspondence. By using this method, you develop the necessary pace and mental set to knock off chores in short order. In contrast, when you flit from one task to another, your efficiency may suffer.

BOUNCE QUICKLY FROM TASK TO TASK

Much time is lost when a person takes a break between tasks. After one task is completed, you might pause for ten minutes to clear your work area and adjust your to-do list. After the brief pause, dive into your next important task. Celebrate your task accomplishment after work, not by taking a break from work during regular working hours.

Incorporating many of the ideas contained in this chapter will help you achieve peak performance or exceptional accomplishment.

Key Terms

Work habits, 483
Productivity, 483
Procrastination, 484
Fear of success, 484
Workaholism, 491
Planning, 492
Time leak, 502

Summary and Review

People with good work habits tend to be more successful in their careers than poorly organized individuals, and they tend to have more time to spend on personal life. Good work habits are more important than ever because of today's emphasis on productivity.

Procrastination is the leading cause of poor productivity and career self-sabotage, and can be viewed as the gap between intention and action. People procrastinate for many reasons, including their perception that a task is unpleasant, is overwhelming, or may lead to negative consequences. Fear of success can also lead to procrastination. Awareness of procrastination can lead to its control.

Seven techniques for reducing procrastination are the following:

- Calculating the cost of procrastination
- Counterattacking the burdensome task
- Jump-starting yourself
- Pecking away at an overwhelming task
- Motivating yourself with rewards and punishments
- Making a commitment to other people
- Expressing a more positive attitude about your intentions

Developing good work habits and time-management practices is often a matter of developing proper attitudes toward work and time. Seven such attitudes and values are these:

- Developing a mission and goals
- Valuing good attendance and punctuality
- Valuing your time
- Valuing neatness, orderliness, and speed
- Working smarter, not harder
- Appreciating the importance of rest and relaxation

Ten skills and techniques to help you become more productive are these:

- Cleaning up and getting organized
- Boosting your energy
- Planning your activities (including the use of time-and-activity charts)
- Getting off to a good start
- Making good use of office technology
- Concentrating on one key task at a time
- Streamlining your work and emphasizing important tasks
- Working at a steady pace
- Creating some quiet, uninterrupted time
- Making use of bits of time and using multitasking for routine work
- Staying in control of paperwork, the inbox, and e-mail

Time wasting is a major problem in the workplace. Seven suggestions for overcoming time wasting are as follows:

- Minimize daydreaming.
- Prepare a time log and evaluate your use of time.
- Avoid unproductive use of computers.
- Keep track of important names, places, and things.
- Set a time limit for certain tasks and projects.
- Schedule similar tasks together (clustering).
- Bounce quickly from task to task.

Check Your Understanding

1. In recent years, companies that sell desk planners and other time-management devices have experienced all-time peak demands for their products. What factors do you think are creating this boom?
2. What have you observed to be two of the most important areas for improvement in work habits and time management for students?
3. Many tidy, well-organized workers never attain much in the way of career success. Which principle of work habits and time management described in this chapter might they be neglecting?
4. How can preparing a personal mission statement help a person become better organized?
5. Why might drastically reducing procrastination often increase a person's income substantially?
6. How might a person use old shoe boxes or plastic trays to enhance his or her productivity?
7. When people learn that a person is self-employed, they often comment, "Oh, that's wonderful, you don't have to worry about time. You can play golf (or engage in some other activity) whenever you want." In what way does this statement misunderstand the importance of time management for the self-employed?
8. A study described under the topic of boosting your energy provided negative results for the use of caffeinated beverages as energy boosters. Would this study deter you, or an energy-drink consumer you might know, to cut back energy drinks and instead focus on the meaning of work and relationships?
9. In what ways has your use of information technology made you more productive?
10. Give an example of how the principles and techniques of good work habits and personal productivity could be applied to a job search.

Web Corner

Procrastination test (must take within forty-eight hours)
www.queendom.com/. Search for the test measuring procrastination tendencies.

Prioritizing effectively:
www.time-management-guide.com/prioritizing.html

National Association of Professional Organizers:
www.napo.net

INTERNET SKILL BUILDER

What Are You Doing with Your Time?

Go to www.businessballs.com to find a basic time-log work sheet. You decide on which activities to enter into the time log. After recording how you are using your time after making the analysis on a few different days, ask yourself, "What have I learned that will enhance my personal productivity?" For example, do you see some slipping away of time that is neither enhancing your productivity directly nor providing you a few moments to refresh?

Developing Your Human Relations Skills

Human Relations Application Exercises

Applying Human Relations Exercise 16-1

Squeezing Productivity Out of Social Networking Sites

The number of people using social networking sites continues to grow explosively, with some people even learning how to use the Internet so they can join a networking site such as Twitter or Facebook. We all know that these sites can be an enjoyable pastime and a distraction from work. The issue we want you to address in small brainstorming groups is how to use social networking sites to improve your work productivity.

After each group has completed its task of brainstorming ways to improve productivity by being a member of a social networking site, you might hold a class discussion of your major findings. See if the class can reach a consensus on whether social networking sites can be a productivity booster or simply a pleasant diversion.

Applying Human Relations Exercise 16-2

My Personal Procrastination Analysis

The purpose of this exercise is to give you practice in understanding why you might have procrastinated in the past and how you might overcome a similar episode of procrastination in the future. To begin, write a twenty-five-word or so description of some important activity on which you have procrastinated in the past. An *important* activity is one that could have a noticeable impact on your mental or financial well-being. Describe also any negative consequences that might have stemmed from the procrastination. Here is an example from an assistant manager at a health club who lives in the state of New York:

I knew my vehicle inspection sticker was due in a month. But I was simply so busy with other things, I couldn't get to it. Also, I figured because it was wintertime, I could spread some snow over the dated sticker, and no police office would catch me. Well, it worked out that I was pulled over for the expired sticker. Unfortunately, the officer also found out I had not renewed my driver's license. My total fines were about $500 plus having to spend loads of time at the motor vehicle bureau straightening out the mess.

Use the following table (or copy the form on your computer) to record your procrastination episode and analyze the cause. After you have checked the most likely cause or causes, make a few notes in the third column as to how you might avoid procrastinating about that situation, or similar situation, in the future.

Procrastination Episode

Reason(s) for Procrastination	Check Each Reason That Applies	Technique I Might Use to Overcome the Procrastination Next Time I Am in That Situation
1. Unpleasant task		
2. Overwhelming task		
3. Possible negative evaluation of my work		
4. Fear of success		
5. Rebelled against being controlled		
6. No meaningful reward		
7. Liked the last-minute rush		
8. I'm a perfectionist		

The assistant manager of the health club admitted that reasons 5 and 6 applied to his situation. He noted that he regards inspection stickers as a form of control over him. He noted also that having the sticker may be important but that he doesn't feel any particular reward for complying with the law. On further reflection, he realizes that some control is necessary in a civilized society. Many uninspected vehicles are a menace on the road. So not getting a sticker has a cost to society as well as to him. He will therefore calculate the personal cost next time. He said, "I know that it is best to tackle a tough task first. It takes a little time and money to get my car inspected, so I should do it first thing on the day set for the inspection."

Human Relations Class Activity

Personal Productivity Checklist

Each class member will use the following checklist to identify the two biggest mistakes per category he or she is making in work habits and time management. The mistakes could apply to work, school, or personal life. In addition to identifying the problems, each student will develop brief action plans about how to overcome them. For instance, "One of my biggest problems is that I tend to start a lot of projects but finish very few of them. Now that I am aware of this problem, I am going to post a sign over my desk that reads, *No one will give me credit for things I never completed.*"

Students then present their problems and action plans to the class. After each student has made his or her presentation, a class discussion is held to reach conclusions and interpretations about the problems revealed. For instance, it might be that one or two time-management problems are quite frequent.

Overcoming Procrastination	**Especially Applicable to Me**
1. Increase awareness of the problem.	________
2. Calculate cost of procrastination.	________
3. Counterattack.	________
4. Jump-start yourself.	________
5. Peck away at an overwhelming task.	________
6. Motivate yourself with rewards and punishments.	________
7. Make a commitment to other people.	________
8. Express a more positive attitude about your intentions.	________
Developing Proper Attitudes and Values	
1. Develop a mission, goals, and a strong work ethic.	________
2. Value good attendance and punctuality.	________
3. Value your time.	________
4. Value neatness, orderliness, and speed.	________
5. Work smarter, not harder.	________
6. Appreciate the importance of rest and relaxation.	________
Time-Management Techniques	
1. Clean up and get organized.	________
2. Plan your activities (including a to-do list with priority setting).	________
3. Boost your energy.	________
4. Get off to a good start.	________
5. Make good use of office technology.	________
6. Concentrate on one key task at a time.	________
7. Streamline your work and emphasize important tasks.	________
8. Work at a steady pace.	________
9. Create some quiet, uninterrupted time.	________
10. Make use of bits of time, and use multitasking for routine work.	________
11. Stay in control of paperwork, the in-basket, and e-mail.	________
Overcoming Time Wasters	
1. Minimize daydreaming.	________
2. Prepare a time log to evaluate your use of time.	________
3. Avoid unproductive use of computers.	________
4. Keep track of important names, places, and things.	________
5. Set a time limit for certain tasks and projects.	________
6. Schedule similar tasks together (clustering).	________
7. Bounce quickly from task to task.	________

Human Relations Case Study 16-1

Josie Struggles to Get It Done

Twenty-six-year-old Josie DiSalvo is intelligent and talented, yet not nearly as successful as she would like to be. In high school and college she too frequently waited too long before preparing papers or studying for exams. As a result, her grades were lower than when she took her time to research and write a paper or study for an exam. At college, she often asked to be given a grade of Incomplete so she could complete a course requirement. Josie's request for a grade of Incomplete was usually refused because she could not provide proof of an emergency to justify an Incomplete.

After graduating from college, six months later than she planned, Josie embarked on a career in sports management. Being energetic, athletic, and personable, Josie soon found employment as a personal trainer at a fitness center. Her intent was to work her way up into a management position at an athletic club. Six months into the program, Josie was told that she was doing a fine job but that she would need to attend a two-week program for certification as a personal trainer in order to stay in her position.

One week later Josie went to the Web site containing the application for the personal trainer certification program. She began answering the easy biographical questions from memory, such as name, e-mail address, and postal address. But the online form also required that Josie track down information from outside sources, such as requesting that a transcript of her grades be sent to the certifying organization. In addition, Josie was asked to write a 200-word essay explaining why she wanted to become a personal trainer.

Josie thought, "I'll just have to get to this later, maybe next week. I've got a lot on my plate already. It's such a bother sending for a transcript and writing a career essay." Two weeks passed, and Josie still had made no more progress with her application.

One morning Josie's supervisor, Lucy, said to her, "I noticed that you did not get your application in on time for the certification training program. This means that we will be taking you off personal trainer status and assigning you to the front desk, in a part-time position."

Josie replied, "Lucy, can you give me one more shot? I've had some personal issues to deal with. Maybe I could take the next program coming up in the fall."

Questions

1. If you were Josie's supervisor, would you grant her "one more shot"? Why or why not?
2. Why might Josie be procrastinating about becoming certified as a personal trainer?
3. What advice can you offer Josie to help her control her procrastination?

Human Relations Role-Playing Exercise

Josie's Boss Attempts to Help Her Overcome Procrastination

The case study about Josie serves as the background and the story line for this role-play. One person plays the role of Josie, who thinks she deserves another chance at attending the certification program for personal trainers. She does not like the idea of being demoted to a part-time front-desk clerk. Her boss, Lucy, will be meeting with Josie in her (Lucy's) office right after the club closes on Tuesday night.

Another person plays the role of Lucy, who wants to help Josie get certified but also recognizes that the club was quite clear with Josie about getting her application in to become certified as a personal trainer. Lucy has noticed that Josie has not been prompt in getting the few reports in on time that she has been requested to prepare.

Observers rate the role-players on two dimensions, using a 1 to 5 scale from very poor to very good. One dimension is "effective use of human relations techniques." For Lucy, focus on how effective she is in helping Josie be more prompt in getting a work obligation completed. For Josie, observe if she can overcome her defensiveness about being a procrastinator. The second dimension is "acting ability." A few observers might voluntarily provide feedback to the role-players in terms of sharing their ratings and observations. The course instructor might also provide feedback.

Human Relations Case Study 16-2

The Busy Office Manager

Mike looked at the kitchen clock, and said to Ruth, his wife: "Oh no, it's 7:25, and my turn to drop off Jason and Gloria at the childcare center. Once again, I'll start my day late for childcare, and just barely making it to work on time."

After getting Jason and Gloria settled at the childcare center, Mike dashed off to the public accounting firm where he worked as the office manager. Mike found an e-mail from Ann Gabrielli, a partner in the firm: "See you today at 11:30 for the review of overhead expenses. Two other partners will be attending."

According to Mike's calendar, the meeting was one week from today. Mike called Ann immediately and said, "My apologies. My schedule says that the meeting is one week from today, at 11:30. I'm just not ready with the figures for today's meeting"

"My calendar says the meeting is today," responded Ann harshly. "I am ready for the meeting, and so are Craig and Gunther (the other partners). This isn't the first time you've gotten your weeks moved up. The meeting will go on, however poorly you have to perform."

"I'll be there," said Mike. "It's just a question of reviewing some figures that I've already collected." Mike calculated that he had less than three hours to prepare a report on overhead. He then glanced at his calendar to see what else he had scheduled for the morning. All was clear excerpt for the entry: "PA/LC." Mike quickly recalled that the initials stood for "performance appraisal with Lucy Cruthers, the head bookkeeper at the firm." He then sent Lucy an e-mail suggesting that they meet the following week at the same time.

Mike had a difficult time locating the computer file he needed. Mike asked Lois, his administrative assistant, to help him locate the file. She scanned about 100 documents, and said "Here's a possibility, a document labeled PTR. The initials could refer to preparing for partners." Lois proved to be correct, and Mike dug into preparing the report, now only two hours away.

At the meeting, the partners accepted his analysis of overhead expenses and said they would study his findings further. As the meeting ended, a senior partner said to Mike, "If you had gotten your weeks straight, I think you would have presented your analysis in more depth."

Mike returned from lunch at 2 p.m., and decided to finish the report on overhead expenses that he had prepared for the partners. By 4 p.m. might was ready to tackle other tasks listed on his daily planner. However, Lois told him that an employment agency representative was in the building so she decided to drop in and talk about their temporary employment services.

"Might as well let her in," said Mike. "We will soon be hiring some temporary bookkeepers. It's getting too late to do much anyway."

On the way home from the childcare center, the oldest child, Gloria, asked if the family could eat at a fast-food restaurant this evening. Mike said, "OK, but I'll have to stop at an ATM first. We'll ask Mom if she wants to eat out tonight before her class." Ruth agreed, and said to Mike, "By the way, how did you day go?

Mike replied, "I just fell one day further behind schedule. I'll have to do some paperwork after the children are asleep. Maybe we can want the late news together. We should both be free by then."

Questions

1. What time-management mistakes does Mike appear to be making?
2. What does Mike appear to be doing right from the standpoint of managing time?
3. What suggestions can you offer Mike to help him get his schedule more under control?

REFERENCES

1. Original story based on facts and observations reported in the following sources: Jane Wooldridge, "The Woman Behind the Cisneros Groups Screens," *The Miami Herald* (www.miamiherald.com), January 23, 2012, pp. 1–5; "Adriana Cisneros: Vice Chairman and Director of Strategy. Cisneros Group of Companies," retrieved March 28, 2012, from: www.Cisneros.com/Executive Profiles; Todd Michael Jamison, "Adriana Cisneros De Griffin, Vice Chairman of the Cisneros Group of Companies, Has Been Selected One of Latin America's Top 50 Business Woman of 2011, *Business Wire*, pp. 1–2, retrieved March 28, 2012, from: www.businesswire.com.
2. Steven Kotler, "Escape," *Psychology Today*, September/October 2009, p. 75.
3. Research of Timothy A. Psychl, reported in Danielle Kost, "Professor Says Putting Off Chores Is a Breakable Habit," *Rochester (NY) Democrat and Chronicle*, September 22, 2002, p. D3.
4. Theodore Kurtz, "Ten Reasons Why People Procrastinate," *Supervisory Management*, April 1990, pp. 1–2.
5. Hara Estroff Marano, "The Making of a Perfectionist," *Psychology Today*, March/April 2008, pp. 80–86.
6. Alan Lakein, *How to Gain Control of Your Time and Your Life* (New York: Wyden Books, 1973), pp. 141–151.
7. Linda Sapadin, *It's About Time! The Six Styles of Procrastination and How to Overcome Them* (New York: Viking, 1996).
8. Stephen R. Covey with Elaine Pofeldt, "Why Is This Man Smiling?" *Success*, January 2000, pp. 38–40.
9. Cited in Alfred A. Edmond, Jr., "Alone in Your Time Zone," *Black Enterprise*, December 2004, pp. 154–155.
10. Dorothy Madden, "Clear Mind of Clutter to Be More Productive," *Democrat and Chronicle*, March 27, 2012, p. 5B.
11. Eric Abrahamson and David H. Freedman, *A Perfect Mess* (Boston: Little, Brown, 2007).
12. Michael Mandel, "The Real Reasons You're Working So Hard... and What You Can Do About It," *Business Week*, October 3, 2005, p. 62.
13. Quoted in Dawn Klingensmith, "Shine—and Rise!" www.philly.com, March 19, 2012, p. 2.
14. Don J. Q. Chen and Vivien K. G. Lim, "Impact of Cyberloafing on Psychological Engagement," paper presented at the Academy of Management annual meeting, August 2011.
15. Quoted in Carrie Ferguson, "The Wages of a Workaholic," Gannett News Service, May 23, 2000; Brenda Goodman, "A Field Guide to the Workaholic," *Psychology Today*, May/June 2006, p. 40.
16. Stewart D. Friedman and Sharon Lobel, "The Happy Workaholic: A Role Model for Employees," *Academy of Management Executive*, August 2003, pp. 87–98.
17. Paul Keegan, "The Master of Getting Things Done," *Business 2.0*, July 2007, p. 77; Ellen Joan Pollock, "How I Got a Grip on My Workweek," *Businessweek*, April 6, 2009, p. 084.
18. Alina Dizik, "Virtual Gofers Tackle Personal To-Do Lists," *The Wall Street Journal*, June 17, 2010, p. D3.
19. Tony Schwartz, "The Productivity Paradox: How Sony Pictures Gets More Out of People by Demanding Less," *Harvard Business Review*, June 2010, pp. 64–69.
20. Charlotte Fritz, Chak Fu Lam, and Gretchen M. Spritzer, "It's the Little Things That Matter," *Academy of Management Perspectives*, August 2011, pp. 28–39.
21. Merrill Douglass, "Timely Time Tips: Ideas to Help You Manage Your Time," *Executive Management Forum*, September 1989, p. 4.
22. Christopher Randler, "The Early Bird Really Does Get the Worm," *Harvard Business Review*, July-August 2010, pp. 30–31.
23. Leigh Gallagher, "How I Managed My Time—the Covey Way," *Fortune*, March 21, 2011, p. 40.
24. Estimate given in Eric Spitznagel, "Any Given Monday," *Bloomberg Businessweek*, September 13–19, 2010, p. 82.
25. Stacy Cowley, "A Guide to Jack Dorsey's 80-hour Workweek," *CNN Money* (http://cnn.money.com), November 14, 2011, pp. 1–2.
26. "Attention Deficit Hyperactivity Disorder: What It Is and Who Is Affected" (www.health.com), January 12, 2009.
27. "Avoid the Burden of 'Workplace ADD,'" *Manager's Edge*, May 2007, p. 7.
28. David Allen, "When Office Technology Overwhelms, Get Organized," *The New York Times* (www.nytimes.com), March 19, 2012, p. 2.
29. Survey cited in "Productivity Declines as the Workday Ends," *Democrat and Chronicle* (Rochester, NY), July 18, 2005, p. 10D.
30. Farhad Manjoo, "An Empty Inbox, or With Just a Few E-mail Messages? Read On," *New York Times* (www.nytimes.com), March 5, 2009.
31. Dan Malachowski, "Wasted Time at Work Costing Companies Billions," updated version retrieved April 20, 2009, from: www.salary.com.
32. Chris Brogran, "The New Attention Deficit," *Entrepreneur*, December 2010, p. 70.

17

Managing Stress and Personal Problems

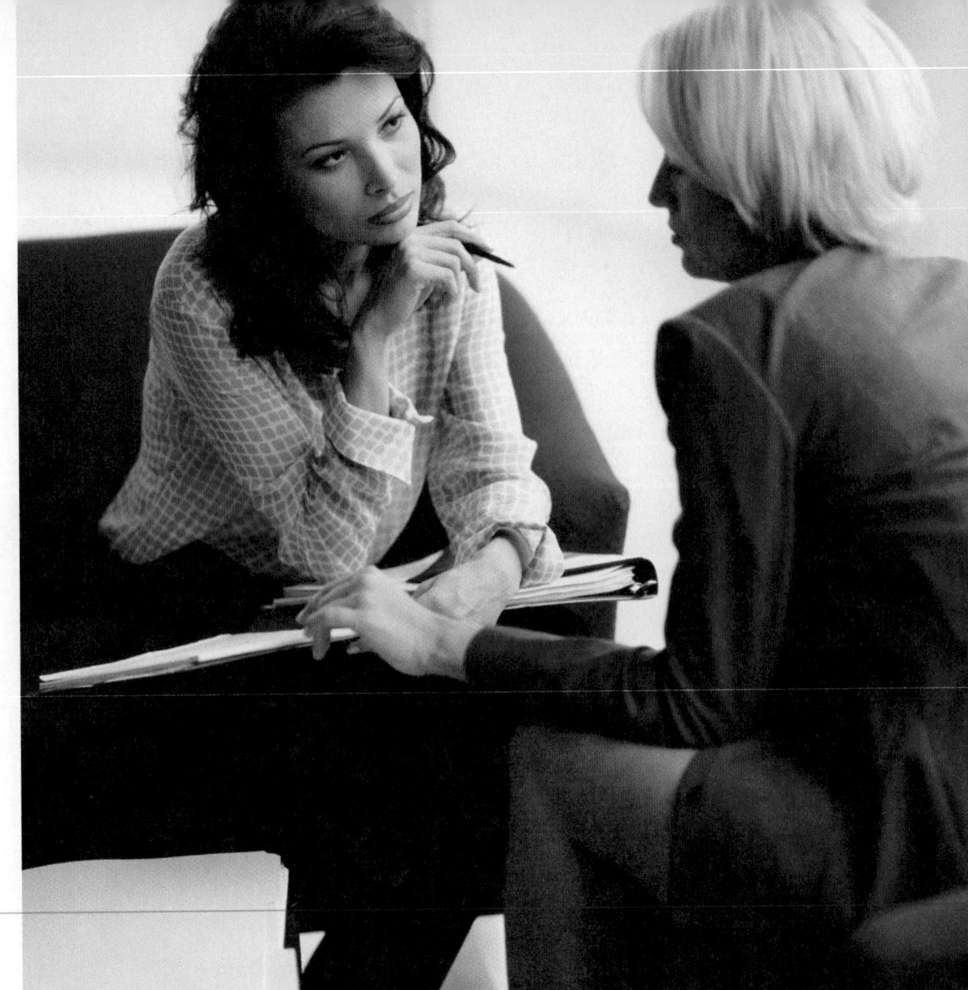

Outline

Max was having difficulty concentrating on his work as the supervisor of order fulfillment at the online department of a national retailer. He was frequently late in submitting sales and shipping data to his manager. When asked a question by one of his group members, Max would often ask the employee to repeat the question because he didn't listen carefully the first time.

Soon, Max's boss, Sara, approached him and explained that she was noticing that he seemed to be too preoccupied to pay full attention to his job. Sara explained to Max that his performance as a supervisor was slipping badly and that he had to improve. Max told Sara, "Yes, I've been facing some personal issues lately that are stressing me out. I'll be back on top of my game as soon as I get my problems under control."

Sara then offered Max the opportunity to visit an employee assistance program the company has to help employees deal with personal problems that interfere with work. Max followed up and asked to see a counselor specializing in financial problems. In speaking with the counselor, Max explained how he and his wife have become overwhelmed by credit card debt and that the associated stress was making it difficult for him to concentrate.

The financial counselor worked with Max to help him cope with the couple's financial problems. An immediate stress reliever for Max was the technique of tackling his smallest debt first—one that required a minimum payment of $55 per month. The counselor explained, "After you conquer this debt, it will seem like a salary increase of $55 per month after taxes." Based on the counseling, Max and his wife also cut way back on expenses by switching to the most basic packages for their cable television and cell phone services, and quit purchasing $4 lattes.

With a financial recovery plan in action, Max reduced his stress level enough to concentrate better on his work. Sara remarked how Max was back to his former self.

Learning Objectives ▸

After studying the information and doing the exercises in this chapter, you should be able to:

1. Describe the meaning of stress and its physiology.
2. Identify several positive and negative consequences of stress.
3. Pinpoint potential stressors in personal life.
4. Pinpoint potential stressors in the workplace.
5. Describe key methods for managing the potential adverse effects of stress.
6. Develop insight into dealing with personal problems through understanding self-defeating behavior and the importance of being resilient.

The story about the distracted supervisor illustrates how companies are concerned about preventing and reducing stress to boost productivity, including having employees overcome personal problems that interfere with work. In this chapter we describe the nature and cause of stress, managing personal and work stress, and the related topic of coping with personal problems.

▶ Learning Objective 1 ▶

What Are the Physiology and Consequences of Stress?

Stress
an internal reaction to any force that threatens to disturb a person's equilibrium; the internal reaction usually takes the form of emotional discomfort

Stressor
the external or internal force that brings about the stress

An important part of learning about stress is to understand its meaning, underlying physiology, and consequences to the person. **Stress** is an internal reaction to any force that threatens to disturb a person's equilibrium. The internal reaction usually takes the form of emotional discomfort. A **stressor** is the external or internal force that brings about the stress. Your perception of an event or thought influences whether a given event is stressful. Your confidence in your ability to handle difficult situations also influences the amount of stress you experience. If you believe you have the resources to conquer the potentially stressful event, you are much less likely to experience stress. A computer whiz, therefore, would not be stressed by the prospect of having to install a new computer operating system. Two key aspects of understanding stress are the accompanying physiological changes and the consequences—including symptoms—of stress.

PHYSIOLOGICAL CHANGES

Fight-or-flight response
the experience of stress prompts the adrenal glands to release a flood of hormones that prepare the body to fight or run when faced with a challenge

The physiological changes taking place within the body are almost identical for both positive and negative stressors. Riding a roller coaster, falling in love, or being fired, for example, make you feel about the same inside. In the long run, however, negative experiences create unpleasant feelings such as anxiety. The stress response begins in the brain, and a number of structures, including the pituitary gland, go on alert. The experience of stress prompts the adrenal glands to release a flood of hormones that prepare the body to fight or run when faced with a challenge. This battle against the stressor is referred to as the **fight-or-flight response.** (The "response" is really a conflict, because you are forced to choose between struggling with the stressor or fleeing from the scene.) It helps you deal with emergencies.

The activation of hormones when the body has to cope with a stressor produces a short-term physiological reaction. Among the most familiar reactions are increases in heart rate, blood pressure, and blood glucose as well as blood clotting. Digestion stops during the stress episode. To help you recognize these symptoms, try to recall the internal bodily sensations you felt if you ever were almost in an automobile accident or if you heard some wonderful news. Less familiar changes are a redirection of the blood flow toward the brain and large-muscle groups and a release of stored fluids from places throughout the body into the bloodstream.

CONSEQUENCES AND SYMPTOMS

If stress is continuous and accompanied by these short-term physiological changes, annoying and life-threatening conditions can occur. A stressful life event usually leads to a high cholesterol level (of the unhealthy type) and high blood pressure. Men who respond most intensely to mental stress run a higher risk of blocked blood vessels. The result is a higher risk of heart attack and stroke. A series of studies indicated that job stressors such as a hostile work environment or excessive hours can enhance a worker's risk for cardiovascular disease. One explanation of this problem is that mental stress, over time, may injure blood vessels and foster the buildup of arterial plaques.[1] Other conditions associated with stress are migraine headaches, ulcers, allergies, skin disorders, and cancer. Stress often results in memory problems, such as forgetting where you put your keys or not remembering an appointment.

Stress symptoms vary considerably from one person to another. A sampling of common stress symptoms is listed in Figure 17-1.

Mostly Physical	
Shaking or trembling	Upper- and lower-back pain
Dizziness	Frequent headaches
Heart palpitations	Low energy and stamina
Difficulty breathing	Stomach problems
Chronic fatigue	Constant cravings for sweets
Unexplained chest pains	Increased alcohol or cigarette consumption
Frequent teeth grinding	Frequent need to eliminate
Frequent nausea and dizziness	Skin eruptions and rashes
Premature aging, including a haggard appearance	
Mostly Emotional and Behavioral	
Difficulty concentrating	Anxiety
Nervousness	Depression
Crying	Forgetfulness
Anorexia	Restlessness
Declining interest in sex and romance	Frequent arguments with others
Feelings of hopelessness, despair, anger, and sadness	Feeling high strung much of the time
	Withdrawal from people and listlessness
	Decrease in job performance, including increased tardiness and absenteeism

FIGURE 17-1

A VARIETY OF STRESS SYMPTOMS

Note: Anxiety is a feeling of distress or uneasiness caused by fear of an imagined or unidentified problem. For example, you might be anxious about meeting your supervisor today, but you have no specific concern in mind.

A major consequence of stress is that it affects our ability to fight infection. Psychology professors Suzanne Segerstrom of the University of Kentucky and Gregory Miller of the University of British Columbia analyzed the results of 293 studies, involving 18,941 individuals, conducted over a thirty-year span. Three major findings emerged from this massive analysis. First, stress does alter immunity—as has been long theorized. Second, short-term stress boosts the immune system, functioning as an adaptive response preparing for injury or infection. Giving a public speech or class presentation are examples of short-term stress for most people. Yet long-term chronic stress causes too much wear and tear, breaking down the immune system. An example of a long-term chronic stress would be long-term unemployment. Third, the immune system of older people, or those who are ill, is more susceptible to stress-related change.[2]

Challenge versus Hindrance Stressors

A useful framework for understanding work-related stressors is that they can have positive or negative consequences. **Challenge stressors** are stressful events and thoughts that have a positive direct effect on motivation and performance. They include work-related stimuli or forces such as a reasonably high workload, times pressures, and a realistic level of responsibility. Workers perceive these stressors as relatively under their control. Challenge stressors also offer the opportunity for personal growth if they are overcome, such as learning a complex new skill.

Challenge stressors stressful events and thoughts that have a positive direct effect on motivation and performance

Hindrance stressors are those stressful events and thoughts that have a negative effect on motivation and performance. They include work-related stimuli or forces such as negative organization politics, bullying by supervisors and coworkers, confusing regulations, and confusion about responsibilities. Hindrance stressors encompass potentially stressful demands usually perceived as beyond the control of the worker and that might block the opportunity for personal growth.[3]

Hindrance stressors stressful events and thoughts that have a negative effect on motivation and performance

The concept of challenge versus hindrance stressors indicates that stress can play a positive role in our lives. The right amount of stress prepares us for meeting difficult challenges and spurs us on to peak intellectual and physical performance. (The findings about the immune system support this conclusion.) An optimum amount of stress exists for most people and most tasks. In general, performance tends to be best under moderate amounts of stress. If stress is too great, people become temporarily ineffective because they may freeze or choke. Under too little stress, people may become lethargic and inattentive. Excessive stress can lower job performance because the stressed person makes errors in concentration and judgment.

The Consequences of Negative Stress

Stress has enormous consequences to employers as well as individuals. It has been estimated that American companies lose about $300 billion annually in accidents, absenteeism, diminished productivity, medical costs, insurance costs, tardiness, and Workers' Compensation claims linked to stress disorders.[4] We emphasize again that positive stress is not associated with negative consequences to the employer.

Evidence suggests that alcohol and illicit drug use might increase when workers experience negative stress. Michael R. Frone, of the State University of New York at Buffalo, studied how the stressors of work overload and job insecurity affected drug use, based on a national sample of U.S. workers. Telephone interviews were the method of data collection. Frone found a positive relationship between these two work stressors to alcohol use before, during, and after work.[5]

A long-term negative consequence to extreme stress is posttraumatic stress disorder in which the person is disturbed by an intense stressor from the past. Some workplace events that are capable of producing posttraumatic stress disorder include being shot by a robber, witnessing or being part of workplace violence, and observing a coworker being killed in an accident. A supervisor and coworkers who communicate an understanding of what the posttraumatic stress disorder sufferer is going through can be helpful.[6]

Overall Relationship Between Stress and Job Performance

Figure 17-2 depicts the relationship between stress and performance, as already suggested by the difference between challenge versus hindrance stressors. Creativity, an important part of performance in many jobs, tends to be higher under conditions of low

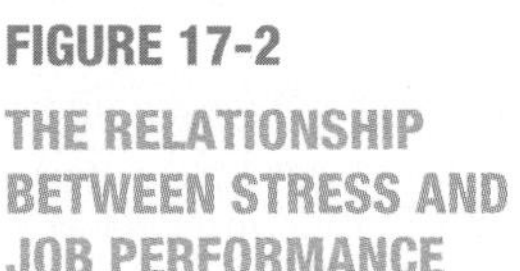

FIGURE 17-2

THE RELATIONSHIP BETWEEN STRESS AND JOB PERFORMANCE

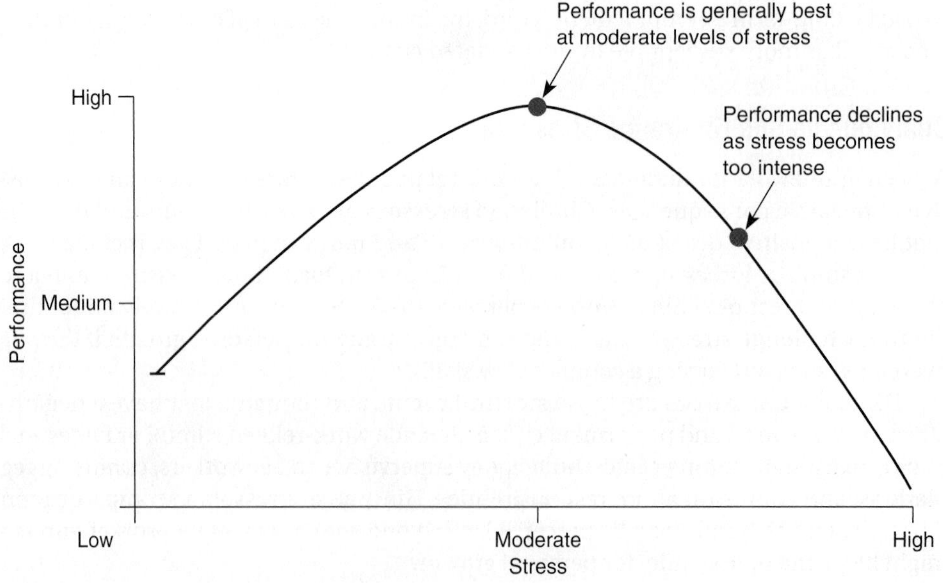

stress (not zero stress). When the stress becomes too high, creative performance is likely to decline.[7]

An exception to this relationship is that certain negative forms of stress are likely to lower performance even if the stress is moderate. For example, the stress created by an intimidating boss or worrying about radiation poisoning—even in moderate amounts—will not improve performance.

Moderate stress is placed in the optimal performance zone as often created by challenge stressors. In this optimal zone the body will experience an increase in heartbeat, breathing, and muscle tension, as well as increased physical strength. The mind will experience enhanced alertness and energy, sharper cognitive skills, more optimism and excitement—all leading to higher job productivity.[8]

Burnout as a Consequence of Long-Term Stress

One of the major problems of prolonged stress is that it may lead to **burnout,** a condition of emotional, mental, and physical exhaustion in response to long-term job stressors. The exhaustion aspect of burnout can be triggered by such factors as a heavy physical workload, time pressures, and shift work.[9] Common symptoms of burnout include the following:

Burnout
a condition of emotional, mental, and physical exhaustion in response to long-term job stressors

- Dreading to go to work in the morning
- Work activities that were enjoyable in the past now feeling like drudgery
- Being envious of other people who are happy at work
- Caring less about doing a good job[10]

The burned-out person often becomes cynical. Burnout is most likely to occur among those whose jobs call for frequent and intense interactions with others, such as a social worker, teacher, or customer service representative. Yet people in other occupations also suffer from burnout, especially when not much support from others is present and the rewards are few.

Also, a hostile work environment, such as being harassed by coworkers and managers, is a major contributor to burnout. Students can also experience burnout because studying and preparing reports is hard work. Conscientiousness and perfectionism also contribute to burnout because people with these characteristics feel stressed when they do not accomplish everything they would like. Similarly, being obsessed about what you are doing can trigger burnout.

Burnout can be treated in many ways, just as with the negative effects of stress. Showing gratitude for hard work by employees is particularly helpful in preventing and treating burnout because many cases of burnout are caused by intense feelings of being unappreciated.

What Are Some Sources of Stress in Personal Life?

◀ Learning Objective 2 ◀

Almost any form of frustration, disappointment, setback, inconvenience, or crisis in your personal life can cause stress. The list is dynamic because new sources of stress emerge continuously. For example, a prolonged downturn in the stock and bond markets can be a stressor for investors who previously paid little attention to how well their investments were performing. Our life stage also helps determine which events are stressors. A person building his or her career is more likely to be more stressed by a limited supply of jobs than a person nearing retirement. Presented next are major categories of stressful events in personal life.

FIGURE 17-3

THE TOP EIGHT STRESSORS AS MEASURED BY LIFE-CHANGE UNITS

Source: Adapted from a portion of the original version in Thomas H. Holmes and Richard H. Rahe, "The Social Readjustment Rating Scale," *Journal of Psychosomatic Research*, 1, 1967, pp. 210–223.

1. Death of a spouse
2. Divorce
3. Marital separation
4. Jail term/imprisonment
5. Death of a family member
6. Personal injury or illness
7. Marriage
8. Fired from a job

1. Significant life change. A general stressor that encompasses both work and personal life is having to cope with significant change. According the pioneering research of Thomas Holmes and Richard Rahe, the necessity of a significant change in an individual's life pattern creates stress. When a major stressor strikes, such as being fired, you have to readjust. The more significant the change you have to cope with in a short period of time, the greater the probability of experiencing a stress disorder, leading to other medical problems.[11] A key point of the Holmes and Rahe research is that stress arises from dramatic, one-time life events. As shown in Figure 17-3, the maximum negative change is the death of a spouse.

2. Low self-esteem. A subtle cause of stress is low self-esteem. People who do not feel good about themselves often find it difficult to feel good about anything. Low self-esteem has several links to stress. One is that being in a bad mood continually functions as a stressor. People with low self-esteem drag themselves down into a funk, which creates stress. Another link between low self-esteem and stress proneness is that people with low self-esteem get hurt more by insults. Instead of questioning the source of the criticism, the person with self-doubt will accept the opinion as valid. An insult accepted as valid acts as a stressor because it is a threat to our well-being.

Low self-esteem is linked to stress in yet another way. People with low self-esteem doubt their ability to work their way out of problems. As a result, minor challenges appear to be major problems. For example, a person with low self-esteem will often doubt he or she will be successful in conducting a job search. As a result, having to conduct a job search will represent a major stressor. A person with high self-esteem might feel better prepared mentally to accept the challenge. (As you will recall, your perception of an event influences whether it is stressful.)

3. Everyday annoyances. Managing everyday annoyances can have a greater impact on your health than major life catastrophes. Among these everyday annoyances are losing keys or a wallet, a hard drive crashing, being stuck in traffic, having your car break down on the way to an important event, and being lost on the way to an important appointment. People who have the coping skills to deal with everyday annoyances are less likely to be stressed out over them. A major reason everyday annoyances act as stressors is because they are frustrating—they block your path to an important goal, such as getting your work accomplished.

4. Social and family problems. Friends and family are the main sources of love and affection in your life, but they can also be the main source of stress. Most physical acts of violence are committed among friends and family members. One of the many reasons we encounter so much conflict with friends and family is that we are emotionally involved with them.

5. Physical and mental health problems. Prolonged stress produces physical and mental health problems, and the reverse is also true. Physical and mental illness can act as stressors—the fact of being ill is stressful. Furthermore, thinking that you might soon contract a life-threatening illness is stressful. If you receive a serious injury, that too can create stress.

6. Financial problems. A major life stressor is financial problems. Although you may not be obsessed with money, not having enough money to take care of what you consider the necessities of life can lead to anxiety and tension. If you do not have enough money to replace or repair a broken or faulty personal computer or automobile, the result can be stressful. A major stressor for recent graduates who move to areas with high costs of living is being unable to afford a comfortable place to live. Figure 17-4 suggests that financial problems are the leading stressor, and that two other top stressors are linked to finances—the economy and housing costs are part of the three leading stressors for Americans. Figure 17-5 presents a budget worksheet that will help many people reduce financial stress. The goal is for monthly income to exceed monthly expenses, or at a minimum for income to meet expenses, including a little money set aside for emergencies.

7. School-related problems. The life of a student can be stressful. Among the stressors to cope with are exams in subjects you do not understand well, having to write papers on subjects unfamiliar to you, working your way through the complexities of registration, and having to deal with instructors who do not see things your way. Another source of severe stress for some students is having too many competing demands on their time. On most campuses you will find someone who works full-time, goes to school full-time, and has a family.

PERSONALITY FACTORS CONTRIBUTING TO STRESS

Some people are more stress prone than others because of personality factors. Three key personality factors predisposing people to stress are type A behavior, a belief that external forces control their life, and negative affectivity.

Type A Behavior and Hostility

People with **type A behavior** characteristics have basic personalities that lead them into stressful situations. Type A behavior has two main components. One is a tendency to try to accomplish too many things in too little time. This leads the type A individual to be impatient and demanding. The other component is free-floating hostility. Because of this combined sense of urgency and hostility, trivial things irritate these people. On the job, people with type A behavior are aggressive and hardworking. Off the job, they keep themselves preoccupied with all kinds of errands to run and things to do.

Type A behavior
personality characteristics that lead a person into stressful situations. Type A behavior has two main components: (1) the tendency to try to accomplish too many things in too little time and (2) free-floating hostility

FIGURE 17-4
CAUSES OF STRESS IN AMERICA

Percentage of people who consider the potential stressor to be somewhat or very significant

Rank	Potential Stressor	Percentage
1	Money	75
2	Work	70
3	The economy	67
4	Relationships (e.g., spouse, children, girlfriend, or boyfriend)	58
5	Family responsibilities	57
6 (tie)	Health problems affecting my family	53
6 (tie)	Personal health concerns	53
7 (tie)	Job stability	49
7 (tie)	Housing costs (e.g., mortgage or rent)	49
10	Personal safety	32

Source: Adapted from "Stress in America 2011 Survey," American Psychological Association, 2012, p. 15.

FIGURE 17-5

BUDGET WORKSHEET TO HELP GET FINANCES UNDER CONTROL

Your Monthly Budget

Monthly Expenses		**Monthly Income**	
Fixed:			
Mortgage or rent	______	Salary	______
Property insurance	______	Tips	______
Health insurance	______	Commissions	______
Auto insurance	______	Bonuses	______
Education	______	Interest and dividends	______
Child support paid	______	Child support received	______
Internet service provider	______	eBay sales	______
Phone (if not bundled with ISP)	______	Other	______
		Total income	
Cable or satellite TV	______		
Federal tax	______	*Summary:*	
State or provincial tax	______	Total income	______
Social Security (FICA)	______	Less total expenses	______
Property tax	______	Balance for savings or deficit	
Vehicle payments	______		
Credit cards and other loans	______		
Set-asides for emergencies	______		
Variable:			
Food in home	______		
Restaurants and other entertainment	______		
Household supplies	______		
Home maintenance	______		
Medical and dental	______		
Clothing and dry cleaning	______		
Hair care	______		
Cosmetics	______		
Gasoline and transportation	______		
Car maintenance	______		
Travel and vacation	______		
Hobbies and clubs	______		
Other	______		
Total expenses	______		

Note: These expense and income general categories may vary with individual circumstances.

Certain features of the type A behavior pattern are related to coronary heart disease. Hostility, anger, cynicism, and suspiciousness lead to heart problems, whereas impatience, ambition, and being work driven are not associated with coronary disease. One study showed that men who received a high score on a personality test about hostility were much more likely to develop coronary heart disease several years later.[12] Many work-driven people who like what they are doing—including many business executives—are remarkably healthy and outlive less competitive people. In reference to heart disease, medical and clinical psychologist David Krantz concluded, "You can be ambitious. You can be time pressured. But if you're not hostile and angry, your risk is lower."[13]

Belief in External Locus of Control

If you believe that your fate is controlled more by external than internal forces, you are probably more susceptible to stress. People with an **external locus of control** believe that external forces control their fate. Conversely, people with an **internal locus of control** believe that fate is pretty much under their control. The link between locus of control and stress works in this manner: If people believe they can control adverse forces, they are less prone to the stressor of worrying about them. For example, if you believe that you can always find a job, you will worry less about unemployment. At the same time, the person who believes in an internal locus of control experiences a higher level of job satisfaction. Work is less stressful and more satisfying when you perceive it to be under your control.

External locus of control individual's belief that external forces control his or her fate

Internal locus of control individual's belief that fate is pretty much under a person's own control

The everyday problem of lost computer files illustrates the importance of an internal locus of control. When a hard drive crashes or a valuable file is lost in some other way, the "external" person blames the computer or the software for the stressful event. An "internal," in contrast, would most likely have created backup files along the way. So when a crash occurs, the person is less stressed because relatively little data have been lost.

What about your locus of control? Do you believe it to be internal? Or is it external?

Negative Affectivity

A major contributor to being stress prone is **negative affectivity**, a tendency to experience aversive (intensely disliked) emotional states. In more detail, negative affectivity is a predisposition to experience emotional stress that includes feelings of nervousness, tension, and worry. Furthermore, a person with negative affectivity is likely to experience emotional states such as anger, scorn, revulsion, guilt, and self-dissatisfaction.[14] Such negative personalities seem to search for discrepancies between what they would like and what exists. Instead of attempting to solve problems, they look for them. Although negative affectivity is a relatively stable personality characteristic, the circumstances a person faces can trigger such behavior.[15] For example, a four-hour wait in an airplane parked on the tarmac might trigger a person's mild tendencies toward negative affectivity.

Negative affectivity a tendency to experience aversive (intensely disliked) emotional states; predisposition to experience emotional stress that includes feelings of nervousness, tension, and worry

What Are Some Key Sources of Work Stress?

Learning Objective 3

No job is without potential stressors for some people. A survey indicated that work is the major source of stress for Americans, with 74 percent of respondents reporting that work is their top stressor.[16] But when work is lacking stressful elements it may not have enough challenge to prompt employees to achieve high performance. Figure 17-6 illustrates six major job stressors you might encounter or have already encountered.

WORK OVERLOAD OR UNDERLOAD

A heavy workload is a widely acknowledged source of job stress. **Role overload**, a burdensome workload, can create stress for a person in two ways. First, the person may become fatigued and thus be less able to tolerate annoyances and irritations. Think of how much easier it is to become provoked over a minor incident when you lack proper rest. Second, a person subject to unreasonable work demands may feel perpetually behind schedule, a situation that itself creates an uncomfortable, stressful feeling.

Role overload a burdensome workload that creates stress for a person in two ways: (1) the person may become fatigued and less able to tolerate annoyances and irritations and (2) a person subject to unreasonable work demands may feel perpetually behind schedule, a situation that itself creates an uncomfortable, stressful feeling

FIGURE 17-6
FREQUENT JOB STRESSORS

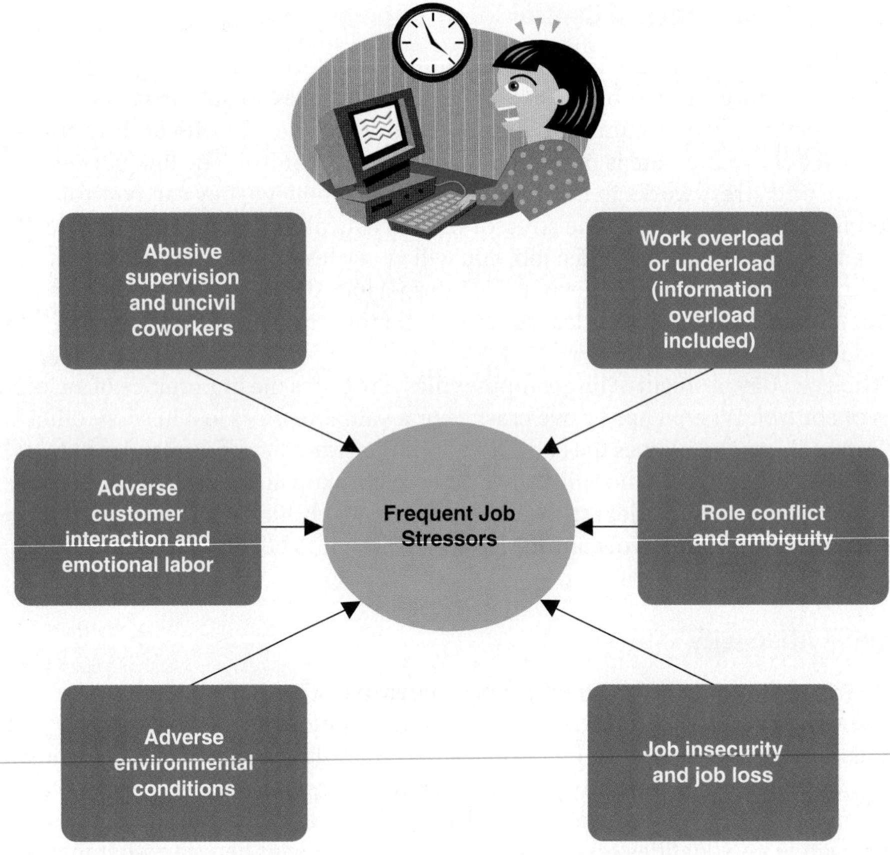

A factor contributing to stress is the work-more economy in which many workers take on extra responsibilities and in some cases perform two jobs yet are paid for one. This approach to workforce management usually comes about because a company has suffered from a business downturn and attempts to control costs by maintaining a lean workforce. Many employers give their employees more responsibility to compensate for the void created by laid-off coworkers, hiring freezes, and new business growth. In 2012, a *Workforce Management* survey indicated that 55 percent of respondents indicated that their job responsibilities had increased as a result of the troubled economy.[17]

Another form of work overload is demanding higher and higher speed from workers. Speed is important to companies because delivering goods and services very quickly brings a competitive edge. The most stressful situation occurs when a company downsizes and the remaining workers are expected to carry a heavier workload at a faster pace than previously. The combination of additional responsibility and high speed can be a major stressor. Among the problems are that hurried employees have very little time to ask for help or to carefully study what they are doing.

A powerful stressor for knowledge workers is information overload. Workers have to process so much information in the form of e-mail messages, text messages, Web sites, written reports, and job-related news that their brain circuits become overloaded, leading to stress and lowered concentration. Many workers encourage overload by multitasking while receiving information.

Role underload
disruptive amount of stress that can occur when people experience too little to do

A disruptive amount of stress can also occur when people experience **role underload,** or too little to do. Some people find role underload frustrating because it is a normal human desire to want to work toward self-fulfillment. Also, making a contribution on the job is one way of gaining self-esteem. Some people, however, find it relaxing not to have much to do on the job. One direct benefit is that it preserves their energy for family and leisure activities.

ROLE CONFLICT AND ROLE AMBIGUITY

Being pulled in two directions is a classic stressor. **Role conflict** refers to having to choose between two competing demands or expectations. Many workers receive conflicting demands from two or more managers. Imagine being told by your manager to give top priority to one project. You then receive an e-mail message from your manager's manager, who tells you to drop everything and work on another project. It's often up to you to resolve such a conflict. If you don't, you will experience stress. Having to choose between taking care of job responsibilities versus personal responsibilities is another potent type of role conflict, such as having to work the night when a good friend is getting married. Do you upset your boss or your good friend?

Role conflict
having to choose between two competing demands or expectations

Not being certain of what they should be doing is a stressor for many people. **Role ambiguity** is a condition in which the job holder receives confusing or poorly defined expectations. A typical complaint is, "I'm not really sure I know what I'm supposed to be doing around here." Role ambiguity is related to job control. If you lack a clear picture of what you should be doing, it is difficult to get your job under control.

Role ambiguity
condition in which the job holder receives confusing or poorly defined expectations

In addition to creating stress, role conflict and role ambiguity can have a negative impact on organizational citizenship behavior, as suggested by a synthesis of forty-two studies. Apparently the anxiety and discomfort associated with role conflict and role ambiguity distracts a person from being a good organizational citizen. The researchers involved in the analysis concluded that employers wishing to encourage more organizational citizenship behavior may want to consider steps to reduce role conflict an ambiguity. Employees should be provided with clearly defined descriptions of job duties and expectations.[18]

JOB INSECURITY AND JOB LOSS

Worrying about losing your job is a major stressor. Even when jobs are plentiful, having to search for another job and facing the prospect of geographic relocation are stressors for many people. Downsizings and corporate mergers—which usually result in downsizing to eliminate duplication in positions—have contributed to job insecurity. The anticipation of layoffs among employees can increase negative stress and lower job performance. In addition, the survivors of a downsizing often experience pressure from the fear of future job cuts, loss of friends, and worry about a sudden increase in workload.

Job loss is a more intense stressor than job insecurity because it is compounded by the stressors of financial problems, decreased status, and blows to the self-esteem. Negative confrontations with creditors might also add to the stress. Furthermore, homelessness might follow job loss, creating a gigantic stressor.

ADVERSE ENVIRONMENTAL CONDITIONS

A variety of adverse organizational conditions are stressors, as identified by the National Institute of Occupational Safety and Health. Several of these adverse conditions are listed below.

1. **Unpleasant or dangerous physical conditions.** Examples are crowding, noise, air pollution, or ergonomic problems. Steady exposure to *noise pollution* has been associated with high blood pressure and fatal heart attacks.[19] Examples of noise pollution include that created by the constant beeping sound required to be emitted from fork-lift trucks and construction vehicles, and the beeping noises of electronic devices.

2. **A sick building.** Sufficiently high levels of polluted air within an office building can create a *sick building,* in which a diverse range of airborne particles, vapors, molds, and gases pollute the indoor environment. The result can be headaches, nausea, and respiratory infections as well as the stress created by being physically ill.

3. **Excessive time in front of a computer monitor.** Working at a computer monitor for prolonged periods of time can lead to adverse physical and psychological reactions. The symptoms include headaches and fatigue, along with eye problems. Common visual problems are dry eyes and blurred or double vision. An estimated one out of five visits to vision care professionals is for computer-related problems. Another vision-related problem is that people lean forward to scan a monitor, leading to physical problems such as back strain.

The neck pain, shoulder strain, and backaches so often associated with people working at computers might also be related to other forms of job stress. As such, working on the computer alone might not be the only cause of the symptoms. Having poor relationships with coworkers and a manager might also contribute to physical problems. A study with call center workers in the United Kingdom found that 45 percent of participants reported upper-body strain, and 34 percent complained of lower-back problems. These same employees reported the most job strain in terms of job-related anxiety and depression.[20] (It is also conceivable that the physical problems could have led to anxiety and depression.)

A repetitive-motion disorder most frequently associated with keyboarding and the use of optical scanners is **carpal tunnel syndrome.** The syndrome occurs when repetitive flexing and extension of the wrist causes the tendons to swell, thus trapping and pinching the median nerve. Carpal tunnel syndrome creates stress because of the pain and misery. The thoughts of having to permanently leave a job requiring keyboarding is another potential stressor. Some of the risk factors for carpal tunnel syndrome include pregnancy, obesity, smoking, and a previous wrist injury, or arthritis.[21]

Carpal tunnel syndrome repetitive-motion disorder most frequently associated with keyboarding and the use of optical scanners; occurs when repetitive flexing and extension of the wrist causes the tendons to swell, thus trapping and pinching the median nerve

Repetitive-motion disorders can be prevented somewhat by computer workers taking frequent rest breaks and using a well-designed combination of the worktable, chair, and monitor. Wearing elasticized wrist bands provides enough support to the wrist tendons to prevent many cases of repetitive-motion disorders. Many people who blame their job for having caused carpal tunnel syndrome fail to recognize that they spend perhaps an additional four hours per evening on the keyboard for purposes such as e-mailing friends and visiting Web sites.

Being comfortable while working prevents much physical strain. Figure 17-7 presents the basics of a workstation designed on *ergonomic* principles. (Ergonomics has to do with making machines and equipment fit human capabilities and demands.)

Adverse environmental conditions can sometimes be overcome. For example, so many workers spend so much time at a computer monitor both on and off the job that many of these people might find a computer monitor (including screens on tablet computers and smart phones) to be a natural way of life. As a result they develop the physical and mental skills to spend extensive time at computers.

ADVERSE CUSTOMER INTERACTION AND EMOTIONAL LABOR

Interactions with customers can be a major stressor. Part of the problem is that the sales associate often feels helpless when placed in conflict with a customer. The sales associate is told that "the customer is always right." Furthermore, the store manager usually sides with the customer in a dispute with the sales associate. Industrial sales representatives might also face adverse customer interaction, such as a customer complaining harshly that a recently purchased machine or software system does not work correctly.

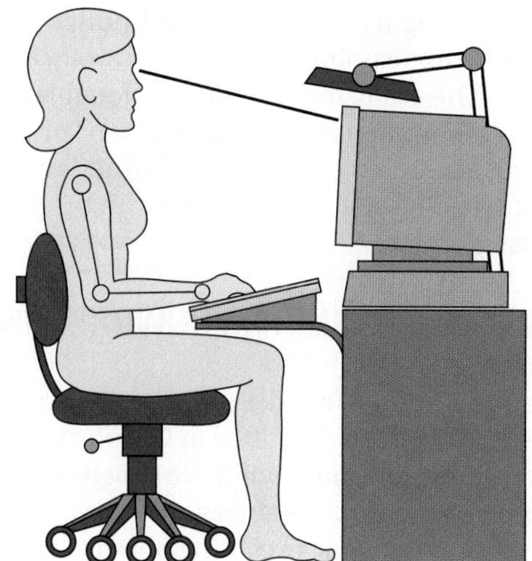

FIGURE 17-7
HOW TO MINIMIZE CUMULATIVE TRAUMA DISORDER

An Ergonomic Workstation

- Keep the screen below your eye level.
- Keep your elbows on the same level with home-key row, with your wrists and lower arms parallel to floor.
- Support your back and thighs with a well-constructed chair.
- Position your feet flat on the floor.
- Use lamp to supplement inadequate room lighting.

Related to adverse customer interaction is the stressor of having to control the expression of emotion to please or to avoid displeasing a customer. Imagine having to smile at a customer who belittles you or makes unwanted sexual advances. Alicia A. Grandey, associate professor of psychology at Penn State University, defines **emotional labor** as the process of regulating both feelings and expressions to meet organizational goals.[22] The process involves both surface acting and deep acting. Surface acting means faking expressions, such as smiling, whereas deep acting involves controlling feelings, such as suppressing anger toward a customer you perceive to be annoying. Deep acting is often better than surface acting in terms of warding off the potential problems of emotional labor. For example, a study with bus drivers indicated that when they engage in surface acting to deal with nasty passengers, the emotional state of the drivers worsened. Yet, when the drivers engaged in deep-level acting, they did not experience many problems of emotional withdrawal from work.[23]

Emotional labor
process of regulating both feelings and expressions to meet organizational goals

Sales workers and customer service representatives often experience emotional labor because so often they have to fake facial expressions and feelings to please customers. Nevertheless, according to one study, the top five occupations in terms of emotional labor demands are (1) police and sheriff's patrol officers, (2) social workers, (3) psychiatrists, (4) supervisors of police and detectives, and (5) registered nurses. Bill and account collectors ranked 15![24]

Engaging in emotional labor for prolonged periods of time can lead to job dissatisfaction, stress, and burnout. A contributing cause is that faking expressions and emotions takes a physiological toll, such as the intestines churning. Workers who engage in emotional labor may also develop cardiovascular problems and weakened immune systems.

Recent research suggests that workers can avoid many of the problems associated with emotional labor if they have good emotional intelligence in the form of being able to recognize the emotions of a customer, client, or patient. For example, if the industrial sales representative can detect that the complaining customer is frightened about a system failure, the representative can reassure the customer that the problem will soon be under control.

A four-week study with eighty-five nurses and police officers in Germany and Holland demonstrated this subtle point about the importance of recognizing the other person's emotional state. The study found that emotional labor did not always lower a worker's engagement (commitment to the organization) providing the police officers and nurses could correctly identify the interaction partner's emotions. (The interaction partner in this case would be the citizen interacting with the police office or the patient interacting with the nurse.)[25]

ABUSIVE SUPERVISION AND UNCIVIL COWORKERS

Being mistreated by a supervisor or coworkers can be a major workplace stressor. Bullying and incivility have already been described in Chapters 9 and 10. Here we mention their stress consequences. What constitutes abusive supervision depends on the perception of subordinates. Supervisors who are abusive are perceived to engage in sustained hostile verbal and nonverbal behaviors, excluding physical contact. Sexual harassment by the supervisor would be considered abusive, as would be insulting a subordinate's appearance. In many cases of supervisors being abusive, the norms of the organization encourage dealing with employees aggressively, including showing very little sympathy.

Recipients of abusive supervision are likely to report greater levels of psychological distress. In addition the recipients of abusive supervision are likely to be irritable, anxious, depressed, and experience physical complaints such as chest pains.[26] A woman in her twenties who reported to a supervisor she perceived to be abusive said: "I think Beth (her supervisor) just hates me. She always finds errors in my work. She wrote me up for wearing clothing to the office that others in the group also wear."

Incivility among coworkers is known to be a major problem in many sectors of the economy. The stress resulting from incivility can result in higher absenteeism, increased turnover, less cooperation, and more complaints to management. Fortunately, incivility and its negative consequences for stress can sometimes be reduced through training. A study, conducted with 1,173 health care workers who underwent a six-month training program to reduce incivility, focused on the health care employees working with facilitators on issues related to civil interactions in their work units. The workers who participated in the program reported greater increases in civility, and decreases in incivility in their work units—compared to those who were not trained.[27]

Learning Objective 4

What Are Several Effective Approaches to Managing Stress?

Because potentially harmful stressors surround us in work and personal life, virtually everybody needs a program of stress management to stay well. Stress management techniques are placed here into four categories: attacking the source of the stress, receiving social support, relaxation techniques, and wellness through proper exercise, diet, and rest. Your challenge is to select those techniques that best fit your circumstances and preferences. At the same time you should be seeking the amount of stress that enables you to capitalize on the benefits of positive stress but not fall prey to the negative symptoms of stress.

DEALING WITH STRESS BY ATTACKING ITS SOURCE

Stress can be dealt with in the short range by indirect techniques such as exercise and relaxation. But to manage stress in the long range and stay well, you must also learn to deal directly with stressors. Many stress-management programs ignore this reality. Several of these techniques are described in the next few paragraphs.

Eliminating or Modifying the Stressor

The most potent method of managing stress is to eliminate the stressor giving you trouble. For example, if your job is your primary stressor, your stress level would be reduced if you found a more comfortable job. At other times, modifying the stressful situation can be equally helpful. Using a problem-solving method, you search for an alternative that will change the stressor.

Placing the Stressful Situation in Perspective

Stress comes about because of our perception of the situation. If you can alter your perception of a threatening situation, you are attacking the source. A potentially stressful situation can be put into perspective by asking, "What is the worst thing that could happen to me if I fail in this activity?" The answer to this question is found by asking a series of questions, starting with the grimmest possibility. For instance, you are late with a report that is due this afternoon. Consider the following questions and answers:

- Will my reputation be damaged permanently? (*No*)
- Will I get fired? (*No*)
- Will I get reprimanded? (*Perhaps, but not for sure*)
- Will my boss think less of me? (*Perhaps, but not for sure*)

Only if the answer is yes to either of the first two questions is negative stress truly justified. This thought process allows stressful situations to be properly evaluated and kept in perspective. You therefore avoid the stress that comes from overreacting to a situation.

An analysis of many studies concludes that the most effective approaches to managing workplace stress are **cognitive-behavioral interventions**—essentially a way of thinking constructively about a problem that includes perspective setting. Cognitive-behavioral interventions teach individuals to recognize how their pessimistic and often distorted thoughts of gloom and doom become stressors. Next, they learn to replace their unrealistic and highly pessimistic thinking with more realistic or more optimistic thinking.[28] Visualize an international marketing director who has a fear of flying, and consequently suffers enormous stress each time she has to take a business trip by airplane. She must learn to conquer her pessimistic outlook on flying with more positive thoughts about airline safety.

Cognitive–behavioral interventions
a way of thinking constructively about a problem that includes perspective setting

Gaining Control of the Situation

Feeling that a bothersome situation is out of control is almost a universal stressor. A key method of stress management is therefore to attack the stressor by gaining control of the situation. A multipurpose way of gaining control is to improve your work habits and time management. By being "on top of things," you can make heavy work and school demands less stressful. A trend related to reducing stress by gaining control is to simplify your life by getting rid of unessential activities and possessions. You will gain control of your life situation by having less clutter.

A note of caution is that an oversimplified life can also be an impoverished life, creating stress of its own. Throw out or give to charity those physical possessions that contribute virtually nothing to your life. Yet save the sources of an enriched life. For example, why give up a smart phone, wide-screen TV, and iPod if all three are major sources of pleasure and satisfaction?

RECEIVING SOCIAL AND ORGANIZATIONAL SUPPORT

Support system
a group of people on whom one can rely for encouragement and comfort

An ideal way to manage stress is one that provides side benefits. Getting close to people falls into this category. You will reduce some stress symptoms and form healthy relationships with others in the process. By getting close to others, you build a **support system,** a group of people on whom you can rely for encouragement and comfort. The trusting relationship you have with these people is critically important. People within your support network include family members, friends, coworkers, and fellow students. In addition, some people in turmoil reach out to strangers to discuss personal problems. According to neuroscientist Steven W. Porges, engaging socially with others triggers neural circuits that calm the heart, relax the intestines, and dampen fear.[29] (Interacting with friendly people is likely to be more beneficial than interacting with hostile individuals.)

The usual method of reducing stress is to talk over your problems while the other person listens. Switching roles can also help reduce stress. Listening to others will make you feel better because you have helped them. Another advantage to listening to the feelings and problems of others is that it helps you to get close to them.

A happy marriage is another support system that can help a worker cope with job stress. According to one study with dual-earner couples, happily married women rebounded quicker from daily stress than women with less blissful unions. Stress was measured by saliva samples of the stress-related hormone cortisol.[30]

Receiving organizational support refers here to using the organization as part of your support system when experiencing heavy stress. The support might come from a friendly supervisor who will listen to the problems you are experiencing and perhaps offer some advice. A widely used form of support is an employee assistance program that offers counseling services for a variety of personal problems that could be impairing performance. (Do you recall Max's situation in the opening case to the chapter?) A large employer might have a full-time employee assistance program, whereas small employers use an outside counseling group.

Wellness program
a company-sponsored activity designed to support employees as they learn and sustain behaviors that reduce health risk, improve quality of life, and enhance personal effectiveness.

Company-sponsored wellness programs have a variety of offerings useful in combatting the adverse effects of stress, including stress management workshops. A **wellness program** is a company-sponsored activity designed to support employees as they learn and sustain behaviors that reduce health risk, improve quality of life, and enhance personal effectiveness. As employees become emotionally and physically healthy, illness-related costs for the employer often decrease.[31] The wellness program focuses on health, whereas an employee assistance program deals with many issues including financial health. Some companies incorporate a separate program into the employee assistance program.

Among the components of a wellness program linked to stress management are onsite physical exercise facilities, smoking cessation programs, nondenominational chaplain service, and nutrition classes. Another approach to most of these activities is to place them online, such as a step-by-step physical exercise program.

The accompanying Human Relations in Practice illustrates how an employer can provide the type of support helpful in managing stress.

RELAXATION TECHNIQUES FOR HANDLING STRESS

"Relax" is the advice many people have always offered the stressed individual. Stress experts give us similar advice but also offer specific techniques. Here we describe three techniques that can help you relax and, consequently, help you reduce stress and its symptoms. In addition, Figure 17-8 lists a variety of "stress busters," many of which are relaxation oriented. Recognize that many of these techniques contribute directly to wellness and that stress management is a major component of wellness. Pick and choose among stress management techniques until you find several that effectively reduce your stress.

Human Relations in Practice

A Stress Prevention Program at a Small Service Organization

A department head in a small public service organization sensed an escalating level of tension and deteriorating morale among her staff. Job dissatisfaction and health symptoms such as headaches also seemed to be on the rise. Suspecting that stress was a developing problem in the department, she decided to hold a series of all-hands meetings with employees in the different work units of the department to explore this concern further. These meetings could be best described as brainstorming sessions where individual employees freely expressed their views about the scope and sources of stress in their units and the measures that might be implemented to bring the problem under control.

Using the information collected in these meetings and in meetings with middle managers, she concluded that a serious problem probably existed and that quick action was needed. Because she was relatively unfamiliar with the job stress field, she decided to seek help from a faculty member at a local university who taught courses on job stress and organizational behavior.

The manager and the professor reviewed the information collected at the brainstorming sessions. They then decided it would be useful for the faculty member to conduct informal classes to raise awareness about job stress—its causes, effects, and prevention—for all workers and managers in the department. It was also decided that a survey would be useful to obtain a more reliable picture of problematic job conditions and stress-related health complaints in the department. The faculty member used information from the meetings with workers and managers to design the survey. The faculty member was also involved in the distribution and collection of the anonymous survey to ensure that workers felt free to respond honestly and openly about what was bothering them. He then helped the department head analyze and interpret the data.

Analysis of the survey data suggested that three types of job conditions were linked to stress complaints among workers:

- Unrealistic deadlines
- Low levels of support from supervisors
- Lack of worker involvement in decision making

Having pinpointed these problems, the department head developed and prioritized a list of corrective measures for implementation. Examples of these actions included (a) greater participation of employees in work scheduling to reduce unrealistic deadlines and (b) more frequent meetings between workers and managers to keep supervisors and workers updated on developing problems.

Source: Case reported in "Stress of Work," *National Institute for Occupational Safety and Health Publication,* No. 99-101, Washington, DC., 1999.

Relaxation Response

Relaxation response
a physical state of deep rest in which one experiences a slower respiration and heart rate, lowered blood pressure, and lowered metabolism; a standard technique for reducing stress

A standard technique for reducing stress is to achieve the relaxation response. The **relaxation response** is a physical state of deep rest in which you experience a slower respiration and heart rate and lowered metabolism. Scientists have shown that the relaxation

FIGURE 17-8
STRESS BUSTERS

- Take a nap when facing heavy pressures. Napping is regarded as one of the most effective techniques for reducing and preventing stress.
- Give in to your emotions. If you are angry, disgusted, or confused, admit your feelings. Suppressing your emotions adds to stress.
- Take a brief break from the stressful situation and do something small and constructive, such as washing your car, emptying a wastebasket, or getting a haircut.
- Get a massage, because it can loosen tight muscles, improve your blood circulation, and calm you down.
- Get help with your stressful task from a coworker, boss, or friend.
- Concentrate intensely on reading, surfing the Internet, a sport, or a hobby. Contrary to common sense, concentration is at the heart of stress reduction.
- Have a quiet place at home and have a brief idle period there every day.
- Take a leisurely day off from your routine.
- Finish something you have started, however small. Accomplishing almost anything reduces some stress.
- Stop to smell the flowers; make friends with a young child or an elderly person.
- Strive to do a good job but not a perfect job.
- Work with your hands, doing a pleasant task.
- Hug somebody you like and who you think will hug you back.
- Become a rag doll by standing with your arms dangling loosely at your sides. Start to shake your hands, then start shaking your arms. Next, sit and repeat the same moves with your legs.
- Find something to laugh at—a cartoon, a movie, a television show, a Web site for jokes, even yourself.
- Minimize drinking caffeinated or alcoholic beverages, and drink fruit juice or water instead. Grab a piece of fruit rather than a can of beer.

response lowers the heart rate, blood pressure, and oxygen consumption. Also, the relaxation response alleviates symptoms associated with many disorders and conditions, including hypertension arthritis, insomnia, depression, infertility, cancer, anxiety, and even aging. By practicing the relaxation response, you can counteract the fight-or-flight response associated with stress.

According to cardiologist and pioneer in mind/body medicine Herbert Benson, four things are necessary to practice the relaxation response: a quiet environment, an object to focus on, a passive attitude, and a comfortable position. You are supposed to practice the relaxation response for ten to twenty minutes, twice a day. To evoke the relaxation response, Benson advises you to close your eyes. Relax. Concentrate on one word or prayer. If other thoughts come to mind, be passive and return to the repetition.

The relaxation response can be released in many ways besides the ritual just described. Among these methods are participating in repetitive sports such as running, progressive muscular relaxation, practicing yoga, and playing a musical instrument.[32]

Similar to any other relaxation technique, the relaxation response is harmless and works for most people. However, some very impatient people find it annoying to disrupt their busy day to work through the relaxation response. Unfortunately, these may be the people who most urgently need to learn to relax.

Meditation

Meditation
a systematic method of concentration, reflection, or concentrated thinking designed to suppress the activity of the sympathetic nervous system

Perhaps the oldest stress management technique of all, mediation is back in vogue. **Meditation** is a systematic method of concentration, reflection, or concentrated thinking designed to suppress the activity of the sympathetic nervous system. The relaxation response is essentially a meditation technique, and napping provides some of the benefits of meditation. The meditator reaches a deep state of mental and physical calmness and relaxation, driving away accumulated stress. Meditation is also recommended as a way of preventing and slowing down and reducing the pain of chronic diseases such as heart disease, AIDS, and cancer. People who meditate learn to tolerate everyday annoyances better. Meditation has been widely researched, and its key benefits in relation to stress include calming the mind and eliminating anxiety.[33]

A very important benefit of mediation as well as other relaxation techniques is that they enhance mental alertness. It would therefore be beneficial to you to meditate shortly before you need to perform at your best, such as giving a presentation to management about your project.

The usual approach to meditation involves four simple steps. First, find a quiet place with a minimum of distractions. Second, close your eyes so that you can close yourself off from the outside world. Third, pick a word whose sound is soothing when repeated. Fourth, say the word repeatedly. For most people, one fifteen-minute session daily will accomplish the benefits of meditation. (You will notice the similarity to the relaxation response, which is a form of meditation.) It is also possible to learn to meditate through online podcasts, videos, and mobile apps. An online search will reveal several of these approaches, for example, www.getsomeheadspace.com.

MANAGING STRESS BY STAYING WELL (PROPER EXERCISE, DIET, AND REST)

A far-reaching strategy for managing stress is to both prevent and reduce negative stress by leading a healthy lifestyle, or being well. Three major components to staying well are proper exercise, diet, and rest. The three components are interrelated because each component facilitates the other: For example, if you exercise enough you tend to prefer healthy food; if you diet properly, physical exercise is easier, and so is obtaining rest. Also, if you rest well you will be in a better frame of mind to exercise, and you will not crave so much caffeine and sugar to stay energized. Proper diet and exercise are also important in helping ward off physical illness that creates stress for the individual. Poor diet and lack of exercise are responsible for almost as many deaths in the United States as smoking, and lead to such problems as cardiac disease and diabetes.

Exercising Properly, Including Yoga

The right amount and type of physical exercise contributes substantially to wellness. Part of the reason exercise is useful for managing stress is that it contributes to relaxation and being better able to cope with frustration. To achieve wellness, it is important to select an exercise program that is physically challenging but that does not lead to overexertion and muscle injury. Competitive sports, if taken too seriously, can actually increase a person's stress level. The most beneficial exercises are classified as aerobic because they make you breathe faster and raise your heart rate. Most of a person's exercise requirements can be met through everyday techniques such as walking or running up stairs, vigorous housework, yard work, or walking several miles per day. Another potential disadvantage of excessive physical exercise is that it makes you so hungry that you overeat.

A major benefit is the euphoria that often occurs when brain chemicals called *endorphins* are released into the body. The same experience is referred to as "runner's high." Other mental benefits of exercise include increased self-confidence; improved body image and self-esteem; improved mental functioning, alertness, and efficiency; release of accumulated tensions; and relief from mild depression.[34]

Millions of people seek to reduce and prevent stress though yoga, which is both physical exercise and a way of developing mental attitudes that calm the body and the mind. During yoga, blood pressure lowers and your heart works more efficiently. One of yoga's many worthwhile goals is to solder a union between the mind and body, thereby achieving harmony and tranquility. Another benefit of yoga is that it helps people place aside negative thoughts that act as stressors. Yoga can therefore reduce anxiety, with the key being deep, slow breathing, as follows:

> Breathe through your nose, drawing air down into your lungs as you expand your diaphragm. As you relax and exhale, the diaphragm contracts. The process controls the pace of your breathing and creates a natural calmness.[35]

Unlike the relaxation response and mild exercise, yoga has some potentially severe negative consequences to the body. Yoga should be first practiced under the guidance of a certified professional to minimize torn muscles and ruptured blood vessels from extreme bending and twisting.[36]

Resting Sufficiently

Rest offers benefits similar to those of exercise, such as stress reduction, improved concentration, improved energy, and better tolerance for frustration. Achieving proper rest is closely linked to getting proper exercise. The current interest in adult napping reflects the awareness that proper rest makes a person less stress prone and enhances productivity. A growing number of firms have napping facilities for workers, and many workers nap at their desks or in their parked vehicles during lunch breaks. Naps of about twenty minutes taken during the workday are used both as energizers and as stress reducers. To keep the effectiveness of workday napping in perspective, workers who achieve sufficient rest during normal sleeping hours have less need for naps during working hours. But the meditation-like benefits of napping offer an advantage even for the person who sleeps adequately at night.

A major purpose of vacations is to attain rest and relaxation. Yet a survey revealed that only 53 percent of working Americans indicate they return from vacation feeling rested and rejuvenated. One problem is attempting to cram too many activities into the vacation, and another is staying wired to the office much of the day and night.[37]

Maintaining a Healthy Diet

Eating nutritious foods is valuable for mental as well as physical health, making it easier to cope with frustrations that are potential stressors. Many nutritionists and physicians believe that eating fatty foods, such as red meat, contributes to colon cancer. Improper diet, such as consuming less than 1,300 calories per day, can weaken you physically. In turn, you become more susceptible to stress. Some non-nutritious foods, such as those laden with caffeine or sugar, tend to enhance stress levels. According to the Dietary Guidelines of the U.S. Department of Agriculture, a healthy diet is one that

- Emphasizes fruits, vegetables, whole grains, and fat-free or low-fat milk and milk products
- Includes lean meats, poultry, fish, beans, eggs, and nuts
- Is low in saturated fats, trans fats, cholesterol, salt (sodium), and added sugars

These recommendations are for the general public over two years of age. Using MyPyramid, the government personalizes a recommended diet, taking into account our age, sex, and amount of physical exercise. Consult www.supertracker.usda.gov.

Alcohol, as in beer, wine, and liquor, consumed in excess is detrimental to physical and mental health. Yet, long-term research at Harvard University and other places as well indicates a key role for the *moderate* use of alcohol. About two alcoholic beverages daily is associated with reduced risk of many causes of mortality and may help to keep cognitive functioning intact with age.[38] (For those opposed to alcohol, the consumption of moderate amounts of dark chocolate apparently provides similar benefits.)

What Are Two Key Perspectives on Understanding and Dealing with Personal Problems?

◀ Learning Objective 5 ◀

Our approach to understanding and overcoming personal problems will be to first describe self-defeating behavior in general and how to reverse the trend. We then emphasize the importance of resilience in dealing with personal problems.

SELF-DEFEATING BEHAVIOR

Many problems on the job and in personal life arise because of factors beyond our control. A boss may be intimidating and insensitive, an employer might lay you off, or your partner might abruptly terminate your relationship. Many personal problems, nevertheless, arise because of **self-defeating behavior.** A person with self-defeating tendencies intentionally or unintentionally engages in activities or harbors attitudes that work against his or her best interest.[39] A person who habitually is late for important meetings is engaging in self-defeating behavior. Dropping out of school for no reason other than being bored with studying is another of many possible examples. In short, self-defeating behavior means the same as being your own worst enemy.

Self-defeating behavior activities or attitudes that work against one's best interest

Counseling specialist Gay Hendricks frames self-defeating behavior as the *upper-limit problem.* Many people reach an upper limit of security in wealth, career, or relationships, and then do something that wrecks it all. An inner thermostat tells us we have reached our limit of attainment, so we retreat to a more comfortable zone.[40] An oft-repeated example is that many lottery winners wind up bankrupt and impoverished because they squander all their winnings—often with the help of friends and family members.

A group of self-defeating behaviors that might escape your attention are **soft addictions,** or ordinary behavior that if done to excess can wreak havoc with your life. Soft addictions often take the form of habit or compulsions that drain your time and money, although they may seem harmless at first.[41] In our complex world, there are extensive opportunities for developing soft addictions. Here are a few examples, and you could probably easily add more to the list:

Soft addiction ordinary behavior that if done to excess can wreak havoc with one's life

- Making a purchase from a soft-drink vending machine or carry-out café several times a day
- Checking e-mail, instant messages, and text messages every few minutes although not required for work or because of an urgent personal problem
- Watching television or playing video games for so many hours that interaction with people and getting household chores done or studying (or self-improvement) suffers
- Engaging in physical exercise so frequently that you suffer frequent injuries and lack the time to get other things in life accomplished
- Devoting endless hours to the Internet, including being in contact with hundreds of "friends" and "followers" on social networking sites
- Daydreaming excessively

To examine your present tendencies toward self-defeating behavior, take the self-sabotage quiz presented in Human Relations Self-Assessment Quiz 17-1. Taking the quiz will help alert you to many self-imposed behaviors and attitudes that could potentially harm your career and personal life.

Human Relations Self-Assessment Quiz 17-1

The Self-Sabotage Questionnaire

Indicate how accurately each of the following statements describes or characterizes you, using a 5-point scale: (0) very inaccurately, (1) inaccurately, (2) midway between inaccurately and accurately, (3) accurately, (4) very accurately. Consider discussing some of the questions with a family member, close friend, or work associate. Another person's feedback may prove helpful in providing accurate answers to some of the questions.

		Answer
1.	Other people have said that I am my own worst enemy.	________
2.	If I don't do a perfect job, I feel worthless.	________
3.	I am my own harshest critic.	________
4.	When engaged in a sport or other competitive activity, I find a way to blow a substantial lead right near the end.	________
5.	When I make a mistake, I can usually identify another person to blame.	________
6.	I have a strong tendency to procrastinate.	________
7.	I have trouble focusing on what is really important to me.	________
8.	I have trouble taking criticism, even from friends.	________
9.	My fear of seeming stupid often prevents me from asking questions or offering my opinion.	________
10.	I tend to expect the worst in most situations.	________
11.	Many times I have rejected people who treat me well.	________
12.	When I have an important project to complete, I usually get sidetracked, and then miss the deadline.	________
13.	I choose work assignments that lead to disappointments, even when better options are clearly available.	________
14.	I frequently misplace things, such as my keys, and then get very angry at myself.	________
15.	I am concerned that if I take on much more responsibility people will expect too much from me.	________
16.	I avoid situations, such as competitive sports, where people can find out how good or bad I really am.	________
17.	People describe me as the "office clown."	________
18.	I have an insatiable demand for money and power.	________
19.	When negotiating with others, I hate to grant any concessions.	________
20.	I seek revenge for even the smallest hurts.	________
21.	I have an overwhelming ego.	________
22.	When I receive a compliment or other form of recognition, I usually feel I don't deserve it.	________
23.	To be honest, I choose to suffer.	________
24.	I regularly enter into conflict with people who try to help me.	________
25.	I'm a loser.	________
	Total Score	________

Scoring and Interpretation:

Total your answers to all the questions to obtain your score.

0–25 You appear to have very few tendencies toward self-sabotage. If this interpretation is supported by your own positive feelings toward your life and yourself, you are in good shape with respect to self-defeating behavior tendencies. However, stay alert to potential self-sabotaging tendencies that could develop at later stages in your life.

26–50 You may have some mild tendencies toward self-sabotage. It could be that you do things occasionally that defeat your own purposes. Review actions you have taken during the past six months to decide if any of them have been self-sabotaging.

51–75 You show signs of engaging in self-sabotage. You probably have thoughts and carry out actions that could be blocking you from achieving important work and personal goals. People with scores in this category characteristically engage in negative self-talk that lowers their self-confidence and makes them appear weak and indecisive to others. People in this range frequently experience another problem. They sometimes sabotage their chances of succeeding on a project simply to prove that their negative self-assessment is correct. If you scored in this range, carefully study the suggestions offered in this chapter.

76–100 You most likely have a strong tendency toward self-sabotage. (Sometimes it is possible to obtain a high score on a test like this because you are going through an unusually stressful period in your life.) Study this section of the chapter carefully and look for useful hints for removing self-imposed barriers to your success. Equally important, you might discuss your tendencies toward undermining your own achievements with a mental health professional.

Overcoming self-defeating behavior requires hard work and patience. Here we present four widely applicable strategies for overcoming and preventing self-defeating behavior. Pick and choose among them to fit your particular circumstance and personal style.

Solicit Feedback on Your Actions

Feedback is essential for monitoring whether you are sabotaging your career or personal life. A starting point is to listen carefully to any direct or indirect comments from your superiors, subordinates, coworkers, customers, and friends about how you are coming across to them. Consider the case of Bill, a technical writer:

> Bill heard three people in one week make comments about his appearance. It started innocently with, "Here, let me fix your collar." Next, an office assistant said, "Bill, are you coming down with something?" The third comment was, "You look pretty tired today. Have you been working extra hard?" Bill processed this feedback carefully. He used it as a signal that his steady late-night drinking episodes were adversely affecting his image. He then cut back his drinking enough to revert to his normal healthy appearance.

Take notes to show how serious you are about the feedback. When someone provides any feedback at all, say, "Please continue. This is very useful." Try not to react defensively when you hear something negative. You asked for it, and the person is truly doing you a favor.

Learn to Profit from Criticism

As the preceding example implies, learning to profit from criticism is necessary to benefit from feedback. Furthermore, to ignore valid criticism can be self-defeating. People who benefit from criticism are able to stand outside themselves while being criticized. It is as if they are watching the criticism from a distance and looking for its possible merits. People who take criticism personally experience anguish when receiving negative feedback.

Ask politely for more details about the negative behavior in question so that you can change if change is warranted. If your boss is criticizing you for being rude with customers, you might respond, "I certainly don't want to be rude. Can you give me a couple of examples of how I was rude? I need your help in working on this problem." After asking questions, you can better determine if the criticism is valid.

Stop Denying the Existence of Problems

Many people sabotage their careers because they deny the existence of a problem and therefore do not take appropriate action. Denial takes place as a defensive maneuver against a painful reality. An example of a self-sabotaging form of denial is to ignore the importance of upgrading one's credentials despite overwhelming evidence that it is necessary. Some people never quite complete a degree program that has become an informal qualification for promotion. Consequently, they sabotage their chances of receiving a promotion for which they are otherwise qualified.

Observe the Discrepancy Between Your Ideal Life and What Exists Now

Motivational speaker Kevin Hogan recommends that you write a description of your ideal life. Describe in specific terms what you would like your life to be now or in the future. Use several senses, including touch, taste, and smell. (For example, what would your log cabin or condominium town home smell like?) Next, write a description of your current self and life. You have a reasonably clear idea of what discrepancies have to be closed to attain you goals.[42] It could be that the discrepancies involve some self-defeating behavior, such as having a low credit score.

Visualize Self-Enhancing Behavior

To apply visualization, program yourself to overcome self-defeating actions and thoughts. Imagine yourself engaging in self-enhancing, winning actions and thoughts. Picture yourself achieving peak performance when good results count the most. A starting point is to identify the next job situation you will be facing that is similar to ones you have flubbed in the past. You then imagine yourself mentally and physically projected into that situation. Imagine what the room looks like, who will be there, and the confident expression you will have on your face. Visualization is akin to watching a video of you doing something right.

DEVELOPING RESILIENCE

Resilience
the ability to withstand pressure and emerge stronger because of an experience; being challenged and not breaking down

In Chapter 2, resilience was described in relation to developing self-confidence. Developing resilience is also a master strategy for dealing with personal problems as well as stress. The ability to overcome setbacks is an important characteristic of successful people. **Resilience** is the ability to withstand pressure and emerge stronger because of the experience. Being resilient also refers to being challenged and not breaking down. The resilient person profits from a setback by learning what to do better next time, such as a sales representative having lost a sale by talking too much and not listening to what the customer really wanted. The ability to bounce back from a setback, or resilience, is another aspect of emotional intelligence. In the context of emotional intelligence, resilience refers to being persistent and optimistic when faced with setbacks.[43]

Human Relations Self-Assessment Quiz 17-2 gives you an opportunity to examine your tendencies toward being resilient. Here we look at a few more aspects of becoming resilient.

1. **The resilient disposition.** People with a resilient disposition are better able to stay calm, and have a healthy level of physical and psychological wellness in the face of challenges.[44] They accept the reality that a problem exists, so they are likely to develop a plan to work their way out of the problem. Assume that Jessica's new boss does not like her because of reasons unrelated to job performance. If Jessica were not resilient, she would become discouraged and think that she is going to experience a setback in her career. If Jessica is resilient, she will develop a few tactics for getting the new boss on her side, such as finding out what tasks her boss thinks should receive the highest priority.
2. **Getting past the emotional turmoil.** An important part of being resilient is to first overcome the emotional turmoil associated with the setback you have encountered,

Human Relations Self-Assessment Quiz 17-2

The Resiliency Quiz

From 1 to 5, rate how much each of the following applies to you (1 = very little, 5 = very much)

1	2	3	4	5	If I have a bad day at work or school, it does not ruin my day.
1	2	3	4	5	After a vacation, I can usually get right back into work at my regular work pace.
1	2	3	4	5	Every "no" I encounter is one step closer to a "yes."
1	2	3	4	5	The popular saying "Get over it" has a lot of merit in guiding your life.
1	2	3	4	5	The last time I was rejected for a job (or assignment) I wanted, it had no particular impact on me.
1	2	3	4	5	I enjoy being the underdog once in a while.
1	2	3	4	5	I enjoy taking risks because I believe that the biggest rewards stem from risk taking.
1	2	3	4	5	I rarely worry about, or keep thinking about, mistakes I have made in the past.
1	2	3	4	5	If I ran for political office and lost, I would be willing to run again.
1	2	3	4	5	When I encounter a major problem or setback, I will talk over the situation with a friend or confidant.
1	2	3	4	5	I am physically sick much less frequently than most people I know, including friends, coworkers, and other students.
1	2	3	4	5	The last time I lost my keys (or wallet or handbag or cell phone), I took care of the problem within a few days and was not particularly upset.
1	2	3	4	5	I get more than my share of good breaks.

Scoring and Interpretation

Add the numbers to get your total score.

60–70 You are highly resilient with an ability to bounce back from setbacks.

45–59 You have an average degree of resiliency when faced with problems.

30–44 Setbacks and disappointments are a struggle for you.

1–29 You may need help in dealing with setbacks.

such as losing a job or being left by a spouse or good friend. Discussing your problem with a friend or counselor is a standard approach for overcoming the emotional turmoil that accompanies a setback. Selecting the right person with whom you can vent your problem is an asset in dealing with your problem. Ideally, you should find someone who can help you help yourself by listening carefully and not jumping in with advice immediately. Remember also to find a good time to discuss your problem with a confidant rather than springing it on him or her.

After some of the emotional trauma from your problem has been reduced, it is time to use your creative problem-solving skills to find a solution—those that you have developed through experience and in your study of other subjects as well as human relations.

"Failure is simply the opportunity to begin again, this time more intelligently."

—Henry Ford

3. **Conduct a failure analysis.** After recognizing that a failure has occurred, resilience is enhanced when the person analyzes why the failure took place. It is best to go beyond the superficial reasons for the failure and to identify root causes, as in problem solving.[45] The root causes get at the true reasons for the failure of a project, task, or interpersonal relationship. Suppose Stacey is bitterly criticized by her boss, the

marketing director for the pet food division of her employer, for having produced a Facebook page that had no impact on sales. Stacey might attribute the failure of the Facebook page to such superficial factors as too much competition, a sluggish economy, and a boss with a tendency to bark at employees. Yet if Stacey digs further into the root causes of her problem, she might admit that the page she developed lacked creativity and spark.

4. **Resilience training.** The purpose of much resilience training is to help people steel themselves against difficult situations instead of becoming overly stressed. At the same time, trainees are taught how to learn from the situation.[46] Part of steeling yourself against a highly challenging situation is to think of what skills you have in your repertoire that will help you work your way out of the problem. Suppose that restaurant manager Gary is witnessing a customer go ballistic right in the restaurant. Instead of being overwhelmed by the problem, Gary reflects, "What conflict-resolution technique do I know that will help me conquer this problem? Maybe disarm the opposition will work here." If Gary is able to calm down the customer, he will have learned from the stressful situation.

Key Terms

Stress, 514
Stressor, 514
Fight-or-flight response, 514
Challenge stressors, 515
Hindrance stressors, 515
Burnout, 517
Type A behavior, 519
External locus of control, 521
Internal locus of control, 521
Negative affectivity, 521
Role overload, 521
Role underload, 522
Role conflict, 523
Role ambiguity, 523
Carpal tunnel syndrome, 524
Emotional labor, 525
Cognitive-behavioral interventions, 527
Support system, 528
Wellness program, 528
Relaxation response, 529
Meditation, 530
Self-defeating behavior, 533
Soft addiction, 533
Resilience, 536

Summary and Review

- The body's battle against a stressor is the fight-or-flight response. Stress always involves physiological changes, such as an increase in heart rate, blood cholesterol, and blood pressure. Men who respond most intensely to mental stress run a higher risk of blocked blood vessels. Stress adversely affects our ability to fight infection.
- Challenge stressors have a positive effect on motivation and performance, whereas hindrance stressors have a negative effect. Negative stress has enormous consequences to individuals and organizations. Alcohol and illicit drug use might increase where workers experience negative stress.
- The existence of challenge stressors suggests that the right amount of stress can be beneficial, such as the right amount of multitasking. Performance tends to be best under moderate amounts of stress, yet certain negative forms of stress almost always decrease performance.
- Prolonged stress may lead to burnout, a condition of emotional, mental, and physical exhaustion in response to long-term job stressors, such as a heavy workload. Occupations that require frequent and intense interaction with others often lead to burnout.
- Almost any form of frustration, disappointment, setback, inconvenience, or crisis in your personal life can cause stress. The categories of situations that can produce stress include significant life changes, low self-esteem, everyday annoyances, social and family problems, physical and mental health problems, financial problems, and school-related problems.
- Personality factors contribute to stress proneness. People with type A behavior are impatient and demanding and have free-floating hostility, all of which leads to stress. People with an external locus of control (believing that external forces control their fate) are more susceptible to stress. Negative affectivity (a predisposition to negative mental states) also contributes to stress.
- Sources of job stress are quite varied. Among them are work overload or underload, role conflict and ambiguity, job insecurity and job loss, adverse environmental conditions including a sick building and carpal tunnel syndrome, and adverse customer interaction and emotional labor (faking expressions and feelings).

To successfully manage stress in the long range, you have to deal with the stressors directly. Three direct approaches are to do the following:

- Eliminate or modify the stressor.
- Place the situation in perspective (cognitive-behavioral approaches to managing stress help with perspective setting).
- Gain control of the situation.

Stress can also be reduced through social support from others, including the organization. Relaxation techniques for handling stress include the relaxation response and meditation. Managing stress by staying well includes proper exercise, diet, and rest. Exercising properly, including yoga, helps reduce and prevent stress. Sufficient rest also helps manage stress. Maintaining a healthy diet makes it easier to cope with frustrations that could be stressful.

Unless personal problems are kept under control, a person's chances of achieving career and personal success diminish. Many personal problems arise out of self-defeating behavior. Soft addictions can be self-defeating. Approaches to overcoming and preventing self-defeating behavior include the following:

- Solicit feedback on your actions.
- Learn to profit from criticism.
- Stop denying the existence of problems.
- Visualize self-enhancing behavior.

Developing resilience is a master strategy for dealing with personal problems as well as stress. To be resilient, it is helpful to get past the emotional turmoil by talking to a confidant and then working to solve the problem.

Check Your Understanding

1. An office manager in an emergency room, and a mother of young triplets, said she knew she was emotionally drained and stressed out because of all her responsibilities. She said she knew that she should manage her stress better, but she simply did not have the time. What advice can you offer this woman?
2. Why might attaining the career goals you have established for the next five years or so be stress-reducing?
3. What is the reason that so many people who win a fortune in a lottery wind up having more stress than in their previous life? (Some big lottery winners become so depressed they commit suicide.)
4. Why do you think having a salaried job and benefits is less stressful for many workers than being self-employed or being paid strictly on commission?
5. Assume that a professional-level worker, such as a customer service representative, is convinced that napping during the workday is an excellent way of managing stress. Where should this person nap?
6. How can a person who becomes stressed from having to interact with coworkers several hours a day compete in the modern world?
7. Why does a simple act like emptying a wastebasket or cleaning out and washing one's car reduce stress for so many people?
8. What is the difference between making a bad mistake once and self-defeating behavior?
9. Give an example of self-defeating behavior engaged in by a business executive or public-office holder. What appear to be the negative consequences to the person's career stemming from the self-defeating behavior?
10. Imagine that a student receives an F in a course. What can he or she do to be resilient?

Web Corner

The Nature of Stress and Stress Management
www.stress.org

Burnout Self-Test
www.mindtools.com/Brn/BurnoutSelfTest.htm

Overcoming Self-Sabotage
www.psychologytoday.com/blog/overcoming-self-sabotage

INTERNET SKILL BUILDER

Employee Assistance Program

Use your favorite search engines to learn about employee assistance programs (EAPs). After visiting several sites, answer these questions: (1) What type of help can an employee expect to receive from an EAP? (2) How does an EAP help with stress management? (3) Does the EAP counselor typically tell the company the nature of the problem facing the employee who sought assistance? (4) What benefits do companies expect from offering an EAP to employees?

Developing Your Human Relations Skills

Human Relations Application Exercises

Applying Human Relations Exercise 17-1

Personal Stress Management Action Plan

Most people face a few powerful stressors in their work and personal life, but few people take the time to clearly identify these stressors or develop an action plan for remedial action. The purpose of this exercise is to make you an exception. Here is an opportunity to inventory your stressors, think through the problems they may be causing you, and develop action plans you might take to remedy the situation. Use the accompanying form or create one with a word processing table or a spreadsheet program.

Work or School Stressor	Symptoms This Stressor Is Creating for Me	My Action Plan to Manage This Stressor
1.		
2.		
3.		

Personal Life Stressor	Symptoms This Stressor Is Creating for Me	My Action Plan to Manage This Stressor
1.		
2.		
3.		

Seven days after preparing this worksheet, observe if any of your stress symptoms have diminished. Also, identify those stressors for which only a long-term solution is possible. One student reported that a major work stressor he faced was that the wanted to work in international business that emphasized doing business with Italian fashion companies. Yet he was experiencing stress because he had almost zero knowledge of the Italian language or culture. (By the way, can you offer this man any suggestions?)

Applying Human Relations Exercise 17-2

Overcoming Self-Defeating Behavior

Most people engage in some behavior that could be self-defeating, sometimes to a major degree. For example, hundreds of otherwise rational people are seriously injured every year because they climb on their roof to clean a gutter or replace a shingle. Also, many people walk out into traffic or bump into a lamppost or building while sending or receiving a text message. Another example is that some well-to-do people cannot resist the urge to shoplift occasionally. If you engage in no self-defeating behavior or behavior that is potentially self-defeating, you are exempt from this exercise. For all others, answer the following four questions:

1. What is my most self-defeating behavior, even if the behavior is infrequent or only has the potential to be self-defeating?
2. If this behavior continues or becomes exaggerated, what are the consequences to my career and personal life?
3. What action steps can I take to overcome this self-defeating behavior?
4. What help can I get to overcome my self-defeating behavior?

Human Relations Class Activity

The Stress-Buster Survey

Each class member thinks through carefully which techniques he or she uses to reduce work or personal stress. Class members then come to the front of the room individually to make brief presentations of their most effective stress-reduction techniques. After the presentations are completed, class members analyze and interpret what they heard. Among the issues to explore are the following:

1. Which are the most popular stress-reduction techniques?

2. How do the stress-reduction techniques used by the class compare to those recommended by experts?
3. For each technique mentioned by a class member, indicate whether you think the method of stress busting will be helpful in the long run or is simply a short-term expedient that might even have negative consequences in the long range. Two examples of the latter are (1) "I like to drink a six pack of beer when I'm stressed out" and (2) "If I'm really uptight, I ride my motorcycle about 75 miles per hour in the middle of the night."
4. Send e-mails or text messages to three class members today or tomorrow indicating what you thought of their methods of stress reduction. If everybody in the class sends e-mail messages to three class members, it is most likely that each student will receive some feedback.

Human Relations Case Study 17-1

Rachel Runs the Treadmill

Six thirty Tuesday morning 38-year-old Rachel Mendez hops out of her bed while her husband Alex Mendez is still sleeping. Rachel's first stop is to wake up her nine-year-old daughter, and encourage her to start getting ready to meet the school bus on time. By 8 a.m. Rachel is in her car and on her way to her job as a business development specialist for a human resource outsourcing company. Her primary responsibility is to entice small- and medium-size companies to turn over most of their human resource functions to her firm.

Just as Rachel begins to manage her e-mail and plan her agenda for the day, she places her right hand about three inches to the right of her heart. Rachel can feel the tightness next to her heart, and in her left arm. She thinks to herself, "This feels like I'm going to have a heart attack, but it doesn't make sense for a woman my age to be a heart attack victim. But I'm happy that I have an appointment at the cardiology center on Thursday."

At the North Side Cardiology Center, Rachel is first interviewed by Nurse Practitioner Janet Trudeau before her interview with Dr. Harry Ching, the cardiologist. Trudeau first took a brief medical history, followed by an interview. Parts of the interview with Trudeau went as follows:

Trudeau: So tell me in more detail why you came to visit our cardiology center.

Mendez: I have these annoying chest pains next to my heart and in my left arm. The pains usually start when I am extremely aggravated and frustrated. I have the pains about once a day.

Trudeau: Do you ever faint or become light-headed during the pains?

Mendez: No, my problem is just the pains. I keep doing whatever I'm doing when the pain hits.

Trudeau: Tell me about the situations you find so aggravating and frustrating.

Mendez: I'm really stressing out. I have a ton of aggravations and worries. To begin my nine-year-old daughter Samantha has seizures. She is under treatment but the problem remains, and its worrisome. I worry every day that Samantha will have a seizure and strike her head or get involved in an accident.

My work is also quite worrisome. I work mostly on commission selling human resource services. Our business has grown rapidly in the last few years, but we have kind of dried up the territory. I have to travel more to find new clients. My earnings are taking a turn downward despite the extra travel.

Trudeau: Are you the sole breadwinner in the family?

Mendez: No, my husband Alex is an assistant manager at a Ruby Tuesday restaurant, and he makes a modest living. But talking about aggravation, my husband is a decent guy but he gives me chest pains. I think he cares much more about professional sports, especially the NFL and the NHL than he does about Samantha and me. If he's watching a game, I can forget about talking about something serious.

And then, of course, Alex works the hours of a restaurant manager, which means that he is often working when I am not working, like on Saturdays and Sundays.

Trudeau: Any other major aggravations in your life?

Mendez: Yes, commuting on busy highways. I can feel my chest pains starting when I think of sitting still for fifteen minutes during rush-hour traffic.

Trudeau: Thank you Rachel. I will be studying this information before your interview with Dr. Ching. Have a seat in the waiting room. He will be with you in about 10 minutes.

Later that day Mendez had an extensive cardiology exam, including an electrocardiogram. Dr. Ching informed her that despite the muscle tension she was experiencing, her heart was in excellent condition.

Questions

1. What sources of stress does Rachel Mendez appear to be facing?
2. What do you recommend Mendez do about the stressors she is facing?
3. Given that Mendez does not have a heart problem, should she be concerned about the stressors in her life? Explain your answer.
4. How might Mendez organize her work and her life better to feel that her life is less out of control?

Human Relations Role-Playing Exercise 17-1

Rachel Discusses Her Stress Problem with Alex

One student plays the role of Rachel who decides to discuss her stress problems with her husband, Alex. She feels that Alex is contributing somewhat to her problems for the reasons described in the case just presented. Another student plays the role of Alex who has some sympathy for Rachel, yet she does not understand that he leads a stressful life also. He believes firmly that watching professional sports provides him effective stress relief. Run the role play for about seven minutes. Observers will decide if the couple is on the way to helping each other lead a less stressful life.

Human Relations Case Study 17-2

*Self-Defeating Sid**

Sid has twenty-five years of experience as a sales representative in the furniture industry. He is an affable, well-educated, and responsible person with excellent sales skills. I first met Sid fifteen years ago when we shared adjacent booths at a furniture show.

Two years later, I was working as a sales manager when I received a call from Sid inquiring about any sales openings we might have. When we met he told me of his disillusionment with promises made to him in his current position that never materialized. A few weeks later, I contacted Sid regarding a position on the West Coast. The hiring manager liked him, and the human resources people checked out his background to their satisfaction, and Sid joined the company as a sales rep in the Pacific Northwest.

In Sid's hands, his sales territory picked up considerably. The regional manager was delighted with the sales results. Nevertheless, he became concerned about Sid's poor attention to planning and paperwork. Sid's chronic complaining about the demands being placed on him by the company also concerned the manager. Because his overall sales performance was still good, we decided to stay in closer touch with Sid and give him support and encouragement in the areas of concern.

Upon contacting Sid myself, I mentioned the need for providing more information from the field. Sid used my phone call as an opening to complain bitterly about his manager and me. He had no specific suggestions other than complaining that he did not have time for such "nonsense." The regional manager and I passed it off as a guy having a bad day.

Because he was becoming more belligerent, we invited Sid to be counseled by a business coach. Through his coaching sessions, as well as feedback from a few business contacts, we discovered a pattern of Sid doing a fine job of selling but only wanting to work on his own terms. We discovered that Sid had been terminated from three previous positions, not because of poor sales results, but his difficulty in working with management.

We eventually had to fire Sid because of his poor teamwork. He soon found a position as a territory manager in the furniture industry, reporting to an old friend who was a regional manager. Within three years, Sid was once again terminated for his inability or unwillingness to work smoothly with management.

Questions

1. In what ways is Sid self-defeating?
2. What can be done to help Sid?
3. If you were Sid's boss, what might you do to help him?

*This story was told by an experienced business owner.

Human Relations Role-Playing Exercise 17-2

Sid's Boss Attempts to Help Him

One person plays the role of Conrad, Sid's current boss. (Sid found new employment selling office furniture.) Conrad notices that Sid is uncooperative in terms of not providing field data the company needs, and not helping other members of the sales team. Conrad wants to get Sid on the right track. Another person plays the role of Sid who believes once again that management is making unreasonable demands upon him.

Observers rate the role players on two dimensions, using a 1 to 5 scale from very poor to very good. One dimension is "effective use of human relations techniques." For Conrad, focus in on how well he communicates his message about Sid needing to become a better team player (more cooperative). For Sid, see if he begins to understand how his behavior might be self-defeating. The second dimension is "acting ability." A few observers might voluntarily provide feedback to the role-players in terms of sharing their ratings and observations. The course instructor might also provide feedback.

REFERENCES

1. Research reviewed in Mark Greer, "Mental Stress Wreaks Physical Havoc on Workers," *Monitor on Psychology,* May 2005, pp. 28–29.
2. Suzanne C. Sergerstrom and Gregory E. Miller, "Psychological Stress and the Human Immune System: A Meta-Analytic Study of 30 Years of Inquiry," *Psychological Bulletin,* 4, 2004, pp. 601–630.
3. J. Craig Wallace et al., "Work Stressors, Role-Based Performance, and the Moderating Influence of Organizational Support,"*Journal of Applied Psychology,* January 2009, p. 255; Nathan P. Podaskoff, Jeffrey A. LePine, and Marcie A. LePine, "Differential Challenge Stressor Relationships with Job Attitudes, Turnover Intentions, and Withdrawal Behavior: A Meta-Analysis," *Journal of Applied Psychology,* March 2007, pp. 438–454.
4. "Job Stress," *The American Institute of Stress,* p. 3, retrieved April 2, 2012, from: www.stress.org.
5. Michael R. Frone, "Are Work Stressors Related to Employee Substance Abuse? The Importance of Temporal Context in Assessments of Alcohol and Illicit Drug Use," *Journal of Applied Psychology,* January 2008, pp. 199–206.
6. Sadie F. Dingfelder, "A Psychodynamic Treatment for PSTD Shows Promise for Soldiers," *Monitor on Psychology,* March 2012, p. 11.
7. Kristin Byron, Shalini Khazanchi, and Deborah Nazarian, "The Relationship Between Stressors and Creativity: A Meta-Analysis Examining Competing Theoretical Models," *Journal of Applied Psychology,* January 2010, pp. 201–212.
8. Research synthesized in Sue Shellenbarger, "When Stress Is Good for You," *The Wall Street Journal,* January 24, 2012, p. D1.
9. Evangelia Demerouti et al., "The Job Demands–Resources Model of Burnout," *Journal of Applied Psychology,* June 2001, p. 502.
10. "Is Your Team Feeling Burned Out?" *Communication Briefings,* December 2010, p. 4. Adapted from Michael Carney and Heather Z. Hutchins, *Tips for Handling Everyday Stress* (London: Global Professional Publishing, 2010).
11. Rabi S. Bhagat, "Effects of Stressful Life Events on Individual Performance and Work Adjustment Processes Within Organizational Settings: A Research Model," *Academy of Management Review,* October 1983, pp. 660–670; Thomas H. Holmes and Richard H. Rahe, "The Social Readjustment Rating Scale," *Journal of Psychosomatic Research,* 11, 1967, p. 213.
12. Research reported in Etienne Benson, "Hostility Is Among Best Predictors of Heart Disease in Men," *Monitor on Psychology,* January 2003, p. 15.
13. Quoted in Nadja Geipert, "Don't Be Mad: More Research Links Hostility to Coronary Risk," *Monitor on Psychology,* January 2007, pp. 50–51.
14. Peter Y. Chen and Paul E. Spector, "Negative Affectivity as the Underlying Cause of Correlations Between Stressors and Strains,"*Journal of Applied Psychology,* June 1991, p. 398.
15. Paul E. Spector, Peter Y. Chen, and Brian J. O'Connell, "A Longitudinal Study of Relations Between Job Stressors and Job Strains While Controlling for Prior Negative Affectivity and Strains," *Journal of Applied Psychology,* April 2000, p. 216.
16. Norman B. Anderson, "Toward Reducing Work Stress," *Monitor on Psychology,* February 2008, p. 9.
17. Ed Frauenheim, "Stressed & Pressed," *Workforce Management,* January 2012, pp. 18–21.
18. Erin M. Eatough, Chu-Hsiang Chang, Stephanie A. Miloslavic, and Russell E. Johnson, "Relationships of Role Stressors With Organizational Citizenship Behavior: A Meta-Analysis," *Journal of Applied Psychology,* May 2011, pp. 619–632.
19. Amy Novotney, "Silence, Please," *Monitor on Psychology,* July/August 2011, p. 47.
20. Christine A. Spring et al., "Work Characteristics, Musculoskeletal Disorders, and the Mediating Role of Psychological Strain: A Study of Call Center Employees," *Journal of Applied Psychology,* September 2007, pp. 1456–1466.
21. Tedd Mitchell, "'Oh, My Aching Wrist!'," *US Weekend,* July 3–4, 2010, p. 16.
22. Alicia A. Grandey, "Emotion Regulation in the Workplace: A New Way to Conceptualize Emotional Labor," *Journal of Occupational Health Psychology,* January 2000, pp. 95–110; Grandey, "When the 'Show Must Go On:' Surface Acting and Deep Acting as Determinants of Emotional Exhaustion and Peer-Related Service Delivery," *Academy of Management Journal,* February 2003, pp. 86–96.
23. Brent A. Scott and Christopher M. Barnes, "A Multilevel Field Investigation of Emotional Labor, Affect, Work Withdrawal, and Gender," *Academy of Management Journal,* February 2011, pp. 116–136.
24. Theresa M. Glomb, John D. Kammeyer-Mueller, and Maria Rotundo, "Emotional Labor Demands and Compensating Wage Differentials,"*Journal of Applied Psychology,* August 2004, p. 707.
25. Myriam N. Bechtoldt, Sonja Rhormann, Irene De Pater, and Bianca Beersma, "The Primacy of Perceiving: Emotional Recognition Buffers Negative Effects of Emotional Labor," *Journal of Applied Psychology,* September 2011, pp. 1087–1094.
26. Simon Lloyd D. Restubog, Kristin L. Scott, and Thomas J. Zagenezyk, "When Distress Hits Home: The Role of Contextual Factors and Psychological Distress in Predicting Employees' Responses to Abusive Supervision," *Journal of Applied Psychology,* July 2011, pp. 713–729.
27. Michael P. Leiter, Heather K. Spence Laschinger, Aria Day, and Debra Gilin Oore, "The Impact of Civility Interventions on Employee Social Behavior, Distress, and Attitudes," *Journal of Applied Psychology,* November 2011, pp. 1258–1274.
28. Katherine M. Richardson and Hannah R. Rothstein, "Effects of Occupational Stress Management Intervention Programs: A Meta-Analysis,"*Journal of Occupational Health Psychology,* January 2008, pp. 69–93.
29. Cited in Stephanie Gold, "A Higher Road to Relaxation," *Psychology Today,* July/August 2007, p. 57.
30. Amy Novotney, "Marital Bliss May Blunt Office Blues," *Monitor on Psychology,* March 2008, p. 11.
31. Leonard L. Berry, Ann M. Mirabito, and William B. Baun, "What's the Hard Return on Employee Wellness Programs?" *Harvard Business Review,* December 2010, p. 106.
32. Herbert Benson (with William Proctor), *Beyond the Relaxation Response* (New York: Berkley Books, 1995), pp. 96–97; Sara Martin, "The Power of the Relaxation Response," *Monitor on Psychology,* October 2008, p. 33.

33. Evidence reviewed in Roger Walsh and Shauna L. Shapiro, "The Meeting of Meditative Disciplines and Western Psychology," *American Psychologist,* April 2006, p. 228; Alina Dizik, "Feeling Transcendent in 10 Minutes or Less," *The Wall Street Journal,* October 27, 2011, p. D2.
34. Beth Azar, "Another Reason to Break a Sweat," *Monitor on Psychology,* June 2010, pp. 36–38.
35. "Yoga Can Reduce Anxiety," *Personal Best Healthlines,* 2007, p. 5. Special Report.
36. Pamela Paul, "When Yoga Hurts," *Time,* October 15, 2007, p. 71.
37. Melinda Beck, "Why Relaxing Is Hard Work," *The Wall Street Journal,* June 15, 2010, p. D1.
38. Stanton Peele, "A Toast to Your Health," *The Wall Street Journal,* February 2, 2011.
39. Mark Goulston, *Get Out of Your Own Way at Work . . . and Help Others Do the Same* (New York: Putnam Adult, 2005); Andrew J. DuBrin, *Your Own Worst Enemy: How to Overcome Career Self-Sabotage* (New York: AMACOM, 1992).
40. Gay Hendricks, *The Big Leap: Conquer Your Hidden Fear and Take Life to the Next Level* (New York: Harper One, 2010).
41. Based on the work of Judith Wright, as reported in Julie Deardorff, "Soft Addictions: You Can Get Hooked in So Many Ways," *Chicago Tribune,* March 18, 2007.
42. Kevin Hogan, "Why Everything Goes to Hell . . . How to Stop Self-Sabotage, NOW and Forever!" (www.kevinhogan.com/selfsabotage.htm), 2009.
43. Daniel Goleman, "Leadership That Gets Results," *Harvard Business Review,* March–April 2000, p. 80.
44. William Atkinson, "Turning Stress into Strength," *HR Magazine,* January 2011, p. 49.
45. Amy C. Edmonson, "Strategies for Learning From Failure," *Harvard Business Review,* April 2011, p. 54.
46. "Resilience Training" (www.mayoclinic.org/resilience-training), 2012.

Appendix A: Comprehensive Assignment for Applying Human Relations Knowledge

A large number of concepts, facts, and skills have been presented in this textbook. To help you develop a master plan integrating much of this information and enhancing your human relations skill at the same time we present the following plan.

First is a large table highlighting the major human relations concepts and skills presented in the text, along with space for you to insert a tentative action plan about how you might use the knowledge or apply the skill in question. Usually it will be necessary to refer back to the appropriate chapter to identify the subtopics under a particular topic, such as looking for specific tactics under "Effective career advancement strategies and tactics."

The topics in the table presented below are often worded in a way that suggests the application of the information. You may not have action plans for every major topic in the text. The action plan might be a sentence long. For example, next to the outline entry "Techniques for resolving conflict," you might insert "Disarming the opposition should work for me. The next time I am criticized, and I am wrong, I will admit what I did wrong and ask for sympathy." To prepare your action plan, it will usually be necessary to refer back to the discussion of the topic within the text.

Second, after you have made action-plan entries for as many concepts and skills that seem relevant for you at the time, write an essay about how to plan to enhance your human relations effectiveness. The raw data for your essay are the action plans you have developed. In other words, your essay about enhancing your human relations effectiveness is a narrative composite of your action plans.

Chapter Number	Concept or Skill	My Action Plan
1	Human Relations and You	
	Use of human relations knowledge	
	How work and personal life influence each other	
	Development of self-understanding	
	Development of human relations movement	
	Major factors influencing job performance and behavior	
2	Self-esteem and Self-confidence	
	Nature of self-esteem	
	Development of self-esteem	
	Consequences of self-esteem	
	Enhancing self-esteem	
	Sources of self-confidence	
	Developing and strengthening self-confidence	
3	Self-motivation and Goal Setting	
	Influence of needs and motives on motivation	
	Contribution of goals to motivation	
	Self-motivation techniques	
	Development of self-discipline	

4	Emotional Intelligence, Attitudes, and Happiness	
	Nature of emotional intelligence	
	Acquiring and changing attitudes	
	How to acquire and enhance happiness	
5	Values and Ethics	
	Understanding values as part of human relations	
	Importance of business ethics	
	Guidelines for making ethical decisions	
	Guidelines for behaving ethically	
6	Problem Solving and Creativity	
	Characteristics related to problem-solving ability	
	Steps in problem solving and decision making	
	Creativity for decision making	
	Improving my creativity	
	Critical thinking for problem solving and creativity	
7	Personal Communication Effectiveness	
	Steps in communication process	
	Interpersonal communication for relationship building	
	Use of nonverbal communication	
	Frequent communication barriers	
	Building bridges to communication	
	Overcoming gender barriers to communication	
	Enhancing listening skills	
8	Communication in the Workplace	
	Use of formal channels of communication	
	Use of informal channels of communication	
	Problems associated with communication technology	
	Performing well in a business meeting	
9	Specialized Tactics for Getting Along with Others in the Workplace	
	Good relationship with manager or team leader	
	Coping with a problem manager	
	Building better coworker relationships	
	Building better relationships with customers	
10	Managing Conflict	
	Reasons for so much conflict	
	Good and bad side of conflict	
	Techniques for resolving conflict	
	Dealing with difficult people	
	Managing anger	
11	Becoming an Effective Leader	
	Traits and characteristics of effective leaders	
	Behaviors and skills of effective leaders	

	Choosing an effective leadership style	
	Getting along well with subordinates	
	Developing my leadership potential	
	Challenges of being a first-time leader	
12	Motivating Others and Developing Teamwork	
	Diagnosing motivation of others	
	Applying two classic motivation theories	
	Empowerment, job design, and positive reinforcement for motivating others	
	Building better teamwork	
	Making use of group dynamics	
	Building an effective work group	
13	Diversity and Cross-Cultural Competence	
	Dimensions of differences in cultural values	
	Approaches to improving cross-cultural relations	
	Overcoming cross-cultural communication barriers	
	Using diversity in the company to advantage	
	My legal rights in a culturally diverse organization	
14	Getting Ahead in Your Career	
	Ideas for conducting a job search	
	Constructing an effective job résumé	
	Performing well in a job interview	
	Effective career advancement strategies and tactics	
	Effective networking skills	
15	Learning Strategies, Perception, and Life Span Changes	
	Major learning strategies and processes	
	Choosing a learning style	
	Making my perceptions more accurate	
	Responding to life span changes and challenges	
	Making a career change	
	Coping with change more effectively	
16	Developing Good Work Habits	
	Overcoming procrastination	
	Proper attitudes and values to develop	
	Effective time-management techniques	
	Overcoming time wasters	
17	Managing Stress and Personal Problems	
	Getting positive consequences from stress	
	Sources of stress in personal life to minimize	
	Sources of work stress to minimize	
	Effective approaches to managing stress	
	Overcoming self-defeating behavior	
	Developing resilience	

Appendix B: The Golden Personality Type Profiler

Why Take the Golden Personality Type Profiler?

Self-awareness is the key to professional development and success. By taking the Golden Personality Type Profiler you will learn about your personality, which is the essence of who you are as a unique individual. It is reflected in what you say, how you feel about yourself, and how you act. Knowing about your personality will help you develop a deeper understanding of your strengths, a clearer picture of how your behavior affects others, and a better appreciation for the interpersonal style of others and how to interact with them more effectively.

The Golden takes about fifteen to twenty minutes to complete and measures five core personality dimensions that describe how you:

- Focus your energy (extraversion/introversion)
- Gather information (sensing/intuition)
- Make decisions (thinking/feeling)
- Approach life (judging/perceiving)
- Respond to stress (tense/calm)

What Will You Learn?

After you complete the assessment, you will receive a personalized Student Feedback Report that explains your five personality scores, your overall personality type, and your preferred

- Learning style
- Communication style
- Approach to teamwork
- Personal motivators
- Leadership style
- Ways to cope with stress

You will also receive a Student Guide to Interpreting Your Golden Results, which will give you a deeper understanding of your results. You will learn about the personality theory of the Golden, how to interpret your scores, and how to relate them to career planning and workplace effectiveness. You will also receive a snapshot description of the sixteen major personality types, so that you can see how you are similar to and different from others.

Learning about your personality will better prepare you for success in school and in your career. You will know more about your strengths, areas to develop further, and what motivates you. You will also gain a better understanding of how to work most effectively with people whose styles are different than your own.

Summary of Global Results

Your global results provide insight to how the four different dimensions of your personality work together to form your personality type. The results indicate your level of preference for each of two opposite scales. A strong preference is not necessarily better than a slight preference, or vice versa - the preferences simply indicate how strongly you favor certain behaviors versus others. You may have relatively equal preference, but slightly favor one scale.

Your Type is ESTZ
Where you focus your energy: Extraverting
How you gather information: Sensing
How you make decisions: Thinking
How you approach life: organiZing

Your test results do not reveal a clear preference.

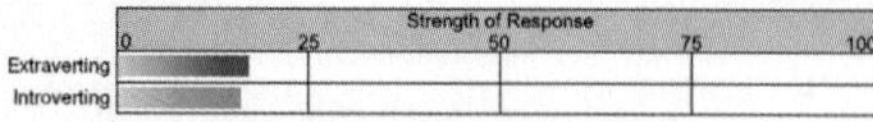

Extraverting
- focuses attention externally toward people and things
- enjoys being sociable, talkative, and gregarious
- enjoys discussions more than reading
- active rather than reflective

Introverting
- focuses attention inward on thoughts and ideas
- prefers a few close friends to many acquaintances
- likes to reflect on ideas before sharing them
- needs quiet time away from action and noise

Summary of Global Results

You have a Slight preference for Thinking.

Strength of Response
0 25 50 75 100
Thinking
Feeling

Thinking
- makes decisions based on logic and rationality
- prefers to deal in objective reason and logic
- does not get personally involved in his/her decisions

Feeling
- focuses on how a decision will impact others
- makes decisions based on person-centered values
- gets personally involved in his/her decisions

Your test results do not reveal a clear preference.

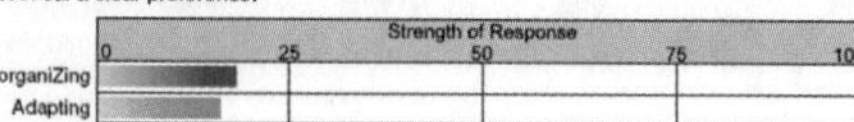

organiZing
- prefers an orderly, organized and planned lifestyle
- likes to make decisions and reach closure
- prefers systematic approaches

Adapting
- prefers a flexible, open-ended and emergent lifestyle
- holds off deciding until there is more information
- prefers spontaneity and limited structure

Access the Golden Personality Type Profiler

If your textbook was not packaged with an access code, you may purchase an access code for the Golden Personality Type Profiler Assessment online at www.pearsonhighered.com.

Glossary

Action plan describes how you are going to reach your goal

Active listener person who listens intensely, with the goal of empathizing with the speaker

Adolescence the period in life from approximately age 13 to 20; from a biological standpoint, adolescence begins with puberty

Affective component (of attitude) the emotion connected with an object or a task

Affirmative action programs that comply with antidiscrimination laws and attempt to correct past discriminatory practices

Aggressive characteristic of people who are obnoxious and overbearing; they push for what they want with almost no regard for the feelings of others

Aggressive personalities people who verbally and sometimes physically attack others frequently

Alternative self an understanding of the self, based on what could have been if something in the past had happened differently

Assertive characteristic of people who state clearly what they want or how they feel in a given situation without being abusive, abrasive, or obnoxious; open, honest, and up-front people who believe that all people have an equal right to express themselves honestly

Attitude a predisposition to respond that exerts an influence on a person's response to a person, a thing, an idea, or a situation

Attribution theory the study of the process by which people ascribe causes to the behaviors they perceive

Autocratic leader leader who attempts to retain most of the authority granted to the group; autocratic leaders make all the major decisions and assume subordinates will comply without question

Backstabbing an attempt to discredit by underhanded means such as innuendo, accusation, or the like

Barriers to communication (or noise) missteps that can occur between encoding and decoding a message; unwanted interference that can distort or block a message

Behavior modification system of motivation that emphasizes rewarding people for doing the right things and punishing them for doing the wrong things

Behavioral component (of attitude) how a person acts

Behavioral interview a candidate is asked how he or she handled a particular problem in the past

Blind area pane of Johari Window that contains information that others are aware of but we cannot see in ourselves in reference to both positive and negative qualities

Brainstorming technique by which group members think of multiple solutions to a problem

Brainwriting arriving at creative ideas by jotting them down

Buddy system the company assigns a new employee a coworker who looks out for his or her welfare, such as explaining company etiquette

Burnout a condition of emotional, mental, and physical exhaustion in response to long-term job stressors

Business etiquette special code of behavior required in work situations

Career path sequence of positions necessary to achieve a goal

Carpal tunnel syndrome repetitive-motion disorder most frequently associated with keyboarding and the use of optical scanners; occurs when repetitive flexing and extension of the wrist causes the tendons to swell, thus trapping and pinching the median nerve

Challenge stressors stressful events and thoughts that have a positive direct effect on motivation and performance

Character doing the right things despite outside pressures to do the opposite; includes leaving enduring marks that set one apart from another; being moral

Character trait an enduring characteristic of a person that is related to moral and ethical behavior that shows up consistently

Charisma type of charm and magnetism that inspires others; important quality for leaders at all levels

Classical conditioning principles stemming from Ivan Pavlov's digestion experiments that help people understand the most elementary type of learning—how people acquire uncomplicated habits and reflexes

Codependency a state of being psychologically influenced or controlled by, reliant on, or needing another person who is addicted to substances such as alcohol and drugs, or behavior such as gambling or Internet use

Cognitive-behavioral interventions a way of thinking constructively about a problem that includes perspective setting

Cognitive component (of attitude) the knowledge or intellectual beliefs an individual might have about an object (an idea, a person, a thing, or a situation)

Cognitive dissonance situation in which the pieces of knowledge, information, attitudes, or beliefs held by an individual are contradictory

Cognitive fitness a state of optimized ability to remember, learn, plan, and adapt to changing circumstances

Cognitive restructuring technique of mentally converting negative aspects into positive ones by looking for the positive elements in a situation

Cognitive skills problem-solving and intellectual skills

Communication the sending and receiving of messages

Communication overload phenomenon that occurs when people are so overloaded with information that they cannot respond effectively to messages

Communities of practice informal employee networks

Conflict condition that exists when two sets of demands, goals, or motives are incompatible

Conflict of interest judgment or objectivity is compromised because of two competing ends that must be satisfied

Confrontation and problem solving the most highly recommended way of resolving conflict; method of identifying the true source of conflict and resolving it systematically

Consensus leader leader who encourages group discussion about an issue and then makes a decision that reflects the consensus of the group members

Consideration the degree to which the leader creates an environment of emotional support, warmth, friendliness, and trust

Consultative leader leader who solicits opinions from the group before making a decision, yet does not feel obliged to accept the group's thinking; this type of leader makes it clear that he or she alone has the authority to make the final decisions

Creative self-efficacy the belief that one has the knowledge and skills to produce creative outcomes

Creativity the ability to develop good ideas that can be put into action

Critical thinking solving problems and making decisions through a systematic evaluation of evidence

Cultural intelligence (CQ) an outsider's ability to interpret someone's unfamiliar and ambiguous behavior the same way that person's compatriots would

Cultural mosaic an individual's unique mixture of multiple cultural identities that yields a complex picture of the cultural influences on that person

Cultural sensitivity an awareness of and a willingness to investigate the reasons why people of another culture act as they do

Cultural training set of learning experiences designed to help employees understand the customs, traditions, and beliefs of another culture

Culture a learned and shared system of knowledge, beliefs, values, attitudes, and norms

Customer service orientation approach of employee whose thoughts and actions are geared toward helping customers

Decision making choosing one alternative from the various alternative solutions that can be pursued

Decoding the process of understanding a message; the receiver interprets the message and translates it into meaningful information

Defensive communication tendency to receive messages in such a way that one's self-esteem is protected

Democratic leader leader who confers final authority on the group; functions as a collector of opinion and takes a vote before making a decision (in extreme sometimes referred to as a free-rein leader)

Denial the suppression of information one finds uncomfortable

Developmental opportunity area for growth or weakness

Diagonal communication the transmission of messages to higher or lower organizational levels in different departments

Difficult people a coworker is classified as difficult if he or she is uncooperative, disrespectful, touchy, defensive, hostile, or even very unfriendly

Disarming the opposition method of conflict resolution in which you disarm the criticizer by agreeing with his or her criticism

Diversity training program that attempts to bring about workplace harmony by teaching people how to get along with diverse work associates; often aimed at minimizing open expressions of racism and sexism

Downward communication the transmission of messages from higher to lower levels in an organization

E-learning an Internet form of computer-based learning

Emotional contagion the automatic and unconscious transfer of emotions between individuals based on cues the one person observes in another

Emotional intelligence the ability to accurately perceive emotions, to understand the signals that emotions send about relationships, and to manage our own and others' emotions

Emotional labor process of regulating both feelings and expressions to meet organizational goals

Empathy understanding another person's point of view

Employee network (or affinity) groups network group of employees throughout the company who affiliate on the basis of a group characteristic such as face, ethnicity, sex, sexual orientation, or physical ability status

Empowerment process by which a manager shares power with team members, thereby enhancing their feelings of self-efficacy

Encoding the process of organizing ideas into a series of symbols, such as words and gestures, designed to communicate with a receiver

Ethical screening running a contemplated decision or action through an ethics test, particularly when a contemplated action or decision is not clearly ethical or unethical

Ethics the moral choices a person makes

Exit strategy determining in advance how to get out of a bad decision, such as having joined a failing family business

Expectancy theory of motivation people will be motivated if they believe that their efforts will lead to desired outcomes

External locus of control individual's belief that external forces control his or her fate

Extinction the weakening or decreasing of the frequency of undesirable behavior by removing the reward for such behavior

Fear of success belief that if one succeeds at an important task, one will be asked to take on more responsibility in the future; a reason some people procrastinate

Feedback information that tells one how well he or she has performed

Fight-or-flight response the experience of stress prompts the adrenal glands to release a flood of hormones that prepare the body to fight or run when faced with a challenge

Flow experience total absorption in work; when flow occurs, things seem to go just right

Formal communication channels the official pathways for sending information inside and outside an organization

Frame of reference model, viewpoint, or perspective

Galatea effect a type of self-fulfilling prophecy in which high expectations lead to high performance

Goal an event, circumstance, object, or condition a person strives to attain

Grapevine major informal communication channel in organizations; the grapevine refers to the tangled pathways that can distort information

Grievance procedure formal process of filing a complaint and resolving a dispute within an organization

Group a collection of people who interact with one another, and are working toward some common purpose; a team approaches being a supergroup

Group dynamics the forces operating in groups that affect how members work together

Group learning A change in the group's repertoire of potential behavior

Group norms unwritten set of expectations for group members—what people ought to do; basic principle to follow in getting along with coworkers

Groupthink a deterioration of mental efficiency, reality testing, and moral judgment in the interest of group solidarity; extreme form of consensus

Hawthorne effect a phenomenon in a work setting or research in which workers or participants employees react positively because management or researchers care about them

Hedonic adaptation the tendency to adapt to regard exciting new aspects of life as routine after a while

Hidden area pane of Johari Window that contains information known to us about ourselves but is hidden from others

Hindrance stressors stressful events and thoughts that have a negative effect on motivation and performance

Horizontal communication sending messages among people at the same organization level

Human relations the art of using systematic knowledge about human behavior to improve personal, job, and career effectiveness

Human relations movement movement that began as a concentrated effort by some managers and their advisers to become more sensitive to the needs of employees or to treat them in a more humanistic manner

Identity crisis adolescent struggle to establish a reliable self-concept or personal identity

Implicit learning learning that takes place unconsciously and without an intention to learn

Informal communication channels unofficial networks of channels that supplement the formal channels

Informal learning planned or unplanned learning that occurs without a formal classroom, lesson plan, instructor, or examination; a way of learning complex skills in the workplace

Ingratiating an attempt to increase one's attractiveness to others to influence their behavior

Initiating structure organizing and defining relationships in the group by engaging in such activities as assigning specific tasks, specifying procedures to be followed, scheduling work, and making expectations clear

Innovation the commercialization or implementation of creative ideas

Insight an ability to know what information is relevant, to find connections between the old and the new, to combine facts that are unrelated, and to see the "big picture"

Intermittent rewards sustaining desired behaviors longer and slowing down the process of behaviors fading away when they are not rewarded

Internal locus of control individual's belief that fate is pretty much under a person's own control

Intranet a company version of the Internet with the basic purpose of giving employees a central place to find what they need amidst a sea of digital information

Intrinsic motivation the natural tendency to seek out novelty and challenges, to extend and use one's capacities, to explore, and to learn

Introspection the act of looking within oneself

Intuition an experience-based way of knowing or reasoning in which weighing and balancing of evidence are done automatically

Job enrichment making a job more motivating and satisfying by adding variety and responsibility

Johari Window a grid showing how much information you know about yourself as well as how much other people know about you

Keywords terms for skills, certifications, job activities, and other qualifications sought for a particular job

Lateral thinking process of spreading out to find many different alternative solutions to a problem

Leader–member exchange (LMX) model leadership model that focuses on the quality of leader–member relations; recognizes that leaders develop unique working relationships with each group member

Leadership the process of bringing about positive changes and influencing others to achieve worthwhile goals

Leadership effectiveness situation in which the leader helps the group accomplish its objectives without neglecting satisfaction and morale

Leadership style a leader's characteristic way of behaving in a variety of situations

Learning generally considered a lasting change in behavior based on practice and experience

Learning style the idea that different people learn best in different ways

Maslow's hierarchy of needs the best-known categorization of needs; according to psychologist Abraham H. Maslow, people strive to satisfy the following groups of needs in step-by-step order: physiological needs, safety needs, social needs, esteem needs, and self-actualizing needs

Meditation a systematic method of concentration, reflection, or concentrated thinking designed to suppress the activity of the sympathetic nervous system

Mentor a more experienced person who guides, teaches, and coaches another individual

Micro-inequity small, semiconscious message sent with a powerful impact on the receiver

Micromanagement the close monitoring of most aspects of group member activities by the manager

Midlife crisis time that adults in their forties face when they feel unfulfilled and search for a major shift in career or lifestyle

Midlife transition adults taking stock of their lives and formulating new goals

Mirroring form of nonverbal communication to overcome communication barriers by subtly imitating another; used to improve rapport with another person

Mixed messages a discrepancy between what a person says and how he or she acts

Mixed signals type of message in which the sender might recommend one thing to others yet behave in another way

Modeling learning a skill by observing another person perform the skill; considered a form of social learning because it is learned in the presence of others

Morals an individual's or a society's determination of what is right and wrong

Motivation concept with two widely used meanings: (1) an internal state that leads to effort expended toward objectives and (2) an activity performed by one person to get another to accomplish work

Motive an inner drive that moves a person to do something

Multicultural identities individuals who incorporate the values of two or more cultures because they identify with both their primary culture and another culture or cultures

Multicultural worker one who can work effectively with people of different cultures

Multiple intelligences theory explaining the idea that people know and understand the world in distinctly different ways and learn in different ways and that they possess eight intelligences, or faculties, in varying degrees

Narcissism an extremely positive view of the self, combined with little empathy for others

Need an internal striving or urge to do something, such as a need to drink when thirsty

Need for achievement the desire to accomplish something difficult for its own sake

Negative affectivity a tendency to experience aversive (intensely disliked) emotional states; predisposition to experience emotional stress that includes feelings of nervousness, tension, and worry

Negative reinforcement taking away something unpleasant from a situation; being rewarded by being relieved of discomfort; form of avoidance learning or motivation

Negotiating and bargaining situation of conferring with another person to resolve a problem

Networking the process of establishing a group of contacts who can help you in your career

Nonassertive characteristic of people who let things happen to them without letting their feelings be known

Nonverbal communication using the body, voice, or environment in numerous ways to help get a message across

Open area pane of Johari Window consisting of information that is known to us and others

Open-door policy communication channel that is structured upward that allows employees to bring a complaint to top management's attention without first checking with the employee's manager

Operant conditioning learning that takes place as a consequence of behavior; a person's actions are instrumental in determining whether learning takes place

Organizational citizenship behavior (OCB) the willingness to go beyond one's job description to help the company, even if such an act does not lead to an immediate reward

Organizational culture values and beliefs of the firm that guide people's actions

Organizational effectiveness the extent to which an organization is productive and satisfies the demands of interested parties, such as employees, customers, and investors

Paraphrase repeating in one's own words what a sender says, feels, and means

Participative leader leader who shares decision-making authority with the group; motivates group members to work as a team toward high-level goals

Passive-aggressive personality a person who appears to enthusiastically and readily respond to another person's request or demand while acting in ways that negatively and passively resist the request

Peak performance exceptional accomplishment in a given task

Peer evaluations system in which teammates contribute to an evaluation of a person's job performance

Perception the various ways in which people interpret things in the external world and how they act on the basis of these perceptions

Perceptual congruence the degree to which people perceive things the same way

Performance standard a statement of what constitutes acceptable performance

Personal brand your distinctive set of strengths, including skills and values

Personal communication style verbal and nonverbal communication style for a unique approach to sending and receiving information

Personal support assisting others in the workplace through the use of interpersonal skills

Personality clash antagonistic relationship between two people based on differences in personal attributes, preferences, interests, values, and styles

Personality disorder a pervasive, persistent, inflexible, maladaptive pattern of behavior that deviates from expected cultural norms

Person–organization fit the compatibility of the individual and the organization

Person–role conflict the demands made by the organization or a superior clash with the basic values of the individual

Planning primary principle of effective time management; deciding what to accomplish and the actions needed to make it happen

Positive psychological capital a positive psychological state of development in which you have a storehouse of hope, self-efficacy, optimism, and resilience

Positive reinforcement increasing the probability that behavior will be repeated by rewarding people for making the desired response; improves learning and motivation

Positive self-talk saying positive things about yourself to yourself

Positive visual imagery picturing a positive outcome in your mind

Private self the actual person an individual may be

Proactive personality characteristic of a person who is relatively unconstrained by forces in a situation and who brings about environmental change; highly proactive people identify opportunities and act on them, showing initiative, and keep trying until they bring about meaningful change

Problem gap between what exists and what you want to exist

Procrastination delaying a task for an invalid or weak reason

Productivity the amount of quality work accomplished in relation to the resources consumed

Prosocial motivation the desire to expend effort to help other people

Psychological hardiness mental state in which the individual experiences a high degree of commitment, control, and challenge

Public self what a person communicates about himself or herself and what others actually perceive about the person

Punishment the introduction of an unpleasant stimulus as a consequence of the learner having done something wrong

Pygmalion effect leader's ability to elevate worker performance by the simple method of expecting them to perform well; the manager's high expectations become a self-fulfilling prophecy

Recognition need the desire to be acknowledged for one's contributions and efforts and to feel important

Relationship management the interpersonal skills of being able to communicate clearly and convincingly, disarm conflicts, and build strong personal bonds

Relaxation response a physical state of deep rest in which one experiences a slower respiration and heart rate, lowered blood pressure, and lowered metabolism; a standard technique for reducing stress

Resilience the ability to withstand pressure and emerge stronger because of an experience; being challenged and not breaking down

Role tendency to behave, contribute, and relate to others in a particular way

Role ambiguity condition in which the job holder receives confusing or poorly defined expectations

Role conflict having to choose between two competing demands or expectations

Role overload a burdensome workload that creates stress for a person in two ways: (1) the person may become fatigued and less able to tolerate annoyances and irritations and (2) a person subject to unreasonable work demands may feel perpetually behind schedule, a situation that itself creates an uncomfortable, stressful feeling

Role underload disruptive amount of stress that can occur when people experience too little to do

Sandwich generation those placed in the middle between the needs of their own children and their aging relatives

Scientific management approach to work that focuses on the application of scientific methods to increase individual workers' productivity

Selective attention giving exclusive attention to something at the expense of other aspects of the environment

Self a complex idea generally referring to a person's total being or individuality

Self-awareness the ability to understand moods, emotions, and needs as well as their impact on others; self-awareness also includes using intuition to make decisions you can live with happily

Self-defeating behavior activities or attitudes that work against one's best interest

Self-determination theory the motivation theory contending that we are most deeply engaged, and do our most creative work, when we feel that we are acting according to our own will and pursuing goals we find meaningful

Self-discipline the ability to work systematically and progressively toward a goal until it is achieved

Self-disclosure the process of revealing one's inner self to others

Self-efficacy confidence in your ability to carry out a specific task in contrast to generalized self-confidence

Self-esteem the experience of feeling competent to cope with the basic challenges in life and of being worthy of happiness

Self-leadership leading oneself; influencing oneself without waiting for an external leader to lead

Self-management the ability to control one's emotions and act with honesty and integrity in a consistent and acceptable manner

Self-respect how you think and feel about yourself

Self-understanding gathering valid information about oneself; self-understanding refers to knowledge about oneself, particularly with respect to mental and emotional aspects

Semantics the study of the meaning and changes in the meaning of words or symbols

Servant leader one who serves group members by working on their behalf to help them achieve their goals, not the leader's goals

Sexual equity parity among heterosexual, gay, lesbian, bisexual, and transgender employees

Sexual harassment unwanted sexually oriented behavior in the workplace that results in discomfort or interference with the job

Shadow organizations where much of the real work gets accomplished, the shadow organization is revealed by social network analysis, which traces who talks to whom

Shared leadership the leader granting group members authority to carry out some of the leadership activities

Skill-benefit statements brief explanations of how an individual's skills can benefit the company

Social awareness having empathy for others and having intuition about work problems

Social intelligence an understanding of how relationships with bosses and colleagues, family, and friends, shape our brains and affect our bodies

Socialization the process of coming to understand the values, norms, and customs essential for adapting to the organization

Social network analysis the mapping and measuring of relationships and links between and among people groups, and organizations that reveals the shadow organization

Soft addiction ordinary behavior that if done to excess can wreak havoc with one's life

Stress an internal reaction to any force that threatens to disturb a person's equilibrium; the internal reaction usually takes the form of emotional discomfort

Stressor the external or internal force that brings about the stress

Success syndrome pattern in which the worker performs one assignment well and then has the confidence to take on an even more difficult assignment

Support system a group of people on whom one can rely for encouragement and comfort

Synergy a product of group effort whereby the output of the group exceeds the output possible if the members worked alone

Team a small number of people who are committed to common goals and approaches to which they hold themselves mutually accountable

Team player one who emphasizes group accomplishment and cooperation rather than individual achievement and not helping others

Teamwork work done with an understanding and commitment to group goals on the part of all team members

Teenage brain a stage of brain development in which people are easily influenced by their environment and more prone to impulsive behavior

Time leak anything you are doing or not doing that allows time to get away from you

Traditional mental set fixed way of thinking about objects and activities

Trust a person's confidence in another individual's intentions and motives and in the sincerity of that individual's words

Two-factor theory of work motivation two different sets of job factors—one set, the motivators, or satisfiers, can motivate and satisfy workers; the other set, dissatisfiers, or hygiene factors, can only prevent dissatisfaction

Type A behavior personality characteristics that lead a person into stressful situations. Type A behavior has two main components: (1) the tendency to try to accomplish too many things in too little time and (2) free-floating hostility

Unknown area pane of Johari Window that contains information that you and others do not know about you

Upward communication the transmission of messages from lower to higher levels in an organization

Value the importance a person attaches to something; values are also tied to the enduring belief that one's mode of conduct is better than another mode of conduct

Variable pay incentive plan that intentionally pays good performers more money than poor performers

Vertical thinking analytical, logical process that results in few answers; the vertical thinker looks for the one best solution to a problem, much like solving an equation in algebra

Webinar a web-based method of holding a seminar

Wellness program a company-sponsored activity designed to support employees as they learn and sustain behaviors that reduce health risk, improve quality of life, and enhance personal effectiveness

Win–win belief that after conflict has been resolved both sides should gain something of value

Workaholism neglecting the normal need for rest and relaxation that can lead to an addiction to work in which not working is an uncomfortable experience

Work engagement high levels of personal investment in the work tasks performed in a job

Work ethic a firm belief in the dignity and value of work and, therefore, important for favorably impressing a manager

Work–family conflict conflict that occurs when an individual has to perform multiple roles: worker, spouse or partner, and often parent

Work habits a person's characteristic approach to work, including such things as organization, priority setting, and handling of paperwork, e-mail, and intranets

Workplace bullying hurtful treatment of others in the workplace that is malicious and typically repeated

Worst-case scenario helpful decision-making aid that involves visualizing what you would do if the alternative chosen proved to be dreadful

Company and Organization Index

Name Index

Subject Index